THE ELGAR COMPANION TO THE EXTRAORDINARY CHAMBERS IN THE COURTS OF CAMBODIA

ELGAR COMPANIONS TO INTERNATIONAL COURTS AND TRIBUNALS

Series Editor: *William A. Schabas, Middlesex University, London, UK*

The Elgar Companions to International Courts and Tribunals series comprises original reference works designed for use by both specialists in the field and more casual readers. Titles in the series combine substance, procedure, descriptive background detail and historical context. Precise scope and coverage varies between volumes and may include sections on history, jurisprudence, procedure, the role of the court in the wider world, and biographies of key figures within the development of the court. Extracts and materials are also included where appropriate.

Titles in the series include:

The Elgar Companion to the International Court of Justice
Robert Kolb

The Elgar Companion to the International Criminal Tribunal for Rwanda
Edited by Anne-Marie de Brouwer and Alette Smeulers

The Elgar Companion to the Extraordinary Chambers in the Courts of Cambodia
Nina H.B. Jørgensen

The Elgar Companion to the Extraordinary Chambers in the Courts of Cambodia

Nina H.B. Jørgensen

Faculty of Law, The Chinese University of Hong Kong

ELGAR COMPANIONS TO INTERNATIONAL COURTS AND TRIBUNALS

EE Edward Elgar PUBLISHING

Cheltenham, UK • Northampton, MA, USA

Published by
Edward Elgar Publishing Limited
The Lypiatts
15 Lansdown Road
Cheltenham
Glos GL50 2JA
UK

Edward Elgar Publishing, Inc.
William Pratt House
9 Dewey Court
Northampton
Massachusetts 01060
USA

A catalogue record for this book
is available from the British Library

Library of Congress Control Number: 2017955175

This book is available electronically in the **Elgar**online
Law subject collection
DOI 10.4337/9781784718077

MIX
Paper from
responsible sources
FSC® C013056
FSC
www.fsc.org

ISBN 978 1 78471 806 0 (cased)
ISBN 978 1 78471 807 7 (eBook)

Typeset by Columns Design XML Ltd, Reading
Printed and bound in Great Britain by TJ International Ltd, Padstow

For Lily, Bear and Pani

'La verité des choses se cachait peut-être ailleurs ...'
Soth Polin, *L'anarchiste*

Contents

Preface

The world has witnessed many atrocities since the followers of the Communist Party of Kampuchea, better known as the Khmer Rouge, marched into Phnom Penh on 17 April 1975 and unleashed a regime of terror of more than three and a half years on the Cambodian people in which an estimated quarter of the population perished. However, the fate that befell this small South-East Asian nation continues to grip and challenge the imagination. Perhaps it is the notion of the State turning on its own people on such an unprecedented scale that is so difficult to fathom. Perhaps it is the tranquil, smiling populace, forging a space in the modern era against the proud backdrop of the ancient Angkorian temples that makes such a dark recent history so improbable. Or perhaps it is the scales of justice, finally weighing in more than 30 years after the crimes that have refocused global attention.

When the film, *The Killing Fields*, was released on video it was made compulsory viewing for all pupils at my middle school in Tokyo. Many of us were not yet teenagers. I recall that a pupil received a heavy scolding for throwing away a half-eaten apple at the entrance to the library where the film was to be screened. Before understanding the context of the reprimand—as the film began and images of scared and starving children were beamed into the safe haven of the library—I reflected on its fairness. Food was prohibited in the library and had the pupil gone to put the remains of the apple in her locker she would have been told off for being late. In retrospect, the incident appeared as an early introduction to the complexities of justice. And the background was the revelation to a child's eyes of the Cambodian 'genocide'.

Little did I know that many years later I would have the opportunity to work for the Extraordinary Chambers in the Courts of Cambodia (ECCC) as the first employee of the United Nations Assistance to the Khmer Rouge Trials in the Pre-Trial Chamber and then to serve as an adviser to the ECCC Supreme Court Chamber. When asked by Edward Elgar Publishers if I would be interested in writing this book as a contribution to their series of *Companions to International Courts and Tribunals*, I felt honoured to take on the task. This book aims to serve as an introduction to the ECCC while also exploring in more depth some of the Court's practical and jurisprudential challenges and outcomes.

I wish to thank friends and colleagues for their inspiration in the optimistic start-up phase of the ECCC, especially the original Pre-Trial Chamber team: Judge Prak Kimsan, Judge Katinka Lahuis, Judge Rowan Downing, Judge Ney Thol, Judge Huot Vuthy, Judge Pen Pichsaly, Anne-Marie Burns, Dirk Jan Laman, Sar Chanrath, Keo Vanny, Chuon Sokreasey, Chuon Sopagna, Lee Kanthoul and the many excellent interns. I also wish to thank Judge Agnieszka Klonowiecka-Milart for her support during the second phase of my involvement with the ECCC.

Ann Hoi Yee Lee did a tremendous job as a student assistant during the final stages of preparation of the manuscript, for which I am very grateful. My thanks also to Crystal Yeung, Polina Malkova and Daley Birkett for research assistance and to the Faculty of Law at the Chinese University of Hong Kong for the facilities to carry out this work.

Finally, thanks are due to Laura Mann and the team at Edward Elgar for their enthusiasm, patience, attentiveness and efficiency at all stages of the process.

Acronyms

CAT	Convention against Torture and Other Cruel, Inhuman or Degrading Treatment or Punishment
CCL 10	Control Council Law No. 10
CNRP	Cambodia National Rescue Party
CPC	Cambodian Criminal Procedure Code
CPK	Communist Party of Kampuchea
CPL	Civil Party Lawyer
CPNLAF	Cambodian People's National Liberation Armed Forces
CPP	Cambodian People's Party
DC-Cam	Documentation Centre of Cambodia
DK	Democratic Kampuchea
DSS	Defence Support Section
ECCC	Extraordinary Chambers in the Courts of Cambodia
ECtHR	European Court of Human Rights
FUNK	National United Front of Kampuchea
GRUNK	Royal Government of National Union of Kampuchea
ICC	International Criminal Court
ICC or Rome Statute	Rome Statute of the International Criminal Court
ICCPR	International Covenant on Civil and Political Rights
ICTR	International Criminal Tribunal for Rwanda
ICTY	International Criminal Tribunal for the former Yugoslavia
ILC	International Law Commission
IMT	International Military Tribunal
IMTFE	International Military Tribunal for the Far East
IR/s	Internal Rule/s
JCE	Joint Criminal Enterprise
KNUFNS	Kampuchean National United Front for National Salvation

KPNLAF	Khmer People's National Liberation Armed Forces
KPRP	Kampuchean People's Revolutionary Party
LCL	Civil Party Lead Co-Lawyers
NATO	North Atlantic Treaty Organization
NGO	Non-Governmental Organization
OCIJ	Office of the Co-Investigative Judges
OCP	Office of the Co-Prosecutors
PRA	People's Representative Assembly
PRK	People's Republic of Kampuchea
PRT	People's Revolutionary Tribunal
PTC	Pre-Trial Chamber
RAK	Revolutionary Army of Kampuchea
SCC	Supreme Court Chamber
SCSL	Special Court for Sierra Leone
SNC	Supreme National Council
SOC	State of Cambodia
STL	Special Tribunal for Lebanon
TC	Trial Chamber
UN	United Nations
UNAKRT	United Nations Assistance to the Khmer Rouge Trial
UNAMIC	United Nations Advance Mission for Cambodia
UNDESA	United Nations Department of Economic and Social Affairs
UNDP	United Nations Development Programme
UNOPS	United Nations Office for Project Services
UNTAC	United Nations Transitional Authority in Cambodia
UNWCC	United Nations War Crimes Commission
US	United States
VSS	Victims Support Section
WESU	Witness and Expert Support Unit

1. Introduction

1. CAMBODIA TODAY

As the story goes, the boundary of Phnom Penh was extended westwards to ensure that the former military complex housing Cambodia's solution to the problem of impunity for the crimes of the Khmer Rouge era would be considered part of the capital city as required under the Law establishing the Extraordinary Chambers in the Courts of Cambodia (ECCC).[1] More than a good story, this extension of the city's limits was formalised in a Royal Decree on the border modification between the Municipality of Phnom Penh and Kandal Province, integrating the villages of Phum Ang, Phum Odem, Phum Angkeo and Phum Prey Svay into Chomchao commune, Dangkor district, Municipality of Phnom Penh.[2]

The ECCC is not far from the centre of Phnom Penh as the crow flies, being located some kilometres further along National Road 4 from what used to be called Pochentong International Airport, now simply Phnom Penh International Airport. In real terms, navigating overloaded motorbikes and lorries on poor roads, which are often flooded in the rainy season, turns each journey there and back on the buses that ferry staff members to and from work into an adventure of an hour or more. It certainly feels as if the ECCC is out of town. After the bottleneck around a lively market, the traffic eventually eases and the approach to the Court complex is lined by rows of newly built, similarly styled houses. The

[1] Law on the Establishment of the Extraordinary Chambers, with inclusion of Amendments, NS/RKM/1004/006, 27 October 2004, Article 43 new: 'The Extraordinary Chambers established in the trial court and the Supreme Court Chamber shall be located in Phnom Penh' ('ECCC Law'); 'The address of the ECCC changed', ECCC, 29 July 2006, <https://www.eccc.gov.kh/en/articles/address-eccc-changed> [accessed 3 June 2017]: 'The address of the Extraordinary Chambers in the Courts of Cambodia changed following the issuance of a Preah Reach Kret (Royal Decree) on extending the boundary of the Municipality of Phnom Penh'.

[2] Preah Reach Kret (Royal Decree) on Border Modification between Municipality of Phnom Penh and Kandal Province, NS/RKT/0706/329, 29 July 2006.

palatial spirals of the rooftops that to the uninitiated give the ECCC buildings the semblance of a temple eventually come into view. An ornamental moat populated by waterlilies separates the main staff entrance from the marshland beyond. There is no physical indication that the Court buildings belong to the regular Cambodian criminal justice structure. Rather, the ECCC appears as a juridical island.

Back in the city centre, the notorious *Toul Sleng* or S-21 prison, once a school and now a museum, is an enduring and visible symbol of the horrors of the Khmer Rouge reign. Tourists, groups of students and foreign officials often combine a visit to S-21 with a trip to the nearby 'killing fields' of *Choeng Ek*, a haunting yet peaceful marker of Cambodia's return to 'Year Zero'. Attending a hearing at the ECCC can these days be added to the itinerary, where albeit late, and albeit in some respects faltering, the wheels of justice began turning in 2006. At the start of the ECCC's operations, five of the primary 'candidates for prosecution'[3] were successfully gathered, including Kaing Guek Eav, or 'Duch', formerly the head of S-21, and members of the Khmer Rouge party leadership and government allegedly most responsible for the 'killing fields', namely Nuon Chea (so-called 'Brother No. 2'), Ieng Sary (former Foreign Minister), Khieu Samphan (former Head of State) and Ieng Thirith (former Minister of Social Affairs and wife of Ieng Sary). While Ieng Sary and Ieng Thirith have since passed away, final convictions have been entered against the remaining three defendants and a second trial against Nuon Chea and Khieu Samphan is in progress. The judicial investigation against Ao An was concluded in December 2016 while the investigation against Yim Tith remained open. Meas Muth who allegedly held a position of influence within the Revolutionary Army of Kampuchea and was commander of the Democratic Kampuchea Navy is also under investigation. The case against Im Chaem, allegedly secretary of Preah Net Preah District in the North-West Zone, was dismissed at the conclusion of the judicial investigation in February 2017.

Now more than ten years old, the ECCC has shown remarkable resilience despite an almost constant bombardment of legal, political and practical obstacles, represented symbolically by nature's revenge in the form of extensive rains which flooded the Court complex so operations were temporarily stalled in 2016. There is little doubt that time is running

---

[3] *See* S. Heder and B. Tittemore, *Seven Candidates for Prosecution: Accountability for Crimes of the Khmer Rouge* (War Crimes Research Office and Coalition for International Justice, June 2001) <http://www.wcl.american.edu/warcrimes/khmerrouge.pdf?rd=1> [accessed 3 June 2017].

out if justice for the victims, perpetrators, Cambodian society and the international community is to be fully achieved.

The purpose of this introductory chapter is to situate the ECCC within the context of relevant developments in Cambodian history in order to explain the Court's mandate and evolution and to allow a proper assessment of its success. This brief narrative recognises that while Cambodia's history is well-known, there is no single version of events, and that the ECCC is itself using the lens of justice to construe the history of the Khmer Rouge period. Criminal justice is essentially backward-looking in that it attempts to uncover the truth of past events as circumscribed by the individualised focus of the criminal process. The workings and revelations of a trial permit new interpretations, understandings and truths to be derived and extracted from the testimony, transcripts and judgments. This chapter also gives a nod to the future where the ECCC's potential legacy will be felt.

2. CAMBODIA YESTERDAY

2.1 The Angkor Period of Greatness

David Chandler's *A History of Cambodia* has been commended for illuminating the culture, politics and history of 'a country long misunderstood'.[4] Apparently Cambodia misunderstood or at least failed to appreciate the significance of its own ancient history of Angkor until it was brought back to life in all its grandeur by the French colonialists.[5] Today, the period spanning 802 to 1431 is considered Cambodia's 'period of greatness'[6] when the country thrived under successive kings. The most revered of these ancient kings is Jayavarman VII who came to power in 1182–83 after defeating the Chams following their 1177 invasion of Cambodia.[7] Jayavarman VII broke with the Hindu tradition and instituted the idea of Buddhist kingship which survived until 1970.[8] Thanks to the account by Zhou Daguan, a Chinese envoy to Cambodia in 1296–97, something is known of the life and customs during the Angkor period. The king, who embodied a sense of just rule, was the point of reference

[4] D. Chandler, *A History of Cambodia* (4th edn, Chiangmai, Silkworm Books, 2008), back cover blurb.

[5] Ibid, p. 2.

[6] Ibid, p. 35.

[7] Ibid, pp. 69–70.

[8] Ibid, pp. 67–8.

for disputes between ordinary people and dispensed royal punishments ranging from fines to the amputation of noses, fingers or toes in respect of the most serious offences.[9] Adultery, theft and disputes between families came under a separate regime and might involve waiting for a 'judgment of heaven' (or, in more pressing cases, sending the disputants into a crocodile pool where the one in the wrong would be eaten), or plunging a suspected thief's hand into boiling oil with guilt being confirmed by the inevitable scalding.[10]

Evidence in the form of Buddhist statuary and inscriptions suggests that Angkor Wat—the major temple in the Angkor complex—remained active between the fifteenth and nineteenth centuries and was never abandoned.[11] Indeed, when the French arrived they found a thriving Buddhist monastery and hundreds of slaves inside the temple.[12]

2.2 Colonisation and Independence

After the Angkor period, Cambodia's centre of gravity began to shift towards Phnom Penh and the country became more vulnerable to outside interference, especially from Thailand and Vietnam. By the 1800s Cambodia was in a situation of 'dual dependency' on these two powers causing King Duang (who in fact enjoyed relative independence during his reign from 1848 until his death in 1860) to reach out to France for protection against the Vietnamese.[13] Cambodia became a French protectorate in 1863 and France steadily consolidated its control, despite a rebellion in 1885 and King Norodom's attempts to block reform. When Norodom died in 1904 and was succeeded by his brother, Sisowath, colonial rule appeared to settle into a rhythm until discontent over high taxes and the income gap between French officials and Cambodians led to the game-changing murder of a French tax collector.[14]

Cambodia's elite became increasingly self-aware during King Monivong's reign in the 1930s and up to the outbreak of the Second World War. Norodom Sihanouk took the throne in 1941 as Cambodian nationalism surged. By this time, the French had distorted the Cambodian

---

[9] Z. Daguan, *A Record of Cambodia, The Land and its People* (translated with an introduction and notes by P. Harris, Chiangmai, Silkworm Books, 2007), pp. 21, 64–5.

[10] Ibid.

[11] Chandler, above n. 4, p. 35.

[12] Ibid.

[13] Ibid, pp. 164–5.

[14] Ibid, pp. 191–4.

economy, profited from rubber production and ceded Battambang and other provinces to Thailand.[15]

After the French were pushed aside by the Japanese, Sihanouk declared Cambodia's independence on 13 March 1945. At the conclusion of the Second World War, however, France re-established colonial control while allowing Cambodians to form political parties. Cambodia's first Constitution was drawn up in 1947, enumerating certain 'freedoms, rights and duties' of Cambodians. In 1952, amid the rise of communism, Sihanouk assumed power as prime minister and pushed harder for independence, finally succeeding in establishing an independent state in 1953.[16] Cambodia, Laos and Vietnam achieved full independence with the adoption of the 1954 Geneva Accords which brought the first Indochina war nominally to an end, separating Vietnam into a northern zone under the control of the Việt Minh and a southern zone known as the State of Vietnam. The Việt Minh who had been fighting the French from Cambodia's eastern areas were required to withdraw in recognition of Cambodia's neutrality and territorial integrity.[17] Sihanouk abdicated the throne in 1955 to participate in elections as an ordinary citizen and monopolised political power right through to 1970 when he was deposed by General Lon Nol.

2.3 The Emergence of the Communist Party of Kampuchea

The Indochina Communist Party, led by Ho Chi Minh, had branches in Vietnam, Laos and Cambodia, and held a Congress in 1951 in which the Cambodian branch was renamed the Khmer People's Revolutionary Party.[18] The Cambodian Communists received no concessions for supporting the Việt Minh in their struggle against the French colonialists and were left out of the Geneva negotiations, which almost resulted in the dissolution of the party in the late 1950s. However, its 'semi-legal

---

[15] C. Etcheson, *The Rise and Demise of Democratic Kampuchea* (Boulder, Colorado, Westview Press, 1984), p. 8.

[16] Chandler, above n. 4, p. 225.

[17] W. Shawcross, *Sideshow: Kissinger, Nixon, and the Destruction of Cambodia* (Revised edn, New York, Cooper Square Press, 2002), p. 48.

[18] *Prosecutor v Nuon Chea* and *Khieu Samphan*, ECCC Case File No. 002/19-09-2007/ECCC/TC, Trial Chamber, Case 002/01 Judgement, 7 August 2014, para. 80 (According to the findings of the ECCC Trial Chamber, this Congress was attended by Nuon Chea. The Trial Chamber relied upon Nuon Chea's testimony and certain documents, including the transcript of a 1998 interview given by Nuon Chea to Khem Ngun, a former assistant to Ta Mok, in establishing the history of the CPK) ('Nuon Trial Judgment').

arm', the Pracheachon, survived Sihanouk's efforts of repression.[19] The Pracheachon became synonymous with 'the communists' from the perspective of the Cambodian government, or the 'Rouges' as Sihanouk began to call them, 'to distinguish them from the "Khmers Roses", the pink liberals in the Democratic Party'.[20] The communists never in fact described themselves as the 'Khmer Rouge'.[21]

In 1960, a revived communist party operating in secret held its First Party Congress and adopted a Party Statute.[22] The new party was named the Communist Party of Kampuchea (CPK). The names of the party leaders only became infamous years later as the CPK strictly followed the mantra: 'If you preserve secrecy, half the battle is already won.'[23]

Saloth Sâr, or Pol Pot—a phantom who changed names with the seasons—was appointed Party Secretary at the Second Party Congress held in Phnom Penh in 1963.[24] Nuon Chea, another mysterious figure who went by the name of Long Rith when serving as a member of the Issarak movement that fought for independence from the French, was appointed as Pol Pot's Deputy.[25]

A 1967 rebellion in Samlaut village in Battambang resulting from land disputes is said to mark the start of the civil war in Cambodia.[26] Subsequent unrest in 1968 led to the establishment of the Revolutionary Army of Kampuchea.[27] The CPK's Third Party Congress was held in the jungle in 1971, formally ratifying the party's name and reiterating the strategic lines set out in the Statute.[28]

The CPK's political ideology was centred on the creation of a totally self-reliant and sovereign Khmer nation, free from any threat posed by encroaching neighbours. This ideology has been described as 'a combination of three elements twisted together almost beyond recognition in a creative, organic synthesis: sociocultural values and dispositions from traditional Khmer culture, certain strands of communist revolutionary

---

[19] P. Short, *Pol Pot: The History of a Nightmare* (London, John Murray Publishers, 2004), p. 114.

[20] Ibid, p. 115.

[21] Nuon Trial Judgment, above n. 18, para. 85.

[22] Nuon Trial Judgment, above n. 18, para. 86.

[23] Short, above n. 19, p. 5.

[24] Nuon Trial Judgment, above n. 18, para. 89.

[25] Short, above n. 19, p. 5.

[26] Nuon Trial Judgment, above n. 18, para. 91.

[27] Ibid, para. 93.

[28] Ibid, para. 95.

thought, and traces of radical Parisian Jacobinism'.[29] It involved an almost total break with the past while at the same time an obsession with certain intrinsic, historical traditions such as a reliance on rice cultivation.[30] The experiment culminated in the destruction of Cambodian society to implement a 'Utopian vision of social order'.[31]

2.4 The Overthrow of Sihanouk

Lon Nol served as Prime Minister under Sihanouk in the late 1960s, having at an earlier stage been appointed Defence Minister and Chief of the General Staff. Cambodia's economy had been faltering under Sihanouk's incompetent management and in 1970, while Sihanouk was travelling abroad, things came to a head. Lon Nol's deputy, Prince Sisowath Sirik Matak, was apparently the main architect of the plot to overthrow Sihanouk and persuaded Lon Nol to sign a decree to this effect, which was followed by a vote of no confidence in Sihanouk in the National Assembly and his removal from office on 18 March 1970.[32] Sihanouk, who was then in Beijing, reacted by creating a political movement known as the National United Front of Kampuchea (FUNK) and a government in exile, the Royal Government of National Union of Kampuchea (GRUNK), while aligning himself with the CPK. Khieu Samphan played the role of liaison between Sihanouk and Pol Pot.[33] Lon Nol abolished the monarchy and the Constitution of the Khmer Republic was declared in 1972.

2.5 The Impact of the Vietnam War

From the mid-1960s, the North Vietnamese Army and Viet Cong forces fighting against South Vietnam were stationed at bases in Cambodia causing Cambodia to be subjected to secret United States (US) mine-laying incursions and air raids.[34] In the year preceding Lon Nol's takeover of power, more than 3,600 B-52 raids were conducted over

[29] Etcheson, above n. 15, p. 28.
[30] Ibid, p. 29.
[31] Ibid, p. 36.
[32] Chandler, above n. 4, pp. 249–50; Nuon Trial Judgment, above n. 18, para. 97.
[33] Nuon Trial Judgment, above n. 18, para. 98.
[34] B. Kiernan, *The Pol Pot Regime: Race, Power, and Genocide in Cambodia under the Khmer Rouge, 1975-79* (3rd edn, New Haven, Connecticut, Yale University Press, 2008), p. 18.

Cambodian territory.[35] The North Vietnamese did not support the CPK during this period, preferring the status quo and the support of Sihanouk's government in the war against the Americans.[36]

The US sent ground troops to Cambodia from April to June 1970 after Sihanouk was deposed.[37] The Khmer Republic was allied to the US in the Vietnam War which fuelled resentment from the CPK that had evolved from being 'largely rural, Buddhist, moderate, and pro-Vietnamese' in the early 1950s to being 'urban, French-educated, radical and anti-Vietnamese' by 1970.[38] Under Pol Pot's leadership, the CPK took advantage of the instability created by US intervention and the devastation caused by American-led carpet bombing of the Cambodian countryside to garner support.[39] Lon Nol's weak, corrupt and disorganised government found itself in a battle against both the North Vietnamese forces and the Khmer Rouge.

US bombings intensified following the signing of a ceasefire agreement between the US and Vietnam in January 1973 since the Khmer Rouge refused to agree to a ceasefire with the Lon Nol government.[40] The US Congress passed a law blocking funding for the continued bombing of Cambodia on 10 May 1973 and the air raids finally ended on 15 August 1973.[41] This was only after a reported 2.7 million tonnes of bombs had been dropped.[42]

The Khmer Rouge gradually consolidated its power and control of territory, and when the time was seen to be ripe to institute the planned nationwide 'agrarian dictatorship',[43] there was little standing in its way. Phnom Penh was at this point overwhelmed with refugees. Lon Nol resigned on 1 April 1975 and went into exile.[44] Sihanouk rejected an

---

[35] Ibid.

[36] Nuon Trial Judgment, above n. 18, para. 94.

[37] Ibid, para. 154.

[38] Kiernan, above n. 34, p. 14.

[39] Ibid, p. 16 (Stating that the carpet bombing of Cambodia's countryside was 'probably the most important single factor in Pol Pot's rise'). *See* also Shawcross, above n. 17, pp. 248–51.

[40] Nuon Trial Judgment, above n. 18, para. 155.

[41] Ibid, para. 156.

[42] Kiernan, above n. 34, p. 19.

[43] *See* L. Phalla, 'Duch's Confession and Apology', *Phnom Penh Post*, 31 March 2009, <http://www.phnompenhpost.com/national/duchs-confession-and-apology> [accessed 3 June 2017].

[44] Nuon Trial Judgment, above n. 18, para. 164.

offer from the leadership of the Khmer Republic of a transfer of power to the GRUNK, insisting on a complete surrender.[45]

2.6 The Khmer Rouge Period

On 17 April 1975, the Khmer Rouge marched into Phnom Penh, took control of the Khmer Republic and re-named it Democratic Kampuchea (DK), triggering the darkest period of Cambodia's history. Children and teenagers were among the Khmer Rouge troops, dressed distinctively in black trousers and shirts, rubber thongs, *kramas* or caps, and carrying weapons.[46] By mid-morning, Phnom Penh had fallen and what at first appeared as a liberation quickly turned into a forceful evacuation of the city.[47] So-called 'new people', in other words the urban population, were forced into the country-side to labour alongside 'veteran people' who had been based in Khmer Rouge zones of control prior to the takeover. These 'new people' faced starvation and execution for stealing and other minor 'offences' or disobedience.[48] Buddhism was suppressed. The total re-organisation of society was accompanied by purges of perceived enemies, involving torture and executions, as well as targeted violence against ethnic minorities such as the Cham Muslims.[49]

The Constitution of Kampuchea declared the State of Kampuchea to be a democratic State 'of the people, workers, peasants and all other Kampuchean labourers' and spoke of a People's Representative Assembly which would elect judges to the 'people's courts' for the administration of justice. Article 10 of the Constitution stated that 'dangerous activities in opposition to the people's State must be condemned to the highest degree', and that 'other cases are subject to constructive re-education in the framework of the State's or people's organizations'. A section on rights and duties emphasised the right to work and the right to equality. The right to practice a religion was purportedly protected, except that

---

[45] Ibid, para. 165.

[46] Ibid, para. 460.

[47] Ibid, para. 464.

[48] *See* S. Heder, 'Reassessing the Role of Senior Leaders and Local Officials in Democratic Kampuchea Crimes: Cambodian Accountability in Comparative Perspective', in J. Ramji and B. van Schaack (eds), *Bringing the Khmer Rouge to Justice: Prosecuting Mass Violence before the Cambodian Courts* (Lewiston, New York, Edwin Mellon Press, 2005), pp. 377–423, p. 393.

[49] S.R. Ratner, J.S. Abrams and J.L Bischoff, *Accountability for Human Rights Atrocities in International Law* (3rd edn, Oxford, Oxford University Press, 2009), pp. 306–14.

'reactionary religions which are detrimental to Democratic Kampuchea and the Kampuchean people are absolutely forbidden'.[50]

The total re-organisation of Cambodian society was supervised by the *Angkar*, an organisation that remained secret until September 1977 when Pol Pot announced in a speech delivered at the Olympic Stadium in Phnom Penh that the *Angkar* was in fact equivalent to the CPK.[51] The term *Angkar* had been widely used by the CPK internally since its establishment but its meaning was unclear, sometimes being code for the top ranks in the party, a synonym for the Standing Committee or Central Committee, a reference to Office 870 in Phnom Penh, shorthand for anyone representing Pol Pot, or an allusion to Pol Pot himself.[52] The Central Committee, disturbed by 'bad elements' holding themselves out as *Angkar*, issued a directive in 1977 stating that:

> 1. The term "*Angkar*" or "Party" is used only for the organization. It shall not be used for any individual.
> 2. For individual (sic): "comrade", "this person's name", or "comrade in this or that position", or "comrade representing *Angkar* at this or that level" shall be used.[53]

Despite this directive, which may not have been communicated to the public, the *Angkar* retained its occult status throughout the Khmer Rouge period.

Following his coming out at the Olympic Stadium, Pol Pot embarked on an official visit to China, hoping for China's support amid growing tension between Cambodia and Vietnam.[54] At the end of 1977, Vietnamese troops crossed into Cambodia causing Cambodia to break off diplomatic relations with Vietnam. Vietnam withdrew shortly afterwards although the Khmer Rouge had suffered the most casualties.[55] It has been commented that 'Pol Pot's purges in 1978 bled Cambodia white'.[56]

---

[50] 'The Constitution of Democratic Kampuchea', in Etcheson, above n. 15, pp. 221–7.

[51] Short, above n. 19, p. 375.

[52] Nuon Trial Judgment, above n. 18, para. 221 (relying on evidence given by Duch and other witnesses); *Prosecutor v Kaing Guek Eav alias 'Duch'*, ECCC Case File No. 001/18-07-2007/ECCC/TC, Trial Chamber, Judgment, 26 July 2010, para. 85 ('Duch Trial Judgment'). *See* also Shawcross, above n. 17, pp. 377–8.

[53] Nuon Trial Judgment, above n. 18, para. 221.

[54] Chandler, above n. 4, pp. 271–2.

[55] Short, above n. 19, p. 378.

[56] Ibid, p. 387.

Training camps for Khmer refugees were established by the Vietnamese and one beneficiary was a young Khmer Rouge military commander, Hun Sen, who had defected in mid-1977.[57] Border clashes continued throughout 1978, culminating in an invasion by Vietnamese forces on Christmas Day, at which point many Cambodians fled the country or were internally displaced. Phnom Penh was captured by the Vietnamese on 7 January 1979. Sihanouk had been flown out with Chinese assistance the previous day, while the Khmer Rouge leadership abandoned ship and scattered across the country, with many heading towards the Thai border.

Although precise figures are not known, it is estimated that up to a quarter of the population perished during the Khmer Rouge regime and the Vietnamese invasion, amounting to between 1.5 and 2 million excess deaths in this period.[58]

2.7 The People's Republic of Kampuchea

The new People's Republic of Kampuchea (PRK) under Vietnamese occupation was a place of civil unrest with various groups being formed to resist the Vietnamese and strive once again for independence. Vietnam put a nominally Cambodian government in place, headed by Heng Samrin who had once been a Khmer Rouge military commander, like his Foreign Minister, Hun Sen.[59] In 1985 Hun Sen took over as Prime Minister. The country was administered by the Kampuchean People's Revolutionary Party (KPRP), which later became the Cambodian People's Party (CPP). The party originally had a Marxist-Leninist political basis but this changed with Cambodia's transitional period beginning in 1989.[60]

---

[57] Ibid, p. 379.

[58] *See* e.g. T. Fawthrop and H. Jarvis, *Getting Away with Genocide? Elusive Justice and the Khmer Rouge Tribunal* (London, Pluto Press, 2004), pp. 3–4; C. Etcheson, 'The Politics of Genocide Justice in Cambodia', in C.P.R. Romano, A. Nollkaemper and J.K. Kleffner (eds), *Internationalized Criminal Courts and Tribunal: Sierra Leone, East Timor, Kosovo and Cambodia* (Oxford/New York, Oxford University Press, 2004), pp. 181–205, p. 181; Heder and Tittemore, above n. 3, p. 3: 'As many as two million people – nearly one-third of the Cambodian population – are believed to have perished at the hands of the CPK when it ruled Cambodia, then called Democratic Kampuchea (DK), from April 1975 to January 1979' <http://www.wcl.american.edu/warcrimes/khmerrouge.pdf?rd=1> [accessed 3 June 2017]; Nuon Trial Judgment, above n. 18, para. 174.

[59] Short, above n. 19, p. 409.

[60] Etcheson, above n. 15, p. 183.

In the meantime, the Khmer Rouge re-grouped close to the Thai border, dissolved the CPK and vowed to continue their armed struggle.[61]

2.8 The People's Revolutionary Tribunal

The immediate reaction of the PRK was to 'demonize the "genocidal Pol-Pot-Ieng Sary clique"'.[62] Pol Pot and his Foreign Minister during the Khmer Rouge era, Ieng Sary, were tried in absentia, convicted of genocide and sentenced to death in 1979 by the People's Revolutionary Tribunal (PRT) established by the PRK.[63] The two accused were charged as 'instigators and planners of genocidal crimes'.[64] The judgment referred to planning at the highest policy level, finding that: 'Pol Pot and Ieng Sary have a record of collusion with each other to oppose the Kampuchean revolution; that they jointly mapped out extremely reactionary domestic and foreign policies and organised and directed the implementation of these policies.'[65] They were held liable as instigators and planners and therefore found to be responsible for all the consequences of their genocidal acts. This was the only formal judicial process in the immediate aftermath of the Khmer Rouge defeat.[66] Vigilante justice was meted out in the 1980s and some of the most feared Khmer Rouge perpetrators were killed.[67]

---

[61] Short, above n. 19, pp. 416–17.

[62] Chandler, above n. 4, p. 280.

[63] 'Decree Law No.1, Preamble', in H.J. de Nike, J. Quigley and K.J. Robinson (eds), *Genocide in Cambodia: Documents from the Trial of Pol Pot and Ieng Sary* (Philadelphia, University of Pennsylvania Press, 2000), p. 45 (The trial was held at the Chaktomuk Theatre in Phnom Penh from 15–19 August 1979). *See* further Fawthrop and Jarvis, above n. 58, Chapter 3.

[64] 'Indictment', in H.J. de Nike, J. Quigley and K.J. Robinson (eds), *Genocide in Cambodia: Documents from the Trial of Pol Pot and Ieng Sary* (Philadelphia, University of Pennsylvania Press, 2000), p. 487.

[65] 'Judgment', in H.J. de Nike, J. Quigley and K.J. Robinson (eds), *Genocide in Cambodia: Documents from the Trial of Pol Pot and Ieng Sary* (Philadelphia, University of Pennsylvania Press, 2000), p. 548.

[66] For an analysis of the process, see T.H. Gutman, 'Cambodia, 1979: Trying Khmer Rouge Leaders for Genocide', in K. Sellars (ed), *Trials for International Crimes in Asia* (Cambridge, Cambridge University Press, 2016), pp. 167–90.

[67] Y. Chhang, 'Anthem Essay: Why the Khmer Rouge Tribunal Matters to the Cambodian Community: Justice for the Future, Not the Victims', *Searching for the Truth*, Documentation Center of Cambodia.

2.9 The State of Cambodia

The PRK amended its 1981 Constitution in 1989, changing the country's name to the State of Cambodia (SOC), just as the last Vietnamese troops finally left Cambodia and the seeds of democratisation began to be sown. 1989 has been described as the 'year of the democratic revolution'.[68] Political and economic reforms in the Soviet Union initiated by Mikhail Gorbachev eliminated the justification for the support by the US and other powers for anti-leftist insurgents in countries such as Cambodia.[69] In Eastern Europe communist regimes were removed and on 9 November 1989 the Berlin Wall fell. Communism no longer posed a threat and by 1991 the Soviet Union had itself collapsed. The withdrawal of the last Vietnamese troops from Cambodia in September 1989 coincided with a sharp reduction in Soviet aid.[70]

The 1989 changes to the Cambodian Constitution were directly influenced by the political climate and arguably marked a tentative step towards limiting the power of the State. A further incentive may well have been to encourage the international community to provide aid and assistance to the government in power, which was concerned about its own survival and still highly vulnerable to outside influence and intervention. A 'diplomatic breakthrough' for Cambodia was on the cards although the precise form it would take was unknown.[71] In anticipation, Cambodia seized an opportune moment to begin demonstrating a commitment to human rights.

Article 35 of the revised Constitution emphasised the basic human rights that had been denied to citizens by successive regimes, most systematically by the Khmer Rouge:

> The State shall ensure the physical inviolability of the individual.
>
> The law shall protect the honour, dignity and life of citizens.
>
> No prosecution, arrest, detention or imprisonment shall be permitted unless authorized by law.

---

[68] B. Holden, *Understanding Liberal Democracy* (2nd edn, New York, Harvester Wheatsheaf, 1993), p. 202.

[69] R.J. McMahon, *The Cold War, A Very Short Introduction* (Oxford/New York, Oxford University Press, 2003), p. 150.

[70] Chandler, above n. 4, p. 285.

[71] Ibid, p. 286.

> Coercion, physical torture or any other punitive act compounding the penalty inflicted on detainees or prisoners are prohibited. Perpetrators, collaborators and accomplices in such acts shall be punished by law.
>
> Confessions extracted by physical or mental coercion shall not be regarded as proof of guilt.
>
> If the accusation is based solely on suspicion, the defendant should be acquitted.
>
> The defendant shall be regarded as innocent until decided otherwise by the court.
>
> The State guarantees to all citizens the right to defend themselves in a court of law.
>
> Capital punishment is abolished.

The protection of the right to life became tangible through the abolition of capital punishment. The desire to break with an oppressive past has been emphasised by the death penalty expert, Roger Hood, as a primary reason for abolition in Cambodia. Hood writes that 'At the end of its civil war and terrible holocaust Cambodia decided to abolish the death penalty completely so as to mark with a powerful symbol the end of the Pol Pot regime'.[72] Similarly, David Johnson and Franklin Zimring note in their comparative study of the death penalty in Asia that the death penalty was abolished in Cambodia 'as part of the process of distancing a new government from the brutality of Pol Pot's regime'.[73] Amnesty International noted that the abolition of the death penalty 'was a major step demonstrating the government's intention to protect the right to life, grossly violated along with almost all other fundamental human rights by the previous Government of Democratic Kampuchea during its time in power'.[74] Chandler states that 'the death penalty was abolished in response to criticism of Cambodia's human rights record'.[75] Abolition of the death penalty formed part of a series of popular reforms including the

[72] R. Hood, *The Death Penalty: A Worldwide Perspective* (3rd edn, Oxford/New York, Oxford University Press, 2002), p. 43.

[73] D.T. Johnson and F.E. Zimring, *The Next Frontier, National Development, Political Change and the Death Penalty in Asia* (Oxford/New York, Oxford University Press, 2009), p. 381 (The authors note (p. 381, footnote 1, citing Short, above n. 19, p. 11) that under Pol Pot, 'Individual rights were not curtailed in favour of the collective, but extinguished altogether').

[74] Amnesty International, Cambodia: Recent Human Rights Developments, ASA 23/007/1990, December 1990, p. 3, <http://www.amnesty.org/en/library/info/ASA23/007/1990/en> [accessed 3 June 2017].

[75] Chandler, above n. 4, p. 285.

reintroduction of Buddhism as the state religion, revision of the national anthem and changes to the flag, and new laws relating to the acquisition and transfer of land.[76]

2.10 The Paris Negotiations and Agreement

The realignment of international politics spurred the reconstitution of Cambodia. The West had supported the Khmer Rouge while the Vietnam-backed regime was in power, fearing that the Vietnamese, supported by the Soviets, had expansionist aims. When the Cold War ended, the United Nations (UN) made a special effort to reconstruct Cambodia. Thus: 'In an unprecedented manner, the UN "took over" responsibility for the country, arranged elections and took the lead in drawing up the new constitution.'[77]

In the latter half of 1989, negotiations took place in Paris, with the participation of the four contending Cambodian parties, representatives of 18 countries including the five permanent members of the Security Council, and the UN Secretary-General. The negotiations were aimed at achieving a settlement and guaranteeing self-determination for the people of Cambodia. A settlement was reached on 28 August 1990 resulting in a framework document. The Supreme National Council (SNC) became the 'unique legitimate body and source of authority in which, throughout the transitional period, the independence, national sovereignty and unity of Cambodia is embodied'.[78]

The following year the Paris Conference reconvened to agree on the UN's role in preparing Cambodia for democratic elections. An Agreement on a Comprehensive Political Settlement of the Cambodia Conflict (Paris Agreement) was concluded on 23 October 1991.[79] The Paris

---

[76] Ibid.

[77] J. Öjendal and M. Lilja, 'Beyond Democracy in Cambodia, Political Reconstruction in a Post-Conflict Society?', in J. Öjendal and M. Lilja (eds), *Beyond Democracy in Cambodia, Political Reconstruction in a Post-Conflict Society* (Copenhagen, Nordic Institute of Asian Studies Press, 2009), pp. 1–30, p. 2.

[78] United Nations General Assembly, The Situation in Cambodia, A/RES/45/3, 15 October 1990, para. 4, <http://www.unhcr.org/refworld/docid/3b00efe53c.html> [accessed 3 June 2017].

[79] The Paris Agreements of 23 October 1991 include (1) Final Act of the Paris Conference on Cambodia; (2) Agreement on a comprehensive political settlement of the Cambodia conflict (with annexes) (hereinafter 'Paris Agreement'); (3) Agreement concerning the sovereignty, independence, territorial integrity and inviolability, neutrality and national unity of Cambodia; and

Agreement contained a number of provisions concerning human rights. According to Article 15(1), all Cambodians shall enjoy the rights and freedoms embodied in the Universal Declaration of Human Rights and other relevant international human rights instruments. Under Article 15(2)(a), Cambodia undertook to take measures to ensure that the policies and practices of the past should never be allowed to return and to adhere to relevant human rights instruments. Under Article 15(2)(b), other signatories equally agreed to promote respect for human rights in Cambodia. The UN Transitional Authority in Cambodia (UNTAC) was to provide human rights education, oversight and investigation, while the UN Commission on Human Rights would continue to follow Cambodia's human rights situation after the transitional period through the appointment of a special rapporteur, if necessary.

The question of accountability did not appear to be a focus of the Paris negotiations. The Cambodian government proposed that the new Constitution should expressly be consistent with the 1948 Genocide Convention, but while Indonesia and France were in favour, the proposal did not meet with widespread approval.[80] The idea of legal action in respect of the Khmer Rouge atrocities had been floated prior to the settlement. One suggestion was to bring a case against Cambodia before the International Court of Justice with the aim of pressurising Cambodia to comply with its obligations to conduct prosecutions, in particular under the Genocide Convention.[81] However, during the negotiations, responsibility for prosecuting offenders was placed upon the future government of Cambodia, falling outside UNTAC's mandate.[82]

The SNC took immediate steps in accordance with the Paris Agreement and acceded to five major human rights treaties in 1992: the International Covenant on Civil and Political Rights, the International Covenant on Economic Social and Cultural Rights, the Convention on the Elimination of Discrimination against Women, the Convention against Torture and the Convention on the Rights of the Child. Special Representatives of the Secretary-General for human rights in Cambodia were appointed from 1993 to 2008 when the role changed its name to Special

---

(4) Declaration on the rehabilitation and reconstruction of Cambodia. *See* United Nations. *Treaty Series*, vol. 1663, 27, 23 October 1991, <https://treaties.un.org/doc/Publication/UNTS/Volume%201663/v1663.pdf> [accessed 3 June 2017].

[80] B. Kiernan and C. Hughes, *Conflict and Change in Cambodia* (London/New York, Routledge, 2007), p. xiv.

[81] Ratner, Abrams and Bischoff, above n. 49, p. 358.

[82] S.R. Ratner, 'The Cambodia Settlement Agreements', *American Journal of International Law*, vol. 87, 1993, pp. 1–41, p. 26.

Rapporteur. The mandate of the six individuals to date who have served as Special Representatives or Rapporteurs derives from the agreements made at Paris and is to monitor, independently, the human rights situation in the country.[83]

The UN Advance Mission for Cambodia (UNAMIC) was succeeded by UNTAC which arrived in Cambodia on 16 March 1992. The UNTAC Law was adopted by the SNC on 10 September 1992, setting out provisions relating to the judiciary, as well as criminal law and procedure applicable in Cambodia during the transitional period.[84] Article 67 of the UNTAC Law reinforced the earlier commitment to abolish the death penalty.

2.11 Cambodia's Seat at the United Nations

A coalition government in exile including the ousted Khmer Rouge and supporters of Sihanouk and his former Prime Minister, Son Sann, continued to represent Cambodia at the UN until the conclusion of the Paris negotiations.[85] Most states refused to recognise the Vietnam-backed government of Prime Minister Hun Sen as legitimate, arguing that the forceful intervention by Vietnam to defeat the Khmer Rouge had been illegal. This meant that Khieu Samphan, then the coalition Vice President and Foreign Minister, appointed a Khmer Rouge supporter named Thiounn Prasith as Cambodia's UN representative while Sihanouk named his deputy.[86]

In 1990, the UN General Assembly adopted a resolution promising that the SNC would 'represent Cambodia externally and occupy the seat of

---

[83] Agreement on a Comprehensive Political Settlement of the Cambodia Conflict, 23 October 1991, Article 17; Agreement Concerning the Sovereignty, Independence, Territorial Integrity and Inviolability, Neutrality and National Unity of Cambodia, 23 October 1991, Article 3. For information on the Special Rapporteur on the situation of human rights in Cambodia, *see* 'Special Rapporteur on the Situation of Human Rights in Cambodia', The Office of the United Nations High Commissioner for Human Rights, <http://www.ohchr.org/EN/HRBodies/SP/CountriesMandates/KH/Pages/SRCambodia.aspx> [accessed 3 June 2017].

[84] For the text of the UNTAC Law, *see Guide to Cambodian Criminal Law* (prepared by the Ministry of Justice, 2005), p. 45.

[85] *See* further Fawthrop and Jarvis, above n. 58, pp. 24–39.

[86] P. Lewis, 'Why Cambodia's UN Seat is "Unattended"', *The New York Times*, 16 December 1990, <http://www.nytimes.com/1990/12/16/world/why-cambodia-s-un-seat-is-unattended.html> [accessed 3 June 2017].

Cambodia at the United Nations'.[87] However, Cambodia's UN seat was reported to be 'temporarily unattended' pending determination of the composition of the SNC.[88] The General Assembly's promise was finally fulfilled after the Khmer Rouge's attempt to sabotage democratic elections in 1993.[89]

2.12 The 1993 Constitution

Funcinpec, the royalist party founded by Sihanouk in the early 1980s, received a majority of the vote in the May 1993 elections. A coalition government was formed with Sihanouk's son, Norodom Ranariddh, as First Prime Minister, and Hun Sen of the CPP as Co-Prime Minister.[90] The monarchy was restored and Sihanouk, who had returned to Phnom Penh in 1991 after the signing of the Paris Agreement, was reinstated as King.

Annex 5 to the Paris agreements entitled 'Principles for a new constitution for Cambodia' emphasised that 'Cambodia's tragic recent history requires special measures to assure protection of human rights' and set out the fundamental rights, including the right to life, that must be included in the Constitution. According to the six basic principles contained in Annex 5, the Constitution (i) would be the supreme law of the land; (ii) would contain a declaration of fundamental human rights; (iii) would declare Cambodia's status as a sovereign, independent and neutral country; (iv) would state that Cambodia would follow a system of 'liberal' democracy, on the basis of pluralism, providing for periodic elections governed by universal suffrage, full participation and secret balloting; (v) would establish an independent judiciary; and (vi) would be adopted by two-thirds of the constituent assembly. It has been suggested that these constitutional principles transcended existing international human rights instruments by going 'beyond recognizing free elections as the sole process for choosing a government after internal strife, and

---

[87] United Nations General Assembly, The Situation in Cambodia, A/RES/45/3, 15 October 1990, para. 5, <http://www.unhcr.org/refworld/docid/3b00efe53c.html> [accessed 3 June 2017].

[88] Lewis, above n. 86.

[89] L. Reydams, J. Wouters, and C. Ryngaert, 'The Politics of Establishing International Criminal Tribunals', in L. Reydams, J. Wouters, and C. Ryngaert (eds), *International Prosecutors* (Oxford, Oxford University Press, 2012), pp. 6–80, p. 47.

[90] Ranariddh was ousted in a 1997 coup but the subsequent elections in 1998 resulted in another coalition between the CPP and Funcinpec, with the CPP exerting greater influence.

beyond committing the elected regime to guaranteeing the human rights of its people, by identifying the path – labelled "liberal democracy on the basis of pluralism" – it is to follow'.[91] The use of this language was apparently proposed by Sihanouk.[92]

The parties represented in the Constituent Assembly drafted a new Constitution which was promulgated on 24 September 1993, establishing a multiparty 'liberal' democracy under a constitutional monarchy. The use of the adjective 'liberal' in this context 'classically implies a concern with individual freedoms that centres on the need to limit the power and authority of the government'.[93] A core concept of liberal democracy in Cambodia was that of the 'people's will'.[94] As Jack Donnelly states, 'the human rights work of most contemporary "democracies" is rooted in substantive adjectives such as "liberal"'.[95]

It has been noted that Sihanouk most likely used the term 'liberal democracy' in the context of the negotiations because it was what the American and other key participants wanted to hear and it did not reflect the government's principles when he was king or prime minister in the 1950s.[96] Indeed, perhaps in part because of the scale of the human rights violations experienced by Cambodia under the Khmer Rouge, a 'human-rights-based concept of sovereignty'[97] was endorsed as a way forward even by states such as China and Vietnam which had not themselves embraced democratic principles. This points to an element of hypocrisy in the path chosen for Cambodia since Cambodia's immediate neighbours were perhaps unlikely to sustain the drive towards genuine respect for human rights.[98] Indeed, the UN-sponsored transition placed Cambodia steps ahead on paper even if there was much human rights work still to be done in practice.

---

[91] Ratner, above n. 82, p. 27.

[92] Ibid, p. 27, footnote 163.

[93] Holden, above n. 68, p. 16.

[94] C. Hughes, 'International Intervention and the People's Will', in B. Kiernan and C. Hughes (eds), *Conflict and Change in Cambodia* (London/New York, Routledge, 2007), pp. 45–68, p. 46.

[95] J. Donnelly, *Universal Human Rights in Theory and Practice* (2nd edn, Ithaca, New York, Cornell University Press, 2003), p. 191.

[96] S.P. Marks, 'The New Cambodian Constitution: From Civil War to a Fragile Democracy', *Columbia Human Rights Law Review*, vol. 26, no. 1, 1994, pp. 45–110, p. 57.

[97] Ratner, above n. 82, p. 40.

[98] Ibid, p. 40 (notes that endorsement of the Paris Agreements by China and Vietnam 'highlights a layer of hypocrisy' in the approach of those states).

The formal transitional period came to an end when the Constituent Assembly became the National Assembly of Cambodia, effectively the new parliament, in accordance with articles 1 and 12 of the Paris Agreement. The country's official name changed to the Kingdom of Cambodia. Article 43 of the 1993 Constitution provides that Buddhism shall be the State religion in Cambodia, making Cambodia one of the world's only predominantly Buddhist States.[99]

2.13 The 1994 Law to Outlaw the Democratic Kampuchea Group

In the 1990s, amnesties became an important tool to reward and reintegrate defecting Khmer Rouge fighters. A Law to Outlaw the Democratic Kampuchea Group was introduced in 1994 as a reaction to the DK group's failure to abide by the terms of the Paris Agreement, in particular by 'violating the articles which called for respect of a ceasefire, the permission to officials and staff of the UN to enter the zones it controlled, for assembly to cantonment, disarmament and demobilization of armed forces, and for respect for the human rights of the Cambodian population.'[100] In addition to violating the Cambodian Constitution, according to the Law the DK group had:

> continually committed criminal, terrorist and genocidal acts which has been a characteristic of the group since it captured power in April 1975 – forcible movement, abduction, killing and subsequently also robbery and banditry, laying mines indiscriminately throughout the plains and forests, destroying public and private property, leading the killing of civilians, forcibly taking and illegally occupying national territory, and selling natural resources by violating the sovereignty of the Kingdom of Cambodia.

The DK group and its armed forces were declared 'outlaws' and property obtained illegally was ordered to be confiscated. DK members who were not leaders could secure an amnesty by returning to live under the control of the Royal Government of the Kingdom of Cambodia. The key

---

[99] I. Harris, '"Onslaught on Human Beings": A Theravāda Buddhist Perspective on Accountability for Crimes Committed in the Democratic Kampuchea Period', in J. Ramji and B. van Schaack (eds), *Bringing the Khmer Rouge to Justice: Prosecuting Mass Violence before the Cambodian Courts* (Lewiston, New York, Edwin Mellon Press, 2005), pp. 59–95, p. 60.

[100] Law on the Outlawing of the 'Democratic Kampuchea' Group, Reachkram No. 01.NS.94, 15 July 1994 (English translation based on the text published by *Phnom Penh Post*, vol. 3, no. 14, 15–28 July 1994).

provisions of the Law addressing the relevant crimes and conditions for the granting of an amnesty were as follows:

> Article 3: Members of the political organization or the military forces of the 'Democratic Kampuchea' group or any persons who commit crimes of murder, rape, robbery of people's property, the destruction of public and private property, etc. shall be sentenced according to existing criminal law.
>
> Article 4: Members of the political organization or the military forces of the 'Democratic Kampuchea' group or any persons who commit
>
> - secession,
> - destruction against the Royal Government,
> - destruction against organs of public authority, or
> - incitement or forcing the taking up of arms against public authority
>
> shall be charged as criminals against the internal security of the country and sentenced to jail for 20 to 30 years or for life.
>
> Article 5: This Law shall grant a stay of six months after coming into effect to permit people who are members of the political organization of military forces of the 'Democratic Kampuchea' group to return to live under the control of the Royal Government in the Kingdom of Cambodia without facing punishment for crimes which they have committed.

As it concerned the Khmer Rouge leadership, Ieng Sary defected in 1996 and was granted by a Royal Decree a pardon in respect of the death sentence imposed by the PRT and an amnesty from prosecution under the 1994 Law.[101] King Norodom Sihanouk's revocation of Ieng Sary's death sentence was at the request of the then Co-Prime Ministers Hun Sen and Prince Norodom Ranariddh.[102] It was Ieng Sary's reward for ensuring the mass defection of Khmer Rouge cadres in two strategic locations which had apparently speeded up the group's final demise.[103] Hun Sen announced that this was the price that had to be paid for the sake of the nation.[104] Ensuring the dissolution of the Khmer Rouge and the reintegration of defectors was at that stage considered to trump punishment as the best way of transitioning to a viable political future. The Royal Decree took into account the Cambodian Constitution but the decision to revoke the application of the death penalty against Ieng Sary was not

---

101 Royal Decree (Reach Kret), NS/RKT/0996/72, 14 December 1996, <http://www.eccc.gov.kh/en/documents/legal/amnestypardon-leng-sary> [accessed 3 June 2017].

102 Fawthrop and Jarvis, above n. 58, p. 137.

103 Ibid.

104 Ibid.

based on the unconstitutionality of the sentence but rather on political considerations.[105] Ieng Sary and his wife, Ieng Thirith, lived in their villa in Phnom Penh until their arrest and transfer to the ECCC in 2007.

2.14 Documentation and Preservation of Evidence

At a session of the Commission on Human Rights held on 7 March 1979, the Chairman of the Sub-Commission on Prevention of Discrimination and Protection of Minorities, Mr. Bouhdiba, presented an analysis of documents that had been received from governments and non-governmental organisations (NGO) on the human rights situation in Democratic Kampuchea. According to a summary of Mr. Bouhdiba's presentation:

> In his analysis, he was not putting an ideology on trial or criticizing a political regime as such. Contrary to normal practice, he had not submitted any conclusions or suggestions, the reason being that the changing situation in Kampuchea made it impossible to propose a constructive solution that would satisfy the expectations of national and international public opinion. However, the events described in the documents were extremely serious – the most serious that had occurred anywhere in the world since Nazism. Of course, there was no proof that they had occurred, since there had been no investigation by the United Nations, but the various accounts were consistent down to the last detail. Even if the events now belonged only to history, it was neither possible nor prudent to pass over them in silence or simply to lay the matter aside.
>
> The first step should be to expose the facts.[106]

Efforts to document crimes and preserve evidence continued during the 'lost' decades when political instability allowed for impunity. Notably in 1994 the US Congress passed the Cambodian Genocide Justice Act marking a shift in US policy from active and later passive support for the Khmer Rouge to active support for efforts to bring former Khmer Rouge members to justice for crimes against humanity committed between 17

---

[105] The abolition of the death penalty would not normally result in those previously sentenced to death walking free, rather, commutation to a term in prison would be the norm. *See Prosecutor v Ieng Sary*, ECCC Case File No. 002/19-09-2007-ECCC/OCIJ (PTC75), Pre-Trial Chamber, Decision on Ieng Sary's Appeal Against the Closing Order, 11 April 2011, para. 192.

[106] United Nations Economic and Social Council, Commission on Human Rights, Thirty-Fifth Session, Summary Record of the First Part (Public) of the 1510th Meeting, E/CN.4/SR.1510, 9 March 1979, paras. 24–5.

April 1975 and 7 January 1979. According to the Act, the US President was urged:

1. to collect, or assist appropriate organizations and individuals to collect relevant data on crimes of genocide committed in Cambodia;
2. in circumstances which the President deems appropriate, to encourage the establishment of a national or international criminal tribunal for the prosecution of those accused of genocide in Cambodia; and
3. as necessary, to provide such national or international tribunal with information collected pursuant to paragraph (1).[107]

State Department lawyers considered the apprehension of the Khmer Rouge leadership to be the priority leading to a chicken or egg scenario in terms of whether arrests or a tribunal should come first.[108] In the meantime, the US provided funding for Yale University's Cambodia Genocide Program which resulted in the establishment of the Documentation Centre of Cambodia (DC-Cam) in 1995. DC-Cam became an independent NGO in 1997 and continues to operate from its base in Phnom Penh, serving as a vital support to the ECCC through its archives, research and other activities.[109]

2.15 The ECCC Negotiations

Hun Sen and Norodom Ranariddh first appealed to the UN for international assistance in conducting a trial of the Khmer Rouge leaders in June 1997, shortly before the coalition government fell apart and fighting broke out in Phnom Penh. In November 1997, once political stability had been regained, the government sent a renewed request to the US asking for the establishment of an international criminal tribunal to bring the Khmer Rouge leadership to trial 'while they are still alive'.[110]

A resolution adopted by the UN General Assembly in February 1998 did not give Cambodia a glowing report on the implementation of human rights norms. The resolution expressed the desire that the 'United Nations respond positively to assist efforts to investigate Cambodia's tragic history, including responsibility for past international crimes, such as acts

---

[107] Cambodian Genocide Justice Act, 22 U.S.C. 2656, 30 April 1994.

[108] D. Scheffer, *All the Missing Souls: A Personal History of the War Crimes Tribunals* (Princeton, Princeton University Press, 2012), pp. 344–5.

[109] Reydams, Wouters, and Ryngaert, above n. 89, p. 47.

[110] Cambodian Prime Ministers Ung Huot and Samdech Hun Sen, 'Letter to United States President Bill Clinton', 27 November 1997, cited in Scheffer, above n. 108, p. 351.

of genocide and crimes against humanity', noted with concern that no Khmer Rouge leader had been brought to account, and expressed grave concern about numerous instances of violations of human rights.[111] While much had been accomplished at least on paper during the Paris negotiations, the problem of impunity continued to loom large.

In a pre-emptive blow to justice, Pol Pot, who was believed to have been captured during internal Khmer Rouge fighting in 1997, died in April 1998.[112] US efforts to obtain a Security Council resolution establishing an International Criminal Tribunal for Cambodia failed. However, the UN Secretary-General appointed a group of experts to evaluate the existing evidence and 'propose further measures as a means of bringing about national reconciliation, strengthening democracy and addressing the issue of individual accountability'.[113]

On 25 December 1998, Khieu Samphan and Nuon Chea surrendered and their armed forces were reintegrated. Their defection was accepted by Hun Sen who famously announced that it was time to 'dig a hole and bury the past'.[114] Nuon Chea was permitted to live near the Thai border.

On 6 March 1999, Ta Mok, a highly feared member of the Democratic Kampuchea Standing Committee, was arrested by the Cambodian authorities and taken to Phnom Penh with a view to a trial before Cambodian domestic courts.

On 15 March 1999, the Report of the Group of Experts recommending the establishment of an international tribunal by the Security Council was presented to both the UN General Assembly and the Security Council.[115] The Cambodian government, which by then favoured a more domestic-oriented approach, was unenthusiastic about the proposal. On 9 May 1999, Duch was arrested and detained on charges under the 1994 Law to

---

111 United Nations General Assembly, The Situation of Human Rights in Cambodia, A/RES/52/135, 27 February 1998.

112 *See* Scheffer, above n. 109, p. 347: (indicating that reports of Pol Pot's whereabouts and capture in this period were misleading).

113 *See* United Nations General Assembly, The Situation of Human Rights in Cambodia, A/RES/52/135, 27 February 1998; and United Nations General Assembly, The Situation of Human Rights in Cambodia, A/RES/53/145, 9 December 1998.

114 S. Berfield, 'Forget the Killing Fields?', *ASIAWEEK*, 8 January 1999, <http://premium.cnn.com/ASIANOW/asiaweek/99/0108/nat6.html> [accessed 3 June 2017].

115 Report of the Group of Experts for Cambodia Established pursuant to General Assembly Resolution 52/135, A/53/850, 18 February 1999, <http://repository.un.org/bitstream/handle/11176/35606/A_53_850%3bS_1999_231-EN.pdf?sequence=21&isAllowed=y> [accessed 3 June 2017].

Outlaw the Democratic Kampuchea Group. By this point trials were on the agenda and King Sihanouk refused to grant further amnesties in view of the discontent of the majority of the Cambodian people.[116]

After renewed calls from Cambodia for domestic trials with international assistance, a local 'Task Force for Cooperation with Foreign Legal Experts and Preparation of the Proceedings for the Trial of Senior Khmer Rouge Leaders' was set up to negotiate with the UN. The Task Force produced a draft law which was presented to the UN but failed to meet with approval. The General Assembly adopted a new resolution appealing to the Cambodian Government 'to ensure that those most responsible for the most serious violations of human rights are brought to account in accordance with international standards of justice, fairness and due process of law' and urging continued cooperation.[117]

In response to foreign pressure, especially by Australia, France and Britain, trials were conducted under domestic criminal law against Khmer Rouge General Nun Paet (in 1999) and Colonel Chhouk Rin and General Sam Bith (in 2002) for an attack in July 1994 on a train in Kampot involving the deaths of 13 Cambodians and a French, Australian and British backpacker. All three accused were sentenced to life imprisonment. Chhouk Rin's trial was held in absentia.[118]

On 10 August 2001, King Norodom Sihanouk signed the Law on the Establishment of the Extraordinary Chambers in the Courts of Cambodia for the Prosecution of Crimes Committed during the Period of Democratic Kampuchea and it was promulgated, a feat which was welcomed by the UN General Assembly.[119] The point of no return appeared to have been reached. Yet on 8 February 2002, the UN announced its withdrawal from negotiations on the basis that the proposed Extraordinary Chambers could not guarantee international standards of justice. The UN required a

---

116 Berfield, above n. 114.

117 United Nations General Assembly, The Situation of Human Rights in Cambodia, A/RES/54/171, 17 December 1999.

118 'Life for Khmer Rouge commander', *BBC News*, 23 December 2002, <http://news.bbc.co.uk/2/hi/asia-pacific/2600171.stm> [accessed 3 June 2017]. For a detailed analysis, *see* J. Hall, 'In the Shadow of the Khmer Rouge Tribunal: The Domestic Trials of Nuon Paet, Chhouk Rin and Sam Bith, and the Search for Judicial Legitimacy in Cambodia', *Columbia Journal of Asian Law*, vol. 20, 2006, pp. 235–97.

119 United Nations General Assembly, The Situation of Human Rights in Cambodia, A/RES/56/169, 19 December 2001.

clear mandate from the General Assembly or Security Council in order for talks to be re-initiated.[120]

A core group of governments, including the US, Canada, Japan, France, Australia and the United Kingdom, called for a resumption of efforts to establish an accountability mechanism for Cambodia.[121] The General Assembly, 'conscious that the opportunity to bring those responsible to justice may soon be lost', passed a resolution welcoming the promulgation of the Law on the Establishment of the Extraordinary Chambers in the Courts of Cambodia and requesting that negotiations proceed.[122] An Agreement between the United Nations and the Royal Government of Cambodia Concerning the Prosecution under Cambodian Law of Crimes Committed during the Period of Democratic Kampuchea (ECCC Agreement) was eventually signed on 6 June 2003.[123] The United Nations Assistance to the Khmer Rouge Trial (UNAKRT) was born. The four cornerstones of the project were: Due Process, International Standards for Court Operations, Security and Safety, and Efficiency and Effectiveness. The draft Law on the Establishment of the Extraordinary Chambers in the Courts of Cambodia was subsequently amended on 6 August 2004 and approved, and the ECCC Agreement came into force.

2.16 The Establishment of the ECCC

The ECCC was formally established in early 2006 and hosted on the premises of the Royal Cambodian Armed Forces High Command Headquarters in Phnom Penh. Construction work commenced to turn a disused military theatre into a state of the art courtroom while temporary facilities were set up for the initial pre-trial hearings. The ECCC Pre-Trial Chamber has noted that: 'The ECCC only existed in any form after the swearing-in of the judges of the ECCC, which took place on 3 July 2006. The ECCC did not exist as an organ before this date.'[124] Ta

---

120 Letter from Kofi Annan to Hun Sen, 12 July 2002.

121 Scheffer, above n. 108, p. 402.

122 United Nations General Assembly, Khmer Rouge Trials, A/RES/57/228, 18 December 2002.

123 Agreement between the United Nations and the Royal Government of Cambodia concerning the Prosecution under Cambodian Law of Crimes Committed During the Period of Democratic Kampuchea, United Nations, Treaty Series, vol. 2329, 117, 6 June 2003, <https://www.eccc.gov.kh/sites/default/files/legal-documents/Agreement_between_UN_and_RGC.pdf> [accessed 3 June 2017] ('ECCC Agreement').

124 *Prosecutor v Kaing Guek Eav alias 'Duch'*, ECCC Case File No. 001/18-07-2007/ECCC/OCIJ (PTC01), Pre-Trial Chamber, Decision on Appeal

Mok died the same month the ECCC formally came into existence. Other possible suspects, such as Son Sen[125] and Kae Pok,[126] had also passed away. The ECCC became fully operational in June 2007 after the adoption of the rules governing its internal procedures by the newly appointed judges.

3. CAMBODIA TOMORROW

Reflecting on his involvement in the ECCC negotiations, David Scheffer, who served as US Ambassador-at-Large for War Crimes Issues at the time and worked tirelessly to sustain US interest has commented that: 'International justice is the art of the possible, and nowhere was that demonstrated more profoundly than in Cambodia.'[127] Just as colonialism revived pride in the long-forgotten Angkor period and an associated hunger for autonomy, the ECCC negotiations revived both international and domestic shame over the Khmer Rouge period and an associated hunger for justice. When the French declared a protectorate in 1863, Cambodia's population was estimated at less than one million. By the time of independence, it had risen to over four million.[128] This was reduced by at least a quarter during the Khmer Rouge period. Cambodia's population is now edging close to 16 million. The majority of this population has no direct memory of the late 1970s. This is worth bearing in mind when assessing the legitimacy and legacy of a criminal justice process focused on events that are sliding behind living memory. For today's younger generation of Cambodia, life navigates the historical landmarks of S-21 and *Choeng Ek* and moves at a fast pace into the future, metaphorically (if not by moped) overtaking the slow bus to the ECCC.

What this future holds remains to be seen. Phnom Penh has developed at a rapid pace in the past decade, readying itself to claim a place as a

---

Against Provisional Detention Order of Kaing Guek Eav alias 'Duch', 3 December 2007, para. 22.

[125] Scheffer, above n. 108, p. 404.

[126] S. Heder and B.D. Tittemore, *Seven Candidates for Prosecution: Accountability for the Crimes of the Khmer Rouge* (2nd edn, Phnom Penh, Documentation Center of Cambodia, 2004), pp. 108–15 (Listed by the authors as a candidate for prosecution), and *see* p. i (Preface to the Second Edition; noting his death).

[127] Scheffer, above n. 109, p. 341 (he writes that there was in fact no coherent US policy, fully backed by top officials in Washington), p. 343.

[128] Chandler, above n. 4, p. 6.

modern Asian city. The *Cambodia Daily* reported in 2015 on plans to further enlarge Phnom Penh by incorporating areas located across the Tonle Sap and Mekong rivers from the Royal Palace for development purposes.[129] Cambodia became a party to the Statute of the International Criminal Court in 2002, exposing itself to the possibility of a future case of crimes against humanity attributed to the ruling elite based on the unlawful dispossession of land.[130]

Cambodia's complex process of democratisation has been described as 'an exercise in political self-determination through a U.N. managed transition to a democratic form of government based on a constitution that both acknowledges Cambodian tradition and current political forces, and establishes a bill of rights and mechanisms for protecting those rights.'[131] It is worth being reminded of the Preamble to the 1993 Constitution which is still in force, subject to amendments:[132]

> We, the Khmer people,
>
> Accustomed to having a grand civilization, a prosperous nation, a very large territory, a prestige glittering like a diamond;
>
> Having fallen into a terrifying decay for the two last decades, when we have been undergoing unspeakable, demeaning sufferings and disasters of the most regrettable way;
>
> In a burst of consciousness, rising up with a resolute determination in order to unite, to strengthen the national unity, to defend the Cambodian territory, to preserve the precious sovereignty and the marvellous civilization of ANGKOR, to re-build the country and become once again an 'Oasis of Peace' based on the system of a liberal multi-party democracy, to guarantee human rights, to ensure the respect of law, to be highly responsible for the destiny of the nation forever evolving toward progress, development and prosperity.

---

[129] K. Sothear, 'Phnom Penh Municipality Plans City Expansion', *The Cambodia Daily*, 21 March 2015, <https://www.cambodiadaily.com/archives/phnom-penh-municipality-plans-city-expansion-80500/> [accessed 3 June 2017].

[130] C. Maza, 'ICC Move Fuels Debate on Cambodian Case', *The Phnom Penh Post*, 19 September 2016, <http://www.phnompenhpost.com/national/icc-move-fuels-debate-cambodian-case> [accessed 3 June 2017].

[131] Marks, above n. 96, p. 47.

[132] The Constitution of the Kingdom of Cambodia, 21 September 1993 (English translation, *see* 'Basic Texts', The Constitutional Council of Cambodia, <http://www.ccc.gov.kh/law_en.php> [accessed 3 June 2017]).

Events since the turn of the century have led local human rights activists to describe Cambodia as being in a freefall from democracy.[133] Protestors took to the streets in 2013 to contest the CPP's victory over the Cambodia National Rescue Party (CNRP), which had made significant gains, arguing that there had been voting irregularities.[134] The promised reforms of the national election commission were slow to materialise and fresh protests in 2014 led to arrests of opposition party and social activists. These developments caused the Asia director of Human Rights Watch to claim that: 'The government's actions in the face of peaceful protest are that of a dictatorship, not a democracy.'[135] In what the international press termed the 'final blow to democracy', legislation was passed in 2017 making it more difficult for opposition parties to function.[136] In anticipation of the new law, and in light of his prior convictions for defamation, the self-exiled leader of the CNRP, Sam Rainsy, resigned to prevent the dissolution of his party. In the same period, garment workers staged repeated protests for higher wages and better conditions and faced violent crackdowns.[137] The 2016 shooting in broad daylight of the popular political commentator, Kem Ley, further mobilised the population especially through social media, and while a man improbably named Chuob Somlab or 'Meet Kill' was convicted of the murder and sentenced to life imprisonment, the trial left questions

---

133 *See* e.g. Joint Organizations, 'Statement: "Cambodia Democracy in Free-fall: Lifting of SRP Parliamentarians Immunity"', Cambodian League for the Prevention and Defence of Human Rights (LICADHO), <http://www.licadho-cambodia.org/pressrelease.php?perm=210> [accessed 3 June 2017].

134 K. Hodal, 'Cambodian Election Protests Grip Phnom Penh', *The Guardian*, 16 September 2013, <https://www.theguardian.com/world/2013/sep/16/cambodia-election-protests-phnom-penh > [accessed 3 June 2017].

135 'Cambodia: New Crackdown on Protesters', Human Rights Watch, 13 November 2014, <https://www.hrw.org/news/2014/11/13/cambodia-new-crackdown-protesters> [accessed 3 June 2017].

136 L. Murdoch, 'Australia Silent as Cambodia's Hun Sen Deals Final Blow to Democracy', *The Sydney Morning Herald*, 22 February 2017, <http://www.smh.com.au/world/australia-silent-as-cambodias-hun-sen-deals-final-blow-to-democracy-20170221-guhorj.html> [accessed 3 June 2017].

137 'Cambodia: Crackdown on Garment Workers Protesting for Higher Wages – Jan 2014', Business and Human Rights Resource Centre, 29 January 2014, <https://business-humanrights.org/en/documents/cambodia-crackdown-on-garment-workers-protesting-for-higher-wages-jan-2014> [accessed 3 June 2017]; E.T. Kim, 'Cambodian Garment Workers Rise up and Face a Crackdown', *Al Jazeera America*, 11 March 2015, <http://america.aljazeera.com/articles/2015/3/11/cambodian-garment-workers-rise-up-and-face-a-crackdown.html> [accessed 3 June 2017].

unanswered.[138] Shortly afterwards a further conviction for 'public defamation and incitement causing turmoil in society' was added to Sam Rainsy's criminal record on the basis that he had claimed the government orchestrated Kem Ley's killing.[139] In an interview for the *Carnegie Council* in 2017, the Cambodian human rights lawyer, Sohporn Sek, who had represented indigenous communities in cases concerning land and natural resources, stated (without 'criticizing the prime minister or any persons') that from his observations in Cambodia, 'democracy is just a term' and at a 'crossroads'. He also observed that most of the State mechanisms, such as the military and judiciary, are controlled by the ruling party and therefore lack independence which is 'dangerous to democracy' and 'not easy to change'.[140]

What is significant, perhaps, is that civil activism has become more of a feature of Cambodian society and an emboldened youth, born after Cambodia's conflicts, are demanding progress. For them the risk that political change might signal a return to war as suggested by Hun Sen may seem remote. More pressing issues include land concessions granted to Chinese and Vietnamese companies, poverty and the growing wealth disparity, and corruption.[141] In 2017, Hun Sen ordered a ban on the export of breast milk to a US-based company, stating that: 'We are not so poor that we have to sell human breast milk.'[142] The mothers who earn

---

138 J. Wallace and N. Vannarin, 'A Life Sentence in Cambodia, but Kem Ley's Murder is Far from Solved', *The New York Times*, 23 March 2017, <https://www.nytimes.com/2017/03/23/world/asia/cambodia-kem-ley-killing-life-sentence.html?rref=collection%2Ftimestopic%2FHun%20Sen&action=click&contentCollection=timestopics&region=stream&module=stream_unit&version=latest&contentPlacement=2&pgtype=collection> [accessed 3 June 2017].

139 O. Sony, 'Rainsy Gets 20 Months for Kem Ley Murder Claim', *The Cambodia Daily*, 31 March 2017, <https://www.cambodiadaily.com/news/rainsy-gets-20-months-for-kem-ley-murder-claim-127323/> [accessed 3 June 2017].

140 D. Stewart, 'Interview with Sophorn Sek: "In Cambodia, 'Democracy' is Just a Term …"', Carnegie Council, 4 April 2017, <https://www.carnegiecouncil.org/studio/multimedia/20170404-sophorn-sek-cambodia-democracy?EMAILTAG> [accessed 3 June 2017].

141 L. H., 'Feeling Cheated', *The Economist*, 29 July 2013, <http://www.economist.com/blogs/banyan/2013/07/cambodias-election> [accessed 3 June 2017].

142 S. David and C. Maza, 'Cambodia Bans Breast Milk Exports after International Media Coverage', *The Phnom Penh Post*, 28 March 2017, <http://www.phnompenhpost.com/national/cambodia-bans-breast-milk-exports-after-international-media-coverage> [accessed 3 June 2017]; T. Wong, 'Cambodia Breast Milk: The Debate over Mothers Selling Milk', *BBC News*, 29 March 2017, <http://www.bbc.com/news/world-asia-39414820> [accessed 3 June 2017]; K. Forster, 'US Company Selling Human Breast Milk Stopped by Cambodia

too little as garment workers to support their families or who lose their jobs when they become pregnant may beg to differ. Nonetheless, an inquiry by the Cambodian Health Ministry into whether the business violated a law on trafficking in human organs suggested that the matter was not being viewed simply as one of national pride. On the twenty-fifth anniversary of the Paris Agreement, the UN Special Rapporteur on Cambodia, Rhona Smith, observed that it was time for Cambodia to fully implement all the rights and freedoms in the various human rights treaties that it had adopted.[143] When the attention of historians turns from the three years and eight months Pol Pot era to the 32 years and counting Hun Sen era there will be a long tale to tell. The next elections are in 2018. Cambodia tomorrow will hopefully be a place where democracy and human rights are mainstreamed as matters of national pride as so eloquently expressed in the Constitution.

Export Ban', *The Independent*, 28 March 2017, <http://www.independent.co.uk/news/world/asia/human-breast-milk-company-ambrosia-labs-selling-us-stopped-cambodia-export-ban-bodybuilders-a7654116.html> [accessed 3 June 2017]; 'This Week in Asia: April 2-8 2017', *South China Morning Post*, p. 5.

[143] 'Time to Move on – UN Expert Urges Cambodia to Fully Implement Rights and Freedoms at Every Level', The Office of the United Nations High Commissioner for Human Rights, 20 October 2016, <http://www.ohchr.org/EN/NewsEvents/Pages/DisplayNews.aspx?NewsID=20718&LangID=E> [accessed 3 June 2017].

2. Legality

1. INTRODUCTION

The Extraordinary Chambers in the Courts of Cambodia (ECCC) came into being 27 years after the Khmer Rouge lost power in Cambodia following a protracted negotiation between Cambodia and the United Nations, resulting in an international agreement between these two parties. This raises the question of the legality of the institution thus created, so long after the events with which it is concerned. The term 'legality' in this context refers to the 'conformity or nonconformity of a body politic, or a national or international mechanism, with the legal rules that regulate its establishment'.[1]

The International Military Tribunals operating at Nuremberg and Tokyo after the Second World War were of dubious legality in spite of their significance as historical precedents, breathing life into the principle of individual criminal responsibility under international law. At those tribunals, the victors sat in judgment over the vanquished, applied substantive law that sometimes crossed the boundary into retroactivity, denied the defendants any right to appeal and proceeded at a pace that placed expediency over due process. The International Criminal Tribunal for the former Yugoslavia (ICTY), established by the UN Security Council in 1993, faced legality objections in its early years of operation revolving around the question whether a political organ had the authority to set up a judicial body. These objections were extensively adjudicated and eventually dismissed by the ICTY Appeals Chamber.[2] There are arguably fewer grounds for challenging the legality of an ad hoc tribunal established by a valid international treaty between a State and the UN, although the resulting tribunal's constitutionality ought nevertheless to be scrutinised. The question whether the Special Court for Sierra Leone (SCSL) was an illegal institution, established unconstitutionally by the

[1] A. Cassese, 'The Legitimacy of International Criminal Tribunals and the Current Prospects of International Criminal Justice', *Leiden Journal of International Law*, vol. 25, 2012, pp. 491–501, p. 492.

[2] *Prosecutor v Tadić*, ICTY Case No. IT-94-1, Appeals Chamber, Decision on the Defence Motion for Interlocutory Appeal on Jurisdiction, 2 October 1995, paras. 26–48.

government of Sierra Leone, was raised by several of the accused in preliminary motions before that court. After determining that it had the jurisdictional competence to determine the lawfulness of its own creation, the SCSL's Appeals Chamber rejected all of the defence arguments and concluded that the SCSL was validly established as a treaty-based, *sui generis* institution.[3]

The legality of a judicial mechanism is to be distinguished from its legitimacy. Legality is a concrete notion that may be assessed by reference to legal instruments and precedents. By contrast, 'legitimacy is fluid and changing—it depends on perceptions and outcomes.'[4] Decisions relating to legality are made by judges, often at the commencement of a legal process, whereas legitimacy is subject to appraisal by all domestic and international stakeholders both during and after—sometimes long after—the process. It has therefore been suggested that: 'While legality is a view from the beginning of a process, legitimacy is a view from the end of the process.'[5] At a certain point issues surrounding legality may morph into, or be overtaken by those relating to legitimacy. An International Commission on Kosovo famously described the NATO intervention against Serbia in 1999 as 'illegal, yet legitimate', suggesting that legitimacy may overrule illegality in certain circumstances.[6] Alternatively, the passage of time may render legality issues less pertinent, such as in the case of the International Military Tribunals which have, in a broad sense, been labelled legitimate in their historical context and in terms of the purposes they were designed to achieve.

The ECCC has not faced direct challenges to its legality but in view of its unique institutional architecture, legality-related issues abound, such as the development and function of 'Internal Rules' specific to the ECCC which supersede Cambodian criminal procedure, the extension of the

---

3 *Prosecutor v Kallon* (SCSL Case No. SCSL-2004-15-AR72(E)), *Norman* (SCSL Case No. SCSL-2004-14-AR72(E)) and *Kamara* (SCSL Case No. SCSL-2004-16- AR72(E)), Appeals Chamber, Decision on Constitutionality and Lack of Jurisdiction, 13 March 2004, paras. 38–62.

4 V. Popovski and N. Turner, 'Legality and Legitimacy in International Order', United Nations University, *Policy Brief*, No. 5, 2008, p. 1, <https://www.ciaonet.org/attachments/860/uploads> [accessed 5 June 2017].

5 V. Popovski, 'Legality and Legitimacy of International Criminal Tribunals', in R. Falk, M. Juergensmeyer and V. Popovski, *Legality and Legitimacy in Global Affairs* (Oxford/New York, Oxford University Press, 2012), pp. 388–413, p. 390.

6 The Independent International Commission on Kosovo, *The Kosovo Report: Conflict, International Response, Lessons Learned* (Oxford/New York, Oxford University Press, 2000), p. 185. *See* also Popovski, ibid, pp. 390–1.

limitation period for certain crimes under domestic Cambodian law to allow prosecution of those crimes before the ECCC, the scope of the Court's personal jurisdiction, and the application of the *principle* of legality or *nullum crimen sine lege* in respect of the relevant substantive international law and modes of liability.

Adopting a viewpoint from the beginning of the process, this chapter will consider the legal basis for the establishment of the ECCC and the consequent legality of the institution, examining the Court's constitutive documents and a series of issues that are tied up with the question of legality. The twin question of the ECCC's legitimacy will be taken up in Chapter 11, taking a viewpoint from the end of the process as described in this book.

2. THE ECCC'S CONSTITUTIVE DOCUMENTS

Three primary documents govern the establishment, legal basis and procedures of the ECCC, namely the Law on the Establishment of the Extraordinary Chambers in the Courts of Cambodia for the Prosecution of Crimes Committed during the Period of Democratic Kampuchea (ECCC Law),[7] the Agreement between the United Nations and the Royal Government of Cambodia (ECCC Agreement),[8] and the Internal Rules.[9]

---

[7] *See* Law on the Establishment of the Extraordinary Chambers, with inclusion of Amendments, NS/RKM/1004/006, 27 October 2004, <https://www.eccc.gov.kh/sites/default/files/legal-documents/KR_Law_as_amended_27_Oct_2004_Eng.pdf> [accessed on 5 June 2017].

[8] The ECCC was established in accordance with the Agreement of 6 June 2003 between the Royal Government of Cambodia and the United Nations. The General Assembly approved the draft Agreement by resolution 57/228(B) of 13 May 2003 and the Agreement entered into force, according to its article 32, on 29 April 2005; *see* Agreement between the United Nations and the Royal Government of Cambodia concerning the Prosecution under Cambodian Law of Crimes Committed During the Period of Democratic Kampuchea, United Nations, Treaty Series, vol. 2329, 117, 6 June 2003, <https://www.eccc.gov.kh/sites/default/files/legal-documents/Agreement_between_UN_and_RGC.pdf> [accessed 3 June 2017]. The Law Approving the Agreement was promulgated on 19 October 2004: *see* Reach Kram, NS/RKM/1004/004, 19 October 2004, <https://www.eccc.gov.kh/sites/default/files/legal-documents/Kram_promulgating_Agreement_19_October_2004-En.pdf> [accessed 5 June 2017].

[9] *See* Extraordinary Chambers in the Courts of Cambodia, Internal Rules (Rev. 9) (revised on 16 January 2015), <https://www.eccc.gov.kh/sites/default/files/legal-documents/Internal_Rules_Rev_9_Eng.pdf> [accessed 5 June 2017] ('Internal Rules').

These documents have been described as the 'three pillars' of the ECCC's constitutional structure.[10]

The ECCC Law was first promulgated (i.e. enacted by the Cambodian legislature under the 1993 Constitution of Cambodia) on 10 August 2001 and amended and further promulgated in 2004 after the ECCC Agreement with the UN was successfully negotiated and signed on 6 June 2003. The 2004 amendments resulted in a number of articles in the ECCC Law being labelled as 'new'.

The constitutionality of the ECCC Law was considered by Cambodia's Constitutional Council at the request of the President of the National Assembly. Notably on the question of key international appointments, such as international judges, the Constitutional Council took the view that 'there is no Article in the Constitution found to prohibit a national institution, in particular the Supreme Council of the Magistracy, from appointing people from the UN, of which Cambodia is a member state'. The constitutionality of permitting international judges to sit on a Cambodian court therefore followed from the fact that the Supreme Council of the Magistracy had the final say over appointments—'the United Nations only provides a list of candidates, and has no decision-making rights'.[11] The ECCC Law was declared to be in accordance with the Constitution, except where it mentioned the death penalty in Article 3 through its reference to the 1956 Penal Code, this penalty having been abolished in Cambodia in 1989.[12]

Articles 30 and 31 of the ECCC Agreement specify that in order to be binding on the parties, the ECCC Agreement must be both approved by the UN General Assembly and ratified by Cambodia in accordance with the relevant Cambodian law regarding competence to conclude treaties. The ECCC Law echoes these requirements.[13] The Instrument of Ratification of the Agreement was done on 19 October 2004 by the Cambodian

---

10 D. Scheffer, 'The Extraordinary Chambers in the Courts of Cambodia', in M.C. Bassiouni (ed), *International Criminal Law, Volume 3: International Enforcement* (3rd edn, Leiden, the Netherlands, Martinus Nijhoff Publishers, 2008), pp. 219–55, p. 239.

11 Decision of the Constitutional Council, No. 040/002/2001, 12 February 2001, <http://www.eccc.gov.kh/sites/default/files/legal-documents/Const_Council_Res_on_KR_Law_12_Feb_2001.pdf> [accessed 6 June 2017] (unofficial translation).

12 A further Decision of the Constitutional Council, No. 043/005/2001 KBT.DH, 7 August 2001 (declaring the revised Article 3 of the ECCC Law to be constitutional).

13 ECCC Law, Article 47 *bis* new.

Minister of Foreign Affairs and International Cooperation.[14] The ECCC Agreement entered into force on 29 April 2005.[15] The Vienna Convention on the Law of Treaties, and in particular its Articles 26 and 27, is stated to be applicable to the ECCC Agreement.[16] Specifically, both the UN and the Cambodian Government must perform the ECCC Agreement in good faith, and the Cambodian Government cannot invoke its domestic laws to justify any failure to perform the ECCC Agreement.[17] Any amendments to the ECCC Law shall always be preceded by consultations between the parties.[18]

The purpose of the ECCC according to the Law is 'to bring to trial senior leaders of Democratic Kampuchea and those who were most responsible for the crimes and serious violations of Cambodian penal law, international humanitarian law and custom, and international conventions recognized by Cambodia, that were committed during the period from 17 April 1975 to 6 January 1979'.[19] The ECCC Agreement is designed

> to regulate [and provide, *inter alia*, the legal basis and the principles and modalities for] the cooperation between the United Nations and the Royal Government of Cambodia in bringing to trial senior leaders of Democratic Kampuchea and those who were most responsible for the crimes and serious violations of Cambodian penal law, international humanitarian law and

[14] Instrument of Ratification on Agreement between the United Nations and the Royal Government of Cambodia concerning the Prosecution under Cambodian Law of Crimes Committed During the Period of Democratic Kampuchea, 19 October 2004, <https://www.eccc.gov.kh/sites/default/files/legal-documents/Instrument_of_Ratification_of_Agreement.pdf> [accessed 5 June 2017].

[15] ECCC Agreement, Article 32; Statement on the Entry into Force of the Agreement between Cambodia and the United Nations on the Khmer Rouge Trials on 29 April 2005, 3 May 2005, <https://www.eccc.gov.kh/sites/default/files/legal-documents/Statement_on_ENTRY_INTO_FORCE_AGREEMENT_29_April_05-Eng.pdf> [accessed 5 June 2017].

[16] ECCC Agreement, Article 2(2).

[17] Vienna Convention on the Law of Treaties, United Nations, *Treaty Series*, vol. 1155, 331, 23 May 1969, Article 26 'Pacta Sunt Servanda': 'Every treaty in force is binding upon the parties to it and must be performed by them in good faith'; Article 27 'Internal Law and Observance of Treaties': 'A party may not invoke the provisions of its internal law as justification for its failure to perform a treaty. This rule is without prejudice to Article 46 'Provisions of Internal Law regarding Competence to conclude Treaties', <https://treaties.un.org/doc/Publication/UNTS/Volume%201155/volume-1155-I-18232-English.pdf> [accessed 5 June 2017].

[18] ECCC Agreement, Article 2(3).

[19] ECCC Law, Article 1.

custom, and international conventions recognized by Cambodia, that were committed during the period from 17 April 1975 to 6 January 1979.[20]

The ECCC Agreement recognises and reaffirms the ECCC's subject-matter and personal jurisdiction as stipulated in the ECCC Law.

3. TEMPORAL JURISDICTION

The temporal jurisdiction of the ECCC—the period from 17 April 1975 to 6 January 1979—is clearly set out in the statement of purposes of both the ECCC Law and the ECCC Agreement. These dates cover precisely the period of Khmer Rouge rule. Some Cambodian officials had sought an earlier starting date to include the US carpet-bombing of Cambodia and events contributing to the rise to power of the Khmer Rouge. Others who were critical of Hun Sen's government sought a later end date so that crimes committed since 1979 that were allegedly attributable to the government were covered.[21] It has been noted that when negotiating the creation of ad hoc criminal tribunals, it is typical for the 'narrow temporal jurisdiction for the most prominent atrocity crimes giving rise to the tribunal' to prevail.[22]

The ECCC's temporal jurisdiction came under scrutiny when two of the defendants suggested that the Trial Chamber acted illegally by relying on facts and conduct that had occurred before 17 April 1975.[23] While this was presented as an issue relating to the Court's temporal jurisdiction, it really concerned the scope and definition of a theory of individual criminal responsibility known as joint criminal enterprise. This theory might be invoked in a situation in which the perpetrators are alleged to have joined together to plan a series of events involving crimes before the period of the court's temporal jurisdiction, and then continue to meet, plan and participate in the unfolding package of criminal conduct during the period of the court's temporal jurisdiction. Clearly the acts constituting the crimes have to be committed within the stipulated time frame but often co-perpetrators contribute in different ways, with some designing and implementing the common criminal plan and others

20 ECCC Agreement, Article 1.
21 Scheffer, above n. 10, p. 239.
22 Ibid.
23 *Prosecutor v Nuon Chea* and *Khieu Samphan*, ECCC Case File No. 002/19-09-2007-ECCC/SC, Supreme Court Chamber, Appeal Judgment, 23 November 2016, para. 211 ('Nuon Appeal Judgment').

physically carrying out the prohibited conduct. The Supreme Court Chamber found that:

> The temporal extent of this cluster of transactions starts with the initial contribution to the common purpose as an expression of the shared criminal intent and ends with either the cessation of any further criminal activity by the enterprise or, as far as individuals contributing to the implementation are concerned, withdrawal from the enterprise, the latter requiring cessation of any further contribution as well as abandonment of the shared criminal intent. From the perspective of the substantive law, therefore, it would be unnatural to break up such a protracted and complex transaction as it is only intelligible if all of its components are considered together.[24]

However, any responsibility for the crimes committed would be 'truncated' in accordance with the Court's temporal jurisdiction.[25]

4. TERRITORIAL JURISDICTION

The territorial jurisdiction of the ECCC is not specified but it must be assumed to be limited to Cambodia in view of the Court's temporal jurisdiction and the fact that the 'Extraordinary Chambers' are considered to be part of the Cambodian court structure.[26]

5. PERSONAL JURISDICTION

The Court's personal jurisdiction is based on both Article 1 of the ECCC Agreement and Articles 1 and 2 (new) of the ECCC Law. Article 2 (new) re-states that 'Extraordinary Chambers shall be established in the existing court structure, namely the trial court and the supreme court to bring to trial *senior leaders of Democratic Kampuchea* and *those who were most responsible* for the crimes and serious violations of Cambodian laws ...'.[27] The article goes on to indicate that: 'Senior leaders of Democratic Kampuchea and those who were most responsible for the above acts are hereinafter designated as "Suspects"'.

The words 'power to bring to trial all Suspects most responsible for' which appear in relation to the crimes mentioned in Articles 7 and 8 of

---

24 Ibid, para. 215.
25 Ibid.
26 *See* also Scheffer, above n. 10, pp. 239–41.
27 *Emphasis added.*

the ECCC Law, but not in relation to Articles 3 to 6, appear superfluous in view of the general reference to the Court's personal jurisdiction over 'senior leaders of Democratic Kampuchea and those who were most responsible for the crimes'. The Supreme Court Chamber has explained that these words are designed to stress that the Co-Investigating Judges and Co-Prosecutors, who are independent in the performance of their functions, are vested with authority to determine whether an investigation or prosecution falls within the scope of the ECCC's personal jurisdiction.[28]

The Group of Experts for Cambodia had previously noted that 'the atrocities that took place in Democratic Kampuchea were committed by thousands of individuals, with varying levels of responsibility across the country.'[29] Against this background, they suggested that it would be best not to equate the term 'leaders' with all persons at the senior levels of the Democratic Kampuchea (DK) Government or even of the Communist Party of Kampuchea. In their view:

> The list of top governmental and party officials may not correspond with the list of persons most responsible for serious violations of human rights in that certain top governmental leaders may have been removed from knowledge and decision-making; and others not in the chart of senior leaders may have played a significant role in the atrocities. This seems especially true with respect to certain leaders at the zonal level, as well as officials of torture and interrogation centres such as Tuol Sleng.[30]

The Group of Experts therefore recommended that an eventual tribunal focus on 'those persons most responsible for the most serious violations of human rights' during the DK period, including senior leaders and others who were directly implicated in the most serious crimes.[31] The Group of Experts also considered that the legal instruments governing the establishment of a tribunal should provide for personal jurisdiction over

---

28 *Prosecutor v Kaing Guek Eav alias 'Duch'*, ECCC Case File No. 001/18-07-2007-ECCC/SC, Supreme Court Chamber, Appeal Judgment, 3 February 2012, para. 64 ('Duch Appeal Judgment').

29 Report of the Group of Experts for Cambodia Established pursuant to General Assembly Resolution 52/135, A/53/850, 18 February 1999, para. 102.

30 Ibid, para. 109.

31 Ibid, para. 110.

anyone whose acts fell within its subject-matter jurisdiction, leaving the prosecutor with full discretion as to which persons to indict.[32]

Meanwhile, in transmitting the report of the Group of Experts to the General Assembly and the Security Council, the UN Secretary-General merged the two categories proposed by the Group of Experts in saying that 'Khmer Rouge leaders responsible for the most serious of crimes should be brought to justice'.[33] The following year, the UN Commission on Human Rights did the same, noting the 'ongoing discussions between the Government of Cambodia and the United Nations Secretariat on standards and procedures for bringing to justice the Khmer Rouge leaders most responsible for the most serious violations of human rights in the years 1975-1979.'[34]

The scope of the ECCC's personal jurisdiction was tested in the first trial before the Court. Kaing Guek Eav *alias* Duch was not charged with being a 'senior leader' of Democratic Kampuchea but rather with being one of those most responsible for the crimes committed during the temporal jurisdiction of the Court, due to 'his formal and effective hierarchical authority and his personal participation as Deputy Secretary then Secretary' of a security centre known as S-21.[35] The national defence counsel raised an objection to the ECCC's personal jurisdiction on behalf of Duch at a very late stage, in fact during closing arguments, when he submitted that 'Duch is not guilty and he shall be free from being prosecuted'.[36] The announcement came as a surprise since Duch had admitted responsibility and expressed remorse throughout his trial, including in his own final submissions. The defence counsel, listing the names of those who ought to fall within the Court's personal jurisdiction,

---

[32] Ibid, para. 111 (the Group noted that it opposed the creation of a tribunal that would explicitly be limited in advance to the prosecution of named individuals).

[33] Identical Letters Dated 15 March 1999 from the Secretary-General to the President of the General Assembly and the President of the Security Council, A/53/850, 15 March 1999.

[34] United Nations Commission on Human Rights, Situation of Human Rights in Cambodia, E/CN.4/RES/2000/79, 27 April 2000, <http://www.refworld.org/docid/3b00f2ba40.html> [accessed 5 June 2017].

[35] *Prosecutor v Kaing Guek Eav alias 'Duch'*, ECCC Case File No. 002/14-08-2006, Office of the Co-Investigating Judges, Closing Order Indicting Kaing Guek Eav alias Duch, 8 August 2008, para. 129.

[36] Preliminary objections would normally be heard at the Initial Hearing. *See Prosecutor v Kaing Guek Eav alias 'Duch'*, ECCC Case File No. 001/18-07-2007-ECCC/TC, E1/80.1, Trial Chamber, Transcript of Proceedings – "Duch" Trial (Trial Day 75), 25 November 2009, p. 114.

argued that Duch was neither a leader nor one of those most responsible for crimes at the relevant time.

In its judgment, the Trial Chamber relied on the report of the Group of Experts as well as the practice of other international tribunals in determining the factors relevant to the gravity of the crimes charged and the level of responsibility of the accused. Considering Duch's role as Chairman of S-21 and the number of victims, among other evidence, the Trial Chamber concluded that he fell within the ECCC's personal jurisdiction. The Trial Chamber also noted that the fact that other individuals may have had similar roles and committed similar crimes in Cambodia during the Court's temporal jurisdiction did not mean Duch was precluded from being one of those most responsible.[37]

The issue came before the Supreme Court Chamber where the defence argued that the term 'senior leaders and those most responsible' referred to only one category of persons, namely, senior leaders who are most responsible. The Supreme Court Chamber first reviewed the history of the negotiations leading to the establishment of the ECCC and found that certain surviving officials of the Khmer Rouge were the intended targets for prosecution, having in mind the ECCC's finite resources.[38] According to the Chamber, the report of the Group of Experts, statements made during negotiations by the Cambodian Deputy Prime Minister Sok An, and comments made subsequently by key participants in the negotiations such as David Scheffer, then US Ambassador-at-Large for War Crimes Issues, all confirmed that:

> the term 'senior leaders of Democratic Kampuchea and those who were most responsible' refers to two categories of Khmer Rouge officials that are not dichotomous. One category is senior leaders of the Khmer Rouge who are among the most responsible, because a senior leader is not a suspect on the sole basis of his/her leadership position. The other category is non-senior leaders of the Khmer Rouge who are also among the most responsible. Both categories of persons must be Khmer Rouge officials and among the most responsible ...[39]

The Supreme Court Chamber proceeded to consider whether the phrase 'senior leaders and those most responsible' constituted a jurisdictional requirement. Following a detailed analysis that applied the rule of

37 *Prosecutor v Kaing Guek Eav alias 'Duch'*, ECCC Case File No. 001/18-07-2007/ECCC/TC, Trial Chamber, Judgment, 26 July 2010, paras. 17–25 ('Duch Trial Judgment').

38 Duch Appeal Judgment, above n. 28, para. 52.

39 Ibid, para. 57.

interpretation in Article 31 of the Vienna Convention on the Law of Treaties to the description of each of the relevant categories of Khmer Rouge officials, as well as the term 'Khmer Rouge official' itself, to determine if they were justiciable,[40] the Chamber concluded that being a Khmer Rouge official was indeed a jurisdictional requirement but 'most responsible' and 'senior leader' were matters for investigative and prosecutorial policy. In particular, the term 'senior leader' was not considered to be necessarily limited to former members of the Communist Party of Kampuchea (CPK) Central and/or Standing Committees. In the light of its assessment, the Supreme Court Chamber concluded that it had not been necessary for the Trial Chamber to go so far as to satisfy itself that Duch was one of those most responsible since the only justiciable issue before the Chambers was his status as a Khmer Rouge official.

Khieu Samphan challenged the ECCC's jurisdiction over him during his trial, arguing that he was neither a political decision-maker during the DK regime, nor did he have effective or operational power when he later became 'nominal' head of State.[41] The Trial Chamber found that Khieu Samphan was a Khmer Rouge official at the relevant time and that the scope of his functions was a matter of fact to be determined during the trial.[42]

On 22 February 2017, the Co-Investigating Judges dismissed the case against Im Chaem on the basis that she was neither a senior leader nor one of the most responsible officials of the Khmer Rouge regime and that she was consequently not subject to the ECCC's personal jurisdiction.[43]

---

40 In the sense of being 'a precise question of historical fact concerning which the Trial Chamber is well suited to answer'. *See* ibid, para. 76.

41 *Prosecutor v Khieu Samphan*, ECCC Case File No. 002/19-09-2007-ECCC-TC, Trial Chamber, Preliminary Objections Concerning Jurisdiction, 14 February 2011, paras. 11–15 (the Trial Chamber deferred consideration of the motion until after the hearing of the evidence in the case).

42 *Prosecutor v Nuon Chea* and *Khieu Samphan*, ECCC Case File No. 002/19-09-2007/ECCC/TC, Trial Chamber, Case 002/01 Judgement, 7 August 2014 ('Nuon Trial Judgment'), para. 14.

43 'Co-investigating Judges Dismiss Case against Im Chaem', Extraordinary Chambers in the Courts of Cambodia, 22 February 2017, <https://www.eccc.gov.kh/en/articles/co-investigating-judges-dismiss-case-against-im-chaem> [accessed on 5 June 2017]; ECCC Case File No. 004/07-09-2009-ECCC-OCIJ, Closing Order (Reasons), 10 July 2017. *See* also ECCC Case File No. 003/07-09-2009-ECCC-OCIJ, Office of the Co-Investigating Judges, Decision on Personal Jurisdiction and Investigative Policy Regarding Suspect, 2 May 2012.

While the ECCC Law and ECCC Agreement may therefore be seen as including language to guide the discretion of the Co-Investigating Judges and Co-Prosecutors, these instruments do not impose a jurisdictional requirement beyond establishing that all accused before the ECCC are former Khmer Rouge officials.[44] The Chambers have confirmed that the suggestion of the Group of Experts to include both leaders and lower-ranking individuals playing a significant role in the commission of serious crimes in the ECCC's jurisdiction was adopted in the ECCC Law.[45] The SCSL, which explicitly had 'the power to prosecute persons who bear the greatest responsibility', may have served as a precedent, recognising the constraints on resources faced by ad hoc tribunals.[46] Reflecting a trend in this direction, the International Criminal Court's (ICC) Office of the Prosecutor has limited its own investigations through its regulations and policy papers to persons who appear to be the most responsible.[47] The ICC Office of the Prosecutor has indicated that 'the notion of the most responsible does not necessarily equate with the de jure hierarchical status of an individual within a structure, but will be assessed on a case-by-case basis depending on the evidence'.[48] Similar to other international or mixed international and domestic tribunals, trust is placed in the investigative and prosecutorial organs of the ECCC to identify the most appropriate candidates for prosecution so that the prosecutorial action is both legal and, as will be further explored in Chapter 11, legitimate.

---

[44] The Co-Investigating Judges 'disagree with the SCC's classification of "personal jurisdiction" as a non-jurisdictional criterion' but have followed the SCC jurisprudence. See ECCC Case File No. 003/07-09-2009-ECCC-OCIJ, Office of the Co-Investigating Judges, Decision on Personal Jurisdiction and Investigative Policy Regarding Suspect, 2 May 2012, para. 10.

[45] *See* also S. Morrison, 'Extraordinary Language in the Courts of Cambodia: The Limiting Language and Personal Jurisdiction of the Cambodian Tribunal,' *Capital University Law Review*, vol. 37, 2008–2009, pp. 583–629, pp. 625–7.

[46] Statute of the Special Court for Sierra Leone, UNSC 1315, 14 August 2000, Article 1 ('SCSL Statute'). For an interpretation of this term by the SCSL, *see Prosecutor v Brima*, SCSL-2004-16-A, Appeal Chamber, Judgment, 22 February 2008, paras. 282–3. *See* also Duch Appeal Judgment, above n. 28, paras. 69 (referring to ICTY and ICTR practice), 73 (referring to SCSL practice).

[47] *See* Regulations of the Office of the Prosecutor, ICC-BD/05-01-09, 23 April 2009, Regulation 34(1). *See* also International Criminal Court, Office of the Prosecutor, Policy Paper on Case Selection and Prioritization, 15 September 2016, para. 42.

[48] International Criminal Court, Office of the Prosecutor, Policy Paper on Case Selection and Prioritization, 15 September 2016, para. 43.

6. SUBJECT-MATTER JURISDICTION

The ECCC's subject matter jurisdiction is set out in general terms in Article 9 of the ECCC Agreement and, with some subtle variations, in more detail in Chapter II, Articles 3 to 8 of the ECCC Law. Article 9 of the ECCC Agreement includes within the Court's jurisdiction 'the crime of genocide as defined in the 1948 Convention on the Prevention and Punishment of the Crime of Genocide, crimes against humanity as defined in the 1998 Rome Statute of the International Criminal Court and grave breaches of the 1949 Geneva Conventions and such other crimes as defined in Chapter II of the Law'. Article 3 of the ECCC Law incorporates certain domestic crimes contained in the 1956 Cambodian Penal Code, namely: Homicide (1956 Penal Code Articles 501, 503–509); Torture (1956 Penal Code Article 500); and Religious Persecution (1956 Penal Code Articles 209 and 210). According to the ECCC Trial Chamber, 'The 1956 Penal Code was the applicable national law governing during the 1975 to 1979 period, as it remained in force following the promulgation of both the Constitution of the Khmer Republic on 10 May 1972 and the DK Constitution on 5 January 1976.'[49] This has also been confirmed by the Supreme Court Chamber.[50]

Articles 4, 5 and 6 of the ECCC Law cover genocide, crimes against humanity and grave breaches of the 1949 Geneva Conventions respectively, using the language of 'committed' for the first two categories of crime and 'committed or ordered' for war crimes. The complete wording of Articles 4 to 6 addressing the core categories of international crime is as follows:

> Article 4
>
> The Extraordinary Chambers shall have the power to bring to trial all Suspects who committed the crimes of genocide as defined in the Convention on the Prevention and Punishment of the Crime of Genocide of 1948, and which were committed during the period from 17 April 1975 to 6 January 1979.
>
> The acts of genocide, which have no statute of limitations, mean any acts committed with the intent to destroy, in whole or in part, a national, ethnical, racial or religious group, such as:
>
> - killing members of the group;
> - causing serious bodily or mental harm to members of the group;

[49] Duch Trial Judgment, above n. 37, para. 29.
[50] Duch Appeal Judgment, above n. 28, para. 92.

- deliberately inflicting on the group conditions of life calculated to bring about its physical destruction in whole or in part;
- imposing measures intended to prevent births within the group;
- forcibly transferring children from one group to another group.

The following acts shall be punishable under this Article:

- attempts to commit acts of genocide;
- conspiracy to commit acts of genocide;
- participation in acts of genocide.

Article 5

The Extraordinary Chambers shall have the power to bring to trial all Suspects who committed crimes against humanity during the period 17 April 1975 to 6 January 1979. Crimes against humanity, which have no statute of limitations, are any acts committed as part of a widespread or systematic attack directed against any civilian population, on national, political, ethnical, racial or religious grounds, such as:

- murder;
- extermination;
- enslavement;
- deportation;
- imprisonment;
- torture;
- rape;
- persecutions on political, racial, and religious grounds;
- other inhumane acts.

Article 6

The Extraordinary Chambers shall have the power to bring to trial all Suspects who committed or ordered the commission of grave breaches of the Geneva Conventions of 12 August 1949, such as the following acts against persons or property protected under provisions of these Conventions, and which were committed during the period 17 April 1975 to 6 January 1979:

- wilful killing;
- torture or inhumane treatment;
- wilfully causing great suffering or serious injury to body or health;
- destruction and serious damage to property, not justified by military necessity and carried out unlawfully and wantonly;
- compelling a prisoner of war or a civilian to serve in the forces of a hostile power;
- wilfully depriving a prisoner of war or civilian the rights of fair and regular trial;
- unlawful deportation or transfer or unlawful confinement of a civilian;
- taking civilians as hostages.

Article 7 provides for jurisdiction in relation to 'the destruction of cultural property during armed conflict pursuant to the 1954 Hague Convention for Protection of Cultural Property in the Event of Armed Conflict', while Article 8 addresses 'crimes against internationally protected persons pursuant to the Vienna Convention of 1961 on Diplomatic Relations'.

The ECCC Law and ECCC Agreement set out broad categories of criminal conduct that may be prosecuted before the Court. The question arises, in particular in relation to crimes against humanity which are not currently the subject of a separate convention[51] and have consistently been evolving, whether the ECCC may in fact exercise jurisdiction over all of the underlying sub-categories. An important restriction on the exercise of jurisdiction is provided by the due process guarantee known as the principle of legality which is outlined below and discussed further in relation to specific substantive crimes and modes of liability in Chapters 7 and 8. It is worth noting at this stage that in relation to crimes against humanity, the ECCC Agreement ambitiously makes reference to the 1998 Rome Statute of the ICC which cannot necessarily be deemed to reflect the law as applicable during the temporal jurisdiction of the ECCC. By contrast, the ECCC Law borrows language from the Statute of the International Criminal Tribunal for Rwanda (ICTR) thereby incorporating a requirement that the attack directed against any civilian population must be on 'national, political, ethnical, racial or religious grounds' while according to the Rome Statute the attack need not necessarily be on any persecutory grounds.

---

[51] *See* generally S.D. Murphy, ILC, Third Report of the Special Rapporteur on Crimes against Humanity, A/CN.4/704, 23 January 2017, <http://legal.un.org/docs/?symbol=A/CN.4/704> [accessed 6 June 2017]. *See* also International Law Commission, Report on the Work of the Sixty-Eighth Session, Chapter VII: Crimes against Humanity, A/71/10, 2016, paras. 77–83 (In addition to the four draft articles and commentaries that were provisionally adopted at the sixty-seventh session, the Commission provisionally adopted draft articles 5 to 10 and their corresponding commentaries at the sixty-eighth session), <http://legal.un.org/docs/?path=../ilc/reports/2016/english/chp7.pdf&lang=EFSRAC> [accessed 6 June 2017]. For the draft Convention on Crimes against Humanity provisionally adopted by the Drafting Committee of the ILC, *see* ILC, Crimes against humanity: Texts and Titles of the Draft Preamble, the Draft Articles and the Draft Annex Provisionally Adopted by the Drafting Committee on First Reading, A/CN.4/L.892, 26 May 2017, <http://legal.un.org/docs/index.asp?symbol=A/CN.4/L.892> [accessed 6 June 2017]. *See* also L.N. Sadat (ed), *Forging a Convention for Crimes against Humanity* (Cambridge, Cambridge University Press, 2011).

Minor differences between the 1948 Genocide Convention, upon which Article 4 of the ECCC Law is based, and the text of Article 4 itself include the use of 'ethnical' rather than 'ethnic' to describe one of the protected groups, most likely copied from the text of the ICTR Statute; the use of 'such as' rather than 'as such' after the phrase 'committed with the intent to destroy, in whole or in part, a national, ethnical, racial or religious group'; and the use of the phrase 'participation in acts of genocide' to encompass complicity and incitement. These discrepancies can probably be explained away as unresolved translation issues resulting from the lengthy negotiation process and do not appear as an attempt to modify the definition of the crime of genocide under customary international law.[52]

The inclusion of grave breaches of the 1949 Geneva Conventions is uncontroversial although this category applies only to international armed conflicts and is therefore relevant, for example, to fighting between the Khmer Rouge and Vietnamese forces and possible ill-treatment of prisoners of war. The ECCC does not have jurisdiction over violations of the laws and customs of war.

Articles 7 and 8 of the ECCC Law are novel in view of the absence of domestic legislation implementing the relevant international treaties at the relevant time and criminalising the destruction of cultural property during conflict and violence against internationally protected persons.[53] The Cambodian negotiators clearly felt that certain conduct within these categories warranted prosecution before the ECCC but perhaps due to anticipated legal challenges, these provisions have remained dead letters.[54]

---

[52] However, it has been noted that the use of 'such as' instead of 'as such' could 'seriously distort the meaning of the crime'. *See* further Scheffer, above n 10, p. 241.

[53] *See* further Scheffer, above n. 10, pp. 243–4; C. Ehlert, *Prosecuting the Destruction of Cultural Property in International Criminal Law with a Case Study on the Khmer Rouge's Destruction of Cambodia's Heritage* (Leiden, the Netherlands, Martinus Nijhoff Publishers, 2013), pp. 198–200.

[54] D. Boyle, 'Past Crimes and the Effect of Statutory Limitations on the ECCC', in S.M. Meisenberg and I. Stegmiller (eds), *The Extraordinary Chambers in the Courts of Cambodia: Assessing their Contribution to International Criminal Law* (The Hague, T.M.C. Asser Press, 2016), pp. 375–85, p. 382.

7. ECCC PROCEDURE AND INTERNAL RULES

The ECCC Agreement states that the applicable procedure before the ECCC 'shall be in accordance with Cambodian law'.[55] However:

> Where Cambodian law does not deal with a particular matter, or where there is uncertainty regarding the interpretation or application of a relevant rule of Cambodian law, or where there is a question regarding the consistency of such a rule with international standards, guidance may also be sought in procedural rules established at the international level.[56]

Article 33 (new) of the ECCC Law is similarly worded. The ECCC Supreme Court Chamber has stated that 'forms of "innovation" authorised under Article 33 (new) of the ECCC Law are decided by way of adopting Internal Rules, which involves a consultative process and endorsement by a majority of the ECCC Judges'.[57] Thus, in the interests of procedural certainty and consistency, the Chambers should limit any ad hoc innovations to 'Chamber-specific procedural technicalities'.[58]

The existing law and procedure is contained in the Cambodian Criminal Procedure Code (CPC) adopted by the National Assembly on 7 June 2007.[59] The ECCC Trial Chamber has confirmed that the CPC governs proceedings before the ECCC.[60] The UN Transitional Authority in Cambodia (UNTAC) Law adopted by the Supreme National Council (SNC) on 10 September 1992, setting out provisions relating to the judiciary, as well as criminal law and procedure applicable in Cambodia during the transitional period, remained in force until the adoption of the new Penal Code in 2009.[61]

---

55 ECCC Agreement, Article 12.

56 Ibid.

57 Duch Appeal Judgment, above n. 28, para. 423.

58 Ibid.

59 For an unofficial English translation of the CPC, *see* Code of Criminal Procedure of the Kingdom of Cambodia (Khmer-English Translation) (1st edn, September 2008), <https://www.unodc.org/res/cld/document/khm/2007/code_of_criminal_procedure_of_the_kingdom_of_cambodia_html/Cambodia_Code_of_Criminal_Procedure_Khmer-English_Translation.pdf> [accessed 5 June 2017].

60 Nuon Trial Judgment, above n. 42, para. 21.

61 For the text of the UNTAC Law, *see Guide to Cambodian Criminal Law* (prepared by the Ministry of Justice, 2005), p. 45. An unofficial translation of the 2009 Penal Code prepared by B. Cheung is available at: http://sithi.org/admin/upload/law/Criminal_Code_Book_with_cover_Jan_2014.pdf [accessed 18 July 2017].

The Internal Rules constitute the main document concerning the organisation and procedures of the ECCC.[62] The purpose of the Internal Rules, which, as their title suggests are drafted and adopted internally by the ECCC and have no direct application outside the ECCC process, 'is to consolidate applicable Cambodian procedure for proceedings before the ECCC and … to adopt additional rules where these existing procedures do not deal with a particular matter, or if there is uncertainty regarding their interpretation or application, or if there is a question regarding their consistency with international standards'.[63] According to the ECCC Trial Chamber, 'The Internal Rules consolidate the Cambodian procedures applicable before the ECCC and adopt international procedure in order to ensure justice, fairness and due process of law.'[64]

The Internal Rules are drafted and agreed during confidential (unless otherwise decided) Plenary Sessions of the main organs of the Court, following specific voting procedures set out in the Rules themselves.[65] The Rules and Procedure Committee, comprised of five national judges and four international judges elected in plenary session and supported by a secretariat, has responsibility for receiving and considering requests for amendments to the Internal Rules and drafting proposals for discussion by the Plenary.[66] The Rules and Procedure Committee is also tasked with adopting Practice Directions relating to the functioning of the ECCC for review by the Plenary.

If there is a lacunae in the Internal Rules, any decision by the judicial organs shall be made in accordance with relevant provisions of the ECCC Agreement and the ECCC Law, having particular regard to certain fundamental principles contained in Rule 21 of the Internal Rules and the

---

62 *See* S. Vasiliev, 'Trial Process at the ECCC: The Rise and Fall of the Inquisitorial Paradigm in International Criminal Law?', in S.M. Meisenberg and I. Stegmiller (eds), *The Extraordinary Chambers in the Courts of Cambodia: Assessing their Contribution to International Criminal Law* (The Hague, T.M.C. Asser Press, 2016), pp. 389–433, p. 394 who argues that the Internal Rules are an act of procedural legislation that exceeds the ECCC's authority.

63 Internal Rules, Preamble, *See* also 'Statement from the Judicial Officers of the ECCC', Extraordinary Chambers in the Courts of Cambodia, Press Release, 7 July 2006, < https://www.eccc.gov.kh/sites/default/files/media/ECCC_Press_Statement_7_July_2006.pdf> [accessed 6 June 2017]; 'ECCC Rules Committee Releases Draft Internal Rules', Extraordinary Chambers in the Courts of Cambodia, Press Release, 3 November 2006, <https://www.eccc.gov.kh/sites/default/files/media/Press_release_on_internal_rules.pdf> [accessed 6 June 2017].

64 Nuon Trial Judgment, above n. 42, para. 21.

65 Internal Rules, Rule 18.

66 Internal Rules, Rule 20.

applicable criminal procedural laws.[67] The opening paragraph of Rule 21 provides that:

> the applicable ECCC Law, Internal Rules, Practice Directions and Administrative Regulations shall be interpreted so as to always safeguard the interests of Suspects, Charged Persons, Accused and Victims and so as to ensure legal certainty and transparency of proceedings, in light of the inherent specificity of the ECCC, as set out in the ECCC Law and the ECCC Agreement.

The validity of Cambodian criminal procedure is preserved although the Internal Rules tend to afford it a residual status. Rule 114, for example, states that 'any procedural action done or order made by the ECCC pursuant to applicable Cambodian criminal law and procedure before the entry into force of these [Internal Rules] shall be deemed to have been validly done'.

Among the ad hoc international or mixed international and domestic tribunals, the new Kosovo Specialist Chambers appear unique in that the Specialist Chamber of the Constitutional Court has 'thirty days to review the Rules of Procedure and Evidence, in order to determine whether they comply with Chapter II of the Kosovo Constitution'.[68] There is no comparable structure for the ECCC's Internal Rules to be vetted by the Cambodian Constitutional Court.

At an early stage of the ECCC proceedings, the Pre-Trial Chamber considered the relationship between the CPC and the Internal Rules and found that:

> The Internal Rules form a self-contained regime of procedural law related to the unique circumstances of the ECCC, made and agreed upon by the plenary of the ECCC. They do not stand in opposition to the [CPC] but the focus of the ECCC differs substantially enough from the normal operation of Cambodian criminal courts to warrant a specialised system. Therefore, the Internal Rules constitute the primary instrument to which reference should be made in determining procedures before the ECCC where there is a difference between the procedures of the Internal Rules and the CPC.[69]

---

[67] Internal Rules, Rule 2.

[68] Law on Specialist Chambers and Specialist Prosecutor's Office, Law No. 05/L-053, 3 August 2015; Kosovo Specialist Chambers, KSC-CC-PR-2017-01, Constitutional Court, Referral of the Rules of Procedure and Evidence Pursuant to Article 19(5) of the Law, 26 April 2017.

[69] *Prosecutor v Nuon Chea*, ECCC Case File No. 002/19-09-2007-ECCC/OCIJ (PTC06), Pre-Trial Chamber, Decision on Nuon Chea Appeal against Order Refusing Request for Annulment, 26 August 2008, para. 14.

Subsequently, a reconsideration of the Pre-Trial Chamber's conclusions concerning the relationship between the Internal Rules and the CPC was requested by the civil parties who sought a ruling that the CPC would prevail over the Internal Rules in case of conflict. The Pre-Trial Chamber declined the request for a reconsideration but noted that the civil parties were entitled to raise the issue of the applicability of the Internal Rules as they deemed necessary in future cases.[70]

The constitutionality of the Internal Rules was raised by Nuon Chea as a preliminary objection before the Trial Chamber. Nuon Chea argued that according to the Cambodian Constitution, law-making authority was vested in the national legislature, that this authority could not be transferred to other entities, and that the Internal Rules exceeded the limits of Article 12(1) of the ECCC Agreement. The Trial Chamber found the motion to be inadmissible, but nevertheless commented on the purpose of the Internal Rules, making reference to the Pre-Trial Chamber's earlier assessment as follows:

> The purpose of the Internal Rules is to consolidate applicable Cambodian procedure, supplemented by international standards where necessary and appropriate. As the Pre-Trial Chamber has previously held, trials at the ECCC differ substantially from cases before ordinary Cambodian courts. Other international courts trying cases similar to those before the ECCC have also adopted Rules of Procedure and Evidence specifically adapted to the requirements of complex international criminal trials. As the Accused acknowledges, the Rules and Procedure Committee referred to those rules in the course of designing the ECCC Internal Rules. These rules represent prevailing international standards in relation to cases adjudicating international crimes and are consonant with the ECCC's obligation, enshrined in Article 33 new of the ECCC Law, to conduct proceedings in accordance with international standards of justice, fairness and due process of law as expressed in Articles 14 and 15 of the ICCPR.[71]

Nuon Chea raised the matter again before the Supreme Court Chamber which found that the Trial Chamber had not erred in making reference to the fact that other tribunals had adopted special rules of procedure and evidence as this merely went to show the 'inherent necessity for

---

70 *Prosecutor v Nuon Chea*, ECCC Case File No. 002/19-09-2007-ECCC/OCIJ (PTC06), Pre-Trial Chamber, Decision on Civil Party Co-Lawyers' Joint Request for Reconsideration on the Legal Status of the Internal Rules, 25 February 2009, paras. 9–13.

71 *Prosecutor v Nuon Chea*, ECCC Case File No. 002/19-09-2007/ECCC/TC, Trial Chamber, Decision on Nuon Chea's Preliminary Objection Alleging the Unconstitutional Character of the ECCC Internal Rules, 8 August 2011, para. 7.

international or hybrid tribunals to have specific sets of rules in order for them to be operational'.[72] In disposing of Nuon Chea's appeal, the Supreme Court Chamber considered both the content of the Internal Rules, and the question whether rules adopted by the plenary were binding upon the organs of the ECCC. Regarding the first issue, the Supreme Court Chamber noted that 'the Internal Rules are not homogenous and contain, in part, a re-statement of the Cambodian law, in part, a re-statement of, and elaboration, upon the international standards and, in part, additional rules.'[73] As to the second question, it was found that the Internal Rules did not have the binding force of general law so that the organs of the ECCC retained 'the power to apply the law as they deem fit in individual instances, including to "innovate" ad hoc, as necessary'.[74] To conclude, the Supreme Court Chamber stated:

> the Internal Rules must be seen primarily as an agreed interpretation of the applicable law, including the necessity of "innovations"; however, their binding force stems from the fact that they offer a persuasive value and, having been adopted in a consultative process and endorsed by the majority of the ECCC Judges, contribute to legal predictability more efficiently than if the ECCC relied exclusively on the individual Chambers' power to close gaps and seek guidance from international rules in specific situations. As such, the Internal Rules are an expression of a consolidation of the applicable legal framework rather than usurpation of legislative powers. The argument that the Internal Rules, as a whole, are unconstitutional must therefore be rejected.[75]

The Internal Rules are naturally the first point of reference in ECCC proceedings, designed as they are to ensure that the ECCC expeditiously fulfils its mandate in accordance with Cambodian law, while upholding the highest fair trial standards. Procedural gaps or uncertainties may be addressed by reliance on the CPC and through a comparative analysis of relevant 'procedural rules established at the international level', as was the case, for example, with the procedures for civil party participation prior to the adoption of more detailed provisions in the Internal Rules.[76] Indeed, when it was decided to introduce Civil Party Lead Co-Lawyers to ensure 'the effective organization of Civil Party representation during the

---

72 Nuon Appeal Judgment, above n. 23, para. 104.

73 Ibid, para. 106.

74 Ibid.

75 Ibid.

76 *See*, eg, *Prosecutor v Nuon Chea*, ECCC Case File No. 002/19-09-2007-ECCC/OCIJ (PTC01), Pre-Trial Chamber, Decision on Civil Party Participation in Provisional Detention Appeals, 20 March 2008, paras. 39–40.

trial stage and beyond', the Internal Rules expressly stated that the Civil Party Lead Co-Lawyers 'derive their powers from these IRs'.[77]

As long as the steady expansion and elaboration of procedures is aimed at ensuring a fairer and more expeditious process with improved checks and balances, without departing significantly from Cambodian procedure in areas that are adequately regulated domestically, there can be little objection. The ECCC is bound generally by the obligation to provide justice and fairness in accordance with international human rights standards so a rule may prove impractical and be amended but it will only impinge on the Court's legality if it is oppressive.

8. DUE PROCESS GUARANTEES

The ECCC Agreement makes explicit reference to the rights of the accused enshrined in Articles 14 and 15 of the 1966 International Covenant on Civil and Political Rights (ICCPR),[78] to which Cambodia became a party in 1992. According to Article 13 of the ECCC Agreement, these rights, including the right to equality before the courts and the prohibition on retroactive law, are to be respected throughout the trial process. Article 33 (new) of the ECCC Law similarly provides that the ECCC 'shall exercise their jurisdiction in accordance with international standards of justice, fairness and due process of law, as set out in Articles 14 and 15 of the 1966 International Covenant on Civil and Political Rights' and states that procedures and conditions for the arrest and custody of suspects 'shall conform to existing law in force'. Article 34 (new) provides that trials shall be public while Article 35 (new) states that the accused shall be presumed innocent until the Court has rendered its 'definitive judgment'. Article 35 (new) goes on to set out the following minimum guarantees to which an accused is entitled in accordance with Article 14 of the ICCPR:

a. to be informed promptly and in detail in a language that they understand of the nature and cause of the charge against them;
b. to have adequate time and facilities for the preparation of their defence and to communicate with counsel of their own choosing;
c. to be tried without delay;

---

77 *See* Internal Rules, Rule 12 *ter* (2).

78 International Covenant on Civil and Political Rights, United Nations, *Treaty Series*, vol. 999, 171, 16 December 1966, Articles 14–15, <https://treaties.un.org/doc/publication/unts/volume%20999/volume-999-i-14668-english.pdf> [accessed 5 June 2017].

d. to be tried in their own presence and to defend themselves in person or with the assistance of counsel of their own choosing, to be informed of this right and to have legal assistance assigned to them free of charge if they do not have sufficient means to pay for it;
e. to examine evidence against them and obtain the presentation and examination of evidence on their behalf under the same conditions as evidence against them;
f. to have the free assistance of an interpreter if the accused cannot understand or does not speak the language used in the court;
g. not to be compelled to testify against themselves or to confess guilt.

The *ne bis in idem* principle, contained in Article 14(7) of the ICCPR and therefore incorporated into the ECCC Law by virtue of Article 33 (new), provides: 'No one shall be liable to be tried or punished again for an offence for which he has already been finally convicted or acquitted in accordance with the law and penal procedure of each country.' This principle is also known as the *res judicata* rule, the rule of *autrefois acquit/autrefois convict* and the protection against double jeopardy in different legal systems.[79] According to Article 37 (new) of the ECCC Law, 'The provision of Article 33, 34 and 35 shall apply mutatis mutandis ... before the Supreme Court.'

The fundamental principles elaborated in Rule 21 of the Internal Rules are as follows:

a) ECCC proceedings shall be fair and adversarial and preserve a balance between the rights of the parties. They shall guarantee separation between those authorities responsible for prosecuting and those responsible for adjudication;
b) Persons who find themselves in a similar situation and prosecuted for the same offences shall be treated according to the same rules;
c) The ECCC shall ensure that victims are kept informed and that their rights are respected throughout the proceedings; and
d) Every person suspected or prosecuted shall be presumed innocent as long as his/her guilt has not been established. Any such person has the right to be informed of any charges brought against him/her, to be defended by a lawyer of his/her choice, and at every stage of the proceedings shall be informed of his/her right to remain silent.

The ECCC's constitutive documents therefore make repeated reference to due process guarantees derived in the first instance from the ICCPR and

[79] C. van den Wyngaert and T. Ongena, '*Ne bis in idem* Principle, Including the Issue of Amnesty', in A. Cassese, P. Gaeta and J.R.W.D Jones (eds), *The Rome Statute of the International Criminal Court: A Commentary, Volume 1* (Oxford/New York, Oxford University Press, 2002), p. 706.

further elaborated in the Internal Rules. Notably, Internal Rule 21(4) states: 'Proceedings before the ECCC shall be brought to a conclusion within a reasonable time.' The question of what is reasonable or unreasonable in terms of the length of proceedings is difficult to answer.[80] So far, no ad hoc tribunal has been established with a firm end date and respect for due process would make inflexible deadlines unworkable. The SCSL's vision of a three-year mandate quickly turned to a fantasy and its eventual ten years of operation could be justified by the significance of the arrest in 2006 of the indicted former Liberian President, Charles Taylor. The estimated duration of an ad hoc process, especially one nestled within the framework of a domestic court structure, has no impact on its legality but a process that endures for so long that it is halted by the deaths of the majority of the actual or potential accused rather than a final verdict may lack legitimacy.

9. THE PRINCIPLE OF LEGALITY

Article 15 of the ICCPR, as incorporated into the ECCC Law by Article 33 (new), provides that 'no one shall be held guilty of any criminal offence on account of any act or omission which did not constitute a criminal offence, under national or international law, at the time when it was committed'. This provision embodies the principle of legality, or *nullum crimen sine lege*. In view of the fact that the ECCC is concerned with acts committed in the 1970s, discussions surrounding the principle of legality have featured prominently in the Court's jurisprudence and the correct application of the principle is of vital importance. A defence argument that the ECCC had no jurisdiction to try crimes against humanity because these crimes were not criminalised under national law at the relevant time and international law was not directly applicable was swiftly dismissed by the Trial Chamber, which emphasised that the Cambodian law-makers intended to give the ECCC jurisdiction over

---

[80] N.H.B. Jørgensen and A. Zahar, 'Deliberation, Dissent, Judgment', in G. Sluiter, H. Friman, S. Linton, S. Vasiliev, S. Zappalà (eds), *International Criminal Procedure: Principles and Rules* (Oxford, Oxford University Press, 2013), pp. 1150–201, pp. 1183–5; 'Statement by Judge Patrick Robinson, President, International Criminal Tribunal for the Former Yugoslavia, to the Security Council', International Criminal Tribunal for the former Yugoslavia, 12 December 2008: 'it must be borne in mind that estimation of the length of a trial, including the delivery of a judgment, is more an art than a science', <http://www.icty.org/en/press/statement-judge-patrick-robinson-president-international-criminal-tribunal-former-yugoslavia> [accessed 8 June 2017].

crimes against humanity as defined in international law and that this definition, as it stood at the time of the criminal conduct, was directly applicable.[81] Further, as a matter of principle dating back to the Nuremberg trials, an accused may be criminally responsible under international law even if the conduct is not proscribed by domestic law.

Notwithstanding the Court's subject-matter jurisdiction, 'each of the charged crimes and forms of responsibility must also conform to the principle of legality.'[82] The Supreme Court Chamber has elaborated:

> The main purpose of the principle of legality ... is protection of individual rights in criminal law. It takes effect in three functional respects. First, it ensures that one who wishes to avoid criminal liability may do so by receiving notice of what acts lawmakers will deem to be criminal. Second, as a procedural matter, the legality principle protects the individual against arbitrary exercise of political or judicial power by preventing legislative targeting or conviction of specific persons without stating legal rules in advance. Third, the principle provides an analogue to the protection afforded by separation of powers in national courts applying national laws. The Supreme Court finds that the restraining function of the international principle of legality is of particular importance in international criminal law as it prevents international or hybrid tribunals and courts from unilaterally exceeding their jurisdiction by providing clear limitations on what is criminal.[83]

It has become well-established that the principle of legality applies to both crimes and modes of participation in crimes, by virtue of its connection to general principles of law prohibiting retroactive crimes and punishments as well as collective punishments.[84] 'Therefore, offences and modes of liability charged before the ECCC must have existed either under national law or international law at the time of the alleged criminal conduct occurring between 17 April 1975 and 6 January 1979.[85] However, the principle of legality neither prevents a Chamber from 'interpreting or clarifying the law or the contours of the elements of a crime' nor from progressively developing the law as long as this does not result in

---

[81] Nuon Trial Judgment, above n. 42, paras 18–19.

[82] Duch Trial Judgment, above n. 37, para. 26. *See* also Nuon Trial Judgment, above n. 42, para. 16.

[83] Duch Appeal Judgment, above n. 28, para. 90.

[84] Ibid, para. 91; Duch Trial Judgment, above n. 37, paras. 28, 473: 'The principle of legality applies to the forms of responsibility, as well as to the substance of the crimes charged. The Chamber must thus establish that the forms of responsibility charged in the Amended Closing Order were recognised under national or international law during the 17 April 1975 to 6 January 1979 period.'

[85] Duch Appeal Judgment, above n. 28, para. 91.

the creation of a new law or an interpretation of existing law that goes beyond 'the reasonable bounds of clarification'.[86] The International Co-Investigating Judge, relying on pronouncements by the European Court of Human Rights, has noted the inevitability of some degree of judicial interpretation to elucidate doubtful points and adapt to changing circumstances.[87] Placing reliance on international jurisprudence that post-dates the ECCC's temporal jurisdiction does not contravene the principle of legality to the extent that this jurisprudence provides 'interpretative guidance as regards the evolving status of certain offences and forms of responsibility under international law'.[88] However, the Supreme Court Chamber has cautioned against over-reliance on ad hoc tribunal jurisprudence, noting that 'these cases are non-binding and are not, in and of themselves, primary sources of international law for the ECCC'.[89] Reliance by the Trial Chamber on decisions of the ICTY and ICTR has been quite extensive and there is sometimes a fine line between interpretation of the law, progressive development and creation of new law. This is manifested in the Court's treatment of crimes against humanity and will be addressed further in Chapter 7.

All of the ad hoc international or mixed domestic and international tribunals have been established after the commission of the crimes at issue and the principle of legality is not seen to pose an obstacle to this ex-post creation of an accountability mechanism in circumstances in which the ordinary domestic courts are ill-equipped for political and/or practical reasons to carry out prosecutions. As the ECCC Trial Chamber has stated, 'the fact that the ECCC was established and conferred with jurisdiction over offences after they were allegedly committed does not violate the principle of legality.'[90] The SCSL had previously reached a

---

[86] Ibid, para. 234 (The Supreme Court Chamber stated at an earlier point in the judgment, para. 95: 'Once a Chamber has determined that a charged offence or mode of liability existed as a matter of national or international law at the time of the alleged criminal conduct, the international principle of legality does not prohibit it from interpreting and clarifying the law or from relying on those decisions that do so in other cases.')

[87] *Prosecutor v Meas Muth*, ECCC Case File No. 003/07-09-2009-ECCC-OCIJ, Office of the Co-Investigating Judges, Notification on the Interpretation of 'Attack against the Civilian Population' in the Context of Crimes against Humanity with regard to a State's or Regime's Own Armed Forces', 7 February 2017, para. 18.

[88] Duch Trial Judgment, above n. 37, para. 34.

[89] Duch Appeal Judgment, above n. 28, para. 97.

[90] Duch Trial Judgment, above n. 37, para. 34.

similar conclusion in addressing a challenge to its legality,[91] as had the ICTY.[92]

The test for compliance with the principle of legality, as established in the international jurisprudence, is whether 'the offence with which an accused is charged was sufficiently foreseeable' and whether 'the law providing for such liability was sufficiently accessible to the accused at the relevant time.'[93] According to the ECCC Supreme Court Chamber, the requirements of foreseeability and accessibility are to be determined through an objective analysis although it is not unreasonable to take account of the senior positions held by the specific accused and this would be consistent with the purpose underlying the principle of legality.[94] The ICTY Appeals Chamber explained further in the *Hadžihasanovic* case that:

> As to foreseeability, the conduct in question is the concrete conduct of the accused; he must be able to appreciate that the conduct is criminal in the sense generally understood, without reference to any specific provision. As to accessibility, in the case of an international tribunal such as this, accessibility does not exclude reliance being placed on a law which is based on custom.[95]

The Supreme Court Chamber has explained its approach to customary international law as follows:

---

[91] *Prosecutor v. Kallon* (SCSL Case No. SCSL-2004-15-AR72(E)), *Norman* (SCSL Case No. SCSL-2004-14-AR72(E)) and *Kamara* (SCSL Case No. SCSL-2004-16- AR72(E)), Appeals Chamber, Decision on Constitutionality and Lack of Jurisdiction, 13 March 2004, para. 82 (citing with approval R. Dixon, K.A.A. Khan and R. May, *Archbold International Criminal Courts: Practice, Procedure and Evidence* (London, Sweet & Maxwell, 2003), paras. 17–29: 'The fact that no court exists with jurisdiction to adjudicate crimes proscribed by international law at the time the offences were committed is not a bar to prosecution and not a violation of the principle *nullum crimen sine lege*').

[92] *Prosecutor v Zejnil Delalić, Zdravko Mucić, Hazim Delić* and *Esad Landžo*, ICTY Case No. IT-96-21-T, Trial Chamber, Judgment, 16 November 1998, para. 313: 'The fact that [the accused] could not foresee the creation of an International Tribunal which would be the forum for prosecution is of no consequence.' (This statement was cited with approval in *Prosecutor v Zejnil Delalić, Zdravko Mucić, Hazim Delić* and *Esad Landžo*, ICTY Case No. IT-96-21-A, Appeals Chamber, Judgment, 20 February 2001, paras. 179–80).

[93] Duch Trial Judgment, above n. 37, para. 28.

[94] Nuon Appeal Judgment, above n. 23, para. 761.

[95] *Prosecutor v. Hadžihasanovic, Alagić* and *Kubura*, ICTY Case No. IT-01-47-AR72, Appeals Chamber, Decision on Interlocutory Appeal Challenging Jurisdiction in Relation to Command Responsibility, 16 July 2003, para. 34.

> [T]he Supreme Court Chamber considers that in evaluating the emergence of a principle or general rule concerning conduct that offends the laws of humanity or the dictates of public conscience in particular, the traditional requirement of 'extensive and virtually uniform' state practice may actually be less stringent than in other areas of international law, and the requirement of *opinio juris* may take pre-eminence over the *usus* element of custom. The Chamber finds this particularly relevant to the question of individual criminal responsibility under international law. Where the *usus* element of an international crime is manifest, in large part, through actual prosecution, one has to bear in mind that this requirement presupposes not only the existence of an established legal norm proscribing the conduct as criminal, but also the record of an infraction, followed by a plethora of complex factors that render the prosecution possible, starting with the identification of the accused, availability of evidence and political will. Taking all of these inherent difficulties into account, a paucity of prosecution cannot be found to disprove automatically the existence of State practice in this regard under international law.[96]

The Supreme Court Chamber has also acknowledged the relationship between treaty law and customary international law, while stating that there is no requirement that the offences or modes of liability at issue be found under each category in order to be charged.[97]

In relation to the accessibility requirement, the Supreme Court Chamber has accepted that treaty laws, laws based on custom or general principles can be relied on equally, and that recourse may also be had to domestic law to establish that the accused could reasonably have known that the crime and its manner of commission were prohibited and punishable.[98] Further, while it would be insufficient to rely exclusively on the immorality or appalling character of an act to determine its criminality, these attributes might help to refute an argument by the alleged perpetrator that he or she did not know the acts were criminal.[99]

---

96 Duch Appeal Judgment, above n. 28, para. 93.

97 Ibid, para. 94.

98 Ibid, para. 96.

99 Ibid. *See* also Nuon Appeal Judgment, above n. 23, para. 762 (the Supreme Court Chamber accepted the Co-Prosecutors' argument that since the crimes for which the accused was convicted 'are some of the gravest known; he cannot seriously contend that he did not understand that his conduct was criminal in the sense generally understood.').

10. LIMITATION PERIODS

The Report of the UN Group of Experts states that 'the passage of time is ... not, in itself, a bar to accountability or justice' and notes the importance of 'keeping the door open to accountability, despite the passage of time' as reflected in the practice of some States and international instruments, such as the 1968 Convention on the Non-Applicability of Statutory Limitations to War Crimes and Crimes against Humanity and the Rome Statute of the ICC.[100] Cambodia is not a party to the Convention on the Non-Applicability of Statutory Limitations to War Crimes and Crimes against Humanity[101] but the rule that statutes of limitation do not apply to these crimes is probably part of customary international law today.[102] Adjudicating core international crimes more than 30 years after their commission is not per se illegal, though for the avoidance of doubt, Articles 4 and 5 of the ECCC Law state that genocide and crimes against humanity have 'no statute of limitations'. This is repeated in the CPC, which additionally includes war crimes.[103] The 1994 Law to Outlaw the Democratic Kampuchea Group also stated in its preamble that the crime of genocide has no statute of limitations. The position may be less clear as it concerns war crimes committed during the period of the ECCC's temporal jurisdiction or the crimes covered by Articles 7 and 8 of the ECCC Law.[104]

The omission of the reference to 'no statute of limitations' in Article 6 of the ECCC Law resulted in defence objections to the Court's jurisdiction over grave breaches of the Geneva Conventions on the basis that the domestic statutory limitation period applied also to international crimes. This argument was deemed inadmissible in the contexts in which it was brought, although the Pre-Trial Chamber confirmed that the Geneva Conventions, 'which are the applicable law under Article 6 of the ECCC Law, provide that war crimes are not subject to any statute of

---

[100] Report of the Group of Experts for Cambodia Established pursuant to General Assembly Resolution 52/135, A/53/850, 18 February 1999, para. 47.

[101] Convention on the Non-Applicability of Statutory Limitations to War Crimes and Crimes Against Humanity, United Nations, Treaty Series, vol. 754, 73, 26 November 1968.

[102] J. Henckaerts and L. Doswald-Beck, *Customary International Humanitarian Law, Volume I: Rules* (Cambridge/New York: Cambridge University Press, 2005), Rule 160, pp. 614–18.

[103] Criminal Procedure Code of Kingdom of Cambodia, 2007, Articles 9, 10 ('CPC').

[104] Boyle, above n. 54, p. 382.

limitations, which indicates that there is no statute of limitations applicable'.[105] As noted in a challenge brought by Meas Muth before the Co-Investigating Judges, the Geneva Conventions are themselves silent on statutes of limitations.[106] The question whether the non-applicability of statutory limitations to war crimes formed part of customary international law in the period from 1975 to 1979 is highly contentious and has not yet been settled by the ECCC.

The question of the legality of the provision in Article 3 (new) of the ECCC Law that the statute of limitations in the 1956 Penal Code shall be extended for an additional 30 years in respect of the *domestic* crimes under the ECCC's jurisdiction has been more fully adjudicated.[107] The 1956 Penal Code provides for a ten-year limitation period in respect of what are defined in the Code as felonies attracting a sentence of at least five years, so the total limitation period of 40 years, counting from the end of the Khmer Rouge period, expires in 2019, by which time all envisaged proceedings before the ECCC will at least have commenced. The Constitutional Council saw no difficulty with extending the limitation period although its reasoning, at least in the English translation of the decision, is ambiguous. The decision notes that a fundamental principle is involved, namely 'the non-retroactivity of any new law over offences committed in the past' and that Cambodia recognises this principle. However, it goes on to say that this fundamental principle is not mentioned in the Constitution and that there may be exceptions to fundamental principles as indicated in the 1956 Penal Code which states that a person cannot be prosecuted for a crime after the introduction of a new law annulling that crime. The Constitutional Council appears to conclude that an extension to the limitation period for domestic crimes is not unconstitutional because the effect of the ECCC Law is to narrow

---

105 *Prosecutor v Ieng Sary*, ECCC Case File No. 002/19-09-2007-ECCC/OCIJ (PTC75), Pre-Trial Chamber, Decision on Ieng Sary's Appeal Against the Closing Order, 11 April 2011, para. 73. *See* further Boyle, above n. 54, p. 383 (discussing the preliminary objections made by the defence on this issue before the Trial Chamber which were not ruled upon as the grave breaches charges were severed from that particular case).

106 *Prosecutor v Meas Muth*, ECCC Case File No. 003/07-09-2009-ECCC/OCIJ, Defence for Meas Muth, Meas Muth's Motion against the Application of Grave Breaches of the Geneva Conventions due to Expiry of the Applicable Statute of Limitations, 12 December 2013, para. 6.

107 The ECCC Law as initially adopted in 2001 extended the limitation period for twenty years and the 2004 amendments to the Law extended the period by a further ten years.

criminal jurisdiction in terms of the culprits, offences and time frame.[108] Alternative approaches would have been to repeal or suspend the statute of limitations for the relevant domestic crimes, as proposed even by the UN Group of Experts,[109] rather than to 'extend' an already expired limitation period. However, the divisions between the ECCC judges on the matter suggest that these options also presented problems.

Initially, the Co-Investigating Judges avoided the issue by deciding in their Closing Order (indictment) against Kaing Guek Eav *alias* Duch that while certain acts identified during the judicial investigation constituted the domestic offences of homicide and torture pursuant to Articles 500, 501, 503, 506 of the 1956 Cambodian Penal Code, under Article 3 of the ECCC Law, 'these acts must be accorded the highest available legal classification', namely crimes against humanity or grave breaches of the 1949 Geneva Conventions.[110] The Pre-Trial Chamber overturned this decision on an appeal by the Co-Prosecutors against the Closing Order, finding that the domestic offences were not subsumed by the international offences as they contained materially distinct elements.[111] The Pre-Trial Chamber noted that it did not 'inherently threaten the *ne bis in idem* principle' to include in the indictment more than one legal offence in relation to the same conduct because this did not involve the actual assignment of liability or punishment.[112] The Pre-Trial Chamber went on to consider whether the crimes of homicide and torture under the 1956 Penal Code were still punishable, but did not address the question of the limitation period in this context, focusing instead on the applicability of

---

[108] Decision of the Constitutional Council, No. 040/002/2001, 12 February 2001, <http://www.eccc.gov.kh/sites/default/files/legal-documents/Const_Council_Res_on_KR_Law_12_Feb_2001.pdf> [accessed 6 June 2017] (unofficial translation).

[109] Report of the Group of Experts for Cambodia Established pursuant to General Assembly Resolution 52/135, A/53/850, 18 February 1999, para. 90 (referring to 'precedents in European States that prosecuted Nazi offenders after the apparent expiration of the prior statute of limitations – in particular Germany and France in the 1960s and 1980s').

[110] *Prosecutor v Kaing Guek Eav alias 'Duch'*, ECCC Case File No. 002/14-08-2006, Office of the Co-Investigating Judges, Closing Order Indicting Kaing Guek Eav alias Duch, 8 August 2008, para. 152.

[111] *Prosecutor v Kaing Guek Eav alias 'Duch'*, ECCC Case File No. 001/8-07-2007-ECCC/OCIJ (PTC 02), Pre-Trial Chamber, Decision on Appeal against Closing Order Indicting Kaing Guek Eav alias "Duch", 5 December 2008, paras. 58–84.

[112] Ibid, para. 88.

subsequent laws, such as the 1992 UNTAC Criminal Code, and concluding that there was no conflict with these laws.[113]

In the early stages of Duch's trial, the defence filed a preliminary motion squarely on the issue of the limitation period. The Trial Chamber's decision on this issue, in which it was unable to reach an affirmative majority, was rendered separately on the same day as the final judgment in the case.[114] The Chamber was unanimous that there was no functioning legal or judicial system in Cambodia between 1975 and 1979 and that the limitation period did not commence between those dates. However, the international and national judges were divided over whether or not the limitation period was interrupted or suspended between 1979 and 1993 (the date of the Constitution of the Kingdom of Cambodia). The Cambodian judges concluded that limitation periods were a procedural and not a substantive matter, and that they were based on an assumption that 'State institutions capable of commencing an investigation or prosecution against the alleged perpetrators of the crimes in question existed'.[115] Tracing the development of Cambodia's judicial system in the period between the end of Khmer Rouge rule and 1993, and considering factors such as the ongoing civil war, transitional period and difficulty of addressing the crimes of the Khmer Rouge era, the Cambodian judges took the view that the limitation period began to run in 1993 and therefore did not preclude the prosecution of Duch for the domestic crimes.

The international judges applied a test based on their interpretation of national practice regarding the interruption or suspension of statutory limitations, namely proof of the 'objective incapacity of the Cambodian legal system to undertake investigation or prosecution in the aftermath of the Democratic Kampuchea regime'.[116] In the opinion of the international judges, this test was not satisfied and they accordingly found that the limitation period had expired by the time of the enactment of the ECCC Law.

The national judges noted that the Constitutional Council had approved the extension to the limitation period and found that they had no

---

113 Ibid, paras. 89–95.

114 *Prosecutor v Kaing Guek Eav alias 'Duch'*, ECCC Case File No. 001/18-07-2007/ECCC/TC, Trial Chamber, Decision on the Defence Preliminary Objection Concerning the Statute of Limitations of Domestic Crimes, 26 July 2010, para. 56.

115 Ibid, para. 16.

116 Ibid, para. 31.

competence to review the correctness of this decision.[117] While the international judges took the view that the retroactive amendment of a statutory limitation period by a national legislature did not expressly contradict international fair trial standards applicable before the ECCC, they disagreed that the decision of the Constitutional Council amounted to such an amendment.[118] The international judges found that it was impossible to 'extend' an already expired limitation period and noted the absence of any indication by the Cambodian legislature that it intended to suspend the applicable limitation period, or to reactivate the right to prosecute domestic crimes after its expiry.[119] They found the decision of the Constitutional Council unhelpful in that it did not indicate that the notion of 'extension' was to be interpreted beyond its ordinary meaning and merely stated that Article 3 (new) of the ECCC Law affected the fundamental principle of non-retroactivity of criminal law without making any further ruling on the impact of this principle.[120] The international judges were willing to consider whether the rights of the Accused to a fair trial as expressed in Article 14 or 15 of the ICCPR would be violated if the decision of the Constitutional Council Decision were nonetheless interpreted as reactivating the right to prosecute. They concluded as follows:

> In general terms, the prohibition against the retroactive application of criminal law protects the values of legal certainty and safeguards the implementation of the principle of impartiality and objectivity by a State in accordance with the rule of law. An interpretation of Article 3 (new) of the ECCC Law as allowing a reinstatement of the right to prosecute domestic crimes in relation to a limited number of individuals and after the expiry of statutory limitations may accordingly be perceived as an infringement of that duty of impartiality and objectivity.[121]

The international judges noted as an aside that due to the 'substantial overlap' between the elements of the domestic crimes and the corresponding international crimes, their finding had no impact on the Chamber's evaluation of the 'totality of the Accused's criminal culpability' or the sentence.[122] As a result of its divided opinion, the Trial Chamber did

[117] Ibid, para. 38.
[118] Ibid, paras. 42–3.
[119] Ibid, para. 45.
[120] Ibid, para. 46.
[121] Ibid, para. 53.
[122] Ibid, para. 55.

not evaluate Duch's responsibility in respect of the national crimes of premeditated murder and torture in the final judgment.[123]

In a subsequent case, the Co-Prosecutors nevertheless asked the Co-Investigating Judges to indict Ieng Sary for the domestic crimes. The national and international Co-Investigating Judges agreed to take this action despite acknowledging differences in their reasoning on the core issue of the limitation period, and noting that they found themselves in a 'procedural stalemate, which is partly due to the hybrid structure of the ECCC'.[124] Ieng Sary raised the matter in an appeal against the Closing Order before the Pre-Trial Chamber which addressed it afresh. The Pre-Trial Chamber took the view that it had no authority to review the legality of the extension of statutes of limitation by the Cambodian National Assembly, or to review the correctness of the decision of the Constitutional Council.[125] However, the Pre-Trial Chamber deemed it appropriate in the light of the ECCC's mandate to exercise its jurisdiction in accordance with international standards of justice, fairness and due process of law, to determine whether the application of Article 3 (new) violated the principle of legality enshrined in Article 15(1) of the ICCPR. This was found not to be the case, as the principle of legality did not include the idea that the time period during which a crime could be prosecuted needed to be foreseeable and accessible to an accused at the time of the commission of the crime. Aligning itself with the conclusion of the national judges in the *Duch* case, the Pre-Trial Chamber considered that statutes of limitation did not run where the judicial institutions were not functioning which meant that in Cambodia they did not begin to run until 24 September 1993 at the earliest.[126] The Pre-Trial Chamber therefore found that the extension to the limitation period did not violate the principle of legality.

The defence for Ieng Sary, Ieng Thirith, Khieu Samphan and Nuon Chea all filed preliminary motions at the start of their joint trial arguing that the jurisdiction of the ECCC over the domestic crimes of murder, torture and religious persecution was time barred. The Trial Chamber skirted the issue of the limitation period, and based its decision on defects in the manner of pleading the domestic offences in the indictment. It decided that due to those defects, the charges concerning

---

[123] Duch Trial Judgment, above n. 37, para. 678.

[124] *Prosecutor v Ieng Sary*, ECCC Case File No. 002/19-09-2007-ECCC/OCIJ (PTC75), Pre-Trial Chamber, Decision on Ieng Sary's Appeal Against the Closing Order, 11 April 2011, para. 272.

[125] Ibid, para. 280.

[126] Ibid, para. 286.

domestic offences could not form the basis of trial proceedings and they were struck out.[127]

On balance, the more restrained approach by the international judges of the Trial Chamber is warranted if legality is the primary consideration, recognising the risk of abuse inherent in retrospective action taken in the absence of any clearly expressed intention to suspend and/or reactivate a limitation period. Notably, the 2007 Code of Criminal Procedure, which adopts lengthier limitation periods than the 1956 Penal Code, provides that 'the statute of limitations for a criminal action … for offences committed before the entry into force of this Code shall be governed by the provisions of the old law' and further that '[w]hen a criminal action is extinguished a criminal charge can no longer be pursued or shall be terminated'.[128] The path for the future with its promise of 'never again' is clear, but it might also be relevant to consider a scenario in which only domestic law was available to prosecute past atrocities. In such circumstances, could the crimes of the Pol Pot era simply be regarded as having 'expired'? The Pre-Trial Chamber and the national judges of the Trial Chamber were arguably also concerned with the legitimacy of the process and the impact of rejecting domestic law entirely after it had been deemed valid and necessary to include it in the ECCC Law in the first place.

11. AMNESTY, PARDON AND *NE BIS IN IDEM*

The ECCC Law provides that the 'Royal Government of Cambodia shall not request an amnesty or pardon for any persons who may be investigated for or convicted of crimes referred to in Articles 3, 4, 5, 6, 7 and 8 of this law'.[129] This provision feeds into the independence of the ECCC and therefore supports its legality, providing further that the 'scope of any amnesty or pardon that may have been granted prior to the enactment of this Law is a matter to be decided by the Extraordinary Chambers'.

---

[127] *Prosecutor v Nuon Chea, Ieng Sary, Ieng Thirith* and *Khieu Samphan*, ECCC Case File No. 002/19-09-2007-ECCC/TC, Trial Chamber, Decision on Defence Preliminary Objections (Statute of Limitations on Domestic Crimes), 22 September 2011, para. 22.

[128] CPC, Articles 7, 10, 612.

[129] ECCC Law, Article 40 new.

The context is the amnesty and pardon that was granted to Ieng Sary prior to the ECCC's establishment. According to the 'unofficial translation' of the Royal Decree available on the ECCC's website, Preah Bat Norodom Sihanouk Varman, King of Cambodia, grants:

> a pardon to Mr Ieng Sary, former Deputy Prime Minister in charge of Foreign Affairs in the Government of Democratic Kampuchea, for the sentence of death and confiscation of all his property imposed by order of the People's Revolutionary Tribunal of Phnom Penh, dated 19 August 1979; and an amnesty for prosecution under the Law to Outlaw the Democratic Kampuchea Group, promulgated by Reach Kram No. 1, NS 94, dated 14 July 1994.[130]

The ECCC Agreement is more explicit in its recognition of the specific context and after repeating the general provision that 'the Royal Government of Cambodia shall not request an amnesty or pardon for any persons who may be investigated for or convicted of crimes referred to in the present Agreement', goes on to say:

> This provision is based upon a declaration by the Royal Government of Cambodia that until now, with regard to matters covered in the law, there has been only one case, dated 14 September 1996, when a pardon was granted to only one person with regard to a 1979 conviction on the charge of genocide. The United Nations and the Royal Government of Cambodia agree that the scope of this pardon is a matter to be decided by the Extraordinary Chambers.[131]

It is appropriate for the ECCC to be given exclusive competence to determine legal questions such as the scope and effect of a pardon or amnesty. Indeed, the provision is perhaps better phrased than its counterpart in the SCSL Statute which simply stated: 'An amnesty granted to any person falling within the jurisdiction of the Special Court in respect of the crimes referred to in articles 2 to 4 of the present Statute shall not be a bar to prosecution'.[132] Not surprisingly, the legality of this provision was challenged before the SCSL as the issue impacted on a number of the defendants before that court.[133]

---

[130] Royal Decree (Reach Kret), NS/RKT/0996/72, 14 September 1996.

[131] ECCC Agreement, Article 11.

[132] SCSL Statute, Article 10.

[133] *Prosecutor v Kallon* (SCSL Case No. SCSL-2004-15-AR72(E)) and *Kamara* (SCSL Case No. SCSL-2004-16-AR72(E)), Appeals Chamber, Decision on Challenge to Jurisdiction: Lomé Accord Amnesty, 13 March 2004, paras. 86–90 (The Appeals Chamber concluded that Article 10 of the SCSL Statute was legally valid and the amnesty granted in the Lomé Agreement did not bar the

The scope and effect of Ieng Sary's amnesty and pardon were extensively debated before the ECCC. The issue first arose before the Co-Investigating Judges who in the context of making an order for Ieng Sary's provisional detention had to consider whether the ECCC proceedings would 'infringe the binding authority of a previous legal decision, under the general principle of criminal law *ne bis in idem*' and, 'assuming that the answer to the first question is negative and providing that the Co-Investigating Judges have the jurisdiction to decide on the scope of the 1996 Royal Decree', whether the pardon and amnesty granted to Ieng Sary were 'opposable to the ECCC'.[134] The Co-Investigating Judges found that the *ne bis in idem* principle was not absolute and would not apply if, for example, the earlier proceedings had been designed to shield the person from prosecution or were not conducted in accordance with the norms of due process. However, they considered that it would be premature to conduct an in-depth analysis of the trial before the People's Revolutionary Tribunal ('PRT') since Ieng Sary had not been charged with genocide before the ECCC at the time of his initial detention. The Co-Investigating Judges also referred to the practice of international tribunals whereby multiple convictions could be imposed under different legal characterisations in respect of the same underlying acts, meaning that, in their view, Ieng Sary could still be convicted of crimes against humanity in a new prosecution even if he had already been convicted of genocide in relation to the same conduct.[135] The ECCC Law was seen to provide the necessary authority for the Co-Investigating Judges to decide on the scope of the amnesty and pardon and since the latter related only to the prior sentence and the offences under the 1994 Law covered by the amnesty did not overlap with the ECCC's subject-matter jurisdiction, the Co-Investigating Judges found there to be no obstacle in the way of Ieng Sary's prosecution before the ECCC.

On an appeal against this decision brought by Ieng Sary, the Pre-Trial Chamber found that the Co-Investigating Judges were correct to examine the issue of the amnesty and pardon since 'the issuance of an arrest or detention order would not be lawful if any circumstance could be foreseen which would evidently or manifestly prevent a conviction by the

---

prosecution of the accused in an international tribunal. In other words, the SCSL had jurisdiction over such accused in spite of the amnesty granted.)

134 *Prosecutor v Ieng Sary*, ECCC Case File No. 002/19-09-2007-ECCC/OCIJ, Office of the Co-Investigating Judges, Provisional Detention Order (Ieng Sary), 14 November 2007, para. 5.

135 Ibid, para. 9.

Trial Chamber'.[136] The discussion in the Pre-Trial Chamber was complicated by the fact that the translation of the Royal Decree that was available to the judges used the word 'amnesty' twice, creating ambiguities over the notions of 'pardon' and 'amnesty', both of which were apparently included within the Khmer term *loekaentoh*, meaning 'to lift guilt'.[137] Although it considered the issues afresh, having given the parties the opportunity to make full submissions, the Pre-Trial Chamber noted that there would be an opportunity for the parties to raise them again at a later stage of the proceedings in accordance with the Internal Rules. Addressing the issue of *ne bis in idem*, the Pre-Trial Chamber noted that the CPC focused on successive prosecutions for the same act (i.e. underlying conduct) while the ICCPR referred to the same offence (i.e. legal characterisation). Having regard both to domestic and international law, the Pre-Trial Chamber found that since the material facts and their legal characterisation alleged against Ieng Sary would not be set out by the Co-Investigating Judges until they issued an indictment, it could only conclude at the provisional detention stage that it would not be manifest or evident that the 1979 trial and conviction would prevent a conviction by the ECCC. As it concerned the 'amnesty' for the death sentence imposed in absentia by the People's Revolutionary Tribunal, the Pre-Trial Chamber found that its validity was too uncertain for it to be manifest or evident that it would prevent a conviction for genocide before the ECCC. Finally, the 'amnesty' in relation to prosecution under the 1994 Law was similarly viewed as not presenting an obstacle to prosecution before the ECCC since the offences mentioned in the 1994 Law were not within the jurisdiction of the ECCC.

As foreseen by the Pre-Trial Chamber, the matter re-surfaced and returned to the same Chamber after the Co-Investigating Judges issued an indictment against Ieng Sary setting out the material facts and their proposed legal characterisation as a basis for the trial.[138] The Pre-Trial

---

[136] *Prosecutor v Ieng Sary*, ECCC Case File No. 002/19-09-2007-ECCC/OCIJ (PTC03), Pre-Trial Chamber, Decision on Appeal against Provisional Detention Order of Ieng Sary, 17 October 2008, para. 16.

[137] *See Prosecutor v Ieng Sary*, ECCC Case File No. 002/10-09-2007/ECCC/TC, Trial Chamber, Decision on Ieng Sary's Rule 89 Preliminary Objections (Ne bis in idem and Amnesty and Pardon), 3 November 2011, footnote 21.

[138] *Prosecutor v Nuon Chea, Ieng Sary, Ieng Thirith* and *Khieu Samphan*, ECCC Case File No. 002/19-09-2007-ECCC-OCIJ, Office of the Co-Investigating Judges, Closing Order (Indictment) in Case 002, 15 September 2010.

Chamber, now in a position to undertake a more comprehensive assessment of the *ne bis in idem* argument, began by analysing the relevant provisions of the CPC since the ECCC constitutive instruments were silent on the effect of prior convictions on proceedings before the ECCC. The CPC was found to be unhelpful in this instance so recourse was had to international rules of procedure, including Article 14(7) of the ICCPR which was deemed to lack a transnational effect in the sense that it only applied to repeat proceedings within a single domestic system.[139] Consequently, Article 14(7) was also deemed unhelpful to a resolution of the matter at hand and the Pre-Trial Chamber turned to a discussion of the 'international *ne bis in idem* principle' as developed in the jurisprudence of the ad hoc tribunals. The international *ne bis in idem* principle is both more protective than the principle contained in Article 14(7) of the ICCPR because its focus is on acts rather than offences, and less protective because it permits a subsequent trial by an 'international' tribunal in certain circumstances. These include situations in which the earlier proceedings were designed to shield the person from criminal liability before the international court, and where the earlier proceedings were not conducted independently or impartially or in accordance with internationally recognised norms of due process. The Pre-Trial Chamber took the opportunity to expound on the rationale behind the international *ne bis in idem* principle as serving a 'dual purpose of protecting the individual against the harassment of the state and being an important guarantee for legal certainty'.[140]

These factors had to be balanced with the interests of the international community and victims in seeing justice done for atrocities. The Pre-Trial Chamber examined the slight difference in wording between Article 10(2)(b) of the ICTY Statute and Article 20(3)(b) of the ICC Statute and rejected the defence argument that the latter provision's reference to defects in the process being 'inconsistent with an intent to bring the person concerned to justice' meant that the prior proceedings had to have been designed to help the person to escape justice. Therefore, according to the international *ne bis in idem* principle:

---

139 *Prosecutor v Ieng Sary*, ECCC Case File No. 002/19-09-2007-ECCC/OCIJ (PTC75), Pre-Trial Chamber, Decision on Ieng Sary's Appeal Against the Closing Order, 11 April 2011, paras. 125, 128.

140 Ibid, para. 142.

> an international or internationalised tribunal shall not exercise jurisdiction in respect of individuals that have already been tried for the same acts by national authorities unless it is established that the national proceedings were not conducted independently and impartially with regard to due process of law.[141]

The Pre-Trial Chamber proceeded to examine the 1979 trial against this standard and found that it did not meet the required guarantees of independence and impartiality. Consequently, it did not provide a barrier to proceedings before the ECCC based on the *ne bis in idem* principle.

Turning to a consideration of the Royal Decree, the Pre-Trial Chamber found that the 'amnesty' (pardon) with respect to the sentence of death imposed on Ieng Sary and the confiscation of his property was designed to 'abolish' and 'forget' the punishment and had no effect on the institution of future proceedings.[142] Regarding what it called the 'second amnesty, i.e. the amnesty from prosecution under the 1994 Law, the Pre-Trial Chamber indicated that it was not clear whether the 1994 Law criminalised membership of the political organisation or military forces of the DK group as a separate offence, but that in any case the 1994 Law created new offences and penalties related to a specific political context rather than an autonomous criminal law regime to prosecute members of the DK group that superseded all other national criminal laws.[143] In other words, the crimes falling within the ECCC's subject-matter jurisdiction were not criminalised under the 1994 Law and would continue to be prosecuted under the relevant domestic or international criminal law irrespective of the status of the perpetrator as a member of the DK group.[144] The Pre-Trial Chamber therefore concluded that the amnesty only prevented Ieng Sary's prosecution for the offences in Article 4 of the 1994 Law concerning State security and for the offence of being a member of the DK group if such membership was indeed criminalised under Articles 1 and 2 of that Law. The Pre-Trial Chamber went on to emphasise Cambodia's international obligations to ensure those alleged to be responsible for serious international crimes were prosecuted and, if applicable, punished.[145]

Despite this comprehensive treatment of the issues by the Pre-Trial Chamber, they arose once more at the start of Ieng Sary's trial, giving the

---

141 Ibid, para. 157.
142 Ibid, paras. 191–4.
143 Ibid, para. 197.
144 Ibid, para. 199.
145 Ibid, para. 201.

Trial Chamber an opportunity to add its reasoning to the mix (although it had invited submissions only on new arguments arising from the Pre-Trial Chamber's decision). The outcome remained unchanged as the Trial Chamber concurred with the Pre-Trial Chamber's findings concerning the deficiencies of the 1979 trial and its disposition of the matter, limiting its own findings to 'an analysis of the consequences of these deficiencies on the effects of the People's Revolutionary Tribunal decision and the applicability of amnesties in relation to serious international crimes'.[146] Despite requesting a new translation of the Royal Decree which clarified that: 'A *pardon* is granted to Mr. IENG Sary … for the sentence of death and confiscation of all his property', the Trial Chamber noted some persisting ambiguities, even when adopting the logical, legal interpretation of the terms 'amnesty' and 'pardon'.[147] The Trial Chamber found that the deficiencies of the 1979 trial 'were so significant that the decision resulting from this trial cannot be characterised as a genuine judicial decision' capable of 'producing valid legal effects'.[148] Moreover, as the trial took place in absentia, the judgment could not be considered final. Agreeing with the Pre-Trial Chamber's reasoning, the Trial Chamber also rejected the idea that the *ne bis in idem* principle prevented the ECCC from exercising its jurisdiction. The Trial Chamber then turned to consider whether any of the international crimes with which Ieng Sary had been charged 'must be excluded from the scope of the Royal Decree on the basis of a treaty or customary rule of international law requiring the prosecution of these crimes or prohibiting amnesties in relation to them'.[149] It concluded that grave breaches of the Geneva Conventions, genocide and torture required prosecution under international law and could not be subject to an amnesty while there was a developing norm to that effect in relation to crimes against humanity.[150] In this respect, the Trial Chamber's approach differed from that of the Pre-Trial Chamber as it bypassed the preliminary question of which offences were potentially

---

146 *Prosecutor v Ieng Sary*, ECCC Case File No. 002/10-09-2007/ECCC/TC, Trial Chamber, Decision on Ieng Sary's Rule 89 Preliminary Objections (Ne bis in idem and Amnesty and Pardon), 3 November 2011, para. 23.

147 Ibid, para. 11 (*Emphasis added*).

148 Ibid, para. 30.

149 Ibid, para. 37.

150 *See* comment on these conclusions by Ieng Sary's international defence lawyer, in M. Karnavas, 'Amnesties and Pardons in International Criminal Law – Part II', International Criminal Law Blog, 22 July 2016, <http://michaelgkarnavas.net/blog/2016/07/22/amnesties-and-pardons-part-ii/> [accessed 6 June 2017]. *See* also S. Williams, *Hybrid and Internationalised Criminal Tribunals: Selected Jurisdictional Issues* (Oxford/Portland, Hart Publishing,

covered by the amnesty in the 1996 Decree and went directly to the question of the validity under international law of amnesties affording immunity from prosecution for the international crimes alleged to have been committed by Ieng Sary. This approach was adopted because the Trial Chamber was unable to exclude the possibility that the purpose of the Royal Decree was to grant Ieng Sary 'general immunity from enforcement of any sentence and from prosecution for any acts committed before 1996, including during the Democratic Kampuchea regime'.[151]

Ieng Sary filed an appeal against the Trial Chamber's decision before the Supreme Court Chamber under Internal Rule 104(4)(a) but this was dismissed by a majority of the judges as inadmissible.[152] The two dissenting judges, Judges Klonowiecka-Milart and Jayasinghe, argued that the appeal should have been heard on an exceptional basis as it concerned an issue 'that would significantly affect the fair and expeditious conduct of the proceedings or the outcome of the trial, and for which an immediate resolution by the Supreme Court Chamber may materially advance the proceedings'.[153] The dissenting judges noted that trials before international or internationalised tribunals tended to be lengthy and that if the Supreme Court Chamber ultimately found in favour of Ieng Sary, 'he will have been subjected to years of baseless and avoidable detention, coupled with occasional physical compulsion to attend at court proceedings'.[154] The two judges refrained from giving their opinion on the merits of the case and Ieng Sary died before there could be a final resolution of the issues concerning his pardon and amnesty before the ECCC's highest Chamber.

2012), p. 350: 'It is certainly arguable that a rule prohibiting blanket, unconditional amnesties, which in effect provide total impunity to offenders, is emerging in international law.'

151 *Prosecutor v Ieng Sary*, ECCC Case File No. 002/10-09-2007/ECCC/TC, Trial Chamber, Decision on Ieng Sary's Rule 89 Preliminary Objections (Ne bis in idem and Amnesty and Pardon), 3 November 2011, para. 29.

152 *Prosecutor v Ieng Sary*, ECCC Case File No. 002/10-09-2007/ECCC/TC/SC(11), Supreme Court Chamber, Decision on Ieng Sary's Appeal Against Trial Chamber's Decision on Ieng Sary's Rule 89 Preliminary Objections (Ne bis in idem and Amnesty and Pardon), 20 March 2012.

153 *Prosecutor v Ieng Sary*, ECCC Case File No. 002/10-09-2007/ECCC/TC/SC(11), Supreme Court Chamber, Dissenting Opinion of Judges Klonowiecka-Milart and Jayasinghe, 20 March 2012, para. 1.

154 Ibid, para. 4.

Despite the absence of a Supreme Court Chamber decision, the ECCC's contribution to the jurisprudence on *ne bis in idem* and amnesties is significant. In particular, the Pre-Trial Chamber developed the idea of an 'international *ne bis in idem* principle', enhancing the understanding of this core human rights principle and providing a springboard for further developments.[155] Notably, the Pre-Trial Chamber and the Trial Chamber agreed that the PRT proceedings did not meet the required standard of fairness so as to bar future proceedings although it should be recognised that it was Ieng Sary's rights that were in fact violated by the hasty, biased trial that led to him being sentenced to death. More could perhaps have been made of the fact that this occurred in absentia, so Ieng Sary remained unaffected, and the verdict was never final. As it concerns the pardon and amnesty, it is unlikely ever to be known for certain whether the King intended to relieve Ieng Sary of all responsibility for crimes, whatever their origin, committed during the DK era as a reward for his defection and supposed contribution to peace and reconciliation. By examining both the ordinary meaning of the Royal Decree, to the extent it is decipherable, and addressing the validity of amnesties for core international crimes under international law, the Pre-Trial Chamber and the Trial Chamber together covered all bases. The emphasis placed on the duty to prosecute in relevant treaties additionally supports the legality of the ECCC in a broader sense as an institution established to assist Cambodia in meeting its international obligations and combating impunity.

12. MAXIMUM PENALTIES

The initial draft of the ECCC Law incorporated the death penalty through its reference to the 1956 Penal Code as providing the basis for the domestic crimes over which the ECCC had jurisdiction. According to the 1956 Penal Code, the 'third degree criminal penalty', in other words

---

155 *See* M. Karnavas, 'Amnesty Part III: Ne Bis in Idem in International Criminal Law', International Criminal Law Blog, 1 August 2016 (who helpfully distils some of the emerging principles in relation to *ne bis in idem*, derived in part from the ECCC's jurisprudence; and states that: 'Despite the trend in Europe toward recognizing a transnational application of the *ne bis in idem* principle, lack of transnational application across domestic States has been identified as a "serious lacuna in international human rights protection," particularly since States are being encouraged or even obliged to introduce universal jurisdiction for international crimes.') <http://michaelgkarnavas.net/blog/2016/08/01/amnesty-part-iii/> [accessed 6 June 2017].

the death penalty, was applicable to certain of these crimes. After the Constitutional Council ruled that the reference to 'third degree criminal penalty' infringed Article 32 of the Cambodian Constitution, the ECCC Law was amended so that life imprisonment became the maximum penalty for both domestic and international crimes provided under the Law.[156] This is specified in Article 38: 'All penalties shall be limited to imprisonment.' The ECCC Agreement contains the same provision.[157]

These provisions on penalties are in line with those of other UN-supported tribunals as well as the ICC. Some domestic tribunals trying international crimes, notably the Iraqi High Tribunal and Bangladesh International Crimes Tribunal, have applied the death penalty. Since Cambodia had previously abolished the death penalty, there was no serious debate about reinstating it in the context of trials of former Khmer Rouge members. The inclusion of the death penalty in the first draft of the ECCC Law appears more as an oversight resulting from the incorporation of crimes under the 1956 Penal code rather than a deliberate attempt to bring back the supreme penalty. The SNC re-affirmed the abolition of the death penalty in Cambodia during the transitional period by providing in article 67 of the 1992 UNTAC Law that: 'The death penalty is abolished in Cambodia'. Article 32 of the 1993 Constitution confirmed that: 'Every Khmer citizen shall have the right to life, personal freedom and security. There shall be no capital punishment.' The 2009 Penal Code similarly makes it clear that the maximum sentence for even the most serious crimes (including genocide, crimes against humanity and war crimes) is life imprisonment.

Had Cambodia been retentionist, like Rwanda was at the time the UN established the ICTR to address the 1994 genocide, the death penalty might have been a further spanner in the works of negotiations over the ECCC. Rwanda was ultimately persuaded that international justice could be achieved despite the court being constrained by maximum sentences of imprisonment. At least from the UN's perspective, as embraced by Cambodia, the absence of the death penalty is a criterion for the legality of the ECCC.

---

[156] Decision of the Constitutional Council, No. 040/002/2001, 12 February 2001, <http://www.eccc.gov.kh/sites/default/files/legal-documents/Const_Council_Res_on_KR_Law_12_Feb_2001.pdf> [accessed 6 June 2017] (unofficial translation); *see* ECCC Law, Articles 3 new, 38–9.

[157] ECCC Agreement, Article 10.

13. WITHDRAWAL AND DISSOLUTION

It has been observed that the ECCC operates 'at greater risk of institutionally collapsing than any other international or hybrid criminal tribunal' having regard to the complex process of negotiation and twin concerns over judicial corruption in Cambodia and political interference by the Cambodian Government.[158] According to Article 25 of the ECCC Agreement, the Cambodian Government 'shall comply without undue delay with any request for assistance by the co-investigating judges, the co-prosecutors and the Extraordinary Chambers or an order issued by any of them, including, but not limited to' matters such as arrests and transfer of suspects. Cooperation was enthusiastic in the ECCC's early days and with respect to the initial arrests, but this enthusiasm turned to frigidity when the international Co-Prosecutor proposed expanding the list of suspects beyond the original five.

The ECCC's fragility might appear at first sight to throw the institution's legality into question. However, the ECCC Law provides for a contingency against the total collapse of the institution, allowing for several stages of withdrawal of key players while nevertheless ensuring that the shell of the ECCC survives. Article 46 (new) states:

> In order to ensure timely and smooth implementation of this law, in the event any foreign judges or foreign investigating judges or foreign prosecutors fail or refuse to participate in the Extraordinary Chambers, the Supreme Council of the Magistracy shall appoint other judges or investigating judges or prosecutors to fill any vacancies from the lists of foreign candidates provided for in Article 11, Article 18, and Article 26. In the event those lists are exhausted, and the Secretary-General of the United Nations does not supplement the lists with new candidates, or in the event that the United Nations withdraws its support from the Extraordinary Chambers, any such vacancies shall be filled by the Supreme Council of the Magistracy from candidates recommended by the Governments of Member States of the United Nations or from among other foreign legal personalities.
>
> If, following such procedures, there are still no foreign judges or foreign investigating judges or foreign prosecutors participating in the work of the Extraordinary Chambers and no foreign candidates have been identified to occupy the vacant positions, then the Supreme Council of the Magistracy may choose replacement Cambodian judges, investigating judges or prosecutors.

While there has been considerable, and sometimes high-profile turnover of international judges and prosecutors, the UN has remained steadfast

---

[158] Scheffer, above n. 10, p. 252.

(whether or not reluctantly) in its support. Article 28 of the ECCC Agreement entitled 'withdrawal of cooperation' provides:

> Should the Royal Government of Cambodia change the structure or organization of the Extraordinary Chambers or otherwise cause them to function in a manner that does not conform with the terms of the present Agreement, the United Nations reserves the right to cease to provide assistance, financial or otherwise, pursuant to the present Agreement.

Article 28 is only concerned with the withdrawal of the UN, but arguably if Cambodia should one day decide to go it alone, the residual domestic structure would be in breach of the ECCC Agreement and lack legality in spite of the contingency plan reflected in Article 46 (new) of the ECCC Law. Once the ECCC has 'definitively concluded' its work, it is designed to 'automatically dissolve' in accordance with Article 47 of the ECCC Law.

3. Structure

1. INTRODUCTION

This chapter takes a clinical look at the framework and unique features of the Extraordinary Chambers in the Courts of Cambodia (ECCC) and provides an overview of the role of its different organs, explaining the overall functioning of the Court. In addition, it considers the ECCC's relationship to the domestic court structure and concludes by assessing what type of judicial mechanism is represented by the ECCC, in other words, whether it is a domestic or an international court, a hybrid or internationalised body, sui generis, specialist, or simply extraordinary. This assessment impacts on how the ECCC's legitimacy is ultimately viewed.

It is common to speak of the 'international side' and the 'national side' of the ECCC to distinguish the UN-administered component from the domestic component and in some departments this division was replicated in the physical layout of the offices at least in its original design. Sometimes the two 'sides' have played as one team, while at other times they have appeared more as opponents. International staffing and technical assistance is administered by the United Nations Assistance to the Khmer Rouge Trial (UNAKRT) which has its own website pointing to its separate identity.[1] UNAKRT comes under the UN Department of Economic and Social Affairs (UNDESA). National staff are appointed by the Cambodian government.

The ECCC is composed of three judicial Chambers: the Pre-Trial Chamber (PTC), the Trial Chamber (TC) and the Supreme Court Chamber (SCC). The Pre-Trial Chamber and Trial Chamber are both constituted by five judges (three Cambodian and two international) as well as two reserve judges, while the Supreme Court Chamber has seven judges (four Cambodian and three international), plus reserve judges.[2] The Office of the Co-Prosecutors (OCP) and Office of the

1 Website of the United Nations Assistance to the Khmer Rouge Trials, <http://www.unakrt-online.org/> [accessed 7 June 2017].

2 ECCC Agreement, Articles 3(2), Article 7(2); ECCC Law, Articles 9 new, 20 new.

Co-Investigative Judges (OCIJ), have a Cambodian Prosecutor and Investigating Judge working alongside an international counterpart, also backed up by reserves. It is worth noting that both the OCIJ and the OCP are considered to be 'judicial offices' in accordance with the Cambodian criminal justice system, which is in turn modelled on the French criminal justice system. A notable feature of the ECCC is the use of official clerks that go by the French name 'Greffier' to assist each of the judicial organs in keeping an accurate and complete record of the proceedings. The structure of the ECCC is represented by an organigram which appears on the Court's website.[3]

The Office of Administration performs functions similar to a registry and provides court management and other services such as translation and interpretation. It is headed by a Cambodian Director, who is supported by an international Deputy Director. The Victims Support Section (VSS) is housed in the Office of Administration and supports victims of the Khmer Rouge who are entitled to participate actively in ECCC proceedings either by filing complaints or applying to be joined as civil parties. The procedures for civil party participation have developed during the life of the Court resulting in the creation of a separate Civil Party Lead Co-Lawyers' Section. The Defence Support Section (DSS) administers the work of the defence as well as providing legal advice, and ensures that defence teams comprise Cambodian and international co-lawyers, duly registered with the Bar Association of the Kingdom of Cambodia. These latter sections enjoy a reasonable degree of autonomy although they nominally fall under the authority of the Director and Deputy Director. According to Article 30 of the ECCC Law, all support staff for the Chambers judges, the investigating judges and prosecutors of the ECCC are supervised by the Office of Administration although in practice staff report in the first instance to supervisors within their respective units.

2. APPOINTMENT OF JUDGES AND PROSECUTORS

Article 3 of the ECCC Agreement specifies that a combination of Cambodian and international judges shall serve in the Chambers. International judges are appointed by the Supreme Council of the Magistracy upon nomination by the Secretary-General of the UN. This procedure is echoed and supplemented by Article 11 (new) of the ECCC Law which

---

3 'Organs of ECCC', Extraordinary Chambers in the Courts of Cambodia, <http://www.eccc.gov.kh/en/organs> [accessed 7 June 2017].

states: 'The Supreme Council of the Magistracy shall appoint at least seven Cambodian judges to act as judges of the Extraordinary Chambers, and shall appoint reserve judges as needed, and shall also appoint the President of each of the Extraordinary Chambers from the above Cambodian judges so appointed, in accordance with the existing procedures for appointment of judges.' Further, according to the same article: 'The Secretary-General of the United Nations shall submit a list of not less than seven candidates for foreign judges to the Royal Government of Cambodia, from which the Supreme Council of the Magistracy shall appoint five sitting judges and at least two reserve judges.' The judges 'shall be persons of high moral character, impartiality and integrity who possess the qualifications required in their respective countries for appointment to judicial offices', and they 'shall be independent in the performance of their functions and shall not accept or seek instructions from any Government or any other source'.[4]

Article 5 of the ECCC Agreement provides that there shall be one Cambodian and one international investigating judge, with a similar appointment process to that of Chambers judges. Article 23 (new) of the ECCC Law elaborates that 'all investigations shall be the joint responsibility of two investigating judges, one Cambodian and another foreign'. According to Article 25 of the ECCC Law, the Co-Investigating Judges are appointed in the first instance from among the currently practising judges, and 'shall have high moral character, a spirit of impartiality and integrity, and experience' and be 'independent in the performance of their functions and shall not accept or seek instructions from any government or any other source'. This mirrors Articles 5(2) and 5(3) of the ECCC Agreement although a caveat to the ethical duty of independence is contained in Article 5(3), namely that:

> It is understood, however, that the scope of the investigation is limited to senior leaders of Democratic Kampuchea and those who were most responsible for the crimes and serious violations of Cambodian penal law, international humanitarian law and custom, and international conventions recognized by Cambodia, that were committed during the period from 17 April 1975 to 6 January 1979.

---

[4] ECCC Agreement, Article 3. (This is echoed and supplemented by ECCC Law, Article 10: 'shall have high moral character, a spirit of impartiality and integrity, and experience.')

It is curious that the ECCC Agreement re-states the limits on the ECCC's personal and subject-matter jurisdiction in the context of judicial independence. This provision was presumably not intended to impose any restrictions on the Co-Investigating Judges in terms of how they carry out their investigation within the scope of the Court's jurisdiction, or to contradict the requirement of acting without 'instructions from any government or any other source' in interpreting the categories of 'senior leaders of Democratic Kampuchea' and 'those most responsible'.

According to Article 6 of the ECCC Agreement, there shall be one Cambodian and one international prosecutor who shall as Co-Prosecutors be responsible for the conduct of the prosecutions. In the same article, it is stated that: 'The co-prosecutors shall be of high moral character, and possess a high level of professional competence and extensive experience in the conduct of investigations and prosecutions of criminal cases.' This requirement for Co-Prosecutors is replicated in Article 19 of the ECCC Law. Also, they shall be 'independent in the performance of their functions and shall not accept or seek instructions from any government or any other source'. Meanwhile, the same qualification on independence as applies in respect of co-investigating judges appears in Article 6(3) of the ECCC Agreement concerning the Co-Prosecutors. Again, this can only be regarded as a reminder to the Co-Prosecutors of the jurisdictional scope of the ECCC. Article 18 (new) of the ECCC Law gives the Supreme Council of the Magistracy the responsibility for appointing Cambodian prosecutors from among the Cambodian professional judges. The foreign prosecutor is appointed by the Supreme Council of the Magistracy upon nomination by the Secretary-General of the United Nations.

The ECCC judges adopted a Code of Judicial Ethics during plenary sessions in 2008.[5] The Cambodian Constitution provides for a separation of powers, including an independent judiciary.[6] However, the domestic judiciary does not have a strong record when it comes to independence.[7]

---

[5] Extraordinary Chambers in the Courts of Cambodia Code of Judicial Ethics, 5 September 2008, <https://www.eccc.gov.kh/en/documents/legal/code-judicial-ethics> [accessed 7 June 2017] ('Code of Judicial Ethics').

[6] Constitution of the Kingdom of Cambodia, 21 September 1999, Article 128, <http://faolex.fao.org/docs/pdf/cam117198.pdf> [accessed 7 June 2017].

[7] As recently as 2016, the Special Rapporteur on Cambodia called for judges to publish reasoning for all decisions in order to strengthen both real and perceived judicial independence, *see* 'Time to Move on – UN Expert Urges Cambodia to Fully Implement Rights and Freedoms at Every Level', The Office of the United Nations High Commissioner for Human Rights, 20 October 2016,

The procedures for seeking the disqualification of judges on grounds of bias go some way towards tackling problems of alleged lack of impartiality and have been extensively invoked in relation to international and national judges alike, as will be discussed further in Chapter 6.

3. OFFICE OF THE CO-PROSECUTORS (OCP)

The OCP is an independent office within the ECCC. Chea Leang has held the position of Cambodian Co-Prosecutor from the outset. Robert Petit (Canada) was the first international Co-Prosecutor and the position has since been held by Andrew T. Cayley (UK) and Nicholas Koumjian (US). William Smith (Australia) has been the deputy international prosecutor throughout.[8] The OCP is staffed by both national and international personnel, including at least one Greffier, in accordance with Article 22 (new) of the ECCC Law and Rule 13 of the Internal Rules.[9]

According to Article 16 of the ECCC Law, all 'indictments' are the responsibility of the Co-Prosecutors 'who shall work together' in their preparation. The Co-Prosecutors do not in fact issue the indictment in the sense of the document containing the formal accusations at the conclusion of an investigation since this is the task of the Co-Investigating Judges. The role of the OCP is rather to prosecute senior leaders of the Khmer Rouge and those most responsible for the crimes committed during the period of Democratic Kampuchea by receiving, considering and processing written complaints or information alleging the commission of crimes within the jurisdiction of the ECCC; conducting a preliminary investigation; ordering the Judicial Police to take suspects into custody as appropriate; initiating a judicial investigation by presenting an Introductory Submission to the Co-Investigating Judges (to be followed by a Supplementary Submission as necessary); participating in judicial investigations conducted by the Co-Investigating Judges; and prosecuting cases through the investigative, pre-trial, trial and appellate stages. It is specified in Article 17 (new) of the ECCC Law that the

<http://www.ohchr.org/EN/NewsEvents/Pages/DisplayNews.aspx?NewsID=20718&LangID=E> [accessed 3 June 2017].

[8] *See* ECCC Law, Article 22 new: 'Deputy foreign prosecutors shall be appointed by the foreign Co-Prosecutor from a list provided by the Secretary-General'.

[9] International personnel are appointed by the United Nations through the United Nations Assistance to the Khmer Rouge Trials ('UNAKRT').

Co-Prosecutors shall have the right to appeal the verdict of the Trial Chamber.

Like other offices of the ECCC, the functioning of the OCP was hampered by the fact that the legal background and experience of national staff tended to be limited and international staff tended not to be versed in Cambodian criminal procedure or to speak Khmer. It should be recalled, however, that one of the main purposes behind the ECCC's unique structure was to allow the transfer and exchange of knowledge and competence. The negotiators of the ECCC Agreement must have been aware that this educational aspect would come at the expense of speed and efficiency, having regard to the amount of patience that had been required to agree to an institution in the first place. As the first international Co-Prosecutor, Robert Petit drew on his experience from the ad hoc tribunals to put in place mixed Cambodian and international teams organised around particular suspects. Prior to taking up the role, he had insisted on including investigative staff within the OCP although in the ECCC system, the OCP only has a limited investigative function.[10]

4. OFFICE OF THE CO-INVESTIGATING JUDGES (OCIJ)

The OCIJ is a unique feature of the ECCC, following the Cambodian/French model of the *juge d'instruction* (investigating judge). This means that pre-trial investigations are carried out primarily by the Co-Investigating Judges and their staff rather than by the OCP, although there is a degree of overlap in the responsibilities of these two organs of the Court. The role of the OCIJ is to collect evidence with a view to determining whether the facts alleged by the Co-Prosecutors in their Introductory and Supplementary Submissions constitute crimes within the jurisdiction of the ECCC (i.e. make a determination on subject-matter jurisdiction); whether the person investigated was either a senior leader or one of the persons most responsible for crimes committed during the Khmer Rouge Regime (i.e. make a determination on personal jurisdiction); and whether the person under investigation is to be indicted and sent to trial, or whether the case against that person should be dismissed.

---

[10] *See* further G. Townsend, 'Structure and Management', in L. Reydams, J. Wouters, and C. Ryngaert (eds), *International Prosecutors* (Oxford, Oxford University Press, 2012), pp. 171–318, p. 301.

Judge You Bunleng has been the national Co-Investigating Judge since the establishment of the ECCC. Judge Marcel Lemonde[11] (France) was the first international Co-Investigating Judge and held the position until late 2010 when he was succeeded by Judge Siegfried Blunk (Germany), followed by Judge Laurent Kasper-Ansermet (Switzerland) acting as reserve Co-Investigating Judge at the time, followed by Judge Mark Harmon (US), and finally Judge Michael Bohlander (Germany). The swift changeover of Co-Investigating Judges in the year following Judge Lemonde's resignation was marked by controversy. Siegfried Blunk resigned over what he described as government pressure after being criticised for closing prematurely one of the judicial investigations.[12] After re-opening the investigation at issue when taking over as reserve Co-Investigating Judge, Laurent Kasper-Ansermet later resigned when it became clear that the Cambodian government refused to recognise his authority and would not endorse his appointment as Co-Investigating Judge.[13] Things assumed a better track with the appointment of Mark Harmon although the fractures within the office were undoubtedly difficult to repair.

5. PRE-TRIAL CHAMBER (PTC)

The judicial investigation is monitored by the PTC, whose jurisdiction was expanded from that of a special Chamber to settle disagreements between national and international Co-Prosecutors and Co-Investigating Judges as envisaged in the ECCC Agreement and ECCC Law, to accord it a similar function to the Cambodian *Chambre d'instruction* (Investigation Chamber). The PTC is comprised of three Cambodian judges and two international judges, presided over by Judge Prak Kimsan.

---

11 Judge Lemonde wrote a book about his experience as Co-Investigating Judge: M. Lemonde and J. Reynaud, *Un Juge Face aux Khmers Rouges* (Paris, Éditions du Seuil, 2013).

12 *See* e.g. S. Mydans, 'Judge Quits Tribunal in Khmer Rouge Inquiry', *The New York Times*, 10 October 2011, <http://www.nytimes.com/2011/10/11/world/asia/judge-quits-cambodia-tribunal.html> [accessed 7 June 2017].

13 'UN Voices Concern as Second Judge Resigns from Cambodia Genocide Court', *UN News Centre*, 19 March 2012, <http://www.un.org/apps/news/story.asp?NewsID=41578#.WQf53tGwc3E> [accessed 7 June 2017]; J. Birchall, 'New Judge will be at Center of Struggle over Khmer Rouge', *International Justice Monitor*, 30 July 2012, <https://www.ijmonitor.org/2012/07/new-judge-will-be-at-center-of-struggle-over-khmer-rouge/> [accessed 7 June 2017].

The ECCC Agreement does not include the PTC as an integral Chamber alongside the Trial Chamber and Supreme Court Chamber. As originally conceived in Article 7 of the ECCC Agreement and Articles 20 (new) and 23 (new) of the ECCC Law, the PTC was to be convened solely for the settlement of differences between the Co-Investigating Judges or the Co-Prosecutors. The detailed procedures for bringing disagreements before the PTC are set out in Internal Rules 71 and 72.

The additional jurisdiction of the Pre-Trial Chamber was agreed in a plenary session of the Court and is set out in Internal Rule 73 as follows:

> In addition to its power to adjudicate disputes between the Co-Prosecutors or the Co-Investigating Judges, as set out in the Agreement and the ECCC Law, the Chamber shall have sole jurisdiction over:
>
> a) appeals against decisions of the Co-Investigating Judges, as provided in Rule 74;
> b) applications to annul investigative action, as provided in Rule 76; and
> c) the appeals provided for in Rules 11(5) and (6); 35(6), 38(3) and 77*bis* of these IRs.

The PTC therefore serves a dual role as a forum for settling disagreements and as a *Chambre d'instruction*. The PTC's expanded role effectively made it a permanent Chamber in view of its consistently heavy workload for the duration of the investigations, although there was resistance to this idea in the early stages of the Court due to the extra resources required for the PTC's successful operation. Indeed, according to Article 27(5) of the ECCC Agreement (which did not envisage the PTC's additional jurisdiction), 'The judges of the Pre-Trial Chamber shall serve only if and when their services are needed' as part of a phased-in approach to the operation of the ECCC presumably geared towards efficiency. As indicated in Internal Rule 73, the PTC hears appeals against decisions of the Co-Investigating Judges and applications to annul investigative action,[14] as well as certain appeals against administrative decisions relating, for example, to the appointment of counsel. Under Internal Rule 74, the Co-Prosecutors may appeal against all orders of the Co-Investigating Judges, including Closing Orders issued at the conclusion of an investigation. The defence may only appeal against ten categories of order, including those confirming the jurisdiction of the Court; refusals of requests for investigative action, the restitution of seized items, expert reports or additional expert investigation; and

---

[14] Internal Rules, Rule 73.

decisions relating to provisional detention or bail. Civil parties may similarly lodge appeals in accordance with Internal Rule 74(4).

According to Article 7 of the ECCC Agreement and Internal Rule 77(13), there is no appeal against decisions of the PTC. However, depending on the nature of the appeal brought against a decision of the Co-Investigating Judges, it is possible for certain fundamental issues, such as those relating to jurisdiction or the characterisation of the facts, to be raised again during trial and revisited by the Trial Chamber and eventually the Supreme Court Chamber.

6. TRIAL CHAMBER (TC)

The Trial Chamber is composed of three Cambodian judges and two international judges and is presided over by Judge Nil Nonn.[15] The main function of the Trial Chamber is to conduct trial proceedings once a case is sent to trial at the conclusion of an investigation and to decide whether an accused person is guilty or not guilty.

7. SUPREME COURT CHAMBER (SCC)

The Supreme Court Chamber is composed of four Cambodian judges and three international judges, presided over by Judge Kong Sim.[16] The main function of the Supreme Court Chamber is to hear appeals against decisions and judgments issued by the Trial Chamber.

There is only one level of review of judgments issued by the Trial Chamber, in contrast to the domestic court structure whereby a Criminal Chamber of the Court of Appeal has the power to decide a case *de novo* and the Supreme Court may then review appeal judgments by a request

---

[15] ECCC Law, Article 9 new: 'The Trial Chamber shall be an Extraordinary Chamber composed of five professional judges, of whom three are Cambodian judges with one as president, and two foreign judges; and before which the Co-Prosecutors shall present their cases. The president shall appoint one or more clerks of the court to participate.'

[16] ECCC Law, Article 9 new: 'The Supreme Court Chamber, which shall serve as both appellate chamber and final instance, shall be an Extraordinary Chamber composed of seven judges, of whom four are Cambodian judges with one as president, and three foreign judges; and before which the Co-Prosecutors shall present their cases. The president shall appoint one or more clerks of the court to participate.'

for cassation.[17] The domestic court structure was replicated in the ECCC Law as originally promulgated in 2001 but the first-tier appeals stage was removed in the amended Law.[18] As a result, the 'remedies available under Cambodian criminal procedure were conflated into one *sui generis* appellate system'.[19] The ECCC Supreme Court Chamber therefore serves as both 'appellate chamber and final instance'.[20]

8. RESERVE JUDGES

Internal Rule 77(7) provides that reserve judges of the Pre-Trial Chamber 'shall be present at all stages of any hearings that the President of the Chamber considers may require a substantial length of time to hear, in particular an appeal against a Closing Order by the Co-Investigating Judges'. Reserve judges of the Trial Chamber are to be present at all stages of proceedings in accordance with Internal Rule 79(3). Both rules specify that reserve judges 'shall not have the right to express any opinion or to make any decision unless and until appointed to replace a sitting judge'. As it concerns Supreme Court Chamber proceedings, the President of the Chamber 'may decide that either or both Reserve Judges shall be present'.[21] The expense of retaining reserve judges at all levels of the Extraordinary Chambers is justified by the need to ensure expeditious, uninterrupted proceedings.

9. SUPER-MAJORITY VOTING

As part of the delicate compromise that brought the ECCC into existence, it was decided that in the absence of unanimity, Chambers decisions should be reached by a super-majority vote (as opposed to a simple

---

17 CPC, Article 417.

18 Reach Kram: Law on the Establishment of Extraordinary Chambers in the Courts of Cambodia for the Prosecution of Crimes Committed during the Period of Democratic Kampuchea, NS/RKM/0801/12, 10 August 2001.

19 *Prosecutor v Kaing Guek Eav alias 'Duch'*, ECCC Case File No. 001/18-07-2007-ECCC/SC, Supreme Court Chamber, Appeal Judgment, 3 February 2012, para. 13 ('Duch Appeal Judgment'); *Prosecutor v Nuon Chea* and *Khieu Samphan*, ECCC Case File No. 002/19-09-2007-ECCC/SC, Supreme Court Chamber, Appeal Judgment, 23 November 2016, para. 93 ('Nuon Appeal Judgment').

20 ECCC Law, Article 9 new.

21 Internal Rules, Rule 108(3).

majority) so as to eliminate the risk of a split vote between national and international judges. The idea was suggested by David Scheffer on the basis that 'some formula had to be developed to ensure the participation of Cambodian judges in the court, but in a way that preserved international influence and oversight.'[22] Scheffer drew an analogy with the requirement of unanimous jury verdicts in common-law trials as compared to the majority votes typically required in civil law jurisdictions and concluded that the supermajority rule 'logically fell within [the] hybrid concept'.[23] At the same time, the rule served to address concerns over possible corruption, whether or not justified.

The starting point according to Article 14 (new) of the ECCC Law (the terms of which are repeated in Article 4 of the ECCC Agreement), is for the judges to attempt to achieve unanimity in their decisions. However, if this is not possible, 'a decision by the [Trial Chamber] shall require the affirmative vote of at least four judges' and 'a decision by the [Supreme Court Chamber] shall require the affirmative vote of at least five judges'. A decision by the PTC requires the affirmative vote of at least four judges.[24] The opinions of the majority and the minority are to be contained in the decision.

If the PTC fails to reach a super-majority in an appeal against the indictment, the default position is that the Trial Chamber is seised on the basis of the Closing Order of the Co-Investigating Judges.[25] If the required majority to enter a conviction is not attained by the Trial Chamber, the accused must be acquitted.[26] If the Supreme Court Chamber notifies the Trial Chamber and the parties that it has not achieved a super-majority, the decision of the Trial Chamber shall stand.[27]

---

[22] D. Scheffer, *All the Missing Souls: A Personal History of the War Crimes Tribunals* (Princeton, Princeton University Press, 2012), p. 387.

[23] Ibid.

[24] ECCC Agreement, Article 7(4).

[25] Internal Rules, Rule 77(13)(b).

[26] Internal Rules, Rule 98(4).

[27] Internal Rules, Rule 108(4) *bis*.

10. JUDICIAL DELIBERATION AND DISSENT

ECCC judges deliberate in camera to reach their decision.[28] The Internal Rules require reasons to be given for any judicial decision or order.[29] The same principles apply in Cambodian criminal procedure.[30] The CPC does not envisage dissenting opinions[31] and in the Cambodian Supreme Court, 'rulings are given by the entire court without identifying the particular views of each individual member of the bench.'[32] Article 24 of the Code of Civil Procedure of Cambodia also provides that the opinions constituting the majority or the minority revealed in deliberations must remain secret.[33]

In contrast, Internal Rule 78 provides that: 'All decisions and default decisions of the [Pre-Trial] Chamber, including any dissenting opinions, shall be published in full, except where the Chamber decides that it would be contrary to the integrity of the Preliminary Investigation or to the Judicial Investigation.' Internal Rule 101 states that: 'Where there is no unanimity, a judge [of the Trial Chamber or Supreme Court Chamber[34]] may write a separate or dissenting opinion, in which case, it shall be attached to the judgment.' In practice, separate or dissenting opinions have commonly been filed by the international judges and occasionally by the national judges. An example of the latter is the brief separate opinion of Judge Thou Mony in connection with disqualification proceedings against the sitting Trial Chamber. Judge Thou Mony lamented the fact that Judge Rowan Downing, who published a powerful dissent in

---

28 Internal Rules, Rules 77(12), 96(1).

29 Internal Rules, Rules 25(2), 25(3), 29(4), 44(2), 50(3), 55(10), 58(6), 59(5), 63(1)(b), 63(7), 64(2), 66(2), 67(4), 68(1), 71(4)(d), 72(4)(e), 77(14), 79(6)(b), 89(3), 99(2), 101(1)(a), 108(4) *bis*, 109(3), 111(5).

30 CPC, Article 337.

31 *See* CPC, Article 357 (on the writing of the judgment).

32 *Prosecutor v Nuon Chea, Ieng Sary, Ieng Thirith* and *Khieu Samphan*, ECCC Case File No. 002/19-09-2007-ECCC/TC, Trial Chamber, Decision on Ieng Thirith and Ieng Sary's Applications for Disqualification of Judge You Ottara from the Special Bench and Requests for a Public Hearing, 9 May 2011, para. 16.

33 Code of Civil Procedure of Cambodia, 26 May 2006, <https://www.jica.go.jp/project/english/cambodia/0701047/materials/c8h0vm000000zsb2-att/01_01e.pdf> [accessed 7 June 2017] (unofficial translation).

34 By virtue of Internal Rules, Rule 104 *bis*, according to which 'the rules that apply to the Trial Chamber shall, mutatis mutandis, also apply to the Supreme Court Chamber'.

the case, had not shared his reasoning with his colleagues.[35] In the event, Judge Downing benefited from having read the reasons provided by the majority, while the majority was deprived of the benefit of seeing his dissenting opinion in advance.[36] Judge Thou Mony stated quite reasonably that:

> I consider that the interests of justice are better served if a Judge shares his or her full written reasoning with colleagues in advance of publication. The sharing of full reasons allows the differences in the approach taken by the different Judges to be clarified, which might assist those seeking to understand the decision. It is possible that a Judge misunderstands or mischaracterises another Judge's approach, inadvertently or perhaps because the language of an opinion could be better expressed. The risk is greater at a court which operates in multiple languages via translations.[37]

Since deliberations are secret, it is impossible to know what really went on behind the scenes. The dissent is dated 23 January 2015 while the majority decision is dated 30 January 2015 so time does not appear to have been the issue. On a matter concerning Ieng Thirith's fitness to stand trial, the Cambodian judges of the Trial Chamber spoke independently. While acknowledging the interests of justice in prosecuting former Khmer Rouge leaders they stated that: 'The integrity of the proceedings and the dignity of a human being preclude the trial of an accused who is in a defenceless position.'[38]

---

[35] *Prosecutor v Nuon Chea* and *Khieu Samphan*, ECCC Case File No. 002/19-09-2007/ECCC/TC, Trial Chamber, Decision on Applications for the Disqualification of Trial Chamber Judges, 14 November 2014; *Prosecutor v Nuon Chea* and *Khieu Samphan*, ECCC Case File No. 002/19-09-2007/ECCC/TC, Trial Chamber, Reasons for Decision on Applications for Disqualification: Separate Opinion from Judge Thou Mony, 30 January 2015.

[36] *See Prosecutor v Nuon Chea* and *Khieu Samphan*, ECCC Case File No. 002/19-09-2007/ECCC/TC, Trial Chamber, Reasons for Decision on Applications for Disqualification: Separate Opinion from Judge Thou Mony, 30 January 2015, *Prosecutor v Nuon Chea* and *Khieu Samphan*, ECCC Case File No. 002/19-09-2007/ECCC/TC, Trial Chamber, Reasons for Decision on Applications for Disqualification: Partly Dissenting Opinion of Judge Rowan Downing, 23 January 2015.

[37] *Prosecutor v Nuon Chea* and *Khieu Samphan*, ECCC Case File No. 002/19-09-2007/ECCC/TC, Trial Chamber, Reasons for Decision on Applications for Disqualification: Separate Opinion from Judge Thou Mony, 30 January 2015, para. 2.

[38] *Prosecutor v Nuon Chea, Ieng Sary, Ieng Thirith* and *Khieu Samphan*, ECCC Case File No. 002/19-09-2007/ECCC/TC, Trial Chamber, Decision on Ieng Thirith's Fitness to Stand Trial, 17 November 2011, para. 63; *see* also R.L.

11. JUDICIAL PRECEDENT

In conformity with general international jurisprudence, there is no principle of *stare decisis* in the ECCC. In other words, a lower Chamber in the ECCC is not bound by a decision made by a higher Chamber, and the Chambers as a whole are not bound by judicial decisions made by any other international or national courts. Normally the Co-Investigating Judges would follow decisions of the Pre-Trial Chamber and all Chambers would follow decisions of the Supreme Court Chamber in the interests of consistency and certainty, or 'practical judicial deference'.[39] As it concerns courts outside the system of the ECCC, their decisions may assist in interpreting the law and assessing the foreseeability requirement as part of the principle of legality.[40]

12. OFFICE OF ADMINISTRATION

Article 31 (new) of the ECCC Law specifies that the Director of Administration, who is responsible for the overall management of the Office of Administration with the exception of UN matters, 'shall be appointed by the Royal Government of Cambodia for a two-year term and shall be eligible for reappointment'. The Director must have significant experience in court administration and fluency in one of the foreign languages used at the ECCC, and 'shall be a person of high moral character and integrity'. The foreign Deputy Director is appointed by the

---

Phillips, 'Frail Accused and Fitness to Stand Trial', in S.M. Meisenberg and I. Stegmiller (eds), *The Extraordinary Chambers in the Courts of Cambodia: Assessing their Contribution to International Criminal Law* (The Hague, T.M.C. Asser Press, 2016), pp. 461–89, p. 478.

[39] ECCC Case File No. 004/07-09-2009-ECCC-OCIJ (*Im Chaem*), Closing Order (Reasons), 10 July 2017, para. 10, also stating that there is no doctrine of *stare decisis* in civil law systems such as Cambodia. See, however, *Prosecutor v Meas Muth*, ECCC Case File No. 003/07-09-2009-ECCC-OCIJ, Office of the Co-Investigating Judges, Decision on Meas Muth's Request for Clarification concerning Crimes against Humanity and the Nexus with Armed Conflict, 5 April 2016, para. 57, where the international Co-Investigating Judge departs from the position of the PTC.

[40] *Prosecutor v Meas Muth*, ECCC Case File No. 003/07-09-2009-ECCC-OCIJ, Office of the Co-Investigating Judges, Notification on the Interpretation of 'Attack against the Civilian Population' in the Context of Crimes against Humanity with regard to a State's or Regime's Own Armed Forces', 7 February 2017, para. 22; Duch Appeal Judgment, above n. 19, para. 97.

Secretary-General of the UN and assigned by the Royal Government of Cambodia. The Deputy Director's responsibilities include the recruitment and administration of all international staff and administering the resources provided through the UN Trust Fund. The first Deputy Director, Michelle Lee, was succeeded in late 2007 by Knut Rosandhaug who has demonstrated his determination to remain in post until the bitter end. The appointed Cambodian Director, Sean Visoth, left on indefinite sick leave in 2008 and his deputy, Tony Kranh, has been acting Director ever since.

The Office of Administration is advised by a Judicial Administration Committee comprised of three national judges and two international judges elected in plenary session, and including the Co-Prosecutors and Director and Deputy Director of Administration in a consultative capacity.[41] The function of the Judicial Administration Committee is to advise the Office of Administration on matters relating to the administrative and judicial support provided to the judicial offices including the budget.

Unusually within the structure of the ECCC, which replicates most roles, the international head of administration is placed in a subservient position to the national head of administration as opposed to having national and international co-directors. It has been suggested that the structure of the ECCC could have been improved by placing a proper registry above the Office of Administration and this was proposed by David Tolbert who served as a UN special expert tasked with advising UNAKRT in 2008.[42] It has been observed that the 'absence of a single responsible registrar has made it unclear which side of the [Office of Administration] has the authority to lead a particular task and who should be held accountable for it'.[43] According to Article 8(1) of the ECCC Agreement, the Office of Administration has the role of *servicing* the Chambers, the OCIJ and the OCP. Judicial officers may not always be the easiest clients but a willingness by the chief administrators to work with, rather than against them, is vital for the effective functioning of a judicial institution whose primary goal is the delivery of justice. While the Office

---

41 Internal Rules, Rule 19.

42 G. Wilkins, 'UN Expert Arrives as US Announces It Might Fund the ECCC', *The Phnom Penh Post*, 27 August 2008, <http://www.phnompenhpost.com/national/un-expert-arrives-us-announces-it-might-fund-eccc> [accessed 7 June 2017]; J.D. Ciorciari and A. Heindel, *Hybrid Justice: The Extraordinary Chambers in the Courts of Cambodia* (Ann Arbor, Michigan, University of Michigan Press, 2014), p. 72.

43 Ciorciari and Heindel, ibid, p. 72.

of Administration was trying to keep its own house in order during the first few years of the ECCC's operation, step by step the cases progressed.

13. DEFENCE SUPPORT SECTION (DSS)

The role of the Defence Support Section, initially headed by Rupert Skilbeck and currently by Isaac Endeley, is to ensure fair trials through effective representation of the accused. Article 24 (new) of the ECCC Law provides that during the investigation 'suspects shall be unconditionally entitled to the assistance of counsel of their own choosing, and to have legal assistance assigned to them free of charge if they cannot afford it, as well as the right to interpretation, as necessary, into and from a language they speak and understand'. This right extends through the entire proceedings and the DSS assists by providing one Cambodian and one international lawyer to serve as Co-Lawyers for each accused as well as by undertaking research and analysis for the Co-Lawyers. The Co-Lawyers are supported by Legal Consultants and Case Managers recruited locally and internationally. The ECCC Legal Assistance Scheme is designed to ensure equality of arms between the defence and prosecution through a fair fee payment scheme. The DSS additionally provides a voice for the defence at outreach or media events and liaises with other tribunals and NGOs.

An occasional frustration for the international defence lawyers, in particular those trained in the common law or other ad hoc tribunal systems, has been the inability to initiate their own investigations. As the Supreme Court Chamber has noted, the ECCC's procedural framework 'does not envisage full-fledged party-driven investigations such as those common to adversarial systems'.[44] However, as long as the defence did not usurp the investigative powers afforded to other Court organs within the ECCC structure, the Supreme Court Chamber could see 'no statutory basis or compelling practical reasons for prohibiting the Defence from undertaking actions aimed at discovering relevant evidence.'[45] The Chamber took the view that a degree of flexibility should be allowed on a case-by-case basis, with the caveat that any investigative action carried out by the defence must not 'lead to witness tampering or any other distortion of evidence'.[46]

---

44 Nuon Appeal Judgment, above n. 19, para. 248.
45 Ibid, para. 249.
46 Ibid.

14. VICTIMS SUPPORT SECTION (VSS)

Victims are entitled to participate in ECCC proceedings by submitting complaints to the Co-Prosecutors, who take their interests into account when considering whether to initiate a prosecution, or by appearing in proceedings as civil parties. The role of the VSS is to inform victims of their rights, help them to exercise those rights effectively, and ensure they have access to a high quality of justice. This means arranging for victims to be represented (when submitting complaints or participating as civil parties) either by a national lawyer acting alone or by an international lawyer acting in conjunction with a national lawyer. Rule 12 *bis* (1)(c) of the Internal Rules states that the VSS shall maintain a list of international and national lawyers who wish to represent Victims or Victims' Associations before the ECCC. The VSS also coordinates the process of seeking reparations and is 'entrusted with the development and implementation of non-judicial programs and measures addressing the broader interests of victims' in collaboration with other organisations as appropriate.[47]

15. CIVIL PARTY LEAD CO-LAWYERS' SECTION

A civil party is defined under the Internal Rules as 'a victim whose application to become a Civil Party has been declared admissible by the Co-Investigating Judges or the Pre-Trial Chamber in accordance with these [Internal Rules]'. In order to be eligible to participate as a civil party, a victim must be 'a natural (living) person or a legal entity who suffered physical, material or psychological harm as a direct consequence of at least one of the crimes alleged' against the person charged before the ECCC.[48]

The Civil Party Lead Co-Lawyers' Section is established by the Office of Administration under Internal Rule 12, which indicates that this section 'shall be autonomous with regard to all substantive matters pertaining to Civil Parties set out in these [Internal Rules]'.[49] Internal

---

47 Internal Rules, Rule 12 *bis* (4).

48 Definition provided in 'Who is Eligible to Become a Civil Party?', Extraordinary Chambers in the Courts of Cambodia, <https://www.eccc.gov.kh/en/victims-support/civil-party-information> [accessed 7 June 2017].

49 Internal Rules, Rule 12 was amended on 9 February 2010 and 17 September 2010.

Rule 12 *ter*[50] explains that 'Civil Party Lead Co-Lawyers shall ensure the effective organization of Civil Party representation during the trial stage and beyond, whilst balancing the rights of all parties and the need for an expeditious trial within the unique ECCC context'. The Civil Party Lead Co-Lawyers (one Cambodian and one international lawyer), derive their powers directly from the Internal Rules.[51]

16. COURT MANAGEMENT SECTION

Apart from submitting complaints or applying to appear as civil parties, victims commonly appear as witnesses. According to Article 33 (new) of the ECCC Law which is mirrored in Article 23 of the ECCC Agreement, the Court 'shall provide for the protection of victims and witnesses' by adopting measures including but not limited to the conduct of in camera proceedings and the protection of the victim's identity. This function is carried out by the Witness and Expert Support Unit (WESU) which forms part of the Court Management Section.

The Court Management Section is a large and important section with multiple units, including, in addition to the WESU, the Audio-Visual Unit, Detention Facility Liaison Unit, Interpretation and Translation Unit, Front Office (Case File Officer), Reproduction and Records Archives Unit and Transcription Unit.

17. OFFICIAL LANGUAGES

According to Article 26(1) of the ECCC Agreement: 'The official language of the Extraordinary Chambers and the Pre-Trial Chamber is Khmer.' The official *working* languages of the ECCC are Khmer, English and French.[52] The Practice Direction on the Filing of Documents, as amended, provides that all documents must be filed in Khmer in addition to one of the international languages.[53] The vast number of documents in the case files and being produced generally by the offices of the Court,

---

[50] Internal Rules, Rule 12 *ter* was adopted on 9 February 2010 and amended on 23 February 2011.

[51] Internal Rules, Rule 12 *ter* (2).

[52] ECCC Agreement, Article 26(2); ECCC Law, Article 45 new.

[53] Practice Direction on Filing Documents before the ECCC (Revision 8), Practice Direction ECCC/01/2007/Rev.8, Articles 2.2, 7 (Some defence teams had elected to file in English only under the old provision).

coupled with extremely limited translation capacity at least in the Court's early stages, provides fertile ground for delays and disruptions to the proceedings. The time taken to produce translations risks creating an imbalance between the international and national components of the Court, although this can largely be overcome by having the necessary linguistic ability reflected in the composition of teams.

These issues came to a head in 2008 when the then international co-lawyer for Khieu Samphan, Jacques Vergès, refused to participate in proceedings on the basis that not all the documents in the case file had been translated into French. This prompted the Co-Investigating Judges to issue a general order concerning the translation rights and obligations of the parties during the investigative phase.[54] The order listed the types of document that a person charged before the ECCC was entitled to receive in his or her own language, which included most importantly the elements of proof on which the indictment relied. In addition, each defence team was offered the assistance of a full-time translator. Attempts to appeal against this order by the defence for Ieng Sary and Khieu Samphan were unsuccessful as the PTC found the appeals to be inadmissible.[55] Nevertheless, the PTC conducted an extensive examination of whether the Charged Person's rights as safeguarded in Internal Rule 21 would require the Chamber to find the appeal admissible, in which it in fact concluded that the Co-Investigating Judges' order was in accordance with international standards.[56] Notably, the PTC found that the defence teams would be in a position to identify exculpatory material and request translation of those specific documents.[57]

---

[54] *Prosecutor v Nuon Chea, Ieng Sary, Ieng Thirith, Khieu Samphan* and *Kaing Guek Eav*, ECCC Case File No. 002/14-08-2006, Office of the Co-Investigating Judges, Order on Translation Rights and Obligations of the Parties, 19 June 2008.

[55] *Prosecutor v Khieu Samphan*, ECCC Case File No. 002/19-09-2007-ECCC/OCIJ (PTC11), Pre-Trial Chamber, Decision on Khieu Samphan's Appeal against the Order on Translation Rights and Obligations of the Parties, 20 February 2009, p. 14; *Prosecutor v Ieng Sary*, ECCC Case File No. 002/19-09-2007-ECCC/OCIJ (PTC12), Pre-Trial Chamber, Decision on Ieng Sary's Appeal against the OCIJ's Order on Translation Rights and Obligations of the Parties, 20 February 2009, p. 13.

[56] *Prosecutor v Ieng Sary*, ECCC Case File No. 002/19-09-2007-ECCC/OCIJ (PTC12), Pre-Trial Chamber, Decision on Ieng Sary's Appeal against the OCIJ's Order on Translation Rights and Obligations of the Parties, 20 February 2009, para. 44.

[57] *Prosecutor v Khieu Samphan*, ECCC Case File No. 002/19-09-2007-ECCC/OCIJ (PTC11), Pre-Trial Chamber, Decision on Khieu Samphan's Appeal

The challenge is to keep all participants linguistically on an equal footing while not adding to the factors that might slow down the proceedings. When reaching its first judgment, the Trial Chamber noted the general rule that documents were required to be available in all three working languages of the ECCC and specified that in light of the requirements of Internal Rule 87, which had been amended in 2009, only those parts of documents which were read out in full or summarised and subjected to examination were considered put before the Chamber.[58]

18. PUBLIC AFFAIRS SECTION

The Public Affairs Section, initially headed by Dr. Helen Jarvis, is the 'external face' of the ECCC, tasked with representing publicly all organs of the Court through various activities such as outreach and public information, coordination with Cambodian and international NGOs, media relations and accreditations, and audio and video records of proceedings. The Public Affairs Section is of particular significance as it concerns the legitimacy and legacy of the ECCC as some of its core functions are to enhance transparency and translate a complex, often dry, legal process into a comprehensible message of justice for victims and all those concerned with or interested in the Court, both nationally and internationally.

19. BUDGET

Article 44 (new) of the ECCC Law describes the financing of the Court which is divided into an international and a national budget, mirroring the staffing structure:

> The expenses and salaries of the Extraordinary Chambers shall be as follows:
>
> 1. The expenses and salaries of the Cambodian administrative officials and staff, the Cambodian judges and reserve judges, investigating judges and reserve investigating judges, and prosecutors and reserve prosecutors shall be borne by the Cambodian national budget;

---

against the Order on Translation Rights and Obligations of the Parties, 20 February 2009, para. 49.

[58] *Prosecutor v Kaing Guek Eav alias 'Duch'*, ECCC Case File No. 001/18-07-2007/ECCC/TC, Trial Chamber, Judgment, 26 July 2010, para. 57 ('Duch Trial Judgment').

2. The expenses of the foreign administrative officials and staff, the foreign judges, Co-investigating judge and Co-prosecutor sent by the Secretary-General of the United Nations shall be borne by the United Nations;
3. The defence counsel may receive fees for mounting the defence;
4. The Extraordinary Chambers may receive additional assistance for their expenses from other voluntary funds contributed by foreign governments, international institutions, non-governmental organizations, and other persons wishing to assist the proceedings.

Article 14 of the ECCC Agreement states that the Cambodian Government shall provide and pay for the premises of the ECCC and the essence of paragraphs one and two of Article 44 (new) of the ECCC Law is repeated in Articles 15 and 16 of the ECCC Agreement. Article 17 of the ECCC Agreement specifies items of UN expenditure such as witness travel from within Cambodia and from abroad and remuneration of defence counsel.

The bifurcated budgetary arrangement presented difficulties from the outset. One problem was the lack of parity in salaries on the international and national sides and in turn the lack of parity in salaries for national staff at the ECCC—which might be up to 50 per cent of international salaries at the same level—and salaries available for similarly qualified persons working for local judicial institutions.

As early as 2003, the UN General Assembly decided that the UN's share of the ECCC's expenses should be paid out of voluntary contributions from the international community.[59] Projections for the combined Cambodian and UN costs of what was expected to be a three-year operation amounted to US$ 57 million.[60] The UNAKRT website sets out ECCC expenditures and donor contributions up to 2013, the biggest donors to UNAKRT being Japan, Australia and the United States and the biggest donors to the Cambodian component being Japan, Cambodia, and the European Union.[61] To date, over 35 countries have contributed.

---

[59] United Nations General Assembly, Khmer Rouge Trials, A/RES/57/228 B, 22 May 2003.

[60] Report of the Secretary-General on the Khmer Rouge Trials, A/59/432, 12 October 2004, para. 45. *See* Report of the Secretary-General on the Khmer Rouge Trials: Addendum, A/59/432/Add.1, 29 November 2004, para. 6: 'the process of setting up the Extraordinary Chambers can only be initiated once sufficient money is in place to fund their staffing and operations for a sustained period of time. I would consider that condition to have been met when pledges for the full three years of the Extraordinary Chambers' operations as well as actual contributions for its first year of operations have been received.'

[61] 'Finances', UNAKRT, <http://www.unakrt-online.org/finances> [accessed 7 June 2017].

Additionally, the ECCC is the first of the ad hoc tribunals to receive contributions from private entities towards its core budget with the Microsoft Corporation contributing $100,000, and Information Today, Inc contributing $500,000.[62] The revised budget for 2017 was US$30.13 million—US$23.76 million for the international component and US$6.37 million for the national component.[63] The international budget is managed by UNDESA whereas the international funds supplied to the national budget were managed by the UN Development Programme (UNDP) as a separate project from UNAKRT until 2009, and are now handled by the UN Office for Project Services (UNOPS) out of its office in Bangkok.

The UN Secretary-General warned in a recent report that in view of the structure of the Court, 'if the operation of either the national or the international component is jeopardized, the overall work of the Court is severely impeded'.[64] He also noted that the ECCC continued to face considerable financial challenges due to the difficulty of attracting sufficient voluntary funding to cover the costs of the international component. Indeed, the General Assembly authorised a subvention to supplement the voluntary contributions so that staff contracts could be extended at least until the end of 2016. By contrast, the funding situation for the national component had stabilised in 2016 thanks to funds provided by Cambodia and the international community.

20. THE NATURE OF THE ECCC

The ECCC's emblem combines a depiction of the administration of justice during the Angkor period of Cambodian history with the wreath

---

62 Information available at 'Finances', UNAKRT, <http://www.unakrt-online.org/finances> [accessed 7 June 2017]. *See* also M. Wierda and A. Triolo, 'Resources', in L. Reydams, J. Wouters, and C. Ryngaert (eds), *International Prosecutors* (Oxford, Oxford University Press, 2012), pp. 113–70, p. 131.

63 'ECCC Revised Budget – 2016/2017', Extraordinary Chambers in the Courts of Cambodia, 28 November 2016, para. 2 and Table 2, <https://www.eccc.gov.kh/sites/default/files/ECCC%20Revised%20Budget-2016-2017.pdf> [accessed 7 June 2017].

64 Report of the Secretary-General: Request for a Subvention to the Extraordinary Chambers in the Courts of Cambodia, A/71/338, 16 August 2016, para. 6.

of olive branches that symbolises peace in the UN system.[65] A figure borrowed from a mural in the former Court of Appeal in Phnom Penh sits on a dais balanced delicately inside the wreath, holding a sword to represent the Court's authority. The wreath is open at the top, and if the figure were to stand up, it could easily step outside the UN's embrace. The emblem therefore symbolises not only hybridity but also singularity both of the institution and its two components. The aim in this section is not to consider the pitfalls of hybridity but to draw some conclusions about the nature of the ECCC based on the Chambers' own discussion of the issue in the various circumstances in which it has impacted on decision-making.

In international criminal justice parlance, a 'hybrid' court is loosely defined as an ad hoc institution designed to determine individual criminal responsibility with reference to particular political and historical circumstances, established with the support and direct involvement of an international organisation, most commonly the UN, including both domestic and international judges and staff, and having jurisdiction over both international crimes and a handful of serious domestic crimes.[66] This type of tribunal may be considered, at least nominally, an integral part of the domestic judicial system or it may be 'grafted' onto the domestic system via a constitutional process. Possible examples that preceded the establishment of the ECCC include the Special Panels for Serious Crimes in East Timor; the Regulation 64 Panels in the courts of Kosovo, and the Special Court for Sierra Leone based in Freetown and subsequently The Hague (for hearings in the *Charles Taylor* case only).[67] While these tribunals all undoubtedly belong to the same ever-growing family, they differ greatly in the degree to which they were initially envisaged to be, or became 'internationalised'. Indeed, the more general term 'internationalised' which is frequently also employed to describe this family of tribunals is perhaps the better term, as it avoids possible

---

[65] 'Introduction to the ECCC', Extraordinary Chambers in the Courts of Cambodia, <https://www.eccc.gov.kh/en/about-eccc/introduction> [accessed 7 June 2017].

[66] *See* S. Williams, *Hybrid and Internationalised Criminal Tribunals: Selected Jurisdictional Issues* (Oxford/Portland, Hart Publishing, 2012), p. 249 (who, after a comprehensive comparative analysis of hybrid and internationalised tribunals concludes that there is no single definition of these tribunals, but several common, defining features).

[67] Later models include the Special Tribunal for Lebanon (based in The Hague), the Extraordinary African Chambers (based in Dakar, Senegal) and the Kosovo Specialist Chambers and Specialist Prosecutor's Office (based in The Hague).

negative connotations of the idea that a tribunal can be half national and half international, in other words split down the middle. The term 'hybrid' is sometimes also replaced by 'mixed' which is a softer word but lacks precision unless the context is explained.

Article 2 (new) of the ECCC Law specifies that 'Extraordinary Chambers shall be established *in* the existing court structure' although physically as well as functionally the Chambers are remote from any existing Cambodian court. The Code of Judicial Ethics makes direct reference to 'the hybrid character' of the ECCC and the need to adopt a code of ethics applying to both Cambodian and international judges, and incorporating both national and international norms.[68] According to the ECCC's own website:

> The hybrid tribunal model is seen as a way to provide full national involvement in the trials while at the same time ensuring that international standards are met. Unlike tribunals for Rwanda or the former Yugoslavia, these trials are not removed from the place where the crimes occurred. They are held in Cambodia, conducted mainly in Khmer, open to participation by Cambodian people and reported via local television, radio and newspapers.[69]

The Office of the High Commissioner for Human Rights freely uses the term 'hybrid', promising assistance to the ECCC in its efforts to promote the rule of law '[i]n keeping with its desire to maximize the legacy of hybrid courts'.[70]

The ECCC clearly belongs to the family of 'hybrid', 'mixed' or 'internationalised' criminal tribunals. If '[i]nternational tribunals are free-standing courts that prosecute international crimes' then the ECCC is not an international tribunal.[71] Structurally it probably comes the closest to being a true hybrid out of the different models that have been or are currently in operation, purely by virtue of the staffing structure which has both a national and an international prosecutor, investigating judge, lead

---

68 Code of Judicial Ethics, Preamble.

69 'Why was This Model Chosen for the ECCC?', Extraordinary Chambers in the Courts of Cambodia, <https://www.eccc.gov.kh/en/faq/why-was-model-chosen-eccc> [accessed 7 June 2017].

70 'Promotion of ECCC Legacy', The Office of the United Nations High Commissioner for Human Rights -Cambodia, 28 September 2015, <http://cambodia.ohchr.org/en/rule-of-law/promotion-eccc-legacy> [accessed 7 June 2017].

71 L. May and S. Fyfe, 'The Legitimacy of International Criminal Tribunals', in N. Hayashi and C.M. Bailliet (eds), *The Legitimacy of International Criminal Tribunals* (Cambridge, Cambridge University Press, 2017), pp. 25–40, p. 25, although the authors include the ECCC in their list.

defence lawyer and lead civil party lawyer working in parallel with each other. The ratio of national to international judges in the Chambers also bears this out, compared to say the SCSL which had only one national judge on each panel, although even at the ECCC it is not 50/50. Moreover, the mirroring of international and national positions at the ECCC occurs not just at the top level but throughout the Court's staffing ladder.

The Pre-Trial Chamber was the first to give the question of the nature of the ECCC detailed consideration in a decision concerning the provisional detention of Duch.[72] In addressing an appeal by Duch against the Co-Investigating Judges' decision to detain him prior to his trial, the Pre-Trial Chamber had to determine whether the ECCC had jurisdiction to review the actions of the Cambodian Military Court which had already detained Duch for more than eight years prior to his transfer to the ECCC. The Pre-Trial Chamber noted the ECCC's distinctive characteristics, especially that it constituted a self-contained system and that its judiciary included both national and foreign judges, and observed that: 'There is no right to have any decision of the ECCC reviewed by courts outside its structure, and equally there is no right for any of its Chambers to review decisions from courts outside the ECCC'.[73] The Pre-Trial Chamber noted the view of the Co-Prosecutors that the ECCC's independence was demonstrated by the following factors: (1) that it was created by an international treaty; (2) that it formed part of the 'machinery of international justice'; (3) that it had different jurisdiction to the national courts of Cambodia, being limited materially, temporally and personally; (4) that there was no possibility of appeal to other courts in Cambodia; (5) that it had a limited lifespan, and (6) that it had unique structural characteristics not found in domestic courts.[74] Reliance was also placed by the Pre-Trial Chamber on the opinion of the Appeals

---

[72] *Prosecutor v Kaing Guek Eav alias 'Duch'*, ECCC Case File No. 001/18-07-2007/ECCC/OCIJ (PTC01), Pre-Trial Chamber, Decision on Appeal Against Provisional Detention Order of Kaing Guek Eav alias 'Duch', 3 December 2007, paras. 18, 19, 21, 22.

[73] Ibid, para. 18.

[74] Ibid, para. 19 (referring to *Prosecutor v Kaing Guek Eav alias 'Duch'*, ECCC Case File No. 001/18-07-07-ECCC-OCJI/PTC01, Pre-Trial Chamber, Report of Examination, 19 November 2007, pp. 7–8, setting out details of the decision appealed against and the facts in issue before the Pre-Trial Chamber by Co-Rapporteurs Judge Rowan Downing and Judge Huot Vuthy).

Chamber of the SCSL in the *Charles Taylor* case, from which the Co-Prosecutors had derived some of their suggested factors. In that case the indicia of an international court included the fact that the court is established by treaty, that it represents an 'expression of the will of the international community', that it is considered to be 'part of the machinery of international justice', and that its jurisdiction involves trying the most serious international crimes.[75] Finding that the ECCC was a 'special internationalised tribunal' by virtue of its independence, for all practical and legal purposes, within the Cambodian court structure, the Pre-Trial Chamber concluded that it had no jurisdiction to judge the activities of other bodies within this structure, including the Military Court.[76] Thus, Duch's prior detention by the Military Court had no bearing on whether the ECCC could order a new period of pre-trial detention under its rules of procedure.

The Pre-Trial Chamber has also stated in the context of disqualification proceedings that 'the ECCC, although it is part of the Cambodian court system, is a separate and independent court with no institutional connection to any other court in Cambodia' and that it is 'a new internationalised court applying international norms and standards'.[77] In yet another context, the Pre-Trial Chamber referred to the ECCC as 'an internationalised court functioning separately from the Cambodian court structure.'[78]

---

[75] *Prosecutor v Kaing Guek Eav alias 'Duch'*, ECCC Case File No. 001/18-07-2007/ECCC/OCIJ (PTC01), Pre-Trial Chamber, Decision on Appeal Against Provisional Detention Order of Kaing Guek Eav alias 'Duch', 3 December 2007, para. 20 (referring to *Prosecutor v Taylor*, SCSL Case No. SCSL-2003-01-01, Appeals Chamber, Decision on Immunity from Jurisdiction, 31 May 2004, paras. 38–9).

[76] *Prosecutor v Kaing Guek Eav alias 'Duch'*, ECCC Case File No. 001/18-07-2007/ECCC/OCIJ (PTC01), Pre-Trial Chamber, Decision on Appeal Against Provisional Detention Order of Kaing Guek Eav alias 'Duch', 3 December 2007, para. 19.

[77] *Prosecutor v Nuon Chea* ECCC Case File No. 002/19-09-2007-ECCC/OCIJ(PTC01), Pre-Trial Chamber, Public Decision on the Co-Lawyers' Urgent Application for the Disqualification of Judge Ney Thol Pending the Appeal against the Provisional Detention Order in the Case of Nuon Chea, 4 February 2008, para. 30.

[78] *Prosecutor v Ieng Sary*, ECCC Case File No. 002/19-09-2007-ECCC/OCIJ (PTC75), Pre-Trial Chamber, Decision on Ieng Sary's Appeal Against the Closing Order, 11 April 2011, para. 131.

The defence challenge as to the lawfulness of Duch's pre-trial detention was renewed before the Trial Chamber at the commencement of the trial. It was argued by the defence that Duch's detention by the ECCC was a continuation of his detention by the Military Court and was therefore unlawful due to the overall length of time served. Rejecting the idea of such continuity, the Trial Chamber affirmed that the ECCC is a 'separately constituted, independent and internationalised court', operating as an 'independent entity' within the existing Cambodian court structure.[79] Further, it was 'a court of special ("extraordinary") and independent character within the Cambodian legal system' with a limited mandate.[80] The Trial Chamber continued:

> The structure of the ECCC is distinct from the structure of other Cambodian courts. While its procedure is in accordance with Cambodian law, the ECCC is entitled to adopt its own Internal Rules in compliance with international standards, which take into account the specific mechanisms necessary to adjudicate mass crimes. It is composed of Cambodian and international staff and judicial officers, who have no competence to appear before or to sit in judgment over a decision by a domestic Cambodian court. Further, Cambodian judges before the ECCC have privileges and immunities additional to those possessed by other Cambodian judges. Whereas Article 11 of the Agreement precludes amnesty or pardon for the crimes within the ECCC's jurisdiction, this may be requested by the Government for sentences imposed by Cambodian courts.[81]

The Trial Chamber also noted that there was no procedural basis for commencing an investigation in the domestic system and concluding it before the ECCC and similarly no line of authority between the domestic courts and the ECCC.[82]

The question of the nature of the ECCC arose once more in the *Duch* case in the context of establishing the relevant legal framework for determining the quantum of sentence. Judge Lavergne, who dissented from the view of the majority of the Trial Chamber, considered the 'reference to Cambodian law ... particularly relevant, owing to the special character of the ECCC, notably because this hybrid court has

---

79 *Prosecutor v Kaing Guek Eav alias 'Duch'*, ECCC Case File No. 001/18-07-2007/ECCC/TC, Trial Chamber, Decision on Request for Release, 15 June 2009, para. 10.

80 Ibid.

81 Ibid, para. 11.

82 Ibid, para. 12.

jurisdiction to prosecute both international and domestic crimes, and because the founding documents make no distinction as to the sentencing regime applicable to these two categories of offences'.[83] In Judge Lavergne's view, 'while this regime may be deemed sui generis, it is difficult to imagine that it is entirely extraneous to domestic law.'[84]

The question whether Duch's prior detention by the Military Court was attributable to the ECCC eventually came before the Supreme Court Chamber, which agreed with the Trial Chamber's assessment as to the ECCC's status as an independent entity.[85] Judges Milart and Jayasinghe dissented from the decision of the majority not to allow Duch a remedy in respect of his prior detention, emphasising the domestic aspects of the ECCC which they deemed to be more relevant to an issue such as detention than its international characteristics. While they recognised that the ECCC had certain international characteristics (evidenced by the ECCC Agreement, the employment of international judges, and the application of international law for some purposes), in their view the ECCC remained a domestic court in key respects. They reasoned as follows:

> First, and most important in this case, the ECCC was established by and within the domestic system. This is plainly evident from the following: (i) the preamble to the Agreement identifies the ECCC as being established 'within the existing court structure of Cambodia'; (ii) the ECCC was established by the ECCC Law, a national statute enacted by the Cambodian legislature, as contemplated by the UN-RGC Agreement; (iii) the phrase 'in the courts of Cambodia' was incorporated into the title of the ECCC Law, and the ECCC Law explicitly refers to the ECCC being 'established in the existing court structure; (iv) earlier versions of the ECCC Law replicated the hierarchy of the Cambodian judiciary; (v) international judges are appointed by the Supreme Council of the Magistracy, a Cambodian institution; and (vi) the ECCC applies national substantive law to the extent delineated in the ECCC Law and UN-RGC Agreement. The domestic character of the Tribunal was, moreover, a heavily negotiated aspect of the ECCC Law and UN-RGC Agreement that was formulated deliberately by its drafters. Indeed, the Cambodian government stood by its position of having a national tribunal with international assistance nearly to the point of rupture.

---

[83] *Prosecutor v Kaing Guek Eav alias 'Duch'*, ECCC Case File No. 001/18-07-2007/ECCC/TC, Trial Chamber, Separate and Dissenting Opinion of Judge Lavergne on Sentence, 26 July 2010, para. 5.

[84] Ibid.

[85] Duch Appeal Judgment, above n. 19, para. 393.

> Furthermore, the framers of the ECCC legal regime intended for Cambodian procedure to be the primary source of procedural law at the ECCC. This is plain from the text of the law: (i) the framers incorporated 'under Cambodian law' into the title of the Agreement; (ii) the phrase 'Cambodian law' is the first source of law listed throughout the Agreement and the ECCC Law; (iii) 'Cambodian law' is explicitly recognized as a primary source of the proceedings in the Agreement and 'existing procedures' are explicitly recognized by the ECCC Law; and (iv) the Court was given the authority to seek guidance in rules established at the international level only where Cambodian law is silent, uncertain or inconsistent with international standards.[86]

The judges went on to say that the domestic nature of the ECCC was especially visible in the context of enforcement of convictions and penalties since these aspects are dealt with by the ordinary prison services. They found it logical that while the applicable law before the ECCC was determined by reference to international authorities, detention matters were governed by domestic law and procedure.[87]

In the different context of reparations, the Supreme Court Chamber recognised the 'hybrid nature' of the ECCC, indicating that notwithstanding this nature, on the legal plane the tribunal acts as an 'emanation of the State of Cambodia and is duty-bound to respect international standards of justice and generally recognised human rights precepts'.[88] Apparently treating 'hybrid' as equivalent to 'internationalised', the Chamber concluded that 'as a criminal tribunal, albeit of an internationalised character, the ECCC is not vested with the authority to assess Cambodia's compliance with these international obligations'.[89]

The national judges of the Pre-Trial Chamber have added their voices separately to the mix in the context of the cases against Meas Muth and others in the second batch of cases before the ECCC. The national component has consistently argued that these cases fall outside the Court's personal jurisdiction. In the view of the national PTC judges:

---

86 *Prosecutor v Kaing Guek Eav alias 'Duch'*, ECCC Case File No. 001/18-07-2007-ECCC/SC, Supreme Court Chamber, Appeal Judgment: Partially Dissenting Joint Opinion of Judges Agnieszka Klonowiecka-Milart and Chandra Nihal Jayasinghe, 3 February 2012, paras. 9–10.

87 Ibid, para. 11.

88 Duch Appeal Judgment, above n. 19, para. 654.

89 Ibid.

> The ECCC is a special court that applies the procedures of prosecution and judicial investigation different from those of Cambodia's national courts. Prosecution and judicial investigation under the national courts merely concern facts, not persons. On the contrary, at the ECCC, prosecution and judicial investigation can proceed only where the two conditions—first, facts 'the crimes and serious violations of Cambodian laws related to crimes, international humanitarian law and custom, and international conventions recognized by Cambodia, that were committed during the period from 17 April 1975 to 6 January 1979' and second, persons 'senior leaders of Democratic Kampuchea and those who were most responsible for the crimes'—are met.[90]

The judges have therefore described in some detail both the international and the national features of the ECCC, sometimes stressing the former, other times the latter, depending on the context.[91] Although not specifically expressed in this way, their analysis may be seen as a means of unpacking the concept of 'extraordinary' which in the ECCC context contains the element of internationalisation. On a political level, both the Cambodian Deputy Prime Minister, Sok An, and the former UN Secretary-General, Ban Ki-moon, have viewed the ECCC as being 'a national court with international characteristics'.[92] The precise terminology may matter less than the question of who is ultimately responsible for the ECCC's success. This is clearly a shared responsibility between the UN and Cambodia. If it is shared equally then 'hybrid' might be the best term to describe the ECCC. But it appears more fluid than that with the stakes perhaps being higher for the UN since it is the internationalised aspect, which lifts the Chambers out of the domestic structure, subjects them to 'international standards' and gives them a *sui generis* status, that defines the 'extraordinary' nature of the domestic Chambers.

---

[90] ECCC Case File No. 004/2/07-09-2009-ECCC/OCIJ (PTC36), Pre-Trial Chamber, Decision on Appeal against the Decision on Tenth Request for Investigative Action: Opinions of Judges Prak Kimsan, Ney Thol and Huot Vuthy, 26 April 2017, para. 17.

[91] The inevitable tendency to cherry-pick laws to achieve desired results has been noted. *See* Ciorciari and Heindel, above n. 42, p. 42.

[92] Ciorciari and Heindel, above n. 42, p. 42.

21. CONCLUSION

The ECCC's structure suggests a degree of unworkability, begging the question why such a model, creating obvious opportunities for obstruction and delay, was agreed to in the first place.[93] Apart from the issue of delay and its cost implications, the greatest vulnerabilities and risks generated by the ECCC's structure, and the ones having potentially the gravest consequences, are those of bifurcation and politicisation.[94] Unfortunately, the ECCC has remained vulnerable throughout and these risks have materialised at various points in its lifespan.

The main participants in the process have had little time to dwell on the question whether the ECCC is structurally sound as once an investigation begins and rooms are filled at the detention centre, proceedings have to take their course because individual rights are at stake. Proceedings flow from the legal and constitutional basis of the Court and are contained within its extraordinary structure. What is perhaps most extraordinary, and an instance of bifurcation tied to politicisation, is that it is structurally possible for proceedings to continue when the national and international components are divided over the question whether it is legally permissible.

---

[93] *See* further Ciorciari and Heindel, above n. 42, p. 44.

[94] On the issue of politicisation, see T. Hamilton and M. Ramsden, 'The Politicisation of Hybrid Courts: Observations from the Extraordinary Chambers in the Courts of Cambodia', *International Criminal Law Review*, vol. 14, no. 1, 2014, pp. 115–47.

4. Procedure

1. INTRODUCTION

Proceedings before the Extraordinary Chambers in the Courts of Cambodia (ECCC) follow a complex route. The action starts in the Office of the Co-Prosecutors (OCP) which is responsible for the preliminary investigation and the preparation and production of an Introductory Submission. This crucial and by default confidential document containing the names of suspects and the outline and theory of the Prosecution's case against them is presented to the Office of the Co-Investigative Judges (OCIJ) and serves both to trigger and provide the framework for the judicial investigation. A case file is built up during the judicial investigation which is forwarded to the OCP when it is complete. The OCP submits a Final Submission informing the Co-Investigating Judges of the Co-Prosecutors' view of the case, and the OCIJ then concludes the investigation with the issuance of a Closing Order either in the form of an indictment or a dismissal of the case. The Closing Order is subject to appeal before the Pre-Trial Chamber (PTC). If an indictment is confirmed, both the Closing Order as amended by the PTC and the case file make their way to the Trial Chamber, heralding the commencement of trial proceedings. A judgment of the Trial Chamber may be appealed before the Supreme Court Chamber (SCC) which has the final word on the case. The parties, including the prosecution, defence and civil parties, have various roles throughout the proceedings as described primarily in the Internal Rules.

Having set out the key procedures applicable to the ECCC, the following chapter will track the cases currently before the Court on their respective journeys through the system.

2. PROCEDURE FROM INITIAL INVESTIGATION TO INDICTMENT

The prosecution of crimes within the jurisdiction of the ECCC is initiated exclusively by the Co-Prosecutors either at their own discretion or on the basis of a complaint by a victim, witness or other person, organisation or source with knowledge of the crime.[1] The aim of the preliminary investigations, carried out by the Cambodian Judicial Police or ECCC investigators at the request of the Co-Prosecutors, is 'to determine whether evidence indicates that crimes within the jurisdiction of the ECCC have been committed and to identify suspects and potential witnesses'.[2] Importantly, at the preliminary investigation stage, the Co-Prosecutors may order the Judicial Police to take a suspect into police custody for a maximum period of 48 hours extendable by a further 24 hours by a new order of the Co-Prosecutors.[3] At the end of this period, the suspect must either be released or brought before the Co-Investigating Judges in accordance with Internal Rule 57 concerning the initial appearance and notification of charges.[4] The judicial investigation is initiated by the filing of a confidential document known as the 'Introductory Submission' containing the result of the Co-Prosecutors' preliminary investigation. The Introductory Submission presents an argument supported by evidence as to the Co-Prosecutors' reasonable belief that crimes within the jurisdiction of the Court have been committed, proposes an appropriate legal characterisation of the facts and identifies suspects and witnesses.[5] The Introductory Submission is accompanied by the case file and all inculpatory and exculpatory evidence in the hands of the Co-Prosecutors.[6] The original submission may be augmented at a later stage by a Supplementary Submission. The Co-Prosecutors can choose to provide a public summary of their submissions.[7] In practice, in the interests of transparency, the OCP has taken the opportunity to provide information to the public as far as possible.

Upon being seized of an Introductory Submission, the Co-Investigating Judges gather further evidence to determine whether the facts contained therein constitute one or more crimes within the jurisdiction of the Court and whether the person under investigation (referred to as the 'Charged Person' in the English version of the Internal Rules or '*la personne mise en examen*' in French) should be indicted and the case forwarded to the Trial Chamber for trial. A core feature of the process is the preparation of a case file containing the full record of the investigation which is intended to form the basis for the trial. The Co-Investigating Judges do

---

1 Internal Rules, Rule 49.
2 Internal Rules, Rules 50(1), (2).
3 Internal Rules, Rules 51(1)–(3).
4 Internal Rules, Rule 51(7).
5 Internal Rules, Rule 53(1).
6 Internal Rules, Rule 53(2).
7 Internal Rules, Rule 54.

not have the power to investigate new facts in the absence of a Supplementary Submission by the Co-Prosecutors. By contrast, the Co-Investigating Judges may place additional suspects under investigation in relation to the facts contained in the Introductory Submission even if they have not been named by the Co-Prosecutors.[8] A Charged Person obtains access to the case file once he or she has been notified of the charges.[9]

The Co-Investigating Judges are considered impartial and tasked with examining both inculpatory and exculpatory material. In this effort, they may undertake any action necessary for the establishment of the truth, such as issuing arrest warrants and detention orders, questioning suspects, interviewing witnesses and victims, seizing exhibits, conducting onsite investigations, requesting expert opinions, granting protective measures, and requesting the cooperation of States or other organs.[10] An order for the provisional detention of a Charged Person may be issued if the conditions set out in Internal Rule 63 are met. During the investigation, the parties may request investigative action and file motions for specific relief. Judicial investigations are confidential 'in order to preserve the rights and interests of the parties', but the Co-Investigating Judges may release information if they deem it essential to keep the public informed of the proceedings.[11]

The Co-Investigating Judges' decision to conclude the judicial investigation shall be made public and at this point the parties may request further investigative action.[12] When the relevant time periods have expired and any appeals to the PTC relating to the Co-Investigating Judges' decisions on further investigative action have been heard, the case file is returned to the Co-Prosecutors for the preparation of their Final Submission. In their Final Submission, the Co-Prosecutors may request either the indictment of the Charged Person/s or the dismissal of the case.[13] The Co-Investigating Judges are not, however, bound by the request of the Co-Prosecutors. A document known as the 'Closing Order' is issued by the Co-Investigating Judges either indicting the Charged

---

[8] Internal Rules, Rule 55.

[9] *Prosecutor v Nuon Chea* and *Khieu Samphan*, ECCC Case File No. 002/19-09-2007/ECCC/TC, Trial Chamber, Case 002/01 Judgement, 7 August 2014, para. 23 ('Nuon Trial Judgment').

[10] Internal Rules, Rule 55(5).

[11] Internal Rules, Rule 56.

[12] Internal Rules, Rule 66(1).

[13] Internal Rules, Rule 66(5).

Person or dismissing the case, with reasons for the decision.[14] In order not to risk being void for procedural defect, the indictment must set out the identity of the accused, a description of the material facts and their legal characterisation, including the relevant criminal provisions and the nature of the criminal responsibility.[15] The Closing Order does not resemble an indictment in the common law system. The concept and the phrase, 'Closing Order', are borrowed from the French legal system.[16] The document contains lengthy legal argument setting the framework for a judge-led trial process.

The Closing Order and all other decisions of the Co-Investigating Judges are subject to appeal by the Co-Prosecutors. The defence and civil parties may appeal against certain orders of the Co-Investigating Judges as set out in Internal Rules 74(3)[17] and 74(4)[18] as well as decisions on applications concerning procedural defects in accordance with Internal Rule 76.[19] These appeals during the investigative phase are heard by the

---

[14] Internal Rules, Rule 67(1).

[15] Internal Rules, Rule 67(2).

[16] L. Nagle, M. Okumura, A. El-Saved, and E. Velivassaki, 'Comparative Research on Procedural Issues concerning the Closing Order and Indictment' (The Documentation Center of Cambodia/International Human Rights Clinic/ School of Oriental and African Studies, University of London, June 2009), p. 46.

[17] Internal Rules, Rule 74(3): 'The Charged Person or the Accused may appeal against the following orders or decisions of the Co-Investigating Judges: a) confirming the jurisdiction of the ECCC; b) refusing requests for investigative action allowed under these IRs; c) refusing requests for the restitution of seised items; d) refusing requests for expert reports allowed under these IRs; e) refusing requests for additional expert investigation allowed under these IRs; f) relating to provisional detention or bail; g) refusing an application to seise the Chamber for annulment of investigative action; h) relating to protective measures; i) declaring a Civil Party application admissible; or j) reducing the scope of judicial investigation under Rule 66 *bis*.'

[18] Internal Rules, Rule 74(4): 'Civil Parties may appeal against the following orders by the Co-Investigating Judges: a) refusing requests for investigative action allowed under these Rules; b) declaring a Civil Party application inadmissible; c) refusing requests for the restitution of seised property; d) refusing requests for expert reports allowed under these IRs; e) refusing requests for further expert investigation allowed under these IRs; f) a Dismissal Order where the Co-Prosecutors have appealed; g) refusing an application to seise the Chamber for annulment of investigative action; h) relating to protective measures; or i) reducing the scope of judicial investigation under Rule 66 *bis*.'

[19] According to Internal Rules, Rule 76(7), the Closing Order shall cure any procedural defects in the judicial investigation so that no issues concerning such procedural defects may be raised before the Trial Chamber or the Supreme Court Chamber.

PTC. If there is no appeal against a Closing Order which issues an indictment, the Co-Investigating Judges seal the case file and forward it to the Greffier of the Trial Chamber.

3. PROCEDURE BEFORE THE PRE-TRIAL CHAMBER

The procedures applicable to the PTC in respect of its function as an investigation chamber are set out in Internal Rules 73 to 78. In the event of an appeal against a decision or order of the Co-Investigating Judges, the Co-Prosecutors or the lawyers for the Charged Person or civil parties shall file a notice of appeal with the Greffier of the Co-Investigating Judges for onward submission to the Greffier of the PTC. Submissions on appeal containing 'the reasons of fact and law upon which the appeal is based together with all supporting documents' are then filed before the PTC in accordance with the time frames set out in Internal Rule 75. Applications brought before the PTC for annulment based on alleged procedural defects in the judicial investigation must pass through an admissibility stage before being determined on the merits in accordance with Internal Rule 76. The PTC has possession of the case file or a 'safeguard copy' while it is hearing appeals.

According to Internal Rule 77(5), hearings before the PTC shall be conducted in camera, although in practice Rule 77(6) has been invoked more often than not, allowing all or part of a hearing to be held in public at the request of any judge or party 'if the Chamber considers that it is in the interests of justice and it does not affect public order or any protective measures authorized by the court'.

The Internal Rules require that one international and one national judge be appointed by the President of the Chamber to serve as co-rapporteurs for each appeal.[20] Their task is to prepare a written report setting out the facts at issue and the details of the decision being appealed. This report is to be placed on the case file and read at the hearing prior to the presentation of observations by the parties. It seems that this procedure may have been dispensed with in practice after the first hearings. The PTC has the power to order the personal appearance of any person, as well as the production of exhibits. At the conclusion of the hearing, the judges deliberate in camera, with the assistance of an interpreter as necessary, to reach their decision.[21] Decisions of the PTC are public, 'except where the Chamber decides that it would be contrary

[20] Internal Rules, Rule 77(10).
[21] Internal Rules, Rule 77(12).

to the integrity of the Preliminary Investigation or to the Judicial Investigation'.[22]

The PTC's workload as an investigation chamber has been immense. In the early days it had to delimit the boundaries of its own unprecedented jurisdiction for example by clarifying the unique procedure for annulment of investigative action.[23] It has been seized of numerous interim appeals on a variety of procedural matters such as the appointment of medical experts.[24] It has also served as a safeguard on defence rights, for example by overturning an order of the Co-Investigating Judges for the *de facto* segregation of the Charged Persons pursuant to a request by Ieng Sary to be permitted to communicate with his wife, Ieng Thirith, in detention.[25]

If there is an appeal against a Closing Order issuing an indictment and the PTC confirms and/or amends the indictment, the case file is forwarded from the PTC to the Trial Chamber.[26]

4. PROVISIONAL DETENTION AND BAIL

The Internal Rules contain detailed provisions concerning provisional detention of a charged person during the investigative phase.[27] The Co-Investigating Judges can issue a reasoned Detention Order after holding an adversarial hearing, during which the Charged Person has the right to be represented by a lawyer.

---

[22] Internal Rules, Rule 78.

[23] *Prosecutor v Nuon Chea*, ECCC Case File No. 002/19-09-2007-ECCC/OCIJ (PTC06), Pre-Trial Chamber, Decision on Nuon Chea Appeal against Order Refusing Request for Annulment, 26 August 2008, paras. 12-6, 21-3.

[24] *See*, e.g., *Prosecutor v Nuon Chea*, ECCC Case File No. 002/19-09-2007-ECCC/OCIJ (PTC07), Pre-Trial Chamber, Decision on Nuon Chea's Appeal regarding Appointment of an Expert, 22 October 2008.

[25] *Prosecutor v Ieng Sary*, ECCC Case File No. 002/19-09-2007-ECCC/OCIJ (PTC05), Pre-Trial Chamber, Decision on Appeal Concerning Contact between the Charged Person and his Wife, 30 April 2008, paras. 14–21. *See* also *Prosecutor v Nuon Chea*, ECCC Case File No.002/19-09-2007-ECCC/OCIJ (PTC09), Pre-Trial Chamber, Decision on Nuon Chea's Appeal concerning Provisional Detention Conditions, 26 September 2008, para. 28 (where the PTC found that while the Co-Investigating Judges had the power to limit contact between detainees in the interests of the investigation, it did not have the power to determine the detention regime).

[26] Internal Rules, Rule 79(1): 'The Trial Chamber shall be seised by an Indictment from the Co-Investigating Judges or the Pre-Trial Chamber.'

[27] Internal Rules, Rule 63.

Provisional Detention may be ordered for a period not exceeding one year (extendable for further one-year periods) in respect of genocide, war crimes and crimes against humanity, and a period not exceeding six months (extendable for further six-month periods) in respect of all other crimes coming within the ECCC's jurisdiction. If at any point the requirements for provisional detention are no longer satisfied, the Co-Investigating Judges may on their own motion or at the request of the Co-Prosecutors order the release of a Charged Person.[28] Similarly, the Charged Person may submit an application for release at any time during his or her provisional detention and if circumstances have changed, the requisite time period between applications for release is reduced.[29]

The Co-Investigating Judges may order that a Charged Person remain at liberty or be released from detention on bail, subject to 'such conditions as are necessary to ensure the presence of the person during the proceedings and the protection of others'.[30] The Charged Person may appeal to the PTC against a Detention Order, an order extending detention, and any other orders of the Co-Investigating Judges concerning detention or bail, as set out in the Internal Rules.

An accused is entitled to remain at liberty while appearing before the Trial Chamber unless provisional detention has previously been ordered. If an accused is in detention at his or her initial appearance, the general position is that he or she shall remain in detention until the delivery of the judgment on the merits of the case.[31] However, after hearing the parties, the Trial Chamber may, at any time during the proceedings, issue an order for the release of an accused, where necessary on bail. If an accused is not detained, the Trial Chamber may issue an order for his or her detention. An accused who requested but was denied release may file further requests for release if circumstances have changed since the last application. All decisions of the Trial Chamber concerning provisional detention are open to appeal before the SCC by the accused or Co-Prosecutors.[32] The Internal Rules provide that an order by the Trial Chamber for the release of an accused shall take immediate effect, unless the President of the SCC, on the request of the Co-Prosecutors, decides to stay the release order until the Co-Prosecutors' appeal against it has been determined. This is to prevent the release of an accused against whom proceedings are not yet complete. Any such decision by the

28 Internal Rules, Rule 64(1).
29 Internal Rules, Rules 64(2), (3).
30 Internal Rules, Rule 65(1).
31 Internal Rules, Rule 82(1).
32 Internal Rules, Rule 82(5).

President of the SCC and the eventual decision on the appeal must be made within strict time frames as set out in the Internal Rules.[33]

5. PROCEDURE BEFORE THE TRIAL CHAMBER

Once the Trial Chamber has been seized by an indictment from the Co-Investigating Judges or the PTC and the case file is formally transferred, the 'Charged Person' is renamed the 'Accused' and the trial is set to start. In practice, as reflected in the amended Rule 69(3), the Trial Chamber may obtain access to the case file prior to any decision by the PTC for the purpose of advance preparation for trial.[34] The accused has on-going access to the case file for the duration of the proceedings.[35] As the Trial Chamber has explained, the 'Case File is the result of the material collated during the judicial investigation phase',[36] but this material 'is considered evidence and relied upon by the Chamber in decision-making only where it is put before the Chamber, subjected to examination, and where it is not excluded on the basis of the criteria contained in Internal Rule 87(3)'.[37] Prior to the Initial Hearing, the Co-Prosecutors must file the lists of witnesses and experts they intend to call, and may be required to provide summaries of the facts on which the witnesses are expected to testify, the points of the indictment to which their evidence relates and the estimated time to be allocated for their testimony.[38] The Co-Prosecutors may also be asked to provide lists of exhibits, an indication of the legal issues they intend to raise, and other information to the Chamber.

Preliminary objections concerning the jurisdiction of the Chamber, any issue requiring the termination of prosecution, or nullity of procedural acts made after the indictment is filed, must be raised no later than 30 days after the Closing Order becomes final.[39] The Chamber may choose

---

33 Internal Rules, Rule 82(6).

34 Internal Rules, Rule 69(3) (which came into force on 21 September 2009, provides that '[t]he filing of an appeal against a Closing Order does not prevent access by the Trial Chamber to the case file for the purposes of advance preparation for trial.') *See* further *Prosecutor v Kaing Guek Eav alias 'Duch'*, ECCC Case File No. 001/18-07-2007/ECCC/TC, Trial Chamber, Judgment, 26 July 2010, para. 37 ('Duch Trial Judgment').

35 Nuon Trial Judgment, above n. 9, para. 23.

36 Duch Trial Judgment, above n. 34, para. 36.

37 Ibid, para. 38. *See* also Nuon Trial Judgment, above n. 9, para. 23.

38 Internal Rules, Rule 80(3).

39 Internal Rules, Rule 89.

to issue its reasoned decision on preliminary objections immediately or wait until its final judgment on the merits of the case.

The trial begins with an initial hearing[40] and proceeds in a manner familiar to the inquisitorial system.[41] The President of the Chamber presides over the proceedings, facilitates interventions by other judges and leads the questioning of the accused and witnesses.[42] With the exception of close relatives of the accused and some other categories, all witnesses take an oath or affirmation prior to giving evidence.[43] In accordance with Cambodian criminal procedure, if they are Buddhist they are asked to appear before a statue of *Lok Ta Dambong Dek*, 'The Lord of the Iron Staff', on the grounds of the ECCC and to swear the following oath:

> I will answer only the truth, in accordance with what I have personally seen, heard, know, and remember. If I answer falsely on any issue, may all the guardian angels, forest guardians and powerful sacred spirits destroy me, may my material possessions be destroyed, and may I die a miserable and violent death. But, if I answer truthfully, may the sacred spirits assist me in having abundant material possession and living in peace and happiness along with my family and relatives forever, in all my reincarnations.[44]

The parties are permitted to ask questions after the judges have concluded their questioning. The judges may order further investigations as appropriate at their own initiative or at the request of the parties.[45] At any point, the Trial Chamber may order the separation of the proceedings relating to one or more of the accused who are being tried jointly if the interests of justice so require.[46]

---

40 Internal Rules, Rule 80 *bis*.

41 *See* analysis by S. Vasiliev, 'Trial Process at the ECCC: The Rise and Fall of the Inquisitorial Paradigm in International Criminal Law?', in S.M. Meisenberg and I. Stegmiller (eds), *The Extraordinary Chambers in the Courts of Cambodia: Assessing their Contribution to International Criminal Law* (The Hague, T.M.C. Asser Press, 2016), pp. 389–433.

42 Internal Rules, Rules 85, 90.

43 Internal Rules, Rule 24.

44 Text available in P. Pizano, '12-Year-Old Girl in 1975: "I Sacrificed Myself So My Family Would be Left Alone"', *Cambodia Tribunal Monitor*, 2 June 2015 (The wording used in the annex to the 2007 CPC differs somewhat from this version but conveys the same message), <http://www.cambodiatribunal.org/2015/06/02/12-year-old-girl-in-1975-i-sacrificed-myself-so-my-family-would-be-left-alone/> [accessed 12 June 2017].

45 Internal Rules, Rule 93.

46 Internal Rules, Rule 89 *ter*.

The scope of the trial, in terms of the factual allegations, may be reduced to ensure 'a fair, meaningful and expeditious judicial process, in consideration of the specific requirements of the proceedings before the ECCC' in accordance with Article 89 *quater*. This is achieved by allowing the Trial Chamber to reduce the scope of the trial by excluding facts set out in the Closing Order and requires the termination of proceedings in respect of those excluded facts.[47] Article 89 *quater* was adopted by the ECCC Plenary on 16 January 2015.[48]

The Trial Chamber may hold 'trial management meetings', in camera if it so decides, in order to 'facilitate the fair and expeditious conduct of the proceedings'. These meetings held with the parties and, where relevant, representatives of other units of the Court, are aimed at setting the dates of hearings, reviewing the status of the case and allowing the accused to raise issues such as medical concerns.[49] For example, in preparation for its second trial, 'having received requests by the parties to hear a cumulative total of 1,054 witnesses and to tender approximately 7,600 documents' the Trial Chamber held such a meeting on 5 April 2011 'with a view to expeditiously commencing trial proceedings'.[50]

As a general rule, the accused shall be tried in his or her presence, however, the Internal Rules contain detailed provisions allowing a trial to proceed in the absence of an accused in the event of that accused's refusal to attend or expulsion from the proceedings.[51] If an accused is unable to attend due to health reasons or other concerns, 'and where the accused's absence reaches a level that causes substantial delay and, where the interests of justice so require', his or her participation can be secured by audio-visual means and questioning may even occur at his or her location.[52] This provision was introduced at the commencement of the trials in 2011 and required the building of holding cells underneath the courtroom equipped with video monitors, telephones and hospital

---

47 Internal Rules, Rule 89 *quater*.

48 'Revision 9 of the ECCC Internal Rules', Extraordinary Chambers in the Courts of Cambodia, <https://www.eccc.gov.kh/en/articles/revision-9-eccc-internal-rules> [accessed 15 June 2017]. This followed the sequence of severance decisions discussed in Chapter 6. *See Prosecutor v Nuon Chea* and *Khieu Samphan*, ECCC Case File No. 002/19-09-2007-ECCC/TC, Trial Chamber, Decision on Additional Severance of Case 002 and Scope of Case 002/02, 4 April 2014.

49 Internal Rules, Rules 79(7), (8).

50 Nuon Trial Judgment, above n. 9, para. 4.

51 Internal Rules, Rules 81(1)–(4).

52 Internal Rules, Rules 81(5), (6).

beds.[53] Internal Rule 81 addresses the issue of the absence of an accused's lawyer.

The trial is public and the hearings are broadcast subject to any protective measures for victims and witnesses that have been adopted in accordance with the Internal Rules. However, if the Chamber considers that a public hearing would be prejudicial to public order, it may issue a reasoned decision ordering that all or part of a hearing should be held in camera.[54] Notwithstanding these possible exceptions, the judgment shall always be announced in a public session.[55]

All evidence is admissible before the Trial Chamber,[56] 'unless it is irrelevant or repetitious, impossible to obtain within a reasonable time, unsuitable to prove the facts it purports to prove, not allowed under the law, or intended to prolong proceedings or frivolous.'[57] Notably, the Trial Chamber may admit new material that is not in the original case file, either on its own motion or at the request of a party.[58] The right to examine witnesses against the accused in accordance with Internal Rule 84(1) and Article 297 of the Cambodian Criminal Procedure Code (CPC) (reflecting Article 14(3)(e) of the International Covenant on Civil and Political Rights (ICCPR)) has been regarded by the Supreme Court Chamber as not being absolute and 'allowing for restrictions in the interest, in particular, of the expeditiousness of the proceedings.'[59]

The appropriateness of permitting 'proofing', whereby witnesses go through their prior statements with the party calling them to refresh their memories, was raised before the SCC which expressed scepticism about the practice while finding that the defence had failed to establish that the Trial Chamber's resort to procedural rules established at the international level in this instance was unreasonable.[60] According to the SCC, 'notwithstanding the absence of a clear prohibition of allowing witnesses to read their statements prior to testifying and to confirm their content in

---

53 *See* further R.L. Phillips, 'Frail Accused and Fitness to Stand Trial', in S.M. Meisenberg and I. Stegmiller (eds), *The Extraordinary Chambers in the Courts of Cambodia: Assessing their Contribution to International Criminal Law* (The Hague, T.M.C. Asser Press, 2016), pp. 461–89, pp. 464–6, 468.

54 Internal Rules, Rule 79(6).

55 Internal Rules, Rule 102.

56 Internal Rules, Rule 87(1).

57 *Prosecutor v Nuon Chea* and *Khieu Samphan*, ECCC Case File No. 002/19-09-2007-ECCC/SC, Supreme Court Chamber, Appeal Judgment, 23 November 2016, para. 284 ('Nuon Appeal Judgment').

58 Duch Trial Judgment, above n. 34, para. 40.

59 Nuon Appeal Judgment, above n. 57, para. 287.

60 Ibid, para. 269.

court, it would be more consistent with the spirit of the Code of Criminal Procedure of Cambodia and with Cambodian judicial tradition not to resort to such practices'.[61] The SCC noted that at the International Criminal Court (ICC), whose procedural model was closest to that adopted by the ECCC Trial Chamber, 'the Witnesses and Experts Support Unit, a neutral organ of the Court, makes the statements available to the witnesses' and that this is seen to 'aid the efficient presentation of the evidence and help the Trial Chamber to establish the truth'.[62] According to the SCC's assessment, however, these two goals—efficiency and truth-finding—might conflict, and therefore the value of proofing practices had to be assessed 'by weighing the in-court time that would be saved against the risk that the spontaneity of the witness' testimony be jeopardised' and an individualised rather than a blanket approach was preferable.[63]

The trial concludes with closing statements by the parties and the accused has the last word.[64] Deliberations of the judges occur in camera and the Internal Rules contain detailed provisions for the preparation and delivery of the judgment.[65] Where there is no unanimity, judges may file separate or dissenting opinions.[66] While the judgment 'shall be limited to the facts set out in the Indictment', it is possible for the Trial Chamber to 'change the legal characterisation of the crime as set out in the Indictment, as long as no new constitutive elements are introduced'.[67]

6. BURDEN AND STANDARD OF PROOF

The burden lies on the Co-Prosecutors to prove the guilt of the accused. In order to convict, the Trial Chamber must 'be convinced of the guilt of the accused beyond reasonable doubt'.[68] As the Trial Chamber has noted, 'Cambodian law derives from civil law and, in particular, from the notion of the judge's *intime conviction*', a notion which is retained in the French version of Internal Rule 87(1) while both the Khmer and English versions

---

[61] Ibid, para. 263.

[62] Ibid, para. 265 (citing *Prosecutor v Lubanga*, ICC Case No. ICC-01/04-01/06, Pre-Trial Chamber I, Decision on the Practices of Witness Familiarisation and Witness Proofing, 8 November 2006, paras. 51–7).

[63] Nuon Appeal Judgment, above n. 57, para. 267.

[64] Internal Rules, Rule 94.

[65] Internal Rules, Rules 101–02.

[66] Internal Rules, Rule 101(2).

[67] Internal Rules, Rule 98(2).

[68] Internal Rules, Rule 87(1).

use the phrase 'convinced beyond a reasonable doubt'.[69] The Trial Chamber has adopted a 'common approach that has evaluated, in all circumstances, the sufficiency of the evidence' with any doubt as to guilt being interpreted in the accused's favour.[70]

Khieu Samphan argued on appeal that the Trial Chamber had erred in reaching its findings against him by applying the civil law concept of *intime conviction* rather than the common law standard of proof beyond reasonable doubt, which he described as being less subjective and more restrictive.[71] The SCC dismissed this argument, pointing out that the Trial Chamber has expressly stated it would adopt the standard of proof beyond reasonable doubt and that a review of the French version of the judgment showed that the Trial Chamber never used the term *intime conviction*, but rather phrases related to the standard as expressed in English such as *il ne fait aucun doute*.[72]

7. PLEAS OF GUILTY

In contrast to some other international or internationalised criminal tribunals, the ECCC procedures do not provide for guilty pleas and the consequent possibility of shortened proceedings and a 'discount' on the sentence are ruled out. This means that the Trial Chamber must 'hear and evaluate all evidence put before it, including in relation to matters not in dispute'.[73] It is, however, possible for the parties to agree facts which can assist in 'identifying the most contentious issues at trial and in streamlining the proceedings'.[74] This is reflected in Internal Rule 87(6), adopted in 2009, which clarifies that: 'Where the Co-Prosecutors and the accused agree that alleged facts contained in the Indictment are not contested, the Chamber may consider such facts as proven.'

69 Duch Trial Judgment, above n. 34, para. 45.
70 Ibid, para. 45; Nuon Trial Judgment, above n. 9, para. 22.
71 Nuon Appeal Judgment, above n. 57, para. 377.
72 Ibid, para. 380.
73 Duch Trial Judgment, above n. 34, para. 48.
74 Ibid.

8. PROCEDURE BEFORE THE SUPREME COURT CHAMBER

Appeals by the accused, the Co-Prosecutors or the civil parties against certain interlocutory decisions and the final judgment are heard by the SCC. The SCC is the court of last resort within the ECCC structure and its decisions are final. The SCC's jurisdiction to decide an appeal against a judgment or a decision of the Trial Chamber is limited to the following grounds: a) an error on a question of law invalidating the judgment or decision; or b) an error of fact which has occasioned a miscarriage of justice. The SCC has an additional jurisdiction to hear an immediate appeal 'based on a discernible error in the exercise of the Trial Chamber's discretion which resulted in prejudice to the appellant'.[75] Immediate appeals may be heard in relation to matters that have the effect of terminating the proceedings and those relating to detention and bail, protective measures and interference with the administration of justice. A decision of the Trial Chamber that has the effect of staying a proceeding which is unlikely to be resumed is also subject to immediate appeal.[76] In respect of all other matters, the appropriate time to lodge an appeal is after the judgment on the merits.

An appeal against the Trial Chamber's judgment may be filed by the Co-Prosecutors and the accused. The civil parties may appeal the decision on reparations but they may only appeal the verdict where the Co-Prosecutors have appealed, and they may not appeal the sentence.[77] The party lodging the appeal files a notice of appeal setting out the grounds and specifying in respect of each ground the alleged errors of law invalidating the decision and the alleged errors of fact occasioning a miscarriage of justice. The notice of appeal is followed by the filing of an appeal brief setting out the arguments and authorities in support of each ground in accordance with the time limits specified in Internal Rule 107.

The general rules concerning proceedings that apply to the Trial Chamber apply, *mutatis mutandis*, to the SCC.[78] It is possible for the SCC to examine evidence on the case file and call new evidence. The SCC is to issue its decision on any appeal against a judgment 'within a

---

75 Internal Rules, Rule 104(4).

76 *Prosecutor v Ieng Thirith*, ECCC Case File No. 002/19-09-2007-ECCC-TC/SC(09), Supreme Court Chamber, Decision on Immediate Appeal against the Trial Chamber's Order to Release the Accused Ieng Thirith, 13 December 2011, para. 15.

77 Internal Rules, Rule 105(1).

78 Internal Rules, Rule 104 *bis*.

reasonable period' while decisions on immediate appeals are in general to be made within three months.[79] Similar to procedures before the PTC, the President of the SCC shall appoint one international and one national judge to be co-rapporteurs for each appeal. The task of the co-rapporteurs is to prepare a written report to be placed in the case file setting out the facts of the case and the details of the decision being appealed so as to provide the SCC full information on the appeal.[80] It is unclear whether this procedure is rigidly adhered to in practice. Hearings of the SCC are broadcast publicly subject to any protective measures in place, although immediate appeals may be determined on the basis of written submissions alone. As with trial proceedings, the accused has the final word during any appeal hearing.[81]

In assessing the scope of its own competence, the SCC has found that 'remedies available under Cambodian criminal procedure were conflated into one *sui generis* appellate system' and that it is therefore authorised by the ECCC Agreement and ECCC Law to 'seek guidance under this system in procedural rules established at the international level, including their interpretation by relevant international judicial bodies'.[82] Noting that the system of appeal in Internal Rule 104(1) retained features of domestic procedures before the Cambodian Court of Appeal and encompassed the grounds for a request for cassation to the Supreme Court of Cambodia, while also reflecting established international criminal law, the ECCC SCC has sought extensive guidance from the practice of the International Criminal Tribunal for the former Yugoslavia (ICTY) and International Criminal Tribunal for Rwanda (ICTR) in interpreting its own appeal procedures.[83]

The SCC has made use of its powers under Internal Rule 93, read with Internal Rule 104 *bis*, to engage in additional investigations and in one instance appointed two 'Delegate Judges' for this purpose.[84] The SCC has also elaborated on the legal framework for additional evidence on

---

79 Internal Rules, Rule 108(4).

80 Internal Rules, Rule 108(5).

81 Internal Rules, Rule 109(9).

82 *Prosecutor v Kaing Guek Eav alias 'Duch'*, ECCC Case File No. 001/18-07-2007-ECCC/SC, Supreme Court Chamber, Appeal Judgment, 3 February 2012, para. 13 ('Duch Appeal Judgment').

83 Ibid.

84 *Prosecutor v Nuon Chea* and *Khieu Samphan*, ECCC Case File No. 002/19-09-2007-ECCC/SC, Supreme Court Chamber, Interim Decision on Part of Nuon Chea's First Request to Obtain and Consider Additional Evidence in Appeal Proceedings in Case 002/01, 1 April 2015, para. 24.

appeal in its judgment in the case against Nuon Chea and Khieu Samphan. As there were no relevant Cambodian rules it looked to procedural rules at the international level and concluded that it would 'call evidence on appeal under Internal Rule 104(1) primarily in circumstances where there is a realistic possibility that the evidence, had it been put before the Trial Chamber, could have led the Trial Chamber to enter a different verdict, in whole or in part'.[85]

The standard of review on appeal varies according to whether the alleged error is one of law or fact. As regards errors of law, the SCC 'reviews the Trial Chamber's findings on questions of law to determine whether they are correct, not merely whether they are reasonable.'[86] After determining the correct legal standard, it reviews the relevant factual findings of the Trial Chamber, applying the correct legal standard to the evidence contained in the trial record and determining whether 'it is itself convinced on the relevant standard of proof as to the factual finding challenged by a party before that finding is confirmed on appeal.'[87] As regards errors of fact, the SCC gives a margin of deference to a finding of fact reached by a Trial Chamber in accordance with international rules of procedure. It is only where the evidence relied on by the Trial Chamber could not have been accepted by any reasonable tribunal of fact or where the evaluation of the evidence is 'wholly erroneous' that the SCC may substitute its own finding for that of the Trial Chamber.[88] A miscarriage of justice is defined as 'a grossly unfair outcome in judicial proceedings' and for the error of fact to be one that occasioned a miscarriage of justice it must have been 'critical to the verdict reached'.[89]

The SCC has recognised its authority in exceptional circumstances to 'raise questions *ex proprio motu* or hear appeals where a party has raised a legal issue that would not lead to the invalidation of the judgement but is nevertheless of general significance to the ECCC's jurisprudence'.[90] It declined to do so when asked by the Co-Prosecutors to answer a single

---

85 Nuon Appeal Judgment, above n. 57, para. 32.

86 Ibid, para. 85.

87 Ibid, para. 86; Duch Appeal Judgment, above n. 82, para. 16.

88 Nuon Appeal Judgment, above n. 57, para. 89.

89 Ibid, para. 99.

90 Duch Appeal Judgment, above n. 82, para. 15 (The SCC cited *Prosecutor v Galić*, ICTY Case No. IT-98-29-A, Appeals Chamber, Judgment, 30 November 2006, para. 6 as the only authority: 'In exceptional circumstances, the Appeals Chamber will also hear appeals where a party has raised a legal issue that would not lead to the invalidation of the judgement but is nevertheless of general significance to the International Tribunal's jurisprudence.')

question on appeal 'in the interests of the law' relating to the mode of liability known as joint criminal enterprise (JCE).[91] The Co-Prosecutors argued that their ground of appeal related to an '*error* of law' but not one which had the effect of invalidating the decision.[92] The existence of a discretionary power to take up pure legal issues is not prescribed in any formal rules of the ECCC or any ad hoc tribunal but was recognised in the international criminal justice context as early as the *Tadić* case before the ICTY and not long afterwards in the *Akayesu* case before the ICTR.[93] This power has been approved in subsequent cases before those tribunals.[94] The authority to entertain important legal questions has also been exercised in the practice of the Special Court for Sierra Leone (SCSL).[95]

---

[91] *Prosecutor v Nuon Chea* and *Khieu Samphan*, ECCC Case File No. 002/19-09-2007-ECCC/SC, Office of the Co-Prosecutors, Co-Prosecutors' Notice of Appeal of a Decision in Case 002/01, 29 September 2014, paras. 2, 7.

[92] *Prosecutor v Nuon Chea* and *Khieu Samphan*, ECCC Case File No. 002/19-09-2007-ECCC/SC, Office of the Co-Prosecutors, Co-Prosecutors' Appeal against the Judgment of the Trial Chamber in Case 002/01, 28 November 2014, para. 6 (*Emphasis added*).

[93] *Prosecutor v Tadić*, ICTY Case No. IT-94-1-A, Appeals Chamber, Judgment, 15 July 1999, paras. 247, 281; *Prosecutor v. Akayesu*, ICTR Case No. ICTR-96-1-A, Appeals Chamber, Judgment, 1 June 2001, paras. 18–28.

[94] *Prosecutor v Galić*, ICTY Case No. IT-98-29-A, Appeals Chamber, Judgment, 30 November 2006, para. 6; *Prosecutor v Kupreškić, Kupreškić, Kupreškić, Josipović* and *Šantić*, ICTY Case No. IT-95-16-A, Appeals Chamber, Judgment, 23 October 2001, para. 22 (The power was recognised but not applied in these two cases). In *Prosecutor v Stakić*, ICTY Case No. IT-97-24-A, Appeals Chamber, Judgment, 22 March 2006, paras. 7 (the Appeals Chamber recognised that: 'In exceptional circumstances, the Appeals Chamber will also hear appeals where a party has raised a legal issue that would not lead to the invalidation of the judgement but is nevertheless of general significance to the Tribunal's jurisprudence.'), 59 (Although no party had appealed the issue of the mode of liability applied by the Trial Chamber (namely, co-perpetration), 'the question of whether the mode of liability developed and applied by the Trial Chamber is within the jurisdiction of this Tribunal is an issue of general importance warranting the scrutiny of the Appeals Chamber *proprio motu*'); *Prosecutor v Brđanin*, ICTY Case No. IT-99-36-A, Appeals Chamber, Judgment, 3 April 2007, para. 361.

[95] *Prosecutor v Brima, Kamara* and *Kanu*, SCSL Case No. SCSL-2004-16-A, Appeals Chamber, Judgment, 22 February 2008, para. 181: 'Notwithstanding the manner in which the Prosecution had classified "Forced Marriage" in the Indictment and the submissions made by the Prosecution on this appeal which is inconsistent with such classification, the Appeals Chamber will consider the submissions made as an issue of general importance that may enrich the jurisprudence of international criminal law.'

The SCC addressed the issue in a roundabout way, stating that the international jurisprudence did not provide a basis for the right of the Co-Prosecutors to appeal but was of 'significance for the discussion of whether the SCC may consider the merits of the appeal even if it were to find it inadmissible'.[96] The appeal was found to be procedurally defective, and while not automatically inadmissible under the Internal Rules, the SCC found there was no need to admit it on an exceptional basis since it could be dealt with in substance under various grounds of appeal raised by the defence in the same case.

The SCC has the power to change the legal characterisation of the crime adopted by the Trial Chamber although it may not introduce new constitutive elements that were not submitted to the Trial Chamber.[97] The judgment on appeal follows a similar format to the trial judgment.[98] Judgments on the merits are not deemed to be final until they have passed through the appellate stage.[99]

9. *AMICUS CURIAE*

An *amicus curiae*, meaning 'friend of the court', is a person or organisation who is not a party to the proceedings but who has special expertise or information to provide on a legal matter arising before the court. 'An *amicus curiae* is traditionally an independent and impartial adviser to the court whose role is simply to inform and not to advocate.'[100] Internal Rule 33 provides for the possibility of the submission of *amicus curiae* briefs as follows:

> 1. At any stage of the proceedings, the Co-Investigating Judges or the Chambers may, if they consider it desirable for the proper adjudication of the case, invite or grant leave to an organization or person to submit an *amicus curiae* brief in writing concerning any issue. The Co-Investigating

---

96 Nuon Appeal Judgment, above n. 57, para. 1139.

97 Internal Rules, Rule 110(2).

98 Internal Rules, Rule 111(1).

99 *Prosecutor v Nuon Chea, Ieng Sary*, and *Khieu Samphan*, ECCC Case File No. 002/19-09-2007-ECCC-TC/SC(18), Supreme Court Chamber, Decision on the Co-Prosecutors' Immediate Appeal of the Trial Chamber's Decision Concerning the Scope of Case 002/01, 8 February 2013, para. 24.

100 *Prosecutor v Nuon Chea* and *Khieu Samphan*, ECCC Document No. E306/3/1, Trial Chamber, Trial Chamber Memorandum Entitled 'Decision on Request for Leave to File *Amicus Curiae* Brief', 4 June 2014, para. 5.

Judges and the Chambers concerned shall determine what time limits, if any, shall apply to the filing of such briefs.

2. Briefs under this Rule shall be filed with the Greffier of the Co-Investigating Judges or Chamber concerned, who shall provide copies to the Co-Prosecutors and the lawyers for the other parties, who shall be afforded the opportunity to respond.

Amicus curiae briefs may be invited on a particular issue,[101] or the *amicus curiae* may request permission from the Chambers to submit a brief.[102] The SCC issued a document entitled 'Information concerning the Submission of *Amicus Curiae* Briefs to the SCC of the ECCC' in which it clarified that: '*Amicus* briefs shall be limited to questions of law and may not include factual evidence relating to elements of a crime charged or indicted.'[103]

Parties and organs of the ECCC have attempted to make creative use of Internal Rule 33. The SCC dismissed a request by the Defence Support Section for *amicus* briefs to be invited in the appeal proceedings concerning Duch.[104] It also dismissed requests by the defence in other cases to intervene or alternatively file an *amicus curiae* brief in the appeal proceedings against Nuon Chea and Khieu Samphan.[105] Similar

---

[101] *See* for example, ECCC Case File No. 07-09-001 ECCC/PTC, Pre-Trial Chamber, Public Notice, 4 September 2007; *Prosecutor v Meas Muth*, ECCC Case File No. 003/07-09-2009-ECCC-OCIJ, Office of the Co-Investigating Judges, Call for Submissions by the Parties in Cases 003 and 004 and Call for *Amicus Curiae* Briefs, 19 April 2016.

[102] *See* for example, *Prosecutor v Kaing Guek Eav alias 'Duch'*, ECCC Case File No. 001/18-07-2007-ECCC-OCIJ(PTC02), Pre-Trial Chamber, Decision on Request for Leave to File *Amicus Curiae* Brief, 2 October 2008; *Prosecutor v Nuon Chea* and *Khieu Samphan*, ECCC Case File No. 002/19-09-2007/ECCC/TC, Trial Chamber, Decision on the Request for Leave to Submit *Amicus Curiae* Brief on Forced Marriage, 13 September 2016.

[103] Supreme Court Chamber, 'Information Concerning the Submission of *Amicus Curiae* Briefs to the Supreme Court Chamber of the ECCC', Extraordinary Chambers in the Courts of Cambodia, 7 March 2011, para. 5, <https://www.eccc.gov.kh/en/documents/legal/information-submission-amicus-curiae-briefs-supreme-court-chamber> [accessed 12 June 2017].

[104] *Prosecutor v Kaing Guek Eav alias 'Duch'*, ECCC Case File No. 001/18-07-2007-ECCC/SC, Supreme Court Chamber, Decision on DSS Request to the Supreme Court Chamber to Invite *Amicus Curiae* Briefs from Independent Third Parties, 3 March 2011, paras. 5–10.

[105] *Prosecutor v Nuon Chea* and *Khieu Samphan*, ECCC Case File No. 002/19-09-2007-ECCC/SC, Supreme Court Chamber, Decision on Renewed Requests to Intervene or Submit *Amicus Curiae* Brief in Case 002/01 Appeal Proceedings, 11 December 2015; *Prosecutor v Nuon Chea* and *Khieu Samphan*,

requests by the defence have also been addressed by the Trial Chamber.[106] The SCC drew a distinction between *amici curiae* and interveners, finding that the former 'are preferably persons or entities with no interest in the outcome of proceedings whereas the latter are those who have such an interest, thereby playing a role akin to the parties to the proceedings'.[107] The SCC added that 'the primary consideration in granting *amicus curiae* status is whether the court's own interest in properly adjudicating the case will be served'.[108]

10. SENTENCING PROCEDURE

In the event of a conviction, the sentence is to be specified in the final disposition of the Trial Chamber.[109] If the sentence handed down is less than or equal to the period of provisional detention already served, then the accused shall be released immediately.[110] If the accused is the only party to appeal against the Trial Chamber's judgment, the SCC may not increase the sentence but may reduce it. If the Co-Prosecutors appeal, the SCC may amend the sentence upwards or downwards.[111] Where the sentence is confirmed on appeal or the SCC sentences an accused to prison, the SCC shall rule on detention matters in accordance with Internal Rule 111(5). Responsibility for the enforcement of sentences lies with the Co-Prosecutors who may seek the assistance of the law enforcement authorities.[112]

ECCC Case File No. 002/19-09-2007-ECCC/SC, Supreme Court Chamber, Decisions on Request to Intervene or Submit *Amici Curiae* Briefs in Case 002/01 Appeal Proceedings, 8 April 2015, para. 15.

[106] *See* for example, *Prosecutor v Nuon Chea* and *Khieu Samphan*, ECCC Document No. E350/7, Trial Chamber, Trial Chamber Memorandum Entitled 'Decision on Requests for Leave to File *Amicus Curiae* Briefs or to Participate as Intervener on the Admissibility and Use of Torture-Tainted Evidence (E350/5 and E350/6)', 23 June 2015.

[107] *Prosecutor v Nuon Chea* and *Khieu Samphan*, ECCC Case File No. 002/19-09-2007-ECCC/SC, Supreme Court Chamber, Decisions on Request to Intervene or Submit *Amici Curiae* Briefs in Case 002/01 Appeal Proceedings, 8 April 2015, para. 11.

[108] Ibid.

[109] Internal Rules, Rule 101(5).

[110] Internal Rules, Rule 99(1).

[111] Internal Rules, Rules 110(3), (4).

[112] Internal Rules, Rule 113.

11. CIVIL PARTY ACTION

Civil parties may participate in criminal proceedings before the ECCC to support the prosecution and seek collective and moral reparations, as described in the 'General Principles of Victims Participation as Civil Parties' contained in Internal Rule 23. The procedures governing civil party participation have evolved to match the Court's experience and to reflect lessons learned in its first case. The most profound changes to the Internal Rules occurred during the ECCC's 7th Plenary Session in February 2010. First, a distinction was made between civil party participation during the judicial investigation stage and the trial stage so that during the investigation, the civil parties participate individually, while at the trial, they form a single group whose interests are represented by the Lead Co-Lawyers for Civil Parties. This is reflected in Rules 12 *ter*, 23(3) and 23 *ter*, according to which civil parties form a 'consolidated group' rather than participating individually at trial. The Trial Chamber commented on the amendment to the Rules as follows: 'Under the applicable legal framework, Civil Parties no longer participate individually on the basis of their particular harm suffered, but instead comprise a consolidated group whose collective interests are represented by the Civil Party Lead Co-Lawyers during the trial stage and beyond.'[113]

Secondly, the admissibility of civil party applications is decided on a case-by-case basis during the judicial investigation stage, rather than at the trial stage. This change, reflected in Rule 23 *bis*, came about as a result of the SCC arriving at a different conclusion on admissibility from the Trial Chamber in the *Duch* case. In that case, the SCC observed that despite the absence of any legal error on the part of the Trial Chamber, there appeared to have been 'a fundamental misunderstanding between the Trial Chamber and the Civil Party Appellants as to the merits and legal effect of the initial review of their applications'.[114] The SCC also recognised that 'the process for the admissibility of civil party applicants and the revocation of their status in the Trial Judgement may have caused anguish and frustration.'[115] To prevent this from occurring in future cases,

113 *Prosecutor v Nuon Chea, Ieng Sary, Ieng Thirith* and *Khieu Samphan*, ECCC Case File No. 002/19-09-2007-ECCC/TC, Trial Chamber, Severance Order pursuant to Internal Rule 89 *ter*, 22 September 2011, para. 8.

114 Duch Appeal Judgment, above n. 82, para. 501.

115 Ibid.

the Internal Rules were amended so that admissibility is determined at the end of the judicial investigation, by separate order, or on appeal to the PTC.

Thirdly, from the issuance of the Closing Order and throughout the trial and appeal stages, civil parties must be represented by a lawyer in order to participate in proceedings and must exercise their rights through their lawyers. They may choose to form groups and be represented by a common lawyer.[116] Alternatively, the Co-Investigating Judges or the Chambers may, in the interests of justice, organise common representation.[117] Victims may organise their action under the umbrella of a Victim's Association and thereby be represented by the association's lawyers.[118] In practice, having legal representation is the only way civil parties can obtain full access to the case file. The right of civil parties to participate in pre-trial appeals was recognised at an early stage,[119] although in order to manage PTC hearings the decision was made to require civil parties to address the Court through their lawyers unless a pre-hearing application to address the Court in person was made by a legitimately unrepresented civil party.[120]

The Civil Party Lead Co-Lawyers are tasked with attempting to reach consensus among the individual Civil Party Lawyers and coordinating the representation of the consolidated group of civil parties at trial.[121] Their functions commence only when the Trial Chamber is seized of a case and include representing the interests of the consolidated group of civil parties and taking responsibility for the overall advocacy, strategy and in-court presentation of the interests of the civil parties during the trial and beyond.[122] The lawyers assigned to individual civil parties or groups support the Civil Party Lead Co-Lawyers in exercising their functions.

---

[116] Internal Rules, Rules 23 *ter* (1), (2).

[117] Internal Rules, Rule 23 *ter* (3).

[118] Internal Rules, Rule 23 *quater*.

[119] *Prosecutor v Nuon Chea*, ECCC Case File No. 002/19-09-2007-ECCC/OCIJ (PTC01), Pre-Trial Chamber, Decision on Civil Party Participation in Provisional Detention Appeals, 20 March 2008, paras. 36, 40–2, 49.

[120] *Prosecutor v Ieng Sary*, ECCC Case File No. 002/19-09-2007-ECCC/OCIJ (PTC03), Pre-Trial Chamber, Decision on Application for Reconsideration of Civil Party's Right to Address Pre-Trial Chamber in Person, 28 August 2008; *Prosecutor v Ieng Sary*, ECCC Case File No. 002/19-09-2007-ECCC/OCIJ (PTC03), Pre-Trial Chamber, Directions on Unrepresented Civil Parties' Right to Address the Pre-Trial Chamber in Person, 29 August 2008, paras. 5–11.

[121] Internal Rules, Rule 12 *ter* (3).

[122] Internal Rules, Rule 12 *ter* (5).

In order for a civil party action to be admissible, the applicant must be clearly identified and demonstrate 'as a direct consequence of at least one of the crimes alleged against the Charged Person, that he or she has in fact suffered physical, material or psychological injury upon which a claim of collective and moral reparation might be based'.[123] The standard for admissibility is that the 'Co-Investigating Judges shall be satisfied that facts alleged in support of the application are more likely than not to be true'.[124] Applications to be joined as civil parties should be submitted in writing to the Co-Investigating Judges no later than 15 days after notification is given of the conclusion of the judicial investigation.[125] A decision to reject a civil party application is subject to expedited appeal before the PTC. The Co-Investigating Judges may decide on the admissibility of all outstanding civil party applications by a separate order at the same time as issuing the Closing Order. This separate order is also open to expedited appeal.[126] Unless and until their applications are rejected, civil party applicants may exercise the rights afforded to civil parties under the Internal Rules. Appeals do not have the effect of staying the trial proceedings. Civil parties may waive the right to request reparations and abandon their action at any time during the pre-trial stage and may withdraw from the consolidated group at the trial stage. Abandonment or withdrawal has no impact on the ongoing criminal prosecution.[127]

Civil parties may not be questioned as simple witnesses in the same case, reflecting Article 312 of the Cambodian Criminal Procedure Code which provides that a 'civil party may never be heard as a witness'.[128] This does not preclude civil parties from testifying on issues relating to the guilt of the accused, indeed, 'the civil party—the individual who claims to be the victim of an alleged crime—will often be particularly well-placed to report on the events that form the basis of the allegation'.[129] Civil parties may provide information to the Trial Chamber in various ways including by testifying, by making a statement outlining

---

123 Internal Rules, Rule 23 *bis* (1).
124 Internal Rules, Rule 23 *bis* (1).
125 Internal Rules, Rule 23 *bis* (2).
126 Internal Rules, Rule 23 *bis* (3).
127 Internal Rules, Rule 23 *bis* (5).
128 Internal Rules, Rule 23(4); Nuon Appeal Judgment, above n. 57, para. 313.
129 Nuon Appeal Judgment, above n. 57, para. 312.

their suffering, and by giving victim impact testimony during a special hearing scheduled for that purpose.[130]

12. REPARATIONS FOR VICTIMS

Internal Rule 23 *quinquies* (1) adopted on 9 February 2009 and amended on 17 September 2010 provides that: 'If an Accused is convicted, the Chambers may award only collective and moral reparations to Civil Parties.'[131] These include measures that: (a) acknowledge the harm suffered by civil parties as a result of the commission of the crimes for which an accused is convicted, and (b) provide benefits to the civil parties which address this harm. Monetary payments to civil parties are excluded.[132] The term 'moral' means repairing moral damages rather than material ones, and the term 'collective' confirms the unavailability of individual financial awards.[133] The Trial Chamber has explained that:

> The redress available before the ECCC differs from that available under a number of international treaties and other instruments, or before certain regional human rights courts, which are instead empowered to adjudicate questions of State responsibility and to order States to make reparation to their citizens where found responsible for gross violations of international human rights law. The Chamber has no jurisdiction to order the implementation or the payment of reparation measures against Cambodian or other national authorities or international bodies. Nor can it properly impose obligations on persons or entities that were not parties to the proceedings before it.[134]

Nevertheless, Internal Rule 23 *quinquies* (3)(b) permits the Chambers within the framework of the Rules to recognise specific projects that contribute to the 'rehabilitation, reintegration and restoration of dignity' of the victims of Khmer Rouge era crimes 'where national or international authorities, non-governmental organisations or other potential donors, provide financial support and other forms of assistance to show solidarity'.[135]

---

130 Ibid, para. 305.

131 C.f. Nuon Trial Judgment, above n. 9, para. 1114.

132 Internal Rules, Rule 23 *quinquies* (1); Nuon Trial Judgment, above n. 9, para. 1115.

133 Nuon Trial Judgment, above n. 9, para. 1115.

134 Ibid, para. 1116.

135 Ibid.

The Civil Party Lead Co-Lawyers must adhere to the pleading requirements set out in Internal Rule 23 *quinquies* (2) and file a single claim for reparations on behalf of the group of civil parties. Their submission shall include a description of the awards sought, a reasoned argument as to how they address the harm suffered, and, in relation to each award, the single, specific mode of implementation sought. In deciding the mode of implementation in accordance with Rule 23 *quinquies* (3), the Chamber may in respect of each award, either (a) order that the costs of the award shall be borne by the convicted person; or (b) recognise that a specific project appropriately gives effect to the award sought by the Lead Co-Lawyers and may be implemented, with the further requirement that such project shall have been designed or identified in cooperation with the Victims Support Section and have secured sufficient external funding. The Chambers have stressed that the two avenues of reparations before the ECCC envisaged in Internal Rule 23 *quinquies* (3)(a) and (b) 'are not only distinct but also mutually exclusive and that the Lead Co-Lawyers shall necessarily select one or the other'.[136]

Internal Rule 100 provides that the Trial Chamber shall make a decision on the civil party claims in the judgment which must not contradict the judgment on the criminal action in the same case. If the accused is the only party to appeal, the SCC may not increase any reparations to be awarded to the civil parties.

13. DISAGREEMENT PROCEDURES

The procedures governing the resolution of disagreements between the Co-Prosecutors and the Co-Investigating Judges are outlined in Article 7 of the ECCC Agreement and addressed in similar terms in Articles 20 (new) and 23 (new) of the ECCC Law. When either the Co-Prosecutors or Co-Investigating Judges require the assistance of the PTC in settling their differences, they should submit written statements of facts and the reasons for their different positions to the Director of the Office of Administration within 30 days of the prosecutorial or investigative action that triggers the dispute, otherwise the action proceeds. The PTC shall then be convened to decide on the matter. The PTC's decision is binding on the parties to the disagreement. If the PTC is unable to reach the super-majority required for any valid decision the result is that 'the investigation or prosecution shall proceed'.

---

136 Ibid, para. 1118.

Internal Rules 71 and 72 give further specificity to these general provisions, stating that as a preliminary measure, either of the Co-Prosecutors or Co-Investigating Judges, or both of them, may record the exact nature of their disagreement in a signed, dated document to be placed in a register of disagreements kept by the Greffier of the relevant office. Within 30 days of the filing of this document in the register of disagreements, either of the Co-Prosecutors or Co-Investigating Judges may seize the PTC of the disagreement by submitting their statement of facts and reasons to the Office of Administration. This statement is not placed on the case file. For as long as the PTC is seized of the disagreement, the disputing parties shall continue to seek consensus. However, in respect of disagreements between the Co-Prosecutors, 'the action or decision which is the subject of the disagreement shall be executed except for disagreements concerning':

> a) an Introductory Submission;
> b) a Supplementary Submission relating to new crimes;
> c) a Final Submission; or
> d) a decision relating to an appeal,
>
> in which case, no action shall be taken with respect to the subject of the disagreement until either consensus is achieved, the 30 (thirty) day period has ended, or the Chamber has been seised and the dispute settlement procedure has been completed, as appropriate.

In respect of disagreements between the Co-Investigating Judges, 'the action or decision which is the subject of the disagreement shall be executed, except for disagreements concerning':

> a) any decision that would be open to appeal by the Charged Person or a Civil Party under these IRs;
> b) notification of charges; or
> c) an Arrest and Detention Order,
>
> in which case, no action shall be taken with respect to the subject of the disagreement until either consensus is achieved, the 30 (thirty) day period has ended, or the Chamber has been seised and the dispute settlement procedure has been completed, as appropriate.

The Internal Rules throw further light on the default decision in the event that the required majority is not achieved before the PTC. With respect to disagreements between the Co-Prosecutors, the default decision shall be that the action or decision done by one Co-Prosecutor shall stand, or that the action or decision proposed to be done by one Co-Prosecutor shall be executed. As it concerns disagreements between the Co-Investigative

Judges, the default decision shall be that the order or investigative act done by one Co-Investigating Judge shall stand, or that the order or investigative act proposed to be done by one Co-Investigating Judge shall be executed. However, where the disagreement concerns provisional detention, there shall be a presumption of freedom.

The Internal Rules provide that the disagreement hearing shall be held and the judgment handed down *in camera*. This seems to contradict the ECCC Agreement and ECCC Law, both of which refer to the decision being 'published' by the Office of Administration and communicated to the Co-Prosecutors or Co-Investigating Judges as appropriate. However, the Internal Rules state that if the disagreement is between Co-Investigating Judges and relates to a decision against which the parties would have the right to appeal, the parties may participate in the disagreement proceedings and the PTC may decide to hold all or part of a hearing in public. In any event, the decision of the PTC is not subject to appeal.

5. Cases

1. THE FIRST INTRODUCTORY SUBMISSION

The first Introductory Submission was filed in the Office of the Co-Investigating Judges on 18 July 2007 stating that according to the preliminary investigation, crimes against humanity, genocide, grave breaches of the Geneva Conventions, homicide, torture and religious persecution occurred in Cambodia during the period of Democratic Kampuchea from 17 April 1975 to 6 January 1979. These crimes were alleged to have been committed as part of a common criminal plan to effect a radical change of Cambodian society along ideological lines. Five suspects were identified.[1] Duch, who was already detained by the Cambodian Military Court, was placed under provisional detention by the Extraordinary Chambers in the Courts of Cambodia (ECCC) on 31 July 2007[2] and the arrest and provisional detention of Nuon Chea,[3] Ieng Sary,[4] Ieng Thirith[5] and Khieu

[1] 'Statement of the Co-Prosecutors', Extraordinary Chambers in the Courts of Cambodia, 18 July 2007, <http://www.genocidewatch.org/images/Cambodia_18_Jul_07_Statement_of_the_Co-Prosecutors.pdf> [accessed 13 June 2017].

[2] *Prosecutor v Kaing Guek Eav alias 'Duch'*, ECCC Case File No. 001/18-07-2007, Office of the Co-Investigating Judges, Order of Provisional Detention (Kaing Guek Eav *alias* Duch), 31 July 2007.

[3] *Prosecutor v Nuon Chea*, ECCC Case File No. 002/19-09-2007, Office of the Co-Investigating Judges, Provisional Detention Order (Nuon Chea), 19 September 2007.

[4] *Prosecutor v Ieng Sary*, ECCC Case File No. 002/19-09-2007-ECCC/OCIJ, Office of the Co-Investigating Judges, Police Custody Decision, 12 November 2007; *Prosecutor v Ieng Sary*, ECCC Case File No. 002/19-09-2007-ECCC/OCIJ, Office of the Co-Investigating Judges, Provisional Detention Order (Ieng Sary), 14 November 2007.

[5] *Prosecutor v Ieng Thirith*, ECCC Case File No.002/19-09-2007-ECCC/OCIJ, Office of the Co-Investigating Judges, Police Custody Decision (Ieng Thirith), 12 November 2007; and *Prosecutor v Ieng Thirith*, ECCC Case File No. 002/19-09-2007-ECCC/OCIJ, Office of the Co-Investigating Judges, Provisional Detention Order (Ieng Thirith), 14 November 2007.

Samphan[6] followed swiftly. In March 2008, the Co-Prosecutors filed a Supplementary Submission based on victim complaints requesting judicial investigation into additional criminal acts.

The separation of the case file concerning Duch's responsibility in respect of S-21 was subsequently ordered.[7] The facts concerning S-21 were then investigated under case file number 001/18-07-2007, often referred to as Case 001. This meant that all other facts related to Duch or the other individuals mentioned in the first Introductory Submission were investigated under case file number 002/19-09-2007, known as Case 002.

2. KAING GUECK EAV ALIAS DUCH (CASE 001)

On the completion of the investigation in Case 001, the Co-Investigating Judges issued a Closing Order indicting Duch for crimes against humanity and grave breaches of the Geneva Conventions of 1949.[8] The Co-Prosecutors filed an appeal against the Closing Order with the Pre-Trial Chamber (PTC) which partially granted the appeal, adding the domestic crimes of torture and premeditated murder as defined by the 1956 Penal Code to the indictment.[9]

The PTC remitted Duch for trial on the basis of the amended Closing Order which alleged that he, as Deputy Secretary or Secretary of S-21, planned, instigated, ordered, committed, or aided and abetted crimes against humanity, grave breaches of the Geneva Conventions of 1949, and the national crimes of premeditated murder and torture, or in the alternative that he was responsible by virtue of his position as a superior. The allegation of crimes against humanity included: (i) murder; (ii) extermination; (iii) enslavement; (iv) imprisonment; (v) torture;

---

[6] *Prosecutor v Khieu Samphan*, ECCC Case File No. 002/19-09-2007-ECCC/OCIJ, Office of the Co-Investigating Judges, Provisional Detention Order (Khieu Samphan), 19 November 2007.

[7] On 19 September 2007. *See* 'Procedural History' in *Prosecutor v Kaing Guek Eav alias 'Duch'*, ECCC Case File No. 002/14-08-2006, Office of the Co-Investigating Judges, Closing Order Indicting Kaing Guek Eav *alias* Duch, 8 August 2008, paras. 4–9.

[8] *Prosecutor v Kaing Guek Eav alias 'Duch'*, ECCC Case File No. 002/14-08-2006, Office of the Co-Investigating Judges, Closing Order Indicting Kaing Guek Eav *alias* Duch, 8 August 2008.

[9] *Prosecutor v Kaing Guek Eav alias 'Duch'*, ECCC Case File No. 001/8-07-2007-ECCC/OCIJ (PTC 02), Pre-Trial Chamber, Decision on Appeal against Closing Order Indicting Kaing Guek Eav *alias* "Duch", 5 December 2008, paras. 104–07.

(vi) rape; (vii) persecution on political grounds; and (viii) other inhumane acts. The allegation of grave breaches of the Geneva Conventions of 1949 included (i) wilful killing; (ii) torture or inhumane treatment; (iii) wilfully causing great suffering or serious injury to body or health; (iv) wilfully depriving a prisoner of war or civilian of the rights of fair and regular trial; and (v) unlawful confinement of a civilian.

An initial hearing took place on 17 and 18 February 2009 and the substantive hearing commenced on 30 March 2009. Four civil party groups comprised of 90 victims participated in the trial through their lawyers. A total of 24 witnesses testified under oath and 22 civil parties provided evidence.[10] Nine expert witnesses appeared before or made submissions to the Trial Chamber. Approximately 1,000 documents were submitted. The trial ended on 17 September 2009.

There has been an on-going fascination with the personality of Kaing Gueck Eav *alias* Duch, since the publication of François Bizot's book *The Gate*, describing the author's experience as Duch's captive under the Khmer Rouge.[11] How did the soft-spoken former school teacher become a notorious torturer, and for how much of Cambodia's tragedy in the 1970s could this individual be held accountable? After Duch was handed over to the ECCC, an attempt to address the first question was made by François Bizot himself in a follow-up to *The Gate* entitled *Facing the Torturer, Inside the Mind of a War Criminal*.[12] Rithy Pran, a well-known Cambodian film-maker and survivor of the Khmer Rouge, confronted Duch while in the ECCC's custody as the basis for his book *The Elimination*. He found that Duch was 'no monster, and he's even less of a demon. He's a man who searches out and seizes upon the weaknesses of others. A man who stalks his humanity. A disturbing man.'[13] The title of Alexander Hinton's book—*Man or Monster?*—is deliberately provocative as the author, who draws on the idea of 'the banality of evil' to frame

---

10 *Prosecutor v Nuon Chea* and *Khieu Samphan*, ECCC Case File No. 002/19-09-2007/ECCC/TC, Trial Chamber, Case 002/01 Judgement, 7 August 2014, para. 30 ('Nuon Trial Judgment').

11 F. Bizot, *The Gate* (London, Vintage Books, 2004).

12 F. Bizot, *Facing the Torturer: Inside the Mind of a War Criminal* (London, Rider Books, 2012).

13 R. Pran and C. Bataille, *The Elimination: A Survivor of the Khmer Rouge Confronts His Past and the Commandant of the Killing Fields* (translated by J. Cullen, New York, Other Press, 2012), p. 34.

his analysis, does not believe Duch's character and conduct can be reduced to these stark alternatives.[14]

The second question is within the ECCC's domain. Hinton notes how the complicated life histories of witnesses and victims are recast as 'testimony' and reduced to a 'truncated and standardized form' in the Trial Chamber's judgment.[15] Duch, who spoke extensively during his trial and whose statements tell their own story, is the person the evidence says he is after a constructed process which takes the man and the monstrous deeds, finds the linkages and determines responsibility, reducing the words spoken during a lengthy trial to a sanitised, selective and arguably digestible narrative. Duch's background and early years were described by the Trial Chamber as follows:[16]

> The Accused was born on 17 November 1942 in Kompong Thom Province, into a family of poor peasants of Chinese origin. He was the eldest of five children and the only son. A good pupil, he completed his schooling at the Kompong Thom junior high school, followed by high school in Siem Reap at the Lycée Sisowath in Phnom Penh, where he passed his baccalaureate. He joined the Khmer Rouge in October 1964. Upon completion of his education, he was appointed as a mathematics teacher at the junior high school in Skoun, Kompong Cham in 1965. He began increasingly dedicating himself to revolutionary activities and left his teaching position to join the underground resistance on 29 October 1967.
>
> The Accused was arrested on 5 January 1968 and later sentenced to 20 years imprisonment for breach of State security. Following his detention in Tuol Kork and Phnom Penh, he was transferred to the army prison at Prey Sar in May 1968, where he witnessed, but was not subjected to, illegal executions and torture. The Accused subsequently was inducted as a full rights member of the CPK, and chose "Duch" as his revolutionary name.
>
> Following the 18 March 1970 coup d'état led by General LON Nol against Prince NORODOM Sihanouk, the Accused was released from prison on 3 April 1970, whereupon he recommenced his activities on behalf of the Khmer Rouge.
>
> He married on 20 December 1975, with his superiors' approval, and had four children, two of whom were born while he was in charge of S-21.

---

[14] A.L. Hinton, *Man or Monster?: The Trial of a Khmer Rouge Torturer* (Durham, Duke University Press, 2016).

[15] Ibid, p. 292.

[16] *Prosecutor v Kaing Guek Eav alias 'Duch'*, ECCC Case File No. 001/18-07-2007/ECCC/TC, Trial Chamber, Judgment, 26 July 2010, paras. 112–14, 122 ('Duch Trial Judgment').

The Trial Chamber rendered its judgment on 26 July 2010. Duch was convicted of persecution on political grounds as a crime against humanity (subsuming the crimes against humanity of extermination (encompassing murder), enslavement, imprisonment, torture (including one instance of rape), and other inhumane acts). He was further convicted of the following grave breaches of the Geneva Conventions of 1949: wilful killing, torture and inhumane treatment, wilfully causing great suffering or serious injury to body or health, wilfully depriving a prisoner of war or civilian of the rights of fair and regular trial, and unlawful confinement of a civilian.[17] Duch's responsibility for the domestic crimes was not addressed due to the Trial Chamber's divided opinion over the question whether the statutory limitation period had expired.[18] He was sentenced to a fixed term of 35 years' imprisonment, with a reduction of five years as compensation for the violation of his rights due to his unlawful prior detention by the Cambodian Military Court.[19] He was additionally given credit for the time already spent in detention, including the period from 10 May 1999 until 30 July 2007 when he was detained by the military court, and the period from 31 July 2007 until the time of a final judgment before the ECCC.[20]

The Co-Prosecutors, the accused, and three civil party groups appealed to the Supreme Court Chamber against the Trial Judgment. The Supreme Court Chamber quashed the Trial Chamber's decision to subsume under the crime against humanity of persecution the other crimes against humanity for which it held Duch responsible, entered additional convictions for the crimes against humanity of extermination (encompassing murder), enslavement, imprisonment, torture, and other inhumane acts, and substituted a sentence of life imprisonment.[21] Additionally, the Supreme Court Chamber granted the appeals from a number of civil parties on the admissibility of their applications and affirmed the Trial Chamber's decision to compile and post on the ECCC's official website all statements of apology and acknowledgements of responsibility made by Kaing Guek Eav during the course of the trial, including the appeal stage.[22]

---

17 Ibid, para. 568.

18 *See* Chapter 2.

19 Duch Trial Judgment, above n. 16, paras. 631–2.

20 Ibid, para. 633.

21 *Prosecutor v Kaing Guek Eav alias 'Duch'*, ECCC Case File No. 001/18-07-2007-ECCC/SC, Supreme Court Chamber, Appeal Judgment, 3 February 2012, pp. 320–1 ('Duch Appeal Judgment').

22 Ibid, p. 321.

Kaing Guek Eav remained under investigation in Case 002 until the Co-Investigating Judges dismissed the charges against him on 14 September 2010.[23]

3. NUON CHEA, KHIEU SAMPHAN, IENG SARY AND IENG THIRITH (CASE 002)

The Closing Order in Case 002 was issued on 15 September 2010, charging Nuon Chea, Khieu Samphan, Ieng Sary and Ieng Thirith with crimes against humanity, genocide, grave breaches of the Geneva Conventions and violations of the 1956 Penal Code.[24] Following an appeal before the PTC, the Closing Order was confirmed with some amendments and the accused were remitted to trial on 13 January 2011. By this time, Nuon Chea was 85 years old, Ieng Sary, 86, Khieu Samphan, 80, and Ieng Thirith, 79.[25]

Ieng Thirith was found unfit to stand trial before the trial proceedings got underway, due to dementia. The Trial Chamber ordered the severance of the charges against her from Case 002, a stay of the proceedings against her and her release.[26] The Co-Prosecutors appealed this and subsequent decisions of the Trial Chamber and the Supreme Court Chamber first ordered additional medical treatment and tests, and later the implementation of a series of post-release conditions.[27] Ieng Sary

---

[23] *Prosecutor v Kaing Guek Eav alias 'Duch'*, ECCC Document No. D420, Office of the Co-Investigating Judges, Dismissal Order, 14 September 2010.

[24] *Prosecutor v Nuon Chea, Ieng Sary, Ieng Thirith* and *Khieu Samphan*, ECCC Case File No. 002/19-09-2007-ECCC-OCIJ, Office of the Co-Investigating Judges, Closing Order (Indictment) in Case 002, 15 September 2010, para. 1613.

[25] *Prosecutor v Nuon Chea, Ieng Sary, Ieng Thirith* and *Khieu Samphan*, ECCC Case File No. 002/19-09-2007-ECCC-OCIJ, Office of the Co-Investigating Judges, Closing Order (Indictment) in Case 002, 15 September 2010, 15 September 2010, paras. 1577, 1585, 1598, 1605.

[26] *Prosecutor v Nuon Chea, Ieng Sary, Ieng Thirith* and *Khieu Samphan*, ECCC Case File No. 002/19-09-2007/ECCC/TC, Trial Chamber, Decision on Ieng Thirith's Fitness to Stand Trial, 17 November 2011, pp. 29–30.

[27] *Prosecutor v Ieng Thirith*, ECCC Case File No. 002/19-09-2007-ECCC-TC/SC(09), Supreme Court Chamber, Decision on Immediate Appeal against the Trial Chamber's Order to Release the Accused Ieng Thirith, 13 December 2011, pp. 24–5; *Prosecutor v Ieng Thirith*, ECCC Case File No. 002/19-09-2007/ECCC/TC, Trial Chamber, Decision on Reassessment of Accused Ieng Thirith's Fitness to Stand Trial Following Supreme Court Chamber Decision of 13 December 2011, 13 September 2012, p. 19; *Prosecutor v Ieng Thirith*, ECCC

died on 14 March 2013, extinguishing all criminal and civil actions against him.[28] Ieng Thirith died on 22 August 2015 having been released from provisional detention on 16 September 2012.[29]

The protagonists in Case 002 do not seem to have inspired quite the same inquiry and body of literature as Duch (or indeed Pol Pot who would presumably have been a co-accused had he survived[30]). David Chandler published *Brother Number One: A Political Biography of Pol Pot* in 1999.[31] The books by Philip Short entitled *Pol Pot, The History of a Nightmare*[32] and Ben Kiernan, *The Pol Pot Regime*,[33] focus more on the history of Cambodia under the Khmer Rouge than on the man himself. The individual motives of these French-educated intellectuals and communist party leaders to return their country to 'Year Zero' are perhaps less intriguing than the policies that drove their actions and the means

---

Case File No. 002/19-09-2007 ECCC-TC/SC (16), Supreme Court Chamber, Decision on Immediate Appeal against the Trial Chamber's Order to Unconditionally Release Ieng Thirith, 14 December 2012, pp. 45–6; *Prosecutor v Ieng Thirith*, ECCC Document No. E138/1/10/1/5/8/3, Trial Chamber, Trial Chamber Memorandum Entitled 'Ieng Thirith Defence Request for Clarification of the Execution of the Supreme Court Chamber's Decision on Immediate Appeal Against the Trial Chamber's Order to Unconditionally Release the Accused Ieng Thirith (E138/1/10)', 27 June 2013, para. 6; *Prosecutor v Ieng Thirith*, ECCC Case File No. 002/19-09-2007/ECCC/TC, Trial Chamber, Order on Measures to be Imposed on Ieng Thirith, 19 July 2013, p. 2.

28 *Prosecutor v Nuon Chea, Ieng Sary*, and *Khieu Samphan*, ECCC Case File No. 002/19-09-2007/ECCC/TC, Trial Chamber, Termination of the Proceedings against the Accused Ieng Sary, 14 March 2013, p. 3.

29 *Prosecutor v Ieng Thirith*, ECCC Case File No. 002/19-09-2007/ECCC/TC, Trial Chamber, Termination of the Proceedings against the Accused Ieng Thirith, 27 August 2015, para. 9, *see* also p. 5: 'the death of the Accused IENG Thirith extinguishes all criminal action against her and ends all civil actions against her at the ECCC.'

30 S. Heder and B. Tittemore, *Seven Candidates for Prosecution: Accountability for Crimes of the Khmer Rouge* (War Crimes Research Office and Coalition for International Justice, June 2001), p. 15, footnote 34: 'The person who would have been the prime target for CPK era crimes, Pol Pot, died in April 1998.' <http://www.wcl.american.edu/warcrimes/khmerrouge.pdf?rd=1> [accessed 3 June 2017].

31 D. Chandler, *Brother Number One: A Political Biography of Pol Pot* (Revised edn, Boulder, Colorado/Oxford, Westview Press, 1999).

32 P. Short, *Pol Pot: The History of a Nightmare* (London, John Murray Publishers, 2004).

33 B. Kiernan, *The Pol Pot Regime: Race, Power, and Genocide in Cambodia under the Khmer Rouge, 1975-79* (3rd edn, New Haven, Connecticut, Yale University Press, 2008).

they used to implement those policies. It is therefore fitting that they were put on trial jointly, for reasons that go beyond legal procedure and the Co-Investigating Judges' charge of a joint criminal enterprise.

Nuon Chea's background and activities prior to the Khmer Rouge era were described by the Trial Chamber as follows:[34]

> NUON Chea, whose birth name is LAO Kim Lorn, was born on 7 July 1926, in Voat Kor Village, Sangkae District, Battambang Province. NUON Chea studied initially in Battambang, continuing his secondary education in Thailand in 1941, and then at the Thammasat University in Bangkok where he started to study law under the name of Runglert Laodi.
>
> NUON Chea joined the then Indochina Communist Party, giving as his reasons his concern at the treatment of Cambodian peasants by French colonial officials and rich Cambodian landowners. From about 1950, NUON Chea's activism intensified as he engaged in propaganda and education activities, which included publishing newspapers and conducting training sessions for peasants in the rural areas.
>
> Around 1951-54, NUON Chea was sent by the Party to study and receive political training in Vietnam. Before settling in Phnom Penh in 1955, NUON Chea moved among different locations in the countryside, such as in Boeng Lvea, along the Stung Chinit River, and in Samlaut, to disguise his active involvement in the revolutionary movement, and ensure his personal security.
>
> In Phnom Penh, NUON Chea continued his underground work for the revolutionary movement as a member of the Party city committee, while working variously as a teacher, a vendor, or a clerk for an import-export company. After POL Pot returned from France in 1955-56, NUON Chea was introduced to him. POL Pot and NUON Chea who were both members of the Khmer People's Revolutionary Party, initially worked together as assistants to TOU Samuth. Later, in 1960, NUON Chea met IENG Sary at the First Party Congress, during which TOU Samuth and NUON Chea were respectively nominated Secretary and Deputy Secretary and the Party was renamed the Workers' Party of Kampuchea.
>
> According to NUON Chea, he met with KHIEU Samphan for the first time near the Aoral Mountain, after Khieu Samphan went to the maquis, but he does not remember when.
>
> From the early 1960s Nuon Chea's political affiliation remained secret. From 1963, NUON Chea travelled to the countryside to meet other leaders of the movement, including POL Pot, IENG Sary and SON Sen.
>
> In 1970, when NORODOM Sihanouk was overthrown, NUON Chea was visiting the East Zone and only managed to return to Phnom Penh after a few months. Once there, he continued to travel to meet POL Pot and IENG Sary

---

[34] Adapted from Nuon Trial Judgment, above n. 10, paras. 305–10, 312.

> to brief them on the situation in Phnom Penh and to receive instructions from POL Pot. As the revolution developed further, however, NUON Chea finally left Phnom Penh and joined the other senior leaders of the Party at S-71.
>
> Throughout the CPK period, NUON Chea was referred to by his surname as "Brother [bang] Nuon," "Uncle [om] Nuon" or "Grand Uncle [om] Nuon" as well as "Comrade Deputy Secretary", or, more generally, "Brother [bang]", "Respected Brother" or "Beloved Brother". While he denied having used or being commonly referred to as "Brother No. 2", several witnesses confirmed that this alias was also used to refer to NUON Chea.

Khieu Samphan wrote a book in 2004, *Cambodia's Recent History and the Reasons behind the Decisions I Made*, apparently keen to present his own image of himself and to defend his role in the Khmer Rouge regime. The book constituted documentary evidence before the Court and was cited numerous times by the Trial Chamber in its judgment. Khieu Samphan's background and activities prior to the Khmer Rouge era were described by the Trial Chamber as follows:[35]

> KHIEU Samphan alias "Haem", "Hem" or "Nan" was born on 27 July 1931 in Chek or Rumchek Commune, Rumduol District, Svay Rieng Province. He attended primary school in Kampong Cham Province, and went on to attend the Preah Sihanouk secondary or junior high school, also in Kampong Cham, where he first met POL Pot (then known as SALOTH Sar). After graduating from Preah Sihanouk School, KHIEU Samphan moved to Phnom Penh to attend the Lycée Sisowath. Following his graduation from the Lycée Sisowath in 1951, he began to study law in Phnom Penh. In 1953, having been awarded a scholarship by the Cambodian government, he travelled to France to study law and economics.
>
> A few months after his arrival in Paris, KHIEU Samphan joined the 'Marxist Circle' founded and regularly attended by other Khmer students in France including IENG Sary, SALOTH Sar, IENG Thirith and SON Sen. Shortly afterwards, KHIEU Samphan left Paris for Montpellier, where he studied law and took classes in economics.
>
> In 1956, KHIEU Samphan returned to Paris to pursue a doctorate in economics. He began to attend regular meetings of the Marxist Circle and, upon the departure of IENG Sary, became its leader. Like other members of the Circle, KHIEU Samphan joined the French Communist Party.
>
> In 1959 KHIEU Samphan presented his doctoral thesis entitled 'L'Economie du Cambodge et ses Problèmes d'Industrialisation' ('The Economy of Cambodia and its Problems of Industrialisation') at the University of Paris.

[35] Adapted from ibid, paras. 351–2, 354–9, 369.

> Not long after his return to Cambodia, KHIEU Samphan founded a French language newspaper called 'L'Observateur'. [...] In 1960, KHIEU Samphan was arrested and detained without charge for over a month and 'L'Observateur' was closed down.
>
> After the closure of 'L'Observateur', KHIEU Samphan joined 'Sangkum Reastr Niyum', the political party founded by NORODOM Sihanouk. In 1962 he was elected to the National Assembly, having been personally endorsed by NORODOM, and appointed Secretary of State for Commerce.
>
> In March 1963, following student demonstrations in Siem Reap, NORODOM Sihanouk – who blamed the riots on communists – broadcast a list of 34 known or suspected 'leftists' (including KHIEU Samphan, POL Pot and IENG Sary), who were condemned as "traitors". KHIEU Samphan nevertheless kept his cabinet post until he was forced to resign in mid-1963.
>
> KHIEU Samphan retained his parliamentary seat upon his resignation from the cabinet, and was re-elected to the National Assembly for a second term in 1966.
>
> In late 1972 or early 1973, KHIEU Samphan married SO Socheat, a cook at S-71.[36] Their first child was born in 1974.

The Trial Chamber did not have the occasion to provide profiles of Ieng Sary and Ieng Thirith due to the termination of proceedings against them. While not judicially verified, Ieng Sary's background and early years were described as follows in an obituary appearing in *The Telegraph*:[37]

> Ieng Sary was born Kim Trang on October 24 1925 in the Tra Ninh province of southern Vietnam, to a Cambodian father and a Chinese mother. He first met Pol Pot in the mid-1940s, when they were classmates at Phnom Penh's elite Lycée Sisowath. Both won government scholarships to study in France, where they joined the French Communist Party.
>
> In 1951, while still in Paris, Ieng Sary married a fellow student, Khieu Thirith, who would become social affairs minister in the Khmer Rouge regime.

---

[36] So Socheat appeared as a witness in the case. *See* M. Kozlovski, 'Prosecution Grills Khieu Samphan's Wife in Extended Cross-Examination', *Cambodia Tribunal Monitor*, 11 June 2013, <http://www.cambodiatribunal.org/2013/06/11/prosecution-grills-khieu-samphans-wife-in-extended-cross-examination/> [accessed 13 June 2017].

[37] 'Obituaries: Ieng Sary', *The Telegraph*, 14 March 2013, <http://www.telegraph.co.uk/news/obituaries/9931092/Ieng-Sary.html> [accessed 13 June 2017]. *See* also D. Chandler, 'Ieng Sary Obituary', *The Guardian*, 14 March 2013, <https://www.theguardian.com/world/2013/mar/14/ieng-sary> [accessed 13 June 2017].

> After returning to Cambodia in 1957, Ieng Sary taught history at a school in Phnom Penh while engaging in clandestine militant activities. In 1963, at a time when suspected communists were being arrested, he and Pol Pot slipped out of the capital to start a guerrilla movement in the countryside. In 1971 he moved to Beijing, where his role was to coordinate the Cambodian resistance. When the Khmer Rouge took power in 1975, Pol Pot was named prime minister and Ieng Sary his deputy prime minister responsible for foreign affairs.

An account of Ieng Thirith's background similarly appeared in an obituary published in *The Telegraph*:[38]

> The youngest of five children of a provincial judge, she was born Khieu Thirith at Phnom Penh on March 10 1932 and educated at the Lycée Sisowath before travelling to Paris with her older sister Khieu Ponnary to take a degree in English Literature at the Sorbonne.
>
> There the sisters joined a Marxist-Leninist study circle that formed the core of what would become the Khmer Rouge, and in 1953 she married a fellow member, Ieng Sary, with whom she had four children. Her sister subsequently married Pol Pot.
>
> Returning to Cambodia in the late 1950s, Ieng Sary and Pol Pot taught in private schools and engaged in underground work while the sisters taught at the Lycée Sisowath. Ieng Thirith also opened an English-language school in Phnom Penh. In 1963, fearing arrest by King Sihanouk's police, Pol Pot and Ieng Sary took shelter in a communist base on the Cambodian-Vietnamese border, where Thirith joined them in 1964, leaving her children in the care of their grandparents.
>
> Before the Khmer Rouge took power in 1975, Khieu Ponnary had been declared insane (she died in 2003) and Pol Pot later remarried. As a result Ieng Thirith became the de facto 'first lady' of the revolution.

An initial hearing took place between 27 and 30 June 2011 where submissions on preliminary objections to jurisdiction were heard, resulting in offences in the 1956 Penal Code being struck out. The Trial

---

[38] 'Ieng Thirith, Khmer Rouge Leader – Obituary: Shakespeare Scholar and "First Lady" of the Khmer Rouge', *The Telegraph*, 25 August 2015, <http://www.telegraph.co.uk/news/obituaries/11823587/Ieng-Thirith-Khmer-Rouge-leader-obituary.html> [accessed 13 June 2017]. *See* also S. Chang, 'Ieng Thirith: Scholar who Became the Highest-Ranked Woman in the Khmer Rouge and Was Later Charged with Genocide', *The Independent*, 24 August 2015, <http://www.independent.co.uk/news/people/news/ieng-thirith-scholar-who-became-the-highest-ranked-woman-in-the-khmer-rouge-and-was-later-charged-10470049.html> [accessed 13 June 2017].

Chamber then decided to divide the proceedings into discrete trials, each comprising distinct charges, and each of which would conclude with a verdict and sentence in the event of a conviction.[39] The first case to proceed, initially against all four accused but finally against Nuon Chea and Khieu Samphan only, became known as Case 002/01.

3.1 Nuon Chea and Khieu Samphan (Case 002/01)

As a consequence of the decision to split Case 002, the allegations in the Closing Order that framed Case 002/01 were as follows:

> [B]etween 17 April 1975 and 6 January 1979, NUON Chea, alias "Brother Number Two", served as Deputy Secretary of the Communist Party of Kampuchea ("CPK") Central and Standing Committees and at times also filled various other roles within the government of Democratic Kampuchea, including Minister of Propaganda and Information, Acting Prime Minister, Chairman of the People's Representative Assembly ("PRA") and Chairman of the Standing Committee of the PRA.
>
> [B]etween 17 April 1975 and 6 January 1979, KHIEU Samphan, alias "Haem", "Hem", "Khang" and "Nan", had various positions and roles in the CPK and Democratic Kampuchea including President of the State Presidium, Chairman of Political Office 870 and member of the CPK Central Committee.
>
> [W]hile serving in these various capacities, the Accused committed (via a joint criminal enterprise) the crimes against humanity of murder, political persecution and other inhumane acts comprising forced transfer and attacks against human dignity during movement of population (phase one); political persecution and other inhumane acts comprising forced transfer and attacks against human dignity during movement of population (phase two); and murder and extermination of Khmer Republic Officials at Tuol Po Chrey.
>
> [T]he Accused planned, instigated, ordered, aided, abetted and/or were responsible as superiors for the following crimes against humanity falling within the scope of Case 002/01: murder; extermination; persecution on political grounds; and other inhumane acts comprising attacks against human dignity, forced transfer and enforced disappearances.[40]

The hearing of evidence in Case 002/01 concluded on 23 July 2013 after 214 hearing days. While Ieng Sary had been present for most of the trial hearings, his death prior to the judgment meant that formally Case 002/01 only concerned the responsibility of Nuon Chea and Khieu Samphan. The parties submitted Closing Briefs on 26 and 27 September

---

39 *See* Chapter 6.

40 Nuon Trial Judgment, above n. 10, paras. 9–11.

2013 and made their Closing Statements between 16 and 31 October 2013. The Trial Chamber heard 58 witnesses (five of whom were character witnesses called on behalf of Khieu Samphan), three experts and 31 civil parties. A total of 1,124 written statements and transcripts in lieu of oral testimony of witnesses and civil parties were admitted along with 5,824 pieces of documentary evidence.[41] The Trial Chamber rendered its judgment on 7 August 2014.

The responsibility of the accused centred on their respective roles in the implementation of a joint criminal enterprise, the common purpose of which as alleged in the Closing Order 'was to implement rapid socialist revolution through a "great leap forward" and defend the Party against internal and external enemies, by whatever means necessary'.[42] The broad joint criminal enterprise (JCE) allegation, which related to the entire scope of allegations in the Closing Order, had to be limited for the purposes of the severed Case 002/01 to the design and implementation of the following policies:

i. The repeated movement of the population from towns and cities to rural areas, as well as from one rural area to another ("Population Movement Policy"), insofar as this policy is relevant to movement of population (phase one) and movement of population (phase two) ... ; and
ii. The targeting of former officials of the Khmer Republic, including both civil servants and former military personnel and their families ("Targeting Policy"), insofar as this policy is relevant to executions of former Khmer Republic officials at Tuol Po Chrey.[43]

The Closing Order identified four phases of the common purpose to liberate Cambodia and create a socialist society: party-building (September 1960–January 1968); initiation of the armed revolution (January 1968–March 1970); the democratic revolution (March 1970–April 1975); and the socialist revolution (April 1975–January 1979).[44] Only the latter phase was directly relevant to the charges but the earlier planning period assisted in explaining how the common purpose came to fruition. The relevant temporal period for Case 002/01 was more limited still, from 17 April 1975 to December 1977.

The factual allegations in Case 002/01 concerned the movement of the Cambodian population from the cities into the countryside immediately after the fall of Phnom Penh:

---

41 Ibid, paras. 32–3.
42 Ibid, para. 722.
43 Ibid, paras. 722–3.
44 Ibid, para. 724.

> Between 17 April 1975 and December 1977 … the Khmer Rouge forcibly transferred the population from cities and towns throughout Cambodia to rural areas and between these rural areas in order to neutralise enemies, both internal and external, and to avert the threat of rebellion; to eliminate and temper the capitalist and feudalist classes; and to build and expand cooperatives. The Party identified the 'New People', including former government officials, intellectuals, landowners, capitalists, feudalists and the petty bourgeoisie, as key enemies of the revolution and collectivisation. To neutralise these enemies, the Khmer Rouge re-educated, moved and eliminated 'New People' and other groups incompatible with building socialism including former Khmer Republic officials and, it is alleged, Buddhists, the Cham and the Vietnamese.[45]

These population movements were alleged to have included at least two million people who were removed from Phnom Penh on 17 April 1975.[46]

The Trial Chamber found that Nuon Chea and Khieu Samphan, through their participation in a joint criminal enterprise, committed the crimes against humanity of murder, political persecution and other inhumane acts (comprising forced transfer and attacks against human dignity) during Phase One of the movement of population; political persecution and other inhumane acts (comprising forced transfer and attacks against human dignity) during Phase Two of the movement of population; and murder and extermination at Tuol Po Chrey.[47] Nuon Chea was also found to have planned, ordered, instigated and aided and abetted the crimes during Phases One and Two of the movement of population and the crimes against humanity of murder, extermination and political persecution committed at Tuol Po Chrey.[48] Additionally, in respect of all of these crimes, Nuon Chea was found responsible for his failure to exercise his duties as a superior to prevent or punish the crimes of his subordinates.[49] Khieu Samphan was found to have planned, instigated and aided and abetted the crimes during Phases One and Two of the population movement but not to have ordered crimes or to have exercised effective control over the perpetrators so as to make him responsible as a superior.[50] Similarly, he was found to have planned, instigated, aided and abetted the crimes against humanity of murder, extermination and political persecution committed at Tuol Po

45 Ibid, para. 169.
46 Ibid, para. 170.
47 Ibid, paras. 877, 996, 1053.
48 Ibid, para. 940, 942.
49 Ibid, para. 941.
50 Ibid, para. 960.

Chrey.[51] Nuon Chea and Khieu Samphan were both sentenced to life imprisonment.[52]

On 29 September 2014, Nuon Chea filed a notice of appeal listing 223 grounds of appeal and Khieu Samphan filed a notice of appeal listing 148 grounds of appeal.[53] The Co-Prosecutors filed a notice of appeal indicating a single ground 'in the interests of law' concerning the Trial Chamber's decision to exclude from consideration an extended form of the joint criminal enterprise doctrine of liability.[54] Pleadings, duly translated, were complete by 12 August 2015. The appeal hearing was scheduled for 16–18 November 2015 but had to be adjourned shortly after it opened since Nuon Chea's Co-Lawyers were not present. This resulted in sanctions for misconduct against Nuon Chea's national Co-Lawyer and a request by the Supreme Court Chamber for the Defence Support Section to appoint a standby counsel for Nuon Chea.[55] The hearing resumed on 16 February 2016 after a standby counsel had been appointed and lasted until 18 February 2016.

In its judgment, the Supreme Court Chamber granted in part and dismissed in part the defence appeals. As it concerned Phase One of the population movement, Nuon Chea's and Khieu Samphan's convictions for the crime against humanity of extermination were reversed, while their convictions for the crimes against humanity of murder, persecution

---

[51] Ibid. paras. 1053–4.

[52] Ibid, paras. 1106–7.

[53] *Prosecutor v Nuon Chea* and *Khieu Samphan*, ECCC Case File No. 002/19-09-2007-ECCC-SC, Defence for Nuon Chea, Nuon Chea's Appeal against the Judgment in Case 002/01, 29 December 2014, pp. i–iv; *Prosecutor v Nuon Chea* and *Khieu Samphan*, ECCC Case File No. 002/19-09-2007-ECCC-SC, Defence for Khieu Samphan, Mr. Khieu Samphan's Defence Appeal Brief against the Judgment in Case 002/01, 29 December 2014, pp. ii–vi.

[54] *Prosecutor v Nuon Chea* and *Khieu Samphan*, ECCC Case File No. 002/19-09-2007-ECCC/SC, Office of the Co-Prosecutors, Co-Prosecutors' Notice of Appeal of a Decision in Case 002/01, 29 September 2014, paras. 2, 7.

[55] *Prosecutor v Nuon Chea* and *Khieu Samphan*, ECCC Document No. 002/19-09-2007-ECCC/SC, Supreme Court Chamber, Decision on the Conduct of the Co-Lawyers for Nuon Chea during the Appeal Hearing of 17 November 2015, paras. 32–33; *Prosecutor v Nuon Chea* and *Khieu Samphan*, ECCC Document No. F30/15, Supreme Court Chamber, Follow-up to Supreme Court Chamber's Instruction to Appoint Standby Counsel for Nuon Chea, 19 November 2015, pp. 3–4; *Prosecutor v Nuon Chea* and *Khieu Samphan*, ECCC Case File No. 002/19-09-2007-ECCC/SC, Supreme Court Chamber, Order Scheduling the Resumption of the Appeal Hearing, 23 December 2015, pp. 2–3.

on political grounds and other inhumane acts were affirmed.[56] As it concerned Phase Two of the population movement, the convictions of the two accused for the crimes against humanity of extermination and persecution on political grounds were reversed, while their convictions for the crime against humanity of other inhumane acts were affirmed, and, on the basis of a re-characterisation of the facts, a conviction for the crime against humanity of murder was entered.[57] As it concerned the events at Tuol Po Chrey, both accused had their convictions for the crimes against humanity of extermination, murder and persecution on political grounds reversed.[58] Despite these modifications, the sentence of life imprisonment for each accused was affirmed.[59] The Co-Prosecutors' appeal was dismissed as being inadmissible.[60] This brought Case 002/01 to finality.

3.2 Nuon Chea and Khieu Samphan (Case 002/02)

In the lengthy proceedings concerning the severance of Case 002, the Supreme Court Chamber had ordered that evidentiary hearings in Case 002/02 should begin as soon as possible after closing arguments in Case 002/01 and that the scope of Case 002/02 should extend at a minimum to charges related to S-21, a worksite, a cooperative and genocide.[61] In view of the urgency of the matter at the time, the Supreme Court Chamber initially issued its reasons in summary form and provided its full reasoned decision on 25 November 2013, after the completion of the trial hearing in Case 002/01. The Trial Chamber held a Trial Management Meeting to consider issues relating to Case 002/02 on 11 December 2013, before issuing a memorandum outlining its work plan for the new trial and inviting written submissions from the parties on the scope of the case. The Trial Chamber then decided to further sever Case 002 and reduce the scope of Case 002/02 so that it did not cover all the remaining charges in the Closing Order. Accepting the essence of a proposal put

---

56 *Prosecutor v Nuon Chea* and *Khieu Samphan*, ECCC Case File No. 002/19-09-2007-ECCC/SC, Supreme Court Chamber, Appeal Judgment, 23 November 2016, p. 519 ('Nuon Appeal Judgment').

57 Ibid, p. 519.

58 Ibid, p. 519.

59 Ibid, para. 1121.

60 Ibid, p. 519.

61 *Prosecutor v Nuon Chea* and *Khieu Samphan*, ECCC Case File No. 002/19-09-2007-ECCC-TC/SC(28), Supreme Court Chamber, Decision on Immediate Appeals against Trial Chamber's Second Decision on Severance of Case 002: Summary of Reasons, 23 July 2013, paras. 11–13.

forward by the Co-Prosecutors, the Trial Chamber determined that the scope of the Case 002/02 crime base should comprise:

> the portions of the Closing Order pertaining to S-21 Security Centre, 1st January Dam Worksite, Tram Kok Cooperative, and genocide (Vietnamese and Cham peoples); …
>
> Kraing Ta Chan Security Centre, Kampong Chhnang Airport Construction site, Au Kanseng Security Centre, Phnom Kraol Security Centre, Trapeang Thma Dam Worksite and the charges of Forced Marriage and Rape (nationwide) and Internal Purges.[62]

All the remaining legal characterisations of the crimes were covered in Case 002/02 despite the removal of certain events and crime sites. The allegations therefore included crimes against humanity, genocide and grave breaches of the Geneva Conventions committed pursuant to the same basic joint criminal enterprise as alleged in Case 002/01. According to an order by the Supreme Court Chamber, all pending proceedings in relation to the charges remaining outside the scope of Cases 002/01 and 002/02 were formally (though provisionally) stayed.[63]

A further Initial Hearing took place on 30 July 2014 and the evidentiary hearings were scheduled to begin on 17 October 2014 on a reduced timetable for the remainder of 2014 to account for the fact that the parties were also preparing their appeals in Case 002/01. During opening statements, however, both Nuon Chea and Khieu Samphan informed the Trial Chamber that they had instructed their Co-Lawyers to boycott the proceedings, whereupon the lawyers walked out of the courtroom. The justifications put forward by the defence included insufficient resources and a pending application to disqualify the bench. Despite being instructed to appear for a Trial Management Meeting on 21 October 2014, the Co-Lawyers were absent on that day. The Trial

---

[62] *Prosecutor v Nuon Chea* and *Khieu Samphan*, ECCC Case File No. 002/19-09-2007-ECCC/TC, Trial Chamber, Decision on Additional Severance of Case 002 and Scope of Case 002/02, 4 April 2014, p. 21 (The decision was upheld by the Supreme Court Chamber: *Prosecutor v Nuon Chea* and *Khieu Samphan*, ECCC Case File No. 002/19-09-2007-ECCC-TC/SC(29), Supreme Court Chamber, Decision on Khieu Samphan's Immediate Appeal against the Trial Chamber's Decision on Additional Severance of Case 002 and Scope of Case 002/02, 29 July 2014, para. 91).

[63] *Prosecutor v Nuon Chea* and *Khieu Samphan*, ECCC Case File No. 002/19-09-2007-ECCC-TC/SC(29), Supreme Court Chamber, Decision on Khieu Samphan's Immediate Appeal against the Trial Chamber's Decision on Additional Severance of Case 002 and Scope of Case 002/02, 29 July 2014, para. 89.

Chamber found that this conduct amounted to an obstruction of the proceedings and issued a warning for misconduct.[64] The Trial Management Meeting was rescheduled for 28 October 2014 and the Co-Lawyers attended on this occasion. The commencement of the evidentiary hearing was rescheduled for 17 November 2014. The defence for Khieu Samphan boycotted the proceedings once again on the instructions of the accused who stated that the team lacked the resources to work on the appeal in Case 002/01 and the evidentiary hearings in Case 002/02 at the same time. The Trial Chamber addressed the problem by changing the status of Khieu Samphan's counsel to 'court appointed counsel', who would be bound by instructions to appear issued by the Chamber and not by instructions to boycott the proceedings issued by the accused.[65] The then 'court appointed counsel' refused to appear and the Trial Chamber decided to appoint standby counsel 'to prepare and maintain the capacity to take over the defence of Khieu Samphan at any time should the Chamber determine it necessary to replace current Counsel'.[66] The international and national co-standby counsel were to remain independent from the existing counsel and not to take instructions from the accused unless ordered to do so by the Court. In the meantime, the proceedings were adjourned until 8 January 2015.

The evidentiary hearing re-commenced as scheduled on 8 January 2015 and concluded on 11 January 2017. The Trial Chamber heard the testimony of 114 witnesses, 63 civil parties and eight experts. Closing

---

64 *Prosecutor v Nuon Chea* and *Khieu Samphan*, ECCC Document No. E320, Trial Chamber, Trial Chamber Memorandum Entitled 'Warning to Counsel for Nuon Chea and Khieu Samphan', 24 October 2014, para. 6.

65 *Prosecutor v Nuon Chea* and *Khieu Samphan*, ECCC Case File No. 002/19-09-2007/ECCC/TC, Trial Chamber, Decision on the Appointment of Court-Appointed Counsel for Khieu Samphan, 21 November 2014, paras. 17–18, and p. 7.

66 *Prosecutor v Nuon Chea* and *Khieu Samphan*, ECCC Case File No. 002/19-09-2007/ECCC/TC, Trial Chamber, Decision on the Appointment of Court-Appointed Standby Counsel for Khieu Samphan, 5 December 2014, paras. 12, 18–19. (Subsequently the conduct of the international counsel for Khieu Samphan was referred to their national bar association, *see Prosecutor v Nuon Chea* and *Khieu Samphan*, ECCC Document No. E330/2, Trial Chamber, Forwarding of ECCC Trial Chamber Decision Entitled 'Order to Refer Conduct of Counsel for Khieu Samphan to Appropriate Professional Bodies', 26 January 2015, p. 2).

arguments were heard in June 2017 with a judgment expected in the second quarter of 2018.[67]

On 27 February 2017, the Trial Chamber issued a decision pursuant to Internal Rule 89 *quater* (1) reducing the scope of Case 002 by excluding all facts set out in the Closing Order in Case 002 that were not included in Case 002/01 or Case 002/02.[68] This meant that there would be no Case 002/03 and that the Closing Order against Nuon Chea and Khieu Samphan was viewed as having been exhausted. In factual terms, it meant no further proceedings in Case 002 with respect to Srae Ambel and Prey Sar worksites; Sang, Koh Kyang, Prey Damrei Srot, Wat Kirirum, North Zone, Wat Tlork, and Kok Kduoch security centres; District 12 (West Zone), Tuol Po Chrey (as it concerns facts that were not adjudicated in Case 002/01), and Steung Tauch Execution Sites; Movement of the Population from the East Zone (Phase 3); Treatment of Buddhists (nationwide); Treatment of the Cham at Kroch Chhmar Security Centre; and Crimes committed by the Revolutionary Army of Kampuchea on Vietnamese territory.[69]

4. THE SECOND AND THIRD INTRODUCTORY SUBMISSIONS

The International Co-Prosecutor, acting individually due to a disagreement with the National Co-Prosecutor, put forward further Introductory Submissions on 20 November 2008. These Submissions called for judicial investigations to be opened into the conduct of five additional suspects. The disagreement between the International and National Co-Prosecutors was submitted to the PTC in accordance with the Internal Rules and as a consequence of the judges being unable to reach the required majority, the action of the International Co-Prosecutor was

---

67 'ECCC Completion Plan – Revision 12', Extraordinary Chambers in the Courts of Cambodia, 31 March 2017, para. 9, <https://www.eccc.gov.kh/en/eccc-completion-plan-revision-12> [accessed 13 June 2017].

68 *Prosecutor v Nuon Chea* and *Khieu Samphan*, ECCC Case File No. 002/19-09-2007/ECCC/TC, Trial Chamber, Decision on Reduction of the Scope of Case 002, 27 February 2017, p. 10.

69 'Trial Chamber Reduces Scope of Case 002', Extraordinary Chambers in the Courts of Cambodia, 27 February 2017, <https://www.eccc.gov.kh/en/articles/trial-chamber-reduces-scope-case-002> [accessed 13 June 2017].

executed.[70] The Second and Third Introductory Submissions were formally filed with the Office of the Co-Investigative Judges (OCIJ) on 7 September 2009.

In a Statement, the Acting International Co-Prosecutor confirmed that the new Introductory Submissions covered crimes that were alleged to have been committed as part of a joint criminal enterprise and identified a total of five suspects. The Statement explains that:

> The Second Introductory Submission requests judicial investigation of eight (8) distinct factual situations of murder, torture, unlawful detention, forced labour and persecution. The factual allegations in this Introductory Submission, if proved, would constitute crimes against humanity, grave breaches of the Geneva Conventions and violations of the 1956 Cambodian Penal Code. The Third Introductory Submission requests judicial investigation of thirty-two (32) distinct factual situations of murder, torture, unlawful detention, forced labour, and persecution. The factual allegations in the Third Introductory Submission, if proved, would constitute crimes against humanity, violations of the 1956 Cambodian Penal Code and genocide.[71]

The Co-Investigating Judges divided the Second and Third Introductory Submissions into what are now referred to as Case 003 and Case 004.

5. MEAS MUTH (AND SOU MET) (CASE 003)

Meas Muth and Sou Met were alleged to have been high-ranking commanders in the Revolutionary Army of Kampuchea. They were both included in Stephen Heder's list of 'Seven Candidates for Prosecution'.[72] Meas Muth allegedly had control of the seaside city of Sihanoukville, including the Wat Eng Tea Nhien Security Centre and Stung Hav Rock Quarry forced labour site, and exercised the authority to send people to S-21. Additionally, he was suspected of having commanded troops in indiscriminate attacks against the Vietnamese in 1977 and 1978. Sou Met was charged in his role as Air Force Commander with using forced

---

[70] ECCC Case File No. 001/18-11-2008-ECCC/PTC, Pre-Trial Chamber, Considerations of the Pre-Trial Chamber Regarding the Disagreement Between the Co-Prosecutors Pursuant to Internal Rule 71, 18 August 2009, para. 45.

[71] 'Statement of the Acting International Co-Prosecutor: Submission of Two New Introductory Submissions', Extraordinary Chambers in the Courts of Cambodia, 8 September 2009, <https://www.eccc.gov.kh/sites/default/files/media/ECCC_Act_Int_Co_Prosecutor_8_Sep_2009_%28Eng%29.pdf> [accessed 13 June 2017].

[72] Heder and Tittemore, above n. 30, pp. 99–113.

labour in the construction of the Kampong Chhnang airport, and with involvement in the S-21 and S-22 detention centres.[73] At the time of the filing of the Introductory Submission, Sou Met was believed to be a Commander of the Royal Cambodian Armed Forces.

On 29 April 2011, the Co-Investigative Judges announced that they had concluded the investigations in Case 003.[74] The International Co-Prosecutor took all available procedural steps to challenge this decision, leading to two appeals before the PTC which resulted in a failure on both occasions to achieve the required majority. In the meantime, the International Co-Investigating Judge who had participated in the decision to conclude investigations in Cases 003, Siegfried Blunk, resigned and was replaced by the International Reserve Co-Investigating Judge, Laurent Kasper-Ansermet. Prior to his own resignation, Judge Kasper-Ansermet issued an order to resume the investigation. Mark Harmon took office as International Co-Investigating Judge on 26 October 2012 and the first of at least three disagreements between the National and International Co-Investigating Judges was filed on 7 February 2013 concerning the continuation of the investigation. It was announced in the media that Sou Met had died on 14 June 2013 and his death was independently confirmed, extinguishing the proceedings against him.[75]

The International Co-Prosecutor filed a Supplementary Submission in Case 003 on 31 October 2014. On 3 March 2015, the Co-Investigating Judge, Mark Harmon, (after signing a further disagreement with the National Co-Investigating Judge) charged Meas Muth with violations of Articles 501 and 506 of the 1956 Penal Code (homicide), grave breaches of the Geneva Conventions, and the crimes against humanity of murder, extermination, enslavement, imprisonment, persecution, and other inhumane acts.[76] On 14 December 2015, announcing that the investigation

---

[73] B. di Certo, 'Meus Muth, Sou Met Among "Most Responsible": Judge', *The Phnom Penh Post*, 3 May 2012.

[74] *Prosecutor v Sou Met* and *Meas Muth*, ECCC Case File No. 003/07-09-2009-ECCC-OCIJ, Office of the Co-Investigating Judges, Notice of Conclusion of Judicial Investigations, 29 April 2011.

[75] *Prosecutor v Sou Met* and *Meas Muth*, ECCC Case File No. 003/07-09-2009-ECCC-OCIJ, Office of the Co-Investigating Judges, Dismissal of Allegations against Sou Met, 2 June 2015, paras. 21–4, 26–7.

[76] *Prosecutor v Meas Muth*, ECCC Case File No. 003/07-09-2009-ECCC-OCIJ, Office of the Co-Investigating Judges, Annex: Notification of charges against Meas Muth, 3 March 2015, paras. 3–11.

was concluded, the International Co-Investigating Judge, Michael Bohlander, rescinded certain charges already laid against Meas Muth and charged him with the crime of genocide, additional counts of crimes against humanity, grave breaches of the Geneva Conventions, and violations of Articles 501 and 506 of the 1956 Penal Code (homicide).[77] The arrest warrant of 4 June 2015 was withdrawn, since Meas Muth appeared voluntarily at the hearing. The International and National Co-Prosecutors filed separate Final Submissions on 14 November 2017, expressing opposing views as to whether Meas Muth should be indicted. The Closing Order is tentatively projected by the first quarter of 2018.[78]

6. IM CHAEM, AO AN AND YIM TITH (CASE 004)

The Third Introductory Submission initiated the judicial investigation into the conduct of the three suspects Im Chaem, Ao An and Yim Tith in what is known as Case 004.[79] The scope of the case was subsequently expanded by Supplementary Submissions filed by the International Co-Prosecutor on 18 July 2011, 24 April 2014, 4 August 2015 and 20 November 2015.

6.1 Im Chaem (Case 004/01)

Im Chaem, also known as 'Grandma Chaem', was living peacefully in Northwestern Cambodia, close to the Thai border, when it was revealed that she was under investigation by the ECCC. She was allegedly secretary of Preah Net Preah District in the North-West Zone of Cambodia under the Khmer Rouge, supervised directly by Ta Mok. It has been asserted that she ran the largest prison in Phnom Trayoung district in which around 40,000 people died either through heavy labour in a quarry or by execution. She allegedly also supervised the construction of huge waterworks to increase rice production, including two dams, one of

---

77 *Prosecutor v Meas Muth*, ECCC Case File No. 003/07-09-2009-ECCC-OCIJ, Office of the Co-Investigating Judges, Notice of Conclusion of Judicial Investigation against Meas Muth, 10 January 2017, paras. 3–5.

78 'ECCC Completion Plan – Revision 12', Extraordinary Chambers in the Courts of Cambodia, 31 March 2017, para. 25(a), <https://www.eccc.gov.kh/en/eccc-completion-plan-revision-12> [accessed 13 June 2017].

79 Following severance decisions, and until the closure of the investigation against him, Yim Tith is the only suspect remaining in the original Case 004.

which 'was built entirely by hand in three months by 1,300 slave labourers subsisting on tiny portions of rice porridge'.[80]

The International Co-Investigating Judge, Mark Harmon, had charged Im Chaem in absentia with violations of Articles 501 and 506 of the 1956 Penal Code (homicide) and the crimes against humanity of murder, extermination, enslavement, imprisonment, persecution on political grounds, and other inhumane acts.[81] The conclusion of the investigation was announced on 18 December 2015 and the case of Im Chaem was severed from Case 004, becoming Case 004/01.[82] On 22 February 2017, the Co-Investigating Judges issued a joint Closing Order with full reasons to follow dismissing the case, on the basis that Im Chaem was found not to be subject to the ECCC's personal jurisdiction, in other words she was neither a senior leader nor one of the most responsible officials of the Khmer Rouge regime.[83]

6.2 Ao An (Case 004/02)

On 27 March 2015, after signing a disagreement with the National Co-Investigating Judge, the International Co-Investigating Judge, Mark Harmon, charged Ao An with violations of Articles 501 and 506 of the 1956 Penal Code (homicide) and the crimes against humanity of murder, extermination, persecution on political or religious grounds, imprisonment or other inhumane acts. On 14 March 2016, the International

---

[80] J. Wallace, 'The Bucollic Life of a Cambodian Grandmother Accused of Mass Killings', *The New York Times*, 24 February 2017, <https://www.nytimes.com/2017/02/24/world/asia/cambodia-khmer-rouge-im-chaem.html> [accessed 13 June 2017].

[81] 'The International Co-Investigating Judge Charges Im Chaem in absentia in Case 004', Extraordinary Chambers in the Courts of Cambodia, 15 February 2016, <https://www.eccc.gov.kh/en/articles/international-co-investigating-judge-charges-im-chaem-absentia-case-004> [accessed 15 June 2017]; *Prosecutor v Im Chaem, Ao An* and *Yim Tith*, ECCC Case File No. 004/07-09-2009-ECCC-OCIJ, Office of the Co-Investigating Judges, Notice of Conclusion of Judicial Investigation against Im Chaem, 18 December 2015, para. 2.

[82] *Prosecutor v Im Chaem, Ao An* and *Yim Tith*, ECCC Case File No. 004/07-09-2009-ECCC-OCIJ, Office of the Co-Investigating Judges, Notice of Conclusion of Judicial Investigation against Im Chaem, 18 December 2015, para. 5.

[83] 'Co-Investigating Judges Dismiss Case Against Im Chaem', Extraordinary Chambers in the Courts of Cambodia, 22 February 2017, <https://www.eccc.gov.kh/en/articles/co-investigating-judges-dismiss-case-against-im-chaem> [accessed 15 June 2017].

Co-Investigating Judge, Michael Bohlander, charged Ao An with genocide, and additional counts of crimes against humanity.[84] The announcement of the same date that the investigation was concluded was signed by both the National and International Co-Investigating Judges.[85] The Co-Investigating Judges subsequently ordered the severance of Ao An from Case 004 in order that the case against him could proceed without undue delay, making him the single subject of Case 004/02.[86] The National and International Co-Prosecutors filed their Final Submissions in the case separately on 18 and 21 August 2017 respectively, with the National Co-Prosecutor taking the view that Ao An did not fall within the ECCC's personal jurisdiction and the International Co-Prosecutor stipulating the crimes for which Ao An should be indicted.

7. CONCLUSION

The Co-Prosecutors made it clear upon the filing of the Second and Third Introductory Submissions that they had no plans to conduct any further preliminary investigations into additional suspects at the ECCC. The cases described in this chapter therefore represent the full extent of proceedings before the ECCC. It remains uncertain whether Cases 003 and 004 will proceed to a trial. In May 2017, it was revealed that the Co-Investigating Judges had sought submissions from the parties on the continuation of those cases in the light of the ECCC's budgetary situation.[87] Currently the final appeal proceedings in Case 002/02 are

---

[84] 'Statement of the International Co-Investigating Judge regarding Case 004', Extraordinary Chambers in the Courts of Cambodia, 14 March 2016, <https://www.eccc.gov.kh/en/document/public-affair/additional-charges-announced-against-ao> [accessed 15 June 2017].

[85] *Prosecutor v Ao An* and *Yim Tith*, ECCC Case File No. 004/07-09-2009-ECCC-OCIJ, Office of the Co-Investigating Judges, Notice of Conclusion of Judicial Investigation against Ao An, 16 December 2016, p. 2.

[86] *Prosecutor v Ao An* and *Yim Tith*, ECCC Case File No. 004/07-09-2009-ECCC-OCIJ, Office of the Co-Investigating Judges, Order for Severance of Ao An from Case 004, 16 December 2016, paras. 4–6.

[87] A. Nachemson and E. Handley, 'Staying Khmer Rouge Tribunal Cases Mulled', *The Phnom Penh Post*, 8 May 2017, <http://www.phnompenhpost.com/national/staying-khmer-rouge-tribunal-cases-mulled> [accessed 13 June 2017]. And *see* Press Release by the Co-Investigating Judges of the same date lamenting the leak of confidential information and clarifying that submissions on the issue had been sought: 'Statement by the Co-Investigating Judges on the Article "Staying Khmer Rouge Tribunal Cases Mulled" in the Phnom Penh Post

projected to conclude in 2020. By that time, the ECCC will have been in operation for 14 years and completed two cases against three accused. The Co-Prosecutors indicated that the last set of cases, i.e. Cases 003 and 004, would lead to a more comprehensive accounting of the crimes committed under the DK regime in the period 1975 to 1979. The snippets of publicly available information concerning the factual allegations in the latter cases certainly point to the validity of this statement but many factors both within and outside the control of the ECCC will influence the Court's willingness and ability to see this commitment through.

of 8 May 2017', Extraordinary Chambers in the Courts of Cambodia, 8 May 2017, <https://www.eccc.gov.kh/en/articles/statement-co-investigating-judges-article-staying-khmer-rouge-tribunal-cases-mulled-phnom-p> [accessed 13 June 2017]. In August 2017, the Co-Investigating Judges deferred a decision on a stay of proceedings as a result of improvements in the Court's funding situation allowing Cases 003, 004 and 004/2 to proceed. See ECCC Press Release, 'Co-Investigating Judges Issue Decision on the Impact of the Funding Situation on Cases 003, 004 And 004/2, 11 August 2017, <https://www.eccc.gov.kh/en/articles/co-investigating-judges-issue-decision-impact-funding-situation-cases-003-004-and-0042 > [accessed 10 December 2017].

6. Proceedings

1. INTRODUCTION

Everything that occurs formally before the Extraordinary Chambers in the Courts of Cambodia (ECCC) in accordance with its constitutive documents constitutes in a sense 'proceedings'. The term covers the entire investigation, trial and appeals process but also discrete matters, often concerning important procedural questions. This chapter serves to highlight certain categories of proceedings that have been of great consequence for the Court, testing its functionality and legitimacy. These include the severance and termination proceedings in Case 002, the disagreement proceedings under the special arrangements set out in the ECCC Law, ECCC Agreement and Internal Rules, the proceedings resulting from the numerous motions requesting the disqualification of judges, and proceedings relating to provisional detention and bail.

2. SEVERANCE OF CASE 002

The Trial Chamber issued its severance order on 22 September 2011 pursuant to Internal Rule 89 *ter*, limiting the scope of the first trial in Case 002 to factual allegations described in the Closing Order as movement of population (Phases One and Two) and crimes against humanity committed in their course.[1] A Decision on Reconsideration followed the initial Severance Order and the Trial Chamber subsequently issued a decision expanding the scope of Case 002/01 to include the executions of former Khmer Republic officials at Tuol Po Chrey as requested by the Co-Prosecutors, at the same time denying other requests for expansion of the case by the Co-Prosecutors.[2] The latter decision resulted in an 'immediate appeal' by the Co-Prosecutors pursuant to

---

[1] *Prosecutor v Nuon Chea, Ieng Sary, Ieng Thirith* and *Khieu Samphan*, ECCC Case File No. 002/19-09-2007-ECCC/TC, Trial Chamber, Severance Order pursuant to Internal Rule 89 *ter*, 22 September 2011, para. 5.

[2] *Prosecutor v Nuon Chea, Ieng Sary*, and *Khieu Samphan*, ECCC Document No. E163/5, Trial Chamber, Trial Chamber Memorandum Entitled 'Notification of Decision on Co-Prosecutions' Request to Include Additional Crime

Internal Rule 104(4) and while the Supreme Court Chamber found it to be admissible, it noted that 'the Impugned Decision is intrinsically linked to the Severance Order and Decision on Reconsideration and forms an episode in a year-long decision-making process that was marked by multiple pronouncements on the same matter in the same factual and legal circumstances'.[3] The Supreme Court Chamber's decision was rendered in February 2013 when proceedings in Case 002/01 were within weeks of the conclusion of the hearing of evidence.

Addressing the merits, the Supreme Court Chamber noted the exceptional nature of the type of severance of a case undertaken by the Trial Chamber:

> Considerations of efficiency and fairness lend support to the general principle, expressed in the laws applicable to the ECCC as well as in international criminal jurisdictions, that charges concerning similar events against several accused should preferably be tried in joint proceedings. Severance of a confirmed indictment is not foreseen under Cambodian law, and the ad hoc international criminal tribunals have been reluctant to grant severance requests. Where severance has been deemed necessary, it has characteristically involved separating an accused person from joint proceedings. As such, decisions on severance constitute exceptions to the general preference for joint trials.[4]

The Supreme Court Chamber also expressed concern over the fact that the parties had not been afforded the opportunity to be heard prior to the Trial Chamber making its decision as to severance, especially in the context of a case as large and complex as Case 002. Further, the Supreme Court Chamber was not just concerned, but 'alarmed' over the 'paucity of reasoning' in the original order, finding that the Trial Chamber had failed to explain how severance of the case 'advances the interest of justice' and that the brief comments provided did not 'satisfy the right to receive a reasoned decision'.[5] Consequently, the Supreme Court Chamber found that the Trial Chamber committed a discernible error in the exercise of its discretion as it had failed to demonstrate through adequate reasoning the

---

Sites within the Scope of Trial in Case 002/01 (E163) and Deadline for Submission of Applicable Law Portion of Closing Briefs', 8 October 2012, paras. 2–3.

[3] *Prosecutor v Nuon Chea, Ieng Sary*, and *Khieu Samphan*, ECCC Case File No. 002/19-09-2007-ECCC-TC/SC(18), Supreme Court Chamber, Decision on the Co-Prosecutors' Immediate Appeal of the Trial Chamber's Decision Concerning the Scope of Case 002/01, 8 February 2013, para. 37.

[4] Ibid, para. 33.

[5] Ibid, para. 41.

interest of justice served in severing the case, had denied the parties their right to be heard, had failed to consider how to render the scope of Case 002/01 reasonably representative of the Indictment and had not developed an adequate plan for handling the remaining sub-cases.[6] Although it declared the severance of Case 002 invalid and annulled the Impugned Decision, the Supreme Court Chamber recognised that severance might be justified and stated:

> Should the Trial Chamber continue to consider the interests of justice to require severance of Case 002, it must first invite the parties' submissions on the terms thereof, and only after all parties' respective interests are balanced against all relevant factors may a severance of Case 002 be soundly undertaken. It is necessary that the Trial Chamber determine, based on its organic familiarity with Case 002, whether the gist of such severance is in judicial manageability, in which case there is necessity for a tangible plan for the adjudication of the entirety of the charges in the Indictment, and not merely a portion thereof. If, however, faced with the deteriorating health of the Co-Accused, the principal motivation is that justice is better served by concluding with a judgement, whether in a conviction or acquittal, of at least one smaller trial on some portion of the Indictment, then the Trial Chamber should state this clearly and give due consideration to reasonable representativeness of the Indictment within the smaller trial(s).[7]

Two months later, having heard the parties,[8] the Trial Chamber issued a new, extensively reasoned decision on severance, limiting the scope of Case 002/01 to crimes against humanity committed during the course of movement of population (Phases One and Two), and the executions of Khmer Republic officials at Tuol Po Chrey, as envisaged in the original, expanded severance order.[9] The Trial Chamber reiterated and elaborated

---

[6] Ibid, paras. 44, 48–9.

[7] Ibid, para. 50.

[8] *Prosecutor v Nuon Chea, Ieng Sary*, and *Khieu Samphan*, ECCC Document No. E163/5/1/13/1, Trial Chamber memorandum entitled 'Directions to the parties in consequence of the Supreme Court Chamber's Decision on Co-Prosecutors' immediate appeal of the Trial Chamber's decision concerning the scope of Case 002/01 (E163/5/1/13)', 12 February 2013, para. 2: 'The immediate consequence of the SCC Decision is that Case 002 is no longer confined in scope and the Trial Chamber cannot presently proceed to a verdict in this case until all factual allegations and charges contained in the Case 002 Closing Order are adjudicated'.

[9] *Prosecutor v Nuon Chea* and *Khieu Samphan*, ECCC Case File No. 002/19-09-2007/ECCC/TC, Trial Chamber, Decision on Severance of Case 002/01 following Supreme Court Chamber Decision of 8 February 2013, 26 April 2013.

on its earlier view that it considered severance to be in the interests of justice because it

> might enable it to issue a multi-Accused verdict following a first trial based on a limited part of the Indictment, thereby 'safeguarding the fundamental interest of victims in achieving meaningful and timely justice [i.e. the rendering of any verdict], as well as the right of all Accused in Case 002 to an expeditious trial'.[10]

Further, the Trial Chamber rejected an application by Khieu Samphan for the severance of his case from that of the other accused, finding that Case 002/01 should continue as a multi-accused trial.[11] The Trial Chamber explained its own understanding of severance and why it was meaningless to speak of 'representative charges' in the ECCC context:

> Under the ECCC legal framework, the indictment is the result of a judicial decision and is final when the Trial Chamber is seised with it. The Co-Prosecutors have no power to withdraw any part of the Indictment and nor can the Trial Chamber use a severance order to reduce or expand the crimes charged. The only purpose of severance at the trial stage is to modify the way in which all charges in the Indictment are to be adjudicated. Charges which would normally be adjudicated in a single trial are separated, to be heard in two or more trials, but otherwise remain unchanged. Legally, severance is exclusively a trial management tool and in the absence of a mechanism for the withdrawal of any charges in the Indictment, all charges will be adjudicated unless an Accused becomes unfit to stand trial or proceedings are terminated by his death.[12]

Nevertheless, the Trial Chamber attempted to construe a workable idea of 'representativeness' applicable in the ECCC context from the jurisprudence of ad hoc tribunals such as the International Criminal Tribunal for the former Yugoslavia (ICTY). It found that the severed Case 002/01 met the criterion of 'reasonable representativeness' of the Case 002 Closing Order in that it covered two of the five main themes in the Closing Order, namely forced movement and execution of purported enemies of the regime while also reflecting the alleged criminality of the policies of the DK regime, incorporating a significant portion of the Closing Order's geographical range and a large percentage of the victimised Cambodian population.[13] Finally, the Co-Prosecutors would be able 'to place these

---

[10] Ibid, para. 8.
[11] Ibid, para. 93.
[12] Ibid, para. 98.
[13] Ibid, para. 118.

offences within the broader context of the joint criminal enterprise in which all Accused are alleged to have participated'.[14] The Trial Chamber concluded that the addition of S-21 to Case 002/01 as urged by the Co-Prosecutors was not essential to ensure representativeness. The Trial Chamber went on to set out the following factors as being relevant to its decision on severance:

(1) the advanced age and physical frailty of the remaining Case 002 Accused;
(2) the public interest in achieving a verdict in relation to at least a portion of the Case 002 Closing Order;
(3) judicial manageability of Case 002/01 in the light of the late stage of trial, including possible prejudice to the Accused that may stem from further expansion of its scope;
(4) the uncertain impact upon the length of proceedings in Case 002/01 should S-21 be added to its scope; and
(5) uncertainty regarding the duration of financial support to the ECCC.[15]

The Trial Chamber analysed each factor in turn and, noting that 'expeditiousness and representativeness are competing considerations', it found that the balance fell in favour of severance without expanding the severed case to include S-21. It declined to set out a precise plan in respect of the remaining charges in Case 002 which were unaffected by the decision.

The Co-Prosecutors and Nuon Chea each filed immediate appeals against the Trial Chamber's 'Second Decision on Severance', both of which were deemed admissible by the Supreme Court Chamber. The Supreme Court Chamber indicated that the Trial Chamber should have sought guidance in procedural rules established at the international level to determining the scope of its discretion under Internal Rule 89 *ter*. Following its own analysis of the position at the international level, the Supreme Court Chamber concluded:

> First, notwithstanding a breadth of discretion vested in a trial court (including the Italian system which favours severance as soon as there is a charge ready for adjudication), a decision on severance of cases is not arbitrary but norm-based and involves balancing different interests rooted in human rights and principles of efficiency. Specific concerns of expeditious proceedings are generally not addressed by adjudicating materially-related charges through multiple trials. Consequently, the effects of severance are assessed in relation to the entirety of charges so reconfigured and not just a portion thereof. As such, where severance is ordered, the status of the entirety of charges

---

14 Ibid, para. 118.
15 Ibid, para. 125.

> encompassed by the indictment is resolved and no criminal procedure that observes the right to a speedy trial and the principle of efficiency permits leaving any severed portion unattended. Rather, depending on factual circumstances and legal ramifications, the separated cases either proceed, or are suspended or dismissed.[16]

According to the Supreme Court Chamber, the Trial Chamber had only carried out the required balancing exercise to a very limited extent when it discussed its five proposed factors and found the fifth factor relating to the ECCC's financial status to be irrelevant to a consideration of the matters at hand. Nevertheless, the Supreme Court Chamber found that the Trial Chamber's repeatedly stated goal in renewing the severance of Case 002, namely to preserve its ability to reach *any* (timely) verdict in the light of the advanced age and physical frailty of the surviving accused, did not constitute an unreasonable exercise of discretion in the circumstances.[17]

The Supreme Court Chamber did not agree with the Trial Chamber that it was meaningless to talk of the representativeness of charges in the ECCC context, finding instead that this was an area in which applying the French/Cambodian principle of legalism (mandatory prosecution) was inappropriate. The ECCC structure required the exercise of prosecutorial and judicial discretion to determine who fell within the Court's personal jurisdiction and whose prosecution would meet the concerns of the international community and contribute to peace and national reconciliation.[18] According to the Supreme Court Chamber:

> The overarching goal of the representativeness criterion is thus to select a minimum quantum of charges that would reasonably reflect the scale and nature of the totality of the alleged criminal acts and individual culpability. As such, underlying the criterion of representativeness is the assumption that the proceedings on the retained charges are capable of bringing about an institutional response that is as relevant to the broad goals of criminal justice as proceedings on the original charges would have been.[19]

The Trial Chamber was found to have erred in law and in the exercise of its discretion by claiming at one and the same time that Case 002 had to

---

[16] *Prosecutor v Nuon Chea* and *Khieu Samphan*, ECCC Case File No. 002/19-09-2007-ECCC-TC/SC(28), Supreme Court Chamber, Decision on Immediate Appeals Against Trial Chamber's Second Decision on Severance of Case 002, 25 November 2013, para. 43.

[17] Ibid, para. 50.

[18] Ibid, para. 61.

[19] Ibid, para. 64.

be severed in the interests of securing at least one timely verdict within the lifespan of the accused, and that the outstanding charges remained active for adjudication in subsequent trials.[20] While the Supreme Court Chamber expressed strong disapproval of the Trial Chamber's reasoning and approach to severance throughout the trial, in order to avoid further inevitable delay it denied the Co-Prosecutors' request to include S-21 in Case 002/01 and Nuon Chea's request to include facts relating to genocide, a cooperative and a worksite. Since the Trial Chamber had not set out its plan for addressing these charges in subsequent proceedings, the Supreme Court Chamber exercised its corrective jurisdiction to indicate that these charges must form the basis of Case 002/02 and that the latter case must commence as soon as possible after the end of closing submissions in Case 002/01.

When it became clear that there would indeed be a trial in Case 002/02, the Trial Chamber decided to further sever Case 002 and reduce the scope of the second case.[21] The Trial Chamber summarised the applicable law on severance as requiring an evaluation of 'legitimate interests rooted in human rights and principles of efficiency', including any potential prejudice to the accused's rights, the efficiency and manageability of the proceedings, avoiding inconsistencies between separate trials, the potential burden on witnesses, and ensuring at least a portion of the charges are adjudicated within the lifespan of frail accused.[22] The Trial Chamber recognised that in defining the scope of the severed trial, it needed to balance the requirements that the trial be both fair and expeditious and 'reasonably representative' of the Closing Order, considering factors such as:

> (i) the crimes charged in the Closing Order; (ii) the classification and nature of the crimes; (iii) the places where the crimes are alleged to have been committed; (iv) the scale of the crimes; (v) the victims of the crimes charged;

---

[20] Ibid, para. 65.

[21] *Prosecutor v Nuon Chea* and *Khieu Samphan*, ECCC Case File No. 002/19-09-2007-ECCC/TC, Trial Chamber, Decision on Additional Severance of Case 002 and Scope of Case 002/02, 4 April 2014, paras. 17, 30, 32, 38 (The decision was upheld by the Supreme Court Chamber: *Prosecutor v Nuon Chea* and *Khieu Samphan*, ECCC Case File No. 002/19-09-2007-ECCC-TC/SC(29), Supreme Court Chamber, Decision on Khieu Samphan's Immediate Appeal against the Trial Chamber's Decision on Additional Severance of Case 002 and Scope of Case 002/02, 29 July 2014, para. 91.)

[22] *Prosecutor v Nuon Chea* and *Khieu Samphan*, ECCC Case File No. 002/19-09-2007-ECCC/TC, Trial Chamber, Decision on Additional Severance of Case 002 and Scope of Case 002/02, 4 April 2014, para. 13.

> (vi) the time period of the crimes charged; and (vii) the fundamental nature of the case.[23]

Under the heading 'Rights of the Accused', the Trial Chamber made the following comment:

> The argument that severance of trials would necessarily create undue delay is not borne out by the experience of Case 002. As noted by the Chamber from the outset of the trial, Case 002/01 will serve as a foundation for a more detailed examination of the remaining charges and factual allegations against the Accused in later trials. By relying on this foundation, Case 002/02 will be streamlined and ensure its expeditious completion. For example, consideration of the admissibility of evidence in Case 002/01 was a time and resource intensive process. The Trial Chamber has clarified that evidence already put before the Chamber in Case 002/01 will be maintained in Case 002/02. This will establish certain efficiencies as the amount of court time and resources necessary to repeat such procedures will therefore be limited in each subsequent trial phase. Furthermore, certain witnesses relevant to the totality of Case 002 were heard in Case 002/01. While the Trial Chamber will make an assessment on a case by case basis, this will reduce the need for certain witnesses to be recalled during subsequent phases of Case 002.[24]

This paragraph rang alarm bells for the Supreme Court Chamber in its consideration of an appeal brought by Khieu Samphan that otherwise endorsed the further severance of Case 002 along the lines proposed by the Trial Chamber (which in any case went beyond the minimum set of charges that the Supreme Court Chamber had ordered to be included in Case 002/01).[25]

In view of the fact that this constituted the third appeal on the issue of severance, the Supreme Court Chamber first launched into an extensive clarification of the nature of severance. In simple terms, severance under Internal Rule 89 *ter* meant a split of the proceedings, whether it involved splitting the accused or the charges and resulted procedurally in the creation of separate and distinct trials.[26] Notably, it assumed divisibility of the case, so that problems related to actual or perceived bias would not

---

23 Ibid, para. 14.

24 Ibid, para. 23.

25 *Prosecutor v Nuon Chea* and *Khieu Samphan*, ECCC Case File No. 002/19-09-2007-ECCC-TC/SC(29), Supreme Court Chamber, Decision on Khieu Samphan's Immediate Appeal against the Trial Chamber's Decision on Additional Severance of Case 002 and Scope of Case 002/02, 29 July 2014, paras. 53–5.

26 Ibid, paras. 42, 70.

arise in subsequent cases concerning related facts.[27] On the question of the risk of delay raised by Khieu Samphan, the Supreme Court Chamber found that both the international jurisprudence and common sense supported 'the factual presumption that a series of severed trials would take longer to adjudicate than a single joint trial'.[28] The core question, however, was whether the predictable delay would be 'undue' and in considering this question the Supreme Court Chamber accepted that the Trial Chamber could prioritise the interest of obtaining a verdict within the lifespan of the co-accused, civil parties and victims in respect of a reasonably representative range of charges.[29] More troublesome were the Trial Chamber's alternate references to 'separate and distinct trials' and 'manageable phases of a single trial' and what this meant in terms of the use of the evidence led in Case 002/01, and factual findings thereon, in Case 002/02.[30] The Supreme Court Chamber observed that although 'evidence remains formally common to the severed cases, this commonality does not extend to findings, and common factual elements in all cases resulting from Case 002 must be established anew'.[31]

In its initial decision, the Supreme Court Chamber had advocated for the establishment by the ECCC of a second trial panel to support the timely adjudication of the remainder of Case 002 in the event of a new severance decision and to alleviate any potential concerns relating to actual or perceived bias of judges arising from the same panel hearing the first and subsequent trials.[32] No party appearing before the Trial Chamber considered this suggestion to be viable.[33] In its second decision, the Supreme Court Chamber stated its view more forcefully that the establishment of a second trial panel was not only practically and financially feasible but had also become imperative. In the event, no such panel was ever established. Having explored the possibility, the President of the Trial Chamber concluded that it was unclear whether legally he had the

---

27 Ibid, para. 45.
28 Ibid, para. 51.
29 Ibid, paras. 55, 62.
30 Ibid, paras. 71–2.
31 Ibid, para. 85.
32 Ibid, para. 51.
33 *Prosecutor v Nuon Chea* and *Khieu Samphan*, ECCC Case File No. 002/19-09-2007/ECCC/TC, Trial Chamber, Decision on Severance of Case 002/01 following Supreme Court Chamber Decision of 8 February 2013, 26 April 2013, para. 84.

power to appoint a second Trial Chamber.[34] Furthermore, he found that it would not be in the interests of justice to appoint new judges and staff since in all likelihood, taking into account a string of practical considerations, this would be less expeditious than proceeding with a single Trial Chamber.[35] In the light of this, the Supreme Court Chamber could only 'assume that the Trial Chamber will not make findings in Case 002/01 which would evince attributing criminal responsibility to the Co-Accused in relation to charges to be adjudicated in subsequent cases'.[36]

The Trial Chamber was clearly in an unenviable position, conducting a trial with elderly and ailing accused, a vast array of facts presented in the Closing Order and pressure from both within and outside the ECCC to proceed expeditiously in the interests of both justice and economy. The Trial Chamber illustrated the scale of the task by citing some facts and figures on witness numbers and noting that the Closing Order was composed of 1624 paragraphs, only 477 of which were included within Case 002/01. In view of the length of the proceedings up to the point of closing arguments in Case 002/01, it seemed impossible for the remainder of Case 002/02 to be heard without further severance.[37] While the judges appeared willing to think creatively and should be commended for exploring the idea of severance, they were at the same time boxed in by their respect based on Cambodian (and French) law for the authority of the Closing Order and related procedures. They were therefore reluctant at an early stage to select representative facts, preferring to start with a segment at the beginning of the Closing Order while recognising that subsequent mini-trials might never become a reality.

The Supreme Court Chamber realised that the normal civil law procedures did not fit the extraordinary circumstances presented and

---

34 *Prosecutor v Nuon Chea* and *Khieu Samphan*, ECCC Document No. E301/4, Trial Chamber Memorandum Entitled 'President's Memorandum on the Proposal to Appoint a Second Panel of the Trial Chamber to Try the Remaining Charges in Case 002', 20 December 2013, para. 3.

35 Ibid, para. 10.

36 *Prosecutor v Nuon Chea* and *Khieu Samphan*, ECCC Case File No. 002/19-09-2007-ECCC-TC/SC(29), Supreme Court Chamber, Decision on Khieu Samphan's Immediate Appeal against the Trial Chamber's Decision on Additional Severance of Case 002 and Scope of Case 002/02, 29 July 2014, para. 85.

37 *Prosecutor v Nuon Chea* and *Khieu Samphan*, ECCC Case File No. 002/19-09-2007-ECCC/TC, Trial Chamber, Decision on Additional Severance of Case 002 and Scope of Case 002/02, 4 April 2014, para. 27.

preferred to seek guidance in the procedural rules established at the international level. The judges were able to take a more global view of the implications of the Trial Chamber's decision for the next phase of the proceedings, warning of future obstacles which the Trial Chamber seemed to put off or ignore. Had the Supreme Court Chamber been able to reach its first decision more quickly, it might have had a greater influence on the Trial Chamber. Proceedings were too far advanced by early 2013 for the Trial Chamber to be expected to backtrack on its outline for a soon to be completed sub-case even if technically, until severance became final, Case 002/01 was not separated from Case 002. The need for the Trial Chamber to re-argue its case for severance cost it extra time and even so, it failed to project a vision for further sub-cases. From an outside perspective, it seemed logical to include S-21 in Case 002/01 to obtain a fuller picture of events in this security centre after the *Duch* case and, in particular, to discover the details of Nuon Chea's involvement.[38] Given the fears at the time that there would be no trial in Case 002/02, let alone a trial judgment or final judgment on appeal, it also made sense to include representative facts relating to genocide, a cooperative and a worksite as proposed by Nuon Chea. However, the Supreme Court Chamber had little choice but to deny these requests when the trial in Case 002/01 had effectively concluded.

The severance decision had various consequences for the factual and legal findings in Case 002/01. On appeal, Nuon Chea argued that the Trial Chamber 'made numerous findings concerning facts and policies outside the scope of Case 002/01'.[39] The Supreme Court Chamber found that the Trial Chamber had a discretion to determine which facts were relevant for determining the charges at hand, even if they might also relate to other charges and this was true of the five Communist Party of Kampuchea (CPK) policies identified in the Closing Order which were not 'clearly distinguishable and mutually exclusive; rather, they are means to structure the analysis of the implementation of the socialist revolution in Cambodia.'[40] Similarly, the severance did not curtail the

---

[38] R. Pran and C. Bataille, *The Elimination: A Survivor of the Khmer Rouge Confronts His Past and the Commandant of the Killing Fields* (translated by J. Cullen, New York, Other Press, 2012), p. 94 (Rithy Panh comments that there are 'hundreds of confessions that bear the following annotation, handwritten by Duch: "to be submitted to Comrade Nuon Chea"').

[39] *Prosecutor v Nuon Chea* and *Khieu Samphan*, ECCC Case File No. 002/19-09-2007-ECCC/SC, Supreme Court Chamber, Appeal Judgment, 23 November 2016, para. 222 ('Nuon Appeal Judgment').

[40] Ibid, para. 227.

Trial Chamber's competence to consider events predating or postdating the charges that might be relevant to establishing the facts underlying the charges, a pattern of conduct, or the accused's mental state at the time of the offence.[41] The Supreme Court Chamber emphasised, however, that 'the Trial Chamber was, in any event, prohibited from attributing criminal responsibility for crimes that fell outside the scope of the charges in Case 002/01'.[42]

A further consequence concerns the approach to be taken to the allegation of an overarching joint criminal enterprise covering all the facts in Case 002. The Trial Chamber was able to address this in Case 002/01 by focusing on only two of the five CPK policies, although separating out interconnected policies in this way presented a challenge even in the first sub-case. The Supreme Court Chamber had repeatedly drawn attention to the 'inappropriateness of treating findings from one case as the "foundation" for another'.[43] This effectively required a fresh start to the establishment of a joint criminal enterprise in Case 002/02.

As a result of the severance saga (and at the initiation of the Co-Prosecutors), the plenary of judges adopted Internal Rule 89 *quater* concerning the reduction of the scope of the trial, drawing directly from the jurisprudence and especially the Supreme Court Chamber's opinions.

3. REDUCTION OF THE SCOPE OF CASE 002

The Co-Prosecutors invoked Internal Rule 89 *quater* to request the termination of the proceedings concerning the facts in the Case 002 Closing Order that had not been covered by Cases 002/01 and 002/02. The Supreme Court Chamber had previously declared a provisional stay of any charges relating to these facts pending appropriate disposal of them by the Trial Chamber. In interpreting Internal Rule 89 *quater*, the Trial Chamber was guided by the Supreme Court Chamber's advice in relation to severance that a balance had to be struck between the interests of a fair and expeditious trial and the need to ensure that the trial is 'reasonably representative' of the indictment.[44] The Trial Chamber was

41 Ibid, paras. 236, 908.

42 Ibid, para. 227.

43 Ibid, para. 228.

44 *Prosecutor v Nuon Chea* and *Khieu Samphan*, ECCC Case File No. 002/19-09-2007/ECCC/TC, Trial Chamber, Decision on Reduction of the Scope of Case 002, 27 February 2017, para. 17.

satisfied that all legal counts in the Closing Order had been covered as well as the most significant events in diverse geographical areas, which 'reasonably reflect the totality of the alleged criminal acts and individual culpability of the Accused'.[45] Paying particular attention to the interests of civil parties who would be directly affected by a termination of proceedings because they suffered harm as a result of the conduct falling outside the scope of Cases 002/01 and 002/02, the Trial Chamber found that a termination 'would objectively be in the interests of a fair, meaningful and expeditious judicial process for the consolidated group of Civil Parties'.[46] Moreover, this would not preclude those civil parties from benefiting from reparations for the benefit of the consolidated group of civil parties. The Trial Chamber therefore decided to exclude the outstanding facts and terminate proceedings in Case 002.

4. THE FIRST DISAGREEMENT PROCEEDINGS

In the early stages of the ECCC proceedings it might have been hoped that the disagreement provisions in the Court's constitutional documents would be dead letters in view of what appeared to be determined and effective cooperation between the two Co-Prosecutors and the two Co-Investigating Judges and their teams. It has been noted that: 'It is commonplace for the staff of any prosecution office to disagree over whom to charge and what charges to file in a given case.'[47] The ECCC negotiators must have predicted that the ECCC's Office of the Co-Prosecutors would be no ordinary prosecution office and that a certain category of disagreement might have to be settled by outside intervention. With hindsight, it appears quite crafty to have designed the system so that the failure by the Pre-Trial Chamber (PTC), one of whose main functions it is to hear disagreement cases, to reach a super-majority would result in the proposed action at the heart of the dispute proceeding. While crafty in one sense, however, the system is also designed so that a genuine deadlock between national and international actors simply endures with potentially serious consequences for the legitimacy of the institution.

---

45 Ibid, para. 18.

46 Ibid, para. 20.

47 G. Townsend, 'Structure and Management', in L. Reydams, J. Wouters, and C. Ryngaert (eds), *International Prosecutors* (Oxford, Oxford University Press, 2012), pp. 171–318, p. 306.

On 8 December 2008, the Co-Prosecutors filed a statement of disagreement in accordance with Internal Rule 71(2) and forwarded it to the Office of Administration for adjudication by the PTC.[48] The disagreement concerned the appropriateness of opening new judicial investigations into crimes alleged to have been committed by certain other senior leaders of the Khmer Rouge or persons most responsible for crimes under that regime. In a subsequent statement, the International Co-Prosecutor gave three reasons for wanting to proceed with the new Introductory Submissions, namely (1) that the crimes described in those submissions were committed, (2) those crimes were within the jurisdiction of the ECCC, and (3) they should be investigated by the Co-Investigating Judges.[49] Further, he expressed his belief that this last set of cases would lead to a more comprehensive accounting for the crimes committed during the Khmer Rouge regime and that he did not believe that such prosecutions would endanger Cambodia's peace and stability. The National Co-Prosecutor took the view that the cases should not proceed on account of Cambodia's past instability and the ongoing need for national reconciliation, the spirit of the ECCC Law and ECCC Agreement, and the limited duration and budget of the Court. While disagreement proceedings are by their nature confidential, the Office of the Co-Prosecutors (OCP) continued to issue press releases to keep the public informed of developments and the international Co-Prosecutor requested that any hearing be held at least partially in public.[50]

The PTC decided not to hold a hearing on the matter, finding that it was sufficiently informed by the written submissions. As a preliminary issue, the PTC commented on the fact that the Co-Prosecutors had issued a series of press statements concerning their disagreement which had

---

[48] 'Statement of the Co-Prosecutors', Extraordinary Chambers in the Courts of Cambodia, 8 December 2008, <https://www.eccc.gov.kh/sites/default/files/media/Statement_of_Co_Prosecutors.pdf> [accessed 19 June 2017].

[49] 'Statement of the Co-Prosecutors', Extraordinary Chambers in the Courts of Cambodia, 5 January 2009, <https://www.eccc.gov.kh/sites/default/files/media/Statement_OCP_05-01-09_EN.pdf> [accessed 19 June 2017].

[50] 'Press Statement of the International Co-Prosecutor', Extraordinary Chambers in the Courts of Cambodia, 24 April 2009, <https://www.eccc.gov.kh/sites/default/files/media/Statement_co_prosecutors_En.pdf> [accessed 19 June 2017]. *See* also 'Statement of the Co-Prosecutors', Extraordinary Chambers in the Courts of Cambodia, 8 December 2008, <https://www.eccc.gov.kh/sites/default/files/media/Statement_of_Co_Prosecutors.pdf> [accessed 19 June 2017]; 'Statement of the Co-Prosecutors', Extraordinary Chambers in the Courts of Cambodia, 5 January 2009, <https://www.eccc.gov.kh/sites/default/files/media/Statement_OCP_05-01-09_EN.pdf> [accessed 19 June 2017].

generated a significant amount of public interest and threatened to undermine the ordinarily confidential disagreement settlement process. However, the PTC recommended the publication of a redacted version of its own findings, taking the view that this would not have an adverse impact on the confidentiality of the investigation.[51] Having been unable to reach an affirmative vote of at least four judges, the PTC issued its 'considerations' on the Co-Prosecutors' disagreement on 18 August 2009, containing joint reasons on the scope of the PTC's review followed by the separate reasons of the international judges and the national judges on the disagreement itself.[52]

The PTC found that the scope of its review was limited to settling the specific issues upon which the Co-Prosecutors disagreed and that it should only consider the facts and reasons raised before it.[53] In view of the fact that the new Introductory Submissions would be forwarded to the Co-Investigating Judges unless at least four judges of the PTC were satisfied that the arguments raised by the National Co-Prosecutor precluded such action, the PTC found that the burden of persuasion was on the National Co-Prosecutor and her arguments should be the main focus of the examination. Indeed, the PTC noted that under normal circumstances the disagreement should have been filed by the National Co-Prosecutor who objected to the decision to file new submissions, rather than by the International Co-Prosecutor who could have proceeded with his proposed action under the ECCC Agreement and ECCC Law after giving 30-day notice to the National Co-Prosecutor.[54]

Judges Prak Kimsan, Ney Thol and Huot Vuthy took the view first, that the preparation of the Second and Third Introductory Submissions was undertaken unilaterally by the International Co-Prosecutor without any discussion with the National Co-Prosecutor, contrary to the ECCC Law, ECCC Agreement and Internal Rules; and second, that the facts and offences described in the Second and Third Introductory Submissions were already covered by the First Introductory Submission and that there was no need to issue the new submissions while the investigation into Case 002 was still ongoing. Judges Lahuis and Downing presented their views on the same two points, finding that the National Co-Prosecutor

---

51 ECCC Case File No. 001/18-11-2008-ECCC/PTC, Pre-Trial Chamber, Considerations of the Pre-Trial Chamber Regarding the Disagreement Between the Co-Prosecutors Pursuant to Internal Rule 71, 18 August 2009, paras. 46–53.

52 Ibid, para. 44.

53 Ibid, para. 24.

54 Ibid, para. 27 (referring to Articles 6(1) and (4) of the Agreement and Articles 16 and 20 (new) 3 of the ECCC Law).

raised the issue of not being informed about the new submissions at a late stage in the disagreement proceedings and it was not an argument that should be considered part of those proceedings; and second, that since the facts set out in the Introductory and Supplementary Submissions define the scope of the judicial investigation, which is supported by the ECCC practice of issuing forwarding orders and supplementary submissions, it would not be correct to say that the First Introductory Submission covered all crimes committed in Cambodia during the ECCC's temporal jurisdiction. Further, while the new submissions contained some facts that overlapped with the earlier submissions, they also contained new facts that could not be investigated in the absence of a new Introductory Submission. The international judges added that in their opinion no discretion could be exercised by the Co-Prosecutors under Internal Rule 53(1) so that if there was reason to believe that crimes within the jurisdiction of the ECCC had been committed, then the Co-Prosecutors were obliged to open a judicial investigation by filing an Introductory Submission.[55] The international judges also debated whether or not the Co-Prosecutors could have proceeded by filing a Supplementary Submission in Case 002 rather than two new Introductory Submissions. They concluded that the new submissions were the proper course, considering that Case 002 had been under investigation for a considerable period of time with four suspects already in custody and that adding new facts would have negative implications for both the existing and new suspects. As the international judges found it futile to provide further reasoning on other aspects of the disagreement, the issue of whether the new suspects came within the ECCC's personal jurisdiction, which later became a core focus of the disagreement, remained up in the air.

5. SUBSEQUENT DISAGREEMENT PROCEEDINGS

The disagreement procedure failed to prove its mettle in the case concerning the Co-Prosecutors. Instead, it simply served to reinforce a growing divide between the international and national judicial officers. It was little surprise that an attempt in early 2012 by the Reserve Co-Investigating Judge, Laurent Kasper-Ansermet, to bring disagreements relating to Cases 003 and 004 before the PTC led to even greater controversy. The Presiding Judge of the PTC, Judge Prak Kimsan, returned the files containing the substance of the disagreement to the

---

55 Ibid, para. 23.

Office of Administration, claiming that Judge Kasper-Ansermet lacked the competence to take any judicial action as he had not been officially nominated by the Supreme Council of the Magistracy of the Kingdom of Cambodia.[56] A subsequent application by Judge Kasper-Ansermet to disqualify Judge Prak Kimsan was 'ruled out' on the same basis.

The two international judges, Judges Rowan Downing and Chang-Ho Chung, nevertheless decided that the PTC was seized of two disagreements between the Reserve Co-Investigating Judge and the National Investigating Judge pursuant to Internal Rule 72. The first concerned the proposal by the Reserve Co-Investigating Judge to issue an order to resume the judicial investigation in Case 003. In their reasoned considerations, the international judges noted that the PTC had not attained the required majority of four affirmative votes in order to reach a decision as to whether or not Judge Kasper-Ansermet had standing to file a disagreement and had adjourned deliberations on the substance of the disagreement.[57] However, according to the international judges, after further inconclusive deliberations, the Presiding Judge of the PTC returned the disagreement file to the Office of the Administration without informing the international judges, treating it as an administrative matter. As a result, finding that questions of admissibility were legal and not administrative matters in the practice of the PTC and being mindful of their ethical duties, the international judges felt compelled to provide a reasoned consideration of the matter. The international judges found that Judge Kasper-Ansermet was validly appointed and exercising his functions as Reserve Co-Investigative Judge and therefore had standing to bring the disagreement.[58] On the merits, they found that Judge Kasper-Ansermet's actions were legally valid until the appointment of a new Co-Investigating Judge and that his power to continue to perform regular

---

[56] 'Clarification of the National Judges of the Pre-Trial Chamber on the Note of Mr. Laurent Kasper-Ansermet, D38, dated 21 March 2012', Extraordinary Chambers in the Courts of Cambodia, 28 March 2012, <https://www.eccc.gov.kh/en/articles/clarification-national-judges-pre-trial-chamber-note-mr-laurent-kasper-ansermet-d38-dated-2> [accessed 19 June 2017].

[57] ECCC Case File No. 003/16-12-2011-ECCC/PTC, Pre-Trial Chamber, Opinion of Pre-Trial Chamber Judges Downing and Chung on the Disagreement between the Co-Investigating Judges pursuant to Internal Rule 72, 10 February 2012, para. 14.

[58] Ibid, para. 39.

duties included the reconsideration of previous decisions including the closure of an investigation provided the test for reconsideration was met.[59]

The second disagreement concerned the proposal by the Reserve Co-Investigating Judge to issue a rogatory letter on the continuation of the judicial investigation in Case 004. The international PTC Judges disposed of it in a similar manner to the first case, except that their conclusion on the merits was simply a reiteration of the default position in case of the failure to reach a super-majority decision on a disagreement, namely that the proposed rogatory letter shall be executed.[60]

6. DISQUALIFICATION PROCEEDINGS

The judges of the ECCC are required to be 'persons of high moral character, impartiality and integrity', who are 'independent in the performance of their functions', and they 'shall not accept or seek instructions from any Government or any other source'.[61] The ECCC Code of Judicial Ethics adopted by the Plenary in 2008 provides in relevant part:

> Article 1. Judicial independence
>
> 1. Judges shall uphold the independence of their office and the authority of the Extraordinary Chambers in the Courts of Cambodia (hereinafter referred to as ECCC) and shall conduct themselves accordingly in carrying out their judicial functions.
> 2. Judges shall not engage in any activity which is likely to interfere with their judicial functions or to affect confidence in their independence.
>
> Article 2. Impartiality
>
> 1. Judges shall be impartial and ensure the appearance of impartiality in the discharge of their judicial functions.
> 2. Judges shall avoid any conflict of interest, or being placed in a situation which might reasonably be perceived as giving rise to a conflict of interest.[62]

---

[59] Ibid, para. 47.

[60] Ibid, para. 38.

[61] ECCC Agreement, Article 3. (This is echoed and supplemented by ECCC Law, Article 10: 'shall have high moral character, a spirit of impartiality and integrity, and experience.')

[62] Code of Judicial Ethics, Articles 1, 2.

The Code goes on to describe the ethical duties of integrity, confidentiality and diligence, and to set out standards relating to conduct during proceedings, public expression and association, and extra-judicial activity. The principles embodied in the Code serve as guidelines only and there is no enforcement mechanism as such.

The Pre-Trial Chamber, Trial Chamber (including specially constituted panels) and Supreme Court Chamber have been seized with at least 14 applications for the disqualification of individual judges or entire benches based on real or perceived bias.[63] A fair amount of judicial attention has therefore been given to a consideration of Internal Rule 34 on 'Recusal and Disqualification of Judges', the core provision of which states:

> Any party may file an application for disqualification of a judge in any case in which the Judge has a personal or financial interest or concerning which the Judge has, or has had, any association which objectively might affect his or her impartiality, or objectively give rise to the appearance of bias.[64]

Rule 34 sets out detailed procedures for disqualification, including that the applicant shall clearly indicate the grounds and provide supporting evidence, and shall file the application as soon as he or she becomes aware of the grounds in question. The admissibility of the application depends on the observance of time limits, for example, if the disqualification of a Co-Investigating Judge is sought, the application must be made before the Closing Order, and if the issue relates to a Trial Chamber judge, the cut-off point is the initial hearing for matters arising before the trial, and the final judgment for matters arising during trial. If the application relates to a Co-Investigating judge it shall be submitted to the PTC, otherwise it is heard before the Chamber in which the judge in

---

[63] For an overview of the jurisprudence up to January 2015, *see* S.M. Torrens, 'Allegations of Political Interference, Bias and Corruption', in S.M. Meisenberg and I. Stegmiller (eds), *The Extraordinary Chambers in the Courts of Cambodia: Assessing their Contribution to International Criminal Law* (The Hague, T.M.C. Asser Press, 2016), pp. 45–75, pp. 52–64. Also, G.G. Escolar, 'Commentary by Gérardine Goh Escolar' in A. Klip and S. Freeland (eds), *Annotated Leading Cases of International Criminal Tribunals – Volume 43: Extraordinary Chambers in the Courts of Cambodia 2007-2010* (Antwerp/New York, Intersentia, 2015), pp. 693–702, p. 693; S. Forder, 'Commentary by Susan Forder' in A. Klip and S. Freeland (eds), *Annotated Leading Cases of International Criminal Tribunals – Volume 44: Extraordinary Chambers in the Courts of Cambodia 11 December 2009 – 23 March 2011* (Antwerp/New York, Intersentia, 2015), pp. 134–8, p. 134.

[64] Internal Rules, Rule 34(2).

question is sitting. Reserve judges may replace the judge whose disqualification is sought for the sole purpose of hearing the application. If the disqualification of more than one member of the Chamber is at issue the Judicial Administration Committee may choose additional judges from amongst the ECCC judges to form a panel. The judge who is the target of the application may submit written submissions to the Chamber or special panel of the Chamber. There is no possibility of appeal against the decision in disqualification cases.

In the event of multiple disqualifications, new judges may be appointed under the relevant ECCC procedures. So far, however, none of the disqualification applications has succeeded. Judge Ney Thol of the PTC, who has been President of the Cambodian Military Court since 1987, recused himself from participation in Duch's appeal against his provisional detention. He went on to recuse himself from the Co-Prosecutors' appeal of the Closing Order against Duch.[65] Although no reasons are given in the judge's letter to the Chamber, it might be assumed that he was concerned about the appearance of bias in view of his role on the Cambodian Military Court and Duch's lengthy prior detention at the hands of the local authorities.

The first formal application for disqualification to be considered before the PTC concerned Judge Ney Thol's participation in Nuon Chea's appeal against his provisional detention. Elaborating on the test for bias contained in Article 34(2), the PTC distinguished actual bias and perceived bias, referred to the presumption of impartiality recognised internationally and domestically, and adopted the standard of a 'reasonable observer' who would be: 'an informed person, with knowledge of all of the relevant circumstances, including the traditions of integrity and impartiality that form a part of the background and appraised also of the fact that impartiality is one of the duties that Judges swear to uphold.'[66]

The PTC applied the same test in dismissing applications by Ieng Sary and Khieu Samphan to disqualify the international Co-Investigating

---

[65] *Prosecutor v Kaing Guek Eav alias 'Duch'*, ECCC Case File No. 001/18-07-2007-ECCC/OCIJ(PTC02), Pre-Trial Chamber, Notification of Recusal of Judge Ney Thol, 13 October 2008, para. 2.

[66] *Prosecutor v Nuon Chea* ECCC Case File No. 002/19-09-2007-ECCC/OCIJ(PTC01), Pre-Trial Chamber, Decision on the Co-Lawyers' Urgent Application for the Disqualification of Judge Ney Thol Pending the Appeal against the Provisional Detention Order in the Case of Nuon Chea, 4 February 2008, para. 21 (citing *Prosecutor v Furundžija*, ICTY Case No. IT-95-17/1-A, Appeals Chamber, Judgment, 21 July 2000, para. 190).

Judge, Marcel Lemonde.[67] In those decisions, reference was also made to the Code of Judicial Ethics of the ECCC and the Bangalore Principles of Judicial Conduct as standard-setting documents.[68] The basis for the alleged bias was a meeting in which Judge Lemonde had, according to one witness, expressed a preference for finding more inculpatory than exculpatory evidence. Ieng Sary's defence lawyers returned to this issue in a subsequent application to disqualify Judge Lemonde as a sanction pursuant to Internal Rule 35 based on an alleged interference in the administration of justice. The PTC found the application to be inadmissible as it could find no procedural rules at the domestic or international level to support the idea of a Chamber having jurisdiction to address disciplinary matters in respect of ECCC judges.[69] This decision was followed by one rejecting an application by Ieng Sary and Ieng Thirith for the disqualification of Judge Lemonde under Rule 34.[70]

The disqualification of the Cambodian Co-Investigating Judge, Judge You Bunleng, was subsequently sought by Nuon Chea on the basis of alleged political interference in certain of the Co-Investigating Judge's decisions. The PTC found that the evidence presented did not establish that Judge You Bunleng had acted or given the appearance of having acted without independence or impartiality.[71] Ieng Sary made a request pursuant to Internal Rule 34 for 'appropriate measures' to be taken

---

[67] *Prosecutor v Ieng Sary*, ECCC Case File No. 002/09-10-2009-ECCC/PTC(01), Pre-Trial Chamber, Decision on Ieng Sary's Application to Disqualify Co-Investigating Judge Marcel Lemonde, 9 December 2009, paras. 16–17; *Prosecutor v Khieu Samphan*, ECCC Case File No. 002/13-10-2009-ECCC/PTC (02), Pre-Trial Chamber, Decision on Khieu Samphan's Application to Disqualify Co-Investigating Judge Marcel Lemonde, 14 December 2009, paras. 24–5.

[68] The Bangalore Draft Code of Judicial Conduct, 2002 (adopted by the Judicial Group on Strengthening Judicial Integrity and revised at the Round Table Meeting of Chief Justices held at the Peace Palace, The Hague, November 25–26, 2002), <http://www.unodc.org/pdf/crime/corruption/judicial_group/Bangalore_principles.pdf> [accessed 19 June 2017].

[69] *Prosecutor v Ieng Sary*, ECCC Case File No. 002/07-12-2009-ECCC/PTC(06), Pre-Trial Chamber, Decision on Ieng Sary's Rule 35 Application for Judge Marcel Lemonde's Disqualification, 29 March 2010, paras. 11–14 (subsequently re-classified as public).

[70] *Prosecutor v Nuon, Chea, Ieng Sary* and *Ieng Thirith*, ECCC Case File No. 002/07-12-2009-ECCC/PTC (05), Pre-Trial Chamber, Decision on Ieng Sary's and on Ieng Thirith Applications under Rule 34 to Disqualify Judge Marcel Lemonde, 15 June 2010, para. 66 and p. 26.

[71] *Prosecutor v Nuon Chea* ECCC Case File No. 002/17-06-2010-ECCC-PTC(09), Pre-Trial Chamber, Decision on Application for Disqualification of Judge You Bunleng, 10 September 2010, paras. 53–5.

against the international judges of the PTC, Judges Katinka Lahuis and Rowan Downing, following statements reportedly made by Prime Minister Hun Sen suggesting his belief that international judges of the ECCC were receiving instructions from their governments. The context was the dissenting opinion by the two international PTC judges on the issue of the investigation of additional suspects before the ECCC which had the effect of allowing the investigations to proceed. The specially constituted panel of the PTC found the motion to be inadmissible.[72]

As proceedings moved to the trial phase, so did the focus of defence attempts to raise concern about possible bias among ECCC judges. Ieng Sary sought the disqualification of the President of the Trial Chamber, Judge Nil Nonn, based on an apparent admission by the Judge in a documentary that he had accepted cash gratuities from litigants while President of the Provincial Court in Battambang. As the relevant video footage had not been obtained, the Defence also sought an order compelling its disclosure. After setting out the relevant legal framework, the Trial Chamber observed, in its rejection of the application, that according to Article 34 and the relevant jurisprudence, 'disqualification pertains to bias against a particular accused in relation to a particular case, and cannot be used to lodge a general complaint about the fitness of an individual to serve as a judge'.[73] It was made clear that the general question whether an individual was qualified to act as a Cambodian judge before the ECCC was a matter for national law.

Subsequently, Ieng Thirith, Nuon Chea and Ieng Sary applied for the disqualification of Judges Nil Nonn, Silvia Cartwright, Ya Sokhan, Jean-Marc Lavergne and Thou Mony, in other words the entire sitting bench of the Trial Chamber, alleging an apprehension of bias due to findings by the same bench in its judgment in Case 001 on issues that would recur in Case 002, as well as findings specific to the accused amounting to a de facto determination of guilt. A specially constituted

---

[72] *Prosecutor v Ieng Sary*, ECCC Case File No. 002/20-10-2009-ECCC/OCIJ(PTC03), Pre-Trial Chamber, Decision on Ieng Sary's Request for Appropriate Measures Concerning Certain Statements by Prime Minister Hun Sen Challenging the Independence of Pre-Trial Chamber Judges Katinka Lahuis and Rowan Downing, 30 November 2009, paras. 13–15 and p. 7.

[73] *Prosecutor v Nuon Chea, Ieng Sary, Ieng Thirith* and *Khieu Samphan*, ECCC Case File No. 002/19-09-2007/ECCC/TC, Trial Chamber, Decision on Ieng Sary's Application to Disqualify Judge Nil Nonn and Related Requests, 28 January 2011, para. 8.

Trial Chamber found that the arguments put forward by the Defence were not substantiated.[74]

In this connection, Ieng Thirith and Ieng Sary also sought to disqualify Judge You Ottara from sitting on the special panel due to his prior role on a panel of the Cambodian Supreme Court which had delivered a decision that was heavily criticised for allegedly pandering to the wishes of the government. Due to the importance of the matter raised, this application was heard and rejected by the ordinary bench of the Trial Chamber after the special panel had rendered its decision and the matter had technically become moot.[75] The same controversial decision by the Cambodian Supreme Court was the basis for an application by Ieng Thirith and Ieng Sary to disqualify Judge Som Sereyvuth from the Supreme Court Chamber of the ECCC which was also rejected.[76]

Applications brought by Nuon Chea, seeking the disqualification of Judge Silvia Cartwright from the Trial Chamber under Internal Rule 34, and Ieng Sary seeking investigative action under Internal Rule 35, on the basis of information obtained by the Defence that meetings had been taking place between the Judge, the international Co-Prosecutor and the Deputy Director of Administration, were similarly rejected.[77] Nuon Chea submitted a further application for Judge Cartwright's disqualification arguing that certain press and in-court statements made by the Judge

---

[74] *Prosecutor v Nuon Chea, Ieng Sary, Ieng Thirith* and *Khieu Samphan*, ECCC Case File No. 002/19-09-2007-ECCC/TC, Trial Chamber, Decision on Ieng Thirith, Nuon Chea and Ieng Sary's Applications for Disqualification of Judges Nil Nonn, Silvia Cartwright, Ya Sokhan, Jean-Marc Lavergne and Thou Mony, 23 March 2011, paras. 17–19. *See* S. Forder, 'Commentary by Susan Forder', in A. Klip and S. Freeland (eds), *Annotated Leading Cases of International Criminal Tribunals – Volume 44: Extraordinary Chambers in the Courts of Cambodia 11 December 2009 – 23 March 2011* (Antwerp/New York, Intersentia, 2015), pp. 134–8, p. 138 (stating that the decision was 'straightforward and convincing').

[75] *Prosecutor v Nuon Chea, Ieng Sary, Ieng Thirith* and *Khieu Samphan*, ECCC Case File No. 002/19-09-2007-ECCC/TC, Trial Chamber, Decision on Ieng Thirith and Ieng Sary's Applications for Disqualification of Judge You Ottara from the Special Bench and Requests for a Public Hearing, 9 May 2011, para. 3.

[76] *Prosecutor v Ieng Thirith*, ECCC Case File No. 002/19-09-2007-ECCC/SC(1), Supreme Court Chamber, Decision on Ieng Thirith's Application to Disqualify Judge Som Sereyvuth for Lack of Independence, 3 June 2011, paras. 11–16.

[77] *Prosecutor v Nuon Chea, Ieng Sary*, and *Khieu Samphan*, ECCC Case File No. 002/19-09-2007/ECCC/TC, Trial Chamber, Decision on Motions for Disqualification of Judge Silvia Cartwright, 2 December 2011, para. 15.

indicated that she had formed an unfavourable view of the accused's case. Once again, the high threshold required to rebut the presumption of impartiality was found not to have been met.[78] In the meantime, Ieng Sary sought an immediate appeal pursuant to Internal Rule 104(4)(d) of the Trial Chamber's decision that had deemed his motion under Internal Rule 35 to be a motion for disqualification. The Supreme Court Chamber found the appeal to be admissible as a request for an investigation into the conduct of Judge Cartwright, Mr. Cayley and Mr. Rosandhaug, however, applying the standard under Rule 35 it dismissed the request on its merits.[79] Ieng Sary subsequently filed an application pursuant to Internal Rule 34 seeking Judge Cartwright's disqualification, putting forward evidence of *ex parte* communications by e-mail between the Judge and the international Co-Prosecutor, but the Defence requests were denied by the Trial Chamber.[80]

Disqualification applications were made by Nuon Chea and Khieu Samphan following the delivery of the Trial Chamber's judgment in Case 002/01 on 7 August 2014 and just as proceedings in the severed Case 002/02 were commencing before the same panel of judges. It was argued that the findings in Case 002/01 revealed actual or perceived bias in relation to future proceedings against the accused. The special panel of the Trial Chamber dismissed the applications by a majority, Judge Rowan Downing dissenting.[81]

---

[78] *Prosecutor v Nuon Chea, Ieng Sary*, and *Khieu Samphan*, ECCC Case File No. 002/19-09-2007/ECCC/TC, Trial Chamber, Decision on Application for Disqualification of Judge Silvia Cartwright, 9 March 2012, para. 20.

[79] *Prosecutor v Ieng Sary*, ECCC Case File No. 002/19-09-2007-ECCC-TC/SC(12), Supreme Court Chamber, Decision on Ieng Sary's Appeal against the Trial Chamber's Decision on Motions for Disqualification of Judge Silvia Cartwright, 17 April 2012, paras. 14–17, 20–3.

[80] *Prosecutor v Nuon Chea, Ieng Sary*, and *Khieu Samphan*, ECCC Case File No. 002/19-09-2007/ECCC/TC, Trial Chamber, Decision on Ieng Sary's Application for Disqualification of Judge Cartwright, 4 June 2012, paras. 6–8, 17–21.

[81] *Prosecutor v Nuon Chea* and *Khieu Samphan*, 002/19-09-2007/ECCC/TC, Trial Chamber, Reasons for Decision on Applications for Disqualification, 30 January 2015, para. 5; *Prosecutor v Nuon Chea* and *Khieu Samphan*, ECCC Case File No. 002/19-09-2007/ECCC/TC, Trial Chamber, Reasons for Decision on Applications for Disqualification: Partly Dissenting Opinion of Judge Rowan Downing, 23 January 2015, para. 1; *Prosecutor v Nuon Chea* and *Khieu Samphan*, ECCC Case File No. 002/19-09-2007/ECCC/TC, Trial Chamber, Decision on Applications for the Disqualification of Trial Chamber Judges, 14 November 2014, pp. 3–4.

The grounds for disqualification proceedings against individual judges have ranged from corruption, to *ex parte* meetings, to improper statements made internally or publicly, to both domestic and foreign political influence. As it concerns entire panels, the issue has been prior judgments which have raised concerns about the same panel's ability to be impartial in subsequent proceedings against the same or different accused. In keeping with the jurisprudence of the ICTY and other international criminal tribunals, the ECCC has set a high standard for disproving the presumption of independence and impartiality.[82] The 'reasonable observer' in the test for an appearance of bias 'must be [an] "informed person, with knowledge of all the relevant circumstances, including the traditions of integrity and impartiality that form a part of the background and appraised also of the fact that impartiality is one of the duties that Judges swear to uphold".'[83]

Further, the ECCC jurisprudence shows that any perceived bias must impact directly on the accused in the case under consideration. The disqualification applications serve as a reminder of international standards of ethics and test the judges' adherence to those standards. In addition, they challenge the Chambers publicly to affirm the independence and impartiality of the judges and to be firm in protecting the proceedings from possible abuse of process. This is not easy given the ECCC's structure and the highly charged political environment in which it operates. Moreover, most of the Cambodian judges continue to hold positions in the domestic system while in post at the ECCC.[84] The decisions refer general questions about the competence and motivation of the Cambodian judiciary back to the domestic system and place under the spotlight some international judges who have apparently come close to 'expressing views which may undermine the standing and integrity of the ECCC'.[85] All of the applications appear to have been taken seriously and the decisions are properly reasoned by the relevant Chamber. Indeed, it

---

[82] *Prosecutor v Nuon Chea* and *Khieu Samphan*, 002/19-09-2007/ECCC/TC, Trial Chamber, Reasons for Decision on Applications for Disqualification, 30 January 2015, para. 33. *See* also Escolar, above n. 63, p. 696.

[83] *Prosecutor v Nuon Chea* and *Khieu Samphan*, 002/19-09-2007/ECCC/TC, Trial Chamber, Reasons for Decision on Applications for Disqualification, 30 January 2015, para. 33.

[84] This does not exclude the applicability of the precedent in *Prosecutor v Zejnil Delalić, Zdravko Mucić, Hazim Delić* and *Esad Landžo*, ICTY Case No. IT-96-21-A, Appeals Chamber, Judgment, 20 February 2001, but represents a practical reality. *See* Escolar, above n. 63, p. 697.

[85] Code of Judicial Ethics, Article 7.

seems that on only one occasion was the Trial Chamber moved to note in its decision that: 'Repetitive or frivolous disqualification motions filed before other international tribunals have resulted in sanction or the threat of sanction.'[86] None of the motions has in fact been deemed frivolous and unanimity in relation to the outcome has been the norm rather than the exception.

Disqualifying a single judge can have a momentous impact on proceedings especially since qualified replacements are not unlimited or, with the exception of reserve judges, on standby. Disqualifying the whole panel of judges from Case 002/02 would have magnified the problem and could have caused the entire Court to fold, taking account of the advanced ages of Khieu Samphan and Nuon Chea, the stage of the proceedings, the controversies over Cases 003 and 004 and the absence of any predisposition on the part of the UN or the Cambodian government to establish a second Trial Chamber. These are practical consequences of a decision to disqualify and while they may help to justify a high standard for proving impartiality they ought not to play into the examination of a concrete case.[87]

Interestingly, the issue that came closest to breaking the Court in the sequence of disqualification decisions was not political interference but the impact of the Trial Chamber's decision to split an unwieldy case into distinct sub-cases with the aim of reaching timely verdicts. The Co-Prosecutors noted that the severance of case 002 created an unprecedented situation in which the same accused were subject to a second trial based on the same charging document.[88] The majority of the special panel of the Trial Chamber hearing the disqualification case carried out a detailed assessment of relevant international jurisprudence, noting that according to the European Court of Human Rights, prior statements by a court short of a pronouncement of guilt do not establish an appearance of bias in relation to an accused. The suggestion that 'successive cases involving common accused and common evidence entail a binary choice

---

[86] *Prosecutor v Nuon Chea, Ieng Sary*, and *Khieu Samphan*, ECCC Case File No. 002/19-09-2007/ECCC/TC, Trial Chamber, Decision on Motions for Disqualification of Judge Silvia Cartwright, 2 December 2011, para. 15.

[87] *See* further *Prosecutor v Nuon Chea* and *Khieu Samphan*, ECCC Case File No. 002/19-09-2007/ECCC/TC, Trial Chamber, Reasons for Decision on Applications for Disqualification: Partly Dissenting Opinion of Judge Rowan Downing, 23 January 2015, paras. 20–2.

[88] *Prosecutor v Nuon Chea* and *Khieu Samphan*, 002/19-09-2007/ECCC/TC, Trial Chamber, Reasons for Decision on Applications for Disqualification, 30 January 2015, para. 34.

between (i) excluding Judges or (ii) excluding evidence such that it is inadmissible' was rejected by the majority.[89] Rather, the test was whether prior judicial findings evinced attributing criminal responsibility in relation to the later case.[90] Applying this test to the Defence assertions of alleged errors in the Case 002/01 judgment, the majority found, for example, that as it concerned the CPK policies, the permissibility of determining the existence of all five policies when the implementation of only two of them was relevant to Case 002/01, and any related inferences of the existence of a joint criminal enterprise, were assertions of factual errors that were matters for appeal rather than a disqualification application. As it concerned assertions of actual prejudgment of guilt based on the Case 002/01 findings, the majority found that Case 002/01 and 002/02 were substantially different and not just in terms of the crime-base evidence, stating that although the judgment in Case 002/01 contained prejudicial findings relating to the participation of the two accused in a JCE and, in the case of Nuon Chea, his effective control of Khmer Rouge cadre, no assessment had been made of the *mens rea* relevant to the Case 002/02 crimes.[91]

Further, the majority pointed out that the judgment had not included findings on whether the joint criminal enterprise 'resulted in and/or involved' the Case 002/02 crimes so there were no findings on the 'ultimate issue of culpability' in relation to Case 002/02.[92] The Defence assertions as to indirect prejudgment of guilt were rejected on a similar basis. Nuon Chea's allegation of bias based on the failure to summons as a witness Heng Samrin, a senior member of the Cambodian government, an issue on which the international and Cambodian judges had been divided, was found to be unsubstantiated. The argument that the Cambodian judges could not be impartial on certain matters because they had lived through the Democratic Kampuchea (DK) regime, an issue that was almost bound to arise at some point during the life of the Court, was also found to be unsubstantiated.

Judge Downing's dissent, limited to the issue of prior findings in the Case 002/01 judgment on factual issues relevant to Case 002/02, suggests that the arguments for or against disqualification of the Trial Chamber judges (with the exception of Judge Claudia Fenz who had merely been reserve judge in Case 002/01) were finally balanced. While Judge Downing concurred with the majority on all other conclusions, he took

---

89 Ibid, para. 54.
90 Ibid, paras. 54, 70.
91 Ibid, para. 94.
92 Ibid.

'the view that the Trial Chamber made findings in the Case 002/01 Judgement on a number of extant and significant issues for determination in Case 002/02, the effect of which is to evince the attribution of individual criminal responsibility to Nuon Chea and Khieu Samphan for crimes charged in Case 002/02'.[93] For a start, he interpreted the applicable law more broadly, stating: 'While factors such as whether a judge has prejudged each and every element of the crime will be instructive in assessing whether a reasonable observer would reasonably apprehend bias, their absence is not determinative.'[94]

In contrast to the majority decision, which relies heavily on the jurisprudence, sometimes stretching the parallels with other cases and obscuring the precise factual context at issue, the dissenting opinion correctly views an appearance of bias as being essentially a matter of fact, requiring a consideration of all relevant factual circumstances. Judge Downing indicates that in view of the lack of specificity in the Defence arguments he has examined the specific factual circumstances *ex officio* and an extensive annex appended to the dissenting opinion contains excerpts from the Closing Order on matters to be adjudicated in Case 002/02, identifying corresponding findings from the judgment in Case 002/01. According to Judge Downing, by finding that between at least June 1974 and December 1977, Nuon Chea and Khieu Samphan participated in a joint criminal enterprise to implement the two policies relevant to Case 002/01, the Trial Chamber necessarily 'made foundational findings on significant, extant issues pertaining to the alleged joint criminal enterprise in Case 002/02'.[95] Indeed, the plurality of persons, common purpose, membership of the accused in the criminal enterprise and existence of such an enterprise had all been established beyond reasonable doubt.

Judge Downing is probably right that due to the overarching nature of the joint criminal enterprise as initially described in the Closing Order and the duty of the Trial Chamber to make all necessary 'foundational findings' in order to be satisfied beyond reasonable doubt, 'it is difficult to imagine how the same judges could bring a mind free of the effect of these conclusions to bear in dealing with the same Accused's alleged responsibility for involvement in the same joint criminal enterprise in a

---

[93] *Prosecutor v Nuon Chea* and *Khieu Samphan*, ECCC Case File No. 002/19-09-2007/ECCC/TC, Trial Chamber, Reasons for Decision on Applications for Disqualification: Partly Dissenting Opinion of Judge Rowan Downing, 23 January 2015, para. 1.

[94] Ibid, para. 16.

[95] Ibid, para. 26.

subsequent trial'.[96] Indeed, as Judge Downing also notes, the Trial Chamber appeared conceptually confused in terms of the impact of severance, suggesting that it had initially hoped to build on its 'foundational findings' in subsequent sub-cases. While the majority view prevails and the sub-cases are proceeding before the same judges, those judges will be expected to pay heed to the Supreme Court Chamber's warning that: 'Even though evidence remains formally common to the severed cases, this commonality does not extend to findings, and common factual elements in all cases resulting from Case 002 must be established anew'.[97] At the same time, the possibility of appealing alleged factual errors, as repeatedly encouraged in the majority decision, should assist in alleviating any lingering concerns over impartiality. It should be readily apparent that efficiency comes second when the fairness and impartiality of the Court is at stake.

On appeal in Case 002/01, Nuon Chea submitted that the Trial Chamber was deeply biased against him and that the judgment 'was a *post facto* rationalisation of a long-held belief that the accused are morally repugnant and deserving of the harshest punishment'.[98] He made reference to excerpts from the interview with Judge Cartwright and Judge Lemonde's book that had been admitted into evidence by the Supreme Court Chamber.[99] The Supreme Court Chamber was not persuaded that Judge Cartwright's public statements gave rise to an appearance of bias as a reasonable observer would have understood her reference to the 'purpose of putting on trial and humiliating tyrants' as being 'more generally to the purpose of judicial reactions to mass atrocities' and not a condemnation of Nuon Chea personally.[100] The Supreme Court Chamber also found that a statement contained in Judge Marcel Lemonde's book that 'all Cambodian judges are ultimately beholden to the government whether because of fear of or proximity to power, and that the [Royal Government of Cambodia] "pulls strings" behind every Cambodian judge' reflected Lemonde's own impression and did not demonstrate a lack of independence on the part of the Trial Chamber.[101] Nuon Chea

---

96 Ibid, para. 27.

97 *Prosecutor v Nuon Chea* and *Khieu Samphan*, ECCC Case File No. 002/19-09-2007-ECCC-TC/SC(29), Supreme Court Chamber, Decision on Khieu Samphan's Immediate Appeal against the Trial Chamber's Decision on Additional Severance of Case 002 and Scope of Case 002/02, 29 July 2014, para. 85.

98 Nuon Appeal Judgment, above n. 39, para. 111.

99 Ibid, para. 64.

100 Ibid, para. 114.

101 Ibid, para. 119.

also argued that the national judges of the Trial Chamber lacked independence because they were 'appointed, promoted, dismissed and disciplined by the Supreme Council of the Magistracy, which includes among its members four individuals appointed by the executive branch, as well as the ECCC's national Co-Prosecutor and national Co-Investigating Judge' and that furthermore, the national judges retain their full time positions in the national judiciary where they are poorly paid, lack security of tenure and are susceptible to corruption.[102] These arguments were rejected by the Supreme Court Chamber on the basis that members of the executive did not participate in the case, that the presence of the national Co-Prosecutor on the Council had had no bearing on decisions made by the Trial Chamber that went against the Co-Prosecutors, and that guarantees had been provided in the ECCC context to insulate judges from corruption.[103] However, the Supreme Court Chamber recognised that certain challenges such as 'limited tenure, funding dependent heavily on interested States and pressure on mandate completion' applied to national and international judges alike and that the appeal did not allege that the ECCC was 'fundamentally flawed in this respect'.[104]

7. PROVISIONAL DETENTION AND RELEASE

The Internal Rules contain provisions on pre-trial detention, bail and release during trial, recognising that Cambodian criminal procedure in this respect may not be entirely suited to the unique framework of the ECCC, especially as it concerns the gravity of the crimes and the anticipated length of each stage of the proceedings.[105] These two factors make it all the more important to ensure that the rights of the accused, and above all the presumption of innocence, are properly respected in accordance with the International Covenant on Civil and Political Rights (ICCPR), which serves as a guiding force behind the entire ECCC process. Article 9 of the ICCPR establishes a presumption of liberty and provides that: 'A person detained under criminal charges shall be tried within [a] reasonable time or shall be released, and it shall not be a

[102] Ibid, para. 125.
[103] Ibid, para. 126.
[104] Ibid.
[105] Ibid, paras. 106–08, 175.

general rule that persons awaiting trial shall be detained in custody'.[106] This means that 'the detention of an accused must at all times have a basis in a judicial decision', in accordance with the law.[107]

Internal Rule 63(1)(a) provides that the Co-Investigating Judges may order the provisional detention of a charged person after an adversarial hearing if the following legal and factual basis for detention set out in Internal Rule 63(3) has been established:

> a) There is well founded reason to believe that the person may have committed the crime or crimes specified in the Introductory or Supplementary Submission; and
> b) The Co-Investigating Judges consider Provisional Detention to be a necessary measure to:
>   i) prevent the Charged Person from exerting pressure on any witnesses or Victims, or prevent any collusion between the Charged Person and accomplices of crimes falling within the jurisdiction of the ECCC;
>   ii) preserve evidence or prevent the destruction of any evidence;
>   iii) ensure the presence of the Charged Person during the proceedings;
>   iv) protect the security of the Charged Person; or
>   v) preserve public order.

This has been described as a 'two pronged detention test—based on "reasonableness" and "necessity"—both of which should be satisfied in order for the detention to be lawful'.[108] The period of provisional detention is limited to one year for genocide, war crimes and crimes against humanity and six months for all other crimes within the ECCC's jurisdiction although a maximum of two extensions for further one year or six month periods are possible. This means that the total maximum period of pre-trial detention in respect of international crimes, i.e. while the case file is in the hands of the Co-Investigating Judges, is three years. Reasoning must be provided in support of any detention order. Under Internal Rule 64, release of a charged person may be ordered by the Co-Investigating Judges on their own motion or that of the charged person or the Co-Prosecutors if the requirements for provisional detention are no longer satisfied. The charged person may also file a further

---

[106] *See* 002/19-09-2007-ECCC-TC/SC(04), Decision on Immediate Appeal by Khieu Samphan on Application for Release, 6 June 2011, para. 46.

[107] Ibid, para. 47.

[108] A. Appazov, 'Commentary by Artur Appazov', in A. Klip and S. Freeland (eds), *Annotated Leading Cases of International Criminal Tribunals – Volume 43: Extraordinary Chambers in the Courts of Cambodia 2007-2010* (Antwerp/New York, Intersentia, 2015), pp. 163–70, p. 165.

application for release not less than three months after the final determination of his or her previous application if his or her circumstances have changed. Internal Rule 65 provides that a charged person may be permitted to remain at liberty or be released from detention under bail conditions, such as the payment of a bail bond. According to Internal Rule 68(1), the issuance of a Closing Order puts an end to provisional detention and bail orders 'once any time limit for appeals against the Closing Order have expired'. However, the Co-Investigating Judges may decide in the Closing Order, by a reasoned decision, to continue provisional detention or bail until the accused is brought before the Trial Chamber. Internal Rule 68(2) further provides that where an appeal is lodged against the indictment, the effect of the Co-Investigating Judges' detention or bail order shall continue until the PTC has made its decision. It is specified that: 'The Pre-Trial Chamber shall decide within four months'. When proceedings move to the Trial Chamber the default position, according to Internal Rule 82(1), is that the accused shall remain at liberty, unless provisional detention has been ordered. If the accused is in detention at the initial appearance before the Trial Chamber, then 'he or she shall remain in detention until the Chamber's judgment is handed down' subject to Internal Rule 82(2) which states that the Trial Chamber may at any time order the release, with or without conditions, or detention of an accused. Thus, it is implied that if detention (as ordered by the Co-Investigating Judges or PTC in the event of an appeal against the Closing Order) was lawful at the time the accused first appears before the Trial Chamber, then detention shall continue throughout the trial unless the accused applies successfully for release.

The Co-Investigating Judges issued detention orders in respect of all five of the original charged persons in Cases 001 and 002 which were duly appealed before the PTC as permitted by Internal Rule 63(4). These appeals were in fact the PTC's first opportunity to determine the scope and nature of its functions as a *Chambre d'instruction*. Being guided by the relevant articles of the Cambodian Criminal Procedure Code (CPC) read together with the Internal Rules, the PTC found that it was directed to review the Provisional Detention Orders of the Co-Investigating Judges by examining: the procedures of the Co-Investigating Judges prior to the Order being issued; the exercise of discretion by the Co-Investigating Judges to consider the application of Internal Rule 63(3); the sufficiency of the facts for ordering detention; whether the circumstances on which the Order was based still existed at the time of the appeal; and other issues.[109] The PTC addressed the conditions under Internal Rule 63(3) describing the 'necessity' of detention in detail, found that provisional detention was warranted in each case under consideration, and substituted its reasons for those of the Co-Investigating Judges.[110] Despite considering all five conditions, the PTC took the view that 'any one of these would have been sufficient to justify the provisional detention of the Charged Person'.[111] The reasoning, though greatly amplifying the conclusions of the Co-Investigating Judges, appears strained at times, as if recognising the limitations of the evidentiary foundation for the exercise of judicial discretion in favour of detention.[112]

The hearing of Khieu Samphan's appeal had been adjourned as a consequence of the International Co-Lawyer, Jacques Vergès, declining to act until all documents in the case file were available in French.[113] Khieu Samphan's appeal against the order on provisional detention was subsequently withdrawn while in the meantime he brought a motion concerning translation rights,[114] twice requested immediate release and

---

109 *Prosecutor v Kaing Guek Eav alias 'Duch'*, ECCC Case File No. 001/18-07-2007/ECCC/OCIJ (PTC01), Pre-Trial Chamber, Decision on Appeal Against Provisional Detention Order of Kaing Guek Eav alias 'Duch', 3 December 2007, para. 8.

110 Ibid, paras. 26–60; *Prosecutor v Nuon Chea*, ECCC Case File No. 002/10-09-2007-ECCC/OCIJ(PTC01), Pre-Trial Chamber, Decision on Appeal against Provisional Detention Order of Nuon Chea, 20 March 2008, paras. 41–83; *Prosecutor v Ieng Thirith*, ECCC Case File No. 002/10-09-2007-ECCC/OCIJ(PTC02), Decision on Appeal against Provisional Detention Order of Ieng Thirith, 9 July 2008, paras. 17–74; *Prosecutor v Ieng Sary*, ECCC Case File No. 002/10-09-2007-ECCC/OCIJ(PTC03), Decision on Appeal against Provisional Detention Order of Ieng Sary, 17 October 2008, paras. 67–117.

111 *Prosecutor v Nuon Chea*, ECCC Case File No. 002/10-09-2007-ECCC/OCIJ(PTC01), Pre-Trial Chamber, Decision on Appeal against Provisional Detention Order of Nuon Chea, 20 March 2008, para. 83 (repeated in the *Prosecutor v Khieu Samphan*, ECCC Case File No. 002/19-09-2007-ECCC-OCIJ, Office of the Co-Investigating Judges, Order Refusing Request for Release (Public Redacted Version), 28 October 2008, para. 14).

112 *See* also Appazov, above n. 108, p. 167.

113 *Prosecutor v Khieu Samphan*, ECCC Case File No. 002/10-09-2007-ECCC/OCIJ (PTC04), Pre-Trial Chamber, Decision on Application to Adjourn Hearing on Provisional Detention Appeal, 23 April 2008, para. 4.

114 *See Prosecutor v Khieu Samphan*, ECCC Case File No. 002/19-09-2007-ECCC/OCIJ (PTC11), Pre-Trial Chamber, Decision on Khieu Samphan's Appeal against the Order on Translation Rights and Obligations of the Parties, 20 February 2009. This issue led to a request by Khieu Samphan for annulment of the judicial investigation based on an abuse of process which was dismissed by

challenged the extension of his provisional detention. While all these matters were pending before the PTC, Khieu Samphan made a further application for release directly to the President of the PTC, claiming he was being held arbitrarily in a process that was 'dogged by delays', but this application was rightly dismissed as inadmissible.[115] The PTC addressed appeals on the second of two orders refusing release[116] and the order extending provisional detention in a consolidated decision. Having examined both the case file and the jurisprudence of international tribunals, the PTC applied the test that release from provisional detention on humanitarian grounds depended on evidence that the health of the individual concerned was 'incompatible with detention'. The request for release was dismissed and the conditions necessitating detention were found still to be met.[117] As it concerned the extension of provisional detention, the PTC chastised the Co-Investigating Judges for failing to provide sufficient details as to why there continued to be 'well-founded reasons to believe that the Charged Person may have committed the crimes with which he has been charged', but found that the evidence supported the Co-Investigating Judges' conclusions.[118] A strong emphasis was therefore placed by the PTC on the need to justify any decision to impose or extend detention, or refuse release, with adequate reasoning.

The issuance of the Closing Order in Case 002, containing a renewed detention order to cover the period between different phases of the proceedings, triggered another series of detention-related appeals. All four defence teams filed appeals against the Closing Order with the PTC and while they did not specifically appeal against the renewed detention

---

the Pre-Trial Chamber: *Prosecutor v Khieu Samphan*, ECCC Case File No. 002/19-09-2007-ECCC/OCIJ(PTC30), Decision on Khieu Samphan's Appeal against the Order on the Request for Annulment for Abuse of Process, 4 May 2010, para. 24.

115 *Prosecutor v Khieu Samphan*, ECCC Case File No. 002/19-09-2007-ECCC/OCIJ(PTC15), Pre-Trial Chamber, Decision on Khieu Samphan's Supplemental Application for Release, 24 December 2008, para. 5.

116 *See Prosecutor v Khieu Samphan*, ECCC Case File No. 002/19-09-2007-ECCC-OCIJ, Office of the Co-Investigating Judges, Order Refusing the Request for Release (Public Redacted Version), 23 June 2008, paras. 33–8 and p. 10 (dismissing Khieu Samphan's request to be treated at home following a cerebral vascular event; Order refusing request for release, 28 October 2008).

117 *Prosecutor v Khieu Samphan*, ECCC Case File No. 002/10-09-2007-ECCC/OCIJ (PTC14 and 15), Pre-Trial Chamber, Decision on Khieu Samphan's Appeals against Order Refusing Request for Release and Extension of Provisional Detention Order, 3 July 2009, paras. 82, 92.

118 Ibid, para. 137.

order, Khieu Samphan, Nuon Chea and Ieng Thirith subsequently invoked the fact that the PTC issued its decision and its reasons on different dates to challenge their continued detention before the Trial Chamber. The Trial Chamber first had to consider whether it was validly seized of the case file by the PTC's decision without full reasoning. This allowed the Trial Chamber an opportunity to stress the importance of fully reasoned decisions with the PTC now being seen as failing to meet this procedural requirement. While the Trial Chamber considered that the PTC's deferral of reasons constituted a procedural defect which 'initially impacted on the Accused's fundamental fair trial guarantees of legal certainty and clarity', this defect was found to be remedied by the subsequent issuance of full reasoning so that the Trial Chamber had been validly seized of the case file.[119] The Trial Chamber found that the 'extreme remedy of immediate release' was not warranted in the circumstances and proceeded to make a cursory assessment of the conditions for detention, finding that detention was primarily necessary to ensure the presence of the accused at trial.[120] In view of the fact that the parties had not made submissions in relation to Internal Rule 63(3), the possibility for the defence to apply for release without demonstrating a change in circumstances under Internal Rule 82(4) was left open. Ieng Sary's motion was addressed separately as the delay between the issuance of the PTC's decision on the appeal against the Closing Order and its reasons had been longer than in the other cases and Ieng Sary also requested release on bail in the form of house arrest. The Trial Chamber affirmed its finding in the related cases that it had been validly seized of the case file but that the PTC's deferral of reasons 'constituted a procedural defect breaching the Accused's fundamental fair trial rights'.[121] Nonetheless, immediate release was not deemed to be a proportionate remedy and the Trial Chamber stated that it 'may consider the appropriateness of other remedies at the conclusion of the trial'.[122] The detention of Ieng Sary was found to be necessary to ensure his presence at trial and the request for release on bail was rejected.

---

119 *Prosecutor v Nuon Chea, Ieng Sary, Ieng Thirith* and *Khieu Samphan*, ECCC Case File No. 002/19-09-2007/ECCC/TC, Trial Chamber, Decision on the Urgent Applications for Immediate Release of Nuon Chea, Khieu Samphan and Ieng Thirith, 16 February 2011, paras. 29, 34.

120 Ibid, paras. 39–41.

121 *Prosecutor v Nuon Chea, Ieng Sary, Ieng Thirith* and *Khieu Samphan*, ECCC Case File No. 002/19-09-2007/ECCC/TC, Trial Chamber, Decision on Ieng Sary's Request for Release, 12 May 2011, para. 12.

122 Ibid, para. 12.

Nuon Chea, Ieng Thirith and Khieu Samphan all filed immediate appeals against the Trial Chamber's decision with the Supreme Court Chamber, asserting multiple grounds. In its decision on the appeals brought by Nuon Chea and Ieng Thirith, the Supreme Court Chamber identified the core issue as being whether the four-month period in Internal Rule 68(2) began to run from the date of the Closing Order or the date of the filing of an appeal. It was clear that the PTC had been concerned about this deadline, apparently erring on the side of caution by issuing its decision on the appeals against the Closing Order as soon as possible with full reasons to follow. The Trial Chamber had been quick to find a procedural defect with potentially serious consequences without embarking on a proper analysis of the procedures and their purpose. According to the Supreme Court Chamber, 'the commencement date of the four-month time limit must be determined through analyses of its systemic context and the purposes of the time limit'.[123] It was readily apparent that the lodging or filing of an appeal activated the time limit, rather than the issuance of the Closing Order. The purpose of the time limit was to 'prevent excessive detention of the Accused' while allowing the defence adequate time to file submissions on appeal and the PTC adequate time to 'examine the case and complete its decision'.[124] Consequently, making the relevant calculations, the Supreme Court Chamber found that the PTC had issued both its decision and its reasoning within the four-month time period. The Supreme Court Chamber viewed this as a 'technical issue of statutory interpretation from which no exercise of fundamental rights arises' since the rule itself reflected a balancing of different interests, including the interest of the accused in having sufficient time to prepare an appeal and to have that appeal properly considered.[125] The Supreme Court Chamber noted that this might come at the expense of lengthening the proceedings and consequently the period of detention, however, 'a legislative or, as in this case, interpretative decision on establishing the starting point of the deadline one month earlier or later in Internal Rule 68 does not disable any of the fundamental rights of the Accused, in particular the right to be tried within a reasonable time'.[126] As a result, the PTC had not

[123] *Prosecutor v Nuon Chea* and *Ieng Thirith*, ECCC Case File No. 002/19-09-2007-ECCC-TC/SC(01/02), Supreme Court Chamber, Decision on Immediate Appeals by Nuon Chea and Ieng Thirith on Urgent Applications for Immediate Release, 3 June 2011, para. 34.

[124] Ibid, para. 34.

[125] Ibid, para. 40.

[126] Ibid.

made a procedural error, there was no breach of the rights of the accused and the question of a remedy did not arise.[127] In its decision on the appeal brought by Khieu Samphan, the Supreme Court Chamber added that the 'sweeping removal' by the Trial Chamber of most of the previously established conditions for detention, 'thus annihilating the presumption of their continuity in the trial phase' had not been adequately substantiated.[128] The Supreme Court Chamber recognised that its competence to consider whether the conditions in Internal Rule 63(3)(b) were met was limited to the scope of the appeal but nevertheless found that the legal basis for the accused's continued detention was valid, considering that: 'The goal of speedy proceedings may be easily frustrated if the Accused goes into hiding, decides to disregard summons or even temporarily is prevented from attending a hearing.'[129] Judge Noguchi dissented on this point, finding that Internal Rule 63(3) did not apply to the accused's continuous detention at the trial phase.[130] There is a certain logic to Judge Noguchi's interpretation of the Internal Rules, in the sense that the start of trial marks a shift to continued detention unless circumstances can be shown to justify a review for release. However, the majority was concerned to ensure that detention was continuously justified and reviewed, especially if there was any doubt as to whether detention had a proper basis at the outset.

Each judicial office has in turn accused another of failing to reason properly on detention matters and scholarly critique has suggested that the reasoning *tout court* is inadequate because there was either insufficient evidence to support the conclusions under each of the five conditions in Internal Rule 63(3) or that addressing all five rather than prioritising a single one was fundamentally the wrong approach.[131] There

---

127 Ibid, para. 47.

128 *See* also *Prosecutor v Khieu Samphan*, ECCC Case File No. 002/19-09-2007-ECCC-TC/SC(04), Supreme Court Chamber, Decision on Immediate Appeal by Khieu Samphan on Application for Release, 6 June 2011, para. 50.

129 *Prosecutor v Khieu Samphan*, ECCC Case File No. 002/19-09-2007-ECCC-TC/SC(04), Supreme Court Chamber, Decision on Immediate Appeal by Khieu Samphan on Application for Release, para. 54.

130 *Prosecutor v Khieu Samphan*, ECCC Case File No. 002/19-09-2007-ECCC-TC/SC(04), Supreme Court Chamber, Partially Dissenting Opinion of Judge Noguchi Decision on Immediate Appeal by Khieu Samphan on Application for Release, 23 June 2011, para. 1.

131 Appazov, above n. 108, p. 167; S. Starygin, 'Judicial Discretion in ECCC Decisions on Pre-Trial Detention against the Backdrop of the Case-law of the International Criminal Tribunals', *International Criminal Law Review*, vol. 11, 2001, pp. 315–58, p. 356.

are many factors that made it arduous to decide on provisional detention or release in the ECCC context. Among these are first the fact that the events occurred so long ago that any assessment of the impact of releasing a well-known former Khmer Rouge member back into society where in most cases he or she had been living relatively peacefully involved a degree of prediction. Judicial predictions without supporting evidence are insufficient, however, under the rules. Second, all of the accused were elderly and either mentally or physically frail at the time of their arrest. There was both a risk of further deterioration in detention and at the same time the possibility for controlled medical care and management of attendance in court. Third, the ECCC's structural location within the Cambodian court system meant that alternatives to detention such as house arrest or other forms of judicial supervision were technically feasible and accessible. The judges unanimously demonstrated a reluctance to test these alternatives. It has been noted that despite being differently situated from the other international or internationalised tribunals, the ECCC has '*de facto* acted as an international tribunal in deciding motions for pre-trial release', making detention the norm and only in one exceptional case eventually granting release.[132]

The exceptional case was that of Ieng Thirith who was diagnosed as suffering from a 'dementing illness probably caused by Alzheimer's disease' when her case was sent to trial in 2011.[133] Medical opinion indicated the probability that her cognitive abilities would decline but that there were nevertheless some drugs and treatments available that could possibly lead to an improvement.[134] She was deemed unfit to stand trial by the Trial Chamber which severed the charges against her in Case 002 and ordered a stay of proceedings. The Trial Chamber had been unable to reach four affirmative votes on the question whether or not Ieng Thirth should be ordered to seek medical treatment or be released without any conditions. Judges Cartwright and Lavergne favoured the latter option, because there was neither a factual basis to suggest the accused might recover sufficiently to stand trial nor a legal basis to impose medical treatment. Due to the split vote, the Trial Chamber had unanimously agreed that unconditional release was the correct remedy as the one which favoured the accused, provoking an immediate appeal by

132 Starygin, ibid, p. 358.

133 *Prosecutor v Ieng Thirith*, ECCC Case File No. 002/19-09-2007-ECCC-TC/SC(09), Supreme Court Chamber, Decision on Immediate Appeal against the Trial Chamber's Order to Release the Accused Ieng Thirith, 13 December 2011, para. 5.

134 Ibid, para. 5.

the Co-Prosecutors. The Supreme Court Chamber could not find any provision for a 'stay of proceedings' in the ECCC's constitutive documents and looked to national and international practice for confirmation that a stay was permissible and functioned as 'a response to certain long-lasting obstacles to the proceedings'.[135] Such a stay would not bar procedural actions to remove the obstacle, however, and obligations to this effect were based on the duty to prosecute, the presumption of innocence, the right to a trial within a reasonable time, and the economy of proceedings.[136] Guided by the international case law, the Supreme Court Chamber noted that 'unconditional release seems only to be exceptionally applied on humanitarian grounds in cases of a *par excellence* terminal condition'.[137] The Supreme Court Chamber found that despite the unanimous opinion within the Trial Chamber that there was a possibility, however remote, that the stay of proceedings might be lifted if the accused became fit to stand trial, they had not imposed any conditions on her release. In the view of the Supreme Court Chamber, '[s]uch an outcome is irreconcilable with the interests of justice from all points of view, including the accused, prosecution, civil parties, and Cambodian society as a whole' and contrary to the 'compelling public interest to prosecute the Accused'.[138] Having established that the stay of proceedings was not permanent, that detention was not precluded during the stay, and that the ECCC had an obligation to exhaust all possibilities for the removal of the obstacle to the continuation of the proceedings, i.e. Ieng Thirith's unfitness, the Supreme Court Chamber ordered the Trial Chamber to request the additional recommended treatment for the accused to be carried out while in detention in a hospital or other appropriate facility with a review after six months. The Supreme Court Chamber had also considered whether judicial supervision would be an option but found that in view of Ieng Thirith's condition she might be unable to fulfil her obligations and that, furthermore, it would not be sufficient to ensure her presence during the proceedings. Judge Jayasinghe dissented from the decision of the majority, finding that 'any form of

---

135 Ibid, para. 18.

136 Ibid.

137 Ibid, para. 25. On the international case law in this context, *see* further Starygin, above n. 131, pp. 334–5.

138 *Prosecutor v Ieng Thirith*, ECCC Case File No. 002/19-09-2007-ECCC-TC/SC(09), Supreme Court Chamber, Decision on Immediate Appeal against the Trial Chamber's Order to Release the Accused Ieng Thirith, 13 December 2011, para. 28.

detention would be contrary to the evidence, to common sense, and to the fair trial rights of the Accused'.[139]

It is questionable whether the imposition of a regime of medical treatment on an accused for the sole purpose of attempting to make that accused fit to stand trial conforms to principles of fairness.[140] Additionally, despite medical advice that three months would be an appropriate period in which to test the effectiveness of the proposed treatment, the Supreme Court Chamber relied on its own review of the medical literature to impose what approximated to a six month 'experiment'. In fact, according to the medical experts, after six months Ieng Thirith's 'dementing illness had progressed' and 'she remained unable to meaningfully assist in the preparation of her defence principally due to her impaired memory', while all treatment options had been exhausted.[141] The Trial Chamber decided to stay the proceedings against her indefinitely, taking the occasion to comment on the presumption in favour of release as follows:

> As the SCC has noted, the Cambodian legal system is also protective of the right to liberty and contains a presumption in favour of release of an Accused pending trial. A fundamental requirement of international human rights norms is also that any deprivation of liberty must be supported by well-founded reasons established by law. In this regard, the European Court of Human Rights ... has held that the reasons for pre-trial confinement may become attenuated over time and that in such circumstances the person concerned should be released. It has held that the gravity of the charges, the public reaction to them, and the severity of a possible sentence can be taken into account in determining to detain an Accused, but these reasons cannot by themselves justify long periods of detention. Furthermore, the rationale for continued detention must be balanced against the risk of an unreasonably long or indefinite deprivation of liberty.[142]

---

[139] *Prosecutor v Ieng Thirith*, ECCC Case File No. 002/19-09-2007-ECCC-TC/SC(09), Supreme Court Chamber, Separate Dissenting Opinion of Judge Nihal Jayasinghe, 13 December 2011, para. 10.

[140] For a fuller analysis, *see* R.L. Phillips, 'Frail Accused and Fitness to Stand Trial', in S.M. Meisenberg and I. Stegmiller (eds), *The Extraordinary Chambers in the Courts of Cambodia: Assessing their Contribution to International Criminal Law* (The Hague, T.M.C. Asser Press, 2016), pp. 461–89, pp. 480–1.

[141] *Prosecutor v Ieng Thirith*, ECCC Case File No. 002/19-09-2007/ECCC/TC, Trial Chamber, Decision on Reassessment of Accused Ieng Thirith's Fitness to Stand Trial Following Supreme Court Chamber Decision of 13 December 2011, 13 September 2012, para. 12.

[142] Ibid, para. 22.

The Trial Chamber considered that continued detention could only be justified if there was a substantial likelihood that Ieng Thirith would become fit to stand trial in the foreseeable future.[143] In the Trial Chamber's view, this time held unanimously, the test was not satisfied and Ieng Thirith's immediate release was ordered. The Co-Prosecutors did not give up, however, and filed an immediate appeal. The Supreme Court Chamber, recognising the complexity of the issue which involved balancing fundamental rights of the accused with the interests of justice, allowed Ieng Thirith's release but imposed judicial supervision and conditions upon her, including the surrender of her passport, monthly security checks and six-monthly medical examinations.[144] In the meantime, Ieng Thirith's daughter, a physician, had been appointed as a legal guardian for her mother by the Phnom Penh Municipal Court and in 2014 the Trial Chamber granted leave for the two of them to travel to Thailand so Ieng Thirith could obtain medical treatment. In the end, therefore, despite the divergent views taken by the Trial Chamber and the Supreme Court Chamber on how best to handle a delicate situation using the mechanisms of the ECCC and domestic procedures, Ieng Thirith was treated humanely and with respect. Notably the issue did not trigger a fundamental divide between national and international judges within the respective Chambers with all judges seemingly at pains to find the right solution. The long drawn out process is perhaps a model from which lessons can be learned rather than one to be mimicked in the future.

After the severance of Case 002, Khieu Samphan made a new request for release, arguing that 'the unlikelihood that the Trial Chamber will render its verdict soon results in an excessively long period of detention, in breach of the Accused's fundamental right to a fair and expeditious trial'.[145] The Trial Chamber re-examined the basis for detention applying the conditions in Internal Rule 63(3), having stated that the 'rationale for continued detention of an Accused must be balanced against the risk of an unreasonable long or indefinite deprivation of liberty'.[146] After undertaking this exercise, the Trial Chamber concluded that all the conditions

---

[143] Ibid, para. 23.

[144] *Prosecutor v Ieng Thirith*, ECCC Case File No. 002/19-09-2007 ECCC-TC/SC (16), Supreme Court Chamber, Decision on Immediate Appeal against the Trial Chamber's Order to Unconditionally Release Ieng Thirith, 14 December 2012, para. 40 and pp. 45–6.

[145] *Prosecutor v Khieu Samphan*, ECCC Case File No. 002/10-09-2007/ECCC/TC, Trial Chamber, Decision on Khieu Samphan's Application for Immediate Release, 26 April 2013, para. 8.

[146] Ibid, para. 15.

remained satisfied and that continued detention was not disproportionate in all the circumstances of the case, having regard to the fact that provisional detention of five years or more had been viewed as justified in cases of comparable complexity.[147] This raises the question of when the balance will eventually tip in favour of liberty. The fact that Khieu Samphan is now serving a sentence as a consequence of the judgment in Case 002/01 means that this question is unlikely ever to be tested before the ECCC.

Duch requested release for the duration of his trial, subject to any conditions imposed by the Trial Chamber, renewing the challenge brought previously before the Co-Investigating Judges and PTC and arguing once again that his detention by the Cambodian Military Court and the ECCC was continuous and exceeded the maximum permitted duration under all relevant laws. The Trial Chamber rejected the idea of continuity of Duch's provisional detention but nonetheless addressed the question whether Duch's prior detention by the Military Court was a violation of his rights for which there should be an appropriate remedy before the ECCC. The Trial Chamber found that 'the Accused's prior detention before the Military Court constitutes a violation of the Cambodian domestic law applicable at the time. It also contravenes his internationally recognized right to a trial within a reasonable time and detention in accordance with the law'.[148] At the same time, the Trial Chamber found that three of the conditions in Internal Rule 63(3) remained applicable, namely the risk of flight, the need to preserve public order, and the protection of the accused's security.[149] Furthermore, Duch's continued detention was justified by the need to ensure his presence at trial and having regard to the gravity of the crimes charged.[150] However, if convicted the Trial Chamber found that Duch would be entitled to credit for the full duration of the period spent in provisional detention under the ECCC's and the Military Court's authority.[151] The Trial Chamber proceeded to rule on whether Duch would be entitled to any remedies in respect of his prior detention in violation of his rights. While these violations could not be attributed to the ECCC and were not found to amount to an abuse of process, the Trial Chamber

147 Ibid, para. 23.

148 *Prosecutor v Kaing Guek Eav alias 'Duch'*, ECCC Case File No. 001/18-07-2007/ECCC/TC, Trial Chamber, Decision on Request for Release, 15 June 2009, para. 21.

149 Ibid, para. 25.

150 Ibid, para. 26.

151 Ibid, paras 27–29.

decided that in the event of a conviction, Duch would be entitled to a remedy 'to be decided by the Chamber at the sentencing stage, for the time spent unlawfully in detention before the Cambodian Military Court between 10 May 1999 and 30 July 2007'.[152] In the event of an acquittal, remedies could be pursued within Cambodian national law.[153] Thus, Duch remained in detention throughout his trial with the expectation of a remedy at its eventual conclusion.

Ultimately, this did not come to pass since the Supreme Court Chamber by a majority overturned the Trial Chamber's decision to grant Duch a reduction in his sentence of five years as a remedy for the violation of his rights.[154] The Supreme Court Chamber could not find a legal basis for a decision that the violations of Duch's rights should be redressed by the ECCC in the absence of evidence establishing either an abuse of process or the responsibility of the ECCC for the infringements.[155] Judges Klonowiecka-Milart and Jayasinghe dissented on this point, referring to a 'shared responsibility' that controlled the question whether a hybrid court ought to be accountable for the acts of the domestic system. In their view, the extent of a tribunal's 'shared responsibility' had to be determined as a matter of fairness.[156] After highlighting the domestic characteristics of the ECCC, especially as it concerned control over detention matters, the dissenting judges found there to be an intimate connection between Duch's prior detention and the ECCC proceedings. Noting that the violation of Duch's rights was 'extreme', they considered that a sentence reduction was the appropriate remedy, as supported by relevant jurisprudence. Since the Supreme Court Chamber substituted a life sentence for the 35-year term imposed by the Trial Chamber it would have been difficult to apply a reduction in any meaningful way. However, for the ECCC finally to have granted Duch a remedy would not seem to have been damaging to its credibility or suggested that it was directly responsible for the conduct of the Military

---

152 Ibid, para. 36.

153 Ibid, para. 37.

154 *Prosecutor v Kaing Guek Eav alias 'Duch'*, ECCC Case File No. 001/18-07-2007/ECCC/TC, Trial Chamber, Judgment, 26 July 2010, paras. 623–4 ('Duch Trial Judgment'); *Prosecutor v Kaing Guek Eav alias 'Duch'*, ECCC Case File No. 001/18-07-2007-ECCC/SC, Supreme Court Chamber, Appeal Judgment, 3 February 2012, paras. 389–99 ('Duch Appeal Judgment').

155 Duch Appeal Judgment, ibid, para. 390.

156 *Prosecutor v Kaing Guek Eav alias 'Duch'*, ECCC Case File No. 001/18-07-2007-ECCC/SC, Supreme Court Chamber, Appeal Judgment: Partially Dissenting Joint Opinion of Judges Agnieszka Klonowiecka-Milart and Chandra Nihal Jayasinghe, 3 February 2012, para. 7.

Court. Those authorities had, after all, at a certain point continued to detain Duch in anticipation of the establishment of the ECCC. Rather, it would have helped to highlight the fact that even individuals accused and convicted of the gravest crimes are entitled to the full exercise of their rights.[157] The ECCC has a duty to uphold the highest standards of due process and fairness in the face of the gravest crimes, both to educate and serve as a model to the ordinary courts. In this respect, it might have missed an opportunity.

[157] *See* further J.D. Ciorciari and A. Heindel, *Hybrid Justice: The Extraordinary Chambers in the Courts of Cambodia* (Ann Arbor, Michigan, University of Michigan Press, 2014), pp. 125–8.

7. Crimes

1. INTRODUCTION

This chapter addresses the legal elements of the crimes charged in Cases 001 and 002 and the development of the law by the Extraordinary Chambers in the Courts of Cambodia (ECCC), both in terms of the customary international law applicable in the period 1975 to 1979 and modern international criminal law. The ECCC is unique among the international and internationalised tribunals in addressing a time frame that falls right in between the trials in the immediate aftermath of the Second World War and the burgeoning of international criminal justice in the mid-1990s. The ECCC judges have had to keep a careful eye on the principle of legality but have at the same time drawn on modern case law as an aid to interpretation. On the one hand, they may be credited with making a significant contribution to the development of the law on crimes against humanity, in particular, both in terms of the contextual elements, including the question whether a nexus with an armed conflict is required, and the underlying crimes, such as extermination. On the other hand, the ECCC has been criticised for its poor record of addressing gender-based violence. Prospectively (since a judgment in Case 002/02 is still pending), the development of the crime of forced marriage as an inhumane act constituting a crime against humanity may mark an important legal advancement in this respect.

Before addressing the legal framework governing the crimes that fall within the ECCC's subject-matter jurisdiction, the facts forming the basis for the findings under different categories of offences as established in the ECCC judgments to date (i.e. in Cases 001 and 002/01) are summarised briefly to provide an impression of what the legal characterisations have sought to capture. A description of the armed conflict in Cambodia provided by the trial judgment in Case 001 is included due to its relevance as a contextual requirement for the category of war crimes.

2. THE FACTUAL CONTEXT OF CASE 001

A feature of Communist Party of Kampuchea (CPK) policy that was central to the *Duch* case was that of 'smashing' enemies. This in fact had its origins in the Democratic Kampuchea (DK) Constitution which under the heading 'Justice' provided that 'violations of the laws of the people's State including dangerous activities in opposition to the people's State must be condemned to the highest degree'.[1] According to Duch himself, to 'smash' meant both physical and psychological destruction by arresting secretly, interrogating using torture, and executing secretly without informing family members.[2] The 'Decision of the Central Committee Regarding a Number of Matters' dated 30 March 1976 was a key document in the trial, giving authority to certain CPK entities to decide on the 'smashing' of enemies. Security centres were established across the country with the purpose of identifying and killing internal enemies, encouraging the act of informing on others and obtaining confessions.

Between 1971 and 1975, Duch directed the security centre known as M-13 where he apparently gained the experience needed for his role at S-21.[3] Duch acknowledged that he served as Deputy and then Chairman of S-21, a security centre tasked with interrogating and executing perceived opponents of the CPK from 1975 to 1979. S-21 became fully operational in October 1975 and included the detention centre itself as well as the surrounding area (Tuol Sleng) and the execution and re-education camp branches of Cheong Ek and Prey Sâr on the outskirts of Phnom Penh. When Duch became head of S-21 after leading the interrogation unit under In Lorn *alias* 'Nat', he reported to Son Sen, who was in charge of internal security, and then later to Nuon Chea.[4] Duch was named Secretary of the S-21 Committee in addition to his role as Chairman of S-21, giving him full authority over all S-21 staff. Duch's deputy was Khim Vak *alias* 'Hor'. Between April 1976 and January 1979, S-21 operated from the premises of the Pohnea Yat Lycée, a high school located between streets 113, 131, 320 and 350, in Phnom Penh, now the site of the Tuol Sleng Genocide Museum. Based on the revised (incomplete) Prisoner List, there were more than 12,273 detainees at S-21, including former Lon Nol cadres and soldiers, DK and CPK high and low-ranking cadres, their family members and affiliates, women, children and foreign nationals. Duch commanded the following units: the

---

1 Democratic Kampuchea Constitution, 5 January 1976, Chapter 7, Article 10, <http://www.d.dccam.org/Archives/Documents/DK_Policy/DK_Policy_DK_Constitution.htm> [accessed 26 June 2017] (unofficial translation).

2 *Prosecutor v Kaing Guek Eav alias 'Duch'*, ECCC Case File No. 001/18-07-2007/ECCC/TC, Trial Chamber, Judgment, 26 July 2010, para. 100 ('Duch Trial Judgment').

3 Ibid, paras. 115, 118.

4 Ibid, para. 131.

Documentation Unit where new detainees were registered and where confessions and other documents were meticulously organised and stored; the Interrogation Unit where confessions were most often violently obtained; the Defence or Military Unit concerned with the security at S-21 and the transportation of detainees to execution sites; and other units such as Photography, Food and Medical Care.[5] Apart from the general supervision of these units, Duch's specific tasks were to recruit and train the staff serving under him, initiate and participate in certain arrests, obtain confessions (regarded as the most important work of S-21) and be solely responsible for their onward transmission to his superiors; and order executions in a system in which all detainees were destined to be executed.[6] Duch also took the decision to relocate executions and burials to Choeung Ek sometime between 1976 and mid-1977.[7] Furthermore, he had authority over the re-education camp known as S-24 or Prey Sar, located outside Phnom Penh near Choeung Ek.[8] S-21 and S-24 were abandoned on 7 January 1979 when Phnom Penh fell to the Vietnamese forces.[9]

3. THE FACTUAL CONTEXT OF CASE 002/01

The evacuation of Phnom Penh occurred in two phases relevant to the factual basis of Case 002/01. Phase One followed immediately after the Khmer Rouge takeover on 17 April 1975. The evacuees suffered violence, abuses and deprivation of food during the operation. The elderly and sick either had to join the evacuation or stay behind in unstaffed hospitals to die. Phnom Penh was largely emptied of its inhabitants within one week of its fall. Senior officials of the ousted Khmer Republic who had not already escaped responded to a radio message to surrender themselves to the Ministry of Information and subsequently disappeared with later reports stating that a certain number of them were executed.[10]

---

5 Ibid, paras. 144–60.

6 Ibid, paras. 161–83.

7 Ibid, paras. 184–6.

8 Ibid, para. 192.

9 Ibid, para. 203.

10 *Prosecutor v Nuon Chea* and *Khieu Samphan*, ECCC Case File No. 002/19-09-2007/ECCC/TC, Trial Chamber, Case 002/01 Judgement, 7 August 2014, para. 503 ('Nuon Trial Judgment').

The evidence showed that numerous other soldiers and civilian officials of the Khmer Republic were executed on the spot in Phnom Penh.[11]

When those who had survived the evacuation arrived in the countryside, they faced resentment fomented by the Khmer Rouge. They were called 'City People', '17 April People' or 'New People' to distinguish them from the local population, known as '18 April People', 'Old People' or 'Base People'.[12] The evacuees were viewed with suspicion as capitalists or feudalists.[13]

At least two million people were transferred from the capital to the countryside.[14] This finding by the Trial Chamber, based on the population of Phnom Penh at that time being two to 2.5 million and the city being 'empty' after the evacuation, withstood appellate review. The Supreme Court Chamber recalled the 'terrifying and violent circumstances' of the evacuation and the Trial Chamber's finding that it happened 'at the peak of the hot season in the general absence of water, food, shelter, hygiene facilities and medical care'.[15] It was also established that civilians were killed and others died because of the conditions of the evacuation.[16]

Phase Two or the 'second wave' of the evacuation began in September 1975 and continued into early 1977.[17] It involved hundreds of thousands of people in the Southwest, West and East Zones (including Kampong Speu, Kandal, Takeo, Prey Veng, Svay Rieng, and Kampong Cham Provinces) who were moved to Battambang and Pursat Provinces (Northwest Zone), Kampong Thom Province (Central (old North) Zone) and Preah Vihear Province (Sector 103).[18] People were transported to assembly points by truck, boat, ox cart and on foot.[19] The population movement was aimed at advancing agricultural production and furthering the class struggle. The 'class struggle' referred to the Party's opposition

---

[11] Ibid, para. 507.

[12] Ibid, para. 517.

[13] Ibid, para. 517.

[14] Ibid, para. 520.

[15] *Prosecutor v Nuon Chea* and *Khieu Samphan*, ECCC Case File No. 002/19-09-2007-ECCC/SC, Supreme Court Chamber, Appeal Judgment, 23 November 2016, para. 655 ('Nuon Appeal Judgment').

[16] Ibid, para. 655 (but not endorsing the Trial Chamber's finding as to the number of deaths: 'The Chamber is satisfied that at least several thousand people died during the transfer of the population from Phnom Penh to the countryside.'). *See* Nuon Trial Judgment, above n. 10, para. 521.

[17] Nuon Trial Judgment, above n. 10, Section 11, paras. 588, 630, 638.

[18] Ibid, paras. 588, 638.

[19] Ibid, para. 591.

to the 'New People'.[20] The 'Old People' were the core in the co-operatives and the 'New People' were to learn from them and be re-fashioned into peasants through hard labour.[21]

From late April 1975, Tuol Po Chrey (Kandieng District, Sector 7, North-west Zone), which included a former Khmer Republic military fort (known as the Po Village Fort), was allegedly used as an execution site for soldiers and civilian officials of the Lon Nol regime with bodies being dumped in a nearby lake.[22]

4. THE ARMED CONFLICT BETWEEN CAMBODIA AND VIETNAM[23]

Cambodia and Vietnam had a volatile relationship during the 1970s which the ECCC Trial Chamber in Case 001 divided into two main phases: (1) the period from the Khmer People's National Liberation Armed Forces's (KPNLAF) entry into Phnom Penh on 17 April 1975 until the DK's severance of diplomatic relations with Vietnam on 31 December 1977; and (2) the period from 31 December 1977 until the fall of Phnom Penh on 7 January 1979, when the DK government fled the capital.[24]

The first phase, during which it was not self-evident that an armed conflict existed, was a direct consequence of territorial disputes over certain islands, including Phu Quoc ('Koh Tral' in Khmer) and Tho Chu ('Koh Krachak' in Khmer). The islands were seized by the Revolutionary Army of Kampuchea (RAK) forces in May 1975 causing numerous casualties and re-taken by the Vietnamese army two weeks later.[25] Later in 1975, there were raids by the Vietnamese army into the Cambodian provinces of Ratanakiri and Mondulkiri and RAK incursions into Vietnamese territory, including into the provinces of Ha Tien, Tay Ninh, Kontum and Darlac. More than 150,000 Vietnamese civilians residing in Cambodia were expelled in the five months after the Khmer Rouge takeover of Phnom Penh and fled to South Vietnam. Border clashes continued throughout 1976 and were addressed in meetings of the CPK Standing Committee where a military response was advocated. Both

---

20 Ibid, para. 613.
21 Ibid, para. 615.
22 Ibid, para. 658.
23 *See* Duch Trial Judgment, above n. 2, paras. 65–81.
24 Ibid, para. 65.
25 Ibid, para. 66.

Vietnam and Cambodia had a policy of secrecy concerning the conflict in place until the severance of diplomatic relations in December 1977, in part to prevent outside interference. This meant that DK raids into Vietnamese territory which culminated in a large-scale attack by the RAK on various Vietnamese townships on 30 April 1977 were not publicised. After unsuccessful attempts at reaching a peace settlement, a second major DK attack occurred on 24 September 1977 in the Tay Ninh Province, resulting in the deaths of hundreds of civilians.[26] The Vietnamese army retaliated in October and November 1977 and launched an extensive attack in December 1977 in the provinces of Kampong Cham, Svay Rieng and Takeo which led to losses on the DK side.[27]

Vietnamese prisoners were first recorded as being present at S-21 in February 1976, although, by Duch's own account, there were Vietnamese detainees also in 1975.[28] Numbers increased in 1978 as the conflict with Vietnam escalated. Vietnamese prisoners at S-21 were divided into the categories of soldiers, spies and civilians and they were interrogated, sometimes tortured, and killed.[29]

The parties in Case 001 did not contest the existence of an international armed conflict between DK and Vietnam from the end of December 1977 to at least 6 January 1979. This period coincided with a DK decision to publicise the war and sever diplomatic ties with Vietnam, resulting initially in the withdrawal of Vietnamese troops from Cambodia. Confessions of Vietnamese prisoners at S-21 started being broadcast for propaganda purposes. In April 1978, Radio Phnom Penh broadcast excerpts from a resolution adopted at a 'Phnom Penh Rally', in which the participants pledged to 'exterminate resolutely all agents of the expansionist, annexationist Vietnamese aggressors from our units and from Cambodian territory forever'.[30] Vietnam went on the offensive in June 1978 and placed troops and artillery along the border.[31] At the same time, the Kampuchean National United Front for National Salvation (KNUFNS) was founded with the aim of overthrowing the DK regime.[32] The Vietnamese army launched its attack in late December 1978 and with the support of the KNUFNS, captured Phnom Penh on 7 January 1979.[33]

---

26 Ibid, para. 73.
27 Ibid, para. 74.
28 Ibid, para. 71.
29 Ibid.
30 Ibid, para. 78.
31 Ibid, para. 79.
32 Ibid.
33 Ibid, para. 80.

5. GRAVE BREACHES OF THE 1949 GENEVA CONVENTIONS

In Case 001, war crimes did not receive quite the same attention as crimes against humanity and since only the latter category featured in Case 002/01, the Trial Chamber's broad-brush approach to the multiple allegations of grave breaches of the Geneva Conventions in Case 001 has been left to stand until an anticipated reassessment of the law in Case 002/02.[34] The principle of legality was not seen to present any obstacle in respect of the war crimes that had been charged as Cambodia and Vietnam had ratified the four Geneva Conventions containing provisions on grave breaches in 1958 and 1957 respectively. In accordance with the Geneva Conventions, an accused may be found responsible for grave breaches only when these are perpetrated against persons or property regarded as 'protected' and within the context of an international armed conflict.

Regarding the contextual elements, the Trial Chamber found that armed hostilities amounting to an international armed conflict existed between Cambodia and Vietnam from 17 April 1975 through 6 January 1979, that Vietnamese detainees were the largest group at S-21 and constituted protected persons under the Geneva Conventions, that the accused was aware of the armed conflict with Vietnam at least from 7 February 1976, and that he knew that S-21 detainees included protected persons.[35] The Trial Chamber found on the basis of the 'Revised S-21 Prisoner List' admitted into evidence that 'no fewer than 345 Vietnamese detainees died or were executed at S-21, in addition to the large but unquantifiable number of Cambodian nationals perceived as Vietnamese sympathisers'.[36]

The following war crimes were found to have been established in Case 001, with the Chamber relying to a large extent on jurisprudence from the International Criminal Tribunal for the former Yugoslavia (ICTY) to define the legal elements: wilful killing, torture and inhumane treatment, wilfully causing great suffering or serious injury to body or health, wilfully depriving a prisoner of war or a civilian of the rights of fair and

---

[34] See further N. Quénivet, 'The Grave Breaches Charges at the ECCC: An Analysis of International Humanitarian Law in the Duch Case' in S.M. Meisenberg and I. Stegmiller (eds), *The Extraordinary Chambers in the Courts of Cambodia: Assessing their Contribution to International Criminal Law* (The Hague, T.M.C. Asser Press, 2016), pp. 353–73.

[35] Duch Trial Judgment, above n. 2, para. 429.

[36] Ibid, para. 436.

regular trial, wilful deprivation of fair trial rights, and unlawful confinement of a civilian.[37]

6. CRIMES AGAINST HUMANITY

In its judgment on appeal in Case 001, the Supreme Court Chamber traced the historical development of crimes against humanity from Hugo Grotius to the 1915 Joint Declaration by France, Great Britain and Russia concerning the Armenians to the Treaty of Versailles to its inclusion in the Nuremberg Charter and crystallisation as positive international law after the Second World War.[38] Crimes against humanity were found to form part of customary international law as a general category of international crimes during the period of the ECCC's temporal jurisdiction.[39] Consequently, charges of crimes against humanity brought under Article 5 of the ECCC Law were seen to accord with the principle of legality. However, the underlying offences also needed to be examined separately to determine whether they too accorded with the principle of legality.[40]

Under Article 5 of the ECCC Law, crimes against humanity are 'any acts committed as part of a widespread or systematic attack directed against any civilian population, on national, political, ethnical, racial or religious grounds'.[41] This definition contains what are sometimes referred to as the contextual or *chapeau* elements of crimes against humanity. According to the ECCC jurisprudence, these requirements may be broken down as follows: '(i) there is an attack; (ii) that is widespread or systematic; (iii) and directed against any civilian population; (iv) on national, political, ethnical, racial or religious grounds; (v) there is a nexus between the acts of the direct perpetrator and the attack; and (vi) the accused or the perpetrator has the requisite knowledge'.[42] On the last requirement, 'The accused needs to understand the overall context in

---

37 Quénivet, above n. 34, pp. 359–61, suggests that the Court relied too heavily on jurisprudence from the ICTY and that its findings reveal problems with the application of the principle of legality.

38 *Prosecutor v Kaing Guek Eav alias 'Duch'*, ECCC Case File No. 001/18-07-2007-ECCC/SC, Supreme Court Chamber, Appeal Judgment, 3 February 2012, paras. 101–03 ('Duch Appeal Judgment').

39 Ibid, para. 104.

40 Nuon Trial Judgment, above n. 10, para. 176.

41 ECCC Law, Article 5.

42 Nuon Trial Judgment, above n. 10, para. 177 (accepted in Nuon Appeal Judgment, above n. 15, para. 707); Duch Trial Judgment, above n. 2, para. 297.

which the acts took place, but need not know the details of the attack or share the purpose or goal behind the attack.'[43]

Various other candidates for inclusion in the definition of crimes against humanity have emerged at different points during the evolution of the concept and the first challenge for the ECCC has been to identify any additional elements that formed part of the definition of crimes against humanity under customary international law in 1975 and which interpretation of the *chapeau* requirements should be applied. For example, an 'attack' is regarded as a 'course of conduct involving the multiple commission of acts of violence'.[44] In Case 001, the attack was found to be constituted by all the events following from the KPNLAF entry into Phnom Penh and seizure of power on 17 April 1975, including the establishment of S-21. This led to the finding that the attack was widespread and systematic *within the boundaries of S-21*, by virtue of the magnitude and number of crimes committed and their organised and prolonged character.[45]

Article 5 includes the following examples of acts which may constitute crimes against humanity if the contextual elements are satisfied: murder, extermination, enslavement, deportation, imprisonment, torture, rape, persecutions on political, racial, and religious grounds, and other inhumane acts. The second challenge for the ECCC has been to determine which of these underlying crimes qualified as crimes against humanity under customary international law in 1975 and how they should be defined.

6.1 Nexus to an Armed Conflict

Article 5 of the ECCC Law does not include a nexus to an armed conflict in its definition of crimes against humanity. The shorthand 'nexus to an armed conflict' derived from the language used in the 1945 Charter of the International Military Tribunal to the effect that acts constituting crimes against humanity must be carried out in execution of or in connection with any crime against peace or any war crime.[46] As the ECCC Supreme Court Chamber has noted, this requirement is technically more onerous

---

43 Duch Trial Judgment, above n. 2, para. 319.

44 Ibid, para. 298.

45 Ibid, para. 321.

46 'Charter of the International Military Tribunal', in Agreement for the Prosecution and Punishment of the Major War Criminals of the European Axis, United Nations, *Treaty Series*, vol. 82, 279, 8 August 1945, pp. 284–300, Article 6(c).

than simply a 'nexus to an armed conflict' because 'it requires a substantive link between the crime alleged and another international crime, either a war crime or a crime against peace'.[47] The most important question to arise in ECCC proceedings concerning the contextual elements for crimes against humanity was whether such a nexus between the crimes and an armed conflict had to be established according to the customary international law applicable in the period 1975 to 1979. This question generated a significant amount of litigation.

The Trial Chamber was the first to offer an answer, concluding after a cursory review of the sources that 'the lack of any nexus with armed conflict in Article 5 of the ECCC Law comports with the customary definition of crimes against humanity during the 1975 to 1979 period'.[48] The question later arose before the Pre-Trial Chamber (PTC) in an appeal by Ieng Thirith against the Closing Order. The PTC found that the Trial Chamber's earlier opinion was *obiter* as the question of a nexus had not been the subject of a specific challenge by the accused in Case 001.[49] This meant that the PTC considered itself free to provide its own reasoning and to reach a different conclusion. According to the PTC:

> in the absence of clear state practice and *opinio juris* from 1975-1979 evidencing severance of the armed conflict nexus requirement for crimes against humanity under customary international law, the principle of *in dubio pro reo* dictates that any ambiguity must be resolved in favour of the accused. Thus, the Pre-Trial Chamber finds that from 1975-1979, the definition of crimes against humanity under customary international law included an armed conflict nexus requirement as articulated in the IMT Charter and Nuremberg Principles, such that there needs to be a link to war crimes or crimes against peace, i.e. a link between the underlying acts charged as crimes against humanity and an armed conflict.[50]

The question subsequently came before the Trial Chamber directly as the substance of a motion brought by the Co-Prosecutors in Case 002. Not surprisingly, the Trial Chamber reached the same conclusion as it had

---

47 Nuon Appeal Judgment, above n. 15, para. 712.

48 Duch Trial Judgment, above n. 2, para. 292.

49 *Prosecutor v Nuon Chea, Ieng Sary, Ieng Thirith* and *Khieu Samphan*, ECCC Case File No. 002/19-09-2007-ECCC/OCIJ (PTC 145 & 146), Pre-Trial Chamber, Decision on Appeals by Nuon Chea and Ieng Thirith against the Closing Order, 15 February 2011, para. 144.

50 Ibid.

done previously but this time provided more extensive reasons.[51] The Trial Chamber stated:

> Having reviewed the pertinent state practice and *opinio juris* between 1945 and 1975, the Trial Chamber concludes that from the earliest inception of crimes against humanity within the Nuremberg Charter and CCL 10, there was already a significant tendency to delink these crimes from armed conflict. This tendency to view crimes against humanity as grave international crimes not inherently connected to armed conflict gained momentum in the aftermath of the Nuremberg era and constituted settled law by 1975.[52]

The decision was framed as a 'reconsideration' of the issue, although all the jurisprudence and legal authorities available to the Chamber remained the same. The Trial Chamber did not specifically grapple with the opposing view that had been taken by the PTC. In its judgment in Case 002/01, the Trial Chamber affirmed its earlier finding that the definition of crimes against humanity under customary international law in 1975 did not require a nexus to an armed conflict.[53]

Prior to the judgment of the Supreme Court Chamber in Case 002/01, the International Co-Investigating Judge found himself in the unusual position of facing uncertainty whether the decision of the PTC or the Trial Chamber was binding or at least more authoritative for the purposes of the Closing Orders in Cases 003 and 004. Determining that neither decision was per se binding, the International Co-Investigating Judge had the opportunity to make his own voice heard by reviewing the 'PTC and Trial Chamber's rulings and the sources they relied upon to reach their different determinations' in order to decide which one to follow.[54] After conducting a comprehensive review of the sources, he favoured the Trial

---

51 Duch Trial Judgment, above n. 2, para. 291; *Prosecutor v Nuon Chea, Ieng Sary, Ieng Thirith* and *Khieu Samphan*, ECCC Case File No. 002/19-09-2007/ECCC/TC, Trial Chamber, Decision on Co-Prosecutors' Request to Exclude Armed Conflict Nexus Requirement from the Definition of Crimes against Humanity, 26 October 2011, para. 12 (finding no basis to reconsider its ruling on the issue in the Duch Trial Judgment).

52 *Prosecutor v Nuon Chea, Ieng Sary, Ieng Thirith* and *Khieu Samphan*, ECCC Case File No. 002/19-09-2007/ECCC/TC, Trial Chamber, Decision on Co-Prosecutors' Request to Exclude Armed Conflict Nexus Requirement from the Definition of Crimes against Humanity, 26 October 2011, para. 33.

53 Nuon Trial Judgment, above n. 10, para. 177.

54 *Prosecutor v Meas Muth*, ECCC Case File No. 003/07-09-2009-ECCC-OCIJ, Office of the Co-Investigating Judges, Decision on Meas Muth's Request for Clarification concerning Crimes against Humanity and the Nexus with Armed Conflict, 5 April 2016, para. 17.

Chamber's ruling over that of the PTC, while in effect 'substituting' his own reasons for those of both the 'higher' Chambers and concluding as follows:

> The Nexus, while present in the definition of crimes against humanity in the Nuremberg Charter and possibly viewed as a constitutive element of the crime by the IMT, was removed from the definition of the crime set forth in Control Council Law No. 10. Although the Nexus was still applicable by virtue of incorporation of the Nuremberg Charter in Control Council Law No. 10, I find it significant that it no longer appeared in the definition of the crime. The vast majority of the Courts that applied that law viewed it merely as a jurisdictional requirement. The Jerusalem District Court in the Eichmann case reached the same conclusion. …
>
> Starting from 1948 with the adoption of the Genocide Convention, and continuing with the Statutory Limitations Convention of 1968 and the Apartheid Convention of 1973, the international community recognised the possibility that crimes against humanity could be committed in times of peace. According to the ICJ, a series of similar resolutions may show the gradual evolution of the *opinio juris* required for the establishment of a new rule.
>
> Finally, the definition of crimes against humanity set forth in the 1954 Draft Code, on which the United Nations' Member States had the opportunity to comment upon, does not contain the Nexus as a constitutive element of the crime.[55]

When the issue eventually reached the Supreme Court Chamber it had become clear that the nexus requirement in the Nuremberg Charter could either be understood as a material element of the definition of crimes against humanity or as a jurisdictional element specifically limiting the International Military Tribunal's competence.[56] The Supreme Court Chamber considered that the jurisprudence emanating from the trials held under Control Council Law No. 10 was inconsistent, but found that the gradual exclusion of the nexus in a series of post-1945 international instruments 'accords with the evolving view that the prohibition of crimes against humanity aims to protect humanity from the commission of atrocities, thus warranting a definition that does not require a nexus to

[55] *Prosecutor v Meas Muth*, ECCC Case File No. 003/07-09-2009-ECCC-OCIJ, Office of the Co-Investigating Judges, Decision on Meas Muth's Request for Clarification Concerning Crimes against Humanity and the Nexus with Armed Conflict, 5 April 2016, paras. 72–5.

[56] Nuon Appeal Judgment, above n. 15, para. 713.

a war crime or a crime against peace'.[57] The Supreme Court Chamber additionally referred to national legislation adopted prior to 1975 which defined crimes against humanity without including a nexus requirement. Consequently, the Supreme Court Chamber concluded that: 'The nexus requirement to a war crime or crime against peace in the Nuremberg Principles was not part of the definition of crimes against humanity by 1975.'[58]

The majority of ECCC judicial opinion therefore favoured the view that the nexus requirement in the Nuremberg Charter was best understood as a jurisdictional element and that in the post-Second World War period and at least by 1975, crimes against humanity stood alone as a category of international crimes capable of commission during times of peace. As the International Co-Investigating Judge indicated, the PTC was correct to find that crimes against humanity were first developed in the context of armed conflicts, but, as ultimately also found by the Supreme Court Chamber, 'starting with the adoption of Control Council Law No. 10 in 1945, crimes against humanity progressively became a discrete category of crimes, distinct from war crimes'.[59] The Trial Chamber was also correct to state that: 'It is undisputed that a nexus to armed conflict is not currently an element of crimes against humanity within customary international law'.[60]

The point of crystallisation of a new norm is always hard to pinpoint in an analysis of the evolution of customary international law. The ICTY Appeals Chamber suggested that even in the Nuremberg Charter the nexus requirement was purely jurisdictional:

> [T]he nexus between crimes against humanity and either crimes against peace or war crimes, required by the Nuremberg Charter, was peculiar to the jurisdiction of the Nuremberg Tribunal. Although the nexus requirement in the Nuremberg Charter was carried over to the 1948 General Assembly resolution affirming the Nuremberg principles, there is no logical or legal basis for this requirement and it has been abandoned in subsequent State practice with

---

57 Ibid, para. 716.

58 Ibid, para. 721.

59 *Prosecutor v Meas Muth*, ECCC Case File No. 003/07-09-2009-ECCC-OCIJ, Office of the Co-Investigating Judges, Decision on Meas Muth's Request for Clarification Concerning Crimes against Humanity and the Nexus with Armed Conflict, 5 April 2016, para. 22.

60 *Prosecutor v Nuon Chea, Ieng Sary, Ieng Thirith* and *Khieu Samphan*, ECCC Case File No. 002/19-09-2007/ECCC/TC, Trial Chamber, Decision on Co-Prosecutors' Request to Exclude Armed Conflict Nexus Requirement from the Definition of Crimes against Humanity, 26 October 2011, para. 10.

> respect to crimes against humanity. Most notably, the nexus requirement was eliminated from the definition of crimes against humanity contained in Article II(1)(c) of Control Council Law No. 10 of 20 December 1945. The obsolescence of the nexus requirement is evidenced by international conventions regarding genocide and apartheid, both of which prohibit particular types of crimes against humanity regardless of any connection to armed conflict.[61]

The inclusion of the nexus requirement in the Nuremberg Principles as produced by the International Law Commission in 1950 casts some doubt on this interpretation of the Nuremberg Charter.[62] However, the ICTY Appeals Chamber was concerned in this context with Article 5 of the ICTY Statute which criminalises as crimes against humanity specified acts 'when committed in armed conflict, whether international or internal in character, and directed against any civilian population'.[63] The ICTY Appeals Chamber found that '[s]ince customary international law no longer requires any nexus between crimes against humanity and armed conflict ... , Article 5 was intended to reintroduce this nexus for the purposes of this Tribunal'.[64] The International Law Commission (ILC) has stated in its current codification work on crimes against humanity that the formulation in Article 5 of the ICTY Statute

> is best understood contextually, having been developed in 1993 with an understanding that armed conflict in fact existed in the former Yugoslavia (which had led to the exercise of the Council's Chapter VII enforcement powers), and as designed principally to dispel the notion that crimes against humanity had to be linked to an international armed conflict.[65]

---

[61] *Prosecutor v Tadić*, ICTY Case No. IT-94-1-AR72, Appeals Chamber, Decision on the Defence Motion for Interlocutory Appeal on Jurisdiction, 2 October 1995, para. 140.

[62] 'Principles of International Law Recognized in the Charter of the Nürnberg Tribunal and in the Judgment of the Tribunal', in ILC, 'Report of the International Law Commission to the General Assembly, A/1316, July 1950', *Yearbook of the International Law Commission*, vol. II, 1950, pp. 364–85, paras. 97-127, Principle VI(c).

[63] Updated Statute of the International Criminal Tribunal for the Former Yugoslavia, September 2009, Article 5, <http://www.icty.org/x/file/Legal%20 Library/Statute/statute_sept09_en.pdf> [accessed 26 June 2017].

[64] *Prosecutor v Tadić*, ICTY Case No. IT-94-1-AR72, Appeals Chamber, Decision on the Defence Motion for Interlocutory Appeal on Jurisdiction, 2 October 1995, para. 78.

[65] S.D. Murphy, ILC, First Report of the Special Rapporteur on Crimes against Humanity, A/CN.4/680, 17 February 2015, para. 40, <http://legal.un.org/ilc/guide/7_7.shtml> [accessed 22 June 2017].

Apart from the absence of the nexus requirement in Control Council Law No. 10 and related jurisprudence supporting its function primarily as a jurisdictional requirement,[66] an identifiable shift occurred in the period between the adoption of the Nuremberg Principles and the debate over the 1954 Draft Code of Offences against the Peace and Security of Mankind which omitted the nexus. As the International Co-Investigating Judge noted, work on the 1954 Draft Code was stalled because of the failure to reach agreement on the definition of aggression and the authoritativeness of this source should not be dismissed as readily as was done by the PTC.[67] It is difficult to fault the PTC for adopting the interpretation that was most favourable to the defence, having been unable to identify a point of crystallisation of the definition of crimes against humanity absent the nexus requirement prior to the adoption of the Rome Statute in 1998. However, on balance, the evidence does support a definite period of crystallisation prior to the ECCC's temporal jurisdiction, especially if due regard is had to the conceptual origins of crimes against humanity, in other words, its core material content. Like genocide, crimes against humanity are often associated with armed conflict but it was never their commission during a 'time of war' that truly defined this species of international crime.

6.2 State Plan or Policy

Another question that arose before the Trial and Supreme Court Chambers was whether the definition of crimes against humanity under customary international law at the relevant time included a State plan or policy contextual requirement. According to the Rome Statute, an 'attack directed against any civilian population' must be 'pursuant to or in furtherance of a State or organizational policy'.[68] However, since the

---

[66] It has been noted that the military tribunals were 'split over whether such a nexus must be read into the definition [of crimes against humanity], or was not required'. *See* R. Cryer, H. Friman, D. Robinson and E. Wilmshurst, *An Introduction to International Criminal Law and Procedure* (2nd edn, Cambridge, Cambridge University Press, 2010), p. 234.

[67] *Prosecutor v Meas Muth*, ECCC Case File No. 003/07-09-2009-ECCC-OCIJ, Office of the Co-Investigating Judges, Decision on Meas Muth's Request for Clarification Concerning Crimes against Humanity and the Nexus with Armed Conflict, 5 April 2016, paras. 56–8; *see* also N.H.B. Jørgensen, *The Responsibility of States for International Crimes* (Oxford/New York, Oxford University Press, 2003), p. 43.

[68] Rome Statute of the International Criminal Court, United Nations, *Treaty Series*, vol. 2187, 3, 17 July 1998, Article 7(2)(a).

Rome Statute was not adopted until 1998, well after the temporal jurisdiction of the ECCC, the task was to identify if, and when, this additional requirement formally became part of the definition of crimes against humanity outside the International Criminal Court (ICC) framework. The Supreme Court Chamber noted that none of the Statutes of the ad hoc tribunals contained such a requirement, nor had it been incorporated via the practice of those tribunals.[69] While recognising some opinion to the contrary, the Supreme Court Chamber agreed with the Trial Chamber's conclusion that '"state practice and *opinio juris* [by 1975] did not clearly support a State or organizational plan or policy requirement" as an independent contextual element of the definition of crimes against humanity'.[70] The existence of such a plan or policy might nevertheless be relevant to establishing the widespread or systematic nature of the attack.[71]

6.3 Attack against Any Civilian Population

By definition, the category of crimes against humanity is aimed at protecting civilians but in practice one and the same attack may affect both civilians and combatants. The ECCC has addressed the question whether the requirement of an 'attack against any civilian population' is satisfied, first in the context of soldiers being present among the civilian population, and second in the context of members of a State's own armed forces being the targets of the attack.

In the first context, former Khmer Republic soldiers were among the targeted group comprised mainly of civilians. According to the Trial Chamber, the phrase 'directed against any civilian population' meant that 'such population must be the primary, as opposed to incidental, target of the attack'.[72] Relying on the jurisprudence of the ICTY and International Criminal Tribunal for Rwanda (ICTR), the ECCC Supreme Court Chamber agreed with the Trial Chamber that in order to qualify as a civilian population for the purpose of crimes against humanity, 'the target population must be of a predominantly civilian nature' and that 'the presence within a population of ... former combatants, who have laid

69 Nuon Appeal Judgment, above n. 15, para. 730.
70 Ibid, para. 732; Nuon Trial Judgment, above n. 10, para. 181.
71 Duch Trial Judgment, above n. 2, para. 301.
72 Nuon Trial Judgment, above n. 10, para. 182.

down their arms, does not alter its civilian characteristic'.[73] The Trial Chamber indicated that where both civilians and soldiers are present, the factors that may be relevant to determining whether the attack was directed at a civilian population include:

> the means and method used in the course of the attack, the status of the victims, their number, the discriminatory nature of the attack, the nature of the crimes committed in its course, and the resistance to the assailants at the time and the extent to which the attacking force may be said to have complied or attempted to comply with the precautionary requirements of the laws of war.[74]

The Trial Chamber in Case 001 found that the 'attack was directed at the entire Cambodian population and did not differentiate between military and civilian personnel. Crimes against humanity were therefore committed against a collectivity of persons at S-21, and were all-encompassing, engulfing both civilian and military elements without distinction.'[75] In Case 002/01, the Supreme Court Chamber upheld the Trial Chamber's finding that 'soldiers *hors de combat* do not qualify as "civilians" for the purposes of Article 5 of the ECCC Law'.[76] Under customary international humanitarian law, a person *hors de combat* is: '(a) anyone who is in the power of an adverse party; (b) anyone who is defenceless because of unconsciousness, shipwreck, wounds or sickness; or (c) anyone who clearly expresses an intention to surrender.'[77] Thus, Khmer Republic soldiers *hors de combat* could not be equated with civilians, but their presence within the civilian population that was the target of a widespread and systematic attack did not deprive that population of its civilian character for the purposes of the definition of crimes against humanity. The question of civilian status arises in respect

---

[73] Nuon Appeal Judgment, above n. 15, para. 738 (citing *Prosecutor v Blaškić*, ICTY Case No. IT-95-14-A, Appeals Chamber, Judgment, 29 July 2004, para. 113); Nuon Trial Judgment, above n. 10, para. 183.

[74] Nuon Trial Judgment, above n. 10, para. 184; Duch Trial Judgment, above n. 2, para. 309.

[75] Duch Trial Judgment, above n. 2, para. 325.

[76] Nuon Appeal Judgment, above n. 15, para. 738; Nuon Trial Judgment, above n. 10, para. 186: 'A member of an armed organisation is not accorded civilian status by reason of the fact that he or she is not armed or in combat at the time of the commission of the crimes.'

[77] Customary International Humanitarian Law, Rule 47, <https://ihl-databases.icrc.org/customary-ihl/eng/docs/v1_rul_rule47> [accessed 22 June 2017].

of the object of the attack and not in respect of individual victims of the underlying crimes.[78]

The second context concerns internal military purges, in other words the Khmer Rouge regime's targeting of its own soldiers. The question in this context is whether the contextual element of an attack directed against any civilian population can be satisfied where members of the armed forces of the State or organisation carrying out the attack are the primary target. This novel issue arose in Cases 003 and 004 and was the subject of a decision by the International Co-Investigating Judge who had sought submissions from the parties as well as issuing an open call for *amicus curiae* briefs.[79] The International Co-Prosecutor and the majority of the 11 *amici curiae* who submitted briefs argued that an attack by a State or organisation against members of its own armed forces could be the basis for a crime against humanity, whereas the defence teams took the contrary position.[80] Certain of the other *amici curiae* submitted that this form of auto-targeting could only constitute a crime against humanity in times of peace while others suggested that it would be limited to the crime against humanity of persecution.[81] The latter argument was rejected outright since despite there being authority for the view that the *chapeau* element of an attack against any civilian population did not apply to 'persecution-type' crimes against humanity, Article 5 of the ECCC Law included this element as a jurisdictional requirement in respect of all crimes against humanity.[82]

---

[78] Nuon Appeal Judgment, above n. 15, para. 76; Nuon Trial Judgment, above n. 10, para. 187: 'Thus, a soldier who is hors de combat may be the victim of an act amounting to a crime against humanity, provided that all other necessary conditions are met.'

[79] *Prosecutor v Meas Muth*, ECCC Case File No. 003/07-09-2009-ECCC-OCIJ, Office of the Co-Investigating Judges, Notification on the Interpretation of 'Attack against the Civilian Population' in the Context of Crimes against Humanity with regard to a State's or Regime's Own Armed Forces', 7 February 2017, paras. 2, 4 (Eleven *Amicus Curiae* briefs were filed).

[80] Ibid, para. 7.

[81] Ibid.

[82] Ibid, paras 33–4 (The Co-Investigating Judge rejected the argument put forward in *Prosecutor v Meas Muth*, ECCC Case File No. 003/07-09-2009-ECCC-OCIJ, *Amici Curiae*, *Amicus Curiae* Brief for Cases 003 and 004 by Catherine Drummond, Philippa Webb and Dapo Akande, 19 May 2016.) *See* Duch Appeal Judgment, above n. 38, para. 233 (The ECCC Supreme Court Chamber had noted that the Legal Committee of the UNWCC referred to two types of crimes against humanity: the 'murder-type' (e.g. murder, extermination,

In his decision, the International Co-Investigating Judge began by identifying the purpose of crimes against humanity under international law as being 'the protection against human rights violations perpetrated on a large scale against individuals including a state's own nationals, who were not otherwise protected by the existing laws and customs of war'.[83] He noted that the jurisprudence of the ad hoc tribunals was of limited use as an interpretative guide since it 'originated in the context of cases where [crimes against humanity] were inextricably linked to an ongoing armed conflict' with the result that those tribunals adopted the meaning of 'civilian' in international humanitarian law.[84] However, three cases of the German Supreme Court operating in the British Zone of Occupation following the Second World War suggested a broader interpretation of 'civilian population' by emphasising the collective and large-scale dimension of crimes against humanity rather than the formal status of the affected persons.[85] In addition, two specific species of crime against humanity—genocide and apartheid—were clearly designed to protect all individuals irrespective of their status in accordance with conventions adopted in 1948 and 1974 respectively.[86] Ultimately, the International Co-Investigating Judge was guided by the need to interpret 'civilian population' in the specific context of crimes against humanity which, as a category of crime, did not depend on a nexus with an armed conflict thus rendering the definition of 'civilian' in international humanitarian law (as favoured by the ICTY Appeals Chamber) inappropriate.[87] In the Judge's view, having regard to the purpose of the law on crimes against humanity, 'a broader definition of civilian population, that of the entire population of a certain country' had to be adopted.[88] He concluded that 'as a matter of principle' between 1975 and 1979 an attack by a state or organisation against its own armed forces, whether carried out in peacetime or during an armed conflict (unless the attacked armed forces were supporting the opposing side) satisfied the *chapeau* requirement of an attack against any

---

enslavement), and the 'persecution-type' committed on racial, political or religious grounds.).

[83] *Prosecutor v Meas Muth*, ECCC Case File No. 003/07-09-2009-ECCC-OCIJ, Office of the Co-Investigating Judges, Notification on the Interpretation of 'Attack against the Civilian Population' in the Context of Crimes against Humanity with regard to a State's or Regime's Own Armed Forces', para. 26.

[84] Ibid, para. 29.

[85] Ibid, para. 43.

[86] Ibid, para. 44.

[87] Ibid, para. 55.

[88] Ibid, para. 55.

civilian population under Article 5 of the ECCC Law.[89] This conclusion was not seen to offend the principle of legality since the interpretation of 'civilian population' based on international humanitarian law became the majority position only after the temporal jurisdiction of the ECCC. In his reaction to various arguments that had been put forward by the defence, the Judge made an impassioned plea to logic and heralded the end of the prioritisation of the arbitrary exercise of state power over the protection of individual rights in the post-Nuremberg legal framework.

The Co-Investigating Judge approached the issue as one of interpretation which was technically correct as the Supreme Court Chamber had already endorsed the existence of the *chapeau* requirements contained in Article 5 of the ECCC Law under customary international law. The Co-Investigating Judge invoked the rule of interpretation in Article 31 of the Vienna Convention on the Law of Treaties as well as the ECCC's practice on interpreting criminal laws.[90] However, it is unclear whether he treated the exercise as one of interpretation of Article 5 of the ECCC Law since he spoke of 'interpreting the law of [crimes against humanity] consistently with [the] objective and purpose [of this law] in a scenario such as that envisaged' in relation to the issue before him.[91] The purpose of the law on crimes against humanity should really have served as a check on the textual interpretation of the words 'any civilian population' in their context in case of any ambiguity. The Co-Investigating Judge proceeded to apply the legality test as a check on his interpretation, effectively addressing the question of the meaning that should be given to the words 'civilian population' according to customary international law at the relevant time.[92] The methodological approach was therefore confusing although in the end the decision covered all bases. One difficulty was that the available evidence of state practice and *opinio juris* as it concerned the possible scope of the impacted group of victims under the emerging law on crimes against humanity was sparse at best. The decision refers to the limited case law as being 'consistent with the objective and purpose of [crimes against humanity]' thus treating the object and purpose of the customary law on crimes against humanity as

---

89 Ibid, paras. 56–7.

90 Ibid, paras. 19–22.

91 Ibid, para. 55.

92 *See* further on the correct analytical approach, *Prosecutor v Ao An* and *Yim Tith*, ECCC Case File No. 003/07-09-2009-ECCC-OCIJ, *Amicus Curiae*, *Amicus Curiae* Brief in Cases 003 and 004 – Professor Ben Saul, 19 May 2016, para. 15.

the guiding light to the interpretation of the contextual elements that also form part of customary law.[93]

The Trial Chamber had previously noted in Case 002/01 that there was no established definition of 'civilian' under customary international law in 1975 and had adopted the ordinary meaning of the term as encompassing persons who are not members of the armed forces.[94] The phrase 'civilian population' therefore included all persons who were not members of the armed forces or otherwise recognised as combatants.[95] The Trial Chamber also reiterated that crimes against humanity may include a state's attack on its own (civilian) population.[96] It did not, however, consider the issue facing the Co-Investigating Judge in Cases 003 and 004 when it made this assessment and assumed a situation of armed conflict. In Case 001, the Supreme Court Chamber noted the distinction drawn at the time of the Nuremberg and Tokyo trials, and recognised in the Nuremberg Principles, between 'murder-type' and 'persecution-type' crimes against humanity.[97] According to this distinction, only the 'murder-type' needed to be directed against a civilian population. However, the Supreme Court Chamber did not dwell on this matter as it was concerned with the definition of the underlying act of persecution. Moreover, Article 5 of the ECCC Law applies the requirement of 'directed against any civilian population' to all types of crimes against humanity.[98]

The jurisprudence of the ad hoc tribunals, as analysed by the Co-Investigating Judge, suggests a narrow interpretation of 'civilian population' applying the meaning of 'civilian' under international humanitarian law, but this jurisprudence needs to be assessed in the context in

---

[93] *Prosecutor v Meas Muth*, ECCC Case File No. 003/07-09-2009-ECCC-OCIJ, Office of the Co-Investigating Judges, Notification on the Interpretation of 'Attack against the Civilian Population' in the Context of Crimes against Humanity with regard to a State's or Regime's Own Armed Forces', para. 43.

[94] Nuon Trial Judgment, above n. 10, para. 185.

[95] This is also reflected in Customary International Humanitarian Law, Rule 5 (Definition of Civilians: 'Civilians are persons who are not members of the armed forces. The civilian population comprises all persons who are civilians.'), <https://ihl-databases.icrc.org/customary-ihl/eng/docs/v1_rul_rule5> [accessed 26 June 2017].

[96] Nuon Trial Judgment, above n. 10, para. 187 (referring to Duch Trial Judgment, above n. 2, para. 312 and *Prosecutor v Kunarac, Kovač* and *Vuković*, ICTY Case No. IT-96-23-T & IT-96-23/1-T, Trial Chamber, Judgement, para. 423).

[97] Duch Appeal Judgment, above n. 38, paras. 232–3.

[98] ECCC Law, Article 5.

which it has evolved.[99] Having regard especially to the ECCC's majority view that the category of crimes against humanity under Article 5 of the ECCC Law does not require a nexus to an armed conflict, it seems appropriate to sever the definition of 'civilian population' from its international humanitarian law roots or associations. If there is no armed conflict it should be unnecessary to speak of civilians or combatants in the first place.[100] It is only when there is an armed conflict and international humanitarian law applies that the distinction between civilians and combatants must be drawn and the parties to the conflict incur obligations both to their own and the enemy's armed forces and civilian populations.[101]

As the Co-Investigating Judge found, the specific situation of the victims rather than their formal status is what counts.[102] The Apartheid Convention, which declares that apartheid is a crime against humanity, refers to 'groups of persons' rather than civilians and 'internal purges' of those serving in state institutions may fall within the scope of apartheid.[103] In this respect, while adopted in the context of institutionalised racism in South Africa, the characterisation of apartheid as a crime against humanity built on the Nuremberg-era condemnation of crimes committed by a state against its own citizens whatever their status, and

---

[99] *Prosecutor v Meas Muth*, ECCC Case File No. 003/07-09-2009-ECCC-OCIJ, Office of the Co-Investigating Judges, Notification on the Interpretation of 'Attack against the Civilian Population' in the Context of Crimes against Humanity with regard to a State's or Regime's Own Armed Forces', para. 55.

[100] *Prosecutor v Meas Muth*, ECCC Case File No. 003/07-09-2009-ECCC-OCIJ, *Amici Curiae*, *Amicus Curiae* Brief Filed by Drs Williams and Grey in Response to Call for *Amicus Curiae* Briefs in Cases 003 and 004, 19 April 2016, para. 19; *Prosecutor v Meas Muth*, ECCC Case File No. 003/07-09-2009-ECCC-OCIJ, *Amici Curiae*, *Amicus Curiae* Brief for Cases 003 and 004 by Catherine Drummond, Philippa Webb and Dapo Akande, 19 May 2016, para. 19.

[101] ECCC Document No. D306/9, *Amicus Curiae*, Brief of Dr. Joanna Nicholson as *Amicus Curiae* in Support of Neither Party, 13 May 2016, para. 2.

[102] *Prosecutor v Meas Muth*, ECCC Case File No. 003/07-09-2009-ECCC-OCIJ, Office of the Co-Investigating Judges, Notification on the Interpretation of 'Attack against the Civilian Population' in the Context of Crimes against Humanity with regard to a State's or Regime's Own Armed Forces', para. 43.

[103] International Convention on the Suppression and Punishment of the Crime of Apartheid, United Nations, *Treaty Series*, vol. 1015, 243, 30 November 1973, Article II: '"the crime of apartheid", which shall include similar policies and practices of racial segregation and discrimination as practised in southern Africa, shall apply to [a list of] inhuman acts committed for the purpose of establishing and maintaining domination by one racial group of persons over any other racial group of persons and systematically oppressing them.'

apartheid has since been incorporated as a crime against humanity into the Rome Statute (with the associated requirement of an attack directed against any civilian population being applicable).[104] Certainly there is a strong argument for including members of the armed forces within the notion of a civilian population in times of peace and, as the Co-Investigating Judge observed, the limited post-Second World War case law addressing the issue as well as the law on apartheid and genocide support a broad understanding of 'civilian'. The ILC's Special Rapporteur on crimes against humanity has also stated that: 'The word "any" indicates that "civilian population" is to have a wide definition and should be interpreted broadly.'[105] The Special Rapporteur has indicated that during a time of peace, 'civilian' includes 'all persons except those individuals who have a duty to maintain public order and have legitimate means to exercise force to that end at the time they are being attacked.'[106] Confusingly, this might include the armed forces as 'civilians' but not the police, whereas the police are generally regarded as civilians.[107] This points towards the need for a situation-specific determination.

It is difficult to envisage a scenario whereby the armed forces of a state or organisation are actively engaged in combat and simultaneously subject to a widespread or systematic attack in the form of an internal purge. In such a scenario, individual members of the armed forces may well be victims of a broader attack on the civilian population whose legal status as such remains unaffected by the presence of a proportion of soldiers. However, the Co-Investigating Judge presumably had in mind

---

104 Nobody has been prosecuted for apartheid as experienced in South Africa. *See* further J. Dugard, 'Convention on the Suppression and Punishment of the Crime of Apartheid', United Nations Audio-Visual Library of International Law, 2008, p. 2, <http://legal.un.org/avl/ha/cspca/cspca.html> [accessed 22 June 2017]. *See* also, United Nations Commission on Human Rights, Implementation of the International Convention on the Suppression and Punishment of the Crime of Apartheid: Study on Ways and Means of Insuring the Implementation of International Instruments such as the Convention on the Suppression and Punishment of the Crime of Apartheid, Including the Establishment of International Jurisdiction Envisaged by the Convention, E/CN.4/1426, 19 January 1981, para. 32.

105 Murphy, above n. 65, para. 135.

106 Ibid (relying on the *Kayishema* case before the ICTR).

107 Nuon Trial Judgment, above n. 10, para. 186: 'As a general presumption, the armed law enforcement agencies of a State are considered to be civilians for purposes of international humanitarian law. A person shall be considered to be a civilian for as long as there is doubt as to his or her status.'

circumstances in which an attack by a state or organisation against its own armed forces could be 'committed during the duration of but not contextually connected to an ongoing armed conflict'.[108] While the precise legal contours of a crime against humanity constituted by an attack directed against members of the armed forces during a time of armed conflict remain to be worked out, the summing up of the general position presented in the amicus brief submitted by Drs. Williams and Grey serves as a useful starting point:

> Applying a functional approach to the term 'civilian' in article 5 of the ECCC Law demonstrates that members of a State's armed forces attacked by their own State should be considered civilian in two circumstances:
>
> a. Where individuals are attacked in the context of an armed conflict due to their perceived allegiance to another party to the conflict or for reasons unconnected to the armed conflict, in particular on discriminatory grounds; and
> b. Where the attack is perpetrated in peacetime.
>
> In addition, members of a state's armed forces may be *victims* of crimes against humanity where the crimes against members of the armed forces form part of a broader attack against a population that is predominantly 'civilian'.[109]

Whether context (a) above warrants prosecution by an international or internationalised tribunal when a broader armed conflict with multiple civilian victims is also at issue will depend on the individual circumstances and their proper characterisation having regard to the full scope

[108] *Prosecutor v Meas Muth*, ECCC Case File No. 003/07-09-2009-ECCC-OCIJ, Office of the Co-Investigating Judges, Notification on the Interpretation of 'Attack against the Civilian Population' in the Context of Crimes against Humanity with regard to a State's or Regime's Own Armed Forces', para. 29.

[109] *Prosecutor v Meas Muth*, ECCC Case File No. 003/07-09-2009-ECCC-OCIJ, *Amici Curiae*, *Amicus Curiae* Brief Filed by Drs Williams and Grey in Response to Call for *Amicus Curiae* Briefs in Cases 003 and 004, 19 April 2016, paras. 28–9 (This does not differ greatly from the conclusion in the *Prosecutor v Meas Muth*, ECCC Case File No. 003/07-09-2009-ECCC-OCIJ, *Amici Curiae*, *Amicus Curiae* Brief for Cases 003 and 004 by Catherine Drummond, Philippa Webb and Dapo Akande, 19 May 2016, para. 22: 'Under customary international law applicable between 1975 and 1979, an attack by a State or organisation against members of its own armed forces may amount to an attack directed against a civilian population for the purpose of Article 5 of the ECCC Law in peacetime, or in armed conflict where: (i) the underlying crime is persecution; or (ii) members of the armed forces are victims of a broader attack directed against a civilian population.').

of the facts. It is perhaps due to the enormity of events before these tribunals and limited resources that the important question raised by the Co-Investigating Judge has become buried.

6.4 Discriminatory Grounds

The Supreme Court Chamber has noted that the formulation 'on national, political, ethnical, racial or religious grounds' that is included in the *chapeau* of Article 5 of the ECCC Law is an element limiting the ECCC's jurisdiction over crimes against humanity.[110] This requirement is not considered to be part of customary international law.[111] According to the Supreme Court Chamber, the jurisdictional requirement entails that the 'attack be founded on a national, political, ethnical, racial or religious basis – but not necessarily on discriminatory grounds'.[112] These words characterise the nature of the attack, but it is not necessary to prove that the perpetrator had a discriminatory intent for all crimes against humanity. If this were the case, the specification of discriminatory grounds for the crime against humanity of persecution would be redundant. The Trial Chamber expressed the position more succinctly: 'The requirement qualifies the nature of the broader attack rather than the individual underlying offences, and consequently does not import a discriminatory intent as a legal ingredient for all underlying crimes against humanity.'[113] In Case 001, the Supreme Court Chamber accepted the conclusion of the Trial Chamber that the relevant attack took place on political grounds. The Trial Chamber had found that the 'justification for the attack was ideologically-driven, seeking to detain, and either reform or eliminate, all real or perceived adversaries of the CPK'.[114]

6.5 Underlying Crimes

6.5.1 Case 001

The Trial Chamber in Case 001 assessed the facts relevant to the underlying acts constituting crimes against humanity at S-21 in general terms as follows. Under the heading of 'Murder and Extermination', the Trial Chamber found that there were numerous executions of foreign nationals, high-ranking CPK cadres and even children, and in some

---

110 Nuon Appeal Judgment, above n. 15, para. 744.
111 Duch Trial Judgment, above n. 2, para. 313.
112 Nuon Appeal Judgment, above n. 15, para. 745.
113 Nuon Trial Judgment, above n. 10, para. 188.
114 Duch Trial Judgment, above n. 2, para. 327.

instances mass executions, sometimes as a result of purges within the CPK and RAK.[115] Under the heading of 'Enslavement', the Trial Chamber found that the detainees especially at S-24 were subjected to long hours of forced labour under constant supervision.[116] Under the heading 'Imprisonment', the Trial Chamber referred to the thousands of individuals who were detained with no legal basis or due process of law at S-21 and S-24.[117] Under the heading 'Torture (Including Rape)', the Trial Chamber found that a variety of interrogation techniques such as beatings, electrocution and water-boarding resulting in severe physical pain and/or mental suffering were applied at S-21 by perpetrators acting in an official capacity, designed to obtain confessions or to punish, and that one incident of rape was proved to have occurred.[118] Under the heading 'Other Inhumane Acts', the Trial Chamber found that all detainees at S-21 and S-24 were deprived of their basic rights, such as the right to adequate food, sanitation and medical treatment and dehumanised by the conditions to which they were subjected.[119] The Trial Chamber noted that all these discrete crimes against humanity were alleged to amount to 'persecution on political grounds' in the sense that they constituted a denial of fundamental rights based upon the victims' real or perceived political beliefs or political opposition to those in power in the CPK.[120]

The Trial Chamber concluded after a cursory assessment that all of these underlying crimes had been recognised since the Nuremberg-era tribunals so as to satisfy the principle of legality.[121] For good measure, the Trial Chamber added that 'the appalling nature of the offences charged pursuant to Article 5 of the ECCC Law helps to refute any claim that the Accused would have been unaware of their criminal nature'.[122] Murder was found to require the death of the victim resulting from an unlawful act or omission by the perpetrator.[123] It had to be shown that the act or omission of the perpetrator was undertaken with the intent either to kill or to cause serious bodily harm in the reasonable knowledge that the

115 Ibid, paras. 209–19.
116 Ibid, para. 231.
117 Ibid, para. 239.
118 Ibid, paras. 241–8, 252–6.
119 Ibid, paras. 259–75.
120 Ibid, paras. 280, 381–90.
121 Ibid, para. 293.
122 Ibid, para. 295.
123 Ibid, para. 331.

act or omission would likely lead to death.[124] Extermination was found to be characterised by an act, omission or combination of each that results in the death of persons on a massive scale.[125] As underlying crimes, murder, extermination and enslavement were considered to be well-established in customary international law and all three crimes were found to be established on the facts. Regarding imprisonment, defined as 'the arbitrary deprivation of an individual's liberty without due process of law', the Trial Chamber explained that in order to amount to a crime against humanity, the deprivation of liberty had to be of similar gravity and seriousness as the other crimes enumerated as crimes against humanity in Article 5 of the ECCC Law.[126] Imprisonment as a crime against humanity was found to have been committed at S-21 and the other detention sites. As it concerned torture, the Trial Chamber adopted the definition contained in the 1984 Convention against Torture, making reference to the case law of ad hoc tribunals.[127] Thus, the crime of torture required that the act or omission was inflicted in order to attain a certain result or purpose.[128] Consistent with the Convention against Torture but contrary to ICTY jurisprudence, the Trial Chamber found 'that in 1975, the involvement of a State official was a requirement for an act to constitute torture under customary international law'.[129] The Trial Chamber found that a range of interrogation techniques amounting to torture were used at S-21 and S-24, and that the conduct alleged to constitute rape satisfied the requirements for both rape and torture.[130] Finding it to be well-established that rape could be characterised as torture, the Trial Chamber proceeded to characterise the one established incident of rape in this way in view of it being an 'egregious component of the prolonged and brutal torture inflicted upon the victim prior to her execution'.[131] Finally, the Trial Chamber found that conditions such as shackling and chaining, blindfolding and handcuffing, severe beatings and corporal punishments, detention in overly small or overcrowded cells, lack of adequate food, hygiene and medical care qualified as separate acts within the category of 'other inhumane acts'.[132]

---

124 Ibid, para. 333.
125 Ibid, para. 334.
126 Ibid, paras. 347, 349.
127 Ibid, paras. 353–8.
128 Ibid, para. 356.
129 Ibid, para. 357.
130 Ibid, paras. 359–60, 366.
131 Ibid, para. 366.
132 Ibid, paras. 372–3.

As it concerned persecution, the Trial Chamber noted that while it had long been proscribed under customary international law, the precise contours of the offence had not been established until the jurisprudence post-1992.[133] Relying on jurisprudence from the ICTY and ICTR, the Trial Chamber found that as early as 1975, persecution included an 'act or omission which … discriminates in fact and which denies or infringes upon a fundamental right laid down in international customary or treaty law'.[134] Thus, acts of persecution included, but were not limited to, the other underlying offences for crimes against humanity, for example murder, extermination, enslavement, imprisonment and torture. Other acts which might amount to persecution if they were of 'equal gravity and severity' to the enumerated acts in the sense of being a 'gross or blatant denial of a fundamental human right' included harassment, humiliation and psychological abuse, confinement in inhumane conditions, cruel and inhumane treatment, deportation, forcible transfer and forcible displacement, and forced labour assignments.[135] The perpetrator must carry out the act or omission deliberately with the intention to discriminate on one of the listed grounds.[136] Having found that the relevant conduct met the gravity threshold for persecution, the Trial Chamber went on to find that all victims were the target of discrimination on political grounds.[137] A majority of the Trial Chamber, Judge Cartwright dissenting, was satisfied that Duch possessed the requisite specific discriminatory intent to support a conviction for persecution.[138] While Judge Cartwright agreed that CPK policy was discriminatory on political grounds, in reaching the conclusion that it had not been proved to the required standard that Duch personally possessed the requisite discriminatory intent, she placed emphasis on the unanimous finding that the CPK, rather than Duch himself, identified 'enemies' and generally ordered arrests.[139]

On appeal in Case 001, the Supreme Court Chamber was concerned with the question whether the underlying crimes against humanity of enslavement, rape, torture and persecution enumerated in Article 5 of the ECCC Law constituted crimes against humanity under customary international law by 1975 and if so, how they should be defined.

---

133 Ibid, para. 375.
134 Ibid, para. 376.
135 Ibid, para. 378.
136 Ibid, para. 379.
137 Ibid, paras. 389–90.
138 Ibid, para. 392.
139 Ibid, paras. 397–9.

6.5.1.1 Enslavement In relation to enslavement, the core issues were first, whether the Trial Chamber erred in the manner in which it defined enslavement as a crime against humanity from 1975–1979; and second, whether the Trial Chamber erred in finding Duch guilty of enslavement only with respect to those S-21 detainees who were subjected to forced labour and not all S-21 detainees. The Supreme Court Chamber undertook an extensive analysis of Nuremberg-era cases to identify the state of the customary law in 1975 and considered that although these cases highlighted the forced and compulsory labour element of enslavement, they also included general statements on treating the victims as commodities. In the view of the Supreme Court Chamber, this confirmed that enslavement as a crime against humanity and the definition of slavery in the 1926 Slavery Convention shared the same roots.[140] The Supreme Court Chamber went on to affirm in substance the definition of enslavement as a crime against humanity suggested by the Trial Chamber as the operative one from 1975–1979, with some adjustment to the wording in recognition of the fact that there is no 'right of ownership over a person' in international law. According to the adjusted definition:

> The *actus reus* of enslavement is 'characterised by [the exercise over a person of any or all powers attaching to the right of ownership]' and the *mens rea* is the intentional exercise of 'any or all of the powers attaching to the right of ownership'.[141]

The Supreme Court Chamber considered that enslavement required an element of seeking an economic benefit or accruing some gain via the exercise of the powers of ownership and control over the victim and concluded that the Trial Chamber had failed to articulate this element.[142] However, the Trial Chamber had impliedly adopted this understanding by relying on 'the exploitation of forced labour in conditions denying the victims any rights and subjecting them to total control'.[143] The gain element should not be regarded as an additional element of the crime but rather the purpose implicit in the ownership powers as such.

In relation to the second issue, the Supreme Court Chamber found that the Trial Chamber had not erroneously read an element of forced labour into the definition of enslavement. In effect, the Trial Chamber had found that 'forced labour is a sufficient but not a necessary prerequisite for

---

140 Duch Appeal Judgment, above n. 38, para. 144.
141 Ibid, paras. 152–3.
142 Ibid, paras. 157–8.
143 Ibid, para. 158.

enslavement as a crime against humanity'.[144] The Trial Chamber had limited itself to the facts in the Closing Order by which enslavement was only alleged where forced labour was present. According to the Supreme Court Chamber, the Trial Chamber could have combined the entire factual record for other indications of enslavement. Relying on its findings as to the purpose implicit in the exercise of ownership powers, the Supreme Court Chamber concluded that the Trial Chamber had not identified any evidence of efforts by the accused to accrue some gain from the totality of S-21 detainees or of otherwise treating them as commodities.[145] Therefore, on the basis of the factual findings, the detainees who were not subjected to forced labour were not victims of enslavement as a crime against humanity.[146]

6.5.1.2 Rape and torture The Trial Chamber had held that the crime of rape as listed in Article 5 of the ECCC Law was a distinct crime against humanity in 1975.[147] However, the Trial Chamber convicted Duch for torture as a crime against humanity, encompassing rape.[148] The Co-Prosecutors appealed against the characterisation of the individual instance of rape as torture.[149] According to the Co-Prosecutors, if rape were to be subsumed within torture it would not reflect the full gravity of the accused's conduct.[150] This raised the question whether rape constituted a distinct crime against humanity in 1975 and whether the Trial Chamber erred in characterising rape as torture.

According to the Supreme Court Chamber, it was clear that rape was well-established as a war crime by 1975 but its status as a crime against humanity was less certain and reliance on the case law of the ICTY, ICTR and Special Court for Sierra Leone (SCSL) created difficulties due to the temporal jurisdiction of those courts.[151] Having regard to that case law, the Supreme Court Chamber observed that even 'by the era of the ad hoc tribunals, rape as a crime against humanity still remained a nascent

---

144 Ibid, para. 126.

145 Ibid, para. 158.

146 Ibid, para. 166.

147 Duch Trial Judgment, above n. 2, paras. 293–4.

148 Ibid, para. 677.

149 *Prosecutor v Kaing Guek Eav alias 'Duch'*, ECCC Case File No. 001/18-07-2007-ECCC/SC, Office of the Co-Prosecutors, Co-Prosecutors' Appeal against the Judgement of the Trial Chamber in the Case of Kaing Guek Eav alias Duch, 13 October 2010, para. 192.

150 Ibid, para. 199.

151 Duch Appeal Judgment, above n. 38, paras. 176–9.

notion'.[152] The Supreme Court Chamber went on to find that 'recognition of rape as a crime against humanity did not begin to take shape until the 1990s, following reports of rape being used as a tool in carrying out widespread or systematic attacks on civilian populations in Haiti, Bosnia, and Rwanda'.[153] Rape was therefore not a distinct crime against humanity at the time relevant to the charges against Duch.[154] Further, the fact of criminalisation of rape at the domestic level was viewed as being insufficient to allow the conclusion that it was a separate crime against humanity.[155] In other words, municipal law could not establish the existence of a crime against humanity but it could help in defining the content of the prohibition. The Supreme Court Chamber therefore found that the Trial Chamber erred in law in concluding that the rape that occurred at S-21 constituted rape as a crime against humanity prohibited under customary international law.[156]

The Supreme Court Chamber proceeded to determine *ex proprio motu* whether the Trial Chamber erred in finding that an act of rape could constitute the crime against humanity of torture during the ECCC's temporal jurisdiction. Torture was found to be a crime against humanity under customary international law by 1975.[157] To define torture, the Supreme Court Chamber gathered the evidence leading up to the 1975 Declaration on Torture, including the jurisprudence under Control Council Law No. 10, the International Committee of the Red Cross Commentary to the 1949 Geneva Convention IV, and the 1969 Greek Case before the European Commission on Human Rights. Taken as a whole, this evidence was seen to support the conclusion that the elements of torture provided in the 1975 Declaration were declaratory of customary international law by the time of the ECCC's temporal jurisdiction.[158] Rape was found to be an act that established per se the suffering of those upon whom it is inflicted and met all the elements of torture. Therefore, the Trial Chamber had not erred in concluding that an instance of rape was covered by the definition of torture that existed under customary international law by 1975. In other words, the act of rape constituted torture.[159]

---

[152] Ibid, para. 179.
[153] Ibid, para. 179.
[154] Ibid, para. 180.
[155] Ibid, para. 182.
[156] Ibid, para. 183.
[157] Ibid, para. 188.
[158] Ibid, paras. 196, 205.
[159] Ibid, para. 213.

6.5.1.3 Persecution In deciding whether persecution was a distinct crime against humanity at the relevant time, the Supreme Court Chamber began as far back as Grotius, but found that it was only after the Second World War that individual criminal responsibility for persecution as a crime against humanity was first invoked. The Supreme Court Chamber therefore concluded that by 1975, persecution on racial, religious or political grounds was recognised as a crime against humanity under customary international law.[160]

In terms of the definition of persecution, there were no clearly articulated elements in the post-Second World War jurisprudence. After going through the relevant sources, the Supreme Court Chamber affirmed the Trial Chamber's articulation of the requisite *mens rea*, and, with some clarifications, the *actus reus*. The Trial Chamber had defined persecution as:

> (i) an act or omission which ... discriminates in fact and which denies or infringes upon a fundamental right laid down in international customary or treaty law (*actus reus*); and
> (ii) deliberate perpetration of an act or omission with the intent to discriminate on political, racial or religious grounds (*mens rea*).[161]

It was the Trial Chamber's interpretation of the 'discriminatory in fact' element that was not accepted by the Supreme Court Chamber.[162] In particular, the Supreme Court Chamber did not agree with the Trial Chamber's statement (relying on ICTY jurisprudence) that where 'the perception of the perpetrator provides the basis of the discrimination in question, the [discriminatory] consequences are real for the victim even if the perpetrator's classification may be incorrect under objective criteria'.[163] The Supreme Court Chamber accepted this statement to the extent that it meant that the perpetrator determines the criteria for targeting on political grounds but rejected it to the extent that it allowed for persecutory intent alone to suffice for establishing the crime of persecution.[164] Consequently:

> for the occurrence of persecution, it is necessary that the act or omission discriminates in fact and discriminates against a discernible group defined pursuant to given criteria. Conversely, there is no discrimination in fact where:

---

160 Ibid, para. 225.
161 Ibid, para. 226.
162 Ibid, para. 275.
163 Ibid, para. 275 (referring to Duch Trial Judgment, above n. 2, para. 317).
164 Ibid, para. 275.

> 1) there is a mistake of fact by the perpetrator as to whether a victim actually belongs to the defined target group; or 2) the perpetrator targets victims irrespective of whether they fall under the discriminatory criterion, in other words, where the targeting is *indiscriminate*.[165]

Finally, the Supreme Court Chamber addressed the question whether the Trial Chamber had erred in finding that *every* individual detained at S-21 was targeted on political grounds and was therefore a victim of persecution. As a result of its interpretation of the *actus reus*, the Supreme Court Chamber found that persecution had not been established in relation to an unspecified number of individuals who had been detained, interrogated, enslaved and executed at S-21 because these crimes were a result of indiscriminate targeting by the Accused and were not committed on political grounds.[166] This meant that Duch's conviction for persecution was struck out although his convictions for extermination, enslavement, imprisonment, torture and other inhumane acts were upheld.

6.5.2 Case 002/01

In its consideration of the movement of the Cambodian population in two phases and the acts alleged to have been committed at Tuol Po Chrey, the Trial Chamber analysed the underlying acts of forced transfer, inhumane acts, murder, extermination and persecution. As it concerned forced transfer, the Trial Chamber found that 'the evacuation of Phnom Penh was not justified on the basis of civilian security or military necessity and, in any event, was not proportional'.[167] The forcible movement of the population involved the following consequences which amounted to other inhumane acts:

> the evacuation of Phnom Penh itself caused the victims long-lasting and serious bodily and mental harm, the effects of which were compounded by the coercive and threatening circumstances in which the evacuation was effected and the inhumane conditions to which the evacuees were subjected during the subsequent journey. These acts were intentional, inhumane and rise to the level of severity of the other crimes against humanity enumerated in the ECCC Law.[168]

The Trial Chamber found that the deaths of those victims who were shot and killed during the evacuation of Phnom Penh, as well as those who

165 Ibid, para. 277.
166 Ibid, para. 284.
167 Nuon Trial Judgment, above n. 10, para. 551.
168 Ibid, para. 552.

died due to the conditions and lack of any assistance, constituted murder.[169] Extermination was also found to have been established, as was persecution on the basis that Khmer Republic officials and city people were targeted on political grounds.[170] The Trial Chamber summed up its findings as follows:

> Based on a complete reading of the Closing Order, the Chamber considers that the various acts charged as political persecution were implemented through a number of crimes. The exclusion of high-ranking Khmer Republic officials was effected by murder. Further, the arrest and execution of low-ranking Khmer Republic officials was effected by murder and/or extermination. Last, the harsher treatment of 'New People' characterised as re-education was effected through forced transfer and the ensuing acts of murder and/or extermination or attacks against human dignity.[171]

The Trial Chamber was also satisfied that movements from the southern to northern regions of Cambodia (Phase Two) were conducted on a massive scale and that at a 'bare minimum, at least 300,000 to 400,000 people were displaced'[172] while 'a very conservative estimate' of the number of people moved within regions was 30,000.[173] According to the Trial Chamber, the crimes against humanity of forced transfer, enforced disappearances, extermination and persecution on political grounds were established. Additionally, attacks against human dignity were found to fall within the ambit of other inhumane acts and resulted from depriving the civilian population of adequate food, shelter, medical assistance, and minimum sanitary conditions during Phases One and Two of the population movements.[174]

In respect of the events at Tuol Po Chrey, the Trial Chamber found that the only reasonable inference to be drawn from the evidence was that a minimum of 250 former Lon Nol officials were transported to Tuol Po Chrey around 25 or 26 April 1975 and executed.[175] In respect of these events, the crimes against humanity of murder, extermination and political persecution through execution were found to be established.

The Supreme Court Chamber upheld the finding of persecution in relation to Phase One, having confirmed the 'possibility that persecution

---

169 Ibid, para. 559.
170 Ibid, paras. 562, 574.
171 Ibid, para. 568.
172 Ibid, para. 580.
173 Ibid, para. 581.
174 Ibid, paras. 456–8.
175 Ibid, para. 681.

as a crime against humanity might target aggregated groups without any common identity or agenda', in other words, groups that were not comprised of members of a political group or those holding political views.[176] However, while the Supreme Court Chamber found that the crime against humanity of other inhumane acts (forced transfer) was established in relation to Phase Two, it considered that the Trial Chamber had erred in finding that persecution was also established.[177] The Supreme Court Chamber also clarified the applicable law relating to murder, extermination and inhumane acts.

6.5.2.1 Murder Nuon Chea argued on appeal that it was necessary to prove direct intent to kill to establish the *mens rea* for murder.[178] The Supreme Court Chamber disagreed, being satisfied on the basis of the post-Second World War jurisprudence that 'it was sufficient to establish that the accused knew that their acts and omissions would likely lead to their victims' death and accepted this result—which corresponds to the notions of *dolus eventualis* and recklessness.'[179] This conclusion was reinforced by domestic practice according to which 'causing of death with less than direct intent but more than mere negligence' was the general approach.[180]

6.5.2.2 Extermination The Trial Chamber had rejected the defence arguments that in order to establish the crime against humanity of extermination it was first necessary to prove that the accused knew that his action was part of 'a vast murderous enterprise' in which a large number of persons were marked for killing and second, to prove an intention to kill persons on a massive scale, or to systematically subject a large number of people to conditions of living that would lead to their deaths *in a widespread or systematic manner*.[181] These matters arose for consideration by the Supreme Court Chamber.

The Supreme Court Chamber found, after examining the relevant post-Second World War jurisprudence, that extermination constituted 'a

---

176 Nuon Appeal Judgment, above n. 15, paras. 678, 680.

177 Ibid, para. 706.

178 *Prosecutor v Nuon Chea* and *Khieu Samphan*, ECCC Case File No. 002/19-09-2007-ECCC-SC, Defence for Nuon Chea, Nuon Chea's Appeal against the Judgment in Case 002/01, 29 December 2014, para. 676.

179 Nuon Appeal Judgment, above n. 15, para. 395.

180 Ibid, para. 409.

181 Nuon Trial Judgment, above n. 10, paras. 417–20.

crime of mass murder, targeting groups or (part of) a population'.[182] The objective of eliminating individuals who are part of a group was seen to be incompatible with the notion of *dolus eventualis*. Mere knowledge that deaths may occur would be insufficient but at the same time knowledge of certain death was not required. Therefore, the *mens rea* of extermination required 'a showing that the killing of members of a group is what was desired by the perpetrator, irrespective of whether he was certain that this would actually happen'.[183] This would amount to a direct intent to kill on a large scale, excluding the possibility of *dolus eventualis*.[184]

In reviewing the Trial Chamber's factual findings on extermination, the Supreme Court Chamber held that the conclusion reached by the Trial Chamber that 'at least several thousand people died' during the evacuation due to 'killings, starvation and exhaustion' was unreasonable.[185] The Supreme Court Chamber had already found in relation to the crime against humanity of murder that there was little reliable evidence of killings of civilians due to the conditions imposed and consequently the evidence of killings on a large scale needed to establish extermination was insufficient.[186] The Supreme Court Chamber reversed the Trial Chamber's finding that extermination occurred during the first phase of the population movement since neither the scale element nor the requisite intent had been established beyond reasonable doubt.[187]

The Supreme Court Chamber reached the same conclusion in relation to the second phase of the population movement, having found that 'evidence of killings and deaths resulting from the conditions imposed during Population Movement Phase Two, particularly the live evidence, was sparse and sometimes vague, also considering that the Trial Chamber found that over 300,000 Cambodians had been affected by the transfers'.[188]

6.5.2.3 Other inhumane acts In the context of Case 002/01, the category of other inhumane acts was invoked as an umbrella category to encompass enforced disappearances, forced transfer and attacks against human dignity. In considering the question whether this category was part of customary international law at the relevant time, the Trial

182 Nuon Appeal Judgment, above n. 15, para. 520.
183 Ibid, para. 520.
184 Ibid, para. 522.
185 Ibid, para. 536.
186 Ibid, para. 536.
187 Ibid, para. 541.
188 Ibid, para. 554.

Chamber stated that 'the principle of legality attaches to the entire category of "other inhumane acts" and not to each sub-category of this offence'.[189] This meant that once this question had been answered in the affirmative, it was only necessary to consider 'whether enforced disappearances, forced transfer and attacks against human dignity are of a similar nature and gravity to the other enumerated offences under the ECCC Law'.[190]

The Supreme Court Chamber agreed in essence with these statements but not with the approach adopted by the Trial Chamber. In the Supreme Court Chamber's view, there was no doubt that under customary international law in 1975, 'other inhumane acts' constituted a residual category of crimes against humanity.[191] The question was whether this category was sufficiently specific to comply with the principle of legality.[192] The Supreme Court Chamber found that despite a natural tension between a clause intended to be residual and the requirement of *lex certa*, 'if interpreted and applied in a way so as to restrain [its] scope … , the notion of other inhumane acts is sufficiently clear and precise to be consistent with the tenets of accessibility and foreseeability deriving from the principle of legality.'[193] The elements of the crime were identified as follows:

> (i) there was an act or omission of similar seriousness to the other acts enumerated as crimes against humanity; (ii) the act or omission caused serious mental or physical suffering or injury or constituted a serious attack on human dignity; and (iii) the act or omission was performed intentionally.[194]

In order to establish that the specific conduct found to constitute an inhumane act violated a basic right of the victims and was of similar nature and gravity to other enumerated crimes against humanity, and thereby ensure respect for the principle of *nullum crimen sine lege certa*, the Supreme Court Chamber emphasised that 'a case-specific analysis of, in particular, the impact of the conduct on the victims and whether the conduct itself is comparable to the enumerated crimes against humanity' was required.[195]

---

189 Nuon Trial Judgment, above n. 10, para. 436.
190 Ibid, para. 440.
191 Nuon Appeal Judgment, above n. 15, para. 576.
192 Ibid, para. 576.
193 Ibid, para. 578.
194 Ibid, para. 580.
195 Ibid, para. 586.

The Supreme Court Chamber found the Trial Chamber's approach to have been methodologically incorrect, in that the Trial Chamber had proceeded to define enforced disappearances and forced transfer by stipulating precise elements even though those crimes had not yet crystallised into separate categories of crimes against humanity in 1975.[196] According to the Supreme Court Chamber:

> stipulating elements of enforced disappearance or enforced transfer as though they constituted separate categories of crimes against humanity was anachronistic and legally incorrect, whereas subsequently analysing the conduct under the same sub-headings as 'legal findings', among other discrete crimes against humanity, was, at a minimum, confusing. Rather, the guiding issue – and indeed the only one of relevance – was whether the conduct in question, in light of all the specific circumstances of the case at hand, actually fulfilled the definition of other inhumane acts.[197]

The Supreme Court Chamber proceeded to consider the conduct during the population movements holistically for each phase in order to determine whether its nature and gravity was similar to that of enumerated crimes against humanity.[198] Based on the facts found by the Trial Chamber, the Supreme Court Chamber concluded that the crime against humanity of 'other inhumane acts' was established in relation to both phases of the population movement.[199]

7. SEXUAL AND GENDER-BASED VIOLENCE

The Co-Prosecutors initially failed to introduce allegations of sexual and gender-based violence into the cases against the five suspects who were the subject of the first Introductory Submission and the Co-Investigating Judges were slow to remedy this omission. The Closing

---

196 Ibid, para. 589. *See* also Nuon Trial Judgment, above n. 10, para. 448 (For example, the Trial Chamber defined the elements of enforced disappearances as follows: 'Enforced disappearances occur when: (i) an individual is deprived of his or her liberty; (ii) the deprivation of liberty is followed by the refusal to disclose information regarding the fate or whereabouts of the person concerned, or to acknowledge the deprivation of liberty, and thereby deny the individual recourse to the applicable legal remedies and procedural guarantees, and (iii) the first and second elements were carried out by state agents, or with the authorisation, support or acquiescence of a State or political organisation.').

197 Nuon Appeal Judgment, above n. 15, para. 589.

198 Ibid, para. 590.

199 Ibid, paras. 655, 657, 660.

Order in Case 001 included one incident of rape but the evidence in support had been obtained almost accidentally during interviews with Duch.[200] In September 2008, one of the Civil Party Lawyers, Silke Studzinsky, announced in an ECCC press statement that the first applicant to be recognised as a civil party on the basis of being a victim of sexual violence had been submitted to the Court's Victims Unit.[201] The Lawyer noted the ECCC's silence and/or confusion surrounding the treatment of such crimes which were commonly perceived to have occurred during the Khmer Rouge regime.[202] The press statement served as an encouragement for other victims to come forward.

Duch was initially charged with rape, torture and persecution as separate crimes against humanity but the Trial Chamber and Supreme Court Chamber differed as to how to characterise the underlying act of sexual violence (in this case, rape) taking account of the customary international law applicable at the relevant time. Thus, the Trial Chamber made a deliberate choice to characterise rape (which in its view, though expressed somewhat ambiguously, could be a separate crime against humanity[203]) as the crime against humanity of torture, it being 'undisputed that rape may also constitute torture where all other elements of

---

[200] *Prosecutor v Kaing Guek Eav alias 'Duch'*, ECCC Case File No. 002/14-08-2006, Office of the Co-Investigating Judges, Closing Order Indicting Kaing Guek Eav alias Duch, 8 August 2008, para. 137 and p. 44; Duch Trial Judgment, above n. 2, para. 246. *See* also V. Oosterveld and P.V. Sellers, 'Issues of Sexual and Gender-Based Violence at the ECCC', in S.M. Meisenberg and I. Stegmiller (eds), *The Extraordinary Chambers in the Courts of Cambodia: Assessing their Contribution to International Criminal Law* (The Hague, T.M.C. Asser Press, 2016), pp. 321–51, pp. 335–6.

[201] 'Press Statement by Civil Parties Lawyer Silke Studzinsky: First Civil Party Application before the Extraordinary Chambers in the Courts of Cambodia (ECCC) on Gender-Based Violence under the Khmer Rouge Regime', Extraordinary Chambers in the Courts of Cambodia, 3 September 2008, <https://www.eccc.gov.kh/sites/default/files/media/PressRelease_1st_civil_party_on_Gender_Based_Violence.pdf> [accessed 22 June 2017].

[202] Ibid, p. 1.

[203] *See* also *Prosecutor v Ieng Sary*, ECCC Case File No. 002/19-09-2007-ECCC/OCIJ (PTC75), Pre-Trial Chamber, Decision on Ieng Sary's Appeal Against the Closing Order, 11 April 2011, para. 364(1) (where the Pre-Trial Chamber states: 'although in section 2.5.3 of the judgment the Trial Chamber enumerates rape as a Crime Against Humanity in its own right, in paragraph 361 of the judgment it only states that rape has 'long been prohibited in customary

torture are established.'[204] Torture was in turn subsumed within the crime of persecution on political grounds, with the result that Duch was convicted of one incident of rape as a form of torture which constituted persecution as a crime against humanity.[205] Although there was evidence before the Trial Chamber of a second incident of rape, this was not found to be proven.[206] A request by the civil parties to have evidence of a further rape put before the Trial Chamber was denied because it had come to light at too late a stage in the proceedings, namely after the civil party who was the alleged victim had appeared in court.[207] On appeal, the Supreme Court Chamber had to consider whether rape was a separate crime against humanity within the ECCC's subject matter jurisdiction between 1975 and 1979 (despite being listed as such in the ECCC Law) because it 'cannot uphold rape as a distinct crime against humanity on the basis of its gravity alone.'[208] Since the Supreme Court Chamber concluded that rape was not a discrete crime against humanity at the time relevant to the charges against Duch, it found it appropriate to characterise rape as torture.

The PTC had reached the same conclusion, prior to the judgment of the Supreme Court Chamber in Case 001.[209] While the PTC found that rape did not exist in its own right as an enumerated crime against humanity under customary international law in 1975, it considered that rape could potentially be characterised as an 'other inhumane act'.[210] The possible characterisation of rape as an 'other inhumane act' became a major issue in the subsequent cases before the ECCC. While Case 001

---

international law and has been described as "one of the worst suffering a human being can inflict upon another"' which, in the understanding of the Pre-Trial Chamber, does not amount to an explicit finding that rape existed by 1975–79 as a Crime Against Humanity in its own right in customary international law.').

204 Duch Trial Judgment, above n. 2, para. 366.

205 Ibid, para. 568.

206 Ibid, para. 247.

207 *Prosecutor v Kaing Guek Eav alias 'Duch'*, ECCC Case File No. 001/1-07-2007/ECCC/TC, Trial Chamber, Decision on Parties Requests to Put Certain Materials before the Chamber pursuant to Internal Rule 87(2), 28 October 2009, para. 14.

208 Duch Appeal Judgment, above n. 38, para. 174.

209 *Prosecutor v Ieng Sang*, ECCC Case File No. 002/19-09-2007-ECCC/OCIJ (PTC75), Pre-Trial Chamber, Decision on Ieng Sary's Appeal Against the Closing Order, 11 April 2011, para. 365: 'With the exception of Control Council No 10, none of the sources indicate that rape was, in its own right, a crime against humanity'.

210 Ibid, para. 371.

was being heard by the Trial Chamber, the Civil Party Lawyers had been focusing their attention on ensuring that sexual violence offences were properly investigated in Case 002. It should be recalled that prior to the decision on severance, Case 002 included the full scope of charges in the first Introductory Submission and that Duch remained as a Charged Person in Case 002 until the dismissal of outstanding charges against him on 14 September 2010. The Civil Party Lawyers were eventually able to persuade the Co-Investigating Judges to issue an order to the Co-Prosecutors to examine the facts surrounding the alleged occurrence of forced marriage and forced sexual relations pursuant to Internal Rule 55(3).[211]

According to Internal Rule 55(3), the Co-Investigating Judges are powerless to investigate 'new facts' unless the investigation into those facts is initiated by the Co-Prosecutors.[212] The Co-Prosecutors duly filed a Supplementary Submission on 30 April 2009 requesting the Co-Investigating Judges to investigate the allegations of forced marriage in certain of the civil party applications.[213] The Co-Prosecutors subsequently clarified that the Co-Investigating Judges could investigate any facts related to forced marriage and forced sexual relations, without there being any necessary linkage between the two, in effect seizing the Co-Investigating Judges of forced marriage, broadly construed, throughout Cambodia.[214] A further clarification followed shortly afterwards, in

---

211 Referred to in *Prosecutor v Nuon Chea, Ieng Sary, Ieng Thirith, Khieu Samphan* and *Kaing Guek Eav alias 'Duch'*, ECCC Case File No. 002/19-09-2007-ECCC-OCIJ, Office of the Co-Investigating Judges, Order on Request for Investigative Action Concerning Forced Marriages and Forced Sexual Relations, 18 December 2009, para. 1.

212 Internal Rule 55(3) provides: 'If, during an investigation, new facts come to the knowledge of the Co-Investigating Judges, they shall inform the Co-Prosecutors, unless the new facts are limited to aggravating circumstances relating to an existing submission. Where such new facts have been referred to the Co-Prosecutors, the Co-Investigating Judges shall not investigate them unless they receive a Supplementary Submission.'

213 *Prosecutor v Nuon Chea, Ieng Sary, Ieng Thirith, Khieu Samphan* and *Kaing Guek Eav alias 'Duch'*, ECCC Document No. D146/3, Office of the Co-Prosecutor, Co-Prosecutors' Response to the Forwarding Order of the Co-Investigating Judges and Supplementary Submission, 30 April 2009 ('Second Supplementary Submission').

214 *Prosecutor v Nuon Chea, Ieng Sary, Ieng Thirith, Khieu Samphan* and *Kaing Guek Eav alias 'Duch'*, ECCC Document No. D146/4, Office of the Co-Prosecutor, Further Authorization pursuant to Co-Prosecutors' 30 April 2009 Response to the Forwarding Order of the Co-Investigating Judges and Supplementary Submission, 5 November 2009 ('Third Supplementary Submission').

which the Co-Prosecutors stated that the alleged incidents of forced marriage and sexual relations to be investigated could be legally characterised as the crimes against humanity of rape and other inhumane acts.[215] The Civil Party Lawyers filed two follow-up requests for investigative action during 2009 arguing that forced marriage was a crime under international law and could be characterised as the crime against humanity of other inhumane acts, rape, enslavement or forced pregnancy and requesting further investigations.[216] While the Co-Investigating Judges did not deem it appropriate to specify the legal characterisation of the charges prior to the issuance of the Closing Order in Case 002, they nevertheless drew attention to the jurisprudence of the SCSL on the matter, in particular the finding of the SCSL Appeals Chamber that forced sexual relations was not a requirement to prove forced marriage.[217] In addition to the characterisation of other inhumane acts applied in the SCSL context, the Co-Investigating Judges suggested that the crimes against humanity of enslavement, imprisonment, torture, rape or forced pregnancy could be relevant, or war crimes such as torture, inhumane treatment, wilfully causing great suffering or serious injury to body or health.[218] The Co-Investigating Judges denied the request of the Civil Party Lawyers for the appointment of qualified experts relating to allegations of forced marriage but invited *amici curiae* briefs on the issue

---

[215] *Prosecutor v Nuon Chea, Ieng Sary, Ieng Thirith, Khieu Samphan* and *Kaing Guek Eav alias 'Duch'*, ECCC Document No. D146/5, Office of the Co-Prosecutor, Further Statement of Co-Prosecutors' Regarding 30 April 2009 Response to the Forwarding Order of the Co-Investigating Judges and Supplementary Submission, 26 November 2009. ('Fourth Supplementary Submission').

[216] Referred to in *Prosecutor v Nuon Chea, Ieng Sary, Ieng Thirith, Khieu Samphan* and *Kaing Guek Eav alias 'Duch'*, ECCC Case File No. 002/19-09-2007-ECCC-OCIJ, Office of the Co-Investigating Judges, Order on Request for Investigative Action Concerning Forced Marriages and Forced Sexual Relations, 18 December 2009, para. 3; *Prosecutor v Nuon Chea, Ieng Sary, Ieng Thirith, Khieu Samphan* and *Kaing Guek Eav alias 'Duch'*, ECCC Case File No. 002/19-09-2007-ECCC-OCIJ (PTC52), Pre-Trial Chamber, Decision on Appeal of Co-Lawyers for Civil Parties against Order Rejecting Request to Interview Persons Named in the Forced Marriage and Enforced Disappearance Requests for Investigative Action, 21 July 2010, para. 5.

[217] *Prosecutor v Nuon Chea, Ieng Sary, Ieng Thirith, Khieu Samphan* and *Kaing Guek Eav alias 'Duch'*, ECCC Case File No. 002/19-09-2007-ECCC-OCIJ, Office of the Co-Investigating Judges, Order on Request for Investigative Action Concerning Forced Marriages and Forced Sexual Relations, 18 December 2009, para. 10.

[218] Ibid, para. 11.

within a tight time frame of several weeks in view of the impending closure of the investigation.[219] The PTC dismissed an appeal by the Civil Party Lawyers against a related Order of the Co-Investigating Judges concerning requests to interview specific persons in connection with the forced marriage charges.[220]

The Closing Order in Case 002 described the regulation of marriages as one of the five DK policies thereby giving the related crimes a central place in the indictment.[221] The legal characterisations were limited to other inhumane acts and rape. It has been noted that the Co-Investigating Judges 'missed the opportunity to capture some of the gender-related nuances of the evidence' by failing to consider options such as political, racial or religious persecution in relation to evidence concerning transgendered individuals, Buddhist monks and female family members of previous employees of Lon Nol.[222] Indeed, the Closing Order charges rape only within the context of forced marriage to match the broader allegation of a joint criminal enterprise based on the implementation of the enumerated policies which included the regulation of marriages but not an overt or separate policy advocating rape. The restrictive approach taken can be explained on the basis of limited time and resources but is nonetheless disappointing in terms of the development of the law. Furthermore, the Supreme Court Chamber's determination that rape was not a separate crime against humanity in 1975 means that other inhumane acts is the only remaining characterisation of the facts relating to forced marriage. As a result of the decision on severance, and despite efforts by the Civil Party Lawyers and Co-Prosecutors to ensure that the charges in Case 002/01 were representative of the indictment as a whole, the facts

---

219 Ibid, paras. 13–14.

220 *Prosecutor v Nuon Chea, Ieng Sary, Ieng Thirith, Khieu Samphan* and *Kaing Guek Eav alias 'Duch'*, ECCC Document No. D310, Office of the Co-Investigating Judges, Order on Request to Interview Persons Named in the Forced Marriage and Enforced Disappearance Requests for Investigative Action, 13 January 2010; *Prosecutor v Nuon Chea, Ieng Sary, Ieng Thirith, Khieu Samphan* and *Kaing Guek Eav alias 'Duch'*, ECCC Case File No. 002/19-09-2007-ECCC-OCIJ (PTC52), Pre-Trial Chamber, Decision on Appeal of Co-Lawyers for Civil Parties against Order Rejecting Request to Interview Persons Named in the Forced Marriage and Enforced Disappearance Requests for Investigative Action, 21 July 2010, p. 25.

221 *Prosecutor v Nuon Chea, Ieng Sary, Ieng Thirith* and *Khieu Samphan*, ECCC Case File No. 002/19-09-2007-ECCC-OCIJ, Office of the Co-Investigating Judges, Closing Order (Indictment) in Case 002, 15 September 2010, paras. 216–17.

222 Oosterveld and Sellers, above n. 200, pp. 329–30.

relating to the regulation of marriages became part of Case 002/02. The Civil Party Lawyers sought re-characterisation of the facts contained in the Closing Order that described rape occurring outside the context of forced marriage as the crimes against humanity of torture, other inhumane acts through rape, or other inhumane acts through attacks against human dignity. The Trial Chamber rejected this request, clarifying that despite findings of rape outside forced marriage, the Closing Order had concluded that rape was not 'one of the crimes used by the CPK leaders to implement the common purpose' and that the legal elements of the crime against humanity of rape had therefore only been established within the context of forced marriage.[223] The Trial Chamber reiterated its consistent understanding that allegations of rape outside forced marriage were not part of Case 002/02.[224] A request by a group of scholars to file an *amicus curiae* brief on the question of the legal characterisation of forced marriage as an inhumane act was granted by the Trial Chamber as the hearing in Case 002/02 drew to an end.[225]

After the experience in Cases 001 and 002, gender-based violence was more clearly a focus of the investigations in Cases 003 and 004 although only in their later stages. The Co-Prosecutors filed a Supplementary Submission in Case 003 on 31 October 2014, referring to evidence that had become available which indicated 'instances where groups of up to 20 couples were forcibly married in a single ceremony, and where women sent from other zones or sectors to Kampong Som were forcibly married to military cadres'.[226] A Supplementary Submission was filed in Case 004 on 24 April 2014 requesting investigations into gender-based

[223] *Prosecutor v Nuon Chea* and *Khieu Samphan*, ECCC Case File No. 002/19-09-2007/ECCC/TC, Trial Chamber, Decision on Lead Co-Lawyers' Rule 92 Submission on the Confirmation of the Scope of Case 002/02 Concerning the Charges of Rape outside the Context of Forced Marriage, 30 August 2016, para. 14.

[224] Ibid, paras. 17–18.

[225] *Prosecutor v Nuon Chea* and *Khieu Samphan*, ECCC Case File No. 002/19-09-2007/ECCC/TC, Trial Chamber, Decision on the Request for Leave to Submit *Amicus Curiae* Brief on Forced Marriage, 13 September 2016, p. 7; *Prosecutor v Nuon Chea* and *Khieu Samphan*, ECCC Case File No. 002119-09-2007 -ECCC/TC, *Amicus Curiae*, *Amicus Curiae* Brief on Forced Marriage, 29 September 2016, para. 1.

[226] Supplementary Submission in Case 003 filed on 31 October 2014. *See* N. Koumjian, 'International Co-Prosecutor Files Supplementary Submission in Case 003', Extraordinary Chambers in the Courts of Cambodia, 4 November 2014, <https://www.eccc.gov.kh/en/articles/international-co-prosecutor-files-supplementary-submission-case-003> [accessed 22 June 2017].

violence extending beyond forced marriages. According to a Press Release by the Co-Prosecutors:[227]

> The allegations include forced marriages, including instances where groups of up to 80 couples were married in a single ceremony. The allegations also include rapes and sexual violence outside the context of forced marriages, including instances where women were raped prior to being executed, and instances where women who reported rapes during the Khmer Rouge period were subsequently executed. The preliminary information available at this time indicates that the forced marriages, rapes, and sexual violence alleged were perpetrated by Khmer Rouge cadre and occurred in areas where named suspects in Case 004 held command or political positions of influence.

In an application brought by one of the Charged Persons in Case 004 requesting the annulment of investigative action concerning forced marriage on the basis that prosecuting acts of forced marriage violated the principle of legality, the International Judges of the PTC, Judges Beauvallet and Baik, had the opportunity to express their opinion on the legal characterisation of the facts relating to forced marriage. They confirmed that the principle of legality attached to the entire category of other inhumane acts and not to each sub-category.[228] Although they stated rather vaguely that '[i]t was clear that conduct of forcing people to act against their will in a way or another could fall under the definition of "other inhumane acts" by judicial clarification based on the use of the doctrine of *ejusdem generis* on a case by case basis', they went on to explain that the criminality of particular acts was not a determinative or sole indicator of gravity and the emphasis should be placed on the inhumanity of the act.[229]

It remains to be seen how the Trial Chamber will characterise the facts relating to the arrangement of marriages within the limits of the customary international law applicable in 1975. The SCSL broke new ground in finding that forced marriage could constitute a separate 'other inhumane act' and was not necessarily subsumed within related categories such as sexual slavery or enslavement.[230] These events post-date

---

[227] Koumjian, ibid.

[228] ECCC Case File No. 004/07-09-2009-ECCC/OCIJ (PTC21), Pre-Trial Chamber, Considerations on Application to Seise the Pre-Trial Chamber with a View to Annulment of Investigative Action Concerning Forced Marriage, 17 May 2016, para. 9.

[229] Ibid, paras. 13, 16.

[230] *See Prosecutor v Brima, Kamara* and *Kanu*, SCSL Case No. SCSL-2004-16-A, Appeals Chamber, Judgment, 22 February 2008, paras. 195–6, 202;

the time frame relevant to the ECCC and the nature and circumstances of forced marriage in the two instances are different. The Co-Prosecutors have nevertheless argued that the 'SCSL jurisprudence is persuasive and applicable authority'.[231] The characterisation of forced marriage as another inhumane act, which was first advocated by the prosecution at the SCSL and later supported by the SCSL Appeals Chamber, aimed to describe the unique suffering of the victims and to capture elements that were not contained in other legal categories.[232] Many of the same facts were additionally characterised as sexual slavery or enslavement in the SCSL cases.[233]

The charges in Case 002/01 describe forced marriage as a state-sanctioned policy which apart from being a core feature of the alleged joint criminal enterprise has a bearing on the legal characterisation of the relevant underlying facts. The Extraordinary Chambers have found that rape was not a separate crime against humanity in 1975 and in the context of Case 002/01, rape is in any event viewed as having a nexus with forced marriage. Assuming forced marriage as an 'other inhumane act' passes the test of legality, a possible outcome would be that rape is subsumed under forced marriage which is in turn subsumed under the heading 'other inhumane acts' constituting a crime against humanity.

Prosecutor v Taylor, SCSL Case No. SCSL-03-01-T, Trial Chamber II, para. 426 (One of the Trial Chambers consistently asserted that the 'term "forced marriage" is a misnomer for the forced conjugal association that was imposed on women and girls in the circumstances of armed conflict, and which involved both sexual slavery and forced labour in the form of domestic work such as cooking and cleaning').

[231] ECCC Case File No. 004/07-09-2009-ECCC/OCIJ (PTC21), Pre-Trial Chamber, Considerations on Application to Seise the Pre-Trial Chamber with a View to Annulment of Investigative Action Concerning Forced Marriage, 17 May 2016, para. 41.

[232] *Prosecutor v Brima, Kamara* and *Kanu*, SCSL Case No. SCSL-2004-16-A, Appeals Chamber, Judgment, 22 February 2008, paras 199–202. *See* also *Prosecutor v Nuon Chea* and *Khieu Samphan*, ECCC Case File No. 002119-09-2007 -ECCC/TC, *Amicus Curiae*, *Amicus Curiae* Brief on Forced Marriage, 29 September 2016, para. 21.

[233] *See* also *Prosecutor v Nuon Chea* and *Khieu Samphan*, ECCC Case File No. 002119-09-2007 -ECCC/TC, *Amicus Curiae*, *Amicus Curiae* Brief on Forced Marriage, 29 September 2016, para. 21 (which states the position that forced marriage should be charged as enslavement, but goes on to conclude that 'international criminal law has evolved to include the "other inhumane act" of forced marriage (along with other crimes) which captures the range and complexity of lived experiences of women and men in different oppressive or conflict situations').

The Supreme Court Chamber has been criticised for misconstruing the principle of legality as it applied to rape in Case 001. The Co-Prosecutors have argued that the key question is whether it was 'reasonably foreseeable and accessible to the Accused that certain acts or omissions would entail international criminal liability' and that a crime does not need to be 'proscribed in the exact and precise terms in which it is later prosecuted'.[234] The drafters of the ECCC Law clearly intended to include rape as a separate crime against humanity and it has been suggested that 'pre-1975 evidence of rape as a crime against humanity *is* available'.[235] Indeed, Control Council Law No. 10 listed rape as a crime against humanity and the post-Second World War jurisprudence did not always draw a clear distinction between crimes against humanity and war crimes. Moreover, it has aptly been pointed out that changing social and political attitudes led to rape being prosecuted more actively as a crime against humanity from the 1990s onwards and that the failure to prosecute in the post-Second World War period does not disprove the existence of the law.[236] Since there is no doubt that rape was punishable at the international level by 1975, the question becomes one of characterisation rather than strict legality. The accused must have proper notice of the charge but in the ECCC system the legal characterisation is subject to change by the judges. Subsuming rape within other categories of crimes against humanity seems to offer little real benefit to the accused, other than a possibly reduced stigma.

However, rape as a crime against humanity clearly lacked a precise definition in 1975. The Trial Chamber wantonly adopted the definition of rape in the *Kunarac* case before the ICTY.[237] This definition has been criticised for narrowly describing 'rape between a perpetrator and a

---

[234] *Prosecutor v Nuon Chea, Ieng Sary, Ieng Thirith* and *Khieu Samphan*, ECCC Case File No. 002/19-09-2007-ECCC/TC, Office of Co-Prosecutor, Co-Prosecutors' Request for the Trial Chamber to Re-Characterize the Facts Establishing the Conduct of Rape as the Crime against Humanity of Rape rather than the Crime against Humanity of other Inhumane Acts, 16 June 2011, para. 7.

[235] R. Killean, 'An Incomplete Narrative: Prosecuting Sexual Violence Crimes at the Extraordinary Chambers in the Courts of Cambodia', *Journal of International Criminal Justice*, vol. 13, no. 2, 2015, pp. 331–52, p. 339. *See* also Oosterveld and Sellers, above n. 200, pp. 340–1 (setting out the evidence).

[236] Oosterveld and Sellers, above n. 200, p. 341.

[237] Duch Trial Judgment, above n. 2, para. 362. *See* Duch Appeal Judgment, above n. 38, para. 182 (The Supreme Court Chamber did not provide a definition of rape, but suggested domestic incorporation of the crime against humanity of rape might be relevant: 'Patterns of criminalisation on the municipal level, on the other hand, might help clarify the definition of rape as a crime against humanity,

victim, and not between two victims, as occurred in forced marriages'.[238] The Co-Investigating Judges preferred the slightly different definition in the *Akayesu* case.[239] In terms of satisfying the test of foreseeability and accessibility to the accused, domestic law on rape, in particular Cambodian law, could have served as a guide. But subsuming rape within another category of crimes against humanity means that the definition of the umbrella crime, whether it be torture or other inhumane acts, is decisive. Technically, therefore, the legal elements of the underlying crime do not need to be set out. From a purely legal perspective this is advantageous for the development of 'forced marriage' under the heading of 'other inhumane acts' as it allows the understanding of 'forced marriage' to be adaptable to different circumstances even though the core features signaling the gravity of the 'inhumane act' must be common to all situations.

8. GENOCIDE

In its early days, the ECCC was often referred to locally as the 'genocide court' and yet more than ten years after the Court's establishment there is surprisingly little to say about the crime of genocide. On the basis of the first Introductory Submission, the Co-Investigating Judges were seized of acts of the CPK targeting the Cham, Vietnamese and Buddhist groups, as well as former officials of the Khmer Republic, occurring throughout Cambodia from before 1975 until at least 6 January 1979. More specifically:

> The Co-Investigating Judges are seized of treatment of the Cham in the Central, East and Northwest Zones; of the Vietnamese in Prey Veng and Svay Rieng Provinces in the East Zone and during incursions into Vietnam; of

---

specifically the actus reus and mens rea, once the existence of rape as a crime against humanity has already been established under municipal or international law.').

[238] Oosterveld and Sellers, above n. 200, p. 337.

[239] *Prosecutor v Nuon Chea, Ieng Sary, Ieng Thirith* and *Khieu Samphan*, ECCC Case File No. 002/19-09-2007-ECCC-OCIJ, Office of the Co-Investigating Judges, Closing Order (Indictment) in Case 002, 15 September 2010, para. 1431.

Buddhists throughout Democratic Kampuchea; and of former officials of the Khmer Republic during the movement of the population from Phnom Penh.[240]

Prior to the issuance of the Closing Order in Case 002, the defence for Ieng Sary filed motions challenging the applicability of the crime of genocide at the ECCC on the basis that genocide was not proscribed under Cambodian criminal law at the relevant time, and seeking clarification as to the elements of the crime.[241] The Co-Investigating Judges reserved their consideration of both matters until the Closing Order, noting only that genocide as recognised in the ECCC Law and ECCC Agreement was a potential legal characterisation of the facts under investigation.[242] As the investigation progressed, the Co-Prosecutors and civil parties sought further investigative action concerning the Khmer Krom minority group in Pursat and Takeo Provinces based on new evidence that came to light suggesting that the Khmer Krom population was targeted as part of the alleged policy of eliminating the Vietnamese. The civil parties argued that the Khmer Krom were perceived to be Vietnamese by the perpetrators and sought the Co-Investigating Judge's confirmation of a subjective approach to the identification of members of the targeted group. The Co-Investigating Judges rejected the requests on the basis that it had not been properly seized of the new evidence by a Supplementary Submission.[243] The Civil Party Lawyers appealed against

---

[240] *Prosecutor v Nuon Chea, Ieng Sary, Ieng Thirith* and *Khieu Samphan*, ECCC Case File No. 002/19-09-2007-ECCC-OCIJ, Office of the Co-Investigating Judges, Closing Order (Indictment) in Case 002, 15 September 2010, para. 206.

[241] *Prosecutor v Ieng Sary*, ECCC Case File No. 002/19-09-2007-ECCC/OCIJ, Defence for Ieng Sary, Ieng Sary's Motion against the Applicability of the Crime of Genocide at the ECCC, 30 October 2009, para. 13.

[242] *Prosecutor v Nuon Chea, Ieng Sary, Ieng Thirith, Khieu Samphan* and *Kaing Guek Eav alias 'Duch'*, ECCC Case File No. 002/19-09-2007-ECCC-OCIJ, Office of the Co-Investigating Judges, Order on Request for Investigative Action on the Applicability of the Crime of Genocide at the ECCC, 28 December 2009, para. 5.

[243] *Prosecutor v Nuon Chea, Ieng Sary, Ieng Thirith, Khieu Samphan* and *Kaing Guek Eav alias 'Duch'*, ECCC Case File No. 002/19-09-2007-ECCC-OCIJ, Office of the Co-Investigating Judges, Combined Order on Co-Prosecutors' Two Requests for Investigative Action regarding Khmer Krom and Mass Executions in Bakan District (Pursat) and the Civil Parties Request for Supplementary Investigations regarding Genocide of the Khmer Krom & the Vietnamese, 13 January 2010, paras. 4–8.

this decision, but any decision by the PTC does not appear to have been made public.[244]

The Closing Order issued on 16 September 2010 charged Nuon Chea, Ieng Sary, Ieng Thirith, and Khieu Samphan with genocide by systematic killings against the Cham and the Vietnamese populations. According to the Closing Order, the Cham are 'an ethnic minority within Cambodia who share a common language, a common culture and Islam as a common religion'.[245] The Closing Order describes the Cham population as an ethnic and religious group while the Vietnamese are considered an ethnic, national and/or racial group.[246] The treatment of Buddhists was characterised as the crimes against humanity of murder and religious persecution.

The genocide charges were addressed by the PTC in its decision on Ieng Sary's appeal against the Closing Order. The PTC cited with approval the Co-Investigating Judges' conclusion that:

> Cambodia acquired sovereign autonomy to accede to the Genocide Convention upon joining the 'French Union' in 1949. The United Nations accepted Cambodia's accession and there is no record of any legal challenge with respect to this accession. The Genocide Convention received the twenty ratifications and accessions required for its entry into force in 1951. Thus, the crime of genocide was part of international law applicable in Cambodia at the relevant time.[247]

---

[244] *Prosecutor v Nuon Chea, Ieng Sary, Ieng Thirith, Khieu Samphan* and *Kaing Guek Eav alias 'Duch'*, ECCC Case File No. 002/19-09-2007-ECCC-OCIJ (PTC 48), Co-Lawyers for Civil Parties, Appeal against Combined Order on Co-Prosecutors' Two Requests for Investigative Action regarding Khmer Krom and Mass Executions in Bakan District (Pursat) and the Civil Parties Request for Supplementary Investigations regarding Genocide of the Khmer Krom & the Vietnamese, 12 February 2010.

[245] *Prosecutor v Nuon Chea, Ieng Sary, Ieng Thirith* and *Khieu Samphan*, ECCC Case File No. 002/19-09-2007-ECCC-OCIJ, Office of the Co-Investigating Judges, Closing Order (Indictment) in Case 002, 15 September 2010, para. 745.

[246] Ibid, para. 791.

[247] *Prosecutor v Ieng Sary*, ECCC Case File No. 002/19-09-2007-ECCC/OCIJ (PTC75), Pre-Trial Chamber, Decision on Ieng Sary's Appeal Against the Closing Order, 11 April 2011, para. 242; *Prosecutor v Nuon Chea, Ieng Sary, Ieng Thirith* and *Khieu Samphan*, ECCC Case File No. 002/19-09-2007-ECCC-OCIJ, Office of the Co-Investigating Judges, Closing Order (Indictment) in Case 002, 15 September 2010, para. 1310.

According to the PTC, the Genocide Convention was 'unquestionably' binding on Cambodia, by its accession prior to the time of the alleged offences, even though the treaty had not been implemented in Cambodian law at that time.[248] The PTC added that 'the *jus cogens* nature of the crime of genocide alleged in the Closing Order is sufficient to justify prosecution, regardless of the specific provisions of Cambodia's domestic law'.[249] The PTC was in no doubt that by 1975 individuals were on notice that genocide was an international crime and therefore there was no violation of the principle of legality in Ieng Sary's case. The PTC also held that the definition of genocide 'has been universal, predictable and constant, being defined identically in the Genocide Convention and the ECCC Law'.[250] This suggests that the PTC regarded the minor discrepancies between the wording of the definition of genocide in the ECCC Law and the Genocide Convention as being inconsequential. The Co-Investigating Judges had adopted the international definition of genocide as follows:

> genocide is defined as the specific intent to destroy, in whole or in part, a national, ethnic, racial or religious group, as such, by means of any of the following acts: killing of members of the group; causing serious bodily or mental harm to members of the group; deliberately inflicting on the group conditions of life calculated to bring about its physical destruction in whole or in part; imposing measures intended to prevent births within the group; or forcibly transferring children from one group to another group.[251]

During the investigation, the Civil Party Lawyers raised the issue of whether genocide should also be charged 'against a subset of, or a substantial part of, the Khmer national group'.[252] According to this argument, the Khmer People constitute a national group and the 'new people' constitute a substantial part or subset of the group. The Civil

---

248 *Prosecutor v Ieng Sary*, ECCC Case File No. 002/19-09-2007-ECCC/OCIJ (PTC75), Pre-Trial Chamber, Decision on Ieng Sary's Appeal Against the Closing Order, 11 April 2011, para. 243.

249 Ibid, para. 244.

250 Ibid, para. 248.

251 *Prosecutor v Nuon Chea, Ieng Sary, Ieng Thirith* and *Khieu Samphan*, ECCC Case File No. 002/19-09-2007-ECCC-OCIJ, Office of the Co-Investigating Judges, Closing Order (Indictment) in Case 002, 15 September 2010, para. 1312.

252 *Prosecutor v Ieng Sary*, ECCC Case File No. 002/19-09-2007-ECCC-OCIJ, Co-Lawyers for Civil Parties, Sixth Investigative Request of Co-Lawyers for Civil Parties Concerning the Charge of Genocide against the Khmer Nationals, 4 February 2010, para. 3.

Party Lawyers requested that the Co-Investigating Judges appoint an independent legal expert to advise on the matter.[253] Any response on this issue does not appear to have been made public. The argument of the Civil Party Co-Lawyers finds support in academic writings. These have been summed up as follows:

> [O]ne line maintains that the Khmer Rouge committed genocide against that portion of the Khmer national group that did not conform to their notions of social and ideological purity. This portion transcended characterization as a political or economic group, neither of which is protected by the Convention, since it represented a far broader segment of the society – basically, that segment that did not fit into the vision of the Khmer nation that the Khmer Rouge sought to impose. Some have contended that the Khmer Rouge committed genocide against the urban Khmer population, the Khmer in the Eastern Zone (who were subjected to brutal treatment in connection with the hostilities with Vietnam and the rebellion in the Zone), or both.[254]

The idea that members of the Khmer national group were targeted on a purely political basis has been challenged, drawing parallels with Nazism and the 'purification of the populace' by the DK government.[255]

The contrasting argument is that even if it is undisputed that the Khmer people constitute a national group, it would be difficult to meet the requirement under the Genocide Convention that the intent be directed against the protected part of the group 'as such' since this requires proof that the members of the group were targeted as members of the Khmer nation. It has been commented that according to the majority of the literature on the Khmer Rouge period, the Khmer Rouge regime targeted the non-minority groups as 'economic, social or political elements whom the Khmer Rouge sought to eradicate but whom the Convention does not protect; or that [members of the Khmer nation] were victims of arbitrary violence and harsh conditions that the government imposed on virtually

---

253 Ibid, para. 42 and p. 16.

254 S.R. Ratner, J.S. Abrams and J.L. Bischoff, *Accountability for Human Rights Atrocities in International Law* (3rd edn, Oxford, Oxford University Press, 2009), p. 321 (citing D. Hawk, 'The Cambodian Genocide', in I. Charny, *Genocide: A Critical Bibliographic Review, Volume 1* (New York: Facts on File Publications, 1988), pp. 137–54, pp. 139–40); B. Kiernan, 'The Cambodian Genocide, Issues and Responses', in G.J. Andreaopolous (ed), *Genocide: Conceptual and Historical Dimensions* (Philadelphia, Pennsylvania, University of Pennsylvania Press, 1997), pp. 191–228, p. 192; H. Hannum, 'International Law and Cambodian Genocide: The Sounds of Silence', *Human Rights Quarterly*, vol, 11, 1989, pp. 82–138, pp. 110–12.

255 Hannum, ibid, p. 89.

the entire country.'[256] So-called 'auto-genocide' whereby the victims are part of the perpetrators' own group is not directly precluded under the Genocide Convention but does not easily meet the strict definition of the crime. The Convention did not envisage the Cambodian situation when it was drafted in the immediate aftermath of the Second World War.[257] It may be speculated whether the mysterious alteration of the order of the words 'as such' to 'such as' in the ECCC Law was intended to remedy this possible gap in the protections provided by the law on genocide. In any case, adopting the ordinary meaning of the words 'such as' in the context of Article 4 of the ECCC Law would most likely fall foul of the principle of legality.[258] Moreover, the ECCC's jurisprudence on persecution, according to which 'New People' were targeted on political grounds and as members of a political group, has now effectively precluded any alternative view of the status of non-minority groups.[259]

---

[256] Ratner, Abrams and Bischoff, above n. 254, p. 322.

[257] *See* also United Nations Economic and Social Council, Commission on Human Rights, Thirty-Fifth Session, Summary Record of the First Part (Public) of the 1510th Meeting, E/CN.4/SR.1510, 9 March 1979, para. 22 (describing the scale of the human rights violations in Democratic Kampuchea as constituting 'nothing less than autogenocide').

[258] This was the view taken by the Co-Investigating Judges in *Prosecutor v Nuon Chea, Ieng Sary, Ieng Thirith* and *Khieu Samphan*, ECCC Case File No. 002/19-09-2007-ECCC-OCIJ, Office of the Co-Investigating Judges, Closing Order (Indictment) in Case 002, 15 September 2010, para. 1311: 'It should be noted that some versions of the definition of this crime in the relevant ECCC instruments could be interpreted as creating an open-ended list of constitutive acts of genocide. In order to avoid a breach of the *nullum crimen sine lege principle*, the Co-Investigating Judges will take into consideration Article 9 of the ECCC Agreement and Article 4 of the ECCC Law which provide that "the Extraordinary Chambers have jurisdiction to prosecute the suspects who have committed crimes of genocide, as defined in the 1948 Convention" and apply the international definition of genocide.'

[259] *See Prosecutor v Nuon Chea, Ieng Sary, Ieng Thirith* and *Khieu Samphan*, ECCC Case File No. 002/19-09-2007-ECCC-OCIJ, Office of the Co-Investigating Judges, Closing Order (Indictment) in Case 002, 15 September 2010, para. 1366: 'In the instant case, the overall attack was based primarily on political grounds. Its implementation entailed dividing the population into categories, which fixed the scope of their rights, with the result that whole segments of the population, whose political or spiritual beliefs were taken to be contrary to the ideological objectives of the Party, were denied their rights.' *See* also Trial Chamber's findings on crimes against humanity in Cases 001 and 002/01 as upheld by the Supreme Court Chamber.

9. DESTRUCTION OF CULTURAL PROPERTY

As a symbol of Cambodia's period of greatness, the temples at Angkor remained unscathed during the Khmer Rouge period.[260] However, the attacks on Buddhism and the Cham people resulted in the destruction of most of Cambodia's 3,000 pagodas and damage to mosques.[261] The Catholic cathedral of Phnom Penh is also reported to have been dismantled, stone by stone.[262]

No charges have been brought pursuant to Article 7 of the ECCC Law which specifically refers to the destruction of cultural property under the 1954 Hague Convention for Protection of Cultural Property in the Event of Armed Conflict. However, destruction of cultural property may be given a different legal characterisation, such as persecution as a crime against humanity, if all elements of that crime are met. For example, the Closing Order in Case 002 states among the allegations concerning the treatment of Buddhists that: 'Many pagodas and sanctuaries were destroyed, or converted for other purposes such as security centres, pig pens, dining halls, hospitals or warehouses. Images of Buddha were destroyed.'[263] As it concerns the Cham people, the Closing Order refers to evidence that 'the CPK banned the practice of Islam and forbade the Cham from praying, seized and burned Qurans, closed or destroyed mosques, or used them for other purposes such as communal dining halls, store houses, or facilities for pigs.'[264] The Closing Order in Case 002 characterises these acts as religious persecution.[265] Another possible characterisation is as a grave breach of the 1949 Geneva Conventions under the heading, 'extensive destruction and serious damage to property,

---

[260] Ratner, Abrams and Bischoff, above n. 254, p. 329, footnote 35 (citing D. Chandler, 'Seeing Red: Perceptions of Cambodian History in Democratic Kampuchea', in D. Chandler, B. Kiernan and A. Barnett (eds), *Revolution and its Aftermath in Kampuchea: Eight Essays* (New Haven, Connecticut, Yale University Southeast Asia Studies, 1983), pp. 34–56, pp. 34–5, 45–6).

[261] Ratner, Abrams and Bischoff, above n. 254, p. 328.

[262] Ibid, p. 329.

[263] *Prosecutor v Nuon Chea, Ieng Sary, Ieng Thirith* and *Khieu Samphan*, ECCC Case File No. 002/19-09-2007-ECCC-OCIJ, Office of the Co-Investigating Judges, Closing Order (Indictment) in Case 002, 15 September 2010, para. 740.

[264] Ibid, para. 756.

[265] Ibid, paras. 1419–21.

not justified by military necessity and carried out unlawfully and wantonly'.[266]

10. DOMESTIC CRIMES

There have been no convictions for the domestic crimes set out in Article 3 of the ECCC Law, but torture and premeditated murder were nevertheless defined by the PTC in its decision on Duch's appeal against the Closing Order.[267] The PTC disagreed with the Co-Investigating Judges that the domestic crimes were subsumed within the international crimes, applying the principles established at the international level on cumulative charging. It was also found that the Co-Investigating Judges had failed to provide reasoning in support of their contention that the international crimes constituted the 'highest available legal classification'.[268]

11. CUMULATIVE CONVICTIONS

The Supreme Court Chamber has addressed the issue of '*concursus delictorum*, the law concerning concurrence or the adjudication of multiple

---

266 Ibid, para. 1317; F. Lenzerini, 'The Role of International and Mixed Criminal Courts in the Enforcement of International Norms Concerning the Protection of Cultural Heritage', in F. Francioni and J. Gordley (eds), *Enforcing International Cultural Heritage Law* (Oxford/New York, Oxford University Press, 2013) pp. 40–64, p. 59.

267 *Prosecutor v Kaing Guek Eav alias 'Duch'*, ECCC Case File No. 001/8-07-2007-ECCC/OCIJ (PTC 02), Pre-Trial Chamber, Decision on Appeal against Closing Order Indicting Kaing Guek Eav alias "Duch", 5 December 2008, paras. 55–107. These definitions were referred to in ECCC Case File No. 004/07-09-2009-ECCC-OCIJ, *Im Chaem*, Closing Order (Reasons), 10 July 2017, paras. 43–56.

268 *Prosecutor v Kaing Guek Eav alias 'Duch'*, ECCC Case File No. 001/8-07-2007-ECCC/OCIJ (PTC 02), Pre-Trial Chamber, Decision on Appeal against Closing Order Indicting Kaing Guek Eav alias "Duch", 5 December 2008, para. 55, citing *Prosecutor v Nuon Chea, Ieng Sary, Ieng Thirith* and *Khieu Samphan*, ECCC Case File No. 002/19-09-2007-ECCC-OCIJ, Office of the Co-Investigating Judges, Closing Order (Indictment) in Case 002, 15 September 2010, para. 152.

offences against one accused with respect to the same set of factual circumstances'.[269] This issue, normally addressed under the heading 'cumulative convictions', is one of both procedure and substance.

In the *Duch* case, the Co-Prosecutors argued that the Trial Chamber erred in failing to convict the accused for all of the crimes for which it found him responsible and instead subsuming those crimes under the crime against humanity of persecution on political grounds. The Supreme Court Chamber therefore had to 'identify the rule for determining concurrence of offences and the appropriate result where the *same* factual conduct fulfils the legal definition of more than one statutory offence under the ECCC law'.[270]

The first question to consider was whether the Trial Chamber had erred in adopting the test for cumulative convictions developed by the ICTY Appeals Chamber in the *Čelebici* case.[271] The Supreme Court Chamber examined this test and looked for other sources, but was unable to identify a general principle of law 'on concurrence of multiple, distinct offences for the same conduct'.[272] Moreover, national approaches were viewed as being difficult to apply to the international system which lacked the same 'level of systemic coherence' as national systems, and the definitions of international crimes, which 'describe multiple categories of conduct, capable of encompassing several criminal transactions, often spanning long periods of time', were 'often broad, complex and imprecise'.[273] The Supreme Court Chamber went on to state:

> In general, the international jurisprudence considers that the *Čelebici* test serves the interests of justice by ensuring that convictions entered against an accused reflect, accurately and in full, the extent of his or her criminal culpability. At the same time, it is recognized that cumulative convictions create three principal dangers to an accused's rights: first, an accused faces the social stigma of being convicted of additional crimes; second, multiple convictions may lead to increased sentencing and negatively affect the possibility of early release under the law of the state enforcing the sentence;

---

269 Duch Appeal Judgment, above n. 38, para. 286.

270 Ibid.

271 *Prosecutor v Zejnil Delalić, Zdravko Mucić, Hazim Delić* and *Esad Landžo*, ICTY Case No. IT-96-21-A, Appeals Chamber, Judgment, 20 February 2001, para. 412: '[M]ultiple criminal convictions entered under different statutory provisions but based on the same conduct are permissible only if each statutory provision involved has a materially distinct element not contained in the other. An element is materially distinct from another if it requires proof of a fact not required by the other.'

272 Duch Appeal Judgment, above n. 38, para. 290.

273 Ibid, para. 292.

and third, there may be a risk of increased sentencing in subsequent convictions based on habitual offender laws.[274]

Dismissing the first two dangers, the Supreme Court Chamber concluded that the Trial Chamber did not err in looking to the *Čelebici* case for guidance.[275] The question whether there could be cumulative convictions for persecution and other crimes against humanity turned on the meaning of the 'materially distinct element' requirement in *Čelebici* and the Supreme Court Chamber, using the example of persecution and extermination, found that there were materially distinct elements in both the *actus reus* and *mens rea*.[276] On the basis of its analysis, the Supreme Court Chamber rejected the idea that: 'The only difference between persecution and the crimes against humanity it subsumes [is] the added, specific requirements of proof of discriminatory animus in the *mens rea* and proof of discrimination in fact in the *actus reus*.'[277] The Supreme Court Chamber also considered that it was the '"abstract" legal elements and the requisite proof of facts under those elements that must be compared when analysing cumulative convictions, rather than the factual circumstances surrounding the underlying conduct.'[278] Consequently, the Supreme Court Chamber entered separate convictions against the accused for extermination (encompassing murder), enslavement, imprisonment, torture and other inhumane acts in addition to persecution.[279]

In Case 002/01, the Trial Chamber considered that extermination, as the more specific offence, subsumed murder, and therefore convicted Nuon Chea and Khieu Samphan of the crimes of persecution on political grounds, extermination, and other inhumane acts (comprising forced transfer, enforced disappearances and attacks against human dignity), on the basis that each offence had a materially distinct element not contained in the others.[280] The convictions for extermination were overturned by the Supreme Court Chamber but the adjustment made to the legal characterisation of the acts of killing during Population Movement Phase Two suggests that the Supreme Court Chamber accepted that murder could be subsumed within extermination.

---

274 Ibid, para. 295.
275 Ibid, para. 298.
276 Ibid, paras. 319–23.
277 Ibid, para. 317.
278 Ibid, para. 324.
279 Ibid, para. 336.
280 Nuon Trial Judgment, above n. 10, para. 1060.

12. CONCLUSION

The definition of crimes against humanity remained fluid even at the time of the adoption of the Statutes of the ICTY, ICTR, SCSL and ICC which all describe the contextual elements slightly differently. In its jurisprudence, the ECCC has accepted that all the elements listed in Article 5 of the ECCC Law must be viewed as jurisdictional requirements even if they were not part of the customary international law definition of crimes against humanity in 1975. At the same time, any candidate requirements that are not listed, such as the nexus with an armed conflict or the existence of a state or organisational policy, have been scrutinised to determine if they should be included. It is clearly no mean feat to decipher the content of the customary international law on crimes against humanity as it existed in 1975. The ECCC Agreement, perhaps carelessly, refers to 'crimes against humanity as defined in the 1998 Rome Statute of the International Criminal Court'.[281] The Rome Statute stipulates the requirement of an attack against any civilian population in respect of all underlying crimes, including persecution and apartheid. The definition of a 'civilian population' as it has emerged in modern jurisprudence is closely tied to the understanding of a civilian in international humanitarian law. This raises a possible concern that the modern conception of crimes against humanity is narrower than the customary law conception in 1975. It may in addition be queried whether the narrower understanding reflects the intention of the drafters of Article 5 of the ECCC Law. The decision of the International Co-Investigating Judge, while of limited authoritative value as the decision of a single judge in the investigative phase of the ECCC process, nonetheless throws light on an important issue with potential ramifications for the current development of the law. It is normally not in the interests of a State or organisation to direct atrocities against members of its own army during a conflict but these circumstances are not impossible. It might even be thought that the use of *Kamikaze* pilots by Japan during the Second World War could fall within this category or the abuse of women who volunteer to fight for the Islamic State, or indeed systematic abuses of conscripted children. The analysis of the issue prompted by the evidence before the ECCC helps to inform the future law and points to the fact that despite numerous legal provisions generating significant problems of cumulative charges and convictions, there are still lacunae and circumstances that have not previously been fully imagined.

---

[281] ECCC Agreement, Article 9.

The timing of the ECCC operations coincides with a global drive to bring attention and an end to sexual violence in conflict.[282] Proper characterisation of sexual violence offences by courts and tribunals functioning in post-conflict situations is important to dispel various myths.[283] First, relevant provisions in the Geneva Conventions and Additional Protocols treat this category of criminality as being about 'honour' or sex rather than about violence. For example, Article 4(2)(e) of Additional Protocol II prohibits 'outrages upon personal dignity, in particular, humiliating and degrading treatment, rape, enforced prostitution and any form of indecent assault'. Second, sexual violence crimes have been considered less grave than other 'grave breaches' of international humanitarian law. Rape, for example, is not listed as a grave breach in the Geneva Conventions or a fundamental guarantee in Additional Protocol I and it was not listed as a crime against humanity in the Nuremberg Charter (although included as such in the subsequent Control Council Law No. 10). Third, sexual violence crimes have often been viewed as opportunistic and committed for personal motives. Finally, these crimes have been treated in isolation from systematic, mass violence.

As a modern 'transitional' justice response in relation to events that are part of increasingly distant history, the ECCC is expected to take into account, even prioritise, the particular suffering of victims of sexual violence. This means viewing the prosecution of crimes against women and girls as a key component of the broader question of redress and

---

[282] *See* e.g. Global Summit to End Sexual Violence in Conflict in London during 10-13 June 2014, in '2014 Global Summit to End Sexual Violence in Conflict', United Kingdom Government, 9 March 2017, <https://www.gov.uk/government/collections/2014-global-summit-to-end-sexual-violence-in-conflict> [accessed 23 June 2017]; International Protocol on the Documentation and Investigation of Sexual Violence in Conflict – Basic Standards of Best Practice on the Documentation of Sexual Violence as a Crime under International Law, Foreign & Commonwealth Office, United Kingdom, June 2014, <http://www.president-ksgov.net/repository/docs/PSVI_protocol_web__3_.pdf> [accessed 23 June 2017]. *See* also International Criminal Court, Office of the Prosecutor, Policy Paper on Sexual and Gender-Based Crimes, June 2014, <https://www.icc-cpi.int/iccdocs/otp/OTP-Policy-Paper-on-Sexual-and-Gender-Based-Crimes–June-2014.pdf> [accessed 23 June 2017].

[283] M. Jarvis and E.M. Salgado, 'Future Challenges to Prosecuting Sexual Violence under International Law: Insights from ICTY Practice', in A. de Brouwer, C. Ku, R. Römkens and L. van den Herik (eds), *Sexual violence as an International Crime: Interdisciplinary Approaches* (Cambridge/Antwerp/Portland, Intersentia, 2013), pp. 101–22, p. 102.

reconciliation. It also includes recognition of the fact that the relevance of gender extends beyond crimes overtly concerned with sexual violence. In the ICTY case of *Krstić*, for example, it was found that while men were more likely to be deliberately killed in the context of the conflict in the former Yugoslavia, women were more likely to be displaced.[284] Taking account of the gender-based suffering of victims, the trend of modern prosecutions is to present allegations of sexual violence as systematic crimes. Where available, the 'umbrella' characterisations are therefore likely to be the crime against humanity of persecution, or the war crime of terrorizing the civilian population. However, it has been observed that 'there can be no complacency that the totality of women's experiences in armed conflict and genocide is captured by existing offences'.[285] This has resulted in new characterisations drawing on customary international law, such as forced marriage as an 'other inhumane act' within the category of crimes against humanity.

It might be argued that the very act of prosecuting sexual violence crimes is recognition of their seriousness irrespective of their characterisation. The Civil Party Lawyers faced an uphill struggle to ensure prosecutions in the early days of the ECCC. Notably, in 2009, there were no gender-trained or female investigators in the Office of the Co-Investigative Judges (OCIJ).[286] Victims may have been unwilling to describe their experience of sexual violence and may not even have known to come forward with their testimony until it was revealed that these acts were under serious investigation. Once prosecutions are on the agenda, characterisation assumes particular significance as it is almost impossible to ignore the current discussion on sexual and gender-based violence in international law in considering whether to subsume a crime of sexual violence within a non-sexual violence category such as torture or even forced marriage. This must be determined amid the tension

---

[284] M. Jarvis, 'Overview: The Challenge of Accountability for Conflict-Related Sexual Violence Crimes', in B.S. Brammertz and M. Jarvis (eds), *Prosecuting Conflict-Related Sexual Violence at the ICTY* (Oxford, Oxford University Press, 2016), pp. 1–18, p. 11.

[285] C. Chinkin, 'Gender-Related Violence and International Criminal Law and Justice', in A. Cassese (ed), *The Oxford Companion to International Criminal Justice* (Oxford/New York, Oxford University Press, 2009), pp. 75–81, p. 78.

[286] *Prosecutor v Nuon Chea, Ieng Sary, Ieng Thirith, Khieu Samphan* and *Kaing Guek Eav alias 'Duch'*, ECCC Case File No. 002/19-09-2007-ECCC-OCIJ, Office of the Co-Investigating Judges, Order on Request for Investigative Action Concerning Forced Marriages and Forced Sexual Relations, 18 December 2009, para. 15.

between presenting a complete picture of criminality based on the facts, the specificity of indictments and the efficiency of proceedings.[287] Modes of liability then come into play as can be seen in Case 002/02 where rape was not part of the policy behind the joint criminal enterprise with the result that rape can only be considered behind the screen of forced marriage.

The ECCC process is less a 'genocide trial' than an exposure of a wide range of crimes against humanity. The seriousness of the crimes will in no sense be diminished if the genocide label is ultimately found to be the incorrect legal fit.[288] Nonetheless, most of the evidence of genocide was heard during 2016 and by this point the overall momentum of the ECCC had been lost. Had Khieu Samphan and Nuon Chea not been such survivors themselves, the ECCC might never have had the opportunity to hear the victims' views on the crime that had come to be seen as synonymous with the Khmer Rouge for many survivors.

In addressing discrete categories of crimes, the judges have sometimes failed to see the broader picture of the Khmer Rouge's conduct. Case 002/01 focussed exclusively on crimes against humanity and yet the idea of a 'civilian' victim of such crimes was viewed by both the Trial Chamber and the Supreme Court Chamber as being intimately connected to the idea of a civilian victim during an armed conflict. The idea initially introduced by the Co-Investigating Judges and adopted by the Chambers that most victims were victimised on political grounds effectively excluded the possibility of a broader, if not creative, approach to genocide.

The Supreme Court Chamber observed in its discussion of cumulative convictions that 'the different categories of crimes have grown ever closer'.[289] This is debatable considering the close relationship between crimes against humanity and war crimes in the post-Second World War

---

287 V. Oosterveld, 'Atrocity Crimes Litigation Year-in-Review (2010): A Gender Perspective', 9 *Northwestern Journal of International Human Rights*, vol. 9, no. 3, 2011, pp. 325–55, p. 355.

288 *See* generally P.M. Wald, 'Judging Genocide', *Justice Initiatives: The Extraordinary Chambers*, 21 April 2006, 85–96, p. 86 <https://www.opensocietyfoundations.org/publications/justice-initiatives-extraordinary-chambers> [accessed 22 June 2017]; T. Fawthrop and H. Jarvis, *Getting Away with Genocide? Elusive Justice and the Khmer Rouge Tribunal* (London, Pluto Press, 2004), p. 223.

289 Duch Appeal Judgment, above n. 38, para. 286.

period. In any event, the ECCC has paid careful attention to legal characterisation and has contributed towards defining the boundaries of the different categories of crimes as they stood in 1975 and as they perhaps still stand today under customary international law.

8. Liability

1. INTRODUCTION

Modes of liability are legal tools to establish the linkage between the crimes proved to have been committed and the alleged perpetrator. Each mode of liability has its own elements often described in terms of an *actus reus* and a *mens rea*. A layering of elements of proof is required before an individual can be convicted of any crime. The modes of liability applicable before the Extraordinary Chambers in the Courts of Cambodia (ECCC) are set out in Article 29 (new) of the ECCC Law as follows:

> Any Suspect who planned, instigated, ordered, aided and abetted, or committed the crimes referred to in article 3 new, 4, 5, 6, 7 and 8 of this law shall be individually responsible for the crime ...

Article 29 (new) also refers to the concept of superior or command responsibility:

> The fact that any of the acts referred to in Articles 3 new, 4, 5, 6, 7 and 8 of this law were committed by a subordinate does not relieve the superior of personal criminal responsibility if the superior had effective command and control or authority and control over the subordinate, and the superior knew or had reason to know that the subordinate was about to commit such acts or had done so and the superior failed to take the necessary and reasonable measures to prevent such acts or to punish the perpetrators.

The complete list therefore includes committing, planning, instigating, ordering or aiding and abetting the crime, and superior responsibility. In Case 001, the Trial Chamber found that these forms of responsibility were also recognised under the 1956 Penal Code, except for planning and superior responsibility. However, according to the Trial Chamber, planning was criminalised by specific domestic provisions and superior responsibility had been established by the Nuremberg-era tribunals.[1] The

[1] *Prosecutor v Kaing Guek Eav alias 'Duch'*, ECCC Case File No. 001/18-07-2007/ECCC/TC, Trial Chamber, Judgment, 26 July 2010, para. 474 ('Duch Trial Judgment').

Trial Chamber found a basis for all forms of responsibility in customary international law. In Case 002/01, the Trial Chamber repeated this position, adding that all the modes of liability were foreseeable and accessible to the accused '[c]onsidering the senior positions held by [them]'.[2] In response to a Defence objection, the Supreme Court Chamber clarified that the question whether the principle of legality had been adhered to must be determined through an objective analysis, although it was not unreasonable to add the subjective element of an accused's senior position as part of the overall assessment.[3]

The Pre-Trial Chamber (PTC) addressed the status of superior responsibility under customary international law in its decisions on appeals against the Closing Order in Case 002.[4] The Pre-Trial Chamber agreed with the Trial Chamber's assessment of the Nuremberg-era jurisprudence in Case 001 and noted that 'the evolution of individual criminal responsibility pursuant to the doctrine of superior responsibility as a customary international law norm was foreshadowed by events in the aftermath of World War I'.[5] Although the Pre-Trial Chamber pointed to the controversies surrounding the post-Second World War case of *Yamashita* which is often held up as the defining moment for the doctrine of superior responsibility,[6] it found it to be 'without question that *Yamashita* serves as precedent for the notion that a superior may be held criminally responsible under international law with respect to crimes committed by

---

2 *Prosecutor v Nuon Chea* and *Khieu Samphan*, ECCC Case File No. 002/19-09-2007/ECCC/TC, Trial Chamber, Case 002/01 Judgement, 7 August 2014, paras. 697 (planning), 699 (instigating), 701 (ordering), 703 (aiding and abetting), 714 (superior responsibility) ('Nuon Trial Judgment').

3 *Prosecutor v Nuon Chea* and *Khieu Samphan*, ECCC Case File No. 002/19-09-2007-ECCC/SC, Supreme Court Chamber, Appeal Judgment, 23 November 2016, para. 761 ('Nuon Appeal Judgment').

4 *Prosecutor v Ieng Sary*, ECCC Case File No. 002/19-09-2007-ECCC/OCIJ (PTC75), Pre-Trial Chamber, Decision on Ieng Sary's Appeal against the Closing Order, 11 April 2011, paras. 413–60; *Prosecutor v Nuon Chea, Ieng Sary, Ieng Thirith* and *Khieu Samphan*, ECCC Case File No. 002/19-09-2007-ECCC/OCIJ (PTC 145 & 146), Pre-Trial Chamber, Decision on Appeals by Nuon Chea and Ieng Thirith against the Closing Order, 15 February 2011, paras. 190–232.

5 *Prosecutor v Ieng Sary*, ECCC Case File No. 002/19-09-2007-ECCC/OCIJ (PTC75), Pre-Trial Chamber, Decision on Ieng Sary's Appeal against the Closing Order, 11 April 2011, para. 421.

6 Trial of General Tomoyuki Yamashita, Case No. 21, United States Military Commission, Manila, 8 October–7 December 1945. See G. Mettraux, *The Law of Command Responsibility* (Oxford, Oxford University Press, 2009), pp. 5–8.

subordinates'.[7] A comprehensive assessment of the sources led the Pre-Trial Chamber to the conclusion that 'the doctrine of superior responsibility was understood not to be strictly limited to military commanders, but it was also extended to include non-military superiors'.[8] Similar issues arose before the Trial Chamber in Case 002/01 but they were swiftly dismissed based on the Pre-Trial Chamber's decisions.[9] Related questions, including whether a superior must have a pre-existing duty to act established in domestic law at the relevant time, and whether a superior is only responsible for the conduct of direct subordinates were answered in the negative by the Trial Chamber.[10] The Chambers have consistently taken the position that in the event of an accused being 'both directly responsible and responsible as a superior in relation to the same conduct', it is appropriate to convict on the basis of the direct from of responsibility and to consider an accused's superior position as an aggravating factor in sentencing.[11]

The Trial Chamber in Case 002/01 found that although the French version of Article 29 (new) of the ECCC Law equated 'aiding and abetting' with *complicité*, the French notion of *aidé et encouragé* should be preferred as it more accurately reflected the notion of aiding and abetting liability in customary international law in addition to according with the English and Khmer versions of the ECCC Law.[12] Khieu Samphan raised three issues relating to the *actus reus* of aiding and abetting, namely whether aiding and abetting could occur by omission; whether an accused's conduct must be 'specifically directed' towards the commission of a crime by the main perpetrator; and whether assistance after the commission of a crime could incur liability.[13] The Trial Chamber relied on Nuremberg-era jurisprudence to find that aiding or abetting could occur by omission;[14] adopted the comprehensive surveys of jurisprudence and instruments contained in the *Šainović* and *Taylor*

[7] *Prosecutor v Ieng Sary*, ECCC Case File No. 002/19-09-2007-ECCC/OCIJ (PTC75), Pre-Trial Chamber, Decision on Ieng Sary's Appeal against the Closing Order, 11 April 2011, para. 427.
[8] Ibid, para. 459.
[9] Nuon Trial Judgment, above n. 2, para. 718.
[10] Ibid, paras. 720–1.
[11] Ibid, para. 688; Duch Trial Judgment, above n. 1, para. 539.
[12] Nuon Trial Judgment, above n. 2, para. 703.
[13] Ibid, para. 705.
[14] Ibid, para. 706.

Appeal Judgments to conclude that 'specific direction' was not a requirement to establish aiding and abetting liability under customary international law;[15] and found that assistance provided exclusively after the perpetration of the crime would not normally satisfy the requirement that the assistance should have a substantial effect on the commission of the crime, but that this would be a matter for the evidence in each case.[16]

The Trial Chamber's findings on specific forms of responsibility have not been given sustained attention by the Supreme Court Chamber due to the overwhelming focus on 'Joint Criminal Enterprise' (JCE) which is said to derive from customary international law and to be incorporated into the notion of 'committing'.[17] This chapter will therefore mainly address the ECCC's jurisprudence on JCE liability as the primary basis for all convictions entered so far by the Court. Indeed, the Chambers, being concerned with 'characterization' of liability in the same way as they have been concerned with characterisation of crimes, have refrained from making exhaustive findings in respect of each form of responsibility and have exercised their discretion to select the one deemed most appropriate.[18] A question running through this chapter is why the ECCC has viewed JCE as being the most appropriate mode of liability among a range of options, including the Cambodian notion of co-perpetratorship with its civil law underpinnings (in contrast to the common law-inspired JCE). The Chambers have not directly answered this question but it may be assumed that the reasons are connected to the established customary international law status of JCE, at least in its first two configurations, combined with the ability of JCE to capture the magnitude of mass atrocity crimes in a manner that arguably cannot be achieved by any other method of attributing responsibility.

---

[15] Ibid, para. 710.

[16] Ibid, para. 713.

[17] *See* Nuon Appeal Judgment, above n. 3, para. 1099: 'The Supreme Court Chamber recalls that it has confirmed the Accused's liability, based on the notion of JCE, in respect of murder, other inhumane acts and persecution in relation to Population Movement Phase One as well as other inhumane acts and murder in relation to Population Movement Phase Two. The Supreme Court Chamber does not consider that it is appropriate to consider the grounds of appeal relating to the other modes of liability, given that these grounds of appeal cannot invalidate the judgement under review or occasion a miscarriage of justice.' In relation to the crimes committed at Tuol Po Chrey, *see* also paras. 1100–1.

[18] Duch Trial Judgment, above n. 1, para. 472.

2. THE CONCEPT OF JOINT CRIMINAL ENTERPRISE

The elements of joint criminal enterprise liability under international law were first identified by the International Criminal Tribunal for the former Yugoslavia (ICTY) Appeals Chamber in its judgment in the case of *Prosecutor v Tadić* delivered in 1999, drawing on the post-Second World War jurisprudence.[19] In terms of the objective requirements, a JCE consists of a plurality of persons who formulate a common plan amounting to or involving the commission of crimes, whereby each participant contributes significantly towards to the accomplishment of the common purpose.[20] Conceptually, JCE may be divided into three categories. The first 'basic' category (JCE I) refers to the situation in which a group of persons, acting pursuant to a common design, possess the same criminal intention. Proof is required that the accused voluntarily participated in one aspect of the common design and, even if not physically committing the crime, nevertheless intended the planned result.[21] The second 'systemic' form (JCE II), most relevant to the ill-treatment of inmates in a concentration camp setting, is based on proof of active participation in the enforcement of a system of repression combined with knowledge of the nature of the system and the intent to further the common concerted design.[22] The third 'extended' category (JCE III), the one in fact applied in *Tadić*, concerns a common design to pursue one course of conduct where one of the perpetrators commits an act which, while outside the common design, was nevertheless a natural consequence of putting that design into effect. The subjective element in the last category is foreseeability—specifically, foreseeing that a crime other than the one agreed upon might be perpetrated, and still willingly taking that risk.[23]

---

[19] *Prosecutor v Tadić*, ICTY Case No. IT-94-1-A, Appeals Chamber, Judgment, 15 July 1999, paras. 185–229 ('Tadić Appeals Judgment'). *See* also Nuon Appeal Judgment, above n. 3, para. 773.

[20] Tadić Appeals Judgment, ibid, para. 227.

[21] Ibid, paras. 196–200.

[22] Ibid, paras. 202–3.

[23] Ibid, paras. 204–19, 228.

3. CHARGING JOINT CRIMINAL ENTERPRISE AT THE ECCC

The Co-Prosecutors presented JCE as a primary mode of liability in the first Introductory Submission. When the Co-Investigating Judges ordered the severance of the case against Duch for a separate trial in Case 001, the Co-Prosecutors put forward a modified JCE theory to describe Duch's participation in an organised system of repression within the S-21 detention centre.[24] The Co-Investigating Judges omitted this theory in the Closing Order in Case 001, leading to an appeal by the Co-Prosecutors to the Pre-Trial Chamber.[25] In its decision, the Pre-Trial Chamber noted that the Co-Investigating Judges should have reasoned why they had turned down the Co-Prosecutors' proposal to include the allegation of a JCE within S-21,[26] but nevertheless rejected this aspect of the appeal, stating:

> … that the significance and exclusivity of the notion of joint criminal enterprise, at least in its basic form, lies in its conceptual underpinning. This allows individual responsibility at the level of a co-perpetrator to be attributed to participants in collective criminal action even though they may be physically divorced from the actual offences. Joint criminal enterprise liability has a subjective focus on the common purpose and the intent of the participant. Thus, if Duch were to be indicted as a participant in a joint criminal enterprise, the perception of the level and extent of his responsibility would differ from the description of his responsibility in the Closing Order. The Closing Order reflects the Introductory Submission which described Duch's personal responsibility in terms of his role in the hierarchical structure of S-21. The Pre-Trial Chamber notes that the alleged S-21 JCE expands the type of conduct attributable to Duch.[27]

---

[24] *Prosecutor v Kaing Guek Eav alias 'Duch'*, ECCC Case File No. 002/14-08-2006/ECCC/OCP, Office of the Co-Prosecutor, Public Information by the Co-Prosecutors pursuant to Rule 54 concerning their Rule 66 Final Submission Regarding Kaing Guek Eav alias 'Duch', 18 July 2008, paras. 241–53.

[25] *Prosecutor v Kaing Guek Eav alias 'Duch'*, ECCC Case File No. 002/14-08-2006, Office of the Co-Investigating Judges, Closing Order Indicting Kaing Guek Eav alias Duch, 8 August 2008.

[26] *Prosecutor v Kaing Guek Eav alias 'Duch'*, ECCC Case File No. 001/8-07-2007-ECCC/OCIJ (PTC 02), Pre-Trial Chamber, Decision on Appeal against Closing Order Indicting Kaing Guek Eav alias 'Duch', 5 December 2008, para. 115.

[27] Ibid, para. 136.

The Pre-Trial Chamber therefore declined to add JCE liability to the Closing Order.[28]

At the initial hearings in Case 001, the Co-Prosecutors notified the Trial Chamber and the parties that they would request the application of JCE to the charges against Duch.[29] They followed up with a written request for the Trial Chamber to declare the general applicability of all three forms of JCE in cases before the ECCC.[30] The Trial Chamber reserved its decision until the final judgment when it invoked Internal Rule 98(2) to re-characterise the facts set out in the Closing Order in order to apply JCE liability. JCE was found to be included in Article 29 (new) of the ECCC Law as a means of 'committing' a crime.[31] The Trial Chamber affirmed the status of JCE I and II in customary international law but declined to pronounce on the customary law status of JCE III in the period 1975 to 1979 since the Co-Prosecutors had only sought to apply JCE III in the alternative.[32] Ultimately, the Trial Chamber convicted Duch on the basis of the 'systemic' category of JCE, i.e. JCE II.[33] The question regarding the applicability of JCE III was not raised before the Supreme Court Chamber in Case 001.

During the investigative phase of Case 002, Ieng Sary challenged the application of JCE before the ECCC.[34] In response, the Co-Investigating Judges held that all three forms of JCE were available.[35] This decision of the Co-Investigating Judges was appealed by Ieng Sary, Ieng Thirith and Khieu Samphan before the Pre-Trial Chamber. On 20 May 2010, the Pre-Trial Chamber rendered its decision in which it found that JCE I and II were recognised forms of responsibility in customary international law

---

28 Ibid, para. 141.

29 Duch Trial Judgment, above n. 1, para. 489.

30 Ibid.

31 Ibid, para. 511.

32 Ibid, paras. 512–13.

33 Ibid, para. 516.

34 *Prosecutor v Ieng Sang*, ECCC Case File No. 002/19-09-2007-ECCC/OCIJ, Defence for Ieng Sary, Ieng Sary Lawyers' Motion against the Application at the ECCC of the Form of Liability Known as 'Joint Criminal Enterprise', 28 July 2008.

35 *Prosecutor v Nuon Chea, Ieng Sary, Ieng Thirith* and *Khieu Samphan*, ECCC Case File No. 002/19-09-2007-ECCC/OCIJ, Office of the Co-Investigating Judges, Order on the Application at the ECCC of the Form of Liability Known as Joint Criminal Enterprise, 8 December 2009, paras. 21, 23.

at the relevant time.[36] However, according to the Pre-Trial Chamber, the authorities relied upon in *Tadić* did not 'constitute a sufficiently firm basis to conclude that JCE III formed part of customary international law at the time relevant to Case 002'.[37] Further, the Pre-Trial Chamber stated that it did not need to decide 'whether a number of legal systems, which can be regarded as representative of the world's major legal systems, recognise that a standard of *mens rea* lower than direct intent may apply in relation to crimes committed outside the common criminal purpose and amount to commission'.[38] This was on the basis that JCE III in any case lacked an underpinning in Cambodian law and was therefore not foreseeable to the accused.[39]

The Closing Order in Case 002 centred the factual allegations on a wide-ranging JCE. According to the Co-Investigating Judges:

> [U]nder international law, Joint Criminal Enterprise (JCE) is a mode of individual criminal responsibility encompassed by the concept of commission. The *actus reus* elements are that the Charged Person, together with a plurality of persons, contributed or participated in a common purpose which resulted in and/or involved the commission of a crime within the ECCC's jurisdiction. The *mens rea* for JCE 1 is a shared intent to contribute to or participate in the implementation of a common purpose.[40]

---

[36] *Prosecutor v Ieng Sary, Ieng Thirith* and *Khieu Samphan*, ECCC Case File No. 002/19-09-2007-ECCC/OCIJ (PTC 35, 37, 38, & 39), Pre-Trial Chamber, Decision on the Appeals against the Co-Investigating Judges' Order on Joint Criminal Enterprise (JCE), 20 May 2010, para. 83.

[37] Ibid, para. 83.

[38] Ibid, para. 87; Nuon Appeal Judgment, above n. 3, para. 774 (The Supreme Court Chamber attributed the finding that Joint Criminal Enterprise ('JCE') III was not applicable in the proceedings before the ECCC as a general principle of law to the Pre-Trial Chamber although the Pre-Trial Chamber did not in fact examine this issue).

[39] *See* further K. Gustafson, 'ECCC Tackles JCE: An Appraisal of Recent Decisions', *Journal of International Criminal Justice*, vol. 8, no. 5, 2010, 1323–32, p. 1329 (who suggests that since the Chamber had already stated that criminalization in domestic law was not essential to meet the test of legality, the Chamber must have taken the view that 'even if JCE III were found to constitute a general principle of law recognized by various legal systems, this could not serve to make this form of liability foreseeable to the suspects, given that it did not have a basis in either customary international law, or domestic Cambodian law.').

[40] *Prosecutor v Nuon Chea, Ieng Sary, Ieng Thirith* and *Khieu Samphan*, ECCC Case File No. 002/19-09-2007-ECCC-OCIJ, Office of the Co-Investigating Judges, Closing Order (Indictment) in Case 002, 15 September 2010, para. 1521.

The Co-Investigating Judges found that there was sufficient evidence to show that Nuon Chea, Ieng Sary, Khieu Samphan and Ieng Thirith not only shared the intent that the crimes alleged in the Closing Order be committed as part of the common purpose, but that 'they were the driving force behind it'.[41] Only JCE I was retained in the Closing Order, on the basis that it was 'most suited for characterizing the criminal responsibility of the Charged Persons for the crimes'.[42]

The Co-Prosecutors subsequently filed a motion before the Trial Chamber to be permitted to use JCE III as an alternative mode of liability in Case 002/01.[43] In its decision, the Trial Chamber adopted the Pre-Trial Chamber's analysis and confirmed that JCE III was inapplicable in proceedings before the ECCC.[44] In this instance, the Trial Chamber offered its views on the post-Second World War cases invoked in support of JCE III both in *Tadić*, and more recently by the Special Tribunal for Lebanon (STL).[45] None of these authorities persuaded the Trial Chamber that JCE III had emerged as a customary international law notion by 1975–1979.[46] The Trial Chamber went on to consider whether JCE III could be supported as a general principle of law, a question that in the Trial Chamber's view had not been answered directly by the Pre-Trial Chamber. It surveyed the law of the United Kingdom, the US, Germany, the Soviet Union, the Netherlands, France and Cambodia and concluded that there was a significant divergence of approach in these jurisdictions and that no general principle could be derived from domestic practice.[47] Regarding Cambodian law specifically, the Trial Chamber noted that none of the forms of responsibility in the 1956 Penal Code, applicable at the relevant time, supported the application of JCE III liability.[48]

---

41 Ibid, para. 1540.

42 Ibid, para. 1541.

43 Ibid, para. 2.

44 Ibid, paras. 22, 26.

45 *Prosecutor v Nuon Chea, Ieng Sary, Ieng Thirith* and *Khieu Samphan*, ECCC Case File No. 002/19-09-2007/ECCC/TC, Trial Chamber, Decision on the Applicability of Joint Criminal Enterprise, 12 September 2011, paras. 30–5; Tadić Appeals Judgment, above n. 19, paras. 205–19; *Prosecutor v Ayyash, Merhi, Oneissi* and *Sabra*, SLT Case No. STL-11-01/I, Appeals Chamber, Interlocutory Decision on the Applicable Law: Terrorism, Conspiracy, Homicide, Perpetration, Cumulative Charging, 16 February 2011, para. 237, footnote 355.

46 *Prosecutor v Nuon Chea, Ieng Sary, Ieng Thirith* and *Khieu Samphan*, ECCC Case File No. 002/19-09-2007/ECCC/TC, Trial Chamber, Decision on the Applicability of Joint Criminal Enterprise, 12 September 2011, paras. 29–35.

47 Ibid, para. 37.

48 Ibid, para. 37, footnote 91.

JCE I formed the basis for the convictions of Nuon Chea and Khieu Samphan in Case 002/01 as imposed by the Trial Chamber and upheld by the Supreme Court Chamber. The Co-Prosecutors raised a single ground of appeal against the Trial Chamber's judgment as a matter of general legal importance, arguing in favour of the applicability of JCE III before the ECCC.

4. JCE I

4.1 JCE I in Customary International Law

The Co-Investigating Judges and all the Chambers have agreed that JCE I was part of customary international law at the relevant time. The Supreme Court Chamber offered a pragmatic account of the limitations of the case law that is typically relied upon in support of JCE, noting that 'the legal categories that the ICTY Appeals Chamber identified in *Tadić* appear to have been based primarily on an assessment of the facts of the underlying cases; the categories were not expressly used in the post-World War II jurisprudence nor are they sharp-contoured legal definitions free from overlap'.[49] The Supreme Court Chamber identified the key question as being

> whether and, if so, to what extent, the applicable law as it stood at the time relevant to the charges provided for individual criminal liability in circumstances where the accused did not carry out the *actus reus* of the international crime charged but had acted in concert with others based on a common purpose and made a contribution to its implementation.[50]

Addressing the argument made by Nuon Chea that an accused would need to commit at least part of the *actus reus* of the crime in question in order for criminal liability to arise, the Supreme Court Chamber stated:

> To the extent that NUON Chea argues that the post-World War II case law often does not even identify the mode of liability relied upon, the Supreme Court Chamber concedes that the jurisprudence is not always clear in this regard – and therefore, needs to be treated with caution. Nevertheless, his argument disregards that the law regarding individual criminal responsibility for international crimes did not come into being by way of a coherent act of legislation. Rather, in the wake of World War II, the atrocities committed

---

49 Nuon Appeal Judgment, above n. 3, para. 775.
50 Ibid.

> during the war were tried by a variety of courts, based on the IMT Statute, the IMTFE Statute, Control Council Law No. 10, and domestic laws. Accordingly, when determining under what circumstances criminal liability for international crimes arises, one has to analyse the post-World War II case law and distil from it the common threads and elements. This is what the *Tadić* Appeal Judgement (ICTY) and subsequent decisions of the ICTY, ICTR, SCSL, STL and indeed the ECCC have done.[51]

The Supreme Court Chamber found it unrealistic to expect that clear distinctions between, for example, the liability of principals and accessories could be derived from such a variety of sources.[52] Indeed, 'even in the jurisprudence of the ICTY, the categorisation of JCE liability as principal as opposed to accessorial liability is of limited relevance'.[53] It is unclear in what sense this categorisation by the ICTY was seen as lacking pertinence as it appears central to the modern concept of JCE. Nevertheless, despite its more cautious treatment of the jurisprudence as compared to the ICTY Appeals Chamber in *Tadić*, the ECCC Supreme Court Chamber concluded that criminal liability could arise 'in circumstances where an individual makes a contribution to the implementation of the common criminal purpose, even if that contribution does not amount to the *actus reus* of the crime and is removed from the commission of the crime itself'.[54] In support of this statement the Supreme Court Chamber referred to the *Almelo*, *Schonfeld*, *Einsatzgruppen*, *RuSHA*, and *Justice* cases.

As it concerned the precise requirements to establish JCE liability, the Supreme Court Chamber emphasised that the participants must 'agree to a common purpose of a criminal character'.[55] In accordance with the *Tadić* case and subsequent jurisprudence, the common purpose must 'amount to' or 'involve' the commission of a crime. The Supreme Court Chamber found that 'the common purpose "amounts to" the commission of a crime if the commission of the crime is the, or among the, primary objective(s) of the common purpose', for example where the common purpose is to kill a group of political enemies.[56] However, the allegation in the Closing Order in Case 002 was as follows:

---

[51] Ibid, para. 776.
[52] Ibid, para. 777.
[53] Ibid, para. 778.
[54] Ibid, paras. 779, 788.
[55] Ibid, para. 789.
[56] Ibid, para. 807.

> The common purpose of the CPK leaders was to implement rapid socialist revolution in Cambodia through a 'great leap forward' and to defend the Party against internal and external enemies, by whatever means necessary. The purpose itself was not entirely criminal in nature but its implementation resulted in and/or involved the commission of crimes within the jurisdiction of the ECCC.[57]

The Supreme Court Chamber accepted that liability could arise in respect of a common purpose that was not overtly criminal, as long as its implementation *involved* the commission of crimes.[58] In relation to this possibility, the Supreme Court Chamber explained:

> [T]he common purpose 'involves' the commission of a crime if the crime is a means to achieve an ulterior objective (which itself may not be criminal). In such a scenario, it is not necessary that those who agree on the common purpose actually desire that the crime be committed, as long as they recognise that the crime is to be committed to achieve an ulterior objective.[59]

It is not immediately obvious what the Supreme Court Chamber meant by marking a difference between 'desiring that the crime be committed' and 'recognising that the crime is to be committed'. The Supreme Court Chamber continued in the following vein:

> This may include crimes that are foreseen as means to achieve a given common purpose, even if their commission is not certain. For instance, if a gang agrees to break into a house to steal and to use, if necessary, deadly force to overcome any resistance that they may encounter, it would be unconvincing to conclude that the eventual murder was not encompassed by the common purpose because it was not certain that murder would actually be committed in the course of the break-in. Rather, in such scenario, the crime of murder was a constituent element of the plan that was conceived, even if the members of the gang did not know whether it would actually be committed. Thus, if attaining the objective of the common purpose may bring about the commission of crimes, but it is agreed to pursue this objective regardless, these crimes are encompassed by the common purpose because, even though not directly intended, they are contemplated by it. Whether a crime was contemplated by the common purpose is primarily a question of fact that – absent an express agreement – has to be assessed taking into account all

---

[57] *Prosecutor v Nuon Chea, Ieng Sary, Ieng Thirith* and *Khieu Samphan*, ECCC Case File No. 002/19-09-2007-ECCC-OCIJ, Office of the Co-Investigating Judges, Closing Order (Indictment) in Case 002, 15 September 2010, para. 1524.

[58] Nuon Appeal Judgment, above n. 3, para. 789.

[59] Ibid, para. 808.

> relevant circumstances, including the overall objective of the common purpose and the likelihood that it may be attained only at the cost of the commission of crimes. What is of note is that the common purpose may encompass crimes in which the commission is neither desired nor certain, just as it is sufficient for the commission of certain crimes that the perpetrator acted with *dolus eventualis* and therefore neither desired that the crime be committed nor was certain that it would happen.[60]

In the Supreme Court Chamber's telling of the 'three people set out to rob a bank' story, all three participants must agree to commit murder if it becomes necessary to kill even though the common purpose is to 'steal'. In the JCE III version of the same scenario, the participants agree to break into a house and steal, but one participant shoots the neighbour who suddenly enters the house while the burglary is in full swing. In the first version, the common purpose has a criminal character—burglary—so the question is whether other crimes may be deemed part of that purpose either from the outset or as the plan evolves. In cases of a non-criminal common purpose it must surely be demonstrated that its achievement *necessarily* involved or contemplated crimes and not merely that they were tacitly understood.[61] The Supreme Court Chamber rescued the analysis to an extent by emphasising that in all the scenarios it had described, 'there is a meeting of minds – express or implicit – in respect of this crime of those who agree on the common purpose'.[62] However, the Supreme Court Chamber went on to say, 'the members of the JCE must accept the commission of the crime either as a goal, as an inevitable consequence of the primary purpose or as *an eventuality treated with*

---

[60] Ibid, para. 808.

[61] *See* also L. Yanev, 'The Theory of Joint Criminal Enterprise at the ECCC: A Difficult Relationship', in S.M. Meisenberg and I. Stegmiller (eds), *The Extraordinary Chambers in the Courts of Cambodia: Assessing their Contribution to International Criminal Law* (The Hague, T.M.C. Asser Press, 2016), pp. 203–54, p. 220: 'in such scenarios where the common purpose has a non-criminal goal, JCE law requires that it *necessarily* involved the commission of a crime (or crimes) as the means agreed amongst the accused to achieve that goal'.

[62] Nuon Appeal Judgment, above n. 3, para. 809. See also ECCC Case File No. 004/07-09-2009-ECCC-OCIJ, *Im Chaem*, Closing Order (Reasons), 10 July 2017, para. 99, where the Co-Investigating Judges state: 'We interpret this holding of the SCC also on the basis of its use of the word "desire" as a clarification that the commission of the crimes need not be the primary objective of the JCE members. However there remains the need to show intent to commit the crimes by the JCE members which is a fundamental requirement of the first type of JCE.'

indifference'.[63] It seems that the Supreme Court Chamber was struggling with the notion of *dolus eventualis* which it had accepted as a correct *mens rea* standard for murder as a crime against humanity.[64] The Supreme Court Chamber's analysis of JCE I is perhaps best understood with reference to its definition of *dolus eventualis* taken from the *Stakić* case before the ICTY: 'if the actor engages in life-endangering behaviour, his killing becomes intentional if he "reconciles himself" or "makes peace" with the likelihood of death'.[65] Thus, the Supreme Court Chamber identified the main difference between the common law notion of recklessness and the civil law notion of *dolus eventualis* as being that the former is 'focused on the cognitive aspect' and the latter on the 'volitional aspect in the perpetrator's attitude toward the result'.[66] Against this background, it becomes easier to see how liability under JCE I could follow from a common plan that involves a crime as an eventuality that is treated with indifference. However, the Pre-Trial Chamber's statement that, conceptually, JCE has a 'subjective focus on the common purpose and the intent of the participant' should also be borne in mind. It would seem like a watering down of the concept of JCE I if the entire basis for liability is a non-criminal common purpose in the achievement of which the participants collectively reconcile themselves with the likelihood that others will commit certain crimes.

The Supreme Court Chamber found sufficient support in the post-Second World War jurisprudence to conclude that individuals could be held criminally liable 'for crimes committed in the course of the implementation of a common purpose to which they had made some kind of contribution beyond being a bystander'.[67] However, it would be insufficient for the implementation of the common purpose merely to *result* in the commission of crimes. The terminology used in the Closing Order and adopted by the Trial Chamber together with its conceptual implications was considered an error of law since it introduced 'a notion of criminal liability that did not exist either under customary international law at the time of the charges or as a general principle of law'.[68] This aspect was addressed in the context of JCE III and will be discussed further in section 6.1 below.

---

[63] Nuon Appeal Judgment, above n. 3, para. 809 (Emphasis added).

[64] Ibid, para. 410.

[65] *Prosecutor v Stakić*, ICTY Case No. IT-97-24-T, Trial Chamber II, Judgment, 31 July 2003, para. 587.

[66] Nuon Appeal Judgment, above n. 3, para. 391.

[67] Ibid, para. 810.

[68] Ibid.

4.2 The Application of JCE I in Case 002/01

The JCE as alleged in Case 002 revolved around the evolution and implementation of five policies, starting prior to 17 April 1975 and continuing throughout the indictment period.[69] These five policies included: (1) the movement of the population from towns and cities to rural areas, as well as from one rural area to another; (2) the establishment and operation of cooperatives and worksites; (3) the re-education of 'bad elements' and killing of 'enemies, both inside and outside the Party ranks'; (4) the targeting of specific groups, in particular the Cham, Vietnamese, Buddhists and former officials of the Khmer Republic, including both civil servants and former military personnel and their families; and (5) the regulation of marriage.[70] Case 002/01 only directly concerned the policies on forced movement and the targeting of former officials of the Khmer Republic and was limited to the time period between 17 April 1975 and December 1977.

4.2.1 Trial Chamber Judgment

The Trial Chamber found it to be established that the Communist Party of Kampuchea (CPK) began to move people from areas under their control into the countryside prior to 1975, with control over the population and the food supply being priorities rather than control over territory. The evacuation of cities was deemed to serve a dual purpose, 'namely to prevent enemies from destabilising CPK forces, and also to prevent cadres from being corrupted by the urban population' and there was an 'economic as well as a political rationale behind these movements'.[71] The process of eliminating private ownership of land and the means of production and replacing it with a system of cooperatives with the State in complete control of commerce began as early as May 1972.[72] The Trial Chamber found that a CPK policy to create cooperatives existed prior to 1975, based on economic as well as ideological reasons.[73] Security centres were established where perceived enemies were interrogated and 'smashed' and the policy of re-education of 'bad elements' and killing of enemies was found to have continued throughout the Democratic Kampuchea (DK) era. The implementation of this policy was to be

[69] Nuon Trial Judgment, above n. 2, para. 102.
[70] Ibid, para. 102.
[71] Ibid, para. 112.
[72] Ibid, para. 113.
[73] Ibid, para. 116.

the subject of Case 002/02.[74] Similarly, the policy of targeting Cham, Buddhist and Vietnamese as alleged in the Closing Order was to be examined in Case 002/02. The Trial Chamber found, however, an increasingly radical CPK policy of targeting groups of individuals considered to be enemies such as former Khmer Republic soldiers or officials, and that thousands of Khmer Republic soldiers were executed after the seizure of Oudong.[75] The Trial Chamber also found that there was 'some evidence of arranged and involuntary marriages', sufficient for it to conclude that 'regulation of marriage was a CPK policy' although the nature and implementation of the policy was a matter for Case 002/02.[76]

The Trial Chamber went on to explain how it was satisfied that the CPK Central Committee made a collective decision to evacuate Phnom Penh's inhabitants by forceful means.[77] The decision to evacuate Phnom Penh was made during a two-week session in June 1974 in Meak village, Prek Kok commune near the bank of the Mekong River, attended by Nuon Chea according to his own admission, and by Ieng Sary and Khieu Samphan according to the Trial Chamber's assessment of the evidence. The Trial Chamber was satisfied that a further meeting to discuss the evacuation of Phnom Penh was held in early April 1975 at B-5, the command centre for the attack on Phnom Penh located in Tang Poun village, Kampong Tralach district, Kampong Chhnang province, attended by Pol Pot, Nuon Chea, Khieu Samphan and other senior leaders. According to the Trial Chamber, these meetings were followed by further meetings with the Khmer Rouge forces in which orders were given to the Revolutionary Army of Kampuchea (RAK) division commanders to evacuate Phnom Penh and other cities. Nuon Chea, Khieu Samphan and Ieng Sary were all found to have participated in the decision to evacuate Phnom Penh and other urban centres.[78]

Despite the policy of secrecy surrounding the CPK and the anonymous organisation that controlled society known as the *Angkar*, the Trial Chamber attempted to reconstruct the CPK's organisational lines. The senior executive organs of the CPK based in Phnom Penh were the Standing Committee, Central Committee, Military Committee, Office 870 (or 'nerve centre' of the Standing Committee),[79] Government Office

[74] Ibid, para. 118.
[75] Ibid, paras. 123, 127.
[76] Ibid, para. 130.
[77] Ibid, para. 132.
[78] Ibid, para. 152.
[79] Ibid, para. 209.

(S-71) and sub-offices of the Government Office, referred to collectively as the 'Party Centre'. Below the level of the Party Centre, Democratic Kampuchea was divided into a hierarchical series of administrative areas with Zones being at the top of the hierarchy, followed by Sectors, Districts and Communes (consisting of cooperatives). All these levels were governed by Committees. The Trial Chamber found it to be established that key decisions were made collectively and not just by Pol Pot.[80]

On 5 January 1976, the new Constitution presented by Khieu Samphan came into effect, heralding the birth of the state of Democratic Kampuchea.[81] The DK Constitution vested legislative power in a People's Representative Assembly (PRA) and provided for a State Presidium to replace the monarchy. On 30 March 1976 the CPK Central Committee nominated Nuon Chea as chairman of the PRA Standing Committee and named Khieu Samphan chairman of the State Presidium (i.e. President of Democratic Kampuchea).[82] The Trial Chamber found that 'the DK was, in the words of KHIEU Samphan, a country where "the party leads the state"'.[83] As it concerned the military structure, the new RAK was formed on 22 July 1975 and headed by Son Sen as commander of the General Staff. The Trial Chamber established the communications structure, including radio, letters, telegrams and means of disseminating propaganda such as CPK Party magazines entitled *Revolutionary Flag* (of which Nuon Chea was found to be a principal author)[84] and *Revolutionary Youth* distributed among party members.

In examining the specific role of the accused, the Trial Chamber found that Nuon Chea's initial role within the CPK included the formulation of Party policies together with Pol Pot and disseminating propaganda. From the First Party Congress in 1960, throughout the DK period, Nuon Chea was Deputy Secretary of the Party. He was also Chairman of the PRA during the DK period and, on occasion, Acting Prime Minister of DK. He was found to have had primary responsibility for propaganda-related and educational matters.[85] The Trial Chamber was unable to conclude beyond reasonable doubt that he was a member of the Military Committee during the DK period.[86] Nuon Chea was however found to have been involved in

80 Ibid, para. 228.
81 Ibid, para. 233.
82 Ibid, para. 235.
83 Ibid, para. 239.
84 Ibid, para. 264.
85 Ibid, para. 347.
86 Ibid, paras. 333, 347.

various military and security matters, such as the procurement of arms and ammunition and the purges of cadres and military from the East Zone. While Duch had given substantial evidence of Nuon Chea's supervision of the operation of S-21, these allegations were severed from Case 002/01 and consequently no findings in this respect were made by the Trial Chamber. The Trial Chamber concluded that Nuon Chea had 'oversight of all Party activities extending beyond the roles and responsibilities formally entrusted to him during the DK period' and 'held and exercised the power to make and implement CPK policies and decisions'.[87]

Khieu Samphan was found to have formally joined the CPK in 1969 after being accused by Norodom Sihanouk of fomenting a peasant uprising and fleeing Phnom Penh to seek the protection of Ta Mok. After Lon Nol came to power in 1970, Khieu Samphan was found to have left Ta Mok's base at Mount Aural and joined the CPK senior leaders at their headquarters at S-71 near the Stung Chinit River.[88] The same year he became Deputy Chairman of the National United Front of Kampuchea (FUNK) and Commander-in-Chief of the Cambodian People's National Liberation Armed Forces (CPNLAF) although he had no direct military authority as Pol Pot was in charge of the CPNLAF forces. He was also Deputy Prime Minister and Minister of National Defence in the Royal Government of National Union of Kampuchea (GRUNK) and admitted to playing an essential role as a liaison between the CPK and Norodom Sihanouk. The Trial Chamber also referred to speeches made by Khieu Samphan on the radio appealing for the overthrow of the Lon Nol regime. These factors caused the Trial Chamber to conclude that Khieu Samphan 'played an important role in winning support for the opposition movement between 1970 and 1975'.[89] In conclusion, the Trial Chamber noted that Khieu Samphan had the trust of the other members of the Party Centre and while his decision-making power was limited to matters of economics and foreign trade, he participated in relevant meetings and had knowledge of CPK's policies and activities.[90]

The CPK leadership was alleged to have pursued a common purpose to liberate Cambodia and create a socialist society in four phases, namely (1) party building (based on three priorities of increasing the people's movements; defensive revolutionary violence and armed struggle; and

---

87 Ibid, para. 348.
88 Ibid, para. 364.
89 Ibid, para. 372.
90 Ibid, paras. 408–09.

building revolutionary bases);[91] (2) initiation of the armed revolution; (3) the democratic revolution (an opportunity provided by the overthrow of Norodom Sihanouk on 18 March 1970 and the establishment by Sihanouk of the GRUNK);[92] and (4) the socialist revolution (beginning with the 'liberation' of Cambodia by the Khmer Rouge on 17 April 1975). As the Trial Chamber noted, the ECCC's jurisdiction is limited to the socialist revolution phase. During this phase, the Trial Chamber found that the CPK's priority was to secure DK from both internal and external threats leading to the implementation of radical policies. 'This Party line, both internally and externally, was based upon the principles of "independence-sovereignty", collectivism and self-reliance.'[93] Nuon Chea, Pol Pot, Khieu Samphan, Ieng Sary and Son Sen were all found to have arrived in Phnom Penh by 25 April 1975, where they formed a Joint Leadership Committee.[94]

The Trial Chamber proceeded to take a somewhat winding and repetitive route towards the establishment of a JCE, acknowledging that certain alleged events had to be excluded due to the severance of charges, and mentioning a number of times that on 17 April 1975, the Khmer Rouge 'liberated' Phnom Penh and began to evacuate the entire population forcibly. Ultimately the Trial Chamber was satisfied that the evidence established a plurality of persons, including the CPK leaders, who shared a common purpose to implement a socialist revolution in Cambodia:

> [a]t the latest, by June 1974 until December 1977, there was a plurality of persons who shared a common purpose to 'implement rapid socialist revolution through a "great leap forward" and defend the Party against internal and external enemies, by whatever means necessary'. Members of the Standing and Central Committees, government ministers, and Zone and Autonomous Sector secretaries, including NUON Chea, KHIEU Samphan, POL Pot, IENG Sary, SON Sen, VORN Vet, Ta Mok, SAO Phim, ROS Nhim, KOY Thuon, KE Pauk, CHANN Sam, CHOU Chet, BOU Phat, YONG Yem, BORN Nan, IENG Thirith and MEY Prang, were part of this group with the specified common purpose.[95]

---

91 Ibid, para. 727.
92 Ibid, para. 732.
93 Ibid, para. 737.
94 Ibid, para. 740.
95 Ibid, para. 777.

The Trial Chamber admitted that this common purpose 'was not in itself necessarily or entirely criminal'.[96] Nonetheless, it found that the Khmer Rouge policies involved the commission of crimes in order to accomplish the common plan.[97] Further:

> These policies resulted in and/or involved the commission of crimes, including forced transfers, murders, attacks against human dignity and political persecution. Both population movements (phases one and two), followed a consistent pattern of conduct in each case including and involving the commission of crimes. This confirms that these policies were criminal and had been adopted beforehand in order to ensure that the common purpose would be achieved.[98]

The Trial Chamber also found that the crimes committed during the first and second phases of the population movement could be imputed to JCE members who used the direct perpetrators to further the common purpose.[99] The Trial Chamber viewed the executions at Tuol Po Chrey as an example of the general pattern of targeting Khmer Republic officials identified under the targeting policy and was satisfied that 'there was a policy to target former Khmer Republic officials which involved the murder and extermination of former Khmer Republic officials at Tuol Po Chrey ... also demonstrated by a consistent pattern of conduct, of which the murders and extermination at Tuol Po Chrey formed part'.[100]

The Trial Chamber was satisfied that Nuon Chea made a significant contribution to the JCE among other ways through his participation in Party Congresses and meetings with other senior CPK leaders, where he played a key role in formulating the content of Party policy[101] and through his role in the propaganda campaign and training of cadres both before and after April 1975.[102] Khieu Samphan was found to have contributed among other ways through his participation in policy meetings, instructional meetings and indoctrination sessions, his involvement in economic affairs and his role as a diplomat. Furthermore, he was found to have given a number of public statements showing that he 'whole-heartedly supported the revolution without a hint of criticism'.[103]

---

[96] Ibid, para. 778.
[97] Ibid, para. 804.
[98] Ibid, paras. 804, 806–07.
[99] Ibid, para. 806.
[100] Ibid, para. 835.
[101] Ibid, para. 869.
[102] Ibid, para. 874.
[103] Ibid, para. 987.

Both accused were found to have shared the intent of the other members of the JCE to bring about the common purpose and to have had the requisite intent to commit the underlying crimes.

4.2.2 Supreme Court Chamber Judgment

The Closing Order in Case 002 did not allege that all crimes were committed through a JCE, and this meant that extermination and the other inhumane act of enforced disappearances committed in the course of Phases One and Two of the population movement fell outside the scope of the JCE in Case 002/01 and were addressed by the Trial Chamber under other modes of liability. The Supreme Court Chamber notified the parties at the outset of a potential change to the 'legal characterisation of the crime', suggesting that all crimes for which convictions were entered could be brought within the JCE.[104]

The Supreme Court Chamber noted that the Trial Chamber had not explicitly found that the relevant policies 'were actually part of the common purpose in the sense of the criminal law' as it had distinguished between the (non-criminal) common purpose and the (criminal) policies.[105] Despite this, the Supreme Court Chamber found it to be clear that the Trial Chamber had viewed the policies as being 'intrinsically linked to the implementation of the socialist revolution in Cambodia'.[106] The Supreme Court Chamber explained further:

> It is in this context that the Trial Chamber's finding that the common purpose was to be implemented 'by all means necessary' has to be understood – the 'means' at issue in the case at hand were the population movement and targeting policies. Thus, while the Trial Chamber's findings may lack precision, there can be no doubt that it was the criminal aspect of the two policies that was at the core of Case 002/01 – and not just 'any means necessary' to implement the socialist revolution. Thus understood, the common purpose of implementing a socialist revolution through these policies was indeed criminal. Put differently, given that the common purpose was to be achieved through the commission of crimes, as encompassed by the policies, the objective of implementing a rapid socialist revolution in Cambodia was indeed criminal.[107]

---

[104] *Prosecutor v Nuon Chea* and *Khieu Samphan*, ECCC Case File No. 002/19-09-2007-ECCC/SC, Supreme Court Chamber, Order Scheduling the Appeal Hearing, 9 October 2015, p. 5.

[105] Nuon Appeal Judgment, above n. 3, para. 815.

[106] Ibid, para. 815.

[107] Ibid, para. 816.

Having found that the Trial Chamber made a legal error in its statement of the applicable standard so as to include crimes that merely resulted from the implementation of the common purpose, the Supreme Court Chamber had to consider which crimes were included within the common purpose applying the correct legal standard.[108] In relation to Phase One of the population movement, murder, other inhumane acts and political persecution were found to be included in the common purpose. The Chamber found that the circumstances surrounding the killing of civilians 'indicate that, implicitly, the common purpose encompassed the anticipation that deadly force could be used by the troops tasked with evacuating the city, should they encounter any resistance'.[109] This meant that the murder of Khmer Republic soldiers was 'implicitly' part of the common purpose, as far as the evacuation of Phnom Penh was concerned.[110] In relation to Phase Two of the population movement, inhumane acts and murder ('implicitly' encompassed by the policy to move the population[111]) were found to be included. After a comprehensive analysis of the Trial Chamber's findings and the evidence on which they were based in relation to Tuol Po Chrey, the Supreme Court Chamber found that it was unreasonable to consider it proven that a policy contemplating the execution of Khmer Republic soldiers and officials existed at the time of those events (as restricted by the severance of the proceedings to the end of April 1975). The convictions of the accused based on JCE in respect of crimes committed at Tuol Po Chrey were therefore overturned.[112]

As it concerned the contribution of the accused to the JCE, the Supreme Court Chamber considered that the Trial Chamber was correct to state that this must be 'significant, but not necessarily indispensable' and that it had properly taken into account the 'totality' of Nuon Chea's and Khieu Samphan's respective activities.[113] The Supreme Court Chamber clarified that 'the contribution must be made to the commission of

---

[108] Ibid, para. 849.
[109] Ibid, para. 857.
[110] Ibid, para. 860.
[111] Ibid, para. 868.
[112] Ibid, paras. 970 (The Supreme Court Chamber found that: 'The Trial Chamber consistently failed to engage with fundamental issues affecting the strength of the evidence, such as the plausibility of alternative explanations concerning the usage of the term "enemy" in the course of an armed conflict, the killing of Khmer Republic soldiers in combat and, generally, evidence lending itself to equivocal interpretation, which the Trial Chamber regularly found to be inculpatory without providing sufficient explanation.'), 972.
[113] Ibid, para. 980.

crimes.'[114] However, it then backtracked a little, recalling that the common purpose 'was the implementation of a rapid socialist revolution in Cambodia, which was intrinsically linked to the criminal policies concerning population movement and targeting of Khmer Republic officials' and acknowledged that given such a non-criminal common purpose, 'even activities that are on their face unrelated to the commission of crimes may be taken into account when determining whether the accused made a significant contribution thereto'.[115]

Although the Supreme Court Chamber did not agree that Nuon Chea had formal responsibility for party discipline, overall it found that the Trial Chamber had not erred in treating the various ways in which Nuon Chea participated in the JCE, viewed in their totality, as a significant contribution.[116] Similarly, while the Supreme Court Chamber considered that some of the Trial Chamber's findings in relation to Khieu Samphan's contribution to the JCE were insufficiently supported by the evidence (for example, his endorsement of the plan to evacuate Phnom Penh at the June 1974 meeting), the conclusion that he made a significant contribution to the common purpose was upheld.[117]

Turning to the *mens rea*, the Supreme Court Chamber agreed with the Trial Chamber that this must cover both the underlying crime and the mode of liability.[118] However, according to the Supreme Court Chamber, the correct *mens rea* standard for JCE I was not a 'substantial likelihood that crimes would be committed' but rather a shared intent to effect the common purpose.[119] In relation to the underlying crimes, the Supreme Court Chamber explained:

> For instance … for the crime against humanity of murder, the requisite mental element is either direct intent or *dolus eventualis*. Thus, if murder is committed through a joint criminal enterprise, it has to be established that the accused had the objective to bring about the death of the victim through the implementation of the common purpose or was aware that the death would be the certain result thereof (direct intent), or was aware that the death of the victim was a possible consequence of the implementation of the common purpose, but proceeded to implement it regardless, having accepted the possible occurrence of deaths (*dolus eventualis*). In contrast, in respect of the crime against humanity of persecution, it has to be established that the

114 Ibid, para. 983 (Emphasis in original).
115 Ibid, para. 984.
116 Ibid, para. 1000.
117 Ibid, para. 1030.
118 Ibid, para. 1053.
119 Ibid, para. 1054.

> accused intended that the implementation of the common purpose would lead to the acts that discriminated against the victims as a discernible group, and that he or she acted with the specific discriminatory intent.[120]

This meant, for example, that in relation to murder during Phase One of the population movement, Nuon Chea was found to possess the requisite intent as it was established that he acted with *dolus eventualis*.[121] While the Trial Chamber was considered to have made certain unreasonable findings concerning Khieu Samphan's *mens rea*, the 'overall conclusion that [he] had prior, contemporaneous and *post-facto* knowledge of the commission of the crimes during Population Movement Phases One and Two' was upheld.[122]

5. JCE II

5.1 JCE II in Customary International Law

In Case 001, the Trial Chamber was satisfied that Internal Rule 98(2) permitted changes to the legal characterisation of both crimes and modes of liability but stressed that it needed to ensure that any change respected the fair trial rights of the accused and that the proposed form of responsibility was applicable before the ECCC.[123] Regarding the impact of re-characterisation on the fair trial rights of the accused, the Trial Chamber found that although the Co-Prosecutors' request to include JCE 'might have been presented in a more timely and coherent manner, and pleaded with greater specificity', the accused had been provided with sufficient notice and opportunity to respond.[124]

In relation to the status of JCE under customary international law, the Trial Chamber emphasised that: 'Joint criminal enterprise is not … a novel creation of the ICTY.'[125] Rather, it could be traced back to Nuremberg-era documents and judgments as well as national legal systems. The Trial Chamber considered that 'in light of the Nuremberg Charter, Control Council Law No. 10 and the subsequent international jurisprudence discussed [by the Trial Chamber], the systemic form of joint criminal enterprise, along with the basic form from which it derives,

---

120 Ibid.
121 Ibid, para. 1061.
122 Ibid, para. 1083.
123 Duch Trial Judgment, above n. 1, para. 496.
124 Ibid, para. 502.
125 Ibid, para. 504.

were part of customary international law during the 1975 to 1979 period'.[126] In the light of this, and taking into account JCE's 'resonance with the Cambodian law concept of co-perpetration applicable at the time', the Trial Chamber found no problem with the principle of legality.[127]

5.2 The Application of JCE II in Case 001

The Trial Chamber referred to its findings regarding the criminal nature of what it described as the 'S-21 system' which was supervised by Duch:

> The Accused acted with [other] individuals, and through his subordinates, to operate the S-21 complex, a facility dedicated to the unlawful detention, interrogation and execution of perceived enemies of the CPK, both domestic and foreign. A concerted system of ill-treatment and torture was purposefully implemented in order to subjugate detainees and obtain their confessions during interrogations … . S-24 was also used as an adjunct facility devoted to forced labour for detainees viewed as suspect by the CPK.[128]

The Trial Chamber went on to find that there was a systemic joint criminal enterprise at S-21, that Duch knew of the criminal nature of the S-21 system and that he acted with intent to further the criminal purpose. As a result of his participation in the systemic joint criminal enterprise at S-21, Duch was found to bear individual criminal responsibility for all the offences that had been established by the evidence.

While this appeared as a classic case in which to apply JCE II, it has been noted that some of the crimes found to have been established, such as the individual instance of rape, did not fit easily into the common purpose as described by the Trial Chamber and more elaborate reasoning on the chosen mode of liability would have been desirable.[129] Nonetheless, the application of JCE II liability by the Trial Chamber was not specifically challenged on appeal.

---

126 Ibid, para. 512.
127 Ibid.
128 Ibid, para. 514.
129 Yanev, above n. 61, pp. 227–9.

6. JCE III

6.1 JCE III in Customary International Law

If it is difficult to identify a clear and consistent approach in the post-Second World War cases to liability pursuant to what is now described as JCE in its first and second forms, the problem is exacerbated in relation to the third or extended form. Each of the ECCC Chambers has been called upon to address the question whether JCE III existed under customary international law in 1975. All three Chambers have answered this question in the negative, whether directly or in a roundabout way. In fact, the Co-Prosecutors' single ground of appeal in Case 002/01 raising the question of the applicability of JCE III in ECCC proceedings was rejected as being procedurally defective by the Supreme Court Chamber in its final judgment on the appeal.[130] This was after full arguments on the merits of the appeal had been submitted by the parties. The Supreme Court Chamber therefore did not address the core issue head on and instead merged its discussion of JCE III with a broader consideration of the Trial Chamber's approach to JCE I, relying on the parties' submissions on the rejected appeal.

The core issue was whether JCE III formed part of customary international law at the time of the conduct relevant to the charges against the accused Nuon Chea and Khieu Samphan so as to be considered as incorporated into Article 29 of the ECCC Law.[131] Indeed, in the judgment of the ICTY Appeals Chamber in *Tadić*, the scope of the word 'committing' in Article 7(1) of the ICTY Statute was seen to be constrained by custom. While the ICTY Appeals Chamber relied on the object and purpose of the Statute and the nature and gravity of international crimes in reaching the conclusion that 'actions perpetrated by a collectivity of persons in furtherance of a common criminal design' were covered by the concept of 'commission', the objective and subjective elements of this form of perpetration, described in terms of three categories of JCE, were derived from customary international law.[132] Definitions and characterisations evolve over time, especially in a system that draws on custom to give legal specificity to prohibited conduct. But

---

[130] Nuon Appeal Judgment, above n. 3, paras 1130–43.

[131] Cf. *Prosecutor v Nuon Chea* and *Khieu Samphan*, ECCC Case File No. 002/19-09-2007-ECCC/SC, Office of the Co-Prosecutor, Co-Prosecutors' Appeal against the Judgment of the Trial Chamber in Case 002/01, 28 November 2014, para. 12.

[132] Tadić Appeal Judgment, above n. 19, para. 193.

this malleable aspect of custom is precisely what makes this source of law controversial as a basis for rules governing criminal liability and highlights the importance of applying the principle of legality correctly.

The Supreme Court Chamber considered that the Trial Chamber erred in law in finding that the relevant policies 'resulted in and/or involved' the commission of crimes, when the correct test for JCE I was whether the crimes were 'intended, contemplated or otherwise encompassed by the common purpose'.[133] One question the Supreme Court Chamber had to address was whether 'an accused may be held liable based on JCE for crimes whose *actus reus* he or she did not commit and which were not encompassed by the common purpose'.[134] In the Supreme Court Chamber's view, imposing liability in these circumstances would be equivalent to applying JCE III. It was not essential for the Supreme Court Chamber to consider the issue of JCE III, as all the crimes found to have been proven were considered to be contemplated by the JCE. Moreover, the analytical framework seems a stretch, as JCE III is concerned with collateral, foreseeable crimes that stem directly from the crimes encompassed by the common purpose. However, the unfortunate terminology of 'resulted in' cast doubt on the rigour of the Trial Chamber's assessment under JCE I and gave the Supreme Court Chamber an opening to express its opinion on JCE III, having rejected the Co-Prosecutors' appeal as inadmissible.

An analysis of the customary international law status of the JCE doctrine traditionally begins with the Charter and Judgment of the International Military Tribunal (IMT) at Nuremberg. The Supreme Court Chamber has recognised that the IMT Judgment does not constitute binding precedent for the ECCC.[135] However, coupled with the IMT Charter and UN General Assembly Resolution 95 (I), which affirmed 'the principles of international law recognized by the Charter of the Nuremberg Tribunal and the judgment of the Tribunal'[136] it may provide evidence of existent and newly emerging principles of international criminal law.[137] The final sentence of Article 6 of the IMT Charter

---

[133] Nuon Appeal Judgment, above n. 3, para. 790.

[134] Ibid, para. 790.

[135] *Prosecutor v Kaing Guek Eav alias 'Duch'*, ECCC Case File No. 001/18-07-2007-ECCC/SC, Supreme Court Chamber, Appeal Judgment, 3 February 2012, para. 110 ('Duch Appeal Judgment').

[136] United Nations General Assembly, Affirmation of the Principles of International Law Recognised by the Charter of the Nüremberg Tribunal, A/RES/1/95(I), 11 December 1946.

[137] Duch Appeal Judgment, above n. 135, para. 110.

notably provides that: 'Leaders, organizers, instigators and accomplices participating in the formulation or execution of a common plan or conspiracy to commit any of the [crimes over which the IMT has jurisdiction] are responsible for all acts performed by any persons in execution of such plan.' Article 5 of the Charter of the International Military Tribunal for the Far East at Tokyo (IMTFE) contains similar wording. The alleged 'common plan or conspiracy' to wage aggressive war was a major focus of both the IMT and the IMTFE and these tribunals accepted the separate allegation of conspiracy as an inchoate crime in relation to wars of aggression, charged as crimes against peace.[138] As it concerned war crimes or crimes against humanity, participation in a common plan or conspiracy was deemed to constitute a mode of liability.[139] Control Council Law No. 10 which was established to provide a uniform legal basis for further prosecutions of alleged war criminals in the Allied zones of occupation in Germany contained a broadly framed provision (Article 2(d)) according to which any person who 'was connected with plans or enterprises involving' the commission of a crime set out in the Law would be punishable.

Principle I of the Nuremberg Principles confirms that: 'Any person who commits an act which constitutes a crime under international law is responsible therefor and liable to punishment.'[140] Principle VII states that 'Complicity in the commission of a crime against peace, a war crime, or a crime against humanity as set forth in Principle VI is a crime under international law.' The Commentary to Principle VII describes the final

---

[138] 'Majority Judgment', in N. Boister and R. Cryer (eds.), *Documents on the Tokyo International Military Tribunal* (Oxford/New York, Oxford University Press, 2008), pp. 71–628, p. 596 (The IMTFE found: 'These far-reaching plans for waging wars of aggression and the prolonged and intricate preparation for and waging of these wars of aggression were not the work of one man. They were the work of many leaders acting in pursuance of a common plan for the achievement of a common object. That common object, that they could secure Japan's domination by preparing and waging wars of aggression, was a criminal object.').

[139] International Military Tribunal (Nuremberg), Judgment, 1 October 1946, p. 449: 'The words are designed to establish the responsibility of persons participating in a common plan.' <http://crimeofaggression.info/documents/6/1946_Nuremberg_Judgement.pdf> [accessed 8 July 2017].

[140] 'Principles of International Law Recognized in the Charter of the Nürnberg Tribunal and in the Judgment of the Tribunal', in ILC, 'Report of the International Law Commission to the General Assembly, A/1316, July 1950', *Yearbook of the International Law Commission*, vol. II, 1950, pp. 364–85, pp. 374–8.

sentence of Article 6 of the Nuremberg Charter, which includes participation in a common plan, as a provision regarding responsibility for complicity.[141] According to the Commentary, when the IMT convicted defendants 'because they gave orders resulting in atrocious and criminal acts which they did not commit themselves', it was applying 'general principles of criminal law regarding complicity', as corroborated by the Tribunal's language in individual cases.[142]

The work of the United Nations War Crimes Commission (UNWCC) provides an important contextual background. The UNWCC was established in London in 1943 and consisted of representatives from 16 countries: Australia, Belgium, Canada, China, Czechoslovakia, France, Greece, India, Luxembourg, the Netherlands, New Zealand, Norway, Poland, the United Kingdom, the US and Yugoslavia.[143] Denmark also joined upon liberation.[144] Its purpose was to investigate war crimes against nationals of the UN and to name and identify the persons allegedly responsible. The UNWCC was later given advisory functions, such as making recommendations to governments on the surrender or capture of suspects and on the mechanisms for trial, following a failed proposal for the creation of a technical-legal committee.[145] A large number of cases of suspected war crimes were examined by the UNWCC—up to 25,000 by February 1947—and the UNWCC claimed to have sufficient evidence to enable the institution of proceedings against 22,500 named individuals.[146] A topic of major concern to the UNWCC

---

141 Ibid, para. 125.

142 Ibid, para. 127.

143 M.E. Bathurst, 'The United Nations War Crimes Commission', *American Journal of International Law*, vol. 39, 1945, pp. 565–70, p. 568.

144 E. Schwelb, 'The United Nations War Crimes Commission', *British Year Book of International Law*, vol. 23, 1946, pp. 363–76, p. 363.

145 Bathurst, above n. 143, p. 569. *See* also Schwelb, above n. 144, p. 364.

146 Schwelb, above n. 144, p. 367 (Schwelb notes the value of the proceedings of the UNWCC in terms of the development of customary international law, stating that on the conclusion of the work of the UNWCC, 'valuable information on state practice applied on an international level through a number of years, in respect of many – sometimes rather involved – questions of international law' will be available. This has been echoed in recent efforts to make all the archive material of the UNWCC available for public use.). *See* 'War Crimes Project: UN the Holocaust & the War Crimes Commission 1943-1948', Centre for International Studies and Diplomacy ('CISD'), University of London School of Oriental and African Studies ('SOAS'), <https://www.soas.ac.uk/cisd/research/war-crimes-project/war-crimes-project-un-the-holocaust-the-war-crimes-commission-1943-1948.html> [accessed 6 July 2017], and United Nations War Crimes Commission,

was the 'phenomenon of mass criminality'.[147] It was recommended to the member governments:

(a) to seek out the leading criminals responsible for the organization of *criminal enterprises* including systematic terrorism, planned looting, and the general policy of atrocities against the peoples of the occupied states, in order to punish all the organizers of such crimes;
(b) to commit for trial either jointly or individually all those who, as members of these *criminal gangs*, have taken part in any way in the carrying out of *crimes committed collectively by groups, formations, or units*.[148]

These recommendations were informed by domestic law concepts such as *associations de malfaiteurs* recognised in the French and Belgian Criminal Codes and also influenced subsequent domestic and international enactments.[149] For example, the Royal Warrant of 18 June 1945 which governed proceedings held by the British in their zones of occupation, including those in Hong Kong and Singapore, provided in Regulation 8(ii) of the annexed Regulations for the Trials of War Criminals:[150]

> Where there is evidence that a war crime has been the result of concerted action upon the part of a unit or group of men, then evidence given upon any charge relating to that crime against any member of such unit or group may be received as prima facie evidence of the responsibility of each member of that unit or group for that crime.
>
> In any such case all or any members of such unit or group may be charged and tried jointly in respect of any such war crime and no application by any of them to be tried separately shall be allowed by the Court.

<http://www.unwcc.org/about/> [accessed 6 July 2017]. *See* also D. Plesch and S. Sattler, 'Changing the Paradigm of International Criminal Law: Considering the Work of the United Nations War Crimes Commission of 1943-1948', *International Community Law Review*, vol. 15, 2013, pp. 203–23, pp. 203–04.

147 Schwelb, above n. 144, p. 374.

148 Ibid, p. 374 (*Emphasis added*).

149 Ibid, p. 374.

150 Royal Warrant 0160/2498, Regulations for the Trial of War Criminals, A. O. 81/1945, 18 June 1945, <https://www.eccc.gov.kh/en/document/court/annex-authority-1-royal-warrant-%E2%80%93-regulations-trial-war-criminals-01602498-14-june-19> [accessed 9 July 2017].

Similar provisions were adopted by Australia, Canada and the US.[151] While the discussions within the UNWCC do not directly support an extended form of JCE, they do indicate a preoccupation with crimes committed jointly as part of a criminal enterprise, a recognition of the need to ensure that all those who participated would be held to account, and a will to discover a correct legal basis for responsibility that would be acceptable to representatives from a variety of legal traditions. Nevertheless, it is not possible to read acceptance of JCE III into the IMT and IMTFE Charters and Control Council Law No. 10. The precise scope of the envisaged liability pursuant to a common design can only be determined by examining the practice of these courts.[152]

The Supreme Court Chamber agreed with the earlier analysis and conclusions of the Pre-Trial Chamber which had examined the cases relied upon in *Tadić* and found that there was an insufficient basis to conclude that the military courts hearing those cases applied a concept equivalent to JCE III. Since the *Essen Lynching* and *Borkum Island* cases have a special place in the *Tadić* conception of JCE III, and since the ECCC may have finally closed the door on further interpretation and analysis, it is worth indulging in one more examination of these historical relics.

---

[151] Schwelb, above n. 144, p. 375 (referring to Australia's Statutory Rules 1945, No. 164, Regulations under the War Crimes Act 1945, 25 October 1945, Rule 12, which contains similar wording to British Royal Warrant 0160/2498, Regulations for the Trial of War Criminals, A. O. 81/1945, 18 June 1945, Regulation 8(ii); and the Canada's War Crimes Act, 1946, Regulations 10(3). Regulation 10(3), of which the effect is substantially the same as that of British Royal Warrant 0160/2498, Regulations for the Trial of War Criminals, A. O. 81/1945, 18 June 1945, Regulation 8(ii), provides: 'Where there is evidence that a war crime has been the result of concerted action upon the part of a formation, unit, body, or group of persons, evidence given upon any charge relating to that crime against any member of such a formation, unit, body, or group may be received as prima facie evidence of the responsibility of each member of that formation, unit, body, or group for that crime; in any such case all or any members of any such formation, unit, body, or group may be charged and tried jointly in respect of any such war crime and no application by any of them to be tried separately shall be allowed by the court.'). *See* 'Annex: Canadian Law Concerning Trials of War Criminals', *Law Reports of Trials of War Criminals*, vol. IV, 1948, pp. 125–30.

[152] *Prosecutor v Ieng Sary, Ieng Thirith* and *Khieu Samphan*, ECCC Case File No. 002/19-09-2007-ECCC/OCIJ (PTC 35, 37, 38, & 39), Pre-Trial Chamber, Decision on the Appeals against the Co-Investigating Judges' Order on Joint Criminal Enterprise (JCE), 20 May 2010, para. 40.

The *Essen Lynching* case was heard before a British Military Court at Essen acting under the June 1945 Royal Warrant pursuant to Control Council Law No. 10.[153] The case was against seven accused jointly charged with a war crime in that they were 'concerned in the killing of three unidentified British airmen, prisoners of war'. The first accused was Heyer, a German Army Captain who gave instructions for three prisoners of war to be taken for interrogation in earshot of a crowd that had gathered. It was alleged that he ordered the escort not to interfere in any way with the crowd if they should molest the prisoners and suggested that the prisoners should be shot. The crowd attacked and eventually killed the prisoners. The second accused was a German private, Koenen, entrusted with the custody of the prisoners but who failed to intervene when they were killed. The remaining accused were civilians involved in the killings. The Prosecution alleged that there were three connected stages in the killings: the incitement at the entrance to the barracks, the beatings and the shootings.

> It was, therefore, the submission of the Prosecution that every person who, following the incitement to the crowd to murder these men, voluntarily took aggressive action against anyone of these three airmen, was guilty in that he was concerned in the killing. It was impossible to separate anyone of these acts from another; they all made up what is known as a lynching. From the moment they left those barracks, the men were doomed and the crowd knew they were doomed and every person in that crowd who struck a blow was both morally and criminally responsible for the deaths of the three men.[154]

Heyer's role was merely verbal but the Prosecution cited a rule of English law to the effect that an instigator may be regarded as a principal (whether or not the person who incited was present when the crime was committed). Koenen was given an order not to interfere which he obeyed, but according to the Prosecution he failed to do what his duty required him to do (i.e. to ensure that the prisoners were not molested). His guilt was not considered by the Prosecution to be as grave as those who took an active part. Heyer was convicted and sentenced to death. Koenan was convicted and sentenced to imprisonment for five years. Three civilians were found guilty: one was sentenced to death and the other two received prison sentences of life and ten years.

---

[153] 'The *Essen Lynching* Case: Trial of *Erich Heyer* and *Six Others*', *Law Reports of Trials of War Criminals*, vol. I, 1947, pp. 88–92, p. 88, <http://www.unwcc.org/wp-content/uploads/2017/04/Law-Reports-Volume-1.pdf> [accessed 9 July 2017].

[154] Ibid, p. 89.

According to the UNWCC's notes on the *Essen Lynching* case, the civilians were found guilty because each of them had in one form or another taken part in the ill-treatment which eventually led to the deaths of the victims, though against none of the accused had it been exactly proved that they had individually shot or given the fatal blows.[155] In *Tadić*, *Essen Lynching* was viewed as being particularly important to JCE III as an example of mob violence where multiple offenders share the same goal but it is impossible to be sure which acts were carried out by which perpetrator.[156] According to *Tadić*, two requirements could be derived from the case, namely 'a criminal intention to participate in a common criminal design and the foreseeability that criminal acts other than those envisaged in the common criminal design are likely to be committed by other participants in the common design.'[157] Since there was no reasoned judgment in the case, the *Tadić* Appeals Chamber deduced from the arguments of the parties and the verdict (that all were guilty of murder) that 'the court upheld the notion that all the accused who were found guilty took part, in various degrees, in the killing; not all of them intended to kill but all intended to participate in the unlawful ill-treatment of the prisoners of war'.[158]

The ECCC Pre-Trial Chamber contrastingly found that although the facts of the case may be directly relevant to JCE III, in the absence of a reasoned judgment 'one cannot be certain of the basis of liability actually retained by the military courts'[159] According to the Pre-Trial Chamber, the case could not by itself warrant a finding that JCE III existed in customary international law.[160] The ECCC Trial Chamber agreed with this assessment, and the Supreme Court Chamber found nothing in the Co-Prosecutors' interpretation of the case to overcome the problems identified by the Pre-Trial Chamber.[161] It is clear from these differing views that the *Essen Lynching* case is open to various interpretations. As already noted, there is no reasoned decision and no summing up by a Judge Advocate in the *Essen Lynching* case. Moreover, there is very little

155 Ibid, p. 91.

156 Tadić Appeals Judgment, above n. 19, paras. 205, 207.

157 Ibid, para. 206.

158 Ibid, para. 209.

159 *Prosecutor v Ieng Sary, Ieng Thirith* and *Khieu Samphan*, ECCC Case File No. 002/19-09-2007-ECCC/OCIJ (PTC 35, 37, 38, & 39), Pre-Trial Chamber, Decision on the Appeals against the Co-Investigating Judges' Order on Joint Criminal Enterprise (JCE), 20 May 2010, para. 79.

160 Ibid, para. 81.

161 Nuon Appeal Judgment, above n. 3, para. 791.

pointing towards the application of a concept of 'common design' akin to JCE III although this concept *could* be applied to the facts. The *Tadić* interpretation is that there was a common plan to ill-treat the prisoners and it was foreseeable that one or more members of the group would kill one or more prisoners. Even the *Tadić* Appeals Chamber recognises, however, that the charge was not murder *per se*, as defined under English law, but 'concern in killings' as a war crime. The Co-Prosecutor did not in fact put forward the theory extracted by the *Tadić* Appeals Chamber as it had done in other cases. Another interpretation is that this was a classic case of co-perpetration where it was unclear who delivered the fatal blow but all were 'concerned' in the ill-treatment that led to the killings (and arguably had the same *mens rea*). Alternatively, Heyer, the instigator of the entire action, may have been treated as the principal, while Koenen aided and abetted by omission and the civilians were accomplices to varying degrees, subject to the same maximum penalty as the principal.

The US participated in war crimes trials under three jurisdictions: the IMT, US Military Tribunals at Nuremberg, and US Army Courts. The *Borkum Island* case was heard by a US Army Court.[162] This is significant because even if it is considered to provide support for JCE III, it is only one case among more than 200 in this category in which about 600 persons, largely German civilians, were prosecuted for the killing of some 1,200 US nationals, mostly airmen. The facts are well-known to JCE scholars. On 4 August 1944, an American flying fortress was hit by flak and forced to land on Borkum Island. The crew consisted of three second lieutenants and four sergeants, all of whom were taken prisoner. Upon his arrival at the scene of the landing, the Military Commander of Borkum Island ordered that the prisoners be marched through the town of Borkum Island to the airfield situated on the other side of the island seven miles away even though it appeared easier for rail transportation to be provided. Seven German soldiers were ordered to march with the

162 '*United States of America v Goebell, Akkermann, Albrecht, Geyer, Heinemann, Krolikovski, Mammenga, Meyer-Gerhards, Pointner, Rommel, Schmitz, Seiler, Weber, Wenzel* and *Witzke*, 1946', *Records of United States Army War Crimes Trials: United States of America v Kurt Goebell et al., February 6-March 21, 1946 and United States of America v August Haesiker, June 26, 1947* (Washington, National Archives and Records Service, 1981), reels 1–7 and '*United States of America v Haesiker*, 1947', *Records of United States Army War Crimes Trials: United States of America v Kurt Goebell et al., February 6-March 21, 1946 and United States of America v August Haesiker, June 26, 1947* (Washington, National Archives and Records Service, 1981), reel 7 (The complete record on 7 reels of microfilm was accessed and studied by the author at the Harvard Law Library in 2015).

prisoners and guard them. At the entrance to the town, the prisoners were forced to march with their hands above their heads and pass between members of the German Labor corps who beat them with spades at the order of their commanding officer. Many civilians also beat them with sticks and fists and threw stones at them. At the centre of town, after the prisoners had been badly beaten, a German soldier ran up and shot one of them in the back of the head. The remaining six continued marching and continued being beaten. Finally, the men collapsed and were killed where they lay by shots through the head.

The trial record includes a 'case analysis' from the Deputy Theater Judge Advocate's Office, War Crimes Branch, US Forces, European Theater, in which the offence is described as 'assault, mistreatment and murder' of seven American airmen. The evidence was considered to point towards a murder plan or plot amongst certain of the 23 alleged perpetrators while the evidence in relation to certain other accused suggested responsibility for beating and assaulting the fliers. The theory of failure to exercise a duty to protect the prisoners also received a mention in relation to two of the accused. The suggested charges against *all* 'perpetrators' were framed as (1) a violation of the laws of war in that they did 'wilfully, deliberately and wrongfully encourage, aid, abet and participate in the killing of [the victims], and (2) a violation of the laws of war in that they did 'wilfully, deliberately and wrongfully encourage, aid, abet and participate in assaults'. The legal theory of the Prosecution was stated to be that Goebell and Akkermann had a plan, to which Wentzel, Seiler and Weber became parties, to create a situation whereby the American fliers would be murdered or beaten to death by the civilian population so that each participant became liable as a principal in the murder. This formulation suggested that within the first charge, certain of the accused were considered principals to murder (as part of a common plan) while others were charged as accomplices. The charges in the case reflected the advice given in the 'case analysis'. Civilians were charged and tried together with military personnel. Captain Kurt Goebell, Commander of Borkum Island Sector, was alleged to have given an order on the basis of a decree by Dr. Joseph Goebbels that military guards were not to protect Allied airmen from civilians if they were taken prisoner. The soldier, Langer, who was believed to have carried out most of the shootings, was not tried.

At the start of the trial, the Defence brought a motion for severance of the trial of the military officers from that of the civilians. The Prosecution responded that the charges and particulars made every accused present at the trial a 'principal and a part of a general act of a whole group.' The motion was denied. After the presentation of the evidence for the

Prosecution, the Defence made two motions for findings of not guilty on behalf of Heineman and Mamenga in relation to Count 1 and on behalf of Rommel and Meyer-Gerhards in relation to Counts 1 and 2. As part of his submissions for the defence, Captain Phelps stated: 'It can be argued that a man is responsible for the reasonable consequences of his actions. Could Heinrich Heinemann have reasonably foreseen that by hitting a flyer on the corner of Franz Habich and Am Bahnhof, that later a Pfc, or whoever it happened to be, jumped out of the crowd and killed these American flyers?' It was in response to these motions that the prosecution first mentioned a theory of common design, quoting extensively from Wharton's *Criminal Law* (Vol. I, section 258):

> All those who assemble themselves together with an intent to commit a wrongful act, the execution whereof makes probable in the nature of things a crime not specifically designed but incidental to that which was the object of the confederacy, are responsible for such incidental crime. ... Hence it is not necessary that the crime should be part of the original design. It is enough if it be one of the incidental probable consequences of the execution of that design and should appear at the moment to one of the participants to be expedient for the common purpose.

The Prosecution went on to quote the law on conspiracy and on riotous assemblies from the same book. On this basis, the Prosecution argued in respect of Heinemann that he not only participated in the assault but was also guilty of Count 1 because he was engaged in a common design. The Prosecution went on to say:

> Yes, there was a common design in this case, all equally guilty. A damnable plan conceived in the mind, first, of Goebell, willingly entered into by the other officers, the guards and civilians with their approval and with their active participation in one degree or another. All did not do the same thing but in the entire plot each played his own part in this common design, and when the whole picture is put together it reveals the part that each man played in this common design, where we get the picture that they designed there to torture, to abuse, and to murder these American flyers.

The Defence responded that there was no evidence of the accused coming together to form an intent to murder the fliers, and even if the accused attached himself to an unlawful association, the Defence questioned the existence of a common object. The Defence also stated that conspiracy law was irrelevant and that under the law relating to riots the offence was participation in the riot and not a felony growing out of that riot. The Court rejected the two motions without providing any reasoning.

Closing remarks on behalf of the Prosecution were made by Captain May and Major Bryan. Bryan first referred to US law to the effect that anyone who aids, abets, counsels, commands, induces or procures the commission of an offence is a principal. May summarised the evidence and the role of each accused, emphasising the importance of determining the guilt of the accused 'in the light of the particular role that each one played'. He continued:

> They did not all participate in exactly the same manner. Members of mobs seldom do. One will undertake one special or particular action and another will perform another particular action. It is the composite of the actions of all that results in the commission of a crime. Now, all legal authorities agree that where a common design of a mob exists and the mob has carried out its purpose, then no distinction can be drawn between the finger man and the trigger man. No distinction is drawn between the one who, by his acts, caused the victims to be subjected to the pleasure of the mob or the one who incited the mob, or the ones who dealt the fatal blows. This rule of law and common sense must, of necessity, be so. Otherwise, many of the true instigators of crime would never be punished.

May noted that there were many things a group or mob would do with mutual encouragement that someone acting alone would not do. At this stage, the Prosecution appeared to have moved away from Wharton's theory of common design and towards a theory of mob violence with each accused participating in an arguably essential way. No mention was made of the common plan or intent. May then stated:

> Yes, may it please the Court, we have the civilians, we have the officers and we have the guards, 'C' for civilians, 'O' for officers, and 'G' for guards, C-O-G, and cogs they were. Cogs in the wheel of common design, all equally important, each cog doing the part assigned to it. And the wheel of wholesale murder could not turn without all the cogs.

In further submissions on behalf of the Prosecution, Bryan returned to the law of conspiracy, stating that all of the accused participated in a conspiracy with the murder of seven American flyers as its ultimate conclusion. Bryan cited section 258 of Wharton again before linking the facts to the war crime of killing or ill-treatment of prisoners of war. Phelps argued on behalf of the Defence that according to his understanding the Prosecution's theory was that all the accused were guilty of murder as part of a mob, commenting: 'If that is the theory then why not try the entire mob?' Phelps then admitted that 'possibly' there was a common design among some of the officers to see that the fliers were beaten by the civilians but continued:

> There is no evidence, however, before this Court which will support a finding of a common design between Akkerman and anyone to have these flyers shot to death. The law is so clear on a common design that I will only discuss it very briefly. When people band themselves together for an unlawful design they are all, both jointly and severally liable for all the unlawful acts of the group in the furtherance of this common design. For example, we will say that there is a common design to rob a bank. All are responsible for a murder committed by any of the bank robbers during the carrying out of this common design. However, if the homicide results because of some independent action by a person not a member of that common design then it is not murder. For example, take the same case of a common design to rob a bank. In the commission of this crime a police officer shoots at one of the bank robbers but misses him and kills the teller of the bank, none of the robbers are in this case guilty of murder. If the common design is to go for a drunken drive and while driving the car in a drunken state you run over a person which results in a homicide, all are jointly and severally liable for this murder. However, if the police in attempting to catch the drunken drivers commits a homicide, then it is not a murder for which any of the occupants of the car driven by the drunken driver can be held responsible.

Phelps went on to argue that Langer, who was not on trial, was not a party to the common design and his actions were those of an outsider. The Defence drew a distinction between aiding and abetting assault (pursuant to a common design) and aiding and abetting murder.

The defence lawyer for Akkermann pointed out that in German law 'one can only be punished for a definite crime if the original connection between his action and the proven success is evident, and furthermore, if the criminal planned this success in his intention, and if this success could have been foreseen by him'. The lawyer questioned whether US law really provided that 'everybody can be punished who was at any time in the company of the murderers'. The defence lawyer for Wentzel argued that 'there always has to be a definite purpose [that a crime be committed] to assume a conspiracy'. Other defence lawyers also challenged the conspiracy argument. Lieutenant Davis, for example, pointed out that the Prosecution had worked hard to establish a conspiracy although this was not mentioned in the charges and that proving murder as a result of a common design was a separate question. Lieutenant Davis went on to say in terms that foreshadowed modern concerns with the specificity of indictments charging broad JCEs that:

> Fundamentally, the Prosecution has to rest its case on the theory that we have here a common design, concurred in by everyone concerned, to do something to the flyers. And let me add that the Prosecution is vague, if not plain coy as to the object and scope of this common design.

According to the Defence, the scope of the common plan, if indeed there was a common plan, did not include the deaths of the flyers. Lieutenant Davis attempted to clarify the law on common design stating there must be evidence of a willing banding together for a common purpose (a criminal intent to join with others for the purpose of committing the crime), in this case an intent to take part in a conspiracy to kill the flyers. He stated: 'Where an act has a simple, normal explanation there are no grounds for torturing it into the mould of a fantastic conspiracy.'

Six defendants were found guilty of both killing and assault charges (five were sentenced to death and one to life imprisonment) while the other nine were found guilty of assault only. In the absence of a reasoned judgment, the precise legal basis upon which the accused were convicted is unclear.[163] The case was reviewed by the Deputy Judge Advocate's Office on 1 August 1947. The review notes that the theory of the case is the same as that in *US v Joseph Hartgen et al.*, known as the *Russelsheim* case.[164] In that case, 'it was alleged that the accused, acting jointly, did wrongfully encourage, aid, abet and participate in the killing of several named American fliers who were then unarmed surrendered prisoners of war.' On this basis, the Judge Advocate was in no doubt that the offence was adequately charged in the *Borkum Island* proceedings. The Prosecution's theory was confirmed. For example, in relation to Wentzel (and repeated in relation to several of the accused):

> All who join as participants in a plan to commit an unlawful act, the natural and probable consequence of the execution of which involves the contingency of taking human life, are legally responsible as principals for a homicide committed by any of them in pursuance of or in furtherance of the plan. The accused very actively furthered and contributed to the plan which resulted in several illegal killings. The sentence [of death] is not excessive.

---

[163] M. Koessler, 'Borkum Island Tragedy and Trial', *Journal of Criminal Law and Criminology*, vol. 47, no. 2, 1956, pp. 183–96, p. 194.

[164] *United States of America v Hartgen, Wust, Witzler, Reinhardt, Wolf, Siepel, Barthel, Daum, Opper, Fugmann* and *Gutlich*, Office of the Staff Judge Advocate, Review of the Staff Judge Advocate, 23 August 1945, section 4, para. a-b (In relation to one of the accused, Fugmann, it was noted in the review of the Staff Judge Advocate that 'A mere bystander in a concerted action of this nature is not guilty of participation.' In relation to the other accused, it seems that all participated in the beatings while only some dealt the fatal blows (or fired the fatal shots), however, 'the conclusion is firm and inescapable that these accused played an active part and that the crimes of all are attributable to each') <https://www.jewishvirtuallibrary.org/jsource/Holocaust/dachautrial/fs112.pdf> [accessed 8 July 2017].

The trial record contains a Memorandum Submitted upon Request of War Crimes Modification Board by Harry D. Pitchford, Department of the Army Civilian Attorney, War Crimes Section.[165] The Memorandum states that the Judge Advocate's description of the law (cited above) 'is in direct conflict with the findings of the court in reference to those accused who were only found guilty of participation in an assault upon the flyers'. The Memorandum also confirms that neither conspiracy nor failure to protect prisoners of war was included in the charges, suggesting that this could not or should not have been part of the Prosecution's theory of the case.

The *Tadić* Appeal Judgment cites extracts from the Closing Arguments[166] of Prosecutor May in *Borkum Island* case and acknowledges that the prosecutor essentially put forward an argument under JCE I, in that all the participants in the common purpose were assumed to share a criminal intent to commit murder.[167] Nonetheless, since some of the defendants were found guilty of both murder and assault while others were found guilty only of assault, the *Tadić* Appeal Chamber inferred that the Court construed the intent behind the common criminal design as being to assault the prisoners of war. It was further presumed that the Court held certain participants responsible also for murder, even where there was no evidence they had carried out the *actus reus*, 'on the basis that the accused, whether by virtue of their status, role or conduct, were in a position to have predicted that the assault would lead to the killing of the victims by some of those participating in the assault'.[168]

The *Tadić* Appeal Judgment concludes its discussion of *Borkum Island* on the above assumption that although the Prosecutor in that case appeared to put forward a notion of common design akin to JCE I, 'it may be inferred' from the verdicts that the Court found a common intention to assault the prisoners and convicted some accused for killing the prisoners on the basis of this being a foreseeable consequence (to those accused) of the common plan to commit assault. The ECCC Pre-Trial Chamber rejected the inferences drawn in *Tadić* in relation to the *Borkum Island* case and stated that it was equally likely, based on the

---

165 Memorandum, 29 June 1950.

166 The extracts quoted in Tadić Appeal Judgment, above n. 19, para. 210, are stated to be from the Prosecutor's opening statement in *Borkum Island* case, but this must be a mistake. At *Borkum Island* case, Trial Record, p. 1177, Prosecutor Bryan begins the task of summing up the evidence and discussing the applicable law. The quoted extracts are from Prosecutor May's speech at *Borkum Island* case, Trial Record, p. 1186.

167 Tadić Appeal Judgment, above n. 19, para. 211.

168 Ibid, para. 213.

Prosecutor's submissions in that case, that those convicted of killing the airmen were found to have the intent to kill (rather than foreseeing this possible outcome).[169]

The Court hearing the *Borkum Island* case has been described as a military commission, none of whose members had legal training.[170] Even if it could be said with confidence that JCE III was applied in this case, as a source of customary international law, it is less authoritative than proceedings before the IMT or pursuant to Control Council Law No. 10. The Prosecution in *Borkum Island* invoked US law (which was also familiar to the American defence lawyers) although a reading of the trial documents suggests that the German defence lawyers accepted the theories of responsibility being put forward as valid (especially as to mob violence) but objected to the manner in which they were being applied by the Prosecution, which was in any case confusing. The best reading of the case may be that a common plan to kill the airmen was found on the part of those convicted under the first count, even though they contributed to this plan in different ways (encouraged, aided, abetted, and participated). According to Koessler, writing about the case contemporaneously:

> Among the legal issues regarding which the position taken by the tribunal is not revealed by its verdict is the extent to which a defendant could be made criminally responsible for an act not directly perpetrated by him. It is a universally recognized principle of criminal law, governing the determination of guilt of an accomplice, that one who knowingly and willingly participates in a criminal design or undertaking is equally with the direct perpetrator or perpetrators responsible for any act in pursuance of that design or undertaking, or which is a natural or probable consequence of it, but only if it was committed after he became a participant to the scheme.[171]

This, according to Koessler, is not the same as US conspiracy doctrine, which (although urged by the Prosecution) could not be applied as this was not a trial under US law: 'only internationally recognized principles of criminal law could properly be applied'.[172] Nonetheless, Koessler suggests the case should be treated with caution since it was debatable

---

169 *Prosecutor v Ieng Sary, Ieng Thirith* and *Khieu Samphan*, ECCC Case File No. 002/19-09-2007-ECCC/OCIJ (PTC 35, 37, 38, & 39), Pre-Trial Chamber, Decision on the Appeals against the Co-Investigating Judges' Order on Joint Criminal Enterprise (JCE), 20 May 2010, para. 80.

170 Koessler, above n. 163, p. 190.

171 Ibid, p. 194.

172 Ibid, p. 195.

whether the evidence was sufficient to justify convictions in respect of the shooting of the prisoners even applying the conspiracy doctrine.[173]

In their appeal before the Supreme Court Chamber, the Co-Prosecutors referred to some additional post-Second World War cases,[174] including

---

[173] Ibid, p. 195.

[174] 'The *Pohl* Case', Trials of War Criminals before the Nuremberg Military Tribunals under Control Council Law No. 10, Vol. V, 1950, pp. 193–1273, pp. 1040–07 (It appears that both Hohberg and Baier were convicted of the full extent of the crimes, including ill-treatment connected to the slave labour regime, on the basis of their knowledge rather than on the basis of foreseeability, consistent with the idea of unlawfully, wilfully, and knowingly participating as leaders, organizers, instigators, and accomplices in the formulation and execution of the common plan as expressed in Control Council Law No. 10); 'The *RuSHA* Case', *Trials of War Criminals before the Nuremberg Military Tribunals under Control Council Law No. 10*, vol. IV, 1950, pp. 597–1185 and vol. V, 1950, pp. 1–192, pp. 116–20, 160–2 (It is possible to read JCE III into the facts relating to Hildebrandt's responsibility for hangings, but the case suggests a closer relationship between knowledge of the meaning of 'special treatment' and direct involvement in special treatment cases); 'The *Einsatzgruppen* Case', *Trials of War Criminals before the Nuremberg Military Tribunals under Control Council Law No. 10*, vol. IV, 1950, pp. 1–598. Among the US trials conducted at Dachau, Germany, the Co-Prosecutors referred to Martin Gottfried Weiss, the '*Dachau Concentration Camp*' case where the prosecution based its entire argument on the notion of common design, however, the case primarily provides support for JCE II despite some ambiguous language used by the Staff Judge Advocate: 'The *Dachau Concentration Camp* Trial: Trial of *Martin Gottfried Weiss* and *Thirty-Nine Others*', *Law Reports of Trials of War Criminals*, vol. XI, 1949, pp. 5–17, p. 5. *See* also *Prosecutor v Nuon Chea, Ieng Sary, Ieng Thirith* and *Khieu Samphan*, ECCC Case File No. 002/19-09-2007/ECCC/TC, Trial Chamber, Decision on the Applicability of Joint Criminal Enterprise, 12 September 2011, para. 34 (The ECCC Trial Chamber considered two further cases relating to Dachau Concentration Camp, namely *United States of America v Ulrich* and *Merkle*, Case No. 000-50-2-17, Deputy Judge Advocate's Office of 7708 War Crimes Group-European Command, Review and Recommendations, 12 June 1947, and *United States of America v Wuelfert* and *Others*, Case No. 000-50-2-72, Deputy Judge Advocate's Office of 7708 War Crimes Group-European Command, Review and Recommendations, 19 September 1947, which do not directly support guilt based on JCE III but at most appear to support JCE I or II). '*Sch. et. al.* case', *Decisions of the Supreme Court for the British Zone*, vol. 2, 1950 (The fact pattern may be consistent with a JCE III finding but the case was only concerned with the question whether Sch's knowing contribution facilitated a crime against humanity and in any case this opinion on review carries little weight in terms of the establishment of a customary norm).

the IMT judgment itself,[175] further illustrating how these cases may be open to different interpretations. In some instances, the Supreme Court Chamber found the interpretation of the Co-Prosecutors to be incorrect or even 'obscure'.[176] The *Hans Renoth* case which was heard by a British Military Court at Elten bore some resemblance to *Essen Lynching* according to the notes provided by the UNWCC in that 'several persons who contributed to the death of a prisoner of war were all held responsible for his murder, though not punished alike.'[177] The Prosecution's case was based on a common design shared by all four accused to commit a war crime but the basis for the convictions could equally have been aiding and abetting liability. Indeed, the UNWCC stated:

> It is impossible to say conclusively whether the court found that the three accused took an active part in the beating or whether they were liable under the doctrine set out by the Prosecutor; it is nevertheless interesting to compare that doctrine with the rule applied in the *Essen Lynching Case*, which made punishable as a war crime the inaction of a soldier who allowed prisoners under his care to be lynched. The *ratio decidendi* would not, of course, be the same in the two cases.[178]

It is furthermore unclear if the Prosecutor's 'doctrine' referred to in the UNWCC notes on the case is that of common design or aiding and

---

[175] '*Sauckel* case' and '*Speer* case', in 'Judicial Decision: International Military Tribunal (Nuremberg), Judgment and Sentences, 1 October 1946', *American Journal of International Law*, vol. 41, no. 1, 1947, 172-333, pp. 311–13, 321–4. (Sauckel was found by the IMT to have been intimately involved in the slave labour programme and his knowledge and intent could be inferred from evidence of his high position, his coordinating role, his own decrees, policies in place, his membership of the Leadership Corps which was established to have been used for criminal purposes, and evidence of reports received by him. Ibid, paras. 254, 256. It is similarly difficult to view Speer's responsibility as being based on a common plan to deport to slave labour with it being foreseeable that ill-treatment would be inflicted on the labourers as his knowledge of the ill-treatment appears to have been established.) Notably, the ICTY Appeals Chamber in the *Šainović* case cited the *Speer* case as one example of a conviction for aiding and abetting based on 'substantially and knowingly contribut[ing] to relevant crimes.': *Prosecutor v Šainović, Pavković, Lazarević* and *Lukić*, ICTY Case No. IT-05-87-A, Appeals Chamber, Judgment, 23 January 2014, para. 1642, footnote 5406.

[176] Nuon Appeal Judgment, above n. 3, para. 793, footnote 2082, and *see* discussion of these cases at paras. 792–4.

[177] 'Trial of *Hans Renoth* and *Three Others*', *Law Reports of Trials of War Criminals*, vol. XI, 1949, pp. 76–8, p. 76.

[178] Ibid, p. 77.

abetting, or a combination of the two. The most that can be said with certainty is that the case demonstrates an attempt by the Prosecutor to put forward the concept of common design. This points towards the availability of the concept, and awareness of its existence, but, as the Supreme Court Chamber found, it is a stretch to conclude that it was actually employed.[179]

The Supreme Court Chamber paid some attention to the trial of Japanese '*heitan* officer', Ikeda, before a Dutch military court in Batavia (Indonesia) on charges of rape, abduction for enforced prostitution and enforced prostitution as war crimes.[180] According to the Co-Prosecutors, the case demonstrated a 'criminal plan' to set up brothels and recruit women to work there, with rape and enforced prostitution being foreseeable consequences of this plan. The military court established the accused's participation in formulating and elaborating a plan to establish brothels in Semarang and to use girls and women from internment camps as prostitutes in these brothels, and also that the accused had knowledge that the plan was carried out. However, the basis for responsibility could equally have been superior responsibility, centred on knowledge and the failure to prevent or investigate. As the Court found,

> the accused – who was also fulfilling the role of a *heitan* officer – by approving a plan of this sort, by participating in the further elaboration of the plan and by failing to check in hindsight how the plan had actually been carried out and how the brothels that had been established on the basis of that plan were operating, must be held liable for the criminal offences committed in the process.[181]

When discussing sentencing, the Court distinguished the accused's responsibility from that of the direct perpetrators (who had already been tried and in some cases sentenced to death), stating that it was less grave:

> Nevertheless the accused is highly culpable, because – as an older senior officer and the main and most influential advisor to the Commander … he should have obstructed the pressure emanating from the officers' group at the cadets' school to get involved in the establishment of brothels staffed by women and girls from internment camps.[182]

---

[179] Nuon Appeal Judgment, above n. 3, para. 792.

[180] *The Queen* v *Shoichi Ikeda*, Temporary Court Martial in Batavia, Case No. 72A/1947, Judgment (Translated Judgment), 30 March 1948, <https://www.legal-tools.org/doc/205dfb/pdf/> [accessed 8 July 2017].

[181] Ibid, p. 8.

[182] Ibid, p. 10.

The Supreme Court Chamber noted the uncertainties as to the basis for liability in the *Ikeda* case and the absence of other supporting State practice, but seemed to acknowledge that the case provided at least some support for the concept of JCE III.

The Supreme Court Chamber re-examined the post-Second World War cases from Italy that were cited in *Tadić* and concluded that those cases did not 'strongly support' JCE III. It also indicated in a footnote that it had reviewed a number of other cases, including the IMTFE Judgement and the *Belsen*, *Farben*, *Hadamar*, *Hostage*, *Mauthausen*, *Ulrich and Merkle* and *Wuelfert* cases.[183] Five further cases were considered worthy of discussion—*Rüsselsheim* (US Military Commission, Germany), *Tashiro* (US Military Commission, Japan), and *Hatakeyama*, *Matsumoto* and *Ishiyama and Yasusaka* (Australian military courts)—but in none of those cases was a concept equivalent to JCE III found to have been applied.[184]

The trials before British Military Courts in Hong Kong constitute an additional group of post-Second World War cases that has been brought to light and analysed after the Pre-Trial Chamber and Trial Chamber rendered their decisions but before the issue was considered by the Supreme Court Chamber. Forty-six trials against 123 individual accused were held in Hong Kong.[185] The trials were governed by the 1945 Royal Warrant and annexed Regulations for the Trial of War Criminals, supported by secondary legislation such as the Instructions issued by Allied Land Forces South-East Asia (ALFSEA).[186] The procedures were derived from the provisions of the British Manual of Military Law 1929 (as amended).[187] Notably, the Manual of Military Law contained a section on responsibility for crimes based on 'common intent' as follows:

---

183 Nuon Appeal Judgment, above n. 3, para. 799, footnote 2107.

184 Ibid, paras. 800–04.

185 *See* Hong Kong's War Crimes Trials Collection, <http://hkwctc.lib.hku.hk/exhibits/show/hkwctc/home> [accessed 7 July 2017].

186 Royal Warrant 0160/2498, Regulations for the Trial of War Criminals, A. O. 81/1945, 18 June 1945; Allied Land Forces South-East Asia War Crimes Instruction No. 1: Investigation of War Crimes and Trial of War Criminals: Policy (2nd edn), WO 203/2080, December 1945, United Kingdom National Archives; Great Britain War Office, *Manual of Military Law 1929* (7th edn, London, H.M.S.O., 1940) (amended in 1936 with the replacement of Chapter XIV and in 1944 with an amendment to para. 443 of Chapter XIV).

187 Great Britain War Office, *Manual of Military Law 1929* (7th edn, London, His Majesty's Stationary Office, 1940) (amended in 1936 with the replacement of Chapter XIV and in 1944 with an amendment to para. 443 of Chapter XIV).

> If several persons combine together for an unlawful purpose or for a lawful purpose to be effected by unlawful means, each is responsible for every offence committed by any one of them in furtherance of that purpose, but not for any offence committed by another member of the party which is unconnected with the common purpose, unless he personally instigates or assists in its commission. Thus, if a police officer goes with an assistant to arrest A in a house and all the occupants of this house combine to resist the arrest, and in the struggle the assistant is killed, the occupants are responsible. But if two persons go out to commit theft and one unknown to the other puts a pistol in his pocket and shoots a man the other is not responsible.[188]

This provision suggests that a concept similar to JCE III was available to the Hong Kong courts but there is little evidence that it was actually applied. Regulation 8(ii) was invoked by the Prosecution in the biggest joint trial—that of Lieutenant Kishi Yasuo and 14 co-accused—charged with committing a war crime by 'being together concerned in the beating, torture and maltreatment of the inhabitants of Silver Mine Bay district of Lantau and in the killing of nine of the said inhabitants'.[189] The Prosecution presented an argument that:

> all the evidence before this court tends to prove that the cruelty, maltreatment, the torture and finally the murder of the unfortunate islanders was not the action of any one individual, however big a part he played in this crime, but was in actual fact the concerted action over a period of one week of a group of individuals belonging to one unit who acted jointly in the continued maltreatment of the civilian inhabitants in their custody and which group or unit having jointly and severally [sic] are thus jointly and severally responsible for the natural consequences of their actions which in this case was the cruel and untimely death of nine of the inhabitants of the said Lantau Island.[190]

---

188 Great Britain War Office, *Manual of Military Law 1929* (7th edn, London, His Majesty's Stationary Office, 1940), p. 107, col. 17 (this paragraph featured in the Great Britain War Office, *Manual of Military Law 1914* (London, H.M.S.O., 1914), p. 89, col. 18) in identical terms save the first phrase which referred instead to 'several persons' going out with 'a common intent to execute some criminal purpose'.) The notion of 'common intent' was known to United States military law as well, *see* United States War Department, *A Manual for Courts-Martial, Courts of Inquiry and of Other Procedure under Military Law* (Washington, D.C., Government Printing Office, 1917), p. 34, col. 69, <http://www.loc.gov/rr/frd/Military_Law/pdf/manual-1917.pdf> [accessed 9 July 2017].

189 'Trial of *Lieutenant Kishi Yasuo and Fourteen Others*', Hong Kong's War Crimes Trials Collection File No WO235/993, *Judge Advocate's Report*, slide 4, para. 1 of the Document.

190 Ibid, slide 550, p. 524 of the Document.

In the absence of a reasoned judgment, however, it is difficult to conclude that the Prosecution's theory was accepted by the Court, even assuming that this theory amounted to a suggestion that all of the accused should be treated as principals to the killings which is by no means clear. In fact, only certain accused were convicted for the killings while others were held liable for maltreatment.[191]

There may still be relevant post-Second World War cases that have not yet been unearthed or analysed. For example, the process of making available the records of trials held in China is ongoing and the jurisprudence from Singapore and the Netherlands is still undergoing scrutiny. It is doubtful whether any of these cases could tilt the balance significantly in favour of a finding that JCE III was part of customary international law by 1975 and it is also questionable whether they could independently be sufficiently authoritative to establish a customary norm. There is nothing that emerges in the cases pursuant to Control Council Law No. 10 and further proceedings before US and British military courts that changes the overall impression that there was no concept bearing a close juridical relationship to JCE III in customary international law at the time relevant to the charges before the ECCC.

As an alternative argument, the Co-Prosecutors had suggested that customary international law could be derived directly from domestic criminal law. This argument was rejected by the Supreme Court Chamber since 'general domestic criminal practice cannot be the basis for establishing a rule of customary international law, given that it lacks an international element'.[192] Indeed, as the STL has observed, albeit in relation to crimes rather than modes of liability:

> To turn into an international crime, a domestic offence needs to be regarded by the world community as an attack on universal values (such as peace or human rights) or on values held to be of paramount importance in that community; in addition, it is necessary that States and intergovernmental organisations, through their acts and pronouncements, sanction this attitude by

---

[191] *See* further N.H.B. Jørgensen, 'On "Being Concerned in Crime": Embryonic Joint Criminal Enterprise?', in S. Linton (ed), *Hong Kong's War Crimes Trials* (Oxford, Oxford University Press, 2013), pp. 137–67; N.H.B. Jørgensen and C. Young, 'Joint and Command Responsibility in Hong Kong's War Crimes Trials: Revisiting the Cases of Kishi Yasuo and Noma Kennosuke', in D. Liu and B. Zhang (eds), *Historical War Crimes Trials in Asia* (Brussel, Torkel Opsahl Academic EPublisher, 2016), pp. 263–87.

[192] Nuon Appeal Judgment, above n. 3, para. 805.

> clearly expressing the view that the world community considers the offence at issue as amounting to an international crime.[193]

The STL was addressing the question whether a customary international rule had evolved defining terrorism. In answering this question in the affirmative, the STL relied on a variety of sources including 'the enactment by States of specific domestic laws and decisions by national courts.'[194] Consistent national legislation, taken together with the other sources, such as adherence to international treaties, was seen to be indicative of the emergence of a customary rule.[195] There is clearly a difference between the incorporation of international criminal law domestically, or the employment of international law in the domestic prosecution of international crimes, and legislation and case law concerning purely domestic criminal law. The former categories are reflective of states' interactions in the international sphere and their use and interpretation of established or emerging international law while the latter category is normally of no relevance to international relations. Thus, even if *all* states consistently applied a notion akin to JCE III in domestic prosecutions of certain crimes such as murder, this would not transform a domestic mode of liability or a *mens rea* standard into a norm of customary international law. The Appeals Chamber in *Tadić* took the view that national legislation and case law served to demonstrate that the three categories of JCE that it deemed to be recognised in international criminal law had an 'underpinning' in many national systems.[196] In that case, the brief analysis of national legislation merely served to enhance the acceptability of the conclusions reached as to the state of customary international law. In the context of the development of custom, domestic legislation and case law can do no more than demonstrate a conceptual 'underpinning' for JCE-related notions.

---

[193] *Prosecutor v Ayyash, Merhi, Oneissi* and *Sabra*, SLT Case No. STL-11-01/I, Appeals Chamber, Interlocutory Decision on the Applicable Law: Terrorism, Conspiracy, Homicide, Perpetration, Cumulative Charging, 16 February 2011, para. 91.

[194] Ibid, para. 87.

[195] Ibid, para. 91.

[196] Tadić Appeal Judgment, above n. 19, para. 225.

6.2 JCE III as a General Principle of Law

Domestic legislation and cases concerning criminal liability can possibly provide the basis for a general principle of law as a source of international law.[197] One reason for the *Tadić* Appeals Chamber's cursory dismissal of the relevance of domestic practice, once it had determined the customary international law status of JCE, was its view that domestic law could not be 'a source of international principles or rules, under the doctrine of the general principles of law recognised by the nations of the world' because it could not be shown that 'most, if not all countries adopt the same notion of common purpose'.[198] The Pre-Trial Chamber observed that the appropriate process to assess the existence of a general principle of law was that suggested in the *Furundžija* and *Kunarac* Trial Judgments before the ICTY. Thus, a 'comprehensive survey of all legal systems of the world'[199] is not required but the 'mechanical importation or transposition from national law into international criminal proceedings' should be avoided.[200] As an example, the Pre-Trial Chamber referred to the *Blaskić* case where the ICTY Appeals Chamber reviewed

---

[197] *See* H. Thirlway, *The Sources of International Law* (Oxford, Oxford University Press, 2014), p. 98, but c.f., *Oil Platforms* case (*Islamic Republic of Iran v United States of America*), Separate Opinion of Judge Simma, ICJ, *Reports*, 2003, p. 358, para. 74 (where Judge Simma conducts a comparative analysis to determine how the problem of multiple tortfeasors is addressed in domestic law, concluding that a general principle of law of joint and several responsibility emerges and states 'On the basis of the (admittedly modest) study of comparative tort law thus provided, I venture to conclude that the principle of joint-and-several responsibility common to the jurisdictions that I have considered can properly be regarded as a "general principle of law" within the meaning of Article 38, paragraph 1 *(c)*, of the Court's Statute.').

[198] Tadić Appeal Judgment, above n. 19, para. 225.

[199] *Prosecutor v Erdemović*, ICTY Case No. IT-96-22-A, Appeals Chamber, Separate Opinion of Judge McDonald and Judge Vohrah, 7 October 1997, para. 57; *Prosecutor v Ayyash, Merhi, Oneissi* and *Sabra*, SLT Case No. STL-11-01/I, Appeals Chamber, Interlocutory Decision on the Applicable Law: Terrorism, Conspiracy, Homicide, Perpetration, Cumulative Charging, 16 February 2011, para. 91. *See* also *Prosecutor v Ieng Sary, Ieng Thirith* and *Khieu Samphan*, ECCC Case File No. 002/19-09-2007-ECCC/OCIJ (PTC 35, 37, 38, & 39), Pre-Trial Chamber, Decision on the Appeals against the Co-Investigating Judges' Order on Joint Criminal Enterprise (JCE), 20 May 2010, para. 86.

[200] *Prosecutor v Furundžija*, ICTY Case No. IT-95-17/1-T, Trial Chamber, Judgment, 10 December 1998, para. 178; *Prosecutor v Kunarac, Kovač* and *Vuković*, ICTY Case No. IT-96-23-T & IT-96-23/1-T, Trial Chamber, Judgment, 22 February 2001, para. 439.

national laws on recklessness and *dolus eventualis* to ascertain the appropriate *mens rea* standard for the mode of liability of 'ordering'.[201] However, the Pre-Trial Chamber concluded that it did not need to undertake an inquiry into whether the *mens rea* standard applicable to JCE III was recognised in a number of national systems representative of the major legal systems of the world because it was in any case not convinced that JCE III was foreseeable and accessible to the charged persons at the relevant time. This conclusion was based on an application of the *nullum crimen* principle which could not be satisfied because no Cambodian law applicable at the relevant time could be identified that would have given notice to the accused that an extended form of JCE liability was punishable.[202]

The Supreme Court Chamber found more directly that domestic legislation and case law was insufficient to establish the existence of a general principle of law as to JCE III. Following a review of domestic practice, the Supreme Court Chamber observed that although some, mainly common law jurisdictions, 'provide for the imputation of crimes that resulted from the implementation of a common purpose even if they were not necessarily part of it', there were limitations.[203] In particular:

> It would appear that in all these jurisdictions, the general principle is that criminal responsibility is ordinarily limited to the perpetrator's own actions; as far as actions of others are concerned, a specific condition for their imputation must be determined by law – for instance that the crime in question was encompassed by an agreement or a common criminal purpose.[204]

The Supreme Court Chamber therefore concluded that 'criminal liability based on making a contribution to the implementation of a common criminal purpose was, at the time relevant to the charges in the case at hand, limited to crimes that were actually encompassed by the common purpose'.[205] This shifted the focus back to the criteria for determining which crimes were encompassed by the common purpose.

---

[201] *Prosecutor v Ieng Sary, Ieng Thirith* and *Khieu Samphan*, ECCC Case File No. 002/19-09-2007-ECCC/OCIJ (PTC 35, 37, 38, & 39), Pre-Trial Chamber, Decision on the Appeals against the Co-Investigating Judges' Order on Joint Criminal Enterprise (JCE), 20 May 2010, para. 86.

[202] Ibid, para. 87.

[203] Nuon Appeal Judgment, above n. 3, para. 806.

[204] Ibid, para. 806.

[205] Ibid, para. 807.

It should be recalled that the Co-Prosecutors had previously argued that JCE III constituted a general principle of law recognized by civilised nations.[206] While the Pre-Trial Chamber did not fully address this assertion, the Trial Chamber rejected it, after surveying seven national legal systems (the United Kingdom, the US, Germany, the Soviet Union, the Netherlands, France and Cambodia) and finding there to be 'a considerable divergence of approach' between these jurisdictions.[207]

In their appeal before the Supreme Court Chamber in Case 002/01, the Co-Prosecutors referred to the domestic law of 40 jurisdictions, including the seven already discussed by the Trial Chamber. Their argument was that this selection would be sufficiently representative to support the existence of a customary norm rather than that it would necessarily be sufficient to establish a general principle of law, the latter issue not being raised directly by the Co-Prosecutors in their appeal. The Defence for Nuon Chea did however respond to the Co-Prosecutors' arguments on the level of general principles as well as customary law.[208]

As indicated by the Pre-Trial Chamber, a comprehensive survey of all the legal systems of the world is not necessarily required to establish a general principle of law. The law and practice of 40 States might be sufficiently representative if all those States consistently adopted the same underlying principle. The materials provided by the Co-Prosecutors provided a cross-section in terms of geographical region as well as legal

---

[206] *Prosecutor v Nuon Chea, Ieng Sary, Ieng Thirith* and *Khieu Samphan*, ECCC Case File No. 002/19-09-2007-ECCC/TC, Office of the Co-Prosecutor, Co-Prosecutors' Request for the Trial Chamber to Consider JCE III as an Alternative Mode of Liability, 17 June 2011, paras. 29, 31. (Indeed, 'The Co-Prosecutors submit that, if the Trial Chamber were to find that JCE III did not form part of customary international law during the relevant time period, it would be appropriate and advisable for the Trial Chamber to request amicus submissions from a qualified academic or research institution on the question of whether JCE III liability could still be applied at the ECCC on the basis of its status as a "general principle of law recognised by civilized nations" during the relevant time period.')

[207] *Prosecutor v Nuon Chea, Ieng Sary, Ieng Thirith* and *Khieu Samphan*, ECCC Case File No. 002/19-09-2007/ECCC/TC, Trial Chamber, Decision on the Applicability of Joint Criminal Enterprise, 12 September 2011, para. 37.

[208] *Prosecutor v Nuon Chea* and *Khieu Samphan*, ECCC Case File No. 002/19-09-2007-ECCC/SC, Defence for Nuon Chea, Nuon Chea's Response to Co-Prosecutors' Appeal against the Trial Judgment in Case 002/01, 28 January 2015, paras. 18–23.

system (common law and civil law).[209] The Defence for Nuon Chea correctly pointed out, referring to Article 21(1)(c) of the Rome Statute, that a 'selective scrutiny' of national systems should include the national law of the State that would normally exercise jurisdiction over the crime.[210] This appears especially important for a court such as the ECCC which is deliberately structured so as to have a close relationship with domestic law.

The Co-Prosecutors divided the law presented into two categories: those States having domestic legislation in force before 1975 that included identical or highly analogous terminology to that of JCE III (23 States); and those States recognising the core concepts underlying JCE III liability—imputation of responsibility for group crimes and also for reasonably foreseeable crimes—while not expressly extending liability to foreseeable crimes outside a common plan (18 States). The criminal laws of a number of States in the first category envisage that where two or more persons form a common intent to carry out a common unlawful purpose, responsibility is incurred for an offence which was the 'probable consequence' of the carrying out of the common purpose.[211] The envisaged responsibility is that of a principal as each participant in the common purpose is deemed to have committed the offence. As elaborated in some of the cited case law, this concept is similar to JCE III although it is framed by a standard of 'probable consequence' which on its face is tighter than 'foreseeable consequence'. With the exception of South Africa (considered a 'hybrid' system), all the States applying this concept follow the common law tradition. The Co-Prosecutors placed civil law countries such as France, Iraq and Italy in the first category but the arguments for their inclusion are unconvincing.

English law applicable at the time relevant to the ECCC's jurisdiction appeared to treat JCE III-related concepts as *exculpatory* in the sense that liability for crimes extraneous to the common goal of an unlawful

---

[209] *Prosecutor v Nuon Chea* and *Khieu Samphan*, ECCC Case File No. 002/19-09-2007-ECCC/SC, Office of the Co-Prosecutor, Co-Prosecutors' Appeal against the Judgment of the Trial Chamber in Case 002/01, 28 November 2014, para. 50.

[210] *Prosecutor v Nuon Chea* and *Khieu Samphan*, ECCC Case File No. 002/19-09-2007-ECCC/SC, Defence for Nuon Chea, Nuon Chea's Response to Co-Prosecutors' Appeal against the Trial Judgment in Case 002/01, 28 January 2015, para. 23.

[211] Paraphrasing Australian (Queensland) Crime Code Act 1899, Section 8. *See* also legislation from Bermuda, Botswana, Canada, Fiji, Israel, Kenya, Malawi, New Zealand, Nigeria, Papua New Guinea, Seychelles, South Africa, Tanzania, Uganda, Western Samoa, Zambia.

enterprise would *only* be incurred if the party to the enterprise actually aided or abetted the extraneous crime.[212] The idea that responsibility may be incurred for collateral crimes falling outside an agreed common purpose in these circumstances was recognised in early English case law as well as in the British Manual of Military Law 1929 applicable at the time of post-Second World War trials.[213] The 'joint enterprise' theory has been controversial in modern English law and was recently subject to a restatement by the Supreme Court and Privy Council.[214]

---

[212] *See* J.F. Stephen. *A Digest of the Criminal Law (Crimes and Punishments)* (St. Louis, F.H. Thomas and Company, 1878), pp. 26–27: 'When several persons take part in the execution of a common criminal purpose, each is a principal in the second degree, in respect of every crime committed by any one of them in the execution of that purpose. If any of the offenders commits a crime foreign to the common criminal purpose, the others are neither principals in the second degree, nor accessories unless they actually instigate or assist in its commission.' The requirement suggested in the case of *R v Anderson* and *Morris* [1966] 2 QB 110 that the party must have authorised the extraneous crimes as being part of the enterprise was clarified (and removed) in the case of *R v Powell (Anthony)* and *Another, R v English* [1999] 1 AC 1.

[213] *Lord Dacre's* case (1542), 1 Hale, P. C. 439; *See* also J. Jervis, *Archbold's Summary of the Law Relating to Pleading and Evidence in Criminal Cases: with the Statutes, Precedents of Indictments, &c., and the Evidence Necessary to Support Them* (11th edn, London, S. Sweet and V. and R. Stevens and G.S. Norton, 1849), pp. 5–6.

[214] The modern English law on what has been termed 'parasitic accessory liability' was laid down by the Privy Council in *Chan Wing-Siu v The Queen* [1985] AC 168. The law was changed in the joint Supreme Court/Privy Council cases of *R v Jogee* [2016] UKSC 8 and *Ruddock v The Queen* [2016] UKPC 7 (The original theory was stated at para. 2 to be: 'if two people set out to commit an offence (crime A), and in the course of that joint enterprise one of them (D1) commits another offence (crime B), the second person (D2) is guilty as an accessory to crime B if he had foreseen the possibility that D1 might act as he did. D2's foresight of that possibility plus his continuation in the enterprise to commit crime A were held sufficient in law to bring crime B within the scope of the conduct for which he is criminally liable, whether or not he intended it.' The Court noted at para. 77 that 'joint enterprise' was not a legal term of art, and at para. 87 that: 'The long-standing pre-*Chan Wing-Siu* practice of inferring intent to assist from a common criminal purpose which includes the further crime, if the occasion for it were to arise, was always a legitimate one; what was illegitimate was to treat foresight as an inevitable yardstick of common purpose.' The Court restated the principles of accessory liability arising from a joint criminal venture, explaining that foresight of what the principal might do was evidence from which the requisite intention for that crime could be inferred.).

In their second category, the Co-Prosecutors attempted to combine two principles which receive separate treatment in the domestic law cited. The first relates to special considerations of responsibility in respect of group crimes and the second to responsibility on the basis of a *mens rea* standard of foreseeability. To derive a general principle applicable to international criminal law from this combination of features would amount to picking and choosing from national law to create a new concept in international law. Such a process would go beyond even the mechanical importation or transposition from national law into international criminal proceedings.

The Defence raised specific objections to the Co-Prosecutors' interpretation of German, Dutch and Cambodian law. These examples point to the undeniable distinctions between legal traditions making it difficult to extract an underlying basis for responsibility that could be seen as a clear precursor for JCE III as currently defined. German law on co-perpetratorship has been considered to influence the ICC's concept of joint commission of a crime under Article 25(3)(a) of the Rome Statute.[215] As elaborated in the jurisprudence of the ICC, the notion of co-perpetratorship is distinct from JCE. There must be a limit to the degree to which the same national provisions can form the basis of divergent international criminal law concepts.[216]

7. THE NON-APPLICATION OF CO-PERPETRATION

The ECCC has proceeded down the road of JCE liability without any sustained consideration of an alternative such as co-perpetration.[217] Indeed, the existence of co-perpetration as a mode of liability in

---

215 *See* e.g. *Prosecutor v Lubanga*, ICC Case No. ICC-01/04-01/06, Trial Chamber I, Judgment pursuant to Article 74 of the Statute: Separate Opinion of Judge Adrian Fulford, 14 March 2012, para. 10 (referring to *Prosecutor v Stakić*, ICTY Case No. IT-97-24-T, Trial Chamber II, Judgement, 31 July 2003 and *Prosecutor v Gacumbitsi*, ICTR Case No. ICTR-2001-64-A, Appeals Chamber, Judgment: Separate Opinion of Judge Schomburg on the Criminal Responsibility of the Appellant for Committing Genocide, 7 July 2006).

216 *See* also M.G. Karnavas, 'Joint Criminal Enterprise at the ECCC: A Critical Analysis of the Pre-Trial Chamber's Decision against the Application of JCE III and Two Divergent Commentaries on the Same', *Criminal Law Forum*, vol. 21, 2010, pp. 445–94, p. 475 (taking the view that 'JCE cannot be assimilated into the Cambodian law of co-perpetration').

217 *See* also N. Jain, 'The Joint Criminal Enterprise Doctrine at the Extraordinary Chambers in the Courts of Cambodia', in K. Sellars (ed), *Trials for*

Cambodian law has been used as an additional justification for the imposition of JCE liability, helping to demonstrate that the possibility of being held responsible for 'committing' crimes pursuant to a JCE was foreseeable and accessible to the accused. As the Pre-Trial Chamber stated:

> In spite of its unique nature, the concept of JCE, at least in its basic and systemic forms (JCE I & II), resembles accountability in traditional civil law in that it treats as co-perpetrators not only those who physically perform the *actus reus* of the crime, but also those who possess the *mens rea* for the crime and participate or contribute to its commission. In this sense, JCE has an underpinning in Cambodian law.[218]

The Trial Chamber also took account of JCE's 'resonance with the Cambodian law concept of co-perpetration applicable at the time' in finding that JCE liability was accessible and foreseeable to the accused.[219]

The 1956 Penal Code provided the basis for these conclusions of the Pre-Trial Chamber and the Trial Chamber. The 1956 Penal Code defines and distinguishes between the concepts of co-perpetration and complicity.[220] Reference is made in Article 82 to co-perpetration as a form of responsibility deriving from direct participation.[221] The perpetrator (*auteur*) is the person who commits the crime, while co-perpetration (*co-action*) requires a common agreement between the co-perpetrators, and complicity covers indirect participation.[222] Direct or indirect voluntary

---

International Crimes in Asia (Cambridge, Cambridge University Press, 2016), pp. 275–300.

[218] *Prosecutor v Ieng Sary, Ieng Thirith* and *Khieu Samphan*, ECCC Case File No. 002/19-09-2007-ECCC/OCIJ (PTC 35, 37, 38, & 39), Pre-Trial Chamber, Decision on the Appeals against the Co-Investigating Judges' Order on Joint Criminal Enterprise (JCE), 20 May 2010, para. 41.

[219] Duch Trial Judgment, above n. 1, para. 512.

[220] *Prosecutor v Ieng Sary, Ieng Thirith* and *Khieu Samphan*, ECCC Case File No. 002/19-09-2007-ECCC/OCIJ (PTC 35, 37, 38, & 39), Pre-Trial Chamber, Decision on the Appeals against the Co-Investigating Judges' Order on Joint Criminal Enterprise (JCE), 20 May 2010, para. 41 (referring to Kai Ambos' *amicus curiae* brief); *Prosecutor v Kaing Guek Eav alias 'Duch'*, ECCC Case File No. 001/8-07-2007-ECCC/OCIJ (PTC 02), Pre-Trial Chamber, Decision on Appeal against Closing Order Indicting Kaing Guek Eav alias 'Duch', 5 December 2008, para. 114, footnote 73.

[221] Duch Trial Judgment, above n. 1, para. 510.

[222] *Prosecutor v Kaing Guek Eav alias 'Duch'*, ECCC Case File No. 001/8-07-2007-ECCC/OCIJ (PTC 02), Pre-Trial Chamber, Decision on Appeal

participants may be equally liable with the principal of the crime.[223] Given that the Cambodian Penal Code was modelled on its French counterpart, the Trial Chamber observed that: 'Relevant French jurisprudence reveals a broad understanding of co-authorship or co-perpetration that may also partially overlap with the notion of joint criminal enterprise.'[224] Unfortunately, no Cambodian jurisprudence on co-perpetratorship could be located. The Trial Chamber, noting that co-perpetratorship in Cambodian law and JCE (in its first and second forms) were not identical, cited with approval the Pre-Trial Chamber's assessment of the relationship between the two forms of responsibility:

> While both require the shared intent by participants that the crime be committed, participation in a JCE, even if it has to be significant, would appear to embrace situations where the accused may be more remote from the actual perpetration of the *actus reus* of the crime than the direct participation required under domestic law.[225]

The Pre-Trial Chamber stressed that JCE was not a 'more severe' form of liability than the domestic notion of co-perpetration, contrary to an argument presented by the defence.[226] The Trial Chamber added that JCE as applied before the ECCC 'follows from customary international law, not national law.'[227]

As the domestic offences under the ECCC's jurisdiction have fallen by the wayside for procedural reasons, any direct juxtaposition of JCE and co-perpetration in ECCC cases is unlikely. The Chambers have not had the opportunity to scrutinise the Co-Investigating Judges' position that JCE is applicable solely to international crimes and is not relevant to the domestic crimes over which the ECCC has jurisdiction.[228] The reverse

---

against Closing Order Indicting Kaing Guek Eav alias 'Duch', 5 December 2008, para. 114, footnote 73.

223 Duch Trial Judgment, above n. 1, para. 510.

224 Ibid.

225 Ibid (citing *Prosecutor v Ieng Sary, Ieng Thirith* and *Khieu Samphan*, ECCC Case File No. 002/19-09-2007-ECCC/OCIJ (PTC 35, 37, 38, & 39), Pre-Trial Chamber, Decision on the Appeals against the Co-Investigating Judges' Order on Joint Criminal Enterprise (JCE), 20 May 2010, para. 41.

226 *Prosecutor v Ieng Sary, Ieng Thirith* and *Khieu Samphan*, ECCC Case File No. 002/19-09-2007-ECCC/OCIJ (PTC 35, 37, 38, & 39), Pre-Trial Chamber, Decision on the Appeals against the Co-Investigating Judges' Order on Joint Criminal Enterprise (JCE), 20 May 2010, para. 41.

227 Duch Trial Judgment, above n. 1, para. 510.

228 *See* further, Yanev, above n. 61, pp. 210–11; N.H.B. Jørgensen, 'Theories of Joint Criminal Responsibility at the Asian Tribunals', in K. Sellars (ed), *Trials*

assertion, that co-perpetration is applicable to the domestic crimes but not to international crimes, has similarly not been considered. In fact, the civil parties appealed against the Co-Investigating Judges Order on JCE that referred to autonomous liability regimes for domestic and international crimes, meaning that JCE was only applicable to international crimes. The Pre-Trial Chamber found that the counter-arguments on appeal failed to demonstrate an error, however, so the matter was not discussed.[229]

It might theoretically have been possible for the Supreme Court Chamber to do the reverse of what the ICTY Appeals Chamber did in the *Stakić* case. In that case, the ICTY Trial Chamber had re-characterised JCE liability as co-perpetration, reading the latter into the word 'committing' just as JCE had previously been read into this word. When the ICTY Appeals Chamber was faced with the choice between JCE and co-perpetration in *Stakić*, it claimed that co-perpetration as defined by the Trial Chamber 'does not have support in customary international law or in the settled jurisprudence of this Tribunal' and applied JCE to the factual findings instead.[230]

The Trial Chamber in the *Lubanga* case observed that although 'both the Romano Germanic and the Common Law legal systems have developed principles about modes of liability' these systems were never intended to address 'the most serious crimes of concern to the international community as a whole'.[231] The ECCC's readiness to adopt the common-law inspired notion of JCE is presumably influenced, indeed dictated by the fact that the doctrine is considered to be part of customary international law. Co-perpetration does not at this stage enjoy the same status. However, the allure of JCE appears to go deeper than the dictates of custom. Both the ECCC Pre-Trial Chamber and the Trial Chamber acknowledged that the concept allows for greater remoteness between the accused and the physical commission of the crime. The Co-Prosecutors

---

for International Crimes in Asia (Cambridge, Cambridge University Press, 2016), pp. 318–40, pp. 327–9. (The 'international' modes of liability such as JCE were in principle found to be applicable also in respect of the domestic crimes before the Special Panels for Serious Crimes in East Timor.)

229 *Prosecutor v Ieng Sary, Ieng Thirith* and *Khieu Samphan*, ECCC Case File No. 002/19-09-2007-ECCC/OCIJ (PTC 35, 37, 38, & 39), Pre-Trial Chamber, Decision on the Appeals against the Co-Investigating Judges' Order on Joint Criminal Enterprise (JCE), 20 May 2010, paras. 98–102.

230 *Prosecutor v Stakić*, ICTY Case No. IT-97-24-A, Appeals Chamber, Judgment, 22 March 2006, para. 62.

231 *Prosecutor v Lubanga*, ICC Case No. ICC-01/04-01/06, Trial Chamber I, Judgment pursuant to Article 74 of the Statute, 04 April 2012, para. 976.

have consistently urged the application of JCE in all its forms before the ECCC, arguing that the crimes were not the isolated acts of individual cadres 'but the result of deliberate criminal policies designed and enforced by the *Khmer Rouge*'.[232] Further, the Co-Prosecutors have asserted that the ECCC could only realise its mandate to try senior leaders and those most responsible if it were able to assign criminal responsibility to those who created and oversaw the implementation of policies.[233] The suggestion is that JCE is uniquely capable of providing the right framework for joint criminal responsibility in cases involving systematic crimes orchestrated at the highest level of decision-making.

8. CONCLUSION

It emerges from the discussion in this chapter that characterisation in terms of liability is at least as important as characterization of crimes and that a considerable amount of the ECCC's judicial effort has been devoted to establishing the appropriate liability framework, matched by a pleading vigour among the parties that only the JCE concept can inspire. JCE, especially in its extended form, goes beyond a mere question of characterisation. In their appeal in Case 002/01, the Co-Prosecutors provided an example from the *Furundžija* case before the ICTY where the underlying conduct consisting of forcible oral sex was already prohibited at the time of its occurrence but charged as sexual assault in some national jurisdictions as opposed to rape which was the preferred ICTY characterisation.[234] In this example, responsibility is incurred in respect of the same underlying conduct even if modern international

---

232 *Prosecutor v Ieng Sary*, ECCC Case File No. 002/19-09-2007-ECCC/OCIJ, Office of the Co-Prosecutor, Response of Co-Prosecutors to Ieng Sary's Lawyers Motion against the Application at the ECCC of the Form of Liability Known as 'Joint Criminal Enterprise', 11 August 2008, para. 13.

233 *Prosecutor v Ieng Sary*, ECCC Case File No. 002/19-09-2007-ECCC/OCIJ, Office of the Co-Prosecutor, Response of Co-Prosecutors to Ieng Sary's Lawyers Motion against the Application at the ECCC of the Form of Liability Known as 'Joint Criminal Enterprise', 11 August 2008, paras. 13–14. *See* also *Prosecutor v Nuon Chea, Ieng Sary, Ieng Thirith* and *Khieu Samphan*, ECCC Case File No. 002/19-09-2007-ECCC/TC, Office of the Co-Prosecutor, Co-Prosecutors' Request for the Trial Chamber to Consider JCE III as an Alternative Mode of Liability, 17 June 2011, para. 16.

234 *Prosecutor v Nuon Chea* and *Khieu Samphan*, ECCC Case File No. 002/19-09-2007-ECCC/SC, Office of the Co-Prosecutor, Co-Prosecutors' Appeal against the Judgment of the Trial Chamber in Case 002/01, 28 November 2014,

criminal law views it as a more serious offence and affords it a different label. As it concerns JCE III as a mode of liability, however, the issue is the *scope* of criminal culpability rather than its characterisation. It is true that JCE III can only be invoked where JCE I exists in the sense of a shared intent to commit certain crimes, but, as also argued by the Defence for Nuon Chea,[235] the effect of applying JCE III is to render an accused criminally responsible for a broader range of conduct, encompassing the conduct of other perpetrators. The real issue, therefore, is not the 'gradual clarification of the rules of criminal liability',[236] but rather the potential for the gradual expansion of the scope of individual criminal responsibility under international law.

The Co-Prosecutors had suggested that the Supreme Court Chamber should take the opportunity to review the issue of JCE III in order to 'harmonise the ECCC's legal position with decisions and final judgments of the ICTY, ICTR, SCSL and STL'.[237] The ECCC stands alone among these tribunals in not accepting the customary international law status of JCE III. While the ECCC's consideration is limited to the law applicable in the period 1975–1979, in reality the jurisprudential foundation of JCE III is contained in the post-Second World War instruments and cases. The Supreme Court Chamber's final assessment may be considered *obiter* since the Co-Prosecutors' appeal was rejected as being inadmissible, but the Supreme Court Chamber nonetheless relied on the arguments of the parties in reaching a clear conclusion on JCE III. Presumably, had it reached a different conclusion, it might have accepted the Trial Chamber's language of 'resulting in' crimes and assessed the contribution of Nuon Chea and Khieu Samphan under JCE III. The interpretation of JCE I adopted by the Supreme Court Chamber is nonetheless relatively broad in that the common purpose is not required to be criminal *per se* as long as it 'amounts to or involves' crimes in the sense that those crimes are 'intended, contemplated or otherwise encompassed by the common

---

para. 17 (citing *Prosecutor v Furundžija*, ICTY Case No. IT-95-17/1-T, Trial Chamber, Judgment, 10 December 1998, para. 184).

[235] *Prosecutor v Nuon Chea* and *Khieu Samphan*, ECCC Case File No. 002/19-09-2007-ECCC/SC, Defence for Nuon Chea, Nuon Chea's Response to Co-Prosecutors' Appeal against the Trial Judgment in Case 002/01, 28 January 2015, para. 12.

[236] *Prosecutor v Nuon Chea* and *Khieu Samphan*, ECCC Case File No. 002/19-09-2007-ECCC/SC, Office of the Co-Prosecutor, Co-Prosecutors' Appeal against the Judgment of the Trial Chamber in Case 002/01, 28 November 2014, para. 18.

[237] Ibid, para. 11.

purpose' and ambiguities remain in relation to the *mens rea* element. In view of the formulation of the JCE in the Closing Order of Case 002, centred on five distinct policies, it is difficult to see what the availability of JCE III could have added.

The Co-Prosecutors invoked policy considerations in favour of allowing JCE III including the need to address the greater social danger of group crimes and the risk that those who participate in criminal enterprises may escape liability. These considerations had been touched on by the STL which stated:

> With regard to the very *raison d'être* of JCEIII, this mode of responsibility is founded on considerations of public policy: that is, the need to protect society against persons who band together to take part in criminal enterprises and, whilst not sharing the criminal intent of those participants who intend to commit *more serious crimes* outside the common enterprise, nevertheless are aware that such objectively foreseeable crimes may be committed and do nothing to oppose or prevent them, but rather continue in the pursuit of the enterprise's other criminal goals.[238]

These are valid concerns but ones that have evolved over time and which are only faintly mirrored in the UNWCC discussions. They are largely irrelevant to the identification of a norm of customary international law even though they may subtly influence the approach taken to the sources.

The ECCC, following the model of the ICTY, has taken care to avoid the 'mechanical importation or transposition from national law into international criminal proceedings … , as well as the attendant distortions of the unique traits of such proceedings.'[239] This may help to explain the ECCC Supreme Court Chamber's reluctance to draw on general principles of law, or to apply concepts of liability existing in Cambodian law. The STL's approach to the definition of terrorism suggests that general principles may evolve into norms of customary international law. For example, the ICTY derived the definition of rape from 'principles of criminal law common to the major legal systems of the world'.[240] This definition, as it has evolved in the practice of the ad hoc tribunals, is arguably now part of customary international law. The idea of an

---

[238] *Prosecutor v Ayyash, Merhi, Oneissi* and *Sabra*, SLT Case No. STL-11-01/I, Appeals Chamber, Interlocutory Decision on the Applicable Law: Terrorism, Conspiracy, Homicide, Perpetration, Cumulative Charging, 16 February 2011, para. 245 (*Emphasis in original*).

[239] *Prosecutor v Furundžija*, ICTY Case No. IT-95-17/1-T, Trial Chamber, Judgment, 10 December 1998, para. 178.

[240] Ibid, para. 177.

evolution from a general principle derived from domestic law to a customary norm also reflects the process of adoption of modes of liability in the post-Second World War jurisprudence. Many of the principles employed were derived from, or heavily influenced by national law and as a result of this large body of jurisprudence it has become possible to distil modes of liability that may now be viewed as part of customary international law. This approach allows for the possibility that JCE has its real basis in domestic law and is today part of customary international law in all its three forms as a consequence of more recent jurisprudence.

9. Sentencing

1. INTRODUCTION

The sentencing practice at the Extraordinary Chambers in the Courts of Cambodia (ECCC) is at this stage limited to the concluded Case 001 against Duch and the concluded Case 002/01 against Khieu Samphan and Nuon Chea. Sentences are intended to reflect the gravity of the crimes proved to have been committed and the individual culpability of the accused. All three convicted accused have been given a sentence of life imprisonment and there is therefore little scope in the ECCC context for a discussion either of a hierarchy in terms of the gravity of the crimes or of visible distinctions in culpability. In the *Duch* case, a fixed term of 35-year imprisonment was initially imposed by the Trial Chamber with a 'discount' of five years as compensation for his prior illegal detention at the hands of the Cambodian Military Court.[1] The Supreme Court Chamber substituted a sentence of life imprisonment.[2] In determining the appropriate sentence to impose on Khieu Samphan and Nuon Chea, the Trial Chamber expressed a degree of irritation with the Supreme Court Chamber's action, as it meant that the Trial Chamber was precluded from reflecting in the sentence what it deemed to be clear differences in culpability between the accused in Case 001 and the accused in Case 002/01.[3]

[1] *Prosecutor v Kaing Guek Eav alias 'Duch'*, ECCC Case File No. 001/18-07-2007/ECCC/TC, Trial Chamber, Judgment, 26 July 2010, paras. 631–2 ('Duch Trial Judgment').

[2] *Prosecutor v Kaing Guek Eav alias 'Duch'*, ECCC Case File No. 001/18-07-2007-ECCC/SC, Supreme Court Chamber, Appeal Judgment, 3 February 2012, para. 383 ('Duch Appeal Judgment').

[3] *Prosecutor v Nuon Chea* and *Khieu Samphan*, ECCC Case File No. 002/19-09-2007/ECCC/TC, Trial Chamber, Case 002/01 Judgement, 7 August 2014, para. 1105 ('Nuon Trial Judgment').

2. LEGAL FRAMEWORK AND SENTENCING PRINCIPLES

The legal framework for sentencing before the ECCC is provided in the ECCC Agreement, which stipulates the maximum penalty of life imprisonment,[4] and the ECCC Law, which states that:

> Those who have committed any crime as provided in Articles 3 new, 4, 5, 6, 7 and 8 shall be sentenced to a prison term from five years to life imprisonment.
>
> In addition to imprisonment, the Extraordinary Chamber of the trial court may order the confiscation of personal property, money, and real property acquired unlawfully or by criminal conduct.
>
> The confiscated property shall be returned to the State.[5]

As the Supreme Court Chamber has noted: 'These provisions empower the Trial Chamber to select any fixed term of imprisonment that is equal to or greater than five years, or to impose a life sentence.'[6] The same sentencing provisions apply to both international and national crimes within the Court's jurisdiction. The Internal Rules simply state that: 'If the Accused is found guilty, the Chamber shall sentence him or her in accordance with the Agreement, the ECCC Law and these IRs'.[7] The constitutional documents are 'otherwise silent as regards the principles and factors to be considered at sentencing' and they do not precisely state whether international or Cambodian law, or a combination of the two, should govern sentencing before the ECCC.[8]

The applicable law at the time of the offences was the 1956 Penal Code which provided for the death penalty in respect of the most serious crimes, a penalty that was subsequently declared unconstitutional. The question whether certain provisions of the 2009 Penal Code applied to the determination of sentences before the ECCC arose before both the Trial Chamber and the Supreme Court Chamber in Case 001. In particular, Article 10(1) provides that a 'new provision which prescribes a lighter penalty shall be applicable immediately' and Article 95 states that where the sentence is life imprisonment, but mitigating circumstances are taken into account, the sentence must be between fifteen and thirty years'

---

4 ECCC Agreement, Article 10.
5 ECCC Law, Article 39.
6 Duch Appeal Judgment, above n. 2, para. 344.
7 Internal Rules, Rule 98(5).
8 Duch Trial Judgment, above n. 1, para. 575.

imprisonment.[9] Further, Article 46 provides that a fixed term sentence longer than 30 years is not permissible.[10]

The Trial Chamber did not dwell on the Cambodian provisions given what it called the 'uncertainties and complexities' in the evolution of Cambodian criminal law since the 1956 Penal Code, and the fact that the 2009 Penal Code was not yet fully in force at the time of the judgment.[11] Judge Lavergne dissented from the decision of the majority to allow an intermediate sentence between 30 years' imprisonment and life,[12] taking the view that Cambodian law should be given more prominence:

> I consider the reference to Cambodian law here particularly relevant, owing to the special character of the ECCC, notably because this hybrid court has jurisdiction to prosecute both international and domestic crimes, and because the founding documents make no distinction as to the sentencing regime applicable to these two categories of offences. Thus, while this regime may be deemed *sui generis*, it is difficult to imagine that it is entirely extraneous to domestic law.[13]

The Judge lamented the fact that by allowing a fixed term of imprisonment greater than 30 years, the majority had taken an approach that neither represented a common standard in international proceedings nor corresponded to modern Cambodian law, and furthermore was the least favourable to the accused.[14]

Contrary to Judge Lavergne's opinion and the arguments presented by the accused on appeal, the Supreme Court Chamber took the view that the relationship between Article 39 of the ECCC Law and Article 46 of the 2009 Penal Code had to be considered in the light of the *lex specialis* principle.[15] As the legislation adopted and designed 'specifically for the unique purposes of the ECCC under its mandate, jurisdiction, character and structure', the ECCC Law was regarded as governing the range of penalties in ECCC proceedings.[16] According to the Supreme Court Chamber, Article 668 of the 2009 Penal Code supported this conclusion,

---

9 Cited in Duch Appeal Judgment, above n. 2, para. 346.

10 Ibid, para. 347.

11 Duch Trial Judgment, above n. 1, para. 577.

12 Ibid, para. 595.

13 *Prosecutor v Kaing Guek Eav alias 'Duch'*, ECCC Case File No. 001/18-07-2007/ECCC/TC, Trial Chamber, Separate and Dissenting Opinion of Judge Jean-Marc Lavergne on Sentence, 26 July 2010, para. 5.

14 Ibid, para. 9.

15 Duch Appeal Judgment, above n. 2, para. 348.

16 Ibid, para. 348.

by stating that 'special criminal legislation' is unaffected by the general provision that the Penal Code prevails over other criminal legislation in the event of a conflict.[17] The Supreme Court Chamber therefore considered that the penalty range before the ECCC could be any fixed term between five years' imprisonment and life imprisonment.

As the ECCC Chambers have noted, there is no uniform approach to sentencing before international tribunals.[18] Some of the main purposes of punishment include recognition of the fact that globally accepted laws have to be obeyed by all and that the sentence must be proportionate to the crime and individualised. Gravity of the crime is the starting point—the 'litmus test for the appropriate sentence'[19]—and all relevant aggravating and mitigating factors must be taken into account. The burden of proof on the defence with regard to mitigating factors is considered to be lighter than the burden of proof on the prosecution with regard to aggravating factors.[20] It has also been seen as appropriate to 'impose a single sentence that reflects the totality of the criminal conduct where an accused is convicted of multiple offences.'[21]

3. SENTENCING IN CASE 001

In Case 001, various unusual factors had to be taken into account by the Trial Chamber in sentencing, including Duch's acknowledgement of his 'legal and moral' responsibility for the crimes at S-21, his last-minute request for an acquittal, and the excessive time spent in pre-trial detention. The Co-Prosecutors requested a sentence of life imprisonment but accepted that this could be converted into a fixed term of 40 years as a remedy for Duch's unlawful detention by the Cambodian Military Court and that a further reduction of five years might be appropriate to take account of mitigating factors.[22]

In terms of the gravity of the crimes, the Trial Chamber noted that Duch had been found criminally responsible for 'crimes of a particularly shocking and heinous character' which 'resulted in the execution of no

---

17 Ibid, para. 351.

18 *See* e.g. Duch Trial Judgment, above n. 1, para. 576.

19 Ibid, para. 582 (citing *Prosecutor v Aleksovski*, ICTY Case No. IT-95-14/1-A, Appeals Chamber, Judgment, 24 March 2000, para. 182).

20 Ibid, para. 584; *see* also Nuon Trial Judgment, above n. 3, paras. 1068–70.

21 Duch Trial Judgment, above n. 1, para. 590; Nuon Trial Judgment, above n. 3, para. 1072.

22 Duch Trial Judgment, above n. 1, para. 569.

fewer than 12,272 victims, the majority of whom were also systematically tortured' and that this had occurred 'in furtherance of a politically-motivated policy of discrimination'.[23] Factors considered to be aggravating included Duch's superior position, the high number of victims, and, in relation to certain offences where it did not constitute a legal ingredient, Duch's discriminatory intent.[24] Superior orders and duress were rejected as mitigating factors while Duch's cooperation with the ECCC afforded him some mitigation.[25] The 'mitigating impact' of Duch's expressions of remorse were found to be 'undermined by his failure to offer a full and unequivocal admission of his responsibility'.[26] Duch's propensity for rehabilitation was also taken into account as a mitigating factor.[27] The Trial Chamber concluded on the basis of expert reports that Duch had 'no psychological or psychiatric impairment relevant to his criminal responsibility' and that he was 'an intelligent, well-educated and methodical individual' who was fully aware of his actions and the degree of his responsibility.[28] Character witnesses had spoken of Duch's strong commitment to his studies, his role as a teacher, and his political and religious beliefs, although the Trial Chamber found nothing in this evidence to excuse Duch's criminal conduct.[29]

The Trial Chamber noted that Duch had been in continuous detention from 10 May 1999 until the date of the judgment.[30] The Chamber had previously ruled that Duch's detention by the Cambodian Military Court between 10 May 1999 and 30 July 2007 was 'unlawful and in violation of his rights to a trial within a reasonable time and detention in accordance with the law' and that if convicted, Duch was to be entitled to full credit for the total amount of time spent in pre-trial detention plus a reduction in his sentence as a remedy for the violation of his rights.[31] The Trial Chamber sentenced Duch to a fixed term of imprisonment of 35

---

23 Ibid, para. 597.
24 Ibid, paras. 601–05.
25 Ibid, paras. 606–09.
26 Ibid, para. 610.
27 Ibid, para. 611.
28 Ibid, para. 616.
29 Ibid, paras. 617–22.
30 Ibid, para. 623.
31 Ibid, para. 624 (referring to *Prosecutor v Kaing Guek Eav alias 'Duch'*, ECCC Case File No. 001/18-07-2007/ECCC/TC, Trial Chamber, Decision on Request for Release, 15 June 2009).

years with a reduction of five years for the violation of his rights and credit for time served until the judgment became final.[32]

The Supreme Court Chamber accepted the standard of review adopted by international tribunals to the effect that it would not revise a sentence unless the Trial Chamber has committed a discernible error in exercising its discretion or had failed to follow the applicable law, with the burden being on the appellant to demonstrate an error.[33] The Supreme Court Chamber took a careful look at the mitigating factors considered by the Trial Chamber and considered that the mitigating impact of these factors was limited at best.[34] It concluded that the Trial Chamber had attached undue weight to the mitigating factors and insufficient weight to the underlying gravity of the crimes and the aggravating factors resulting in the imposition of a sentence that did not reflect the gravity of the crimes.[35] Since this error of law invalidated the sentence, the Supreme Court Chamber conducted its own assessment and found that the combination of the high number of deaths for which Duch was responsible and the extended period over which the crimes were committed 'undoubtedly place this case among the gravest before international criminal tribunals'.[36] Duch's leadership role at S-21 and his dedication to his tasks were also emphasised.[37] In conclusion, the Supreme Court Chamber stated:

> The crimes committed by KAING Guek Eav were undoubtedly among the worst in recorded human history. They deserve the highest penalty available to provide a fair and adequate response to the outrage these crimes caused in victims, their families and relatives, the Cambodian people, and all human beings. The Co- Prosecutors did not exaggerate when they referred to S-21 as the 'factory of death.' KAING Guek Eav commanded and operated this factory of death for more than three years. He mercilessly terminated the lives of at least 12,272 individuals, including women and children.[38]

The Supreme Court Chamber noted that the fact that more than 30 years had passed since the commission of the crimes did not lessen the need for a high penalty and imposed a sentence of life imprisonment on

---

[32] Ibid, paras. 631–3.
[33] Duch Appeal Judgment, above n. 2, para. 354.
[34] Ibid, para. 371.
[35] Ibid, para. 373.
[36] Ibid, para. 376.
[37] Ibid, para. 377.
[38] Ibid, para. 380.

Duch.[39] As it concerned the remedy granted by the Trial Chamber, the Supreme Court Chamber found by a majority that in the absence of an abuse of process or responsibility of the ECCC for the infringements there were no legal grounds for awarding compensation.[40] Judges Klonowiecka-Milart and Jayasinghe agreed with the life sentence but would have allowed a remedy in the form of a reduction in sentence.[41] After some discussion and in the light of Cambodian and international law and practice, the Supreme Court Chamber unanimously awarded Duch credit for the entirety of his time spent in detention from 10 May 1999 to the date of the judgment on appeal.[42]

3.1 Public Reaction to the Sentence in Case 001

When the Trial Judgment in Case 001 was handed down, many ordinary citizens who had been anxiously awaiting the first verdict of the ECCC were puzzled by the final figure of 19 years to be served by Duch after the subtraction of the length of his pre-trial detention, as well as the period of compensation awarded in respect of its partial illegality. In their call for the imposition of life imprisonment on appeal, the Co-Prosecutors argued that the 'sentence is manifestly inadequate, given the inherent inhumanity of this factory of torture and death that the Respondent assisted in establishing and presided over for nearly three years'.[43] The Supreme Court Chamber based its re-evaluation of the sentence on purely legal considerations but it may be speculated whether the public sentiment played into their thinking.

Victims and the general public were interviewed to determine their reactions to the sentence. There was general confusion over the precise length of time Duch was actually to serve. Dissatisfaction stemmed from the realisation that Duch might not end up dying in jail, a factor of some importance to survivors of the regime. The findings of a survey of reactions to the verdict in the provinces were summed up as follows:

---

39 Ibid, para. 381.

40 Ibid, para. 390.

41 *Prosecutor v Kaing Guek Eav alias 'Duch'*, ECCC Case File No. 001/18-07-2007-ECCC/SC, Supreme Court Chamber, Appeal Judgment: Partially Dissenting Joint Opinion of Judges Agnieszka Klonowiecka-Milart and Chandra Nihal Jayasinghe, 3 February 2012, paras. 1, 31. See further Chapter 6.

42 Duch Appeal Judgment, above n. 2, para. 404.

43 *Prosecutor v Kaing Guek Eav alias 'Duch'*, ECCC Case File No. 001/18-07-2007-ECCC/SC, Office of the Co-Prosecutor, Co-Prosecutors' Appeal against the Judgment of the Trial Chamber in the Case of Kaing Guek Eav alias Duch, 13 October 2010, para. 8.

> First, many who reject the 35-year sentence feel that the brutal acts of Duch deserve a harsher sentence such as life imprisonment. Second, those that accept the 35-year sentence do so because they think that he will die in prison. Among those that reject the 19-year sentence, many feel 19 years is vastly disproportionate to his crimes and that he could possibly live after serving his sentence. The few that accept the 19-year sentence cite being sympathetic to his age, believe that he will die in prison, or reason according to the teachings of Buddhism. Lastly, as more information on the mitigating factors, which reduced the sentence to 19 years, became available, the majority of people (… who believed that the sentence is 35 years and were satisfied), instantly became dissatisfied with the 19 years. Overall, there is a feeling of dissatisfaction and to a lesser extent, anger, among survivors of the Pol Pot regime.[44]

Notably, most of those who were dissatisfied with the term of 35 years favoured life imprisonment although there were a few calls for the death penalty, mainly from people who were unaware that it was constitutionally prohibited. Kim Hauoy of Rumlech commune, Pursat province, accepted the 35-year sentence not because she wanted Duch to die in prison, but because she never believed there would be a tribunal in the first place and because she wanted reconciliation. She observed: 'If Duch were executed that would not bring back my parents.'[45] Another interesting observation was that of Pel Kimlang of Svay Khleang Commune, Kampong Cham province, who explained:

> We follow the Buddha, and he asks that we forgive, so if there are three choices of release, execution, or imprisonment, I would choose the middle choice of imprisonment so that Duch can have a few years to be with his family and die at home because he also has a wife and children.[46]

Following the Trial Chamber's verdict, Youk Chhang, the Director of the Documentation Centre of Cambodia commented:

> The Duch verdict is not incorrect. Frustration with the sentence was bound to run high. Had the sentence been a bit longer, it would perhaps have provided greater satisfaction to the majority of the survivors, but nothing would have satisfied them completely. You could sentence him to more than 14,000 years, for each life, and even that wouldn't make it fair. But, finally, there's official

---

[44] D.Q. Keo, 'Disarray and Disappointment after Duch Verdict', *Searching for the Truth* (Magazine of the Documentation Center of Cambodia), Third Quarter 2010, pp. 5–12, p. 8, <http://www.d.dccam.org/Projects/Magazines/Image_Eng/pdf/3rd_Quarter_2010.pdf> [accessed 30 June 2017].

[45] Ibid, p. 9.

[46] Ibid, p. 10.

> accountability. Now it is necessary to conduct meaningful outreach about the verdict to increase support for the Court in advance of Case 002, the next and most important trial.[47]

Reactions of victims to the life sentence substituted by the Supreme Court Chamber suggested that there was a greater sense of justice having been done while the violation of Duch's own rights remained a matter of concern for some local and international NGOs.[48]

4. SENTENCING IN CASE 002/01

In Case 002/01, the Trial Chamber was guided by the Supreme Court Chamber's legal assessment in Case 001 and noted that factors relevant to an evaluation of the gravity of the crimes included 'the large number of victims, the brutal and inhumane circumstances of the offences, the lasting impact of these crimes on the Cambodian people, and the key role of both Accused in the preparation and commission of the crimes'.[49] The Trial Chamber focused on the large number of victims of crimes during the first two phases of the movement of population—between 2,330,000 to 2,430,000 people—'among the highest of any decided case concerning international crimes'.[50] Moreover, these crimes had been committed across a broad geographical area, namely the whole of Cambodia, over a period of almost two years. General aggravating circumstances included the fact that the crimes were committed against vulnerable and defenceless individuals.[51] More specifically, Nuon Chea and Khieu Samphan were both seen to have abused their positions of authority and influence.[52] Moreover, they were well-educated individuals who understood the consequences of their actions.[53] Limited weight as mitigating factors

---

[47] Cited in D.Q. Keo and S. Nhean, 'Duch Can Never be a Free Man: Youk Chhang', *Searching for the Truth* (Magazine of the Documentation Center of Cambodia), Third Quarter 2010, p. 3, p. 3, <http://www.d.dccam.org/Projects/Magazines/Image_Eng/pdf/3rd_Quarter_2010.pdf> [accessed 30 June 2017].

[48] J.D. Ciorciari and A. Heindel, *Hybrid Justice: The Extraordinary Chambers in the Courts of Cambodia* (Ann Arbor, Michigan, University of Michigan Press, 2014), p. 132.

[49] Nuon Trial Judgment, above n. 3, para. 1073 (citing arguments of the Co-Prosecutors).

[50] Ibid, para. 1075.

[51] Ibid, para. 1082.

[52] Ibid, para. 1081.

[53] Ibid, paras. 1086, 1089.

was given in respect of the cooperation of both accused with the ECCC and their advanced ages, as well as Khieu Samphan's purported good character.[54]

The Trial Chamber took the view that Nuon Chea's criminal responsibility exceeded that of Khieu Samphan but that a life sentence was the appropriate penalty for both accused.[55] The Trial Chamber went on to note that there were factors such as the much greater number of victims, and the greater number of crimes and their gravity, that indicated 'far greater culpability' on the part of Nuon Chea and Khieu Samphan as compared to Duch.[56] However, the Trial Chamber found itself unable to reflect these distinctions in the sentences imposed as a result of the 'precedent' set by the Supreme Court Chamber.[57]

The Supreme Court Chamber upheld the sentences despite having overturned certain legal and factual findings of the Trial Chamber. In particular, it found that the Trial Chamber's assessment of the gravity of the crimes remained apt.[58] The Supreme Court Chamber also took into account Nuon Chea's and Khieu Samphan's 'complete lack of consideration for the ultimate fate of the Cambodian people, especially the most vulnerable groups, the fact that the crimes were not isolated events but occurred over an extended period of time' and their significant roles in the commission of these crimes.[59]

4.1 Confiscation of Assets in Case 002/01

The Trial Chamber was unable to identify any personal property or money in the possession of Nuon Chea or Khieu Samphan that had been acquired unlawfully or by criminal conduct. There were therefore no assets that could be the subject of a confiscation order under Article 39 (new) of the ECCC Law.[60] The accused in Case 002 had been found to be indigent.[61]

---

[54] Ibid, paras. 1090–8.

[55] Ibid, paras. 1105–07.

[56] Ibid, para. 1105.

[57] Ibid.

[58] Ibid, para. 1120.

[59] Ibid.

[60] Ibid, para. 1108.

[61] Ibid, para. 1124, footnote 3225, mentioning that the 'Co-Investigating Judges and the Pre-Trial Chamber have both denied Civil Parties' requests to undertake investigative action concerning properties owned by the Charged Persons including measures to preserve such properties for the purpose of reparations'.

5. CONCLUSION

Sentencing is not an exact science and the ECCC is not alone among international or internationalised tribunals in failing to establish any meaningful scale of punishment, which in any case would be impossible given the small number of cases. Penalties reflect individual facts and circumstances and vary widely from the death penalty where it is available (for example, in the proceedings concerning international crimes in Iraq and Bangladesh) to single figure terms of imprisonment for crimes against humanity or even genocide.[62] The most interesting aspect of the ECCC's sentencing practice, which does not in fact relate directly to sentencing, is the ultimate decision by a majority of the Supreme Court Chamber to deny Duch a remedy in respect of his unlawful detention by the Cambodian Military Court. This decision was criticised by NGOs who observed that it 'may be perceived as a case of public opinion trumping human rights'.[63] While the majority's decision is legally supportable, it tends to confirm the ECCC's detachment from the domestic criminal process when there were shared goals and, as the dissenting judges observed, a degree of 'shared responsibility' concerning Duch's trial.

There is a possible correlation between the recognition of Buddhism as the State religion in Cambodia and the abolition of the death penalty in 1989. Punishments in ancient times appeared strongly retributive. Ven Tep Vong, an influential monk in Cambodia who was re-ordained in 1979 following the Vietnamese defeat of the Khmer Rouge, was a witness in the 1979 trial of Pol Pot and Ieng Sary. He stated at the time that the perpetrators had 'lost their "human nature"' from the Buddhist perspective, and concluded: 'these savage beasts should be turned upside down like bats, with their legs in the air above their heads, and once they have

---

[62] *See* further, S. D'Ascoli, *Sentencing in International Criminal Law: the UN Ad Hoc Tribunals and Future Perspectives for the ICC* (Oxford/Portland, Oregon, Hart Publishing, 2011).

[63] 'Cambodia: Khmer Rouge Judgment Welcome, But Raises Human Rights Concerns', Amnesty International, 3 February 2012, <https://www.amnesty.org/en/latest/news/2012/02/cambodia-khmer-rouge-judgment-welcome-raises-human-rights-concerns/> [accessed 29 June 2017]. *See* also Open Society Justice Initiative, 'Report: Recent Developments at the Extraordinary Chambers in the Courts of Cambodia', Cambodia Tribunal Monitor, February 2012, <http://www.cambodiatribunal.org/sites/default/files/reports/cambodia-eccc-20120223.pdf> [accessed 29 June 2017].

fallen they will be condemned to hell.'[64] He appeared to soften his approach in later years and feared that a tribunal would be based on a 'politics of anger' (retribution) and not lead to the truth. According to Ian Harris, the contemporary Cambodian Buddhist view on accountability is that it should conform to *Theravāda* principles and reconciliation should take precedence over retribution.[65] Justice in the next life in the context of Buddhist cosmology does not exclude human justice and punishment in this life. There is a commonly-held belief that Khmer Rouge members who perpetrated crimes will be reborn as cockroaches which may assist in providing a coping mechanism for victims, especially in the absence of 'human justice' in respect of lower level perpetrators.

It remains to be seen how the Trial Chamber will approach sentencing in the event of convictions in Case 002/02. While it has been established that a single sentence may be imposed to reflect the totality of the criminal conduct in the event of convictions for multiple offences in the same case, it is unclear whether the same principle applies to convictions in two separate cases. The Trial Chamber could refrain from imposing an additional penalty in Case 002/02 and simply record any increased culpability of the accused. Or it could impose penalties to be served concurrently. This situation does not appear to have arisen directly in international or internationalised proceedings.[66] It could potentially have

---

[64] I. Harris, '"Onslaught on Human Beings": A Theravāda Buddhist Perspective on Accountability for Crimes Committed in the Democratic Kampuchea Period', in J. Ramji and B. van Schaack (eds), *Bringing the Khmer Rouge to Justice: Prosecuting Mass Violence before the Cambodian Courts* (Lewiston, New York, Edwin Mellon Press, 2005), pp. 59–95, p. 83 (citing 'Document 2.1.2.03: Tep Vung, Buddhist Superior', in H.J. de Nike, J. Quigley and K.J. Robinson (eds), *Genocide in Cambodia: Documents from the Trial of Pol Pot and Ieng Sary* (Philadelphia, Pennsylvania, University of Pennsylvania Press, 2000), pp. 149–53, p. 152).

[65] Harris, ibid, p. 82 (Harris suggests that Article 27 of the Cambodian Constitution which permits the King to grant partial or complete amnesty should be understood against the historical background of Buddhist approaches to crime and punishment).

[66] A. Heindel, 'Managing Enormous Mass Crimes Indictments: The ECCC Severance Experiment', in S.M. Meisenberg and I. Stegmiller (eds), *The Extraordinary Chambers in the Courts of Cambodia: Assessing their Contribution to International Criminal Law* (The Hague, T.M.C. Asser Press, 2016), pp. 435–59, p. 437: 'The ECCC is the first mass crimes court to proceed with consecutive trials based on one indictment.' *Prosecutor v Nuon Chea* and *Khieu Samphan*, ECCC Case File No. 002/19-09-2007-ECCC/TC, Office of the Co-Prosecutors, Co-Prosecutors' Response to Khieu Samphan's Request for Stay of Proceedings or Disqualification of Judges, 4 September 2014, para. 17: 'The severance of

arisen in the proceedings against Saddam Hussein before the Iraqi High Tribunal as these were divided from the outset into separate cases concerning different events, but Saddam Hussein was hanged after his conviction in the first trial so no further trials could be held. Guidance may be sought in domestic practice and parallel contempt proceedings against persons on trial for international crimes before international tribunals.[67]

Case 002 has created a unique situation in international criminal law. Never before have accused persons at an international or internationalized criminal tribunal been subject to a second trial based on separate factual allegations that are part of the same charging document.'

[67] For example, Vojislav Šešelj was convicted three times of contempt and sentenced to periods of 15 months, 18 months and two years' imprisonment respectively while on trial before the ICTY. See ICTY Press Release, 'Vojislav Šešelj sentenced to two years imprisonment for Contempt of the Tribunal', 28 June 2012 <http://www.icty.org/en/press/vojislav-%C5%A1e%C5%A1elj-sentenced-two-years-imprisonment-contempt-tribunal> [accessed 19 July 2017].

10. Victims

1. INTRODUCTION

The first international Co-Prosecutor, Robert Petit, once noted in an interview that regardless of the 'types of crimes and the sheer magnitude of them and the sheer horror of them ... it still remains the same principle. You're representing the victims. The pressure is the same in that you have a responsibility to represent the voices [of] the victims'.[1] In Extraordinary Chambers in the Courts of Cambodia (ECCC) proceedings, the victims may additionally speak for themselves and participate as civil parties. This feature of the ECCC has presented a major challenge in terms of achieving the appropriate balance between the fair trial rights of the accused and the rights of the civil parties, while simultaneously ensuring that trials proceed expeditiously.[2]

The procedures for civil party participation and reparations claims were outlined in Chapter 4. One notable aspect of these procedures has been their evolution during the lifespan of the Court. Accommodating civil parties under the relatively open scheme originally envisaged by the Internal Rules and based on Cambodian practice was just about manageable in Case 001. Indeed, at the time the Pre-Trial Chamber (PTC) rendered its decision to allow civil parties to participate during the judicial investigation, only four civil parties had been admitted by the Co-Investigating Judges.[3] The Pre-Trial Chamber considered that it would be improper to speculate about the implications of its decision for

---

[1] 'Canadian Takes Key Role in Cambodia Tribunal', *Embassy*, 28 June 2006, <https://www.globalpolicy.org/component/content/article/163/28910.html> [accessed 3 July 2017].

[2] For a comprehensive study see FIDH report (authored by International Civil Party Lead Co-Lawyer M. Guiraud), *Victims' Rights before the Extraordinary Chambers in the Courts of Cambodia, A Mixed Record for Civil Parties*, 2012, <https://www.fidh.org/IMG/pdf/eccc_victrights_rep_nov2012_en_web.pdf> [accessed 19 July 2017].

[3] *Prosecutor v Nuon Chea*, ECCC Case File No. 002/19-09-2007-ECCC/OCIJ (PTC01), Pre-Trial Chamber, Decision on Civil Party Participation in Provisional Detention Appeals, 20 March 2008, para. 3.

the future.[4] Civil party participation threatened to overwhelm the proceedings in Case 002 due to the sheer number of victims who were potentially eligible. In fact, a total of 3,869 civil parties were finally admitted in Case 002.[5] It is therefore little surprise that the ECCC felt compelled to 'streamline' procedures and reign in participatory rights via changes to the Internal Rules adopted by the plenary of judges and to some extent through its jurisprudence.[6] The purpose of these amendments was 'to meet the requirements of trials of mass crimes *and* to ensure that ECCC proceedings responded more fully to the needs of victims'.[7] The Supreme Court Chamber has referred to the 'mosaic of the civil party regime in the ECCC Internal Rules and numerous revisions to that regime'.[8] The first main change concerned the admissibility of civil party claims, which would be determined entirely during the investigative phase, following the negative experience in Case 001 where the Trial Chamber was called upon to determine both the admissibility of civil party claims and their substance. The second main change was to require the formation of a consolidated group of civil parties during the trial phase whose interests at trial would be represented exclusively by the Civil Party Lead Co-Lawyers.

The Pre-Trial Chamber has observed that 'the inclusion of civil parties in proceedings is in recognition of the stated pursuit of national reconciliation'.[9] National reconciliation is not something the ECCC can achieve on its own. The involvement of victims in the ECCC process has

---

4 Ibid, para. 48.

5 *Prosecutor v Nuon Chea* and *Khieu Samphan*, ECCC Case File No. 002/19-09-2007-ECCC/SC, Supreme Court Chamber, Appeal Judgment, 23 November 2016, para. 1111 ('Nuon Appeal Judgment').

6 *Prosecutor v Nuon Chea* and *Khieu Samphan*, ECCC Case File No. 002/19-09-2007/ECCC/TC, Trial Chamber, Case 002/01 Judgement, 7 August 2014, para. 1109 ('Nuon Trial Judgment').

7 Ibid, para. 1109 (*Emphasis added*).

8 *Prosecutor v Kaing Guek Eav alias 'Duch'*, ECCC Case File No. 001/18-07-2007-ECCC/SC, Supreme Court Chamber, Appeal Judgment, 3 February 2012, para. 412 ('Duch Appeal Judgment').

9 *Prosecutor v Nuon Chea*, ECCC Case File No. 002/19-09-2007-ECCC/OCIJ (PTC01), Pre-Trial Chamber, Decision on Civil Party Participation in Provisional Detention Appeals, 20 March 2008, para. 37 (referring to United Nations General Assembly, Khmer Rouge Trials, A/RES/57/228, 18 December 2002, which is in turn mentioned in the preamble to the Internal Rules as recognizing 'the legitimate concern of the Government and the people of Cambodia in the pursuit of justice and national reconciliation, stability, peace and security').

depended heavily on the support of civil society. Local NGOs have played a significant role in raising awareness, providing information and encouraging victims to come forward in cooperation with the ECCC's Victims Support Section. It has been estimated that about 84 per cent of victim application forms were submitted to the ECCC through intermediary NGOs.[10] Furthermore, since there was initially no legal aid scheme in place for civil parties, NGOs arranged for legal representation, often on a *pro bono* basis.[11] Managing the expectations of victims has been a key issue for both the ECCC and collaborating NGOs, and while there has been a genuine earnestness to deliver on all fronts, there is at the same time a manifest potential for the emergence of mixed or even conflicting messages.

This chapter highlights some of the developments in the ECCC's jurisprudence concerning civil parties, as they reflect and intersect with the relevant rule changes, focusing on admissibility, participation and reparations. The chapter concludes with a tentative assessment of the success of the ECCC's civil party participation scheme.

2. ADMISSIBILITY OF CIVIL PARTY CLAIMS

According to Internal Rule 23 *bis* (1):

> In order for Civil Party action to be admissible, the Civil Party applicant shall:
>
> a) be clearly identified; and
> b) demonstrate as a direct consequence of at least one of the crimes alleged against the Charged Person, that he or she has in fact suffered physical, material or psychological injury upon which a claim of collective and moral reparation might be based.

The essence of this definition of a civil party (originally contained in Internal Rule 23(2)) has survived the amendments to the Internal Rules,

---

[10] C. Sperfeldt, 'Cambodian Civil Society and the Khmer Rouge Tribunal', *The International Journal of Transitional Justice*, vol. 6, 2012, pp. 149–60, p. 151; K. Tibori-Szabó and M. Hirst (eds), *Victim Participation in International Criminal Justice, Practitioners' Guide* (The Hague, T.M.C Asser Press, 2017), pp. 91–93.

[11] Sperfeldt, ibid, p. 151.

'thus confirming its lasting validity before the ECCC'.[12] It is based on Article 13 of the Cambodian Criminal Procedure Code (CPC), which mirrors Article 2 of the French Code of Criminal Procedure. The Supreme Court Chamber had the occasion to address the question of who may be admitted as a civil party before the ECCC in the appeal in Case 001. It should be recalled that in Case 001, the Trial Chamber had determined the issue of admissibility. The Trial Chamber considered that the injury suffered by the victim must be the direct consequence of the criminal conduct of the accused as also provided in Article 13 of the CPC.[13] The Trial Chamber considered in detail whether Duch could be found responsible for the harm alleged by the civil parties who claimed to be survivors of S-21 or S-24, or alternatively who claimed kinship or special bonds of affection of dependency in relation to the immediate victims of S-21 or S-24.[14] Two questions arose before the Supreme Court Chamber concerning the notion of a victim, namely whether immediate family members of a direct victim were automatically included in this notion, and whether special bonds of affection or dependency needed to be demonstrated in the case of non-immediate family of the deceased direct victims.[15]

The Supreme Court Chamber emphasised that the notion of a victim and hence the admissibility of a civil party claim had to be interpreted in accordance with Cambodian procedure. It was only if Cambodian procedure failed to provide an answer to a relevant question that guidance could be sought in procedural rules established at the international level.[16] Neither Article 13 of the 2007 Code of Criminal Procedure nor the original Internal Rule 23(2) was seen to contravene international standards and the scope of the term 'civil party' at the ECCC was therefore governed by these provisions.[17]

According to the Supreme Court Chamber, '[c]ritical to the definition of the civil party in these legal instruments is not a formal designation of a specific class of persons, but the substantive criterion of an actual

---

[12] Duch Appeal Judgment, above n. 8, para. 412. *See* also *Prosecutor v Kaing Guek Eav alias 'Duch'*, ECCC Case File No. 001/18-07-2007/ECCC/TC, Trial Chamber, Judgment, 26 July 2010, para. 640, footnote 1072 ('Duch Trial Judgment').

[13] Duch Trial Judgment, ibid, para. 642.

[14] Ibid, paras. 644, 650.

[15] Duch Appeal Judgment, above n. 8, para. 408.

[16] Ibid, para. 414.

[17] Ibid.

injury resulting as a direct consequence of the crime'.[18] Any injury (whether physical, material or psychological) resulting from the crime, as the defining (and limiting) criterion for admissibility was seen to include anatomical or functional biological damage such as a wound, mutilation, disfiguration, disease, loss or dysfunction of organs, or death; a material object's loss of value, such as complete or partial destruction of personal property, or loss of income; or mental disorders or psychiatric trauma, such as post-traumatic stress disorder.[19]

The Supreme Court Chamber used the term 'direct victim' to refer to 'persons whose rights were violated or endangered by the crime charged' which in Case 001 included the 12,273 detainees at S-21.[20] An 'indirect victim' would be a person who suffered injury as a direct consequence of the crimes committed against the direct victim(s), such as psychological harm.[21] The Supreme Court Chamber found that direct and indirect victims had autonomous rights, that persons within each category could meet the requirement of injury as a direct consequence of the offence, and that the category of indirect victims was not restricted to a particular class of persons such as family members.[22] As it concerned the question whether indirect victims who were not immediate family members needed to prove 'special bonds or affection or dependence' with the direct victim in order for their civil party applications to be admissible, the Supreme Court Chamber found that this purported requirement was rather a 'discretionary presumption' inherent in the notion of an injury to indirect victims and foreseeable to any proposed civil party.[23] Immediate family might be presumed to have a special bond of affection with the direct victim and therefore discharged of the burden of proving an injury.[24]

In Case 001, the civil parties appealed against the 'two-step review process' applied by the Trial Chamber to determine admissibility, consisting of an initial assessment prior to, during, or shortly after the Initial Hearing and a final assessment in the trial judgment.[25] The result had been that some victims who participated actively in the trial proceedings lost their civil party status at the very end of the process. Another

---

18 Ibid, para. 410.
19 Ibid, para. 415.
20 Ibid, para. 416.
21 Ibid, para. 417.
22 Ibid, para. 418.
23 Ibid, para. 447.
24 Ibid, para. 448.
25 Ibid, para. 453.

unfortunate effect was that victims who had lost their civil party status in the trial judgment would be time-barred from appealing against the Trial Chamber's decision on reparations even if they succeeded in having their civil party status reassigned on appeal. In many, but not all, of these instances, the victim's civil party status had been challenged by the defence during the trial. The Trial Chamber had taken the position that despite a declaration of admissibility at an early stage of the proceedings, it was only at the end of the hearing that it could establish the 'existence of wrongdoing attributable to the Accused which has a direct causal connection to a demonstrable injury personally suffered by the Civil Party'.[26]

The Supreme Court Chamber turned first to the CPC which envisaged that a civil party claim would be examined on the merits at the same time as the determination on criminal responsibility of an accused and that civil parties effectively participated in the trial at their own risk of a negative outcome. In contrast, the ECCC process provided for judicial scrutiny over the admissibility of civil party applications from the investigative phase. Nonetheless, since neither the granting of interim recognition by the Co-Investigating Judges nor a decision on admissibility by the Trial Chamber were envisaged under the Internal Rules as originally formulated, these actions were open to different interpretations. The Supreme Court Chamber looked to the practice of the International Criminal Court (ICC), and noted that in contrast to victim participation at the ICC, the ECCC conferred full participation rights.[27] The ICC Chambers were seen to have a wide discretion in deciding victim participation at different stages of the proceedings and ultimately the practice of the ICC was not considered to provide helpful guidance.[28] The Supreme Court Chamber took the view that considering different factors, 'including the right to representation, fairness, legal certainty, and economy of proceedings, there is a legal interest in having the full "cast"

---

26 Duch Trial Judgment, above n. 12, para. 639.

27 Duch Appeal Judgment, above n. 8, para. 478. For a comparison of the ECCC and ICC practice, *see* B. Zhang, 'Recognizing the Limits of Victims Participation: A Comparative Examination of the Victim Participation Schemes at the ECCC and the ICC', in S.M. Meisenberg and I. Stegmiller (eds), *The Extraordinary Chambers in the Courts of Cambodia: Assessing their Contribution to International Criminal Law* (The Hague, T.M.C. Asser Press, 2016), pp. 515–34.

28 Duch Appeal Judgment, above n. 8, paras. 484, 486.

in the proceedings established as much as possible before the commencement of trial'.[29] Although the Trial Chamber was not found to have acted outside the Internal Rules, which in any case were lacking at the time, they were found to have applied a legal framework that was 'patently obscure'.[30] The Supreme Court Chamber did not consider that the Trial Chamber had committed an error of law by evaluating civil party status in the trial judgment. However, in view of the 'fundamental misunderstanding between the Trial Chamber and the Civil Party Appellants as to the merits and legal effect of the initial review of their applications', the Supreme Court Chamber allowed the appellants to submit additional evidence on appeal and conducted a fresh review of their applications.[31] This required establishing the correct standard of proof for assessing the criteria of admissibility at the reparations phase of proceedings. The Supreme Court Chamber decided, after reviewing the limited existing practice, that the standard of 'more likely than not' that had subsequently been incorporated into the Internal Rules with respect to admissibility decisions taken during the investigative phase was the correct one.[32] Applying this standard, the Supreme Court Chamber reversed the Trial Chamber's decisions in respect of the admissibility of certain civil parties.

The extensive debate over the admissibility of civil party claims in Case 001 exposed several *lacunae* in the legal framework and missteps by the Trial Chamber which could only partly be redressed by the Supreme Court Chamber's analysis. The Internal Rules had already been amended by the time the Supreme Court Chamber heard the appeal in Case 001 so that the admissibility of civil parties in Case 002 was entirely within the domain of the Co-Investigative Judges and the Pre-Trial Chamber.

At the conclusion of the investigation in Case 002, the Pre-Trial Chamber was required to determine a significant number of appeals by civil parties against decisions by the Co-Investigating Judges denying their civil party status. In one instance, in which 95 civil party appeals were joined, the Pre-Trial Chamber reviewed the applications afresh having found that the Co-Investigating Judges erred in failing to provide

---

[29] Ibid, para. 489.
[30] Ibid, para. 493.
[31] Ibid, para. 501.
[32] Ibid, paras. 523, 531. *See* Internal Rules, Rule 23 *bis* (1), final sentence: 'When considering the admissibility of the Civil Party application, the Co-Investigating Judges shall be satisfied that facts alleged in support of the application are more likely than not to be true'.

adequate reasons for its decisions, in viewing the causal link as being between the harm and the facts investigated rather than between the harm and any of the crimes alleged, and applying an approach to the term 'injury' that was too restrictive, especially given the nature of victimisation from mass atrocities.[33] The Pre-Trial Chamber regarded Internal Rule 23 *bis* (1) as including:

- The existence of a causal link between the crimes and the injury;
- Injury;
- Proof of identification;
- Level of proof.[34]

Regarding the first element of a causal link, the Pre-Trial Chamber noted the collective dimension of the alleged crimes which spanned the whole of Cambodia and the modes of liability which included a joint criminal enterprise, as well as their collective (and not merely individual) effect.[35] The Pre-Trial Chamber agreed with the Co-Investigating Judges (and the ICC) that an injury must be personal but does not necessarily have to be direct and considered that the cultural context needed to be taken into account.[36] The Pre-Trial Chamber applied a presumption of collective injury in cases in which a civil party applicant suffering psychological injury could not substantiate a close relationship with the immediate victim.[37] The level of proof—more likely than not to be true—was set out in the Internal Rule 23,[38] and the Pre-Trial Chamber took a flexible approach to proof of identity. According to the Pre-Trial Chamber,

---

33 *Prosecutor v Nuon Chea, Ieng Sary, Ieng Thirith* and *Khieu Samphan*, ECCC Case File No. 002/19-09-2007-ECCC/OCIJ (PTC76, PTC112, PTC113, PTC114, PTC115, PTC142, PTC157, PTC164, PTC165 and PTC172), Pre-Trial Chamber, Decision on Appeals against Orders of the Co-Investigating Judges on the Admissibility of Civil Party Applications, 24 June 2011, paras. 37, 39, 42, 44. *See* also *Prosecutor v Nuon Chea, Ieng Sary, Ieng Thirith* and *Khieu Samphan*, ECCC Case File No. 002/19-09-2007-ECCC/OCIJ (PTC 47 and 53), Pre-Trial Chamber, Decision on the Reconsideration of the Admissibility of Civil Party Applications, 1 July 2011.

34 *Prosecutor v Nuon Chea, Ieng Sary, Ieng Thirith* and *Khieu Samphan*, ECCC Case File No. 002/19-09-2007-ECCC/OCIJ (PTC76, PTC112, PTC113, PTC114, PTC115, PTC142, PTC157, PTC164, PTC165 and PTC172), Pre-Trial Chamber, Decision on Appeals against Orders of the Co-Investigating Judges on the Admissibility of Civil Party Applications, 24 June 2011, para. 57.

35 Ibid, para. 42.

36 Ibid, para. 83.

37 Ibid, para. 93.

38 Ibid, para. 94.

admitting a larger number of civil parties under its more generous approach would not have an adverse effect on the rights of the accused especially in view of the 'simplified purpose of civil party action at trial' envisaged by the amended rules.[39] Following its *de novo* review, the Pre-Trial Chamber allowed all but one of the appellants' applications.[40] Judge Marchi-Uhel dissented in relation to a large proportion of these applications, finding that a *de novo* review was not warranted and that the majority's expansive approach was not justified.[41]

In Case 002, there was no possibility for the question of admissibility to arise before the Supreme Court Chamber as a result of the amendments to the rules. Indeed, a shortcoming of the revised system for determining admissibility is the short time frame in which civil parties can appeal against the rejection of their applications and in which the defence can appeal against the decisions to admit certain civil parties.[42] It is also difficult for civil parties to demonstrate that they have suffered an injury as a consequence of one of the crimes alleged against the accused when the investigation is still ongoing.

3. ROLE AND RIGHTS OF CIVIL PARTIES

In the ECCC's first significant decision on civil party participation, the Pre-Trial Chamber permitted the four civil parties then admitted in Case 001 to participate in pre-trial proceedings, including those relating to detention.[43] *Amicus curiae* briefs on the matter were even sought and five

39 Ibid, para. 97.

40 Ibid, pp. 51–5.

41 *Prosecutor v Nuon Chea, Ieng Sary, Ieng Thirith* and *Khieu Samphan*, ECCC Case File No. 002/19-09-2007-ECCC/OCIJ (PTC76, PTC112, PTC113, PTC114, PTC115, PTC142, PTC157, PTC164, PTC165 and PTC172), Pre-Trial Chamber, Decision on Appeals against Orders of the Co-Investigating Judges on the Admissibility of Civil Party Applications: Separate and Partially Dissenting Opinion of Judge Catherine Marchi-Uhel, 24 June 2011, paras. 2, 6.

42 K.A.A. Khan and D. Rudy, 'The Right of the Civil Parties to Participate v. the Right of the Accused to a Fair and Expeditious Trial: Challenges at the ECCC?', *Oxford Transitional Justice Research Working Paper Series: Justice and Reconciliation in Cambodia*, 10 June 2010, pp. 4–5, <https://www.law.ox.ac.uk/sites/files/oxlaw/khanandrudy_therightofcivilpartiesvtherightoftheaccused1.pdf> [accessed 3 July 2017].

43 *Prosecutor v Nuon Chea*, ECCC Case File No. 002/19-09-2007-ECCC/OCIJ (PTC01), Pre-Trial Chamber, Decision on Civil Party Participation in Provisional Detention Appeals, 20 March 2008, paras. 36, 38, 40–2, 49.

were received.[44] The Pre-Trial Chamber found that the Cambodian Criminal Procedure Code envisaged the participation of civil parties during the investigation.[45] Reference was also made to 'international standards' supportive of this position. The Pre-Trial Chamber interpreted the right of civil parties to participate in criminal proceedings by supporting the prosecution to mean participation in all criminal proceedings including appeals against provisional detention. Thus, 'Civil Parties have active rights to participate starting from the investigative phase of the procedure.'[46] The fact that civil parties could participate in appeals against provisional detention even though they did not participate in the initial detention hearing (as they had not been notified of the judicial investigation until the detention order was issued) was not seen to create a problem as any imbalance between the rights of the parties could be addressed by allowing the defence adequate opportunity to respond. In contrast to ICC procedures, there was no need for civil parties before the ECCC to show a special interest in any stage of the proceeding.

The Supreme Court Chamber noted in Case 001 that once admitted in the proceedings, a civil party acquires a number of procedural rights and may:[47]

(i) be afforded protective measures;
(ii) be represented by lawyers;
(iii) be questioned in the presence of their lawyer;
(iv) request investigative actions;
(v) lodge appeals;
(vi) participate as a party in appeals generally;
(vii) support the prosecution;
(viii) make a claim for moral and collective reparations;
(ix) participate in trial proceedings;
(x) call witnesses;
(xi) access the case file;
(xii) respond to preliminary objections;
(xiii) question the accused;
(xiv) exercise the right of audience;
(xv) make written submissions; and
(xvi) make closing statements.

---

44 Ibid, para. 14.
45 Ibid, para. 29.
46 Ibid, para. 36.
47 Duch Appeal Judgment, above n. 8, para. 488.

The participatory rights of civil parties during the pre-trial stage have remained largely unaffected by the rule changes. However, during the trial phase, civil parties have to some extent lost their individual voices as they must form a consolidated group whose interests are collected, coordinated and represented by a national and an international Lead Co-Lawyer. In both Cases 001 and 002, the civil parties were not permitted to make opening remarks as there was no provision for them to do so in the Internal Rules[48] and were denied (by a majority) the opportunity to make submissions on sentencing.[49] Nonetheless, civil parties (through the Lead Co-Lawyers) are the first to make their closing statement under Internal Rule 94(1), have equivalent rights to other parties when it comes to questioning witnesses and the accused, and were in fact frequently given the floor in Case 002 to make submissions or question witnesses through their own lawyers.[50] While there has been an undeniable shift from the more individualised participation in Case 001 to the more collective participation in Case 002 it is difficult to see how the trial in Case 002/01 could have proceeded without a degree of 'streamlining'.

The streamlined procedures were aimed at preserving a balance between the rights of the parties and ensuring manageability and efficiency. From a defence perspective, the changes arguably did not go far enough, as although having one consolidated group of civil parties led by the Lead Co-Lawyers undoubtedly reduced the length of the trial, the scope of civil party participation remained open.[51] From the perspective of the civil parties, or at least their lawyers, the shifting nature of their role and rights and status as an unequal player was a source of frustration. As Zhang has noted, it is possible to admit the need for

---

48 *See* I. Stegmiller, 'Legal Developments of Civil Party Participation at the ECCC', in S.M. Meisenberg and I. Stegmiller (eds), *The Extraordinary Chambers in the Courts of Cambodia: Assessing their Contribution to International Criminal Law* (The Hague, T.M.C. Asser Press, 2016), pp. 535–50, pp. 540–1 (especially footnote 29).

49 Nuon Trial Judgment, above n. 6, para. 1064 (citing *Prosecutor v Kaing Guek Eav alias 'Duch'*, ECCC Case File No. 001/18-07-2007/ECCC/TC, Trial Chamber, Decision on Civil Party Co-Lawyers' Joint Request for a Ruling on the Standing of Civil Party Lawyers to Make Submissions on Sentencing and Directions Concerning the Questioning of the Accused, Experts and Witnesses Testifying on Character, 9 October 2009).

50 *See* Zhang, above n. 27, p. 524.

51 *See* Khan and Rudy, above n. 42, p. 2.

improvements within the new framework while at the same time recognising that the efficiency of a criminal trial must be guaranteed.[52] It would be too much to expect the ECCC to design a perfect system from the outset, but the envisaged lifespan of the Court does not allow much time for experimentation.

4. REPARATIONS

Civil party participation before the ECCC includes a right to pursue a civil action for collective and moral reparations against an accused for harm that is directly attributable to the crimes for which the accused is convicted.[53] In Case 001, the Trial Chamber granted reparations in the form of a compilation of all statements of apology and acknowledgements of responsibility made by Duch during the course of the trial to be posted on the ECCC's official website within 14 days of the date of the judgement becoming final.[54] All other civil party claims were rejected.[55]

On appeal in Case 001, the Supreme Court Chamber first outlined the legal framework applicable to reparations before the ECCC, noting that Internal Rule 23(11) and (12) covered reparations but did not provide an extensive guide as to how they should be awarded.[56] The Supreme Court Chamber observed that while the notion of reparations before the ECCC drew on Cambodian criminal procedure concerning civil party claims and international human rights law on reparations, these sources were of limited relevance since the Internal Rules 'delineate a specific reparation regime that has been tailored to the ECCC's *sui generis* mechanism and mandate'.[57] In particular, civil party participation under Cambodian law was much broader than under the ECCC regime.[58] The Supreme Court Chamber accepted the Trial Chamber's statement that 'departures from national law were considered necessary in view of the large number of Civil Parties expected before the ECCC and the inevitable difficulties of quantifying the full extent of losses suffered by an indeterminate class

52 Zhang, above n. 27, p. 525.
53 Duch Trial Judgment, above n. 12, para. 660.
54 Ibid, para. 683.
55 Ibid, para. 683.
56 Ibid, para. 639.
57 Ibid, para. 641.
58 Duch Appeal Judgment, above n. 8, para. 643.

of victims'.[59] The Supreme Court Chamber proceeded to analyse the right to a remedy in international law, although in a different context from criminal proceedings. It was noted that the Internal Rules provided for reparations to be 'awarded against' and 'borne by convicted persons', and that there was therefore no standing to bring a claim against the Cambodian State.[60]

In addressing the question of what was meant by 'collective and moral' reparations, the Supreme Court Chamber referred to Internal Rule 23(12) which mentions the publication of the judgment, financing a non-profit activity or service beneficial to victims, and 'other appropriate and comparable forms of reparation'. The word 'moral' meant repairing moral rather than material damages while the word 'collective' confirmed 'the unavailability of individual financial awards'.[61] This did not mean that all measures requiring financing in order to be implemented were excluded or that moral reparations entailing individual benefit could not be awarded as long as the award was available for victims as a collective.[62] Awards should benefit as many victims as possible[63] and should also serve a reconciliatory function.[64] In the Supreme Court Chamber's view:

> Acknowledging the limitations of the above outlined framework of the ECCC … although collective and moral reparations may not reinstate the victims of human rights abuses either physically or economically, other general purposes of reparations are fulfilled before the ECCC to the extent the reparation responds to 'the psychological, moral, and symbolic elements of the violation.' This is achieved through the 'verification of the facts and full and public disclosure of the truth' as fostered by the findings of the Co-Investigating Judges and three Chambers, through the access and participation of victims to proceedings, and through victims' identification and individual recognition in the final judgement that represent a public acknowledgement of their suffering.[65]

The Supreme Court Chamber also considered that its acknowledgement of a proposed award as an appropriate reparation measure might in itself be a form of satisfaction and redress and inspire efforts to ensure the

---

59 Duch Trial Judgment, above n. 12, para. 661, footnote 1144; Duch Appeal Judgment, above n. 8, para. 644.
60 Duch Appeal Judgment, above n. 8, para. 656.
61 Ibid, para. 658.
62 Ibid.
63 Ibid, para. 659.
64 Ibid, para. 660.
65 Ibid, para. 661.

realisation of the award.[66] However, since the ECCC had no authority to compel the State of Cambodia to administer or implement an award, any claim requiring the State's intervention, such as a request for a State apology, had to be rejected.[67] The Supreme Court Chamber considered that the Civil Party Appellants had put forward numerous requests for appropriate forms of reparation, including the provision of medical and psychological treatment for direct and indirect victims, naming public buildings after victims and installation of informative plaques, holding commemorative ceremonies, and erection of memorials such as pagodas, pagoda fences and monuments.[68] The Supreme Court Chamber found itself unable to grant these requests due to the constraints imposed by the ECCC's reparation framework coupled with Duch's indigence.[69] Instead it called on national authorities, the international community, and other potential donors to provide the necessary financial and other forms of support to take forward those civil party requests found to amount to appropriate forms of reparations.[70] This meant that like the Trial Chamber, which was found to have provided inadequate reasoning, the Supreme Court Chamber had to reject the civil party requests related to:

- Compilation and Dissemination of Apologetic Statements Including Civil Parties' Comments Thereon;
- Letter Requesting an Apology from the Government;
- Installation of Memorials at Tuol Sleng and Choeung Ek and Transformation of Prey Sâr into a Memorial Site;
- Paid Visits for Civil Parties to Memorial Sites;
- Provision of Medical Treatment and Psychological Services for Civil Parties;
- Production and Dissemination of Audio and Video Material about Case 001;
- Naming 17 Public Buildings after the Victims and Associated Ceremonies;
- Writing an Open Letter to the RGC Requesting Part of the Entrance Fees to be Used to Fund Reparations.

In Case 002, the Trial Chamber was operating under the amended rules and had to decide only on the substance of the civil parties' consolidated

---

66 Ibid.
67 Ibid, para. 664.
68 Ibid, para. 717.
69 Ibid.
70 Ibid.

claim for reparations. The amendments to the Internal Rules (Internal Rule 23 *quinquies* (3)(b)) had created an additional reparations avenue:

> This alternative permits the Civil Party Lead Co-Lawyers to request the Trial Chamber to recognize that specific reparations measures, designed or identified in coordination with the Victims Support Section, are appropriate for implementation using external resources. Over the course of the trial in Case 002, this enabled the Victims Support Section and Lead Co-Lawyers to seek funding for reparations from donor contributions and to develop these projects in collaboration with governmental and non-governmental organizations external to the ECCC.[71]

Although the two possible modes of implementation of the awards envisaged by Internal Rule 23 *quinquies* (3)(a) and (b) are intended to be distinct as well as mutually exclusive, the Civil Party Co-Lawyers appeared to invoke both modes by requesting that the cost of reparations be borne by the accused and at the same time that costs be externally funded by third parties.[72] The Trial Chamber decided to consider the requests under Internal Rule 23 *quinquies* (3)(b) in view of the indigence of the accused.[73] The following projects were judicially endorsed by the Trial Chamber:

- A National Remembrance Day on 20 May agreed to by the government of Cambodia;
- The creation of a group of sculptures within the *Stat Chas* (Old Stadium) roundabout park in front of Bun Rany Hun Sen High School in Phnom Penh by Séra, a French-Cambodian artist, with the inauguration intended to take place on 17 April 2015;
- 'Testimonial therapy' consisting of psychological support for victims;
- The establishment of self-help groups;
- A permanent public exhibition;
- A Mobile Exhibition and Education Project: Exploring History and Transitional Justice;
- Inclusion of a chapter on forced population movement and executions at Tuol Po Chrey within the Cambodian school curriculum;
- The establishment of a community peace learning centre at Samraong Khnong, in Battambang Province which would conduct

71 Nuon Trial Judgment, above n. 6, para. 1113.
72 Ibid, para. 1123.
73 Ibid, para. 1124.

seminars and training on Khmer Rouge era crimes and the work of the ECCC;
- A booklet on Facts Adjudicated in Case 002/01 and Civil Party Participation;
- Publication and distribution of two Khmer language editions of the Case 002/01 verdict, one being the entire judgment and the other a summary version of it;
- Inclusion of Civil Party names on the ECCC website.[74]

Two projects were not endorsed due to insufficient information on the budget and other details:

- Around five public memorial sites;
- Construction of a stupa in the pagoda at Vincennes, Paris, to serve as a place of remembrance and acknowledgment for the Cambodian Civil Parties living in France.[75]

The Trial Chamber found that the civil parties and many other victims had suffered 'immeasurable harm, which includes physical suffering, economic loss, loss of dignity, psychological trauma and grief arising from the loss of family members or close relations' as a consequence of the crimes for which the accused were convicted.[76] The Trial Chamber noted its general support for memorialisation, psychological assistance, documentation and education and welcomed 'any initiative that offers support to the victims, keeps their memory alive, acknowledges their suffering and awakens public awareness to avoid repetition of acts such as those that occurred.'[77] There was an open invitation to donors to support other measures that had not been specifically endorsed in the judgement.

5. CONCLUSION

In its consideration of the appeal in Case 001, the Supreme Court Chamber asked, rhetorically, 'whether a regime that so broadly embraces victims, yet is so heavily dependent on proving an injury, is compatible with criminal proceedings concerning core international crimes and mass

---

74 Ibid, paras. 1126, 1129, 1131, 1133–40, 1153, 1155, 1160.
75 Ibid, paras. 1127, 1130, 1161–3.
76 Ibid, para. 1150.
77 Ibid, para. 1164.

victimisation'.[78] The PTC's generous approach to admissibility perhaps provides a partial answer. Victims were always envisaged to play a prominent role in ECCC proceedings, both as a reflection of Cambodian procedures and in recognition of the Court's role in promoting national reconciliation. Victims may influence the charges by providing information to the Co-Prosecutors, support the prosecution in the proceedings because they share the same goal—a conviction of the accused—and at the same time represent their own interests in order to achieve the separate goal of obtaining reparations.

It would be unrealistic to expect the ECCC to serve as a one stop shop for all purposes of retributive and restorative justice. Moreover, the disproportionate number of accusers positioned opposite the defence lawyers at the Co-Prosecutors' and civil party lawyers' benches in the courtroom might instinctively suggest an imbalance in terms of protecting the fair trial rights of the accused. A streamlined system was unavoidable and has broadly served its function. Although there has been a shift away from a genuine system of civil party participation, it would be going too far to suggest that civil party rights have been sacrificed on the altar of efficiency.

The tasks of civil party lawyers and the relationship between the lawyers representing individual civil parties or groups of civil parties and the Civil Party Lead Co-Lawyers introduced under the amended Internal Rules are complex.[79] The Rules tend to assume that civil parties and their lawyers will speak with one voice and that this voice will echo that of the prosecution, but in reality there are bound to be different interests, strategies and agendas at play.[80] It is a challenging situation for all concerned and creates a type of hierarchy of legal representation, placing civil party lawyers in a subordinate position to the Civil Party Lead Co-Lawyers who have a coordinating function rather than a truly representative one.

---

[78] Duch Appeal Judgment, above n. 8, para. 424.

[79] See Stegmiller, above n. 48, p. 542, who suggests that the Internal Rules should have included provisions for the settlement of disputes between civil party lawyers and Civil-Party Lead Co-Lawyers.

[80] It has also been noted that 'the more the participation is conducted by representatives at the expense of the victims' personal involvement, the greater are the risks of victims' disappointment, detachment from the process, and even "secondary victimization"'. See A-M. de Brouwer and M. Heikkilä, 'Victim Issues: Participation, Protection, Reparation and Assistance, in G. Sluiter, H. Friman, S. Linton, S. Vasiliev, S. Zappalà (eds), *International Criminal Procedure: Principles and Rules* (Oxford, Oxford University Press, 2013), pp. 1299–374, p. 1350.

The revised scheme for reparations has helped to catalyse action and cooperation more broadly in society. While to an extent the Chambers have outsourced the reparations programme to external actors, the advantage is that victims who did not participate as civil parties may also benefit from measures that could only ever provide 'moral' relief.

11. Legitimacy

1. INTRODUCTION

With the benefit of hindsight, would the Cambodian government and the international community have joined hands and built the Extraordinary Chambers in the Courts of Cambodia (ECCC)? Possibly not. The Court has received more criticism than acclaim and is generally touted as a model not to be followed.[1] A more complete transitional justice process for Cambodia might have included a form of truth commission, and less of a wait for justice. But hindsight is not always helpful. Cambodia was not properly at peace until 1999 when for 'the first time in decades its government was not dependent on a predominant foreign patron.'[2] The ECCC was to some degree an experiment, informed by the earlier experiments in international or 'hybrid' justice. It was tailor made for a particular community in a domestic political context known for its reticence, and at the same time had to be tailored to meet international standards and reflect global political interests. It is unlikely to be able to dispense 'perfect justice', whatever that phrase may imply, but can it nevertheless enjoy legitimacy?

The question of the legitimacy of international courts and tribunals has been receiving increased attention in the scholarly literature with attempts being made to place the *concept* of legitimacy in a coherent theoretical and analytical framework. This framework necessarily varies

---

1 See e.g. D. Cohen, M. Hyde and P. van Tuyl, 'A Well-Reasoned Opinion? Critical Analysis of the First Case against the Alleged Senior Leaders of the Khmer Rouge (Case 002/01)', East-West Center, 2015, <https://krttrialmonitor.files.wordpress.com/2015/11/cohen-wellreasoned2015.pdf> [accessed 12 July 2017]; C. Campbell, 'Cambodia's Khmer Rouge Trials Are a Shocking Failure', *Time*, 13 February 2014, <http://time.com/6997/cambodias-khmer-rouge-trials-are-a-shocking-failure/> [accessed 12 July 2017]; J.A. Hall, 'Trial on Trial', *The New York Times*, 10 March 2009 (stating in the context of corruption allegations that 'the nature of this dirty laundry suggests that the UN-backed tribunal is so deeply flawed that its very existence needs to be re-evaluated'), <http://www.nytimes.com/2009/03/10/opinion/10iht-edhall.1.20723411.html> [accessed 12 July 2017].

2 D. Chandler, *A History of Cambodia* (4th edn, Chiangmai, Silkworm Books, 2008), p. 292.

according to the object of the study, whether it be the legitimate exercise of power and authority in the global sphere, the substantive content of international law, a group of courts with connected features or a single institution.[3] It has been observed that '[w]here power is acquired and exercised according to justifiable rules, and with evidence of consent, we call it rightful or legitimate' but that we also need to explain 'what makes it so, and why it matters'.[4] Adopting a viewpoint from the end phase of the process as indicated in the discussion of legality at the beginning of this book, this chapter will first briefly explore the concept of legitimacy as it pertains to the ECCC. Drawing on this exploration, a series of topics that help to inform the overall assessment of the Court's legitimacy will be discussed. These topics include hybridity and independence, transparency, fairness, efficiency, accessibility and answerability. Finally, the chapter will offer some tentative conclusions as to the legitimacy of the ECCC, noting that a complete study of this important question is best reserved for a time when hindsight has reached maturity.

---

[3] See e.g. R. Falk, M. Juergensmeyer and V. Popovski, *Legality and Legitimacy in Global Affairs* (Oxford, Oxford University Press, 2012); N. Hayashi and C.M. Bailliet (eds), *The Legitimacy of International Criminal Tribunals* (Cambridge, Cambridge University Press, 2017); G. Boas, W.A. Schabas and M.P. Scharf (eds), *International Criminal Justice: Legitimacy and Coherence* (Cheltenham, Glos/ Northampton, Massachusetts, Edward Elgar Publishing, 2012); L.H. Meyer (ed), *Legitimacy, Justice and Public International Law* (Cambridge, Cambridge University Press 2009); R. Wolfrum and V. Röben (eds), *Legitimacy in International Law* (Berlin/Heidelberg, Max-Planck-Gesellschaft zur Förderung der Wissenschaften e.V., 2008); S. Wheatley, *The Democratic Legitimacy of International Law* (Oxford/Portland, Oregon, Hart Publishing, 2010); Y. Shany, 'How Can International Criminal Courts Have a Greater Impact on National Criminal Proceedings? Lessons From the First Two Decades of International Criminal Justice in Operation', *Israel Law Review*, vol. 46, no. 3, November 2013, pp. 431–53, pp. 449–50; A. von Bogdandy and I. Venzke, 'In Whose Name? An Investigation of International Courts' Public Authority and its Democratic Justification', *European Journal of International Law*, vol. 23, no. 1, 2012, pp. 7–41, pp. 9–10; M. Glasius, 'Do International Criminal Courts Require Democratic Legitimacy?', *European Journal of International Law*, vol. 23, no. 1, 2012, pp. 43–66, pp. 43–5; A. Buchanan and R. Keohane, 'The Legitimacy of Global Governance Institutions', *Ethics & International Affairs*, vol. 20, no. 4, 2006, pp. 405–37, p. 405; M. de S.-O.-L'E. Lasser, *Judicial Deliberations: A Comparative Analysis of Judicial Transparency and Legitimacy* (Oxford, Oxford University Press, 2004).

[4] D. Beetham, *The Legitimation of Power* (Basingstoke, Macmillan, 1991), p. 3.

2. ANALYSING LEGITIMACY IN THE ECCC CONTEXT

Legitimacy is a fluid, adaptable and relative notion which is related to legality, justice and fairness but more easily perceived than measured. As a concept, it is of interest to moral and political philosophers, social and political scientists and lawyers, and incorporates political, sociological, criminological and victimological perspectives. It is 'highly subjective', and may include 'ethical, religious, rational, or even subconscious' considerations.[5] For philosophers, 'legitimacy entails the *moral justifiability* of power relations'.[6] Social scientists study legitimacy in particular social contexts and concern themselves with societal expectations and the '*belief in legitimacy* on the part of the relevant social agents'.[7] Chinkin notes from a lawyer's perspective that legitimacy is 'the normative belief that a rule or institution ought to be obeyed' and provides a 'pull factor' for compliance.[8] Legitimacy is made up of objectively measurable 'characteristics of a system of power' and the subjective 'beliefs people hold about it'.[9] Indeed, these two aspects have been labelled descriptive, empirical or sociological legitimacy, referring to how a court is perceived, and normative legitimacy, asking whether the court meets definite standards.[10]

If legality concerns a court's authority to exist, legitimacy is about recognising the validity of the process. Thus, 'legitimacy is equivalent to

---

5 V. Popovski, 'Legality and Legitimacy of International Criminal Tribunals', in Falk, Juergensmeyer and Popovski, above n. 3, pp. 388–413, p. 389.

6 Beetham, above n. 4, p. 5 (*Emphasis* in original).

7 Ibid, pp. 6 (*Emphasis* in original), 8 (referring to Max Weber's definition of legitimacy).

8 C. Chinkin, 'U.N. Human Rights Council Fact-Finding Missions: Lessons from Gaza', in M.H. Arsanjani, J. Cogan, R. Sloane and S. Wiessner (eds), *Looking to the Future: Essays on International Law in Honor of W. Michael Reisman* (Leiden/Boston, Martinus Nijhoff Publishers, 2011), pp. 475–98, p. 483 (*Emphasis added*).

9 Beetham, above n. 4, p. 9.

10 S.A. Langvatn and T. Squatrito, 'Conceptualising and Measuring the Legitimacy of International Criminal Tribunals', in Hayashi and Bailliet, above n. 3, p. 43; S. Vasiliev, 'Between International Criminal Justice and Injustice: Theorising Legitimacy', in Hayashi and Bailliet, above n. 3, pp. 66–91, pp. 74, 78; D. Bodansky, 'Legitimacy in International Law and International Relations,' in J.L. Dunoff and M.A. Pollack (eds), *Interdisciplinary Perspectives on International Law and International Relations: The State of the Art* (Cambridge, Cambridge University Press, 2013), pp. 321–41, pp. 326–7.

legal validity' but not to legality.[11] Legitimacy is not identical to justice, the latter being an 'ideal standard' while the former 'expresses a threshold value, in a non-ideal world, for the conditions under which an institution has the right to rule'.[12] A process may be legitimate because, or despite the fact that, a jury returns the verdict: 'My Lord, we find the defendant who stole the horse not guilty.'[13] Thomas Franck assimilates legitimacy with justice and fairness.[14] The principle of legality, or *nullum crimen sine lege*, afforded such prominence by the ECCC Chambers, might be seen as an expression of this assimilation.

According to a theory of legitimacy tailored to international courts and tribunals in general, and built on justifications for the acceptance of authority, 'an international court is legitimate when it is (1) fair and unbiased, (2) interpreting and applying norms consistent with what states believe the law is or should be, and (3) transparent and infused with democratic norms'.[15] Antonio Cassese identified four categories of legitimacy relevant to international *criminal* courts and tribunals.[16] First is 'consent legitimacy' which refers to the moral and psychological acceptance of an institution by the affected population.[17] Second is 'purposive legitimacy', derived from the values, principles and goals shared by a majority of the institution's constituency which provide it with 'legitimating grounds'.[18] Third is 'universal values legitimacy' which looks to the values of the international community as expressed in

---

[11] Beetham, above n. 4, p. 4 (although Beetham also describes legality as 'an important component of legitimacy' and one which does not depend on beliefs), 12. *See* also Vasiliev, above n. 10, p. 76 (suggesting that 'legitimacy is a complement and a *corrective* to legality') (*Emphasis* in original).

[12] A. Buchanen and R.O. Keohane, 'The Legitimacy of Global Governance Institutions', in Wolfrum and Röben, above n. 3, pp. 25–62, p. 34.

[13] Cited by T.M. Franck, *Fairness in International Law and Institutions* (Oxford, Oxford University Press, 1998), p. 34.

[14] Franck, ibid, pp. 7–9, 25–6. *See* also A. Pellet, 'Legitimacy of Legislative and Executive Actions of International Institutions', in Wolfrum and Röben, above n. 3, pp. 63–82, pp. 67–8; T.M. Franck, *The Power of Legitimacy Among Nations* (New York, Oxford University Press, 1990), p. 16.

[15] N. Grossman, 'Legitimacy and International Adjudicative Bodies', *George Washington International Law Review*, vol. 41, no. 1, 2009, pp. 107–80, p. 115.

[16] A. Cassese, 'The Legitimacy of International Criminal Tribunals and the Current Prospects of International Criminal Justice', *Leiden Journal of International Law*, vol. 25, 2012, pp. 491–501, p. 492.

[17] Ibid.

[18] Ibid.

jus cogens or Rawls's 'principles of justice as fairness'.[19] Fourth is 'performance legitimacy' which includes factors such as an institution's '*answerability* to a founding authority; the *transparency* of its decision-making … and its *accountability to the institution's constituency*.'[20] Another framework for an assessment of the legitimacy of an international criminal tribunal, combining descriptive and normative characteristics, focuses on the court's pedigree (how it came into being), its process (how decisions are made) and its results (whether justice is produced).[21]

The turn of the last millennium has been described as the 'honeymoon period for [international criminal justice] and the cluster of values that support it'[22] but the suggestion that these values are changeable or even dissolving should be countered if legitimacy in this context is to have any fixed point of reference. All of the proposed theoretical frameworks for assessing the legitimacy of a court such as the ECCC contain common features and combine values grounded in international human rights law and ethical principles with the transitional or post-conflict justice needs and expectations of a particular society. Legitimacy is not welded to the broader goals of the court being scrutinised, but those goals necessarily inform the assessment.[23] The ECCC Supreme Court Chamber has itself stated that:

> This Court's very existence and its perseverance through the negotiation process as an idea and its subsequent operation as an institution are a testament to the great public interest in the prosecution of the persons and crimes within its jurisdiction and to prevent impunity and foster national reconciliation.[24]

On a different occasion, the Supreme Court Chamber stressed that the task of the ECCC is 'not only seek the truth about what happened in Cambodia, but also to pay special attention and assure a meaningful

---

[19] Ibid.

[20] Ibid, p. 493 (*Emphasis* in original).

[21] Langvatn and Squatrito, above n. 10, p. 52.

[22] D. Luban, 'After the Honeymoon: Reflections on the Current State of International Criminal Justice', *Journal of International Criminal Justice*, vol. 11, no. 3, 2013, pp. 505–15, p. 506.

[23] Langvatn and Squatrito, above n. 10, p. 56.

[24] *Prosecutor v Ieng Thirith*, ECCC Case File No. 002/19-09-2007-ECCC-TC/SC(09), Supreme Court Chamber, Decision on Immediate Appeal against the Trial Chamber's Order to Release the Accused Ieng Thirith, 13 December 2011, para. 28.

participation for the victims of the crimes committed as part of its pursuit for national reconciliation'.[25] As a process, the ECCC is designed to go beyond bare criminal justice and promote reconciliation, physical and psychological rehabilitation of victims and the discovery of the truth for the benefit of Cambodians and the entire international community whose conscience was 'shocked' by the atrocities and haunted by the long period of inaction.

3. HYBRIDITY AND INDEPENDENCE

The bifurcated structure of the ECCC, and the problem of a structure that could easily bifurcate was examined in chapter 3. This structure was a direct result of the push by the international community for proceedings that could be guaranteed to meet international standards of justice and fairness and the pulling away by the Cambodian government which favoured a domestically dominated court but recognised that it needed financial and expert assistance. Hun Sen reportedly stated: 'I do not wish a foreign woman to come to Cambodia and dress up in a Khmer dress. I want a Khmer woman to dress in a Khmer dress and for foreigners to come and help put on the make-up.'[26] The international community was seen to lack the moral authority to impose its demands, having largely remained silent about Khmer Rouge crimes through to the end of the 1980s while legitimising the former regime by allowing it to represent Cambodia at the UN.[27] There was a sense 'this was Cambodia's genocide and Cambodians were in the best position to judge crimes against their own people'.[28] At the same time, Cambodia was ill-equipped to handle the trials alone due to its 'corrupt and under-resourced judicial system' and poor human rights record, the lack of funds and the fact that many government officials had once been members of the Khmer Rouge.[29]

---

[25] *Prosecutor v Nuon Chea, Ieng Sary, Ieng Thirith* and *Khieu Samphan*, ECCC Case File No. 002/19-09-2007-ECCC/OCIJ (PTC76, PTC112, PTC113, PTC114, PTC115, PTC142, PTC157, PTC164, PTC165 and PTC172), Pre-Trial Chamber, Decision on Appeals against Orders of the Co-Investigating Judges on the Admissibility of Civil Party Applications, 24 June 2011, para. 65.

[26] Y. Chhang, 'The Thief of History – Cambodia and the Special Court', *International Journal of Transitional Justice*, vol. 1, 2007, pp. 157–72, p. 167.

[27] Ibid.

[28] Ibid.

[29] Ibid, p. 168 (Chhang notes that only about 20 members of Cambodia's judiciary survived Democratic Kampuchea).

It has been suggested that a tribunal with mixed panels of international and domestic (or regional) judges (and arguably by the same token a mixed staffing structure) is likely to be regarded as more legitimate than a purely international tribunal on the basis that 'judges should mirror the society over which they exercise jurisdiction'.[30] In this context, it has aptly been remarked that: 'Too often, the "local" judge is deeply personalized and contextualized to the point of suspicion of bias, corruption, or incompetence, while the "international" judge is entirely abstracted, neutralized, and decontextualized as expert.'[31] The hybrid model aims to break down these perceived divisions. Cambodian judges at the ECCC have mostly been receptive to international input on complex legal questions while international judges have remained loyal to the core conception of the ECCC, namely of establishing extraordinary chambers *within* the courts of Cambodia. Indeed, the Supreme Court Chamber, speaking with one voice, has noted that no judicial system is perfect and that 'the relation between the judiciary and the other branches of government remain marked by conflict and tension, including in modern democracies aspiring to the highest Rule of Law standards'.[32] The Supreme Court Chamber added:

> Without diminishing the importance of judicial reform in the direction of strengthening autonomy and independence, it would, nevertheless, be inappropriate to refuse … legitimacy to a trial before the ECCC based on abstract discord between the institutional design of the Cambodian judiciary and international standards. Advancing this proposition further would effectively question the *raison d'être* of hybrid criminal tribunals – a conclusion unacceptable for institutions operating under the auspices of the United Nations.[33]

Independence is a professional virtue of all participants in the process, including judges, prosecutors, defence lawyers and victims' lawyers. The virtue of independence in the sense of being free from corruption or

---

[30] H. Hobbs, 'Hybrid Tribunals and the Composition of the Court: In Search of Sociological Legitimacy', *Chicago Journal of International Law*, vol. 16, no. 2, 2016, pp. 482–522, p. 495 (referring to the International Project of Judicial Independence of the International Association of Judicial Independence and World Peace, Mount Scopus International Standards on Judicial Independence, 19 March 2008, Article 2.15).

[31] Hobbs, ibid, p. 487.

[32] *Prosecutor v Nuon Chea* and *Khieu Samphan*, ECCC Case File No. 002/19-09-2007-ECCC/SC, Supreme Court Chamber, Appeal Judgment, 23 November 2016, para. 126 ('Nuon Appeal Judgment').

[33] Ibid.

outside influence is equally applicable to court administrators, especially at the senior level.

The push and pull between the international community represented by the UN and Cambodia represented by its government has continued throughout the life of the Court. Perhaps as a result, the ECCC has avoided becoming overly internationalised or overly domesticated but has instead come close to reaching a stalemate. Bringing former Khmer Rouge leaders to trial in a context in which international standards are enforced is surely part of the government's strategy for legitimacy. But the ECCC needs space to prove its own independence if it is to serve as a model for an independent domestic judiciary. In order for the trials to be truly transitional and to earn legitimacy 'they must offer elements from which a renewed national identity can be constructed.'[34] The hybridity of the ECCC and the safeguarding of independence afford it legitimacy, but it in practice is a fragile balance.

4. TRANSPARENCY

Judicial investigations are in principle confidential but the Co-Investigating Judges may issue information deemed essential to keep the public informed.[35] This is specified in the Internal Rules[36] and elaborated in Article 3.12 of the Practice Direction on Filing of Documents before the ECCC[37] which states that the filing party may indicate its view as to the public or confidential nature of a document but that the judges have the sole power to review the document and determine its status. The principle of the confidentiality of the case file caused certain defence teams consternation in the early days of the Court's operation, especially

---

[34] D. PoKempner, 'The Tribunal and Cambodia's Transition to a Culture of Accountability', in J. Ramji and B. van Schaack (eds), *Bringing the Khmer Rouge to Justice: Prosecuting Mass Violence before the Cambodian Courts* (Lewiston, New York, Edwin Mellon Press, 2005), pp. 333–58, p. 353.

[35] Internal Rules, Rule 56.

[36] Internal Rules, Rules 54 (concerning Introductory, Supplementary and Final Submissions of the Prosecutor), 56 (concerning public information by the Co-Investigative Judges), 77(5)–(6) (concerning hearings before the Pre-Trial Chamber).

[37] Practice Direction on Filing Documents before the ECCC (Revision 3), Practice Direction ECCC/01/2007/Rev.3, Article 3.12, <https://www.eccc.gov.kh/sites/default/files/documents/courtdoc/PD_Filing_Revision_3_final_Eng.pdf> [accessed 12 July 2017].

where documents marked public by the defence and considered not to breach any confidentiality nonetheless failed to be published on the Court's official website. The problem escalated and eventually resulted in a comprehensive 'Order on Breach of Confidentiality' by the Co-Investigative Judges.[38] The Supreme Court Chamber has since reiterated that the 'disclosure of classified documents, if established beyond reasonable doubt, is an offence under Rule 35(1)(a), possibly leading to a sanction in accordance with Cambodian law and/or a finding of misconduct against a lawyer' and emphasised that the proper action is for a party seeking re-classification of a document to apply to the relevant Chamber.[39]

From its first proceedings, the Pre-Trial Chamber developed a practice of reversing the presumption of *in camera* hearings and publishing pleadings as far as the need to ensure the integrity of the investigation would permit. This approach helped to provide the public with a window into the Court's operations and to sustain interest until the opening of the first trial. Hearings before the Trial Chamber are conducted in public, subject to protective measures.[40] Retaining the confidentiality of sensitive information pertaining to victims and witnesses is largely uncontroversial and, indeed, procedurally necessary. The Court has worked consistently to amend and improve its confidentiality policies to enhance transparency and the Co-Investigating Judges have published an increasing number of documents.[41] In relation to Case 002/01, the Trial Chamber noted that at the conclusion of closing submissions, 5,102 documents and materials before the Trial Chamber remained 'confidential' and ruled of its own motion that confidentiality was no longer justified for any information

[38] *Prosecutor v Ieng Sary*, ECCC Case File No. 002/19-09-2007-ECCC/OCIJ, Office of the Co-Investigating Judges, Order on Breach of Confidentiality of the Judicial Investigation, 3 March 2009.

[39] *Prosecutor v Nuon Chea*, ECCC Case File No. 002/19-09-2007-ECCC-TC/SC(08), Supreme Court Chamber, Decision on Immediate Appeal by Nuon Chea against the Trial Chamber's Decision on Fairness of the Investigation, 27 April 2012, para. 36.

[40] Internal Rule, Rule 79(6).

[41] *See* 'The Co-Investigating Judges Publish a Number of Documents', Extraordinary Chambers in the Courts of Cambodia, 26 March 2009, <https://www.eccc.gov.kh/sites/default/files/media/Press_Release_OCIJ_EN_0.pdf> [accessed 13 July 2017].

publicly disclosed in the trial judgment.[42] Defence lawyers have persistently requested oral hearings in disqualification matters but these requests have consistently been rejected, with the Chambers finding that the interest of transparency would be ensured by the re-classification of all relevant filings as 'public'.[43]

Arguably, it was the absence of transparency and the delayed reaction to corruption allegations against senior Cambodian administrative staff which threatened to discredit the entire process more than the suspicion of kickbacks itself.[44] Defence lawyers legitimately questioned whether the fair trial rights of the defendants could have been impacted by any malpractice.[45] The allegations resulted in a temporary freeze on disbursements administered by the United Nations Development Programme

---

[42] *Prosecutor v Nuon Chea* and *Khieu Samphan*, ECCC Case File No. 002/19-09-2007/ECCC/TC, Trial Chamber, Case 002/01 Judgement, 7 August 2014, para. 39 ('Nuon Trial Judgment').

[43] *Prosecutor v Nuon, Chea, Ieng Sary* and *Ieng Thirith*, ECCC Case File No. 002/07-12-2009-ECCC/PTC (05), Pre-Trial Chamber, Decision on Ieng Sary's and on Ieng Thirith Applications under Rule 34 to Disqualify Judge Marcel Lemonde, 15 June 2010, para. 34.

[44] A headline in *The Economist* read 'The Court on Trial' and warned of the risks of a cover up: 'The Court on Trial: the Khmers Rouges and Justice', *The Economist*, 4 April 2009, pp. 49–50.

[45] The issue was brought before the Co-Investigating Judges: *Prosecutor v Nuon, Chea, Ieng Sary, Ieng Thirith* and *Khieu Samphan*, ECCC Case File No. 002/19-09-2007-ECCC/OCIJ, Defence for Nuon Chea, Eleventh Request for Investigative Action, 27 March 2009. The Request was joined by the other Charged Persons in Case File 002. The Co-Investigative Judges found that they did not have jurisdiction to conduct the action requested by the defence: *Prosecutor v Nuon, Chea, Ieng Sary, Ieng Thirith* and *Khieu Samphan*, ECCC Case File No. 002/19-09-2007-ECCC/OCIJ, Office of the Co-Investigating Judges, Order on Request for Investigative Action, 3 April 2009, p. 4. All four Charged Persons appealed, *see*, *Prosecutor v Nuon, Chea, Ieng Sary, Ieng Thirith* and *Khieu Samphan*, ECCC Case File No. 002/19-09-2007-ECCC/OCIJ(PTC 20), Defence for Ieng Sary, Ieng Sary's Appeal against the Co-Investigating Judges' Order on Request for Investigative Action regarding Ongoing Allegations of Corruption & Request for an Expedited Oral Hearing, 4 May 2009; *Prosecutor v Nuon, Chea, Ieng Sary, Ieng Thirith* and *Khieu Samphan*, ECCC Case File No. 002/19-09-2007-ECCC-OCIJ-PTC19, Defence for Ieng Thirith, Ieng Thirith Appeal against Office of the Co-Investigating Judges' 'Order on Request for Investigative Action' of 3 April 2009, 4 May 2009; *Prosecutor v Nuon, Chea, Ieng Sary, Ieng Thirith* and *Khieu Samphan*, ECCC Case File No. 002/19-09-2007-ECCC/OCIJ (PTC-21), Defence for Nuon Chea, Appeal against Order on Eleventh Request for Investigative Action, 4 May 2009; and *Prosecutor v Nuon, Chea, Ieng Sary, Ieng Thirith* and *Khieu Samphan*, ECCC Case File No.

(UNDP) for the payment of salaries for domestic staff. Eventually, the UN Office of Internal Oversight Services conducted an investigation which resulted in the preparation of a report, the existence of which was made known although its contents remain confidential to this day. The Trial Chamber denied a request by the civil party lawyers to facilitate the disclosure of the report.[46] The core question was considered to be whether there was a 'nexus between the allegations of corruption, which concern whether certain national administrative officials of the ECCC paid money to obtain their positions, and the judicial decision-making functions of the ECCC'.[47] The Trial Chamber was satisfied that the allegations of corruption had no bearing on the fair trial rights of the parties and that the non-disclosure of the report would not impact on the transparency of the proceedings. While facilitating disclosure fell outside the Trial Chamber's purview, it noted that similar requests had been filed with the Cambodian courts and with the UN itself.

The UN and Cambodia agreed to establish an office of the Independent Counsellor to receive allegations of corruption within the ECCC, building on the structure already in place of national and international ethics monitors and with the aim of protecting staff against any possible retaliation for good faith reporting of wrongdoing.[48] The Auditor General of Cambodia, H.E. Mr. Uth Chhorn, was appointed to the role. As communications are received on a confidential basis, it is difficult to assess whether this has been a much used or effective solution. It did at least seem adequate to calm the situation and perhaps restore any lost legitimacy. The challenge of rescuing the Court's reputation while sweeping nothing under the carpet and simultaneously saving face cannot be underestimated. It is impossible to know whether it would have been more or less damaging for the UN to publish the contentious report.

002/19-09-2007-ECCC/OCIJ (PTC22), Defence for Khieu Samphan, Appeal by Defense for Khieu Samphan against the Co-Investigating Judges' Order on Request for Investigative Action Dated 3 April 2009, 4 May 2009.

46 *Prosecutor v Kaing Guek Eav alias 'Duch'*, ECCC Case File No. 001/18-07-2007/ECCC/TC, Trial Chamber, Decision on Group 1 – Civil Parties' Co-Lawyers' Request that the Trial Chamber Facilitate the Disclosure of an UN-OIOS Report to the Parties, 23 September 2009, para. 19 and p. 8.

47 Ibid, paras. 5, 16.

48 Office of Legal Affairs, 'Joint Statement on Establishment of Independent Counsellor at the Extraordinary Chambers in the Courts of Cambodia', United Nations Assistance to the Khmer Rouge Trials, 12 August 2009, <http://www.unakrt-online.org/articles/joint-statement-establishment-independent-counsellor-extraordinary-chambers-courts-cambodia> [accessed 12 July 2017].

An actively interested press and academic community serves to enhance transparency by questioning the lack of access to materials where an abuse of secrecy is suspected and commenting, speculating and criticising. The effect of this interaction is sometimes to provoke the Court into making clarifying statements.[49] A highly critical report on the trial judgment in Case 002/01[50] triggered not only academic commentary on the critique[51] but an online reaction by the international Civil Party Co-Lawyer concerned by the possible impact of the report on the proceedings.[52] All this attention perhaps gave more credence to the report than it deserved but nonetheless internal and external actors were engaged in a transparent debate about perceived shortcomings in the trial judgment. The extent to which internal actors should participate in external discussions is part of the flip side of transparency which requires the preservation of the integrity of the Court and maintenance of the ethical duty of non-communication when the circumstances so dictate. Transparency can be used effectively in the interests of fairness, as when Judge Lemonde published the names of six summonsed witnesses who refused to appear.[53]

---

[49] 'Statement by the Co-Investigating Judges on the Article "Staying Khmer Rouge Tribunal Cases Mulled" in the Phnom Penh Post of 8 May 2017', Extraordinary Chambers in the Courts of Cambodia, 8 May 2017, <https://www.eccc.gov.kh/en/articles/statement-co-investigating-judges-article-staying-khmer-rouge-tribunal-cases-mulled-phnom-p> [accessed 12 July 2017].

[50] Cohen, Hyde and van Tuyl, above n 1.

[51] *See* e.g. M. Newton, 'East-West Center's "A Well-Reasoned Opinion?" Professor Michael A. Newton Offers Expert Analysis', *Cambodia Tribunal Monitor*, 18 February 2016, <http://www.cambodiatribunal.org/2016/02/18/professor-michael-a-newton-offers-his-expert-analysis-of-the-east-west-centers-well-reasoned-opinion/> [accessed 12 July 2017].

[52] M. Guiraud, 'A Well-Reasoned Critique? – Marie Guiraud Responds to East-West Center Report', Cambodia Tribunal Monitor, 6 January 2016, <http://www.cambodiatribunal.org/2016/01/06/a-well-reasoned-critique-marie-guiraud-responds-to-east-west-center-report/> [accessed 12 July 2017].

[53] *See* Open Society Justice Initiative, 'Political Interference at the Extraordinary Chambers in the Courts of Cambodia', Open Society Foundations, July 2010, p. 27 (referring to 'Letter from Judge Marcel Lemonde to Summon Senate President Chea Sim, National Assembly President Heng Samrin, Foreign Minister Hor Namhong, Finance Minister Keat Chhon and Two CPP Senators', *International Criminal Law Bureau*, 25 September 2009 (no longer on ECCC website but available on the International Criminal Law Bureau blog), <http://www.internationallawbureau.com/index.php/eccc-update-decision-on-civil-parties-closing-statements-in-duch-trial-nuon-chea-provisional-detention-allegations-of-bias-against-investigating-judge/> [accessed 12 July 2017]), <https://www.opensociety

5. FAIRNESS

The ideal of fairness is contained within the notion of 'international standards' and permeates the entire process before the ECCC. It is difficult to contest that the judges have striven to uphold due process even though certain decisions may seem suspect to the aggrieved party or an outside observer. In this respect, the opportunity to mount a challenge, assert a right and to have it deliberated upon is at least as important as the outcome which can never be guaranteed. Much turns on the adequacy of the justification for the outcome and the Supreme Court Chamber has stressed that an important element of a fair trial is sufficiently reasoned decisions.[54] Sufficient reasoning in the ECCC context includes refraining from over-reliance on the jurisprudence of the ad hoc tribunals especially when applying the principle of legality in view of the ECCC's temporal jurisdiction. Therefore, 'careful, reasoned review' of the findings of these tribunals 'is necessary for ensuring the legitimacy of the ECCC and its decisions'.[55] As the Supreme Court Chamber has explained:

> the reasoning required to ensure fairness of the proceedings will always depend on the specific circumstances of the case. This does not mean that a chamber has to mechanically work through each and every argument that a party has raised in the course of the trial, or that failure to do so automatically leads to a finding that the right to a reasoned decision has been violated. Of most importance is that it is comprehensible how the chamber evaluated the evidence and reached its factual and legal conclusions.[56]

The Supreme Court Chamber has not been afraid to identify instances of inadequate reasoning on the part of the Trial Chamber. For example, it found that civil parties enjoyed the right to a reasoned decision on their reparation claims and that this had been infringed because the civil party

---

foundations.org/reports/political-interference-extraordinary-chambers-courts-cambodia> [accessed 12 July 2017]. *See* also S. Rith and S. Strangio, 'KR Tribunal Summons Top Officials', *The Phnom Penh Post*, 8 October 2009, <http://www.phnompenhpost.com/national/kr-tribunal-summons-top-officials> [accessed 12 July 2017]; C. Sokha and J. O'Toole, 'Minister Explains KRT Snub', *The Phnom Penh Post*, 16 June 2010, <http://www.phnompenhpost.com/national/minister-explains-krt-snub> [accessed 12 July 2017].

[54] Nuon Appeal Judgment, above n. 32, para. 202.

[55] *Prosecutor v Kaing Guek Eav alias 'Duch'*, ECCC Case File No. 001/18-07-2007-ECCC/SC, Supreme Court Chamber, Appeal Judgment, 3 February 2012, para. 97 ('Duch Appeal Judgment').

[56] Nuon Appeal Judgment, above n. 32, para. 207.

appellants were unable to 'unambiguously identify the reasoning pertinent to certain reparation requests'.[57] The Pre-Trial Chamber has similarly chastised the Co-Investigating Judges for failing to provide proper reasoning.[58]

Numerous assertions of the violation of the right to a fair and impartial investigation and trial were raised during the course of Case 002, and while these allegations ranged from unfairness arising from selective prosecution to systematic flaws in the conduct of the judicial investigation, a focus was the possible tainting of the proceedings by political interference. The question of political interference was extensively litigated but neither the Trial Chamber nor the Supreme Court Chamber considered that this issue had an actual bearing on the proceedings so as to prejudice the rights of the accused.[59]

---

[57] Duch Appeal Judgment, above n. 55, para. 671. *See* also *Prosecutor v Nuon Chea*, ECCC Case File No. 002/19-09-2007-ECCC-TC/SC(08), Supreme Court Chamber, Decision on Immediate Appeal by Nuon Chea against the Trial Chamber's Decision on Fairness of the Investigation, 27 April 2012, para. 28: 'The Trial Chamber committed an error of law by failing to provide stand-alone reasons for its rejection of the Rule 35 Request'.

[58] *See*, e.g., *Prosecutor v Kaing Guek Eav alias 'Duch'*, ECCC Case File No. 001/8-07-2007-ECCC/OCIJ (PTC 02), Pre-Trial Chamber, Decision on Appeal against Closing Order Indicting Kaing Guek Eav alias "Duch", 5 December 2008, para. 115; and *Prosecutor v Khieu Samphan*, ECCC Case File No. 002/10-09-2007-ECCC/OCIJ (PTC14 and 15), Pre-Trial Chamber, Decision on Khieu Samphan's Appeals against Order Refusing Request for Release and Extension of Provisional Detention Order, 3 July 2009, para. 137.

[59] Nuon Trial Judgment, above n. 42, paras. 42–3. *See* also *Prosecutor v Nuon Chea, Ieng Sary, Ieng Thirith* and *Khieu Samphan*, ECCC Case File No. 002/19-09-2007-ECCC/TC, Trial Chamber, Decision on Ieng Sary's Motion for a Hearing on the Conduct of the Judicial Investigations, 8 April 2011, p. 2; *Prosecutor v Nuon Chea*, ECCC Case File No. 002/19-09-2007/ECCC/TC, Trial Chamber, Decision on Nuon Chea Motions regarding Fairness of Judicial Investigation (E51/3, E82, E88 and E92), 9 September 2011, paras. 17–18, 21–3; *Prosecutor v Nuon Chea*, ECCC Case File No. 002/19-09-2007-ECCC-TC/SC(08), Supreme Court Chamber, Decision on Immediate Appeal by Nuon Chea against the Trial Chamber's Decision on Fairness of the Investigation, 27 April 2012, paras. 32–4; *Prosecutor v Nuon Chea*, ECCC Case File No. 002/19-09-2007-ECCC-TC/SC(20), Supreme Court Chamber, Decision on Nuon Chea's 'Immediate Appeal against Trial Chamber Decision on Application for Immediate Action pursuant to Rule 35', 25 March 2013, paras. 22–7; *Prosecutor v Nuon Chea*, ECCC Case File No. 002119-09-2007-ECCC-TC/SC(15), Supreme Court Chamber, Decision on Nuon Chea's Appeal against the Trial Chamber's Decision on Rule 35 Applications for Summary Action, 14 September 2012, paras. 68–9.

One aspect of the alleged political interference that could not so easily be dismissed was its impact on the availability of certain defence witnesses. In its final judgment in Case 002/01, the Trial Chamber considered that all parties had been afforded the opportunity to propose the witnesses they deemed most important to their case and in the event such a witness was not called, to put alternative evidence before the Chamber.[60] At an earlier stage of the proceedings, the international and Cambodian judges had been divided over whether to summons the witnesses with the pseudonyms TCW-223 and TCW-494, acknowledged to be government officials (and later revealed to be Ouk Bunchhoen and Heng Samrin respectively), with the result that these witnesses could not be called.[61] The international judges asserted that trials before the ECCC were 'intended to promote national reconciliation, heightening the duty to serve justice to which Cambodian officials are presumably not indifferent'.[62] The Supreme Court Chamber took the view that Heng Samrin's testimony could have been relevant to Case 002/01 'in light of his former position as Deputy Division Commander of the Eastern Zone and as one of highest-ranking individuals still alive who were involved in the evacuation of Phnom Penh' and his potential knowledge of a meeting in Phnom Penh on 20 May 1975 at which the Communist Party of Kampuchea (CPK)'s policies were disseminated.[63] However, the Supreme Court Chamber decided that although the Trial Chamber had erred, it had not been established that the failure to call Heng Samrin resulted in 'a grossly unfair outcome in the judicial proceedings'.[64] This was also found to be true for proposed witnesses Ouk Bunchhoen and Robert Lemkin.

Other issues of concern to the defence included the availability of time and facilities, equality of arms and the right to examine witnesses on the same basis as the Co-Prosecutors. The Trial Chamber found that the accused had availed themselves of opportunities to make statements and

---

[60] Nuon Trial Judgment, above n. 42, paras. 50–4.

[61] *Prosecutor v Nuon Che* and *Khieu Samphan*, ECCC Case File No. 002/19-09-2007-ECCC-TC, Trial Chamber, Final Decision on Witnesses, Experts and Civil Parties to be Heard in Case 002/01, 7 August 2014, Section 3.2.8, paras. 87–111 (*see* separate opinions).

[62] *Prosecutor v Nuon Che* and *Khieu Samphan*, ECCC Case File No. 002/19-09-2007-ECCC-TC, Trial Chamber, Final Decision on Witnesses, Experts and Civil Parties to be Heard in Case 002/01: Opinion of Judges Silvia Cartwright and Jean-Marc Lavergne, 7 August 2014, para. 109.

[63] Nuon Appeal Judgment, above n. 32, para. 145.

[64] Ibid, para. 145.

respond to questions,[65] that adequate relief had been provided where it was in the interests of justice and that any curtailment of the questioning of witnesses was in the interests of efficiency and the ascertainment of the truth.[66]

Fairness applies also to civil parties although the 'fair trial rights' of victims are less well-developed than those of the accused.[67] In the ECCC process, civil parties require facilities and access to the case materials in order to fulfil their purpose under the Internal Rules. The careful balancing of the rights of all participants in the process has been a particular challenge for the ECCC, especially to avoid prioritising the accusers (prosecution and civil parties) over the accused when at least visually the courtroom often appeared crammed with lawyers on one side while one or two defence teams sat on the other and the accused was sometimes absent, watching via video-link from a bed in the holding cells below. The manner in which the various organs of the Court have accommodated and developed the notion of civil party participation while retaining the focus on the rights of the accused overall affords it legitimacy.

6. EFFICIENCY

Fairness and expeditiousness are not competing objectives. They are part of the same complex equation formulated to throw out a result that equals justice. When considering the question of additional evidence sought by Nuon Chea on appeal, the Supreme Court Chamber disagreed with the Trial Chamber's statement that the fairness of the proceedings must be *balanced* with the requirement to hold an expeditious trial, finding that 'the Chambers of the ECCC are under an obligation to ensure that proceedings are *both* fair and expeditious'.[68] The Supreme Court Chamber was addressing two aspects of a fair trial in this context, namely the right of the accused to be tried without undue delay and the right to

---

65 Nuon Trial Judgment, above n. 42, paras. 74–8.

66 Ibid, paras. 44, 60.

67 *See* e.g. A. Pues, 'A Victim's Right to a Fair Trial at the International Criminal Court?: Reflections on Article 68(3)', *Journal of International Criminal Justice*, vol. 13, no. 5, 2015, pp. 951–72.

68 *Prosecutor v Nuon Chea* and *Khieu Samphan*, ECCC Case File No. 002/19-09-2007-ECCC/SC, Supreme Court Chamber, Interim Decision on Part of Nuon Chea's First Request to Obtain and Consider Additional Evidence in Appeal Proceedings in Case 002/01, 1 April 2015, para. 22 (*Emphasis added*).

secure the attendance and examination of witnesses in his defence. As the Supreme Court Chamber found:

> In respect of the first aspect, the probative value of proposed evidence *in support of* the charges may be balanced against the time required to obtain it, where it would put in peril the right of the accused to be tried without undue delay. The right to be tried without undue delay, however, does not limit the right of the accused to obtain evidence on his behalf. Rather, general concerns of expeditiousness circumscribe the right of the accused to obtain evidence where the motion for evidence would *de facto* not serve the defence ...[69]

Certain procedural adjustments or even innovations may be acceptable, however, as long as they can guarantee fairness along with expeditiousness. From June 2012 onwards, in the interests of expeditiousness, the President of the Trial Chamber had begun asking witnesses and civil parties who testified to affirm the accuracy of their prior statements made during the investigative phase so that questioning could be limited to matters that had not adequately been covered and to credibility.[70] The biggest innovation in the interests or perhaps naïve expectation of efficiency was undoubtedly the decision to sever Case 002. The implications of this decision both for fairness and expeditiousness have been profound, irrespective of the sound intentions that guided the Trial Chamber towards this solution.

Operating in three official languages may be deemed essential for the ECCC's legitimacy but translation issues have been a constant source of delay. The Court lacked qualified translators and interpreters in the early days of its operation and training and recruitment was barely sufficient to keep up with the ever-growing volume of documentation and the demands of the hearings, not to mention judicial deliberations and collaboration between international and Cambodian prosecutors and lawyers. The translation issue resulted in Khieu Samphan's appeal against his provisional detention being stalled and ultimately withdrawn.[71] A subsequent hearing on the appeal against the order for

---

69 *Prosecutor v Nuon Chea* and *Khieu Samphan*, ECCC Case File No. 002/19-09-2007-ECCC/SC, Supreme Court Chamber, Interim Decision on Part of Nuon Chea's First Request to Obtain and Consider Additional Evidence in Appeal Proceedings in Case 002/01, 1 April 2015, para. 22 (repeated with *emphasis added* in Nuon Appeal Judgment, para. 162).

70 Nuon Trial Judgment, above n. 42, para. 31.

71 *Prosecutor v Khieu Samphan*, ECCC Case File No. 002/19-09-2007-ECCC/OCIJ (PTC04), Pre-Trial Chamber, Decision relating to Notice of Withdrawal of Appeal, 15 October 2008. *See* also *Prosecutor v Khieu Samphan*,

extension of provisional detention and order refusing the request for release was also adjourned due to the absence of the international co-lawyer. The effect of the lawyer's protest was in fact to delay the opportunity of his own client to exercise the right to challenge his ongoing detention. At the same time, the Charged Person's insistence on the participation of his international co-lawyer would have presented the judges with a dilemma had they been inclined to proceed regardless.[72]

The Supreme Court Chamber has clarified that all documents before the ECCC must be filed in Khmer as well as in English *or* French, and that parties may seek translation into the other language.[73] Attempts were made to ensure that throughout the investigation and trial, all parties had capabilities in all three official languages of the ECCC and that the defence had equal access to interpreters and translators.[74] The parties were ordered by the Trial Chamber to ensure that all admitted evidence was available in all three official languages by the time of the filing of Closing Briefs in Case 002/01. Since this did not occur, the Trial Chamber only relied on the evidence that was not available in all three languages where it was corroborated by another reliable source.[75]

An outside observer reportedly suggested that 'the slow pace of the trial fed on itself, creating a kind of complacency, "a sense that the money will go on forever and people's patience will go on forever."'[76] This criticism is often levelled at ad hoc tribunals but to the contrary, most participants in the ECCC process seem acutely aware that the money could run out at any point. Indeed, Cambodian staff often had to wait months for their salaries due to cash flow or funding issues and

---

ECCC Case File No. 002/19-09-2007-ECCC/OCIJ (PTC15), Pre-Trial Chamber, Decision on Khieu Samphan's Supplemental Application for Release, 24 December 2008.

72 *Prosecutor v Khieu Samphan*, ECCC Case File No. 002/19-09-2007-ECCC/OCIJ (PTC04), Pre-Trial Chamber, Decision on Application to Adjourn Hearing on Provisional Detention Appeal, 23 April 2008, para. 15.

73 *Prosecutor v Khieu Samphan*, ECCC Case File No. 002/19-09-2007-ECCC-TC/SC(18), Supreme Court Chamber, Decision on Request by the Defence for Khieu Samphan for Trilingual Notification of the Supreme Court Chamber's Decisions, 30 April 2013, para. 8.

74 Nuon Trial Judgment, above n. 42, para. 38.

75 Ibid, para. 36.

76 S. Mydans, '11 Years, $300 Million and 3 Convictions. Was the Khmer Rouge Tribunal Worth It?', *The New York Times*, 10 April 2017, <https://www.nytimes.com/2017/04/10/world/asia/cambodia-khmer-rouge-united-nations-tribunal.html?smid=nytcore-ipad-share&smprod=nytcore-ipad&_r=0> [accessed 12 July 2017].

demonstrated considerable dedication in remaining in their posts. However, the Supreme Court Chamber deemed it inappropriate for the Trial Chamber to rely on the ECCC's 'financial malaise' in considering whether severance of the proceedings was justified, holding that '[w]hile Judges are at all times certainly obligated to be mindful of the efficiency of proceedings, they must always act within the *sacrum* sphere of the law, the tenets of which cannot be overridden by the *profanum* of budgetary savings'.[77] According to the Supreme Court Chamber:

> in international criminal proceedings financial policies may legitimately enter into equation and affect the scope of the charges in three ways: by legislative decisions shaping personal and subject-matter jurisdiction; by efficiency-driven prosecutorial decisions on which cases to prosecute; and, eventually, by efficiency-driven decisions on the withdrawal or reduction of charges, the latter however being necessarily predicated upon the criterion of reasonable representativeness of the indictment.[78]

The Supreme Court Chamber referred to the ECCC's 'funding crisis' affecting the entire institution and called on donor countries and the UN to act so as to 'guarantee a trial driven by law', otherwise 'all ECCC proceedings must be terminated and the court must close down'.[79] Funding has continued to be provided, in fits and starts, and the Court's financial woes have not appeared to make it more, or less efficient.

7. ACCESSIBILITY

The ECCC's location in Cambodia helps to ensure physical accessibility for the victims, relatives of the accused and interested parties and is a distinct advantage also in keeping down costs. There has been a keen interest in proceedings from the outset and the Court has facilitated access by arranging buses for attendance at hearings and conducting an extensive outreach programme. It has been estimated that more than

---

77 *Prosecutor v Nuon Chea* and *Khieu Samphan*, ECCC Case File No. 002/19-09-2007-ECCC-TC/SC(28), Supreme Court Chamber, Decision on Immediate Appeals against Trial Chamber's Second Decision on Severance of Case 002, 25 November 2013, para. 75.

78 Ibid.

79 Ibid.

236,000 people have attended the proceedings.[80] There has been intense local press interest in the proceedings and NGOs have played an indispensable role, 'designing and distributing specialized information materials, radio call-in shows, websites, films, public forums and community based outreach sessions'.[81] The existence of the ECCC triggered creative educational and rehabilitative ideas and initiatives, which, while serving a different purpose from the criminal trials, help to lend legitimacy to the trial process and its broader goals.

Whether or not the ECCC's immense documentary output is accessible to ordinary citizens is open to question. The Pre-Trial Chamber began its first decision by noting 'the significant public interest in the proceedings and the need for members of the public, without legal training, to understand and appreciate the meaning of its decision' and claimed to be 'writing in a style reflecting this need.'[82] This need, to the extent it was ever real, was gradually forgotten. Sections of the judgments of the Supreme Court Chamber unsurprisingly read like academic papers with heavily footnoted reasoning on the law. As part of a treatise on the law of presumptions in the section of the Duch Appeal Judgment concerning civil party appeals it is stated that: 'Notice may not be required where a presumption reflects probability that is strongly supported by pressing conjecture.'[83] Even if the meaning of this sentence were clear, such language might be difficult to translate into French, never mind Khmer. Furthermore, a significant amount of Latin is used to describe concepts that may not be familiar to all legal systems. Relatively straightforward examples include *Lex Certa*, *Ejusdem Generis* and *Lex Mitior*, while *Allegans Contraria* and *Non-Est Audiendus* may be harder to grasp. Co-Investigating Judge Michael Bohlander was moved to quote Dickens in one of his decisions and while a degree of personal flare may enhance

---

[80] *See* N. Koumjian, 'Khmer Rouge Tribunal: A U.N. Prosecutor's View', *The New York Times*, 13 April 2017, <https://www.nytimes.com/2017/04/13/opinion/khmer-rouge-tribunal-a-un-prosecutors-view.html?mcubz=0> [accessed 12 July 2017].

[81] C. Sperfeldt, 'Cambodian Civil Society and the Khmer Rouge Tribunal', *The International Journal of Transitional Justice*, vol. 6, 2012, pp. 149–60, p. 151.

[82] *Prosecutor v Kaing Guek Eav alias 'Duch'*, ECCC Case File No. 001/18-07-2007/ECCC/OCIJ (PTC01), Pre-Trial Chamber, Decision on Appeal Against Provisional Detention Order of Kaing Guek Eav alias 'Duch', 3 December 2007, p. 2.

[83] Nuon Appeal Judgment, above n. 32, para. 438.

readability, there is a risk that the message becomes lost in translation.[84] By contrast, the Special Court for Sierra Leone (SCSL), which only had English as an official language, attempted to promote accessibility by banning the use of Latin. Outreach activities are of course designed to render complex legal analysis accessible to the public and the development of child or school friendly versions of the ECCC's judgments would be a worthwhile endeavour.

8. ANSWERABILITY

Answerability raises two questions. First, who is answerable before the ECCC? Second, to whom is the ECCC answerable? Both questions relate to the broader issue of which justice needs of the Cambodian and international community the ECCC is called upon to address. As it has been noted, 'When laws serve only themselves, there is a lack of legitimacy.'[85]

Even if the continuation of Cases 003 and 004 were not in doubt, it is debatable whether the ECCC cast a wide enough net over potential perpetrators. It has tried a smaller handful of individuals than any other international or internationalised tribunal. Indeed, its final record may add up to only three convictions out of five persons sent for trial, and no acquittals, though one of the total of ten persons investigated was not sent for trial. In transmitting the report of the Group of Experts to the General Assembly and the Security Council, the UN Secretary-General indicated that the cause of justice and accountability would best be served if both Khmer Rouge military commanders and the political leadership were tried.[86] In his closing statement in Case 001, the national lawyer representing Duch asked if Article 31 of the Cambodian Constitution was

---

84 *Prosecutor v Meas Muth*, ECCC Case File No. 003/07-09-2009-ECCC-OCIJ, Office of the Co-Investigating Judges, Notification on the Interpretation of 'Attack against the Civilian Population' in the Context of Crimes against Humanity with regard to a State's or Regime's Own Armed Forces', 7 February 2017, para. 68.

85 V. Popovski and N. Turner, 'Legality and Legitimacy in International Order', United Nations University, *Policy Brief*, no. 5, 2008, p. 1, <https://www.ciaonet.org/attachments/860/uploads> [accessed 12 July 2017].

86 Identical Letters Dated 15 March 1999 from the Secretary-General to the President of the General Assembly and the President of the Security Council, A/53/850, 15 March 1999.

being upheld when 'amongst the 196 prison chairmen, only the S-21 prison chairman is being prosecuted.'[87]

The question of whom and how many should answer for crimes before the ECCC in order to assure its legitimacy has no easy answer. On the one hand, if the International Co-Prosecutor had stopped with the five initial suspects, there might never have been the damaging split between the international and national judicial organs, thereby rendering the process swifter, more efficient, cheaper, and in some senses more legitimate. On the other hand, such a decision would have opened the Court up to criticism that it was playing into the Cambodian government's hand and trying the already earmarked scapegoats, thereby rendering it a flawed, pre-determined and ultimately illegitimate process. Having regard to the goals of the ECCC, its financial precariousness and the age and fragility of the accused and witnesses, and leaving aside political considerations, the middle ground adopted by the International Co-Prosecutor is defensible although the figure most frequently suggested was about 15.[88] Certainly many more are answerable for the crimes of the Khmer Rouge period but, alas, will not be tried by the ECCC or at all. The Co-Investigating Judges have referred to the 'massive impunity gap for crimes committed during the DK era'[89] and viewed the effect of the ECCC Law on personal jurisdiction as being to restrict the ECCC's own jurisdiction to those most responsible while also excluding personal or subject-matter jurisdiction by the ordinary Cambodian courts over crimes within the ECCC's temporal jurisdiction.[90]

The potential impunity gap extends beyond Khmer Rouge officials. The ECCC is also known as the 'Khmer Rouge Tribunal' and the acronym UNAKRT stands for 'UN Assistance to the Khmer Rouge Trials'. The emphasis is squarely on the period of Khmer Rouge rule. But there were crimes committed by others in the same decade. The Court has only considered the US bombing of Cambodia between 1969 and 1973 peripherally in Case 002/01, as part of the historical context within

---

87 *Prosecutor v Kaing Guek Eav alias 'Duch'*, ECCC Case File No. 001/18-07-2007-ECCC/TC, E1/80.1, Trial Chamber, Transcript of Proceedings – 'Duch' Trial (Trial Day 75), 25 November 2009, p. 103.

88 *See* also D. Scheffer, 'How Many are Too Many Defendants at the KRT?', *Phnom Penh Post*, 8 January 2009, <http://www.phnompenhpost.com/national/how-many-are-too-many-defendants-krt> [accessed 12 July 2017].

89 ECCC Case File No. 004/07-09-2009-ECCC-OCIJ, *Im Chaem*, Closing Order (Reasons), 10 July 2017, para. 25.

90 Ibid, para. 23.

the limits of the Closing Order.[91] Notably, the defendants at Nuremberg were tried for conduct for which the Allies might also be deemed responsible, such as the bombardment of undefended cites including Dresden and Hiroshima. Where a modern tribunal focuses narrowly on one side to a conflict, as for example was the case with the International Criminal Tribunal for Rwanda (ICTR), a shadow may be cast over its legitimacy.

A separate question is to whom the court is answerable. Although ordinary citizens were not consulted during the process of the ECCC's establishment, when negotiations appeared doomed to failure, '[p]rotests and demands to restart negotiations poured in from genocide victims at home and abroad, and received ample coverage in the media.'[92] According to research carried out by NGOs, Cambodians had a strong sense of an absence of justice, both in relation to the crimes of the Khmer Rouge and in their society as a whole, an overwhelming desire for accountability, and a wish to participate in their own legal system.[93] Studies carried out so far suggest that the ECCC has met with a broadly positive reaction among the general public.[94] Ian Harris notes that 'if we want to understand Cambodian attitudes toward the applicability of "western" concepts of criminal justice to offences committed during the Democratic Kampuchea period, our discussion needs to be set firmly within the

---

91 Nuon Trial Judgment, above n. 42, paras. 55–8 (rejecting the defence argument that the accused's crimes should be placed in the context of the American bombing of Cambodia between 1969 and 1973 and the living conditions in Cambodia prior to 1975).

92 Chhang, above n. 26, p. 165.

93 Ibid, p. 169.

94 P. Pham, P. Vinck, M. Balthazard and S. Hean, 'After the First Trial: A Population-Based Survey on Knowledge and Perceptions of Justice and the Extraordinary Chambers in the Courts of Cambodia', University of California, Berkeley, School of Law, Human Rights Center, June 2011 p. 26, <https://www.law.berkeley.edu/files/HRC/Publications_After-the-First-Trial_06-2011.pdf> [accessed 12 July 2018]; K. Hale, 'Khmer Rouge Tribunal Is a Success, Even If Others Have Trouble Admitting It', *HuffPost*, <http://www.huffingtonpost.com/kip-hale/khmer-rouge-tribunal-a-su_b_5695307.html#> [accessed 13 July 2017]; Open Society Justice Initiative, 'Performance and Perception: The Impact of the Extraordinary Chambers in the Court of Cambodia', Open Society Foundations, February 2016, p. 102: 'The response of Cambodians to the court is generally positive' and 'A majority of Cambodians sees the court as positively contributing, finally, to a sense of justice about the Khmer Rouge atrocities; they believe it has a positive impact on their society or their personal healing.', <https://www.opensocietyfoundations.org/sites/default/files/performance-perception-eccc-20160211.pdf> [accessed 14 July 2017].

Cambodia Buddhist context'.[95] Buddhism is more than just a religion in Cambodia. It is an integral part of the culture and provides a moral framework and focal point for everyday life. It is said that 'the monastic order is the most well-regarded and least corruptible segment of Cambodian society'.[96] Cambodia has been influenced by Buddhist thought and practice for most of its history and Theravāda Buddhism, known for its gentility, has dominated since the end of the Angkorian period.[97] In view of the Khmer Rouge's attempt to eradicate Buddhism, its subsequent revival may be expected to influence and be influenced by the ECCC process.

When reflecting on the crimes of the Khmer Rouge, the question 'why' is the recurring one amongst ordinary citizens. There may be a misconception that a judicial process can get to the bottom of this eternal question. It has been noted that although the majority of the population favoured a trial, they were mostly interested in its public and confrontational nature, and a show of remorse on the part of the guilty.[98] Over two-thirds of those surveyed in one study for their attitudes towards the establishment of the ECCC indicated that they were not looking for revenge, but also could not forgive the cadres who made them suffer.[99] Over 70 per cent in the same group favoured a tribunal with UN participation.[100] The UN Secretary-General made the following statement in his 'Millennium Report':

> [E]ven though the United Nations is an organization of states, the Charter is written in the name of 'we the peoples'. It reaffirms the dignity and worth of the human person, respect for human rights and the equal rights of men and women, and a commitment to social progress as measured by better standards of life, in freedom from want and fear alike. Ultimately, then, the United Nations exists for, and must serve, the needs and hopes of people everywhere.[101]

---

[95] I. Harris, '"Onslaught on Human Beings": A Theravāda Buddhist Perspective on Accountability for Crimes Committed in the Democratic Kampuchea Period', in J. Ramji and B. van Schaack (eds), *Bringing the Khmer Rouge to Justice: Prosecuting Mass Violence before the Cambodian Courts* (Lewiston, New York, Edwin Mellon Press, 2005), pp. 59–95, p. 60.

[96] Ibid, pp. 61, 80.

[97] C. Etcheson, *The Rise and Demise of Democratic Kampuchea* (Boulder, Colorado, Westview Press, 1984), p. 11.

[98] PoKempner, above n. 34, p. 351.

[99] Chhang, above n. 26, p. 171.

[100] Ibid.

[101] K.A. Annan, *We the Peoples: The Role of the United Nations in the 21st Century* (New York, United Nations, Department of Public Information, 2000), p. 6.

The idea of 'We the peoples' implies that the ECCC is answerable both to Cambodians and to the international community and that domestic and international legitimacy are connected. Both 'sides' have a jointly vested interest in a credible court that delivers on its promises.

9. CONCLUSION

Reference has been made to the 'legitimacy-related anxiety'[102] surrounding international and internationalised criminal tribunals and nowhere is this more keenly felt than in relation to the ECCC. Possible legitimacy detractors include structural bifurcation, corruption, the small number of accused, political interference impacting on independence, inefficiency and, as a consequence of the slow pace and gradual fading of the accused and witnesses, a growing irrelevance. Legitimacy indicators include the successful arrests, investigations and completed trials, the contribution to the discovery of the truth, the participation of victims and the award of reparations, the upholding of fair trial rights and the reinforcement of the principle that nobody is above the law and everybody is entitled to their rights on an equal basis. To an extent, the ECCC has managed to overcome the legitimacy detractors by concentrating on its core function of conducting criminal investigations and trials in accordance with the Court's objectives and constitutive documents.

From the perspective of the mixed composition of the bench, it has been suggested that hybrid tribunals 'are positioned to offer greater sociological legitimacy than purely international tribunals'.[103] Supermajority voting in the Chambers was envisaged to promote legitimacy as it was designed to ensure that the voice of 'we the peoples' could not be expressed by the national or international judges acting alone. However, the effect has been to allow separate voices to resonate in relation to Cases 003 and 004 and for the investigations in those cases to be largely an international endeavour. Sooner or later the proceedings are likely to be stalled, whether through lack of funding or persistent divided opinions in Cases 003 and 004 making a trial all but impossible. It should not be forgotten that the ECCC was designed with this type of eventuality in mind, hence the detailed disagreement procedures, and the fact that the system has been tested, even to breaking point, does not necessarily detract from legitimacy and may even be a positive indicator. Legitimacy

---

102 Vasiliev, above n. 10, p. 71.
103 Hobbs, above n. 30, p. 488.

'can be gained and it can be lost. It evolves over time and its maintenance requires constant effort.'[104] The ECCC process is not over yet.

104 Popovski and Turner, above n. 85, p. 4.

12. Legacy

1. INTRODUCTION

It has been noted that '*Angkor*, *Angkar* and *Angko* are the three quintessential themes of Cambodian history'.[1] *Angkar* 'is the story of a search for Utopia, and the discovery of something quite different'.[2] *Angkor* relates to a bygone era when civilisation flourished. *Angko* means rice, which is the staple food in Cambodia.[3] As Cambodia comes to terms with the catastrophe of the Khmer Rouge period, recovers the spirit of its ancient past and prospers, what will be the enduring legacy of the Extraordinary Chambers of the Courts in Cambodia (ECCC)?

It is easy to point first to the price tag on the trials—around US$300 million—and the small number of individuals held to account for the deaths of at least 1.7 million people.[4] But the cost and conviction rate are not necessarily fair or comprehensive measures of success. It should rather be asked: 'To what extent has this tribunal contributed to beginning the process of embedding the idea of justice, the absence of impunity, into public consciousness, to help Cambodia transition to a better

---

[1] H. Jarvis, *Cambodia (World Bibliographical Series: Volume 200)* (Oxford/Santa Barbara, California, Clio Press, 1997), p. xiii (This work constitutes an impressive bibliography of material covering all aspects of Cambodian history, religion, politics and culture, including sections on literature and film, pre-dating the establishment of the ECCC.).

[2] C. Etcheson, *The Rise and Demise of Democratic Kampuchea* (Boulder, Colorado, Westview Press, 1984), p. xiii.

[3] For a modern take on these themes, *see* the lyrics to Cambodian-American rapper Prach Ly's song 'Power, Territory and Rice', Frontline World, <http://www.pbs.org/frontlineworld/stories/cambodia/ly.html> [accessed 17 July 2017].

[4] S. Mydans, '11 Years, $300 Million and 3 Convictions. Was the Khmer Rouge Tribunal Worth It?', *The New York Times*, 10 April 2017, <https://www.nytimes.com/2017/04/10/world/asia/cambodia-khmer-rouge-united-nations-tribunal.html?smid=nytcore-ipad-share&smprod=nytcore-ipad&_r=0> [accessed 12 July 2017]. *See* also reaction by N. Koumjian, 'Khmer Rouge Tribunal: A U.N. Prosecutor's View', *The New York Times*, 13 April 2017, <https://www.nytimes.com/2017/04/13/opinion/khmer-rouge-tribunal-a-un-prosecutors-view.html?smid=nytcore-ipad-share&smprod=nytcore-ipad&_r=1> [accessed 17 July 2017].

place?'[5] It is also worth remembering that without any accountability mechanism, the senior Democratic Kampuchea (DK) leaders would have seen out their twilight years in peaceful retirement. There would have been no proper opportunity to address the crimes of the past, and the majority of survivors may well have taken the secrets of their suffering to the grave, leaving Cambodia's youth unknowing and unencumbered. The ECCC was not about creating the 'perfect formula for justice' but rather about 'building a court that can *deliver* such justice'.[6] Whatever its flaws, the *Duch* trial showed that the ECCC was capable of establishing a historical record of events for both a domestic and global audience.[7] The ECCC Supreme Court Chamber has noted that the 'root causes and the consequences of certain actions may be suitable subjects of historical analysis, but have no bearing on an individual's criminal, as opposed to moral, responsibility.'[8] The causes of Cambodia's tragedy are multifaceted, and there are 'many actors amongst whom responsibility must be shared'.[9] The ECCC has a limited mandate and can only find one truth. But it is an important truth.

Legacy is a concept as much as a word signifying something handed down to the next generation. It can incorporate the 'broader sociological or philosophical aims of justice for mass atrocities' but also describes the 'concrete measures that positively impact on justice sector reform'.[10] Like legitimacy, it has a domestic and an international component. This concluding chapter will take up various themes relating to the ECCC's legacy, including the impact of the ECCC's proceedings on the rule of law in Cambodia, restorative justice, the development of domestically applicable international fair trial standards, the contribution of the ECCC's jurisprudence to the evolution of the substantive law, and finally, the value of the ECCC precedent as a model for future internationalised criminal justice processes.

---

5 Mydans, ibid.

6 D. Scheffer, *All the Missing Souls: A Personal History of the War Crimes Tribunals* (Princeton, Princeton University Press, 2012), p. 392.

7 Ibid, p. 405.

8 *Prosecutor v Nuon Chea* and *Khieu Samphan*, ECCC Case File No. 002/19-09-2007-ECCC/SC, Supreme Court Chamber, Appeal Judgment, 23 November 2016, para. 82 ('Nuon Appeal Judgment').

9 P. Short, *Pol Pot: The History of a Nightmare* (London, John Murray Publishers, 2004), p. 4.

10 'Promotion of ECCC Legacy', The Office of the United Nations High Commissioner for Human Rights -Cambodia, 28 September 2015, <http://cambodia.ohchr.org/en/rule-of-law/promotion-eccc-legacy> [accessed 7 June 2017].

2. DOMESTIC LEGACY

Being a 'hybrid' court and based 'in-country', there were great hopes for the ECCC in terms of 'developing the rule of law, capacity-building, and "legacy" in general'.[11] Additionally, it was expected that the Court would contribute towards reconciliation and stability as envisaged under the ECCC Agreement.[12] The ECCC was to be a role model for domestic courts in Cambodia 'by evincing the independence and impartiality of proceedings and the credibility of its process' and by transferring and exchanging knowledge and skills through judicial and other training.[13]

The various organs of the ECCC, sometimes in cooperation with the UN or local and international NGOs and universities, have organised specialised training programmes for judges, prosecutors, lawyers, journalists, judicial police, translators and archivists. The judges had the opportunity to visit the International Criminal Court (ICC) and other institutions in The Hague. On one occasion, the ECCC attracted a visit

---

[11] D. Cohen, '"Hybrid" Justice in East Timor, Sierra Leone, and Cambodia: "Lessons Learned" and Prospects for the Future', *Stanford Journal of International Law*, vol. 15, no. 1, 2007, pp. 1–38, p. 36. Cf. J.D. Ciorciari and A. Heindel, *Hybrid Justice: The Extraordinary Chambers in the Courts of Cambodia* (Ann Arbor, Michigan, University of Michigan Press, 2014), p. 248: 'Proximity to the survivor population and local judiciary can backfire and create a negative or "reverse" legacy …'

[12] Cf. J.N. Clark, *International Trials and Reconciliation: Assessing the Impact of the International Criminal Tribunal for the Former Yugoslavia* (Abingdon, Oxon/New York, Routledge, 2014), p. i (arguing on the basis of an empirical study that reconciliation is not a realistic aim for a criminal court).

[13] 'Promotion of ECCC Legacy', The Office of the United Nations High Commissioner for Human Rights – Cambodia, 28 September 2015, <http://cambodia.ohchr.org/en/rule-of-law/promotion-eccc-legacy> [accessed 7 June 2017]. *See* also *Prosecutor v Nuon Chea, Ieng Sary, Ieng Thirith* and *Khieu Samphan*, ECCC Case File No. 002/19-09-2007/ECCC/TC, Trial Chamber, Decision on Ieng Sary's Application to Disqualify Judge Nil Nonn and Related Requests, 28 January 2011, para. 14 (the ECCC 'may, as a model court, nonetheless serve to encourage and underscore the significance of institutional safeguards of judicial independence and integrity'); M. Kaing, 'Khmer Rouge Sentence a Milestone, but Cambodia's Justice System Remains Fragile', *The Asia Foundation Blog*, 3 September 2014, <http://asiafoundation.org/2014/09/03/khmer-rouge-sentence-a-milestone-but-cambodias-justice-system-remains-fragile/> [accessed 19 July 2017]; M.G. Karnavas, 'Bringing Domestic Cases into Compliance with International Standards', (2014) *The Cambodia Law and Policy Journal*, vol. 3, <http://cambodialpj.org/article/bringing-domestic-cases-into-compliance-with-international-standards/> [accessed 19 July 2017].

by ten delegates from the Kenyan Judicial Service Commission who sought to learn from a 'trailblazer' court which combined 'elements of Cambodian civil law with internationally-applied common law'.[14] ECCC employees are trained on the job, gaining skills to take back to their parallel functions in the domestic system. There has been no absence of capacity-building and exchange activity although there is always more that could have been done.[15] It has been observed that 'the natural advantages that [the ECCC's] location and composition afford have been tempered by shortcomings in its institutional design, endowment and political will'.[16] In particular, the ECCC lacked a dedicated outreach office with relevant functions being split between the Public Affairs Section and the Victims Support Section.[17] This meant outsourcing core outreach tasks to NGOs. While in certain respects this reflected a weakness in the Court's institutional design, it could also be seen as a strength as it encouraged ownership of the ECCC by civil society.

The Chambers have stressed the desirability of having a broader impact on the capacity and independence of the domestic judiciary, reconciliation and respect for human rights but have also noted that they face limitations. In the context of disqualification proceedings against Judge Nil Nonn, the Trial Chamber commented that weaknesses within the Cambodian judiciary were one of the reasons for the ECCC's establishment.[18] However, insofar as the question concerned the fitness of a judge to serve in the domestic courts, recourse had to be made to 'domestic mechanisms designed to uphold standards of judicial integrity within the Cambodian judiciary'.[19] All that the Trial Chamber could do was to emphasise the need for 'such mechanisms to operate effectively and equitably in order to safeguard public confidence in the judiciary and to strengthen the rule of law within Cambodia'.[20]

As it concerned Judge You Ottara's participation in a controversial Cambodian Supreme Court decision, the Trial Chamber took the view

---

[14] T. Stevenson, 'Kenya's Judiciary Seeks Experiences from ECCC', Extraordinary Chambers in the Courts of Cambodia, 30 May 2013, <https://www.eccc.gov.kh/en/blog/topic/1279> [accessed 17 July 2017].

[15] *See* further Ciorciari and Heindel, above n. 11, pp. 249–53.

[16] Ibid, p. 233.

[17] *See* further, Ciorciari and Heindel, above n. 11, pp. 235–6.

[18] *Prosecutor v Nuon Chea, Ieng Sary, Ieng Thirith* and *Khieu Samphan*, ECCC Case File No. 002/19-09-2007/ECCC/TC, Trial Chamber, Decision on Ieng Sary's Application to Disqualify Judge Nil Nonn and Related Requests, 28 January 2011, para. 13.

[19] Ibid, para. 16.

[20] Ibid.

that much of the criticism in the reports before it were 'directed toward the substance of Cambodian criminal defamation law and its effect on the right of free speech in Cambodia', and this was beyond the scope of the subject-matter jurisdiction of the ECCC.[21] The Supreme Court Chamber adopted a similar approach in a related application to disqualify Judge Som Sereyvuth which it found 'in fact targets the legal system of Cambodia and all judges who participated in the [Mu Sochua case]'.[22]

Reconciliation is a possible offshoot of all aspects of the ECCC process but perhaps most closely attached to sentencing and the longer-term rehabilitation of victims. National reconciliation with a country's own brutal history, such as occurred in Germany after the Second World War, might be easier to achieve through the ECCC process than individual forgiveness of perpetrators by their victims. It must not be forgotten that reintegration of the Khmer Rouge into society is an aspect of reconciliation.[23] This goal was behind the 1994 Law to Outlaw the Democratic Kampuchea Group and may help to explain the absence of any domestic effort to bridge the impunity gap as it concerns lower-ranking former Khmer Rouge officials.

In his closing speech in Case 001, the International Co-Lawyer François Roux likened the trial of Duch to proceedings before a truth and reconciliation commission. He commented that: 'It is to the honour of Cambodia that this country has been able to allow so many people to follow and observe these proceedings through the television and to witness what is being said in this trial.'[24] To that extent, the trial served

---

21 *Prosecutor v Nuon Chea, Ieng Sary, Ieng Thirith* and *Khieu Samphan*, ECCC Case File No. 002/19-09-2007-ECCC/TC, Trial Chamber, Decision on Ieng Thirith and Ieng Sary's Applications for Disqualification of Judge You Ottara from the Special Bench and Requests for a Public Hearing, 9 May 2011, para. 14.

22 *Prosecutor v Ieng Thirith*, ECCC Case File No. 002/19-09-2007-ECCC/SC(1), Supreme Court Chamber, Decision on Ieng Thirith's Application to Disqualify Judge Som Sereyvuth for Lack of Independence, 3 June 2011, para. 15.

23 The Co-Investigating Judges have noted that 'the goal of peace and reconciliation which entails reintegration of the Khmer Rouge into society was [a] paramount motivation of the Cambodian government' in limiting the personal jurisdiction of the ECCC. ECCC Case File No. 004/07-09-2009-ECCC-OCIJ, *Im Chaem*, Closing Order (Reasons), 10 July 2017, para. 16.

24 *Prosecutor v Kaing Guek Eav alias 'Duch'*, ECCC Case File No. 001/18-07-2007-ECCC/TC, E1/81.1, Trial Chamber, Transcript of Proceedings – 'Duch' Trial (Trial Day 76), 26 November 2009, pp. 7–8, <https://www.eccc.gov.kh/sites/default/files/documents/courtdoc/E1_81.1_TR001_20091126_Final_EN_Pub.pdf> [accessed 17 July 2017].

as a model from Roux's perspective. In the same case, the International Co-Prosecutor urged the application of an appropriately severe sentence, arguing that a heavily reduced sentence based on the special features of the case would 'hamper and not help the attainment of national reconciliation in Cambodia'.[25] Further, while recognising that national reconciliation was a legitimate consideration for the ECCC, he stressed that it was 'a by-product of a criminal trial, not its purpose' and that the central purpose would always be the ascertainment of the truth.[26] However, the simple knowledge that the surviving senior DK leaders will see out their days in prison is unlikely to be sufficient to address the healing aspect that underlies reconciliation.

When Duch was asked by the Trial Chamber whether he taught S-21 staff how to execute detainees, he chillingly cited a Khmer saying to the effect that, 'I do not need to teach crocodiles how to swim, because the crocodiles already know how to swim'.[27] It was never envisaged to be part of the ECCC's legacy to reach all levels of perpetrator and combat impunity in a comprehensive manner. However, the Court has gone some way towards demonstrating that there is no impunity for those who play a leading role in the commission of international crimes. The Supreme Court Chamber commented on the daily reminders as Case 002/01 unfolded of the need to realise 'the deterrence purpose of punishment for crimes against humanity', referring to 'reports of foreign governments turning against their constituent peoples, and the increasing caseload of the ICC'.[28] In the Supreme Court Chamber's view, 'the passage of time neither leads to impunity nor undue leniency'.[29] At the same time, the ECCC's inability to secure the attendance of politically-connected witnesses and the stalling of Cases 003 and 004 casts doubt on the veracity of the statement that nobody is above the law.

---

[25] *Prosecutor v Kaing Guek Eav alias 'Duch'*, ECCC Case File No. 001/18-07-2007-ECCC/TC, E1/80.1, Trial Chamber, Transcript of Proceedings – "Duch" Trial (Trial Day 75), 25 November 2009, p. 31.

[26] Ibid, pp. 30–1.

[27] *Prosecutor v Kaing Guek Eav alias 'Duch'*, ECCC Case File No. 001/18-07-2007/ECCC/TC, Trial Chamber, Judgment, 26 July 2010, para. 222 ('Duch Trial Judgment').

[28] *Prosecutor v Kaing Guek Eav alias 'Duch'*, ECCC Case File No. 001/18-07-2007-ECCC/SC, Supreme Court Chamber, Appeal Judgment, 3 February 2012, para. 382 ('Duch Appeal Judgment').

[29] Ibid.

A 2010 report of the Human Rights Council stated that 'democratisation has not yet fully taken root' in Cambodia.[30] This may be in part due to the 'highly truncated time-scale'[31] in which paradigmatic shifts, including multi-lateral intervention and a universal demand for democratisation have occurred.[32] The fact that the role of Special Rapporteur on the human rights situation in Cambodia is still deemed necessary is an indication that Cambodia's transition to a liberal democracy with its associated human rights goals as outlined at Paris is not considered by the UN to be complete. This is despite Cambodia's enthusiastic and commendable ratification of various human rights treaties, including the Rome Statute in 2002. It remains to be seen whether the ECCC experience can further inspire the actual promotion of respect for human rights even in the limited context of fair and transparent judicial proceedings.

3. RESTORATIVE LEGACY

The ECCC's potential to provide restorative justice for victims is contained in its mechanisms for civil party participation in proceedings and awards of reparation as discussed in Chapter 10. The Supreme Court Chamber has observed that the ECCC's criminal proceedings 'ought to be considered as a contribution to the process of national reconciliation, possibly a starting point for the reparation scheme, and not the ultimate

---

[30] S.P. Subedi, Human Rights Council, Report of the Special Rapporteur on the Situation of Human Rights in Cambodia, A/HRC/15/46, 16 September 2010, p. 1, <https://documents-dds-ny.un.org/doc/UNDOC/GEN/G10/161/45/PDF/G1016145.pdf?OpenElement> [accessed 17 July 2017]. *See* also S.P. Subedi, Human Rights Council, Report of the Special Rapporteur on the Situation of Human Rights in Cambodia, A/HRC/18/46, 2 August 2011, para. 64 (in which the Special Rapporteur states: 'Cambodia needs to accelerate the process of democratization in the country.'), <https://documents-dds-ny.un.org/doc/UNDOC/GEN/G11/153/63/PDF/G1115363.pdf?OpenElement> [accessed 17 July 2017].

[31] I. Harris, '"Onslaught on Human Beings": A Theravāda Buddhist Perspective on Accountability for Crimes Committed in the Democratic Kampuchea Period', in J. Ramji and B. van Schaack (eds), *Bringing the Khmer Rouge to Justice: Prosecuting Mass Violence before the Cambodian Courts* (Lewiston, New York, Edwin Mellon Press, 2005), pp. 59–95, p. 81.

[32] L. McGrew, 'Re-Establishing Legitimacy through the Extraordinary Chambers in the Courts of Cambodia', in J. Őjendal and M. Lilja (eds), *Beyond Democracy in Cambodia: Political Reconstruction in a Post-Conflict Society* (Copenhagen, Nordic Institute of Asian Studies Press, 2009), pp. 250–96, p. 251.

remedy for nation-wide consequences of the tragedies during the DK'.[33] The judges might have wished they could do more, as they went on to state a little defensively that 'the ECCC cannot be overloaded with utopian expectations that would ultimately exceed the attainable goals of transitional justice'.[34] Clearly, they felt constrained by their narrow mandate.

A study based on interviews with civil parties and their representatives carried out in 2011 found that high on the list of requests for collective and symbolic reparations were a memorial, stupa or funeral monument in each province to remember the victims, health and mental health services, and a museum and alms house.[35] In their submissions on reparations, the lawyers for the civil parties indicated the importance of memorialisation not just for survivors but also to educate and sensitise future generations to prevent the atrocities of the Khmer Rouge period from ever recurring.[36] Broadly, the reparations awarded in Case 002/01 match the priorities of the civil parties although due to inadequate evidence of funding, the Trial Chamber refused the request for the establishment of memorial sites. As this request was stated to have the support of the government,[37] it is to be hoped that it will be followed up.

In addition to judicial measures, the Victims Support Section (VSS) is 'entrusted with the development and implementation of non-judicial programs and measures addressing the broader interests of victims'.[38] These non-judicial measures were anticipated to be a 'major legacy' of the ECCC.[39] It seems, however, that the judicial and non-judicial

---

33 Duch Appeal Judgment, above n. 28, para. 655.

34 Ibid.

35 N. Kirchenbauer, M. Balthazard, L. Ky, P. Vinck and P. Pham, 'Baseline Study of the Cambodian Human Rights and Development Association's Civil Party Scheme for Case 002: Victims Participation before the Extraordinary Chambers in the Courts of Cambodia', Cambodian Human Rights and Development Association and Harvard Humanitarian Initiative, January 2013, p. 39, <https://www.eccc.gov.kh/sites/default/files/Victims-participation-before-ECCC-Baseline-Study-Jan-2013.pdf> [accessed 17 July 2017].

36 *Prosecutor v Nuon, Chea* and *Khieu Samphan*, ECCC Case File No. 002/19-09-2007-CETC/CPI, Civil Parties, Deuxième Complément D'Informations À La Demande Définitive De Réparations des Co-Avocats Principaux Pour Les Parties Civiles En Application De La Règle 80bis Du Règlement Intérieur Et Annexes Confidentielles, 31 March 2014, paras. 7–14.

37 Nuon Appeal Judgment, above n. 8, para. 1127.

38 Internal Rules, Rule 12 *bis* (4).

39 Ciorciari and Heindel, above n. 11, p. 228 (citing Judge Silvia Cartwright at the opening of the ECCC's 7th Plenary Session on 2 February 2010).

measures became largely indistinguishable as a result of changes to the rules on reparations to accommodate the large numbers of civil parties in Case 002.[40] Nonetheless, the VSS initiated certain activities, in particular those focusing on women and the consequences of sexual and gender-based violence. A long-term project entitled 'Promoting Gender Equality and Improving Access of Justice for Female and Gender-based Violence Survivors of the Khmer Rouge Regime', conducted in cooperation with the Transcultural Psychosocial Organization, attracted funding from the UN Trust Fund to End Violence against Women.[41]

At the commencement of the ECCC proceedings, the Pre-Trial Chamber expressed the concern that:

> the passage of time has not diminished the impact of the Democratic Kampuchea regime on society. It is believed that a proportion of the population that lived through this period from 1975 to 1979 suffers from Post-Traumatic Stress Disorder. Specialists believe that the commencement of judicial activities before the ECCC 'may pose a fresh risk to the Cambodian society'. It may 'lead to the resurfacing of anxieties and a rise in the negative social consequences that may accompany them'.[42]

The reparations projects adopted in the context of Case 002/01 and the non-judicial measures may go some way towards providing psycho-social support to victims, but they come at a late stage. One observer has suggested that the post-traumatic stress suffered by survivors was re-awakened by the outreach activities undertaken by local NGOs who lacked the requisite expertise and resources.[43] This is a difficult assertion to test but represents an important area requiring further attention and study.

---

[40] Ibid, pp. 227–9.

[41] *See* Gender-Based Violence under Khmer Rouge Information Platform, <http://gbvkr.org/> [accessed 27 July 2017]; and 'Victims Support Section of the ECCC Secures Funds from UN Trust Fund to End Violence against Women', Extraordinary Chambers in the Courts of Cambodia, 28 January 2016, <https://www.eccc.gov.kh/en/articles/victims-support-section-eccc-secures-funds-un-trust-fund-end-violence-against-women> [accessed 17 July 2017].

[42] *Prosecutor v Kaing Guek Eav alias 'Duch'*, ECCC Case File No. 001/18-07-2007/ECCC/OCIJ (PTC01), Pre-Trial Chamber, Decision on Appeal Against Provisional Detention Order of Kaing Guek Eav alias 'Duch', 3 December 2007, para. 50 (citing R. Savage, 'Post Traumatic Stress Disorder: A Legacy of Pain and Violence', *Monthly South Easter Globe*, July 2007, pp. 24–7).

[43] J. Brinkley, *Cambodia's Curse: The Modern History of a Troubled Land* (New York, PublicAffairs, 2011), pp. 316–36.

4. PROCEDURAL LEGACY

The nascent state of the Cambodian Criminal Procedure Code, adopted only in August 2007, meant that the domestic and internationalised procedures could to some extent develop in tandem. There was clearly the potential for 'international standards' to filter down to domestic courts while the domestic criminal justice system was being overhauled. At the same time, the right balance had to be found between internationalising the ECCC process on the one hand and staying true to Cambodian processes on the other. This required genuine cooperation between the national and international judges and staff.[44] Duch's lawyer referred at the opening of the trial to the benefits of the procedures which had allowed the case file to include a 're-enactment' at S-21 and Choeng Ek, where Duch had met his former victims.[45] Marcel Lemonde, the Co-Investigating Judge who initiated this process (described in French as a *reconstitution*), has explained that it is a common investigative procedure in France, which involves taking the accused and witnesses to the scene of the crime to clarify each one's role.[46] It is open to question whether this was ultimately a worthwhile use of precious investigative time. Cinematic re-enactments had already been made, though without Duch's participation.[47] From a legacy perspective, re-enactments bring the past alive in the present in the hope of finally extinguishing painful memories.[48] However, although the ECCC's re-enactment was filmed, the

---

44 Any purely independent action by international lawyers on behalf of their clients would appear to offend the spirit if not the letter of the Internal Rules. *See* Internal Rules, Rule 22(1)(c): 'A foreign lawyer shall work in conjunction with a national lawyer in the defence of their client before the ECCC.'

45 *Prosecutor v Kaing Guek Eav alias 'Duch'*, ECCC Case File No. 001/18-07-2007-ECCC/TC, E1/6.1, Trial Chamber, Transcript of Proceedings – 'Duch' Trial (Trial Day 2), 31 March 2009, p. 90, <https://www.eccc.gov.kh/sites/default/files/documents/courtdoc/E1_6.1_TR001_20090331_Final_EN_Pub.pdf> [accessed 17 July 2017].

46 M. Lemonde and J. Reynaud, *Un Juge Face aux Khmers Rouges* (Paris, Éditions du Seuil, 2013), p. 108.

47 *See* e.g. *S-21: The Khmer Rouge Killing Machine*, dir. Rithy Panh, Cambodia/France, Institut national de l'audiovisuel and First Run Features (which brought survivors Vann Nath and Chum Mey together with some of their former captors).

48 *See* further A.C.H. Lim, *Cambodia and the Politics of Aesthetics* (Abingdon, Oxon/New York, Routledge, 2013), p. 125 (who notes that in the film *S-21: The Khmer Rouge Killing Machine*, Chum Mey expresses doubts about the

confidential nature of the case file means that the video has not yet been made available to the public.[49]

The reasoning of the Chambers on a variety of issues from pre-trial detention to admissibility of appeals suggests that careful consideration was given to the relationship between Cambodian criminal procedure and international standards, the latter phrase becoming a buzzword in the early days of the Pre-Trial Chamber which was tasked with clarifying a wide range of preliminary procedures. The ECCC was also poised to demonstrate the practical application of the rights contained in the ICCPR, serving an important educative function.

One important procedural and evidential issue that has generated a considerable amount of litigation is the admissibility of evidence obtained by torture. The issue was first raised before the Co-Investigating Judges by Ieng Thirith's defence lawyers who argued that evidence obtained by torture was inadmissible in ECCC proceedings except against the torturer to show that the statement had been made. The debate centred on Article 15 of the Convention against Torture and Other Cruel, Inhuman or Degrading Treatment or Punishment (CAT), according to which:

> Each State Party shall ensure that any statement which is established to have been made as a result of torture shall not be invoked as evidence in any proceedings, except against a person accused of torture as evidence that the statement was made.[50]

Among other factors, this 'exclusionary rule' is designed to prevent the admission of inherently unreliable evidence. The Co-Investigating Judges accepted the applicability of Article 15, and found that the limited exception applied to superiors as well as direct perpetrators given the purposes of the CAT, which included prohibiting the use of a confession obtained under torture against the victim and deterring those higher up

---

possibility of reconciliation while Vann Nath states that it is essential to preserve the memory of events at S-21).

[49] *See* also C. Barton, 'Duch to "Re-enact" S-21 Crimes', *The Phnom Penh Post*, 22 February 2008, <http://www.phnompenhpost.com/national/duch-re-enact-s-21-crimes> [accessed 17 July 2017]. Controversially, a French film crew also filmed the re-enactment. *See* Marcel Lemonde's reflections in his book, Lemonde and Reynaud, above n. 46, pp. 120–7.

[50] Convention against Torture and Other Cruel, Inhuman or Degrading Treatment or Punishment, United Nations, *Treaty Series*, vol. 1465, 85, 10 December 1984, Article 15, <http://www.ohchr.org/Documents/Professional Interest/cat.pdf> [accessed 17 July 2017].

the chain of command from authorising torture.[51] The Co-Investigating Judges also allowed for the limited use of torture-tainted evidence to provide investigative leads.[52]

The Trial Chamber adopted the position that evidence produced by torture was inadmissible in all circumstances for the truth of its contents.[53] This holding was challenged by the Defence for Nuon Chea who argued that torture-tainted evidence could be used in defence of the accused.[54] When the issue arose on appeal, the Supreme Court Chamber had to consider first, whether it had been established that statements made at S-21 resulted from torture, second, whether those statements could be used by Nuon Chea to assist his defence, and third, whether the Co-Prosecutors could use them to prove facts unrelated to the truth of their contents.[55] The use of torture-tainted evidence had in the meantime

---

51 *Prosecutor v Ieng Thirith*, ECCC Case File No. 002/19-09-2007-ECCC-OCIJ, Office of the Co-Investigating Judges, Order on Use of Statements Which Were or May Have Been Obtained by Torture, 28 July 2009, paras. 16–30. *See* also *Prosecutor v Ieng Thirith*, ECCC Case File No. 002/19-09-2007-ECCC/OCIJ(PTC26), Pre-Trial Chamber, Decision on the Admissibility of the Appeal against Co-Investigating Judges' Order on Use of Statements Which Were or May Have Been Obtained by Torture, 18 December 2009, para. 30 (where despite finding the appeal against the order of the Co-Investigating Judges to be inadmissible, the PTC stated: 'Article 15 of the CAT is to be strictly applied' and there is no room for a determination of the truth of the statement). For commentary, *see* D. McKeever, 'Evidence Obtained Through Torture before the Khmer Rouge Tribunal: Unlawful Pragmatism?', *Journal of International Criminal Justice*, vol. 8, no. 2, 2010, pp. 615–30.

52 For commentary, *see* T. Thienel, 'The Admission of Torture Statements into Evidence', in S.M. Meisenberg and I. Stegmiller (eds), *The Extraordinary Chambers in the Courts of Cambodia: Assessing their Contribution to International Criminal Law* (The Hague, T.M.C. Asser Press, 2016), pp. 491–513, pp. 499–501 (also discussing the 'fruit of the poisonous tree' doctrine).

53 *Prosecutor v Nuon Chea* and *Khieu Samphan*, ECCC Case File No. 002/19-09-2007/ECCC/TC, Trial Chamber, Case 002/01 Judgement, 7 August 2014, para. 35: 'certain evidence admitted for a limited purpose, such as proof that a statement was obtained through torture, may be relied upon only for that limited purpose and not as to the truth of the statement' ('Nuon Trial Judgment'). *See* also *Prosecutor v Nuon, Chea* and *Khieu Samphan*, ECCC Case File No. 002/19-09-2007/ECCC/TC, Trial Chamber, Decision on Evidence Obtained through Torture, 5 February 2016, para. 20. For commentary *see* Thienel, ibid, p. 498.

54 Nuon Appeal Judgment, above n. 8, paras. 241, 362.

55 *Prosecutor v Nuon, Chea* and *Khieu Samphan*, ECCC Case File No. 002/19-09-2007-ECCC/SC, Supreme Court Chamber, Decision on Objections to Document Lists: Full Reasons, 31 December 2015, para. 30.

become a live issue once more in Case 002/02.[56] Interestingly, both Prosecution and Defence sought to limit the extent of the prohibition on torture-tainted evidence for their respective purposes, arguing that their proposed uses of such evidence would not undermine Article 15 of the CAT.

The Supreme Court Chamber began by noting that Cambodia had ratified the CAT in 1992 and that the normative content of Article 15 was sufficiently precise for implementing legislation to be unnecessary.[57] Furthermore, the CAT was deemed to be directly applicable in accordance with Article 31(1) of the Cambodian Constitution.[58] The Supreme Court Chamber examined relevant domestic law and referred to Article 38 of the Cambodian Constitution which provided that '[c]onfessions obtained by physical torture or mental pressure shall not be admissible as evidence of guilt'.[59] Further, according to Article 321 of the Cambodian Criminal Procedure Code, '[u]nless it is provided otherwise by law, in criminal cases all evidence is admissible', and '[a] confession shall be considered by the court in the same manner as other evidence'. However, the same article states that '[a] declaration given under the physical or mental duress shall have no evidentiary value'.[60] Taking the domestic provisions together with the more specific Article 15 of the CAT, the Supreme Court Chamber concluded after a comprehensive analysis that the latter was clear: 'A party requesting the use of evidence derived from torture or wishing to tender such evidence must first demonstrate that it is being introduced only for the reason permitted by Article 15 of the CAT'.[61] In its judgment on appeal in Case 002/01, the Supreme Court Chamber confirmed its previous position, accepting the Co-Prosecutors' point that any contrary decision might have the effect of encouraging torture.[62]

In the period between the Supreme Court Chamber's decision on the use of documents in the Case 002/01 appeal proceedings and its final judgment on appeal, the Trial Chamber had proceeded to issue a new decision in relation to Case 002/02. The Trial Chamber took the view that since the Supreme Court Chamber had only been concerned with Case 002/01, it had not interpreted the limited exception contained in Article

56 Ibid, para. 27.
57 Ibid, para. 34.
58 Ibid.
59 Ibid, para. 31.
60 Ibid.
61 Ibid, para. 69.
62 Nuon Appeal Judgment, above n. 8, para. 364.

15 of the CAT or examined the precise context of documents from Kraing Ta Chan and other security centres.[63] Following a thorough analysis of Article 15 of the CAT in the context of ECCC proceedings, the Trial Chamber attempted to offer principled guidance on the use of torture-tainted evidence. By a super-majority, it concluded, in essence, that 'the exception to the exclusionary rule in Article 15 of the CAT permits the use of torture-tainted evidence against a person accused of torture for purposes other than proving the truth of the matter asserted in the statement'.[64] Applying the principles suggested by the Trial Chamber, any proposed use of such evidence would be evaluated on a case-by-case basis.[65]

Judge Fenz dissented from the decision of the majority on the basis that 'the exception has been changed from allowing the use of a statement obtained by torture for one purpose to allowing the use of such statement for all purposes but one (i.e. to establish its truth).'[66] Judge Fenz also warned that a case-by-case approach would result in a 'highly-fragmented and potentially inconsistent body of jurisprudence' which would not serve the deterrent purpose of the CAT due to its ambiguous signals.[67] In her view, the prohibition in Article 15 of the CAT was absolute and she indicated that to find otherwise would set the jurisprudence on a slippery slope towards weakening one of the most important protections in international law.[68]

It was to be expected that the problem of torture-tainted evidence would arise before the ECCC in view of the evidentiary emphasis on events at S-21 and other security centres. As the Trial Chamber noted, Case 001 established that 'torture was used to obtain confessions at S-21, … where prisoners did not give satisfactory confessions more torture was ordered, and … much of the information contained in the confessions

---

[63] *Prosecutor v Nuon, Chea* and *Khieu Samphan*, ECCC Case File No. 002/19-09-2007/ECCC/TC, Trial Chamber, Decision on Evidence Obtained through Torture, 5 February 2016, para. 3.

[64] 'Disposition', in *Prosecutor v Nuon, Chea* and *Khieu Samphan*, ECCC Case File No. 002/19-09-2007/ECCC/TC, Trial Chamber, Decision on Evidence Obtained through Torture, 5 February 2016, p. 34.

[65] *Prosecutor v Nuon, Chea* and *Khieu Samphan*, ECCC Case File No. 002/19-09-2007/ECCC/TC, Trial Chamber, Decision on Evidence Obtained through Torture, 5 February 2016, para. 88.

[66] *Prosecutor v Nuon, Chea* and *Khieu Samphan*, ECCC Document No. E350/S.1, Trial Chamber, Reasons for Partially Dissenting Opinion of Judge Fenz, 11 March 2016, para. 5.

[67] Ibid, para. 11.

[68] Ibid, paras. 25–6.

was fabricated'.[69] It could therefore be said that the findings in Case 001 and the assessment of the Co-Investigating Judges in Case 002 demonstrated a real risk that torture was used to obtain confessions at S-21 as well as other security centres for the purposes of Case 002/02.[70] This context might help to explain the Trial Chamber's approach, but its most recent decision sends a mixed and potentially perilous signal to both domestic and international courts. The text of Article 15 of the CAT is unambiguous and it is questionable whether the forced interpretation and expansion of its terms by the Trial Chamber was justified. The Trial Chamber referred to the 'absence of consistent international jurisprudence' on the matter and found that 'an international standard concerning the use of evidence derived from torture has not yet been established'.[71] This remains true and the jurisprudence may yet be developed further before the ECCC. In the meantime, the ambiguous position is unhelpful as a legacy for domestic courts.

5. JURISPRUDENTIAL LEGACY

The ECCC has a rich jurisprudential legacy as it concerns the definition and development in customary international law of crimes against humanity and war crimes, and modes of liability such as joint criminal enterprise. These contributions to the international jurisprudence were discussed in Chapters 7 and 8. The ECCC has a unique role in undertaking both an historical inquiry into international law as it existed in 1975–1979 and in addressing issues at the cutting edge of international criminal law. While existing and future international and internationalised courts as well as domestic courts may choose to distinguish the ECCC's findings and take a different approach on individual issues, the ECCC's statement of the applicable law in the period 1975 to 1979 deserves to be taken seriously.

At the time of writing, due to the severance decision and slow pace of Cases 003 and 004, the ECCC had not rendered a decision on the law of genocide and had only addressed a fraction of relevant issues relating to grave breaches of the Geneva Conventions. The Trial Chamber continues to face a challenge in terms of how to approach an overarching Joint

---

[69] *Prosecutor v Nuon, Chea* and *Khieu Samphan*, ECCC Case File No. 002/19-09-2007/ECCC/TC, Trial Chamber, Decision on Evidence Obtained through Torture, 5 February 2016, para. 79.

[70] Ibid, para. 79.

[71] Ibid, para. 69.

Criminal Enterprise (JCE) within the limited factual scope of Case 002/02. In the interests of fairness and in view of the age and health condition of the surviving accused, it might have been desirable to break the JCE down into smaller components, recognising that the court had its own precedent in the form of the 'S-21-JCE'. As a concept, JCE in its first and second forms only becomes objectionable when it is viewed as being overly expansive. If co-perpetration under Cambodian law had been used more directly to inform the approach to JCE then it could also have served a restraining function.

The ECCC's JCE chapter is not yet closed and JCE appears to remain central to prosecutorial strategy in all outstanding cases. The eagerness of defence lawyers in Cases 003 and 004 to intervene in matters concerning the applicability of JCE in Case 002 points to the jurisprudential importance attached to this mode of liability and the consequences of failing to construe it correctly. The Co-Prosecutors expressed the intention to introduce JCE III as an alternative mode of liability in Case 002/02[72] although this idea may have been dropped as a result of the Supreme Court Chamber's decision in Case 002/01. The concept would indeed seem relevant in the scenario suggested by the Co-Prosecutors whereby 'an accused who contributes to a criminal enterprise to enslave and persecute civilians, including girls and young women, or to force couples into marriages against their will, can be held responsible for the rapes that the accused could reasonably foresee could result from the implementation of that plan'.[73] Arguably other modes of liability could also capture this scenario but the debate nevertheless points to the significance of the legal issue and its direct relevance to the ECCC's jurisprudence and legacy.

---

72 *Prosecutor v Nuon, Chea* and *Khieu Samphan*, ECCC Case File No. 002-02/19-09-2007-ECCC/TC, E1/240.1, Trial Chamber, Transcript of Proceedings: Initial Hearing, 30 July 2014, pp. 33–40 (at 10:12:15).

73 *Prosecutor v Nuon Chea* and *Khieu Samphan*, ECCC Case File No. 002/19-09-2007-ECCC/SC, Office of the Co-Prosecutors, Co-Prosecutors' Appeal against the Judgment of the Trial Chamber in Case 002/01, 28 November 2014, para. 21. Apparently the Deputy Co-Prosecutor hinted in an e-mail to the press that this was an important reason for recognising JCE III, *see Prosecutor v Nuon Chea* and *Khieu Samphan*, ECCC Case File No. 002/19-09-2007-ECCC/SC, Defence for Case 003, Case 003 Defence Request to Intervene in the Appeal Proceedings in Case 002/01 for the Purpose of Addressing the Applicability of JCE III at the ECCC or, in the Alternative, Request for Leave to Submit *Amicus Curiae* Brief on JCE III Applicability, 12 January 2015, para. 4.

6. INSTITUTIONAL LEGACY

When its structure and functions were finally agreed, the ECCC appeared at least on paper to have 'a credible institutional character' with the capability to conduct fair trials according to international standards.[74] In principle, the judicial investigation made sense as this conformed to Cambodian criminal procedures and had the potential to speed up the gathering of evidence while at the same time leading to a shorter trial. In fact, the judicial investigation was not particularly swift and trials have taken as long as comparable trials before other ad hoc tribunals, possibly longer, due in part to the need for truncated trial sessions to accommodate the fragile health of the accused. It was almost impossible to imagine a 'genuine civil law process' in an internationalised tribunal with actors from a range of legal systems.[75] Indeed, for a period even the International Co-Investigating Judge came from a common law system.[76] The confidential nature of the investigation was also a source of frustration, especially for some defence lawyers and for the interested public. The public might have considered itself to be short-changed without an in-depth adversarial hearing at the conclusion of the investigation. If time had not been of the essence, the parallel functions of a full judicial investigation overseen by the Pre-Trial Chamber and a complete adversarial trial with the possibility of appeals to the Supreme Court Chamber would seem to promote rather than detract from fairness. The fact that the Co-Investigating Judges, Pre-Trial Chamber, Trial Chamber and Supreme Court Chamber have all rendered decisions on the most fundamental issues before the Court, such as Ieng Sary's pardon and amnesty, JCE III and torture-tainted evidence is not *per se* problematic. To the contrary, despite this duplication of efforts, the judges at all levels have demonstrated that they can issue independent and well-reasoned opinions on a range of complex issues. However, for the ECCC and most tribunals operating in similar circumstances, time *is* of the essence.

---

[74] D. Scheffer, 'The Extraordinary Chambers in the Courts of Cambodia', in M.C. Bassiouni (ed), *International Criminal Law, Volume 3: International Enforcement* (3rd edn, Leiden, the Netherlands, Martinus Nijhoff Publishers, 2008), pp. 219–55, pp. 219–20.

[75] *See* Ciorciari and Heindel, above n. 11, p. 47 (citing Marcel Lemonde who indicated that a 'genuine civil law process didn't happen').

[76] Mark Harmon, an American lawyer, served as International Co-Investigating Judge from 2012 to 2015, suggesting that the French model was not integral to a process that had become increasingly internationalised.

While it would be unfair to suggest that the inquisitorial model of internationalised justice has been completely discredited by the ECCC experience, the ECCC is unlikely to be replicated in full. It has been suggested that the ECCC itself provides the 'first empirical insight into how the "inquisitorial" model of criminal process can be expected to fare when grafted onto a hybrid criminal jurisdiction adjudicating international crimes committed in the distant past'.[77] The inquisitorial model is in fact the basis for the ECCC and it is the features grafted onto this model, combined with their interactions or reactions, that have challenged its functioning. Paring it down and reducing its complexity would be a desirable start for any future copycat model. As it concerns civil party participation, it has been suggested that allowing groups rather than individuals to participate might be preferable, although the ECCC moved close to this option in Case 002.[78] Another suggestion has been for a separate restitution hearing at the conclusion of the trial.[79] It should also be recalled that the establishment of an international or internationalised tribunal is often preceded by a lengthy investigation as occurred in the case of the Special Tribunal for Lebanon (STL) with replication of investigative efforts. This does not justify any inefficiency on the part of the ECCC, but suggests that the creation of an ideal model remains a pipedream.

The biggest problem with the ECCC's institutional design was arguably the risk of bifurcation which became an unfortunate reality as Cases 003 and 004 proceeded. As a result, it may be questioned whether in its sunset period the Court has indirectly prioritised the needs of the international community over the domestic population, forging ahead

---

[77] S. Vasiliev, 'Trial Process at the ECCC: The Rise and Fall of the Inquisitorial Paradigm in International Criminal Law?', in S.M. Meisenberg and I. Stegmiller (eds), *The Extraordinary Chambers in the Courts of Cambodia: Assessing their Contribution to International Criminal Law* (The Hague, T.M.C. Asser Press, 2016), 389–433, pp. 392, 393, 396 (although the author acknowledges at p. 393 that 'the adoption of a non-adversarial approach to the ECCC process was dictated neither by an abstract and theoretical consideration of its relative advantages nor by an intention to stage a procedural experiment' but rather rooted in the complex negotiation process. He also goes on to state at p. 396 that 'it is generally correct to characterize the system as resting on an inquisitorial foundation').

[78] Ciorciari and Heindel, above n. 11, p. 230 (citing an interview with Jeanne Sulzer, former Legal Officer in the ECCC Civil Party Lead Co-Lawyers Section).

[79] Ibid (referring to a suggestion made by ECCC defence lawyer Michael Karnavas).

with decisions signed only by the International Co-Investigating Judge leading to repeated, futile and time-wasting split votes in the Pre-Trial Chamber. Ironically, but understandably, the UN does not wish to lose face or see the ECCC fail after its many accomplishments, while it seems to be business as usual for government structures.

7. CONCLUSION

New internationalised tribunals have been established or are under discussion for the Central African Republic, Kosovo, South Sudan, Sri Lanka, Syria and the Democratic Republic of the Congo. It has been suggested that 'before rushing headfirst into a second era of hybrid criminal justice, it is important to take stock'.[80] Lessons can and should be learned and the ECCC has an important place in the evolution of 'hybrid justice' both in terms of the Court's domestic and international legacy. While models of internationalised justice should not be 'simply constructed as *sui generis* "expedient stopgaps" or as generic imitations of other hybrid courts'[81] they should ideally remain true to their domestic foundations and must to an extent be tailor made. The fact of being anchored in a domestic system does not inherently afford them greater legitimacy.[82] However, these forms of specialised justice are in a sense halfway houses towards full implementation of the ICC's complementarity principle which sees accountability for international crimes moving towards the domestic sphere.

Expectations for the ECCC were set high because the crimes of the Khmer Rouge were so momentous. The Trial Chamber cited Jon Swain who described the exodus from Phnom Penh in 1975 as a 'great caravan of human misery'.[83] Without the ECCC, there would have been no real legal reckoning in respect of this indelible stain on humanity's history. It has not been a perfect process and the ECCC will have a mixed legacy. But to be unduly critical would be to undermine the efforts of all those,

---

[80] H. Hobbs, 'Hybrid Tribunals and the Composition of the Court: In Search of Sociological Legitimacy', *Chicago Journal of International Law*, vol. 16, no. 2, 2016, pp. 482–522, p. 488.

[81] Ibid, p. 486.

[82] P. McAuliffe, 'Hybrid Tribunals at Ten: How International Criminal Justice's Golden Child Became an Orphan', *Journal of International Law and International Relations*, vol. 7, 2011, pp. 1–65, p. 2.

[83] Nuon Trial Judgment, above n. 53, para. 482.

internationally and domestically, who have committed themselves to the success of the project.

A modern Cambodian play, *Breaking the Silence*, ends with the chorus:

> Transform the River of Blood into a River of Reconciliation.
> A River of Responsibility.
> Transform the River of Blood into a River of Reconciliation.
> A River of Responsibility.[84]

The silence is broken, the actors leave the stage and the river runs clean again.

---

[84] 'Epilogue', in A. Prins, *Breaking the Silence: A New Cambodian Play* (Phnom Penh, Documentation Center of Cambodia, 2009), p. 23, <http://www.d.dccam.org/Projects/Radio/pdf/DCCAM_BREAKING_THE_SILENCE_%20FINAL.pdf> [accessed 17 July 2017].

Index